Rotary Tiller

SERVICE MANUAL ■ *3RD EDITION*

Rotary Tiller Manufacturers:

- Ariens
- Atlas
- BCS
- Clinton
- John Deere
- Feldmann

- Ford
- Gilson
- Haban
- Hoffco
- Homelite

- Honda
- International
- Kubota
- Lazy Boy
- Merry
- Mighty Mac

- MTD
- Murray
- J.C. Penney
- Roper
- Roto-Hoe

- Sears
- Snapper
- Troy-Bilt
- Wards
- Wheel Horse
- White

Engine Manufacturers:

- Acme
- BCS
- Briggs & Stratton

- Clinton
- Honda

- Kawasaki
- Kohler
- Kubota

- Lombardini
- Tecumseh

- Wisconsin Robin

Cover photograph courtesy of: Kubota Tractor Corporation, 3401 Del Amo Boulevard, Torrance, CA 90509-2992

©Copyright 1989 by Intertec Publishing   Printed in the United States of America
Library of Congress Catalog Card Number 89-046263

Intertec Publishing
P.O. Box 12901 ■ Overland Park, KS 66282-2901

CONTENTS

GENERAL

Drive Belt Chart 150

Maintenance Log 278

Metric Conversion 277

VEHICLE SERVICE SECTIONS

ARIENS
   RT214, RT320, RT324, RT424, RT424X,
   RT424CI, RT524, RT524S, RT524C, RT5020,
   SRT5020, RT7020, RT8020, RT8028,
   RT7927 4

ATLAS
   12-2100, 12-3010, 12-3011, 12-3100,
   12-3150, 12-5012, 12-5013, 12-5015,
   12-5016, 12-5021, 12-5022, 12-5100,
   12-5300 12

BCS
   204, 205, 715, 725, 735, 745 16

CLINTON
   500-T-14 29

JOHN DEERE
   216, 324, 524, 624 30

FELDMANN
   73335, 83335 34

FORD
   1005, 1013, 1023, 1094, 1105, 1114A,
   1134, 1183, 1200 .35

GILSON
   51081, 51088, 51097, 51174 42
   51082, 51085 44
   51083 46
   51094, 51096, 51106 48
   51080, 51084 50
   51095, 51170, 51105 52
   51114, 51134, 51159, 51175, 51175A,
   51176A, 51135, 51179, 51179A 55
   51104, 51171, 51171A, 51181, 51116,
   51158, 51142, 51143, 51172, 51173 63

HABAN
   861-002 68

HOFFCO
   Li'l Hoe 71

HOMELITE
   MTC-12, FT-5, RT-5 73

HONDA
   F210, F401AD, F401A2, F501A1, F501A2 76

INTERNATIONAL
   526, 526A 78

KUBOTA
   AT25, AT55 80
   AT60, AT70S, AT70S-E 85

LAZY BOY
   T5500, LB200GT, 3LBCT, S265, 756T,
   LB5RT, LB8RT, Max 89

MERRY
   Custom G-77, Custom G-78, Custom 7300,
   Exporter G-90, Exporter G-91, Exporter G-92,
   Exporter 7600, Exporter 7601, Exporter 7602,
   International 7600, International 7601,
   Minnie MM-1, Minnie 2000, Minnie 2001,
   Minnie 3200, Minnie 7100, Professional G-83,
   Professional G-84, Professional G-87,
   Professional G-88, Professional 7500,
   Professional 7501, Professional 7502,
   Scotsman G-76, Scotsman 7200, Suburban G-80,
   Suburban G-82, Suburban 7400, Suburban 7402,
   Suburban 7480, Suburban Rev. 7401,
   Suburban Rev. 7403 93

MIGHTY MAC
   324, 524, 524R, 822RT 97

MTD
   030, 320, 355, 385, 386, 405, 408, 409 98
   410A, 412A, 418A 103

MURRAY
   1000, 1190, 1202, 1203, 1290, 1302, 1303 105

J.C. PENNEY
   3040, 3041, 3046 108

ROPER
   RF300, RF500, RF550, RT130, RT150, RT180 109

ROTO-HOE
   SP, 220, 904, 910, 990 113

SEARS
   29852, 29936, 29937, 29943, 29945, 29958,
   29966, 29968, 299130, 299150, 299382 116

SNAPPER
   300T, 301T, 301TR, 401T, 401TR, 401TCR,
   500T, 501T, 501TC, 501TR, 501TCR 123
   RT5, RT5X, RT8, RT8S, R5000, R5001, R5002,
   R5002R, R8000, R8001, R8001S, R8002,
   R8002S 126

TROY-BILT
   Econo-Horse, Horse, Junior, Pony, PTO Horse,
   Tuffy 130

WARDS
   1580, 39000, 39008, 39011, 39023, 39025,
   39031, 39032, 39095, 39098, 39103 138
   39083, 39084, 39096, 39097 138

WHEEL HORSE 142

WHITE
   Roto Boss 200, Roto Boss 300, Roto Boss 350,
   Roto Boss 500, Roto Boss 800, Roto Boss 802 145

ENGINE SERVICE SECTIONS

ACME
   A 220 B 154
   ALN 290 WB, ALN 330 WB 158
   VT 88 WB 162
   SERVICING ACME ACCESSORIES 165
   ACME SPECIAL TOOLS 165

BCS
   180 166
   SERVICING BCS ACCESSORIES 169
   BCS SPECIAL TOOLS 169

BRIGGS & STRATTON
   60000, 80000, 90000, 110000, 130000,
   170000, 190000 .170
   SERVICING BRIGGS & STRATTON
   ACCESSORIES 182
   BRIGGS & STRATTON SPECIAL TOOLS 18

CLINTON
   500-0100-000 187
   CLINTON SPECIAL TOOLS (500 Series) 190
   498-0301-000 191

CLINTON (Cont.)
SERVICING CLINTON ACCESSORIES 195
CLINTON SPECIAL TOOLS (498 Series) 195

HONDA
GV100 196
GX110, GX140 200
SERVICING HONDA ACCESSORIES 204

KAWASAKI
FA130 205

KOHLER
K91 212
K-141, K-161, K-181, K-241 216
M8, M14 224
SERVICING KOHLER ACCESSORIES 230

KUBOTA
GS90V, GS200, GS230, GS280 232
SERVICING KUBOTA ACCESSORIES 236
KUBOTA SPECIAL TOOLS 239

LOMBARDINI
3LD510 240
6LD360 247

TECUMSEH
(2-STROKE)
TC200 253
(4-STROKE) 256
SERVICING TECUMSEH ACCESSORIES 264

WISCONSIN ROBIN
EY18W 266
W1-145V, W1-185V 270
SERVICING WISCONSIN ROBIN ACCESSORIES . .274

DUAL DIMENSIONS

This service manual provides specifications in both the Metric (SI) and U.S. Customary systems of measurement. The first specification is given in the measuring system used during manufacture, while the second specification (given in parenthesis) is the converted measurement. For instance, a specification of ''0.28 mm (0.011 inch)'' would indicate that the equipment was manufactured using the metric system of measurement and U.S. equivalent of 0.28 mm is 0.011 inch.

ARIENS

ARIENS COMPANY
655 West Ryan Street
Brillion, WI 54110-1098

Model	Engine Make	Engine Series	Power Rating	No. of Forward Speeds	Power Reverse?	Tilling Width	Drive Type
RT214	B&S	60000	2 hp (1.49 kW)	1	No	14 in. (35.5 cm)	Gear
RT320	B&S	80000	3 hp (2.24 kW)	1	No	20 in. (51 cm)	Gear Gear
RT324	B&S	80000	3 hp (2.24 kW)	1	No	24 in. (61 cm)	Gear
RT424	B&S	110000	4 hp (3.0 kW)	1	Yes	24 in. (61 cm)	Gear
RT424X	B&S	110000	4 hp (3.0 kW)	1	Yes	24 in. (61 cm)	Gear
RT424CI	B&S	110000	4 hp (3.0 kW)	1	Yes	24 in. (61 cm)	Gear
RT524	B&S	130000	5 hp (3.73 kW)	2	Yes	24 in. (61 cm)	Gear
RT524S	B&S	130000	5 hp (3.73 kW)	2	Yes	24 in. (61 cm)	Gear
RT524C	B&S	130000	5 hp (3.73 kW)	1	No	24 in. (61 cm)	Chain
RT5020	Tec.	H50	5 hp (3.73 kW)	2	Yes	24 in. (61 cm)	Gear
SRT5020	Tec.	H50	5 hp (3.73 kW)	2	Yes	24 in. (61 cm)	Gear
RT7020	Tec.	H70	7 hp (5.22 kW)	4	Yes	24 in. (61 cm)	Gear
RT8020	Kohler	K181	8 hp (5.96 kW)	4	Yes	24 in. (61 cm)	Gear
RT8028	Kohler	K181	8 hp (5.96 kW)	4	Yes	28 in. (71 cm)	Gear

LUBRICATION

ENGINE

All Models

Refer to appropriate Briggs & Stratton, Tecumseh or Kohler engine section for engine lubrication specifications.

WHEELS AND CONTROLS

All Models

Transport wheels on front tine models should be removed at least once a year and repacked with a multipurpose grease. Pivot shaft on swing handle models should be greased at least once a year with Ariens Moly-Lithium grease or suitable equivalent.

TINE CHAIN CASE

Model RT524C

Chain case oil on early models (A— Fig. AR1) should be checked every 10 to

Fig. AR1—View of chain case assemblies used on early (A) and late (B) RT524C models. Refer to text for lubrication specifications.

15 hours of operation. Recommended lubricant is Ariens L-2 gear lube or suitable equivalent.

To check oil level in early chain case, place tiller on a level surface. Clean dirt from chain case housing and remove oil

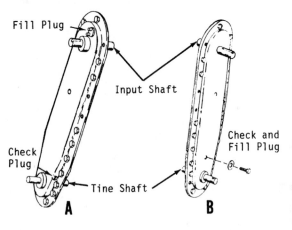

level check plug. Oil level should be at bottom of plug hole. If oil level is low, remove fill plug and add oil slowly until it starts to run out of check plug hole, then reinstall plugs. Late model chain case (B) is lubricated and sealed during production and should not require additional lubrication, unless disassembled for repair. Fill late model case with 8 ounces (236.5 mL) of Ariens Liquid Grease, part 000070 or suitable equivalent.

TINE GEARCASE

All Models So Equipped

Gearcase oil should be checked at least every 10 hours of operation. Recommended lubricant is Ariens L-2 gear lube or suitable equivalent.

To check gearcase oil, place tiller on a level surface. Clean dirt from around oil level plug (1—Fig. AR2) and remove plug. Oil level should be at bottom of plug hole. If oil level is low, add oil through level hole until oil is flush with bottom of plug hole. Reinstall and tighten plug.

WHEEL DRIVE GEARCASE

Models RT5020, RT7020, RT8020 and RT8028

Gearcase oil should be checked at beginning of every day and should be changed at the end of first season of operation. Recommended lubricant is Ariens L-2 gear lube or suitable equivalent.

To check gearcase oil, place tiller on a level surface. Clean dirt from top of gearcase and remove oil level dipstick (1—Fig. AR3). Oil level should be at full line (2) on dipstick. Add oil through hole if oil level is low. Reinstall dipstick and tighten.

MAINTENANCE

Inspect all fasteners for looseness and retighten as needed. Check control levers, linkage and cables for freedom

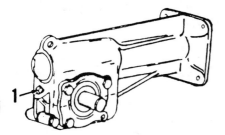

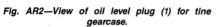

Fig. AR2—View of oil level plug (1) for tine gearcase.

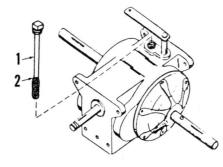

Fig. AR3—View of oil level dipstick (1) for cast iron wheel drive gearcase used on early models. Aluminum gearcase used on late models is similar. Oil should be maintained at full mark (2).

of movement and excessive play. Inspect drive belt(s) for excessive stretching, wear, cracks or any other damage. Install new belt(s) if needed. Inspect all belt pulleys and renew if damaged or excessively worn.

ADJUSTMENT

CLUTCH CONTROL

Front Tine Models Except RT524S

Adjust clutch by repositioning clutch spring in clutch cable chain (Fig. AR4). Clutch spring should stretch slightly

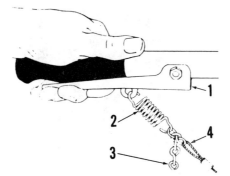

Fig. AR4—View of clutch control components for front tine tillers except Model RT524S.

1. Clutch lever
2. Spring
3. Chain
4. Clutch cable

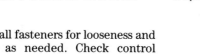

Fig. AR5—View of clutch adjusting nuts (2) on RT524S swing handle models. Refer to text for adjustment procedure.

1. Idler pulley
2. Adjusting nuts
3. Clutch cable

when clutch lever (1) is pulled up against handle bar. Chain should be shortened if spring does not stretch when clutch lever is pulled up. Adjust reverse clutch, on models so equipped, following the same procedure.

If proper clutch adjustment cannot be obtained and spring (2) is hooked into the last link of chain (3), loosen idler pulley retaining nut and slide pulley assembly in slotted bracket. Tighten idler pulley retaining nut and readjust clutch chain as previously outlined.

Model RT524S

Adjust clutch by raising or lowering adjusting nuts (2—Fig. AR5). Idler pulley (1) should be tight against belt with clutch handle depressed and should fall away from belt when clutch handle is released.

Adjust idler pulley up or down in slotted bracket if proper clutch adjustment can not be obtained. In extreme cases, it may be necessary to add or subtract shims under engine to obtain proper clutch adjustment.

Rear Tine Models

FORWARD CLUTCH SPRING. Engage main clutch lever in forward position and measure length of spring (4—Fig. AR6). Spring length with forward clutch engaged should be 15/16 to 1-1/16 inches (23.8-27.0 mm) on Models RT5020, SRT5020 and RT7020, or 2-11/16 to 2-13/16 inches (68.3-71.4 mm) on all other models. Disconnect link (3) and turn in or out on threaded rod as necessary to obtain correct length. Note that spring (4) is compressed when clutch is applied on Models RT5020, SRT5020 and RT7020, while spring is stretched on Models RT8020 and RT8028.

REVERSE IDLER. On early Models RT5020, SRT5020 and RT7020, adjust

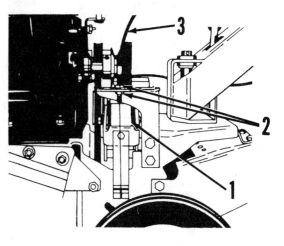

reverse clutch control by moving idler pulley (5—Fig. AR6) in or out in idler bracket slot. Loosen nut (6) and adjust pulley (5) as necessary to obtain proper reverse and neutral operation.

On all other models, move fixed idler pulley (11—Fig. AR7) up or down in slotted bracket (12) to obtain correct reverse idler (5) travel distance (D). Travel distance (D) should be approximately one inch (25.4 mm) on late RT5020, SRT5020 and RT7020, or approximately 1-1/4 inches (31.7 mm) on all other models.

Fig. AR6—View of clutch control components and drive belt(s) arrangement for early Models RT5020, SRT5020 and RT7020. Later models and RT8020 and RT8028 models are similar.

1. Forward idler pulley assy.
2. Cotter pin
3. Adjustment link
4. Clutch spring
5. Reverse idler pulley assy.
6. Retaining nut
7. Reverse drive belt
8. Forward drive belts

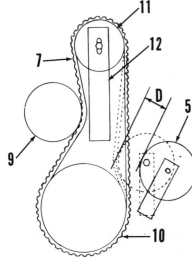

Fig. AR7—Adjust reverse idler pulley (5) by moving fixed reverse idler (11) up or down in slotted bracket (12) as necessary to obtain correct travel distance (D). Refer to text.

5. Reverse idler pulley
7. Reverse belt
9. Engine pulley
10. Transmission pulley
11. Fixed reverse idler pulley
12. Bracket

DRIVE BELT

Front Tine Models With Slotted Idler Brackets

If proper clutch adjustment cannot be obtained by lengthening or shortening clutch chain, loosen idler pulley retaining nut and slide pulley assembly in slotted bracket. Tighten idler pulley retaining nut and readjust clutch chain. Refer to CLUTCH CONTROL under ADJUSTMENT section for adjusting procedure.

Rear Tine Models

To adjust belt center distance, loosen four cap screws (2—Fig. AR8) securing frame to wheel drive gearcase. Turn adjustment screw (1) to tighten or loosen drive belts, then retighten four cap screws. Refer to CLUTCH CONTROL under ADJUSTMENT section to readjust forward clutch spring and reverse idler.

TINE GEARCASE ADJUSTMENT

Rear Tine Models

Loosen adjustment cap (24—Fig. AR13) retaining set screw. Tighten cap until snug, then back off cap approximately 60 degrees. Retighten set screw.

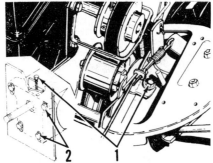

Fig. AR8—View of belt(s) center distance adjustment parts for Models RT5020, SRT5020, RT7020, RT8020 and RT8028.

1. Adjustment screw
2. Cap screws

Fig. AR9—View of wheel drive and tine engagement levers and operating procedure.

1. Wheel drive engagement lever
2. Tine engagement lever

CHANGING FORWARD SPEEDS

Models RT524, RT524S, RT5020, SRT5020, RT7020, RT8020 and RT8028

PULLEY SPEED POSITIONS. Front tine models have one forward drive belt. Rear tine models have two forward drive belts. Inside pulley grooves are for low speed and outside grooves for high speed.

To change belt position, disconnect spark plug lead from spark plug, then remove drive belt guard. Start belt out of pulley groove and pull starter rope to assist in removing belt. Reposition belt and pull starter rope to help roll belt in pulley groove. For rear tine models, both drive belts must be removed and repositioned. Reinstall drive belt guard, then reconnect spark plug lead.

TRANSMISSION SPEED POSITIONS. Rear tine tiller Models RT7020, RT8020 and RT8028 have a high and low speed position in a drive clutch assembly. Refer to Fig. AR9 for lever identification and speed positions. Disengage main clutch lever then select desired wheel drive speed. Engage tine lever, then engage main clutch lever.

OVERHAUL

ENGINE

All Models

Engine model number is stamped on blower housing for Briggs & Stratton engines. Engine make and series number is marked on data plate attached to engine for Kohler and Tecumseh engines. Refer to appropriate Briggs & Stratton, Kohler or Tecumseh engine section for overhaul procedures.

CHAIN CASE

Model RT524C

OIL SEAL INSTALLATION. Remove tines from tine shaft, then use seal puller to remove outer and inner seals from case hub. Clean tine shaft with emery cloth. Install inner seal with lip facing toward inside and outer seal with lip facing toward outside. Drive new seals in until outer seal is flush with case hub.

INSPECTION. Refer to Fig. AR10 for parts breakdown and identification. Inspect and renew all components that are worn or damaged. Install new gasket and seals. Lubricate chains, sprockets and bearings with a light film of gear lube during reassembly. Keep all dirt and foreign matter out of chain case during reassembly. Refer to LUBRICATION section for lubrication requirements after reassembly and installation.

TINE GEARCASE

Models RT214, RT320, RT324 and RT424.

OIL SEAL INSTALLATION. Remove tines from tine shaft. Using a screwdriver, pry seal out of case hub. Clean tine shaft with emery cloth. Drive new seal in until seal face is flush with case hub.

INSPECTION. Refer to Fig. AR11 for parts breakdown and identification. Remove bearing flange (9) securing bolts and remove flange (9) and gasket (8). Remove oil level plug (11), then turn adjustment plug (17) out of gearcase. Remove Woodruff key (21) from worm shaft (20) and push worm shaft assembly out of gearcase. Remove tine shaft (5) and gear (4) from gearcase. Be sure that gasket (16) is removed.

Inspect and renew all components that are worn or damaged. Install new gaskets and seals. Lubricate gears and bearings with a light film of gear lube during reassembly. Keep all dirt and foreign matter out of gearcase during reassembly. Adjust worm shaft end play by turning adjustment plug (17) in until gasket (16) is compressed, then continue to tighten until plug identation is aligned with hole for oil level plug (11). Do not back off adjustment plug to obtain alignment. Refer to LUBRICATION section after reassembly and installation.

Models RT424X, RT424CI, RT524 and RT524S

OIL SEAL INSTALLATION. Remove tines from tine shaft, then remove seal

from case hub. Clean tine shaft with emery cloth. Drive new seal in until seal face is flush with case hub.

INSPECTION. Refer to Fig. AR12 for parts breakdown and identification.

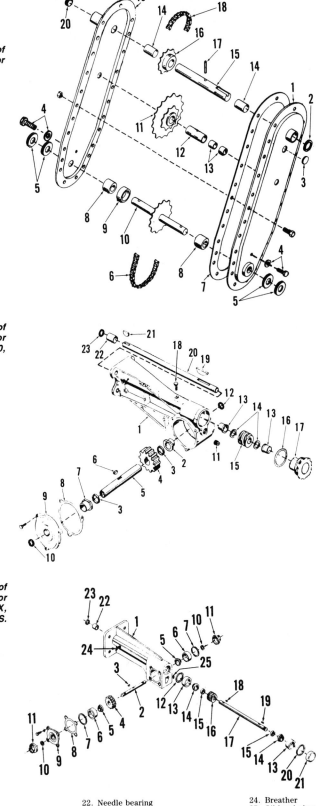

Fig. AR10—Exploded view of chain case components for tiller Model RT524C.

1. Chain case, L.H.
2. Oil seal
3. Oil fill plug
4. Check plug & gasket
5. Oil seals
6. Chain
7. Gasket
8. Needle bearing
9. Spacer
10. Tine shaft assy.
11. Idler sprocket
12. Bearing race
13. Needle bearings
14. Bushing
15. Input shaft
16. Sprocket
17. Roll pin
18. Chain
19. Chain case, R.H.
20. Expansion plug

Fig. AR11—Exploded view of gearcase components for tiller Models RT214, RT320, RT324 and RT424.

1. Gearcase (Aluminum)
2. Bushing
3. Washer
4. Bronze gear
5. Tine shaft
6. Woodruff key
7. Bushing
8. Gasket
9. Bearing flange
10. Seal
11. Oil level plug
12. Seal
13. Bushing
14. Washers
15. Worm gear
16. Gasket
17. Adjustment plug
18. Cap screw
19. Woodruff key
20. Worm shaft
21. Woodruff key
22. Needle bearing
23. Seal

Fig. AR12—Exploded view of gearcase components for tiller Models RT424X, RT424CI, RT524 and RT524S.

1. Gearcase (Cast iron)
2. Tine shaft
3. Woodruff key
4. Bronze gear
5. Bearing cone
6. Bearing cup
7. Snap ring
8. Gasket
9. Bearing flange
10. Seal
11. Dust cover
12. Snap ring
13. Bearing cup
14. Bearing cone
15. Bearing spacer
16. Worm gear
17. Worm shaft
18. Woodruff key
19. Straight key
20. Snap ring (various thicknesses)
21. Dust cap

Remove bearing flange (9) securing bolts and remove flange (9) and gasket (8). Remove tine shaft (2) assembly. Pry dust cap (21) out of gearcase, then remove snap ring (20). Tap input end of worm shaft and remove bearing cup (13) and

22. Needle bearing
23. Seal

24. Breather
25. Oil level plug

worm shaft assembly from gearcase. Caution should be used during disassembly, excessive effort applied on internal case parts could result in damage and renewal of part(s).

Inspect and renew all components that are worn or damaged. Install new gaskets and seals. Lubricate gears and bearings with a light film of gear lube during reassembly. Keep all dirt and foreign matter out of gearcase during reassembly. Use a press to remove and install shaft bearings. Press bearing (22) into case (1) with lettered side of bearing facing rear of case. Press bearing (14) 3/32 inch (2.4 mm) from knurled end of worm shaft (17). To adjust end play clearance between bearing cones and cups on input worm shaft, thickness of snap ring (20) is changed. Vary thickness of snap ring (7) to adjust tine shaft (2) end play. Install thickest snap ring possible to provide shaft with recommended zero end play. Refer to LUBRICATION section after reassembly and installation.

Models RT5020, SRT5020, RT7020, RT8020 and RT8028

OIL SEAL INSTALLATION. Remove tines from tine shaft, then remove seals from case hub. Clean tine shaft with emery cloth. Install inner seal with lip facing toward inside and outer seal with lip facing toward outside. Drive new seals in until outer seal is flush with case hub.

INSPECTION. Refer to Fig. AR13 for parts breakdown and identification. Remove bolts and lockwashers securing bearing flange cover (9) to gearcase. Remove flange cover and gasket(s) noting number of gasket(s) removed. Withdraw tine shaft (6), worm gear (7) and bearing cones (2) from housing. Loosen Allen head set screw (15) and turn adjusting cap (24) out of housing. Remove bearing cup (17) by tapping it out with worm shaft, then remove worm shaft assembly from gearcase housing. Caution should be used during disassembly, excessive effort applied on internal case parts could result in damage and renewal of part(s).

Inspect and renew all components that are worn or damaged. Worm (23) and worm gear (7) must be renewed as a set. Install new gaskets and seals. Lubricate gears and bearings with a light film of gear lube during reassembly. Press bearing (10) into housing (1) from lettered side of bearing. Preload between bearing flange cover (9) and bearings (2) should be 0.001-0.005 inch (0.03-0.13 mm). Obtain correct preload by installing flange cover on gearcase without gaskets. Tighten screws which retain cover (9) evenly un-

til cover is snug, then measure distance between cover and gearcase with a feeler gage. Remove cover and install gaskets (8) less than measured gap to provide correct preload on bearings. Gaskets (8) are available in 0.005 inch (0.13 mm), 0.010 inch (0.25 mm) and 0.015 inch (0.38 mm) thicknesses. Refer to TINE GEARCASE ADJUSTMENT under ADJUSTMENT section for worm shaft end play adjusting procedure. Refer to LUBRICATION section for lubrication requirements after reassembly and installation.

CAST IRON WHEEL DRIVE GEARCASE

Early Models RT5020, RT7020, RT8020 and RT8028

INSPECTION. Refer to Fig. AR14 for parts breakdown and identification. Inspect and renew all components that are worn or damaged. Install new gaskets and seals. Lubricate gears and bearings with a light film of gear lube during reassembly.

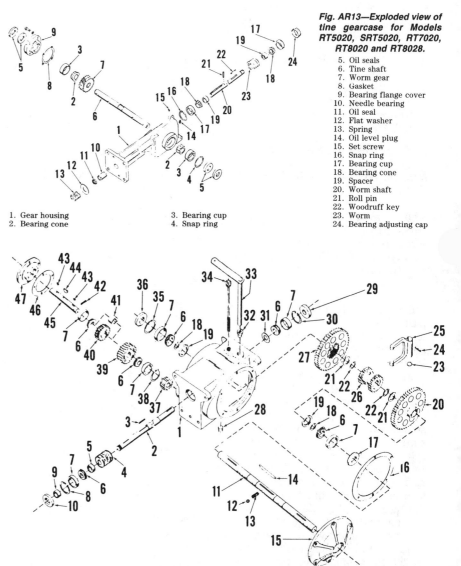

Fig. AR13—Exploded view of tine gearcase for Models RT5020, SRT5020, RT7020, RT8020 and RT8028.

5. Oil seals
6. Tine shaft
7. Worm gear
8. Gasket
9. Bearing flange cover
10. Needle bearing
11. Oil seal
12. Flat washer
13. Spring
14. Oil level plug
15. Set screw
16. Snap ring
17. Bearing cup
18. Bearing cone
19. Spacer
20. Worm shaft
21. Roll pin
22. Woodruff key
23. Worm
24. Bearing adjusting cap

1. Gear housing
2. Bearing cone
3. Bearing cup
4. Snap ring

Fig. AR14—Exploded view of wheel drive gearcase assembly for Models RT5020, SRT5020, RT7020, RT8020 and RT8028. High gear (27) is absent and replaced with a spacer (not shown) on Models RT5020 and SRT5020.

1. Transmission housing	13. Spring	24. Roll pin	37. Low speed pinion gear
2. Worm shaft	14. Woodruff key	25. Clutch yoke	38. Snap ring
3. Woodruff key	15. Bearing flange cover	26. Sliding hub	39. Worm gear
4. Worm	16. Gasket	27. High gear assy.	40. High speed pinion gear
5. Spacer	17. Oil seal	28. Oil drain plug	41. Spacer
6. Bearing cone	18. Snap ring	29. Seal	42. Roll pin
7. Bearing cup	19. Spacer	30. Snap ring	43. Woodruff key
8. Snap ring	20. Low gear assy.	31. Spacer	44. Woodruff key
9. Spacer	21. Spacer	32. Bushing	45. Pinion shaft
10. Seal	22. Snap ring	33. Yoke shaft & lever	46. Gasket
11. Axle shaft	23. Plug	34. Dipstick	47. Pinion flange
12. Steel ball		35. Snap ring	
		36. Seal	

End play of worm shaft (2) should be 0.002 inch (0.05 mm). Thickness of snap ring (8) determines amount of worm shaft end play.

End play in pinion shaft (45) should be 0.001-0.005 inch (0.03-0.13 mm). To measure for correct end play, install flange cover (47) without gaskets and tighten retaining screws evenly until cover is snug, then measure distance between cover and gearcase with a feeler gage. Remove cover and install gaskets which provide correct end play.

Preload between bearing flange cover (15) and bearings (6) should be 0.001-0.005 inch (0.03-0.13 mm). To measure for correct preload, install flange cover (15) on gearcase without gaskets. Snug down cover with securing screws and measure distance between cover and gearcase with a feeler gage. Remove cover and install correct number of gaskets to apply a 0.001-0.005 inch (0.03-0.13 mm) preload on bearings.

Refer to LUBRICATION section for lubrication requirements after reassembly and installation.

TINE CLUTCH

Early Models RT5020, RT7020, RT8020 and RT8028 With Cast Iron Wheel Drive Gearcase

Refer to Fig. AR15 for exploded view of tine clutch assembly. To disassemble clutch, separate rear jaw (3) from yoke (4). Front jaw is secured on wheel drive gearcase main shaft with two sets of set screws (7 and 10). Remove top set screw (7) and loosen bottom set screw (10) to remove jaw (9) from shaft. Drive out roll pins (5) to remove yoke (4) and shaft (2).

Inspect all components for excessive wear or other damage and renew as necessary. Reassembly is the reverse of disassembly noting the following: Coat clutch jaws (3 and 9) with a suitable bearing grease. Install yoke (4) with flat side facing front of case (1). Be sure yoke (4) properly engages annular groove in jaw (3). Install jaw (9) on wheel drive gearcase shaft so outer surface of jaw is 1-11/16 inches (42.8 mm) from face of wheel drive case.

ALUMINUM TRANSMISSION AND TINE CLUTCH ASSEMBLY

Late Models RT5020, SRT5020, RT7020 and RT8020

Refer to Fig. AR16 for exploded view of aluminum transmission assembly. To disassemble transmission, remove top cover (60) and note position of clutch lever (48) and yoke (61). Drive out roll pins (62) and remove clutch yoke (61) and

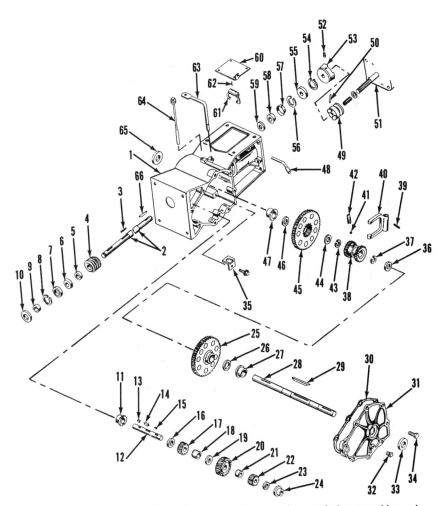

Fig. AR16—Exploded view of aluminum wheel drive and tine clutch transmission assembly used on late Models RT5020, SRT5020, RT7020 and RT8020. High gear (45) is absent on RT5020 and SRT5020 models.

1. Housing	18. Spacer	35. Retainer	51. Tine gearcase
2. Worm shaft	19. Washer	36. Shim(s)	52. Set screw
3. Woodruff key	20. Worm gear	37. Snap ring	53. Front clutch jaw
4. Worm	21. Spacer	38. Hub	54. Snap ring
5. Spacer	22. Low pinion gear	39. Roll pin	55. Seal
6. Bearing cone	23. Washer	40. Shift yoke	56. Snap ring
7. Bearing cup	24. Bushing	41. Steel ball	57. Bearing cup
8. Snap ring	25. Low gear	42. Spring	58. Bearing cone
9. Bushing	26. Washer	43. Snap ring	59. Washer
10. Seal	27. Bushing	44. Shim(s)	60. Cover
11. Bushing	28. Axle shaft	45. High gear	61. Clutch yoke
12. Pinion shaft	29. Woodruff key	46. Washer	62. Roll pin
13. Woodruff key	30. Gasket	47. Bushing	63. Shift lever
14. Woodruff key	31. Cover	48. Tine clutch lever	64. Dipstick
15. Woodruff key	32. Plug	49. Rear clutch jaw	65. Seal
16. Washer	33. Seal	50. Roll pin	66. Woodruff key
17. High pinion gear	34. Cap screw		

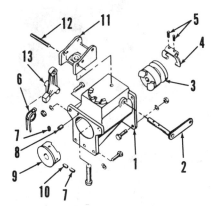

Fig. AR15—Exploded view of tine clutch assembly used on early models with cast iron wheel drive gearcase.

1. Case	8. Pin
2. Yoke shaft	9. Front clutch jaw
3. Rear clutch jaw	10. Bottom set screw
4. Clutch yoke	11. Bracket
5. Roll pin	12. Pin
6. Spring	13. Latch
7. Top set screw	

rear clutch jaw (49). Remove two set screws (52) and slide front clutch jaw (53) off shaft (2). Remove snap ring (54). Remove bushing (9), seal (10) and snap ring (8). Remove side cover (31). Slide washer (26) and low gear (25) off axle (28). Noting position of shift lever (63), drive out roll pin (39), remove lever (63), shift yoke (40) and pull axle shaft (28) from housing (1). Remove snap ring (37) and slide hub (38) off shaft (28). Do not lose spring (42) and ball (41) when sliding hub (38) off shaft (28). Remove high gear (45), shim(s) (44) and washer (46). Drive worm shaft (2) out front of housing (1). Drive out seal (55), remove snap ring (56) and drive out bearing cup (57). Remove pinion shaft (12). Low pinion gear (22) and high pinion gear (17) are a light press fit on shaft (12).

Inspect all components for excessive wear or other damage. Renew all gaskets and seals. Reverse disassembly procedure to reassemble transmission.

DRIVE BELTS

Model RT524C

Remove drive belt cover. Remove belt from pulleys and install new belt. Drive belt size is ½ inch x 32 inches long. Refer to Fig. AR17 for belt routing and parts identification. Refer to CLUTCH CONTROL ADJUSTMENT section for adjusting procedure. Reinstall drive belt cover.

Models RT214 and RT320

Refer to Fig. AR18 for belt routing and parts identification. Disconnect wire from spark plug, then remove drive belt guard. Remove cap screw (3) and swing belt finger (1) clear of belt. Unhook clutch chain from lever. Loosen idler pulley retaining nut and slide pulley clear of belt. Remove belt from pulleys and install new belt. Drive belt size is ½ inch x 32-1/4 inches long. Refer to DRIVE BELT and CLUTCH CONTROL under ADJUSTMENT section for belt

adjusting procedures. Reinstall cap screw and adjust belt finger to provide 1/16 to 1/8 inch (1.6-3.2 mm) clearance between belt and finger when clutch is engaged. Reinstall belt cover, then reconnect spark plug wire.

Model RT324

Refer to Fig. AR19 for belt routing and parts identification. Disconnect wire from spark plug, then remove drive belt guard. Remove cap screw (5) and swing belt finger (6) clear of belt. Unhook clutch chain from lever. Loosen idler bracket cap screw (4) enough to allow belt to slide clear of pulley. Remove belt from pulleys and install new belt. Drive belt size is ½ inch x 32 inches long. Retighten cap screw (4). Refer to CLUTCH CONTROL under ADJUSTMENT section for adjusting procedure. Reinstall cap screw (5) and adjust belt finger to provide 1/16 to 1/8 inch (1.6-3.2 mm) clearance between drive belt and finger when clutch is engaged. Reinstall belt cover, then reconnect spark plug wire.

Models RT424, RT424X, RT424CI, RT524 and RT524S

Refer to Fig. AR20 for routing belts and parts identification. Disconnect wire from spark plug, then remove drive belt guard. Remove forward drive belt wire finger and securing bolt. Unhook clutch chain from lever. Tip forward idler away from belt and remove belt from pulleys. Forward drive belt size is ½ inch x 32 inches long. To replace reverse belt, loosen forward engine pulley (2) set screws and remove pulley from shaft. Unhook reverse clutch chain from lever. Remove reverse belt finger securing nuts and washers and swing belt finger clear of belt. Loosen idler arm cap screw (6) enough to allow belt to slide clear of pulley. Remove belt from pulleys and install new belt. Reverse drive belt size is 3/8 inch x 32 inches long. Reassemble in reverse order of

disassembly. Refer to CLUTCH CONTROL under ADJUSTMENT section for adjusting procedure. Adjust belt fingers

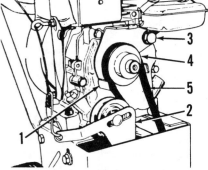

Fig. AR18—View of drive belt and components for Models RT214 and RT320.

1. Belt finger
2. Idler pulley assy.
3. Cap screw
4. Engine pulley
5. Drive belt

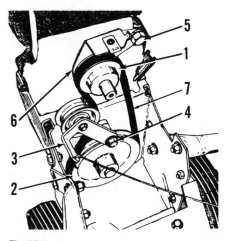

Fig. AR19—View of drive belt and components for Model RT324.

1. Engine pulley
2. Gearcase pulley
3. Idler pulley assy.
4. Idler bracket cap screw
5. Belt finger cap screw
6. Belt finger
7. Drive belt

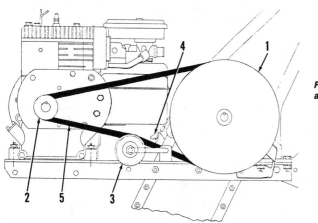

Fig. AR17—View of drive belt and components for tiller Model RT524C.

1. Chain case drive pulley
2. Engine pulley
3. Idler pulley assy.
4. Cable lever
5. Drive belt

Fig. AR20—View of belt arrangement and components for tiller Models RT424, RT424X, RT424CI, RT524 and RT524S.

1. Reverse engine pulley
2. Forward engine pulley
3. Reverse idler assy.
4. Forward idler assy.
5. Gearcase pulley
6. Idler arm cap screw
7. Reverse drive belt
8. Forward drive belt

to provide 1/16 to 1/8 inch (1.6-3.2 mm) clearance between drive belt and fingers when clutch is engaged. Reinstall belt cover, then reconnect spark plug wire.

Models RT5020, SRT5020, RT7020, RT8020 and RT8028

Refer to Fig. AR6 for routing belts and parts identification. Disconnect wire from spark plug, then remove drive belt guard. Unbolt and remove forward drive belt wire finger. Remove cotter pin (2) from adjustment link (3) and remove link from idler bracket. Swing idler assembly clear of drive belts and remove belts. Forward drive belt(s) size is ½ inch x 32 inches long. To replace reverse belt, remove reverse belt finger securing nuts and washers and swing belt finger clear of belt. Remove cotter pin from reverse idler linkage rod, then remove linkage rod from idler bracket. Swing idler assembly clear of belt and remove belt from pulleys. Reverse drive belt is 3/8 inch x 31 inches. Replace belts and reassemble in reverse order of disassembly. Refer to CLUTCH CONTROL under ADJUSTMENT section for adjusting forward clutch spring and reverse idler. Adjust belt fingers to provide 1/16 to 1/8 inch (1.6-3.2 mm) clearance between drive belt and fingers when clutch is engaged. Reinstall belt cover, then reconnect spark plug wire.

ATLAS

ATLAS POWER EQUIPMENT CO.
P.O. Box 70
Harvard, IL 60033

Model	Engine Make	Engine Series	Engine Horsepower	No. of Forward Speeds	Power Reverse?	Tilling Width (In.)	Drive Type
12-2100	B&S	60000	2	1	No	10.5-18.5	Chain
12-3010	B&S	80000	3	1	No	14-24	Gear
12-3011	B&S	80000	3	1	No	14-24	Gear
12-3100	B&S	80000	3	1	No	14-24	Chain
12-3150	B&S	80000	3	1	No	10.5-18.5	Chain
12-5012	B&S	130000	5	1	No	9.75-26	Gear
12-5012	Tec.	H50	5	1	No	9.75-26	Gear
12-5013	B&S	130000	5	1	No	9.75-26	Gear
12-5013	Tec.	H50	5	1	No	9.75-26	Gear
12-5015	B&S	130000	5	1	Yes	9.75-26	Gear
12-5016	B&S	130000	5	1	Yes	9.75-26	Gear
12-5021	B&S	130000	5	2	Yes	9.75-26	Gear
12-5022	B&S	130000	5	2	Yes	9.75-26	Gear
12-5100	B&S	130000	5	1	Yes	14-26	Chain
12-5300	B&S	130000	5	1	No	14-26	Chain

LUBRICATION

ENGINE

All Models

Refer to appropriate engine section for engine lubrication requirements. Recommended fuel is regular or unleaded.

WHEELS AND CONTROLS

All Models

A few drops of oil should be placed oc-

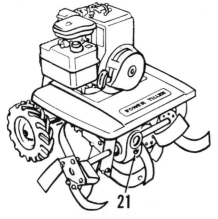

Fig. AT1 — View of gear box oil fill plug (21) location on models so equipped.

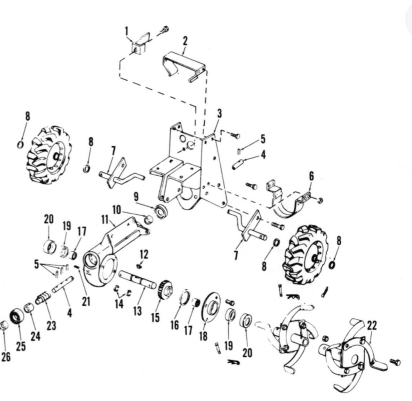

Fig. AT2 — Typical exploded view of tiller gear box and frame assemblies used on all gear-drive models. Refer to Figs. AT7, AT8 and AT9 for drive belt arrangement.

1. Belt guide	8. Washer	15. Bronze gear	22. Tine assy.
2. Belt retainer	9. Oil seal	16. "O" ring	23. Worm gear
3. Frame	10. Sleeve bearing	17. Needle bearing	24. Center worm spacer
4. Worm shaft	11. Gear housing	18. Gear housing cover	25. Ball bearing
5. Roll pin	12. Key	19. Oil seal	26. End worm spacer
6. Belt guard	13. Output shaft	20. Dust shield	27. Snap ring
7. Axle	14. Retainer ring	21. Oil level plug	28. End cover

casionally on all movable parts such as wheel bearings and idler roller arms. Caution should be used in not getting oil on drive belts.

GEAR DRIVE

All Models So Equipped

Manufacturer recommends AMOCO worm gear oil, however, SAE 140 EP oil, may be used if AMOCO oil is unavailable. Proper gear housing oil level is approximately ½-inch (12.7 mm) below bottom of filler plug opening (21 – Fig. AT1 or AT2) with gear housing in level position. Oil level should be checked after every 5 hours of operation. Renew oil after every 50 hours of operation.

CHAIN DRIVE

All Models So Equipped

Models 12-2100 and 12-3150 are lubricated during assembly and do not require periodic lubrication. All other chain drive models are lubricated by SAE 50 oil poured through oil fill plug (15 – Fig. AT3) opening. With tiller setting in normal position, oil level should be approximately ½-¾ inch (12.7-19.1 mm) below bottom of fillter plug hole. Oil level should be checked every 5 hours and added as necessary.

MAINTENANCE

Check condition of control levers, linkage and cables and renew if excessive play or binding prohibits easy, complete engagement of drive mechanism. Inspect drive belt(s) and renew if frayed, cracked, burnt or otherwise damaged. Inspect belt pulley(s) and renew if damaged or worn excessively. Output shaft dust shields should be checked and renewed if cracked, split or otherwise damaged.

ADJUSTMENT

DRIVE BELTS

Models 12-3100, 12-5100, 12-5300

With engagement lever (5 – Fig. AT4) in drive position adjust turnbuckle (13) until spring (10) has slight tension and

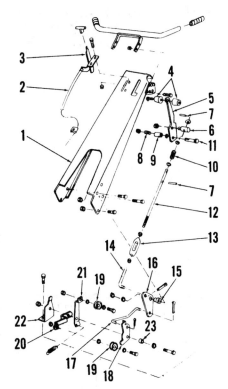

Fig. AT4 – Exploded view of Models 12-3100, 12-5100 and 12-5300 handle assembly.

1. Handle frame	13. Turnbuckle
2. Throttle cable	14. Lower control rod
3. Throttle lever	15. Bushing
4. Knob	16. Bellcrank
5. Drive lever	17. Idler control rod
6. Stud	18. Idler pulley plate
7. Pin	19. Idler pulley
8. Spring	20. Forward idler arm
9. Spacer	21. Reverse arm
10. Spring	22. Idler bracket
11. Bolt	23. Spacer
12. Upper control rod	

gap between pin (7) and stud washer (24 – Fig. AT5) is approximately 1/16-inch (1.6 mm).

Models 12-2100, 12-3150

Adjust bolt (B – Fig. AT6) on engagement lever (L) until cable (C) is tight and there is slight tension on spring (S) with lever in off position.

All Other Models

To adjust engagement lever on Models 12-5012, 12-5013, 12-5015, 12-5016, 12-5021 and 12-5022, rotate turnbuckle on engagement rod. For initial setting pull back on engagement lever until lever is approximately 3/16 inch (4.8 mm) from top end of slot when pulled on with moderate hand pressure. Tighten both locknuts at turnbuckle. If rod bends excessively the turnbuckle is adjusted too tight.

If belt slack is excessive on gear-drive models, install washers between engine and tiller hood on each engine mounting bolt. Total thickness of washers at each bolt should be equal so engine is level. Repeat adjustment procedure on Models 12-5012, 12-5013, 12-5015, 12-5016, 12-5021 and 12-5022.

OVERHAUL

ENGINE

All Models

Engine model no. is stamped on blower housing for Briggs and Stratton

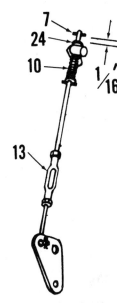

Fig. AT5 – Drawing of turnbuckle adjustment on Models 12-3100, 12-5100 and 12-5300. Refer to Fig. AT4 for parts identification except for: 24. Stud washer.

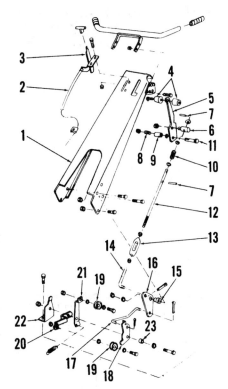

Fig. AT3 – Exploded view of chain drive components on Models 12-3100, 12-5100 and 12-5300.

1. Pulley	8. Sleeve	14. Upper intermediate sprocket	18. Inner tine & hub assy.
2. Roll pin	9. Output shaft & sprocket	14A. Lower intermediate sprocket	19. Outer tine & hub assy.
3. Oil seal	10. Spacer	15. Oil fill plug	20. Chain (no. 35)
4. Bushing	11. Bushing	16. Plate	21. Chain (no. 420)
5. Chain case	12. Seal	17. Gasket	22. Chain (no. 50)
6. Input shaft & sprocket	13. Dust seal		
7. Bushing			

engines. Engine make and series no. is marked on data plate attached to engine for Tecumseh engines. Refer to appropriate Briggs and Stratton or Tecumseh engine section for overhaul procedures.

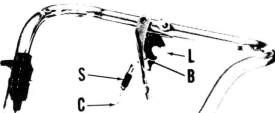

DRIVE BELTS

Models 12-3010, 12-3011, 12-5012, 12-5013

To renew belt, remove lower belt

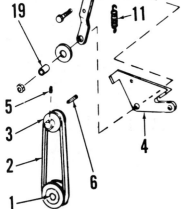

Fig. AT6—Adjust drive belt on Models 12-2100 and 12-3150 by turning bolt (B) as outlined in text.

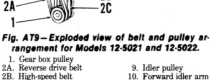

Fig. AT7—Exploded view of belt and pulley arrangement for Models 12-3010, 12-3011, 12-5012 and 12-5013. Refer to Fig. AT9 for parts identification except for: 2. Drive belt; 19. Spacer.

Fig. AT9—Exploded view of belt and pulley arrangement for Models 12-5021 and 12-5022.

1. Gear box pulley	
2A. Reverse drive belt	9. Idler pulley
2B. High-speed belt	10. Forward idler arm
2C. Low-speed belt	11. Spring
3. Forward engine pulley	12. Reverse engine pulley
4. Idler arm plate	13. Woodruff key
5. Set screw	14. Nut
6. Key	15. Low-speed arm
7. Idler arm spring	16. Reverse idler arm
8. Washer	17. Idler arm spacer

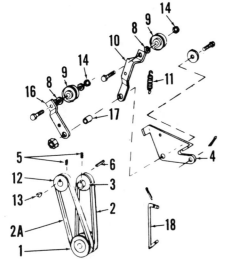

Fig. AT8—Exploded view of belt and pulley arrangement for Models 12-5015 and 12-5016. Refer to Fig. AT9 for parts identification except for: 2. Forward drive belt; 18. Link.

guard (6–Fig. AT2) then remove belt from lower and upper pulleys (1 and 3–Fig. AT7). Install belt by reversing removal procedure. Drive belt size is ½-inch x 31 inches long. After belt installation be sure belt guide (1–Fig. AT2) is properly installed and idler pulley is on outside of belt. Refer to **ADJUSTMENT** section for belt adjustment. It may be necessary to remove washers between engine and tiller hood to permit proper adjustment.

Models 12-5015, 12-5016

To renew belts remove lower belt guard (6–Fig. AT2) then remove forward drive belt (2–Fig. AT8) from upper and lower pulleys. To remove reverse belt (2A) both engine drive pulleys (3 and 12) must be removed. Unscrew set screws (5) and slide or pull the forward drive pulley off the shaft, then remove the reverse drive pulley and belt. Install belts by reversing removal procedure. Drive belt(s) size is ½-inch x 31 inches long. After belt installation be sure belt guide (1–Fig. AT2) is properly installed and idler pulley is on outside of belt. Refer to **ADJUSTMENT** section for belt adjustment. It may be necessary to remove washers between engine and tiller hood to permit proper adjustment.

Models 12-5021, 12-5022

To renew belts remove lower belt guard (6–Fig. AT2), then remove high speed drive belt (2B–Fig. AT9) from lower and upper pulleys (1 and 3). If

Fig. AT10—Exploded view of frame assembly used on Models 12-2100, 12-3150. Refer to Fig. AT11 for parts identification except for: 35. Idler pulley; 36. Bracket; 37. Idler arm; 38. Control cable.

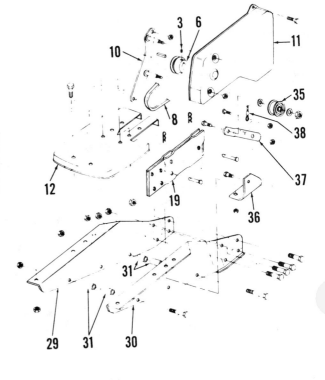

other belts are to be removed then engine pulleys (3 and 12) must be removed. Loosen set screws, then slide pulleys with belts from shafts. Install belts by reversing removal procedure. Drive belt(s) size is ½-inch x 31 inches long. Refer to **ADJUSTMENT** section for belt adjustment. It may be necessary to remove washers between engine and tiller hood to permit proper adjustment.

Models 12-2100, 12-3100, 12-3150, 12-5100 and 12-5300

To renew belts remove belt guard assembly (11 – Fig. AT10 or AT11). Relieve idler pulley tension then slip belts off pulleys. To install belts reverse removal procedure. Models 12-2100, 12-3100, 12-3150 and 12-5300 drive belt size is ½-inch x 36 inches long. For Model 12-5100 forward drive belt size is ½-inch x 36 inches long. Reverse drive belt size is ½-inch x 32 inches long.

CHAIN CASE

All Models

INSPECTION. For Models 12-2100 and 12-3150 refer to Fig. AT12 for parts breakdown and identification. For Models 12-3100, 12-5100 and 12-5300 refer to Fig. AT3 for parts breakdown and identification. A ½-inch x 13 thread per inch screw is used as a jackscrew for removal of input shaft pulley on Models 12-2100 and 12-3150. Drive cross pin (2 – Fig. AT12) out of drive pulley (1) and input shaft, then thread screw into pulley hub until it bottoms against end of input shaft. Continue to turn screw until pulley is removed from shaft.

Inspect and renew all components that are worn or damaged. Install new gasket and seals. Lubricate chains, sprockets and bearings with a light film of oil during reassembly. Keep all dirt and foreign matter out of chain case during reassembly. Models 12-2100 and 12-3150 do not require any lubrication other than the light film of oil. For Models 12-3100, 12-5100 and 12-5300 refer to **LUBRICATION** section for lubrication requirements after reassembly and installation.

GEAR CASE

All Models

INSPECTION. Refer to Fig. AT2 for parts breakdown and identification. Inspect and renew all components that are worn or damaged. Install new seals. Lubricate gears and bearings with a light film of oil during reassembly. Keep all dirt and foreign matter out of gear case during reassembly. Refer to **LUBRICATION** section for lubricating requirements after reassembly and installation.

Fig. AT11 – Exploded view of frame assembly used on 12-5100. Models 12-3100 and 12-5300 are similar except for absence of reverse drive parts.

1. Deflector
2. Reverse drive belt
3. Set screw
4. Reverse engine pulley
5. Woodruff key
6. Forward engine pulley
7. Key
8. Forward drive belt
9. Handle brace cover
10. Belt guide
11. Belt guard
12. Hood
13. Handle support
14. Drag bracket pivot pin
15. Drag bar depth pin
16. Spring
17. Spacer
18. Washer
19. Drag bracket pivot
20. Drag bar
21. Plate
22. Spring
23. Spacer
24. Washer
25. Wheel height pin
26. Spring
27. Spacer
28. Bracket
29. Frame rail, right
30. Frame rail, left
31. Spacer
32. Wheel bracket
33. Spacer
34. Washer

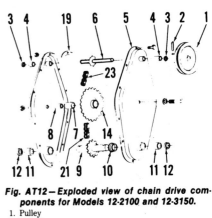

Fig. AT12 – Exploded view of chain drive components for Models 12-2100 and 12-3150.

1. Pulley
2. Roll pin
3. Oil seal
4. Bushing
5. Chain case
6. Input shaft & sprocket
7. Bushing
8. Sleeve
9. Output shaft & sprocket
10. Spacer
11. Bushing
12. Seal
14. Intermediate sprocket
19. Gasket
21. Chain (no. 420)
23. Chain (no. 42)

BCS

BCS MOSA
13601 Providence Road
P.O. Box 1739
Matthews, NC 28105

Model	Engine Make	Engine Series	Power Rating	No. of Forward Speeds	Power Reverse?	Tilling Width	Drive Type
204	BCS	180	5 hp (3.7 kW)	2	Yes	20 in. (51 cm)	Gear
205	BCS	180	5 hp (3.7 kW)	2	Yes	18 in. (46 cm)	Gear
715	Acme	A220	6 hp (4.5 kW)	3	Yes	8-26 in. (20-66 cm)	Gear
715	Acme	ALN290	8 hp (6.0 kW)	3	Yes	8-26 in. (20-66 cm)	Gear
715	Acme	ALN330	10 hp (7.5 kW)	3	Yes	8-26 in. (20-66 cm)	Gear
725	Acme	ALN290	8 hp (6.0 kW)	5	Yes	20-30 in. (51-76 cm)	Gear
725	Acme	ALN330	10 hp (7.5 kW)	5	Yes	20-30 in. (51-76 cm)	Gear
725	Lombardini (Diesel)	6LD 360	8 hp (6.0 kW)	5	Yes	20-30 in. (51-76 cm)	Gear
735	Acme	ALN330	10 hp (7.5 kW)	5	Yes	20-30 in. (51-76 cm)	Gear
735	Lombardini (Diesel)	3LD 510	10 hp (7.5 kW)	5	Yes	20-30 in. (51-76 cm)	Gear
745	Acme	VT88	16 hp (12.0 kW)	5	Yes	33 in. (84 cm)	Gear
745	Lombardini (Diesel)	3LD 510	14 hp (10.4 kW)	5	Yes	33 in. (84 cm)	Gear
745	Kohler	M14	14 hp (10.4 kW)	5	Yes	33 in. (84 cm)	Gear

LUBRICATION

ENGINE

All Models

Refer to appropriate Acme, BCS, Lombardini or Kohler engine section for engine lubrication specifications. Recommended oil is a good quality SAE 10W-40 engine oil. Recommended fuel for gasoline powered models is regular gasoline. Recommended fuel for diesel powered models is number 1 diesel fuel.

TRANSMISSION

All Models

Oil level in transmission should be checked after 50 hours of operation or every six months. With tiller in a level position, oil level should be even with oil level plug hole (1—Fig. B1) on side of transmission on Models 204 and 205, or

between lines (4 and 5—Fig. B2) on dipstick (2) located on top of transmission on all other models. Transmission oil should be changed at one year intervals. Recommended oil is a good quality SAE 80W-90 EP gear lubricant.

Fig. B1—Transmission oil level should be even with level plug hole (1) on Models 204 and 205.

TINE GEARCASE

All Models

Check oil level in tine gearcase every 50 hours of operation on Models 204 and 205, or every 100 hours on all other models. With tiller on level surface, oil level should be approximately 50 mm (2 in.) from top of fill plug hole on 204 and 205 models, or near the top of fill hole on all other models. Fill plug is located on top of tine gearcase on all models. Change oil in tine gearcase at one year intervals. Recommended oil is a good quality SAE 80W-90 EP gear lubricant.

MAINTENANCE

All Models

Inspect all fasteners for looseness and tighten as necessary. Check control levers, linkage and cables for freedom of movement and excessive play. Apply a suitable lubricant on control cables and linkage after 50 hours of operation on 204 and 205 models, or yearly on all other models. Periodically check tires for specified inflation pressure of 98 kPa (14.2 psi). On Models 715, 725, 735 and 745, check clutch cable adjustment after every 50 hours of operation. Refer to ADJUSTMENT section.

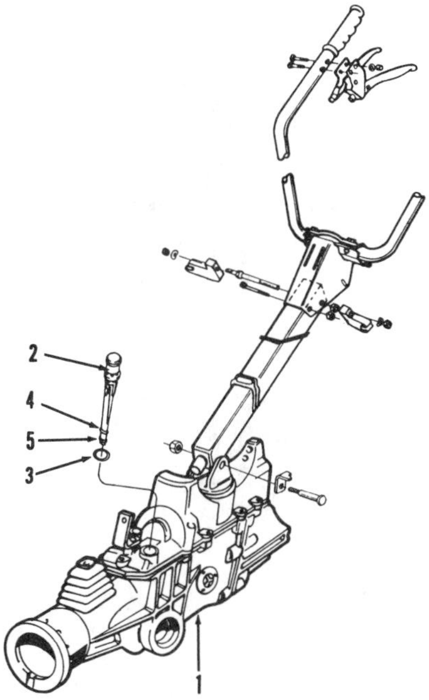

ADJUSTMENT

CONTROL CABLES

Models 204 and 205

Free play in control levers (3—Fig. B3) should be 6-13 mm (0.25-0.5 in.). To adjust levers, loosen jam nut (2) and turn adjusting nut (1) to obtain correct free play. Tighten jam nut, start engine and operate unit to check adjustment. Make certain that simultaneous engagement of forward and reverse gears is not possible. Refer to Figs. B4 and B5 for exploded views of handlebar and control assemblies.

CLUTCH CABLE

Models 715, 725, 735 and 745

To adjust clutch cable, hold cable nut (2—Fig. B6) from turning with a suitable wrench. Rotate adjustment nut (1) to obtain a 13 mm (0.5 in.) deflection (D) in cable (3).

TRANSMISSION CONTROL

Models 715, 725, 735 and 745

Place transmission into the neutral position. Push tiller to ensure that transmission is in neutral. Loosen nuts (3—Fig. B7) and move indicator bracket (1) as necessary to align lever (2) with neutral position on indicator bracket (1).

Fig. B2—On Models 715, 725, 735 and 745, transmission oil level should be between lines (4 and 5) on dipstick (2).

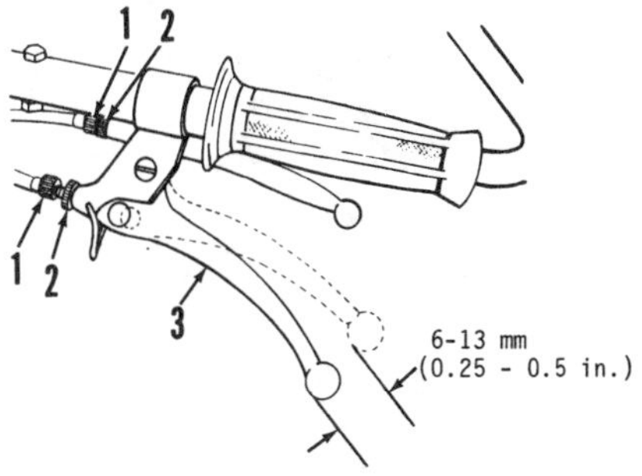

Fig. B3—To adjust control cables, loosen jam nut (2) and turn adjusting nut (1) to obtain proper control lever (3) free play.

6-13 mm
(0.25 - 0.5 in.)

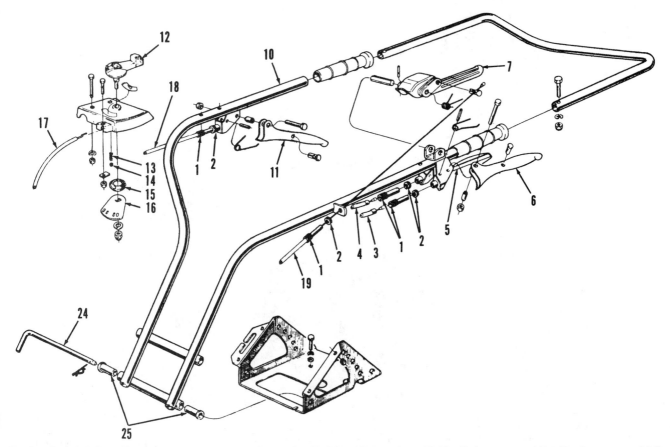

Fig. B4—Exploded view of handlebar and control assemblies used on Model 204. Refer to legend in Fig. B5 for component identification except rod (24) and bushings (25).

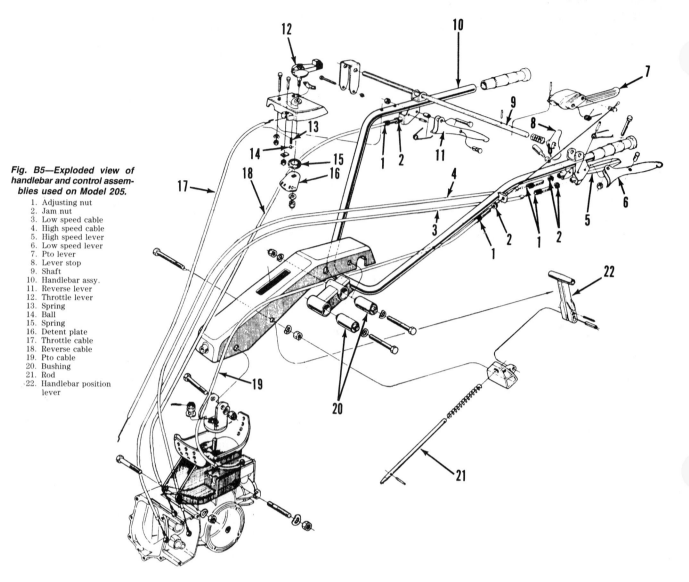

Fig. B5—Exploded view of handlebar and control assemblies used on Model 205.

1. Adjusting nut
2. Jam nut
3. Low speed cable
4. High speed cable
5. High speed lever
6. Low speed lever
7. Pto lever
8. Lever stop
9. Shaft
10. Handlebar assy.
11. Reverse lever
12. Throttle lever
13. Spring
14. Ball
15. Spring
16. Detent plate
17. Throttle cable
18. Reverse cable
19. Pto cable
20. Bushing
21. Rod
22. Handlebar position lever

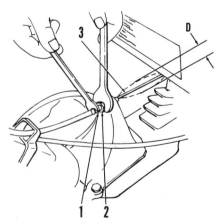

Fig. B6—On Models 715, 725, 735 and 745, deflection (D) in clutch cable (3) should be 13 mm (0.5 in.). Hold cable nut (2) and turn adjusting nut (1) to adjust clutch cable.

1. Adjustment nut
2. Cable nut
3. Cable
D. Deflection

DIFFERENTIAL LOCK

Models 735 and 745

Loosen jam nut (22—Fig. B8) and turn adjusting screw (21) to adjust cable.

Fig. B7—To adjust transmission control on Models 715, 725, 735 and 745, loosen nuts (3) and move indicator bracket (1) to align lever (2) with neutral position on indicator bracket (1).

1. Indicator bracket
2. Lever
3. Nut

Start engine and operate unit to check adjustment. Differential should lock in two-wheel drive when lever (20) is pulled back. Make sure differential unlocks when lever (20) is released.

OVERHAUL

ENGINE

All Models

Engine type is marked on data plate attached to blower housing and serial number is stamped in engine block below data plate on Acme engines. On BCS engines, serial number is marked on plate attached to cylinder air baffle above ignition coil. Model, specification and serial numbers are marked on tag located on carburetor side of blower housing on Kohler engines, and on tag

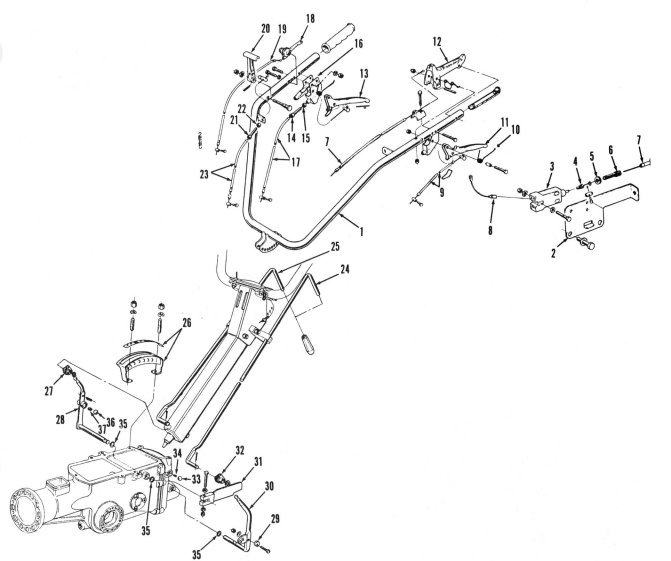

Fig. B8—Exploded view of handlebar and control assemblies typical of Models 715, 725, 735 and 745. Engine kill switch (3), lever (12), cable (7) and ground lead (8) are absent on early models.

1. Handlebar assy.	9. Clutch cable assy.	17. Brake cable assy.
2. Bracket	10. Spring	18. Throttle lever
3. Kill switch	11. Clutch lever	19. Throttle cable assy.
4. Spring	12. Kill switch lever	20. Differential lock
5. Jam nut	13. Brake lever	lever
6. Adjusting screw	14. Adjusting screw	21. Adjusting screw
7. Cable assy.	15. Jam nut	22. Jam nut
8. Ground lead	16. Bracket	23. Cable assy.

24. Pto control rod	31. Lockout lever
25. Shift rod	32. Knuckle
26. Indicator bracket	33. Ball
27. Knuckle	34. Spring
28. Shift lever	35. "O" ring
29. Pto lockout cam	36. Ball
30. Pto lever	37. Spring

located on flywheel side of blower housing on Lombardini engines. Refer to appropriate Acme, BCS, Kohler or Lombardini engine section for overhaul procedure.

TINE GEARCASE

Model 205

NOTE: Tiller gearcase used on Model 205 is equipped with a shock absorbing clutch assembly (9, 10, 11, 12 and 13—Fig. B9). If tiller tines do not rotate under load, inspect unit for worn or damaged clutch components.

Fig. B9—Exploded view of tine gearcase used on Model 205.

1. Case
2. Bearing
3. Snap ring
4. Seal
5. Flange
6. Washer
7. Nut
8. Tine shaft
9. Ring gear
10. Clutch cone
11. Belleville springs
12. Spacer
13. Ring nut
14. Seal
15. Snap ring
16. Washer
17. Bearing
18. Snap ring
19. Bushing
20. Pinion shaft
21. Cover
22. Gasket
23. Plug
24. Bearing

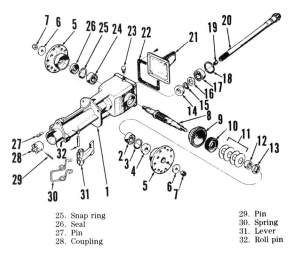

25. Snap ring	29. Pin
26. Seal	30. Spring
27. Pin	31. Lever
28. Coupling	32. Roll pin

DISASSEMBLY. Remove nuts (7—Fig. B9), washers (6) and tine flanges (5). Remove cover (21) and drain oil. Remove seals (4 and 26) and snap rings (3 and 25). Lock rotation of tine shaft (8) and unscrew ring nut (13). Nut (13) has right-hand threads. Press tine shaft out of case (1) from opposite end of ring gear (9) and remove shaft and related components as shown in Fig. B10. Remove snap ring (18—Fig. B9). Properly support case (1) and drive out pin (29). Separate coupling (28) from pinion shaft (20), pull shaft (20) from case (1) and remove seal (14).

INSPECTION. Inspect all components for excessive wear or damage. Inspect case for metal shavings indicating excessive wear of clutch cone (10—Fig. B9). Make sure cone (10) does not bottom out inside ring gear (9) by placing cone (10) inside gear (9) and measuring thickness as shown in Fig. B11. Renew clutch cone and ring gear if thickness (T) is less than 31.394 mm (1.236 in.).

Belleville springs (11—Fig. B9) should be approximately 4.25 mm (0.167 in.) thick. Renew Belleville springs (11) if flattened out or damaged.

REASSEMBLY. Renew all seals and gaskets. Coat all components with a film of gear lube during reassembly. Use a suitable seal protector on splines of pinion shaft (20—Fig. B9) to prevent damage to seal (14). Install tine shaft (8) into case (1) in opposite direction of removal (Fig. B10). Refer to (inset—Fig. B12) and install Belleville springs (11) as shown. Tighten ring nut (13) as tight as possible. Install seals (4 and 26—Fig. B9) with lips facing inward. Refer to LUBRICATION section for lubrication requirements after reassembly.

Models 715, 725, 735 and 745

DISASSEMBLY. Refer to Fig. B13 or B14 for appropriate exploded view of tine gearcase. Remove cover (19) and drain oil. Unbolt side cover (3) and

remove cover (3) and tine shaft (7).

On Models 715, 725 and 735, remove seal (11—Fig. B13), snap ring (12) and pinion shaft (17). On Model 745, remove screw (22-Fig. B14), washer (21), coupling (20), seal (11), snap ring (12) and pinion shaft (17).

INSPECTION. Inspect all components for excessive wear or damage and renew as necessary. Two sizes of tine shaft (7—Fig. B13) have been used on Models 715, 725 and 735. Measure shaft diameter at point shown in Fig. B15 before ordering parts. Early shaft diameter is 20.218 mm (0.796 in.) and later shaft diameter is 24.993 mm (0.984 in.).

REASSEMBLY. Renew all gaskets and seals. Lubricate components with a light film of oil during reassembly. Install bearings (6 and 8—Fig. B13 or B14) on shaft (7) prior to installing shaft (7) into case (14). Use suitable seal protectors when installing shafts (7 and 17) to prevent damage to seals. Tighten side cover (3) attaching nuts to 24.4 N·m (18 ft.-lbs.). Tighten screw (22—Fig. B14) to 10.8 N·m (8 ft.-lbs.). On early Models 715, 725 and 735 equipped with 20.218 mm (0.796 in.) diameter tine shaft

Fig. B10—On Model 205, remove shaft (8) as shown. Refer to legend in Fig. B9 for component identification.

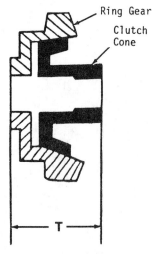

Fig. B11—To check clutch wear on Model 205, assemble ring gear and clutch cone as shown. Minimum thickness (T) is 31.394 mm (1.236 in.). Refer to text.

Fig. B12—On Model 205, install Belleville springs (11) as shown (inset). Refer to legend in Fig. B9 for component identification.

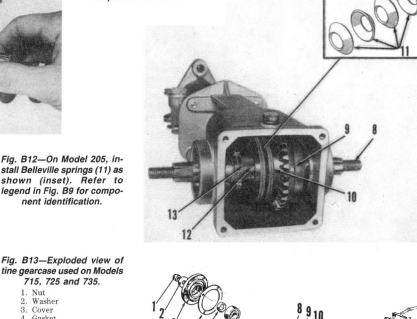

Fig. B13—Exploded view of tine gearcase used on Models 715, 725 and 735.

1. Nut
2. Washer
3. Cover
4. Gasket
5. Seal
6. Bearing
7. Tine shaft & gear assy
8. Bearing
9. Seal
10. Plug
11. Seal
12. Snap ring
13. Bearing
14. Case
15. Tine flange
16. Bearing
17. Pinion shaft
18. Gasket
19. Cover

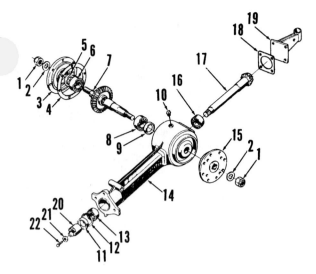

Fig. B14—Exploded view of tine gearcase used on Model 745. Refer to legend in Fig. B13 for component identification except coupling (20), washer (21) and screw (22).

(7—Fig. B13), tighten nuts (1) to 85.4 N·m (63 ft.-lbs.), or 135.6 N·m (100 ft.-lbs.) on later models equipped with 24.993 mm (0.984 in.) diameter tine shaft (7). On Model 745, tighten nuts (1—Fig. B14) to 274 N·m (202 ft.-lbs.). Refer to LUBRICATION section for lubrication requirements after reassembly.

WHEEL REVERSERS

Model 205

Model 205 is equipped with planetary wheel reversing units to change drive direction to accommodate various tiller attachments.

To disassemble reverser unit, remove cap screws (9—Fig. B16) and separate flange (5) along with planetary gears (4) from hub (2). Remove cap (1) and crown gear (3) from hub (2).

Inspect all components for excessive wear or damage and renew as necessary.

Reassembly is the reverse of disassembly procedure. Apply a liberal amount of a suitable bearing grease on planetary gears (4), crown gear (3) and hub (2) during reassembly.

CLUTCH

Models 715, 725 and 735

To disassemble clutch, remove engine from tiller. Using a 5 mm Allen wrench

(3—Fig. B17), remove screw (2). Clutch is a taper fit on crankshaft. Use BCS tool 521.48980.2 as shown in Fig. B17 to break loose taper fit. If BCS tool 521.48980.2 is not available, remove clutch by striking side of clutch with a soft-faced mallet. Place clutch in a vise as shown in Fig. B19 and remove three screws (1).

WARNING: Spring (6—Fig. B18) is under considerable load when compressed. Use caution when releasing vise to prevent damage to unit or personal injury.

Carefully release vise and separate hub (3) and ring (10). All other components can now be removed.

Inspect all components for excessive wear or any other damage and renew as necessary. Renew spring (6) if free length is less than 83.8 mm (3.3 in.). Make sure retainer (4) slides freely inside spring seat (7).

Three clutch designs have been used. Early models used a clutch assembly with an 18 degree cone (9) and ring (10). Later models used a 12 degree "C"

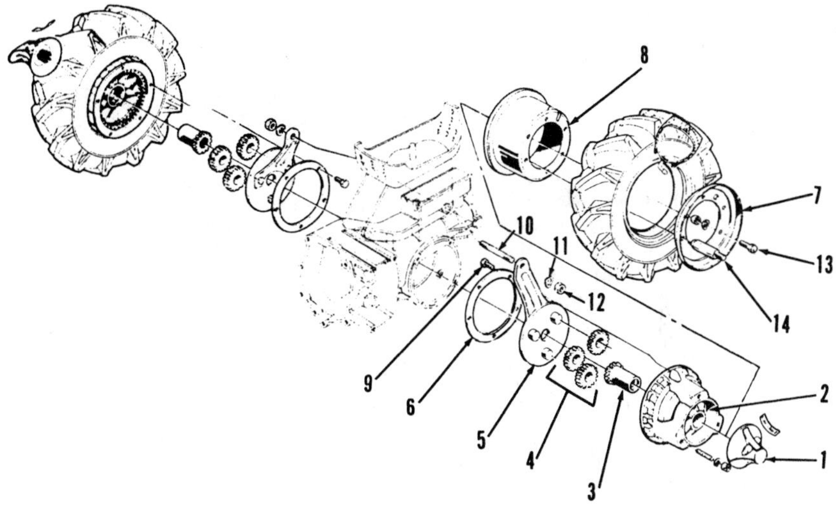

Fig. B16—Exploded view of wheel reversers used on Model 205.

1. Cap	5. Flange	8. Drum	11. Washer
2. Hub	6. Ring	9. Cap screw	12. Nut
3. Crown gear	7. Plate	10. Stud	13. Cap screw
4. Planetary gears			14. Stud

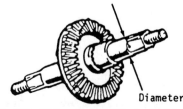

Fig. B15—When ordering parts for Models 715, 725 or 735, measure tine shaft diameter at point shown. Shaft diameter is 20.218 mm (0.796 in.) on early models and 24.993 mm (0.984 in.) on later models.

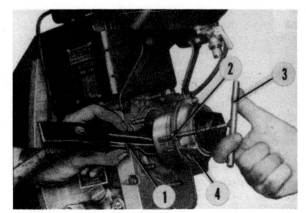

Fig. B17—Clutch assembly is a taper fit on engine crankshaft on Models 715, 725 and 735. Remove Allen screw (2) and break taper fit with BCS tool 521.48980.2 (1), or by striking side of clutch with a soft-faced mallet.
1. BCS tool 521.48980.2
2. Allen screw
3. 5 mm Allen wrench
4. Clutch assy.

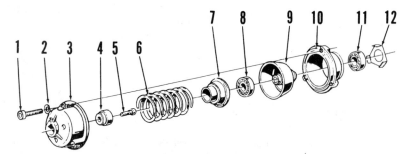

Fig. B18—Exploded view of 12 degree "L" clutch assembly used on current production Models 715, 725 and 735. Note direction of screws (1). On earlier models equipped with 12 degree "C" clutch assembly, screws (1) face opposite direction and thread into hub (3).

1. Screw	4. Retainer	7. Spring seat	10. Ring
2. Washer	5. Screw	8. Bearing	11. Bearing
3. Hub	6. Spring	9. Cone	12. Retainer

Inspect all components for excessive wear or damage and renew as necessary. Renew spring (10) if spring free length is less than 83.8 mm (3.3 in.). Check friction lining in clutch rings (8 and 12) as shown in Fig. B22.

Reassemble clutch assembly and loosely install screws (6—Fig. B21) and nuts (15). Install clutch assembly on transmission mainshaft to align cones (9 and 11) and tighten screws (6) to 10.8 N·m (8 ft.-lbs.). Install centering screw (5) and tighten to 24.4 N·m (18 ft.-lbs.). Install bell (1) on engine crankshaft and tighten nut (3) to 146.4 N·m (108 ft.-lbs.).

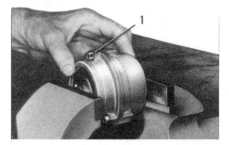

Fig. B19—Place clutch assembly in a vise as shown and remove screws (1). Use caution when releasing vise as spring (6—Fig. B18) is under high load.

Fig. B20—View A is 12 degree "C" clutch ring used on Models 715 up to serial number 68724 and 725 and 735 models up to serial number 68428. View B is 12 degree "L" clutch ring used on current production 715, 725 and 735 models. Check lining wear by measuring diameter at points shown.

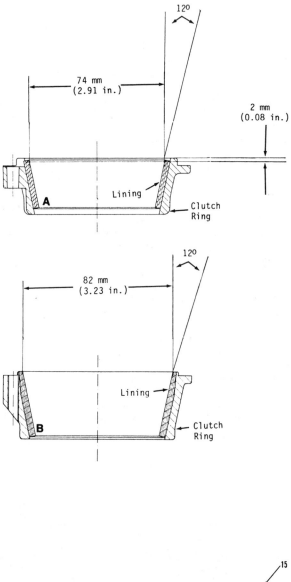

(View A—Fig. B20), and current production models are equipped with a 12 degree "L" (View B) clutch assembly. Refer to Fig. B18 or B20 to identify clutch used on later models.

Inspect friction lining in clutch ring by measuring diameter as shown in Fig. B20 and renew clutch ring if necessary. If an early 18 degree clutch requires renewal, use the later 12 degree design.

Reverse disassembly procedure to reassemble clutch. Tighten screws (1—Fig. B18) to 10.8 N·m (8 ft.-lbs.). Tighten screw (5) to 24.4 N·m (18 ft.-lbs.).

Model 745

To disassemble clutch, remove engine from tiller. Remove nut (3—Fig. B21) and lockwasher (2). Loosen bell (1) on tapered shaft by striking side of bell with a soft-faced mallet. Remove centering screw (5) and pull clutch assembly off transmission mainshaft. Place clutch in a vise as shown in Fig. B19 and remove nuts (15—Fig. B21) and screws (6).

WARNING: Spring (10) is under considerable load when compressed. Use caution when releasing vise to prevent damage to unit or personal injury.

Fig. B21—Exploded view of clutch assembly used on Model 745.

1. Bell
2. Lockwasher
3. Nut
4. Bearing
5. Centering screw
6. Screw
7. Lockwasher
8. Ring
9. Fixed cone
10. Spring
11. Movable cone
12. Ring
13. Bearing
14. Retainer
15. Nut

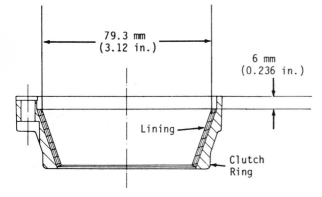

Fig. B22—On Model 745, check condition of clutch friction lining in rings (8 and 12—Fig. B21) by measuring at point shown. Diameter should be approximately 79.3 mm (3.12 in.).

TRANSMISSION

Models 204 and 205

DISASSEMBLY. Remove control cables and springs at transmission. Separate engine from transmission and remove tine gearcase on 205 models. Drive out roll pin (31—Fig. B23) and lift out pto control pin (34). Pull coupling

(39) with shoe (8) from pto shaft (3). Pull pto shaft (3) from case (1). Drive out roll pins (14 and 17) and remove control pins (13 and 16) along with shoes (8). Remove reverse gear (20), sliding gear (19) and hub (21). Remove snap ring (22), thrust washer (23) and idler gear (24). Pull seal (40) and remove snap ring (43). Locate shoulder on worm shaft (28) as shown in Fig. B24 and remove shaft (28). Take

out four screws, remove cover (not shown) and remove shaft and gear assembly (35 and 36).

INSPECTION. Inspect all components for excessive wear or damage and renew as necessary. Check control pins (13, 16 and 34—Fig. B23) for acceptable fit in case (1). Make sure pivot flange (15) is a tight fit on control pin (13). Inspect machined surface of pto shaft (3) and machined surface inside worm shaft (28) for seizing, scoring or overheating. Inspect all gears for broken teeth or oth-

Fig. B24—Shoulder (S) must be positioned as shown when removing or installing worm shaft (28). Refer to legend in Fig. B23 for component identification.

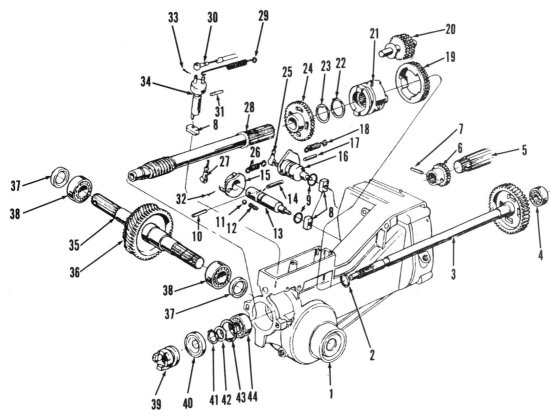

Fig. B23—Exploded view of transmission assembly used on Models 204 and 205.

1. Case	9. "O" ring	16. Reverse control pin	23. Thrust washer
2. Thrust washer	10. Roll pin	17. Roll pin	24. Idler gear
3. Pto shaft	11. Ball	18. Spring	25. Reverse cable
4. Bearing	12. Spring	19. Sliding gear	26. Spring
5. Drive shaft	13. Speed control pin	20. Reverse gear	27. Forward speed
6. High speed gear	14. Roll pin	21. Sliding hub	control
7. Roll pin	15. Pivot flange	22. Snap ring	28. Worm shaft
8. Shoe			

29. Spring	37. Seal
30. Pto cable	38. Bearing
31. Roll pin	39. Coupling
32. Cotter pin	40. Seal
33. Cotter pin	41. Snap ring
34. Pto control pin	42. Washer
35. Shaft	43. Snap ring
36. Gear	44. Bearing

er damage. Inspect bearings for roughness.

REASSEMBLY. Reverse disassembly procedure to reassemble transmission. Renew all gaskets and seals. Use suitable seal protectors when installing shafts to prevent damage to seals. Install worm shaft (28—Fig. B23) into case (1) from pto end of case with shoulder (S—Fig. B24) positioned as shown. Lubricate spline on worm shaft (28—Fig. B23)

with a suitable grease prior to installing idler gear (24). Make sure sliding gear (19) works freely on hub (21) and properly engages reverse gear (20) after installation. Refer to LUBRICATION section for lubrication requirements after reassembly.

Models 715, 725 and 735

DISASSEMBLY. Remove engine and handlebar assembly. Drain oil and

remove reverse idler assembly (26—Figs. B25 and 26). Drive out pins (22). Slide out pto engagement lever (not shown). Do not lose spring (39) or ball (40) when removing lever. Remove shift lever (21) and slider (18). Unbolt and remove cover (37).

On Model 715, pull out shafts (12 and 14—Fig. B25) from cover (37) end of case (1). Drive out pins (6). Avoid dropping pins (6) into final drive housing through oil holes in case. Slide gear shift handle out of case (1), remove lever (7) and shoe (8), sliding gear (11) and low gear (10).

On Models 725 and 735, pull out pto shaft (14—Fig. B26) along with gears (15 and 16). Slide out clutch shaft (12). Drive out pins (6), remove lever (7) and shoe (8). Drive out pins (33) and remove lever (29). Do not lose spring (32) or ball (31). Remove lever (34) and shoe (35). Slide gears (11 and 10) off worm shaft (2).

INSPECTION. Inspect all components for excessive wear or damage and renew as necessary. Check bearings for roughness and gears for broken teeth or other damage. Renew springs (39—Figs. B25 and B26) and springs (32—Fig. B26) if free length is less than 8.9 mm (0.35 in.). If spline on worm shaft (2) is excessively worn, final drive assembly should be overhauled and worn components renewed.

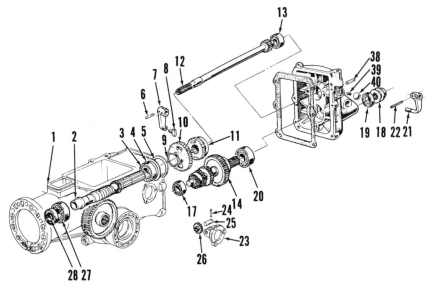

Fig. B25—Exploded view of transmission used on Model 715. Refer to legend in Fig. B26 for component identification.

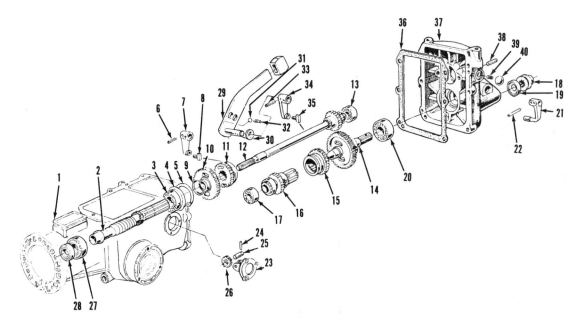

Fig. B26—Exploded view of transmission used on Models 725 and 735.

1. Case	8. Shoe	15. Reduction gear	21. Lever	28. Seal	34. Lever
2. Worm shaft	9. Thrust washer	16. Triple gear	22. Roll pin	29. Reduction gear	35. Shoe
3. Bearing	10. Low gear	17. Bearing	23. Flange	lever	36. Gasket
4. Washer	11. Sliding gear	18. Slider	24. Roll pin	30. Seal	37. Cover
5. Snap ring	12. Clutch shaft	19. Seal	25. Pin	31. Ball	38. Pin
6. Roll pin	13. Bearing	20. Bearing	26. Reverse idler	32. Spring	39. Spring
7. Lever	14. Pto shaft		27. Bearing	33. Roll pin	40. Ball

REASSEMBLY. Renew all gaskets and seals. Reverse disassembly procedure to reassemble transmission. Lubricate bearings and shafts with Molykote or a suitable equivalent grease during reassembly. Tighten cover (37—Figs. B25 and B26) attaching bolts to 24.4 N·m (18 ft.-lbs.). After reassembly, seat clutch shaft and bearings by lightly tapping clutch shaft as shown in Fig. B27.

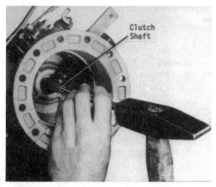

Fig. B27—After transmission reassembly on Models 715, 725 and 735, seat clutch shaft and bearings by tapping on clutch shaft as shown.

Refer to LUBRICATION section for lubrication requirements after reassembly.

Model 745

DISASSEMBLY. Remove engine from tiller. Refer to CLUTCH section and remove clutch assembly and drain oil. Drive out pins (21—Fig. B28) and slide out lever (22). Be sure to catch ball (23) and spring (24). Remove lever (20) and coupler (19). Unbolt and remove cover (17). Refer to FINAL DRIVE section and remove brake and gear reduction assemblies. Remove snap ring (13) and pull shafts (12 and 26) from cover (17). Remove pins (6) and slide out lever (57), catching ball (59) and spring (58). Do not allow pins (6) to fall into final drive housing through oil holes in case (1). Remove lever (7), shoe (8) and gears (10 and 11). Drive out pins (56), remove lever (51), spring (53), ball (52), lever (55) and shoe (28). Remove sliding gear (27) and triple gear (29).

INSPECTION. Inspect all components for excessive wear or damage and renew as necessary. Check bearings for roughness and gears for broken teeth or other damage. Renew springs (24 and 53—Fig. B28) if free length is less than 8.9 mm (0.35 in.). Renew spring (58) if free length is less than 24.4 mm (0.96 in.). If spline on worm shaft (2) is excessively worn or damaged, final drive assembly should be overhauled and worn components renewed.

REASSEMBLY. Reverse disassembly procedure to reassemble transmission. Renew all seals and gaskets. Lubricate bearings and shafts with Molykote or a suitable equivalent grease during reassembly. Shafts (12 and 26—Fig. B28) may require tapping into cover (17) with a soft-faced mallet. Tighten cover (17) attaching bolts to 24.4 N·m (18 ft.-lbs.). Refer to LUBRICATION section for lubrication requirements after reassembly.

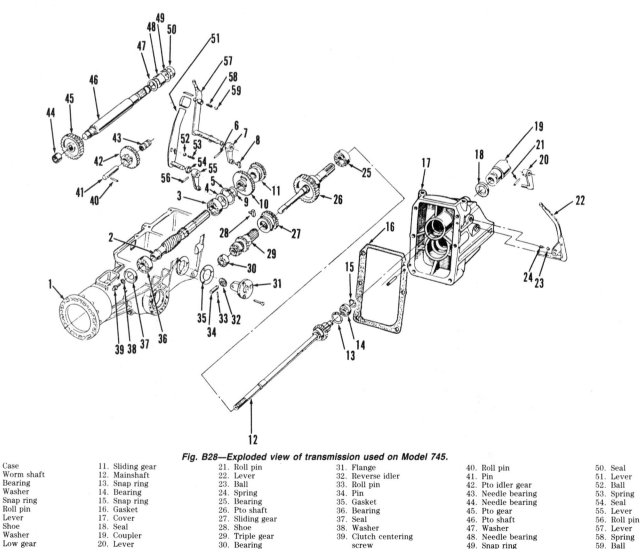

Fig. B28—Exploded view of transmission used on Model 745.

1. Case	11. Sliding gear	21. Roll pin	31. Flange
2. Worm shaft	12. Mainshaft	22. Lever	32. Reverse idler
3. Bearing	13. Snap ring	23. Ball	33. Roll pin
4. Washer	14. Bearing	24. Spring	34. Pin
5. Snap ring	15. Snap ring	25. Bearing	35. Gasket
6. Roll pin	16. Gasket	26. Pto shaft	36. Bearing
7. Lever	17. Cover	27. Sliding gear	37. Seal
8. Shoe	18. Seal	28. Shoe	38. Washer
9. Washer	19. Coupler	29. Triple gear	39. Clutch centering
10. Low gear	20. Lever	30. Bearing	screw

40. Roll pin	50. Seal
41. Pin	51. Lever
42. Pto idler gear	52. Ball
43. Needle bearing	53. Spring
44. Needle bearing	54. Seal
45. Pto gear	55. Lever
46. Pto shaft	56. Roll pin
47. Washer	57. Lever
48. Needle bearing	58. Spring
49. Snap ring	59. Ball

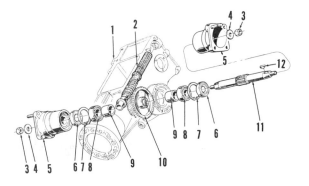

Fig. B29—Exploded view of final drive assembly used on Models 715 and 725.

1. Case
2. Worm shaft
3. Nut
4. Washer
5. Hub
6. Seal
7. Snap ring
8. Bearing
9. Spacer
10. Ring gear
11. Wheel shaft
12. Woodruff key

FINAL DRIVE

Models 715 and 725

DISASSEMBLY. Remove engine, handlebar assembly and drive wheels. Remove wheel brakes if so equipped. Remove case top cover and disassemble transmission as outlined in TRANSMISSION section. Remove worm shaft (2—Fig. B29) by tapping out with a punch as shown in Fig. B30. Remove nuts (3—Fig. B29). Using a soft-faced mallet, strike hubs (5) on the side to loosen hubs on shaft (11). Pry out seals (6) and remove snap rings (7). Position case (1) on its side and drive out shaft (11) through ring gear (10) and out of case (1). Use a wooden block or a suitable brass punch to prevent damage to shaft (11).

INSPECTION. Inspect all components for excessive wear or damage and renew as necessary. Check bearings for roughness and gears for broken teeth or other damage.

REASSEMBLY. Renew all seals and gaskets. Install one snap ring (7—Fig. B29) and one bearing (8) into case. Place one spacer (9) and ring gear (10) into case and install wheel shaft (11). Install remainder of bearings, snap rings and seals. Install worm shaft (2). Tighten nuts (3) to 85.4 N·m (63 ft.-lbs.). Tighten drive wheel nuts to 50 N·m (37 ft.-lbs.).

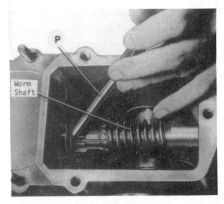

Fig. B30—On Models 715 and 725, tap out worm shaft with a punch (P) as shown. Use caution not to damage shaft or bearing.

Refer to TRANSMISSION section and reassemble transmission assembly. Refer to LUBRICATION section for lubrication requirements after reassembly.

Model 735

DISASSEMBLY. Remove engine, handlebar assembly and drive wheels. Remove brake drum (24—Fig. B31), shoes (23) and backing plate (22). Disassemble transmission as outlined in

TRANSMISSION section. Remove cover (21). Refer to Fig. B26 and remove snap ring (5) and thrust washer (9) from transmission end of case. Lift worm shaft (2) with bearing (3) out top of case. Remove hub assemblies (2 through 9—Fig. B31). Properly support hubs (6) in a suitable press and press out shaft (9). Remove bearing (2), snap ring (3) and seal (8) from hub (6). If necessary, remove nut (14) and remove rod (19) from cover (21). Note position of rod (19) and spring (17) for reference during reassembly.

INSPECTION. Inspect all components for excessive wear or damage and renew as necessary. Make sure rivets in differential (10—Fig. B31) are tight. Spring (13) should have a free length of approximately 25.4 mm (1 in.).

REASSEMBLY. Reassembly is the reverse of the disassembly procedure. Renew all gaskets and seals. Reassemble hub assemblies (2 through 9—Fig. B31)

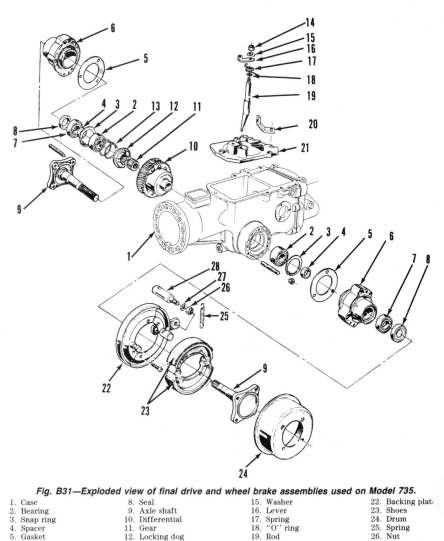

Fig. B31—Exploded view of final drive and wheel brake assemblies used on Model 735.

1. Case	8. Seal	15. Washer	22. Backing plate
2. Bearing	9. Axle shaft	16. Lever	23. Shoes
3. Snap ring	10. Differential	17. Spring	24. Drum
4. Spacer	11. Gear	18. "O" ring	25. Spring
5. Gasket	12. Locking dog	19. Rod	26. Nut
6. Hub	13. Spring	20. Bracket	27. Washer
7. Bearing	14. Nut	21. Cover	28. Anchor

and place differential into case. Install hub assemblies making sure axle shafts (9) properly engage differential (10). Tighten hub attaching nuts to 24.4 N·m (18 ft.-lbs.). To install cover (21), first disengage differential lock by locating locking dog (12) in the position shown in Fig. B32. Rotate lever (16) fully counterclockwise and set cover (21) on case (1). Tighten cover attaching nuts to 50 N·m (37 ft.-lbs.). Refer to TRANSMISSION section and reassemble transmission. Refer to LUBRICATION section for lubrication requirements after reassembly.

Model 745

DISASSEMBLY. Remove engine and handlebar assemblies. Refer to CLUTCH section and remove clutch. Remove drive wheels and brakes. Disassemble

Fig. B32—Before installing cover (21—Fig. B31), make sure differential lock is in the disengaged position by locating dog as shown.

transmission as outlined in TRANSMISSION section. Position differential lock lever in disengaged position and note location of lever for reference upon reassembly. Remove gearcase cover. Remove nuts (20—Fig. B33) and gear reduction housings.

Refer to Fig. B26 and remove snap ring (5) and lift worm shaft (2) out top of case. Lift differential (10—Fig. B33) from case (1).

Drive out two pins (14) from reduction housing and remove cover (6). Place flange of axle shaft (19) into a vise and tap reduction housing (9) with a soft-faced mallet to remove axle shaft (19). Place shaft (4) into a vise and tap reduction housing (9) with a soft-faced mallet to remove shaft (4). Use care not to damage spline on shaft (4).

INSPECTION. Inspect all components for excessive wear or damage and renew as necessary. Check bearings for roughness and gears and shafts for broken teeth or other damage. Make sure rivets in differential (10—Fig. B33) are tight. Spring (13) should have a free

length of approximately 25.4 mm (1 in.).

REASSEMBLY. Renew all gaskets and seals. Reassembly is the reverse of disassembly noting the following: Press bearing (18—Fig. B33) on axle shaft (19) with thin side of bearing toward flange of shaft (19). Renew spacers (17). Assemble bearings (2 and 5) on shaft (4) and drive shaft with bearings into reduction housing (9) with a soft-faced mallet. Fill reduction housing (9) with a suitable bearing grease. Place reduction gear (16) into housing (9) and install axle shaft (19) with bearing (18) into reduction housing (9). Make sure axle shaft (19) properly engages reduction gear (16). Place differential (10) into case and install reduction units on case. Tighten nuts (20) to 24.4 N·m (18 ft.-lbs.). Install worm shaft (2—Fig. B26) into case. Disengage differential lock as shown in Fig. B32. Install cover and tighten attaching nuts to 24.4 N·m (18 ft.-lbs.). Refer to TRANSMISSION section and reassemble transmission. Refer to LUBRICATION section for lubrication requirements after resembly.

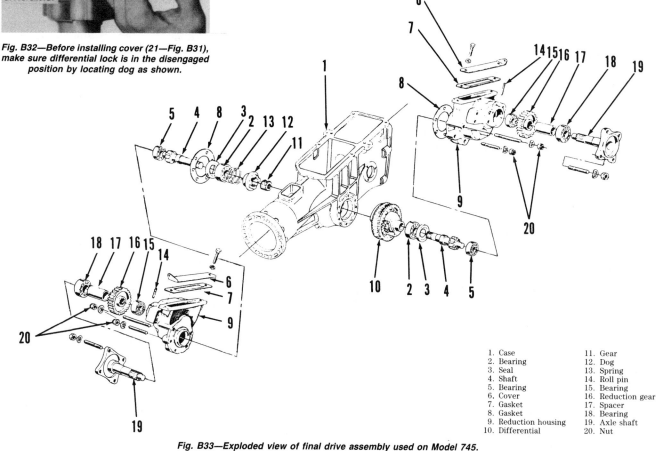

1. Case	11. Gear
2. Bearing	12. Dog
3. Seal	13. Spring
4. Shaft	14. Roll pin
5. Bearing	15. Bearing
6. Cover	16. Reduction gear
7. Gasket	17. Spacer
8. Gasket	18. Bearing
9. Reduction housing	19. Axle shaft
10. Differential	20. Nut

Fig. B33—Exploded view of final drive assembly used on Model 745.

SYNCHRONIZED PTO

Models 735 and 745

DISASSEMBLY. Remove cover (13—Fig. B34). Remove roll pin (5), idler shaft (4) and idler gear (3). Remove seal (6), snap ring (7) and pull pto shaft (10) and gear (11) from cover (13). Remove nut (21), lever (23) and rod (16).

INSPECTION AND REASSEMBLY. Inspect all components for excessive wear or damage and renew as necessary. Lubricate bearings, seals, shafts and gears with Molykote or a suitable equivalent during reassembly. Disengage differential lock as shown in Fig. B32 and install cover (13). Tighten cover attaching nuts to 24.4 N·m (18 ft.-lbs.). Make sure lever (23) is in the correct location to enable rod to engage differential lock device.

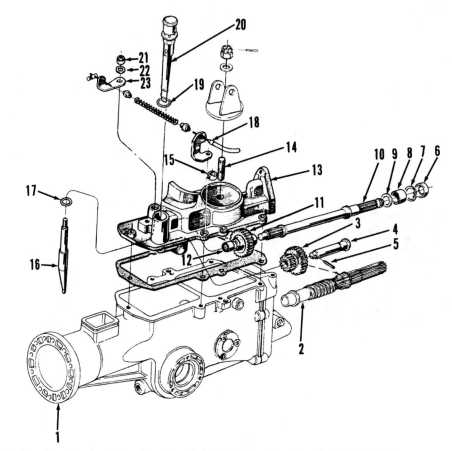

1. Case
2. Worm shaft
3. Idler gear
4. Idler shaft
5. Roll pin
6. Seal
7. Snap ring
8. Needle bearing
9. Washer
10. Pto shaft
11. Gear
12. Needle bearing
13. Cover
14. Stud
15. Spacer
16. Rod
17. "O" ring
18. Differential lock cable
19. "O" ring
20. Dipstick
21. Nut
22. Washer
23. Lever

Fig. B34—Exploded view of synchronized pto unit used on Model 735. Pto unit used on Model 745 is similar.

CLINTON

CLINTON ENGINE CORPORATION
Maquoketa, Iowa 52060

Model	Engine Make	Engine Series	Engine Horsepower	No. of Forward Speeds	Power Reverse?	Tilling Width (In.)	Drive Type
500-T-14	Clinton	500	3	1	No	14	Chain

LUBRICATION

ENGINE

Mix ¾ pint of SAE 30 two stroke (or high quality outboard) oil with each gallon of gasoline (approximately 10:1 ratio).

CHAIN DRIVE

Chain case contains approximately ¼ pint of 140 EP gear lube. To check oil level clean dirt from case housing, then remove plug (15–Fig. CL2). Oil should come to the bottom of the level plug hole. If oil level is low remove fill plug (16). Add oil through fill plug hole (16) until it begins to run out of level check hole. Reinstall and tighten plugs.

MAINTENANCE

Inspect all bolts and nuts for looseness

and retighten as necessary. Inspect drive belt for excessive stretching, wear, cracks or any other damages. Install new belt if needed. Inspect wheel bearings for excessive wear, lubricate wheel bearings occasionally with SAE 30W oil to prevent premature bearing failure.

Inspect all pulleys for damage and excessive wear. Renew as needed. Inspect operation of clutch cable, tension adjustment on spring and freedom of movement of all linkage.

CLUTCH CONTROL ADJUSTMENT

If tines do not disengage when clutch lever is released, adjust by inserting spring (2–Fig. CL1) in a higher chain link (3), so that there is no tension on spring when clutch lever (1) is released. If belt slippage occurs, adjust by attaching spring (2) to a lower link of chain (3) until there is tension on spring when clutch lever (1) is engaged. Clutch cable adjustment is necessary after installing a new drive belt or to compensate for normal belt stretching.

OVERHAUL

ENGINE

Engine make and series no. is marked on data plate attached to engine. Refer to appropriate Clinton engine section for overhaul procedures.

CHAIN CASE

INSPECTION. Refer to Fig. CL2 for parts breakdown and identification. Inspect and renew all components that are worn or damaged. Install new gaskets and seals. Lubricate gears, chains and bearings with a light film of oil during reassembly. Keep all dirt and foreign matter out of chain case during reassembly. Refer to **LUBRICATION** section for lubrication requirements after reassembly and installation.

DRIVE BELT

Remove drive belt guard. Remove belt from input shaft pulley and engine pulley. Install new belt on pulleys. Drive belt size is ⅜-inch x 27 inches long. Manufacturer recommends using a notched belt. Refer to **CLUTCH CONTROL ADJUSTMENT** section for adjusting procedure. Reinstall belt guard cover.

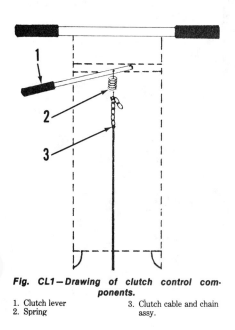

Fig. CL1 – Drawing of clutch control components.

1. Clutch lever
2. Spring
3. Clutch cable and chain assy.

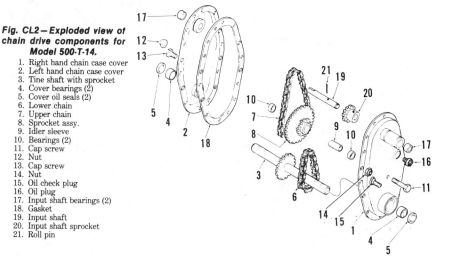

Fig. CL2 – Exploded view of chain drive components for Model 500-T-14.

1. Right hand chain case cover
2. Left hand chain case cover
3. Tine shaft with sprocket
4. Cover bearings (2)
5. Cover oil seals (2)
6. Lower chain
7. Upper chain
8. Sprocket assy.
9. Idler sleeve
10. Bearings (2)
11. Cap screw
12. Nut
13. Cap screw
14. Nut
15. Oil check plug
16. Oil plug
17. Input shaft bearings (2)
18. Gasket
19. Input shaft
20. Input shaft sprocket
21. Roll pin

JOHN DEERE

DEERE & COMPANY
John Deere Road
Moline, Illinois 61265

Model	Engine Make	Engine Series	Engine Horsepower	No. of Forward Speeds	Power Reverse?	Tilling Width (In.)	Drive Type
216	B&S	60000	2	1	No	16	Chain
324	Tec.	H35	3.5	1	Yes	13-24	Gear
524	Tec.	H50	5	1	Yes	13-24	Gear
624	Tec.	H60	6	1	Yes	13-34	Gear

LUBRICATION

ENGINE

All Models

Refer to appropriate Briggs and Stratton or Tecumseh engine section for engine lubrication specifications. Recommended oil grade is SAE 30 or equivalent. Recommended fuel is either regular or low-lead gasoline having an octane rating of 90 or higher. The use of non-leaded gasolines reduces cylinder head deposits, but could shorten engine valve life if carburetor is adjusted too lean.

WHEELS AND CONTROLS

All Models

Wheel bolts (Fig. JD3) should be removed and lubricated with SAE multipurpose grease at least once a year. All moveable parts should be lubricated occasionally with a few drops of oil. Caution should be taken in not getting oil on drive belts.

CHAIN DRIVE

All Models So Equipped

Chain case oil should be checked weekly or every 25 hours depending upon the amount of operation. Recommended oil for chain case is SAE 30 engine oil.

To check oil level in chain case place tiller on a level surface. Clean dirt from chain case housing and remove oil level plug (Fig. JD1). Oil level should be at bottom of plug hole. If oil level is low remove rubber fill plug from side of chain case (Fig. JD2). Add oil slowly until it starts to run out of level plug hole. Reinstall plugs.

Fig. JD1 – View of oil level plug for Model 216.

Fig. JD2 – View of oil fill plug for Model 216.

Fig. JD3 – View of oil level plug for Models 324, 524 and 624.

GEAR DRIVE

All Models So Equipped

Oil level in gear case should be checked at the beginning of each season or after every 25 hours of operation. Recommended gear case oil is SAE 90 gear lubricant or equivalent SCL multipurpose type gear oil. Gear case capacity is 8 ozs. or 0.237 liter.

To check oil level in gear case, place tiller on a level surface. Clean surface around oil level plug (Fig. JD3) and remove plug. Oil level should be at bottom of plug hole. If oil level is low add oil through plug hole until it begins to run out, then reinstall plug.

MAINTENANCE

Inspect all fasteners for looseness and retighten as needed. Check control levers, linkage and cables for freedom of movement and excessive play. Inspect drive belt(s) for excessive stretching, wear, cracks or any other damage. Install new belt(s) if needed. Inspect all pulleys and renew if damaged or excessively worn (Fig. JD4).

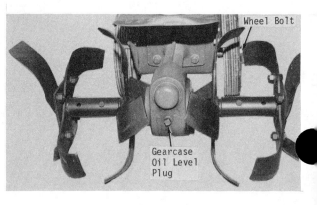

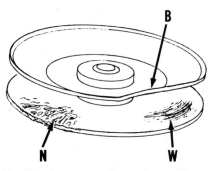

Fig. JD4—Damage to pulley such as rough surface (N), cupped surface (W) or bent sides (B) will quickly wear belt out.

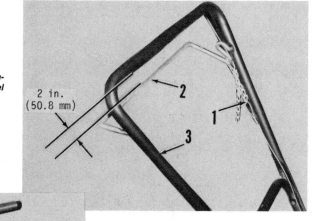

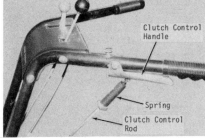

Fig. JD5—View of clutch control components for Model 216.

1. Control cable hook
2. Drive control rod
3. Control handle

Fig. JD6 — View and identification of clutch control components for Models 324, 524 and 624.

ADJUSTMENT

CLUTCH CONTROL

Model 216

Adjust by lengthening or shortening chain on control cable hook (1 – Fig. JD5). Clearance between drive control rod (2) and bottom of tiller control handle (3) should be approximately two inches when idler pulley begins to tighten drive belt. Drive belt should slip on all pulleys when drive control is released. To check, disconnect wire from spark plug and pull recoil starter. If tiller creeps, provide more slack in cable by lengthening chain at hook.

Models 324, 524 and 624

Adjust by turning clutch spring (Fig. JD6) up or down on clutch rod to change belt tension. If forward drive belt slips on pulleys when clutch handle is raised, increase spring tension by disconnecting spring from clutch control handle. Turn spring down on control rod one or two turns, then reconnect spring to handle. Spring should stretch ½-inch (12.7 mm) when handle is raised. Continue procedure until ½-inch (12.7 mm) stretch is obtained.

OVERHAUL

ENGINE

All Models

Engine model no. is stamped on blower housing for Briggs and Stratton engines. Engine make and series no. is marked on data plate attached to engine for Tecumseh engines. Refer to appropriate Briggs and Stratton or Tecumseh engine section for overhaul procedures.

CHAIN CASE

Model 216

OIL SEAL INSTALLATION. Installation of tine shaft oil seals (19 – Fig. JD7) may be done without removing chain case from tiller. Remove tines from shaft. Use seal puller or use a sharp punch to split oil seal, then pry seal from chain case hub. Clean tine shaft with emery cloth. Drive new seal in until it bottoms out in case hub.

REMOVE AND DISASSEMBLE. Drain fuel from tank and engine oil from crankcase. Unhook clutch cable chain. Remove lower handle bar "U" bolts, handle bars, drive belt cover, drive belt, transport wheel assembly and tines. Remove four engine attaching bolts, then remove engine. Remove one remaining bolt which attaches tine shield to frame, then remove shield. Remove two bolts which attach chain case to

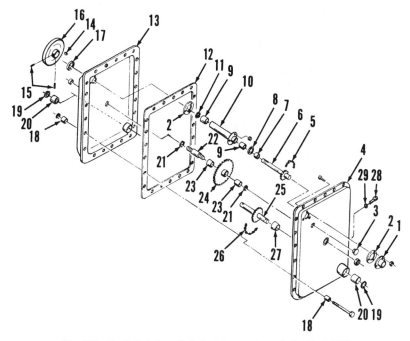

Fig. JD7 — Exploded view of chain drive components for Model 216.

1. Right hand tube	7. Spacer	14. Woodruff key	22. Threaded shaft
2. Gasket (2 used)	8. Washer	15. Set screws	23. Bushing (2 used)
3. Oil plug	9. Bushings	16. Drive pulley	24. Sprocket
4. Right hand chain case half	10. Flange tube	17. Spacer	25. Tine shaft
5. Chain	11. Oil seal	18. Spacer (4 used)	26. Chain
6. Input shaft and sprocket	12. Gasket	19. Oil seal (2 used)	27. Spacer
	13. Left hand chain case half	20. Bearing (2 used)	28. Self-tapping screw
		21. Washer	29. Cork washer

frame, then withdraw chain case toward front.

Refer to Fig. JD7 for parts breakdown and identification. Loosen the two drive pulley set screws and slide pulley from input shaft. Clean surfaces of tine shaft with emery cloth. Remove chain case bolts and center chain case hex nut. Split chain case, then remove input shaft and sprocket assembly. Withdraw chain and sprocket assemblies from case for inspection. Completion of disassembly may be done with referral to Fig. JD7. Thoroughly clean all parts with suitable cleaning solvent. Inspect sprockets for excessive wear or broken teeth. Inspect chains for loose or binding links. Inspect sprocket shafts for excessive wear. Clearance between bearings and shaft should be 0.005-inch (0.13 mm). Reassemble in reverse order of disassembly. Install new oil seals and gaskets. Refer to **LUBRICATION** section for lubrication requirements after reassembly and installation.

GEAR CASE

Models 324, 524 and 624

OIL SEAL INSTALLATION. Installation of tine shaft oil seals (1 – Fig. JD8) may be done without removing gear case from tiller. Remove tines from shaft. Use a seal puller or use a sharp punch to split oil seals and pry seals from side cover and case. Clean tine shaft with emery cloth. Press new seals in cover and case hub until seal face is flush with outside of castings. Reassemble in reverse order of disassembly. Refer to **LUBRICATION** section for lubrication requirements.

REMOVE AND DISASSEMBLE. Remove engine and tines. Remove idler pivot bolt (Fig. JD9) and lift out idler assemblies and belts. Loosen drive pulley set screw. Remove four bolts securing gear case to frame. Slide gear case forward sharply to knock drive pulley from shaft. Remove gear case from frame.

Refer to Fig. JD8 for parts breakdown and identification. Remove dust cap (9), oil level plug (17) and drain oil. Remove cotter pin (10), nut (11), washer (12) and bearing (13) from input shaft. Tap input shaft rearward to remove oil seal from case. Remove snap ring (22—Fig. JD8) from input shaft. Remove bolts securing tine shaft cover (3). Remove cover and tine shaft (8) from gearcase. Align worm gear (16) with outer race (14) and press input shaft and race out of gear case using a suitable press and holding fixtures. Drive groove pin (15—Fig. JD8) out of input shaft assembly. Remove worm gear from shaft. Clean all parts with suitable cleaning solvent and inspect closely. Inspect bearings and races for excessive wear. Renew both bearing and race if either is found to be bad. Inspect gears for worn, broken or damaged teeth. Bronze gear may be pressed off of tine shaft if replacement is necessary.

REASSEMBLE AND REINSTALL. Press rear roller bearing back on input shaft past snap ring groove. Reinstall snap ring and press bearing back up in contact with snap ring. Install new tine shaft oil seals. Install outer race in case. Install Woodruff key on input shaft and slide shaft in case through worm gear. Drive groove pin through worm gear

and shaft. Install thrust washer on each side of bronze gear and install tine shaft assembly in case. Install side cover (3 – Fig. JD8) with new gasket. Install input shaft lower bearing (13), washer (12) and nut (11). Tighten nut until snug, then back off until shaft has 0.002-0.012 inch (0.05-0.31 mm) end play. Install cotter pin and dust cap. Install upper seal (23) being careful not to cut seal on input shaft keyway. Drive seal in until flush with casting.

Install gear case in frame reversing order of removal. Clearance between drive pulley and ½-inch bolt heads should be 1/16-inch (1.6 mm). Tighten drive pulley set screw. Install drive belts, idler assemblies and idler pivot bolt. Install belts on pulleys and check adjustment. Refer to **CLUTCH CONTROL ADJUSTMENT** section for adjusting procedure. Refer to **LUBRICATION** section for lubrication requirements.

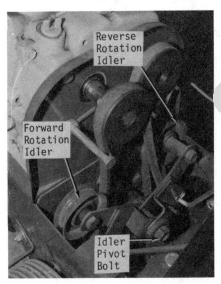

Fig. JD9 – View of idler assemblies for Models 324, 524 and 624.

DRIVE BELT

Model 216

Remove drive belt cover. Remove belt from pulleys and install new belt. Drive belt size is 17/32-inch x 49 inches long. Loosen engine mounting bolts, slide engine until distance between shafts Fig. JD12) is 15¼ inches (38.7 cm), then retighten engine mounting bolts Reinstall belt cover and check clutch adjustment. Refer to **CLUTCH CONTROL ADJUSTMENT** section for adjusting procedure.

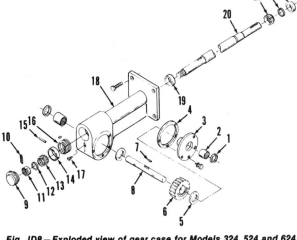

Fig. JD8 – Exploded view of gear case for Models 324, 524 and 624.

1. Oil seal	6. Bronze gear	12. Washer	18. Gear case
2. Needle bearing	7. Woodruff key	13. Tapered roller bearing	19. Bearing cup
3. Gear case cover	8. Tine shaft	14. Bearing cup	20. Input shaft
4. Gasket	9. Dust cap	15. Groove pin	21. Tapered roller bearing
5. Thrust washer (2 used)	10. Cotter pin	16. Worm gear	22. Snap ring
	11. Slotted nut	17. Oil level plug	23. Seal

Fig. JD12—Drive belt arrangement and adjustment setting for Model 216.

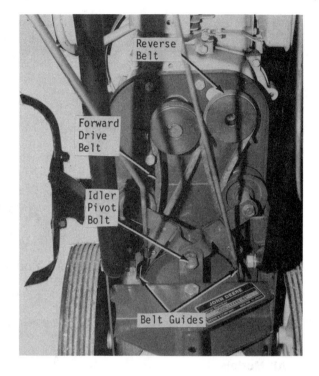

FORWARD DRIVE BELT. Remove belt guard from rear of engine. Loosen belt guides (Fig. JD13) and swing clear of belts. Remove belt from pulleys and install new belt. Drive belt size is ½-inch x 33 inches long. Reposition belt guides. Clearance between belts and guides should be ⅛-inch (3.2 mm) when belt is engaged. Reinstall belt guard. Refer to **CLUTCH CONTROL ADJUSTMENT** section for adjusting procedure.

Fig. JD13—Drive belt arrangement and attaching parts for Model 324.

REVERSE DRIVE BELT. Remove and reinstall forward drive belt as outlined in **FORWARD DRIVE BELT** section. Loosen engine crankshaft pulley set screws, then use a suitable puller to partially remove pulley. Install new reverse belt. Drive belt size is ½-inch x 33 inches long. Reinstall pulley back in original position, then tighten pulley set screws.

Models 524 and 624

Remove belt guard from rear of engine. Loosen belt guides (Fig. JD14) and swing clear of belts. Remove belts from pulleys and install new belts. Forward drive belt size is ½-inch x 33 inches long. Reverse drive belt size is ½-inch x 32 inches long. Reposition belt guides so that clearance between belts and guides is ⅛-inch (3.2 mm) when belt is engaged. Reinstall belt guard. Refer to **CLUTCH CONTROL ADJUSTMENT** section for adjusting procedures.

Fig. JD14—Drive belt arrangement and attaching parts for Models 524 and 624. Belt guides are located as called out in Fig. JD13.

FELDMANN

FELDMANN ENGINEERING AND MANUFACTURING CO., INC.
Box 153
Sheboygan Falls, WI 53085

Model	Engine Make	Engine Series	Engine Horsepower	No. of Forward Speeds	Power Reverse?	Tilling Width (In.)	Drive Type
73335	B&S	60000	2	1	No	6-18	Chain
83335	B&S	80000	3	1	No	6-18	Chain

LUBRICATION

ENGINE

All Models

Refer to Briggs and Stratton engine section for engine lubrication requirements. Recommended oil grade is SAE 30 or equivalent. Recommended fuel is either regular or low-lead gasoline having an octane rating of 90 or higher.

WHEELS AND CONTROLS

All Models

Lubricate transport wheels, idler pulley and pivot points at least every 10 hours of operation with SAE 30 oil. Do not allow oil on drive belts.

CHAIN DRIVE

Check oil in chain case every 10 hours of operation or at lease once a year. Recommended lubricant is SAE 90 gear oil.

To check oil level in chain case, place tiller on a level surface. Clean dirt from chain case housing and remove oil level plug at bottom of housing on left side. Oil level should be at bottom of plug hole. If oil level is low, add oil slowly until it starts to run out of plug hole, then reinstall plug.

MAINTENANCE

Inspect all fasteners for looseness and retighten as needed. Check control levers, linkage and cables for freedom of movement and excessive play. Inspect drive belt(s) for excessive stretching, wear, cracks and any other damage. Install new belt(s) if needed. Inspect all belt pulleys and renew if damaged or excessively worn.

ADJUSTMENT

CLUTCH CONTROL CABLE

All Models

For initial adjustment, allow 24 inches of cable between spring and handle, then lengthen or shorten cable to provide proper tension of idler pulley on belt.

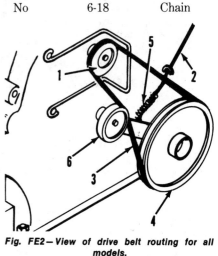

Fig. FE2 — View of drive belt routing for all models.

1. Engine pulley	4. Transmission pulley
2. Control cord	5. Spring
3. Belt	6. Idler pulley

Fig. FE1 — Exploded view of chain drive for all models.

1. Washer		10. Intermediate sprocket
2. Felt washer	5. Gasket	8. Washers	11. Tine shaft & sprocket
3. Seal	6. Chain	9. Input shaft & sprocket	assy.
4. Chain case	7. Bronze bearings	assy.	12. Spacers

FORD

FORD TRACTOR OPERATIONS
Troy, Michigan 48084

Model	Engine Make	Engine Series	Engine Horsepower	No. of Forward Speeds	Power Reverse?	Tilling Width (In.)	Drive Type
1005	B&S	190000	8	2	Yes	12-26	Gear
1013	B&S	130000	5	1	No	12-26	Chain
1023	B&S	130000	5	1	Yes	12-26	Gear
1094	B&S	90000	3.5	1	No	12-26	Gear
1105	B&S	90000	3.5	1	Yes	7-22	Gear
1114A	B&S	130000	5	1	Yes	1	Chain
1134	B&S	13000	5	1	Yes	18	Chain
1183	B&S	13000	5	1	Yes	18	Chain
1200	B&S	8000	3	1	No	7-22	Gear

LUBRICATION

ENGINE

All Models

Refer to appropriate Briggs and Stratton engine section for engine lubrication specifications. Recommended oil grade is SAE 30 or equivalent. Recommended fuel is either regular or low-lead gasoline having an octane rating of 90 or higher. The use of non-leaded gasolines reduces cylinder head deposits, but could shorten engine valve life if carburetor is adjusted too lean.

WHEELS AND CONTROLS

All Models

Transport wheels on models so equipped should be lubricated occasionally with SAE 30 oil. Drive belt idler pulley shafts and all other pivot joints should be lubricated at least every 8-10 operating hours with SAE 30 oil. Caution should be taken in not getting oil on drive belts.

CHAIN DRIVE

Model 1013

Chain case oil should be checked at least every 10 hours of operation. Recommended oil is lead base (EP) SAE 140 heavy duty gear oil.

To check oil level, clean case and remove oil level plug (18–Fig. F17). Tilt rear of tiller up so that center gear bolt (27) and oil fill plug (28) are parallel with ground. Oil level should be at bottom of plug hole (18). Add oil if level is low, then reinstall plugs.

Models 1114A, 1134 and 1183

Wheel drive case and tine drive case

should be checked at least every 25 hours of operation. Recommended oil is lead base (EP) SAE 140 heavy duty gear oil.

To check oil level of wheel drive case, clean case and remove level and fill plug (Fig. F1). Set depth control lever at shallowest setting. Oil level should be at

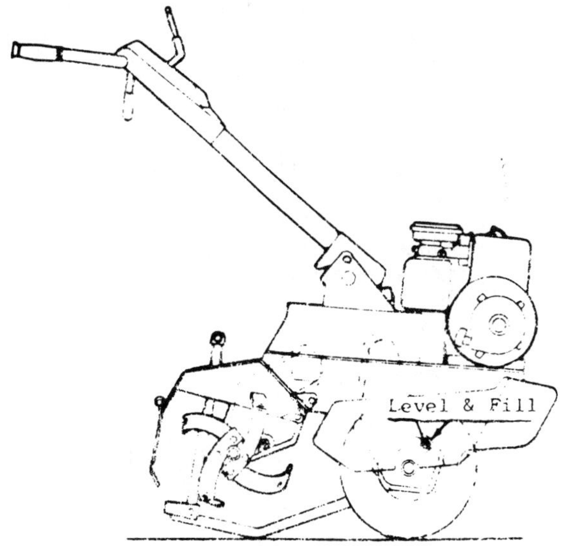

Fig. F1—Wheel drive oil level plug for Models 1114A, 1134 and 1183.

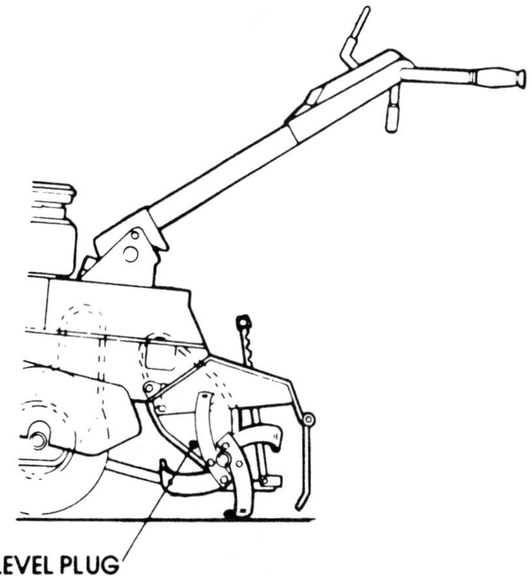

Fig. F2—Tine drive oil level plug for Models 1114A, 1134 and 1183.

OIL LEVEL PLUG

bottom of plug hole. If necessary, add oil until flush with bottom of plug hole, then reinstall oil level plug.

To check oil level of tine drive case, clean case and remove level plug (Fig. F2). Set depth control lever at deepest setting. If oil level is below bottom of plug hole, remove fill plug (Fig. F3). Add oil until oil begins to run out oil level hole (Fig. F2), then reinstall and tighten plugs.

GEAR CASE

Models 1105 and 1200

Recommended oil is lead base (EP) SAE 140 heavy duty oil.

To check gear case oil level tip tiller on its left side. Clean case and remove oil fill screw (Fig. F4). Case should be completely full of oil. If case is low add oil, then reinstall oil fill screw.

Model 1094

Recommended oil is lead base (EP) SAE 140 heavy duty oil. Oil level should be checked at least every 25 hours of operation. Gear case bushing (Fig. F5) should be greased with #2 wheel bearing grease at least every 10 operating hours.

To check gear case oil place tiller on a level surface, clean dirt from around oil level plug (Fig. F5) and remove plug. Oil level should be at bottom of plug hole. If oil level is low add oil through level hole until oil begins to run out, then reinstall and tighten plug.

Model 1023

Recommended oil is lead base (EP) SAE 140 heavy duty oil. Oil level should be checked at least every 25 hours of operation.

To check gear case oil place tiller on a level surface. Clean dirt from front of

gear case and remove oil level plug (Fig. F6). Oil level should be at bottom of plug hole. If oil level is low remove oil fill plug (Fig. F6), add oil until oil begins to run out level hole, then reinstall and tighten plugs.

Model 1005

Recommended oil is lead base (EP) SAE 140 heavy duty oil. Oil level should be checked at least every 25 hours of operation.

To check gear case oil, block up tiller wheels until center line of level plug is parallel to ground (Fig. F7). Clean dirt from front of gear case and remove oil level plug. Oil level should be at bottom of plug hole. If oil level is low, remove oil fill plug (Fig. F7). Add oil until oil begins to run out level hole, then reinstall and tighten plugs.

MAINTENANCE

Inspect all fasteners for looseness and retighten as needed. Check control levers, linkage and cables for freedom of movement and excessive play. Inspect drive belt(s) for excessive stretching, wear, cracks, or any other damage. Install new belt(s) if needed. Inspect all pulleys and renew if damaged or excessively worn.

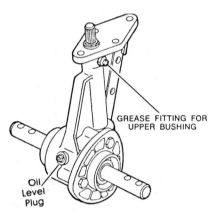

Fig. F5—Gear case oil level plug for Model 1094.

Fig. F6—Gear case oil level and fill plug for Model 1023.

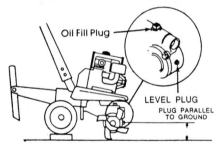

Fig. F7—Gear case oil level and fill plug for Model 1005.

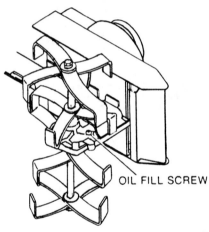

Fig. F4—Gear case oil fill screw for Models 1105 and 1200.

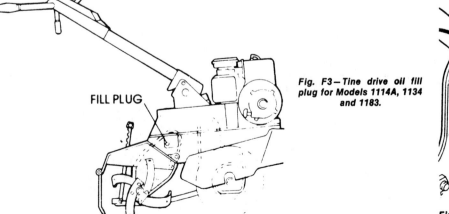

Fig. F3—Tine drive oil fill plug for Models 1114A, 1134 and 1183.

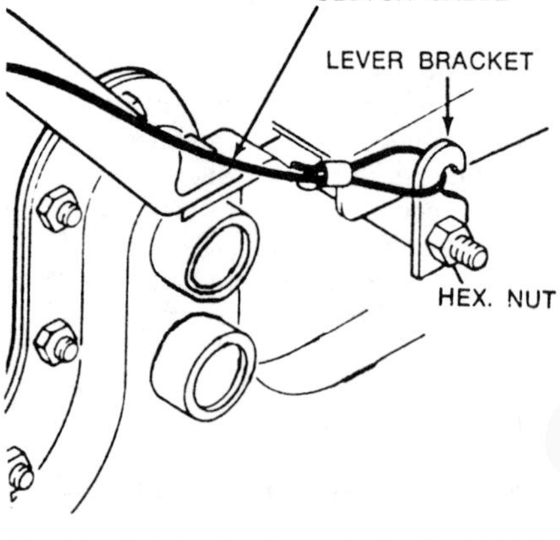

Fig. F8—Clutch adjusting parts for Model 1013.

ADJUSTMENT

CLUTCH CONTROL

Model 1013

Loosen hex nut at end of lever bracket (Fig. F8). Move idler arm until there is a clearance of ¼-inch (6.4 mm) between belt and pulley, move lever bracket (Fig. F8) forward until clutch cable is tight, then retighten hex nut.

Models 1114A, 1134 and 1183

Adjust handle bar to lowest position. Loosen adjustment nut (Fig. F9), move clutch control lever on handle bar until it is centered in neutral position, then retighten adjustment nut.

Models 1105 and 1200

Push the clutch control handle to the forward position. Loosen set screw (Fig. F10), move cam (Fig. F10) until clearance between cam and pad is 3/16-inch (4.8 mm), then retighten set screw.

Model 1094

Adjustment is made by raising or lowering clevis pin position in control rod (Fig. F11). If tines turn when control rod is in neutral position, install clevis pin in a higher hole of control rod. Continue this procedure until tines do not turn in neutral position.

Models 1005 and 1023

Adjustment is made by raising or lowering stop collar on control rod (Fig. F12). With clutch control lever in forward position, clearance between pivot bushing and stop collar should be ¼-inch (6.4 mm). If clearance is incorrect loosen set screw (Fig. F12), move stop collar, then retighten set screw.

BELT ADJUSTMENT

Model 1013

Loosen engine bolts and slide engine forward. Refer to **CLUTCH CONTROL ADJUSTMENT** section for readjustment of clutch lever.

Models 1114A, 1134 and 1183

TINE DRIVE BELT. To adjust, loosen clamp cap screws (Fig. F13), then rotate chain case assembly. Clearance between inside surfaces of belt (Fig. F14) should be ¾-inch (19 mm) when clutch control lever is in forward position. Retighten clamp cap screws, then check to see if tines turn in neutral position. If tines do not turn in neutral position, adjustment is complete. If tines rotate, readjust belt to increase slack slightly.

WHEEL DRIVE BELT. Clearance between upper idler and belt should be ¼-inch (6.4 mm) with clutch control lever in neutral position (Fig. F15). If adjustment is incorrect, idler (Fig. F15) must be repositioned by removing machine screw and reinstalling in another of the four adjustment locations. Install new belt if correct adjustment is not possible.

Models 1005 and 1023

Adjustment is accomplished by installing shims between engine and tine shield. Install shims until 1/16-1/8-inch (1.6-3.2 mm) clearance is obtained between input pulley belt finger (Fig. F16) and belt when belt is fully engaged.

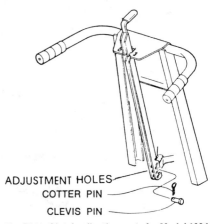

ADJUSTMENT HOLES
COTTER PIN
CLEVIS PIN

Fig. F11 – Clutch adjusting parts for Model 1094.

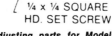

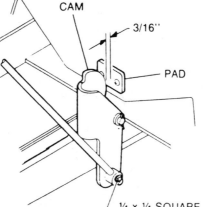

CAM

3/16"

PAD

¼ x ¼ SQUARE
HD. SET SCREW

Fig. F10 – Clutch adjusting parts for Models 1105 and 1200.

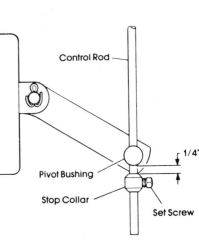

Control Rod

Pivot Bushing

Stop Collar

Set Screw

1/4"

Fig. F12 – Clutch adjusting parts for Models 1023 and 1005.

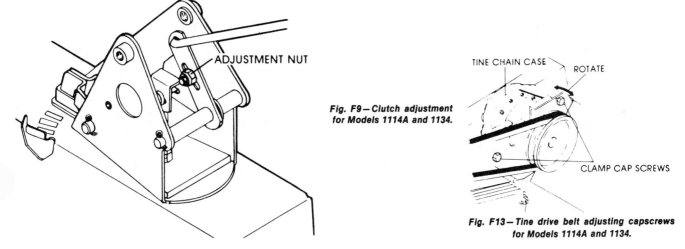

ADJUSTMENT NUT

Fig. F9 – Clutch adjustment for Models 1114A and 1134.

TINE CHAIN CASE

ROTATE

CLAMP CAP SCREWS

Fig. F13 – Tine drive belt adjusting capscrews for Models 1114A and 1134.

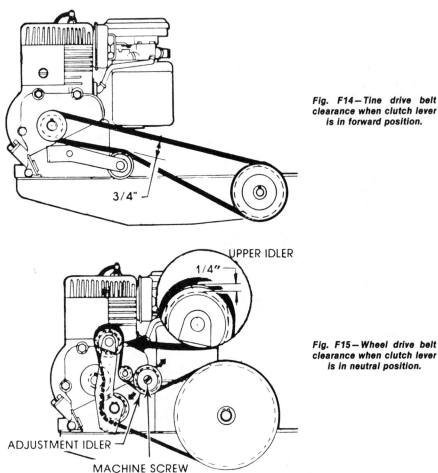

Fig. F14—Tine drive belt clearance when clutch lever is in forward position.

Fig. F15—Wheel drive belt clearance when clutch lever is in neutral position.

CHANGING FORWARD SPEEDS

Model 1005

The engine drive pulley and input pulley have 3 V-belt grooves. The inside 2 grooves are for forward speed adjustment. Groove closest to engine will provide fastest tine speed. If belt is new or tight, it may be necessary to loosen engine bolts, then tilt engine back to change pulley grooves.

OVERHAUL

ENGINE

All Models

Engine model number is stamped on blower housing. Refer to appropriate Briggs and Stratton engine section for overhaul procedures.

CHAIN CASE

Model 1013

OIL SEAL INSTALLATION. Remove tines from tine shaft. Use a suitable tool to remove oil seal from chain case hub. Clean tine shaft with emery cloth. Drive new seal in until bottomed in case hub.

GEAR CASE ADJUSTMENT

Models 1005, 1023 and 1094

Remove cotter pin (15–Fig. F19 or 4–Fig. F20) and tighten worm shaft adjustment plug (16–Fig. F19 or 21–Fig. F20) until snug, then back off one notch and reinstall cotter pin.

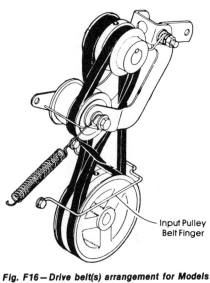

Fig. F16—Drive belt(s) arrangement for Models 1023 and 1005.

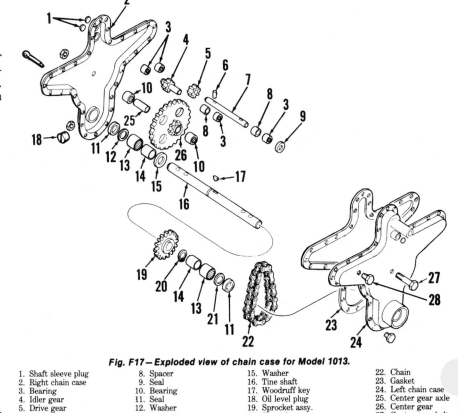

Fig. F17—Exploded view of chain case for Model 1013.

1. Shaft sleeve plug	8. Spacer	15. Washer	22. Chain
2. Right chain case	9. Seal	16. Tine shaft	23. Gasket
3. Bearing	10. Bearing	17. Woodruff key	24. Left chain case
4. Idler gear	11. Seal	18. Oil level plug	25. Center gear axle
5. Drive gear	12. Washer	19. Sprocket assy.	26. Center gear
6. Pin	13. Bearing	20. Snap ring	27. Center gear bolt
7. Input shaft	14. Inner race	21. Washer	28. Oil fill plug

INSPECTION. Refer to Fig. F17 for parts breakdown and identification. Inspect all components and renew all that are worn or damaged. Install new gaskets and seals. Lubricate gears, chains and bearings with a light film of oil during reassembly. Keep all dirt and foreign matter out of chain case during reassembly. Refer to **LUBRICATION** section for lubrication requirements.

Models 1114A, 1134 and 1183

Tine Drive and Wheel Traction Chain Cases

OIL SEAL INSTALLATION. Remove tines or wheels from output shaft. Use a suitable tool to remove oil seal from chain case hub. Clean shaft with emery cloth. Drive new seal in until bottomed in case hub.

INSPECTION. Wheel traction chain case is factory sealed and must be renewed as a complete unit. Refer to Fig. F18 for tine chain case parts breakdown and identification. Inspect all components and renew all that are worn or damaged. Install new gaskets and seals. Lubricate gears, chains and bearings with a light film of oil during reassembly. Keep all dirt and foreign matter out of chain case during reassembly. Refer to **LUBRICATION** section for lubricating requirements after reassembly and installation.

GEAR CASE

Models 1105 and 1200

OIL SEAL INSTALLATION. Remove tines from output shaft. Use a suitable tool to remove oil seal from gear case hub. Clean shaft with emery cloth. Drive new seal in until bottomed in case hub. Refer to **LUBRICATION** section for lubricating requirements.

Gear case is factory sealed and must be replaced as a complete unit if service is required.

Model 1094

OIL SEAL INSTALLATION. Remove tines from output shaft. Remove bolts securing side cover (17 – Fig. F19) to gear case and remove cover. Remove old seal (20), install new oil seal, then reinstall side cover and bolts. On opposite side of gear case hub (5), pry seal from hub and drive new seal in until bottomed in bore of case hub.

INSPECTION. Refer to Fig. F19 for gear case parts breakdown and identification. Inspect all components and renew all that are worn or damaged. In-

stall new gaskets and seals. Lubricate gears and bearings with a light film of oil during reassembly. Refer to **GEAR CASE ADJUSTMENT** section for end play adjusting procedure. Refer to **LUBRICATION** section for lubrication requirements.

Models 1005 and 1023

OIL SEAL INSTALLATION. Remove tines from output shaft. On Model 1005 remove bolts securing cover (31 – Fig. F20) to gear case and remove cover. On Model 1023 remove cotter pin (36) and lock cover (35), then withdraw

cover (33) from gear case. Remove and replace oil seal. Reinstall cover and securing parts. On opposite side, pry oil seal out of hub, then drive new seal in until bottomed in bore of case hub.

INSPECTION. Refer to Fig. F20 for gear case parts breakdown and identification. Inspect all components and renew all that are worn or damaged. Install new gaskets and seals. Lubricate gears and bearings with a light film of oil during reassembly. Keep all dirt and foreign matter out of gear case during reassembly. Refer to **GEAR CASE AD-**

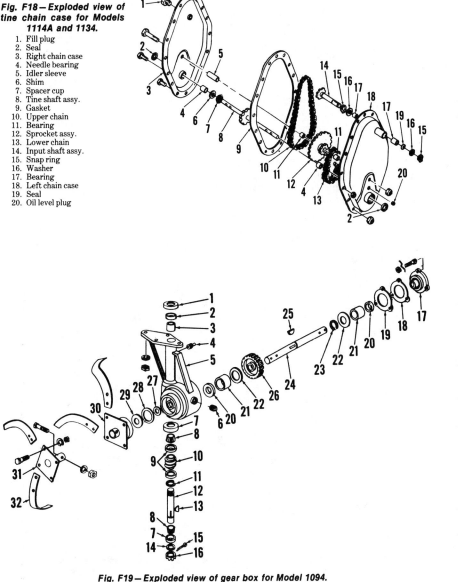

Fig. F18 – Exploded view of tine chain case for Models 1114A and 1134.

1. Fill plug
2. Seal
3. Right chain case
4. Needle bearing
5. Idler sleeve
6. Shim
7. Spacer cup
8. Tine shaft assy.
9. Gasket
10. Upper chain
11. Bearing
12. Sprocket assy.
13. Lower chain
14. Input shaft assy.
15. Snap ring
16. Washer
17. Bearing
18. Left chain case
19. Seal
20. Oil level plug

Fig. F19 – Exploded view of gear box for Model 1094.

1. Alignment bushing	9. Worm spacer	17. Gear case cover
2. Felt wick	10. Worm	18. Cover gasket
3. Worm shaft bushing	11. Snap ring	19. Cover gasket
4. Grease fitting	12. Worm shaft	20. Tine shaft seal
5. Gear case	13. Hypro key	21. Bushing
6. Oil level plug	14. "O" ring	22. Washer
7. Worm shaft bearing cup	15. Cotter pin	23. Snap ring
8. Bearing cone	16. Adjustment plug	24. Tine shaft

25. Woodruff key
26. Worm wheel
27. Intermediate felt seal
28. Inner felt seal
29. Washer
30. Inner tine hub assy.
31. Outer tine hub assy.
32. Tine

JUSTMENT section for end play adjusting procedure. Refer to **LUBRICATION** section for lubrication requirements.

CLUTCH CONE ASSEMBLY

Model 1094

To renew clutch assembly, engine must be removed from engine base (2 – Fig. F21) and bell housing (8). Disconnect throttle control (11), remove the three 5/16 x 1⅞ inch bolts securing engine to base and bell housing, then remove engine. Inspect upper cone (4) and clutch cone assembly (5) for excessive wear, renew as necessary. Inspect condition of spring (6) and renew if stretched or broken. Clutch yoke (13), rollers (16), clutch cone and worm shaft splines should be cleaned and lubricated with SAE 30 oil. Reassemble in reverse order of disassembly.

DRIVE BELTS

Model 1013

Remove drive belt cover. Remove belt from pulleys and install new belt. Drive belt size is ½-inch x 29 inches long. Loosen engine mounting bolts and slide engine. Belt should slip on pulleys when idler pulley is not engaged. Reinstall belt cover and check clutch adjustment.

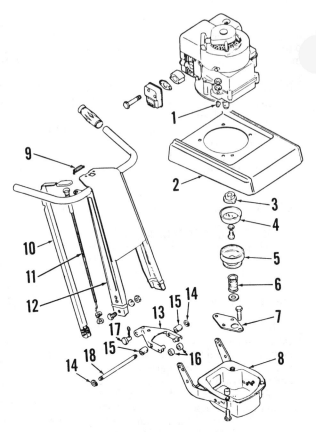

Fig. F21 – Exploded view of upper body for Model 1094.
1. Hypro key
2. Engine base
3. Cone clutch hub
4. Upper cone
5. Clutch cone assy.
6. Clutch spring
7. Reinforcement plate
8. Bell housing assy.
9. Spring
10. Clutch rod
11. Throttle control
12. Handle assy.
13. Clutch yoke
14. Retaining ring
15. Pivot pin spacer
16. Clutch roller
17. Clevis pin
18. Pivot pin

Refer to **CLUTCH CONTROL ADJUSTMENT** section for adjusting procedure.

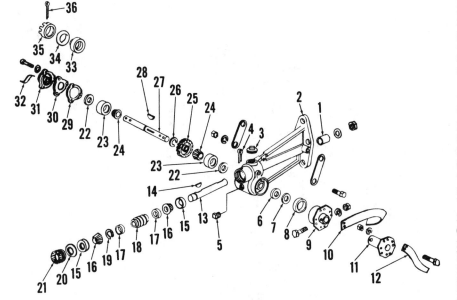

Fig. F20 – Exploded view of gear box used on Models 1023 and 1005. Parts 29 through 32 are used on 1005 models and parts 33 through 36 are used on 1023 models.

1. Bushing	10. Tine, R.H.	19. Snap ring	28. Hypro key
2. Gear box housing	11. Outer hub	20. Seal	29. Gasket
3. Oil fill plug	12. Tine, L.H.	21. Adjustment plug	30. Gasket
4. Cotter pin	13. Worm shaft	22. Seal	31. Cover
5. Oil level plug	14. Hypro key	23. Cup	32. Lock plate
6. Inner felt seal	15. Cup	24. Cone	33. Cover
7. Washer	16. Cone	25. Bronze worm wheel	34. Seal
8. Intermediate felt seal	17. Spacer	26. Snap ring	35. Lock cover
9. Inner hub	18. Worm gear	27. Tine shaft	36. Cotter pin

Models 1114A, 1134 and 1183

TINE DRIVE BELT. Refer to Fig F22 for correct belt routing. Place clutch lever in neutral position. Remove drive belt cover and belt guide (7). Slip belt (13) from pulleys and install new belt. Drive belt size is ⅜-inch x 38 inches long. Reinstall belt guide. Refer to **BELT ADJUSTMENT** section for belt adjusting procedure. Reinstall drive belt cover.

WHEEL DRIVE BELT. Remove tine drive belt as outlined in previous paragraph. Remove retaining ring (4 – Fig. F22) from idler arm shaft. Remove belt from wheel drive case pulley (12). Remove retaining ring (10) from wheel drive case pulley shaft, then remove pulley taking care not to lose Woodruff key. Remove cotter pin (6) from link (5). Slide idler arm assemblies (3) out until spacer (2) can be withdrawn from between idler arms, then remove belt (14). Reverse removal procedure to install belt. Drive belt size is ⅜-inch x 46 inches long. Reinstall tine drive belt. Refer to **BELT ADJUSTMENT** section for adjusting procedure.

Models 1105 and 1200

Place control lever in neutral, remove bolts securing engine to tiller, then remove engine. Remove belt by slipping it over input pulley (I – Fig. F23). Install belt by reversing removal procedure making certain belt is installed inside pins (P). Drive belt size is ⅜-inch x 20 inches long. Reinstall engine.

Models 1023 and 1005

Remove belt guard and unhook spring (6–Fig. F24) from idler arm assembly. Remove input pulley belt guide (7) and idler roller belt guide (4). Remove

reverse drive belt (2) noting its position. Remove forward drive belt (1). Install new belts by reversing removal procedure. Model 1023 forward drive belt size is ½-inch x 35 inches long and reverse drive belt size is ⅜-inch x 37 inches long. Model 1005 forward drive belt size is ½-inch x 37 inches long and reverse drive belt size is ⅜-inch x 39 inches long. Refer to **BELT ADJUST-MENT** section for adjusting procedure.

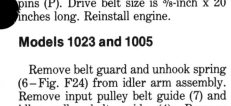

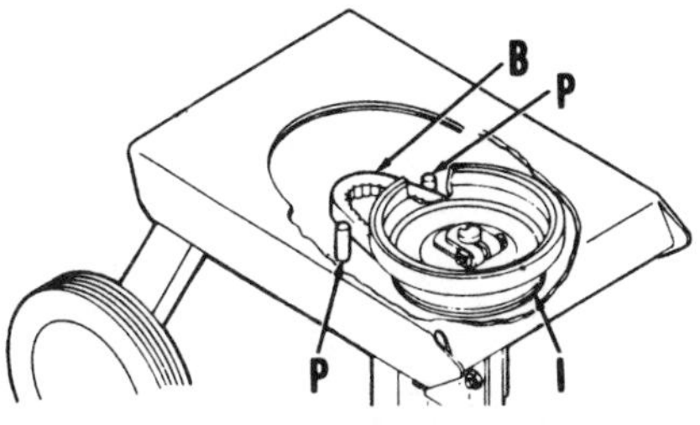

Fig. F23 – View of proper belt arrangement for Models 1105 and 1200.

P. Belt guide pins
I. Input pulley

B. Drive belt

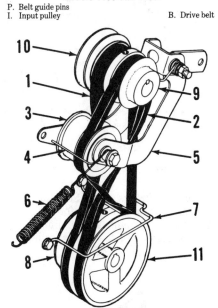

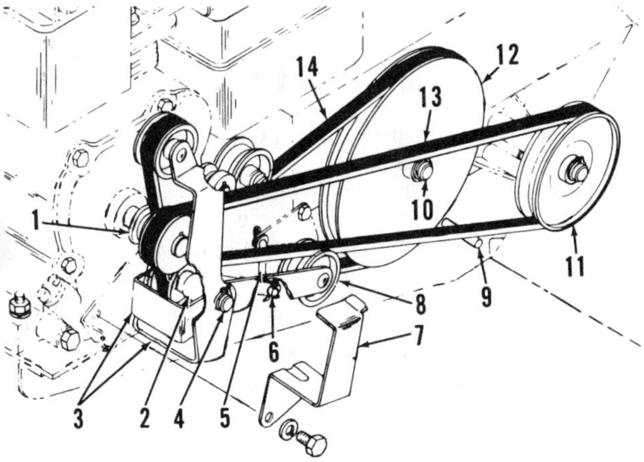

Fig. F22 – View of proper belt arrangement and attaching parts for Models 1114A and 1134.

1. Engine pulley
2. Spacer
3. Idler arm assemblies
4. Retaining ring
5. Idler arm link
6. Cotter pin
7. Belt guide
8. Tine drive idler pulley
9. Belt guide pin
10. Retaining ring
11. Tine drive case pulley
12. Wheel drive case pulley
13. Tine drive belt
14. Wheel drive belt

Fig. F24 – View of belt and pulley system for Models 1023 and 1005. High speed pulleys (8 and 10) are only used on Model 1005.

1. Forward drive belt
2. Reverse drive belt
3. Idler roller
4. Idler roller belt guide
5. Idler arm assy.
6. Idler spring
7. Input pulley belt guide
8. High speed pulley groove
9. Engine pulley
10. High speed pulley groove
11. Input pulley

GILSON

LAWN-BOY PRODUCT GROUP
Box 152
Plymouth, WI 53073

Model	Engine Make	Engine Series	Engine Horsepower	No. of Forward Speeds	Power Reverse?	Tilling Width (In.)	Drive Type
51081	B&S	130000	5	1	Yes	12-26	Gear
51088	Tec.	H60	6	1	Yes	12-26	Gear
51097	B&S	130000	5	1	Yes	12-26	Gear
51174	B&S	13000	5	1	Yes	12-26	Gear

LUBRICATION

ENGINE

All Models

Refer to Briggs and Stratton or Tecumseh engine section for engine lubrication requirements. Recommended fuel is regular or low lead gasoline.

Fig. G1 — View of gear box oil fill plug (F) and oil level plug (L) location.

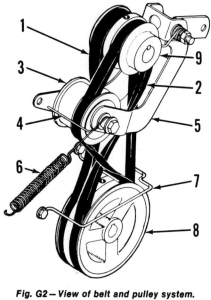

Fig. G2 — View of belt and pulley system.

1. Forward drive belt
2. Reverse drive belt
3. Idler roller
4. Idler roller belt guide
5. Idler arm assy.
6. Idler spring
7. Input pulley belt guide
8. Input pulley
9. Engine pulley

GEAR DRIVE

Oil level in gear housing should be

Fig. G3 — Drawing of clutch control lever adjustment. Refer to text for procedures.

1. Control rod
2. Pivot bushing
3. Stop collar
4. Set screw

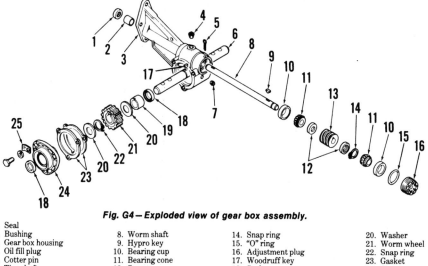

Fig. G4 — Exploded view of gear box assembly.

1. Seal
2. Bushing
3. Gear box housing
4. Oil fill plug
5. Cotter pin
6. Tine shaft
7. Pipe plug
8. Worm shaft
9. Hypro key
10. Bearing cup
11. Bearing cone
12. Spacer
13. Worm
14. Snap ring
15. "O" ring
16. Adjustment plug
17. Woodruff key
18. Seal
19. Bushing
20. Washer
21. Worm wheel
22. Snap ring
23. Gasket
24. Cover
25. Lock tab

checked at least every 25 hours of operation. Gear housing oil level should be even with oil level plug hole (L – Fig. G1) with tiller in level position. If oil level is low, then add oil through fill plug hole (F) until oil runs out level hole. Recommended oil is SAE 140EP.

MAINTENANCE

Inspect belt pulleys and renew if damaged or worn excessively. Check condition of control levers and linkage and renew if excessive play or binding prohibits easy, complete engagement of drive mechanism. After every 8 to 10 hours of operation the idler roller (3 – Fig. G2) should be removed and bearing wick saturated with SAE 30 oil. Periodically lubricate wheel bushings with SAE 30 oil.

ADJUSTMENT

CLUTCH CONTROL LEVER. Move clutch control lever forward (in the drive position), slide stop collar (3–Fig. G3) up to ¼ inch (6.4 mm) from pivot bushing (2), then tighten set screw (4). Place control lever in neutral then pull on engine recoil starter with spark plug wire disconnected to check that belts slip on all pulleys and tiller does not creep. If tiller moves forward in the neutral position loosen set screw and move stop collar upward slightly. If tiller moves backward slide stop collar downward slightly. Retighten set screw.

Repeat procedure until tiller does not creep in neutral.

GEAR CASE BEARING ADJUSTMENT. After many hours of operation, end play may develop in worm shaft bearings (11–Fig. G4). To adjust, remove cotter pin (5) from gear housing and turn adjustment plug (16) in as far as possible then back off one notch and install cotter pin.

BELT ADJUSTMENT. Engine shims (20–Fig. G5) or washers may be used to compensate for belt stretch. Add shims or washers between engine and tine shield (23) until proper belt tension is attained.

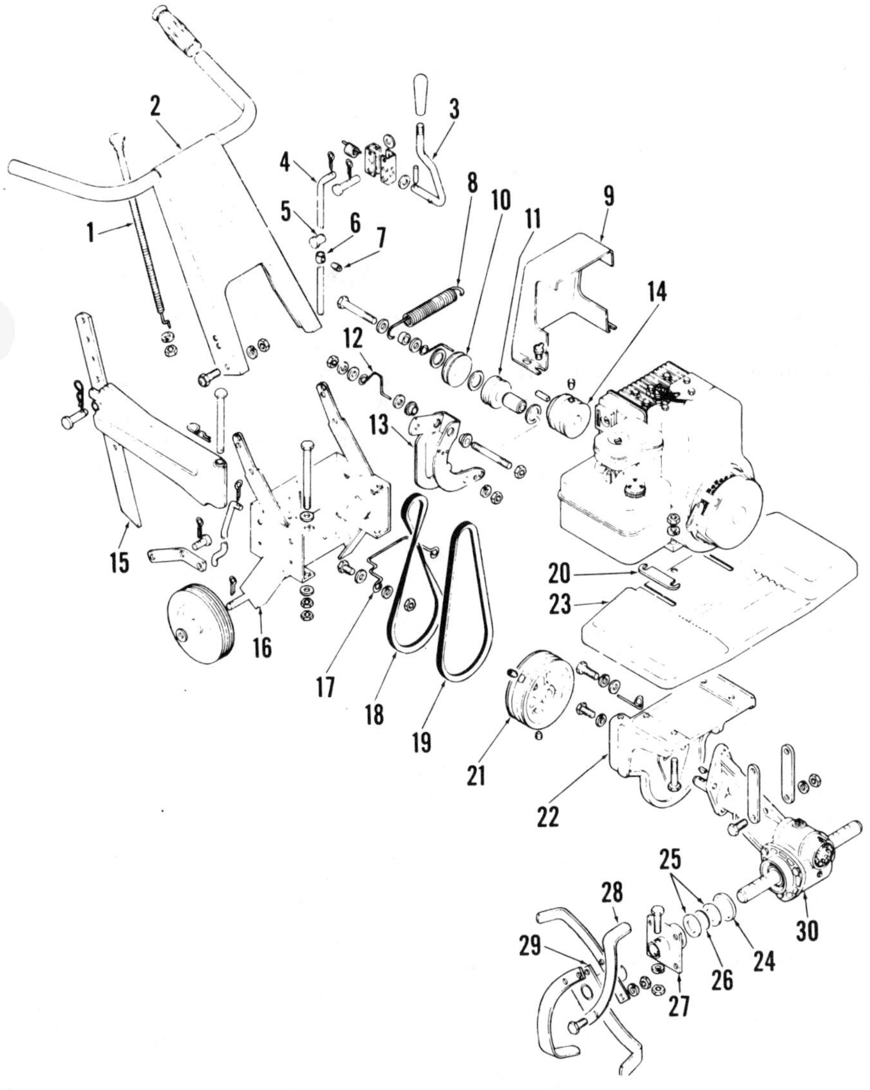

OVERHAUL

ENGINE

All Models

Engine model no. is stamped on blower housing for Briggs and Stratton engines. Engine make and series no. is marked on data plate attached to engine for Tecumseh engines. Refer to appropriate Briggs and Stratton or Tecumseh engine section for overhaul procedures.

DRIVE BELTS

To renew belts, remove belt guard (9–Fig. G5) and unhook spring (6–Fig. G2) from the idler arm assembly. Remove input pulley belt guide (7) and idler roller belt guide (4). Remove reverse drive belt, noting its position. Remove forward drive belt, then install new belts by reversing removal procedure. Manufacturer recommends Gilson No. 6163 for reverse drive belt and Gilson No. 1110 for forward drive belt. After installation belt guides (4 and 7) should be adjusted 1/16/1/8 inch (1.6-3.2 mm) from pulleys.

GEAR BOX

Overhaul of gear box assembly is evident after inspection of unit and referral to Fig. G4. Clean gear box housing thoroughly before disassembling to prevent dirt from entering unit. Examine bronze gear and renew if teeth are broken, chipped or excessively worn. Inspect bearings and cones and renew if chipped, pitted or discolored. Always install complete new bearing assembly if either cone or cup is damaged. Remove rust and burrs from areas of shaft where seals contact using #400 emery cloth. Do not damage shaft by over-polishing because leakage may result. Inspect shaft especially around seal contact surfaces and around hypro key for cracking, galling or other damage. Renew or repair shaft if necessary. Center bronze gear over key to maintain proper alignment with worm gear. Always renew gaskets and seals when overhauling unit.

Fig. G5 – Exploded view showing drive components.

1. Throttle control			
2. Handle assy.	9. Belt guard	16. Frame	23. Tine shield
3. Control lever	10. Reverse idler assy.	17. Belt guide	24. Intermediate felt sea.
4. Control rod	11. Idler assy.	18. Reverse belt	25. Inner felt seal
5. Pivot bushing	12. Belt guide	19. Forward belt	26. Washer
6. Stop collar	13. Idler arm assy.	20. Engine spacer shims	27. Inner tine hub assy.
7. Set screw	14. Engine pulley	21. Input pulley	28. Tine
8. Spring	15. Depth control stake	22. Engine base	29. Outer tine hub assy.

GILSON

Model	Engine Make	Engine Series	Engine Horsepower	No. of Forward Speeds	Power Reverse?	Tilling Width (In.)	Drive Type
51082	B&S	130000	5	2	Yes	12-26	Gear
51085	B&S	190000	8	2	Yes	12-26	Gear

LUBRICATION

ENGINE

All Models

Refer to Briggs and Stratton engine section for engine lubrication requirements. Recommended fuel is regular or low lead gasoline.

GEAR DRIVE

Oil level in gear housing should be checked at least every 25 hours of operation. Gear housing oil level should be

Fig. G10 — View of gear box oil fill plug (F) and oil level plug (L) location.

even with oil level plug hole (L—Fig. G10) with tiller in level position. It may

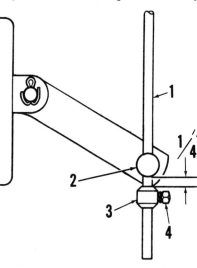

Fig. G12 — Drawing of clutch control lever adjustment. Refer to text for procedures.
1. Control rod
2. Pivot bushing
3. Stop collar
4. Set screw

be necessary to place boards under tiller wheels to level unit. If oil level is low, add SAE 140 EP oil through fill plug hole (F) until oil runs out level hole.

MAINTENANCE

Inspect belt pulleys and renew if damaged or worn excessively. Check condition of control levers and linkage and renew if excessive play or binding prohibits easy, complete engagement of drive mechanism. Each year the idler roller (3—Fig. G11) should be removed and the bearing wick saturated with SAE 30 oil. Periodically lubricate the wheel bushings with SAE 30 oil.

ADJUSTMENT

CLUTCH CONTROL LEVER

Move clutch control lever forward (in the drive position), slide stop collar (3—Fig. G12) up to ¼ inch (6.4 mm) from

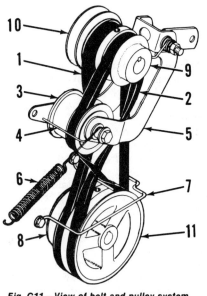

Fig. G11 — View of belt and pulley system.
1. Forward drive belt
2. Reverse drive belt
3. Idler roller
4. Idler roller belt guide
5. Idler arm assy.
6. Idler spring
7. Input pulley belt guide
8. High speed pulley groove
9. Engine pulley
10. High speed pulley groove
11. Input pulley

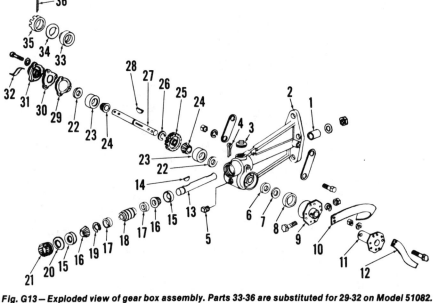

Fig. G13 — Exploded view of gear box assembly. Parts 33-36 are substituted for 29-32 on Model 51082.
1. Bushing
2. Gear box housing
3. Oil fill plug
4. Cotter pin
5. Oil level plug
6. Inner felt seal
7. Washer
8. Intermediate felt seal
9. Inner hub
10. Tine, R.H.
11. Outer hub
12. Tine, L.H.
13. Worm shaft
14. Hypro key
15. Cup
16. Cone
17. Spacer
18. Worm gear
19. Snap ring
20. Seal
21. Adjustment plug
22. Seal
23. Cup
24. Cone
25. Bronze worm wheel
26. Snap ring
27. Tine shaft
28. Hypro key
29. Gasket
30. Gasket
31. Cover
32. Lock tab
33. Cover
34. Seal
35. Lock cover
36. Cotter pin

pivot bushing (2), then tighten set screw (4). Place control lever in neutral and disconnect wire from spark plug, then pull recoil starter to check that belts slip on all pulleys and tiller does not creep. If tiller moves forward in neutral position, then loosen set screw and move stop collar upward slightly. If tiller moves backward slide stop collar downward slightly. Retighten set screw. Repeat procedure until tiller does not creep in neutral.

CHANGING SPEEDS

Forward speed ranges are low and high. The forward drive belt (1–Fig. G11) must be relocated on pulleys to shift forward speed from low to high or vice versa. To change belt from low to high move belt (1) to pulleys (8 and 10). If belt is too tight to change pulley positions, loosen engine to base bolts and tilt engine back, then relocate belt.

DRIVE BELT

Engine shims (11–Fig. G14) or washers may be used to compensate for belt stretch. Add shims or washers between engine and tine shield until proper belt tension is attained.

GEAR CASE BEARING

After many hours of operation, end play may develop in the worm shaft bearings. To adjust, remove cotter pin (4–Fig. G13) from gear housing and turn adjustment plug (21) in as far as possible then back off one notch and install cotter pin.

OVERHAUL

ENGINE

All Models

Engine model no. is stamped on blower housing. Refer to appropriate Briggs and Stratton engine section for overhaul procedures.

DRIVE BELTS

To renew belts, remove belt guard (50–Fig. G14) and unhook spring (6–Fig. G11) from the idler arm assembly. Remove input pulley belt guide (7) and idler roller belt guide (4). Remove reverse drive belt (2), noting its

position. Remove forward drive belt, then install new belts by reversing removal procedure. Manufacturer recommends Gilson No. 6163 for reverse drive belt and Gilson No. 1110 for forward drive belt. After installation, belt guides (4 and 7) should be adjusted 1/16-1/8 inch from pulleys.

GEAR BOX

Overhaul of gear box assembly is evident after inspection of unit and referral to Fig. G13. Clean gear box housing thoroughly before disassembling to prevent dirt from entering unit. Examine bronze gear and renew if teeth are broken, chipped or excessively worn. Inspect bearings and cones and renew if chipped, pitted or discolored. Always install complete new bearing assembly if either cone or cup is damaged. Remove rust and burrs from areas of shaft where seals contact using #400 emery cloth. Do not damage shaft by over-polishing because leakage may result. Inspect shaft especially around seal contact surfaces and around hypro key for cracking, galling or other damage. Renew or repair shaft if necessary. Center bronze gear over key to maintain proper alignment with worm gear. Always renew gaskets and seals when overhauling unit.

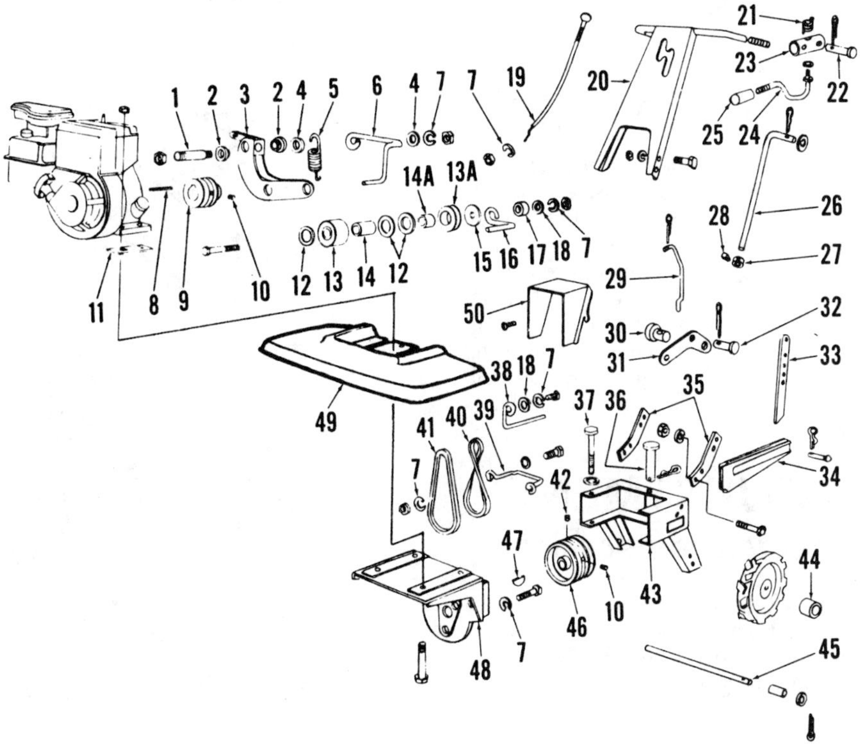

Fig. G14 – Exploded view of typical drive components.

1. Idler arm shaft	13A. Reverse idler assy.	25. Knob	38. Belt guide
2. Bushing	14. Idler shaft	26. Control rod	39. Belt guide
3. Idler arm	14A. Reverse idler shaft	27. Stop collar	40. Reverse belt
4. Washer	15. Washer	28. Set screw	41. Forward belt
5. Idler spring	16. Belt guide	29. Link	42. Set screw
6. Belt guide	17. Bushing	30. Pivot bushing	43. Main frame
7. Lock washers	18. Washer	31. Pivot arm	44. Wheel bushing
8. Key	19. Throttle control	32. Clevis pin	45. Axle
9. Engine pulley	20. Handle assy.	33. Depth control	46. Input pulley
10. Set screw	21. Lever spring	34. Tailpiece assy.	47. Hypro key
11. Engine shim	22. Control pin	35. Handle bracket	48. Engine base
12. Washer	23. Control tube	36. Hanger pin	49. Tine shield
13. Idler roller	24. Control lever	37. Bolt	50. Belt guard

GILSON

Model	Engine Make	Engine Series	Engine Horsepower	No. of Forward Speeds	Power Reverse?	Tilling Width (In.)	Drive Type
51083	B&S	190000	8	4	Yes	12-26	Gear

LUBRICATION

ENGINE

Refer to Briggs and Stratton engine section for engine lubrication requirements. Recommended fuel is regular or low lead gasoline.

GEAR DRIVE

Oil level in gear housing should be checked at least every 25 hours of operation. Gear housing oil level should be even with oil level plug hole (L–Fig. G20) with tiller in level position. It may be necessary to place boards under the tiller wheels to level unit. If oil level is low, add oil through fill plug hole (F) until oil runs out level hole. Recommended oil is SAE 140 EP.

MAINTENANCE

Inspect belt pulleys and renew if damaged or worn excessively. Check condition of control levers and linkage and renew if excessive play or binding prohibits easy, complete engagement of drive mechanism. After each 8-10 hours of operation the idler roller (31–Fig. G21) should be removed and the bearing wick saturated with SAE 30 oil. Periodically lubricate wheel bushings with SAE 30 oil.

ADJUSTMENT

CLUTCH CONTROL ROD

With clutch control lever in neutral position, tiller should not creep to reverse or forward. Check by disconnecting spark plug wire and pulling recoil

starter. If tiller moves forward in the neutral position, loosen jam nut (7–Fig. G23) remove spring clip (5A) and rotate control rod (6) clockwise one or two turns into ball joint assembly (8). If tiller moves backward turn control rod (6) counter-clockwise one or two turns out of ball joint assembly (8). Recheck for improper engagement in neutral, then retighten jam nut (7) against ball joint assembly (8) when proper adjustment is attained.

BELT

To compensate for belt stretch loosen jam nut (7–Fig. G23), remove spring clip (5A) and rotate control rod (6) counter-clockwise out of ball joint assembly (8) two turns then retighten jam nut (7). Check for correct neutral

adjustment as outlined in previous section.

GEAR CASE BEARING

After many hours of operation end play may develop in worm shaft bearings (8–Fig. G22). To adjust, remove cotter pin (6) from gear housing and turn adjustment plug (14) in as far as possible then back off one notch and reinstall cotter pin.

OVERHAUL

ENGINE

Engine model no. is stamped on

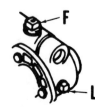

Fig. G20 – View of gear box oil fill plug (F) and oil level plug (L) location.

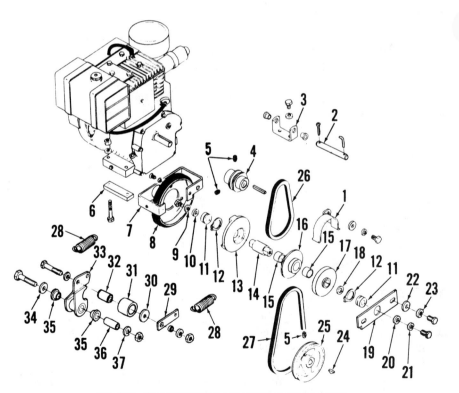

Fig. G21 – Exploded view of belt, pulley and drive system.

1. Belt guide	11. Bearing	20. Spacer	29. Spring bracket
2. Pivot shaft	12. Snap ring	21. Lockwasher	30. Washer
3. Pivot bracket	13. Reverse pulley half	22. Washer	31. Idler roller
4. Engine pulley	14. Drive shaft	23. Lockwasher	32. Idler shaft
5. Set screw	15. Bushing	24. Hypro key	33. Idler arm assy.
6. Engine block	16. Pulley center	25. Input pulley	34. Washer
7. Drive support bracket	17. Pulley half	26. Upper drive belt	35. Bushing
8. Friction wheel roller	18. Washer	27. Lower drive belt	36. Spacer
9. Lockwasher	19. Drive support plate	28. Spring	37. Lockwasher
10. Spacer			

blower housing. Refer to appropriate Briggs and Stratton engine section for overhaul procedures.

DRIVE BELTS

To renew belts remove belt guard (2 – Fig. G23) and unhook spring (28 – Fig. G21) from idler roller assembly. Remove two bolts securing drive support plate (19 – Fig. G21) to drive support bracket (7) and rotate support plate (19) 90-degrees from secured position. Remove lower drive belt (27) from input pulley (25). Remove upper drive belt after removing belt guide (1). Install new belts by reversing removal procedure. Manufacturer recommends Gilson No. 26345 for lower drive belt and Gilson No. 26344 for upper drive belt. After installation, belt guide (1) should be adjusted 1/16-1/8 inch (1.6-3.2 mm) from pulleys.

GEAR BOX

Overhaul of gear box assembly is evident after inspection of unit and referral to Fig. G22. Clean gear box housing thoroughly before disassembling to prevent dirt from entering unit. Examine bronze gear and renew if teeth are broken, chipped or excessively worn. Inspect bearings and cones and renew if chipped, pitted or discolored. Always install complete new bearing assembly if either cone or cup is damaged. Remove rust and burrs from areas of shaft where seals contact using #400 emery cloth. Do not damage shaft by over-polishing because leakage may result. Inspect shaft especially around seal contact surfaces and around hypro key for cracking, galling or other damage. Renew or repair shaft if necessary. Center bronze gear over key to maintain proper alignment with worm gear. Always renew gaskets and seals when overhauling unit.

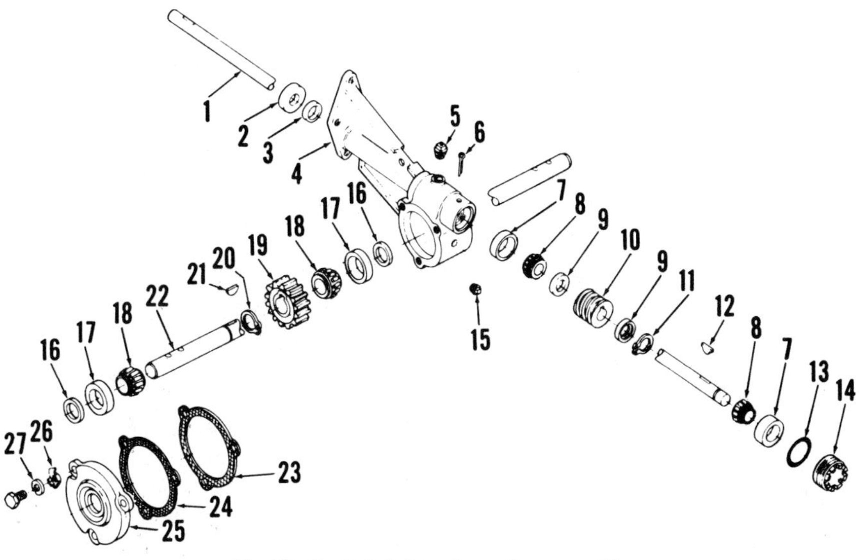

Fig. 22 – Exploded view of gear box assembly.

1. Worm shaft	8. Cones	15. Oil level plug	22. Tine shaft
2. Ball bearing	9. Spacers	16. Seals	23. Gasket
3. Gasket	10. Worm gear	17. Cups	24. Gasket
4. Gear box housing	11. Snap ring	18. Cones	25. Cover
5. Vent plug assy.	12. Hypro key	19. Bronze worm wheel	26. Washer
6. Cotter pin	13. "O" ring	20. Snap ring	27. Lockwasher
7. Cups	14. Adjusting plug	21. Key	

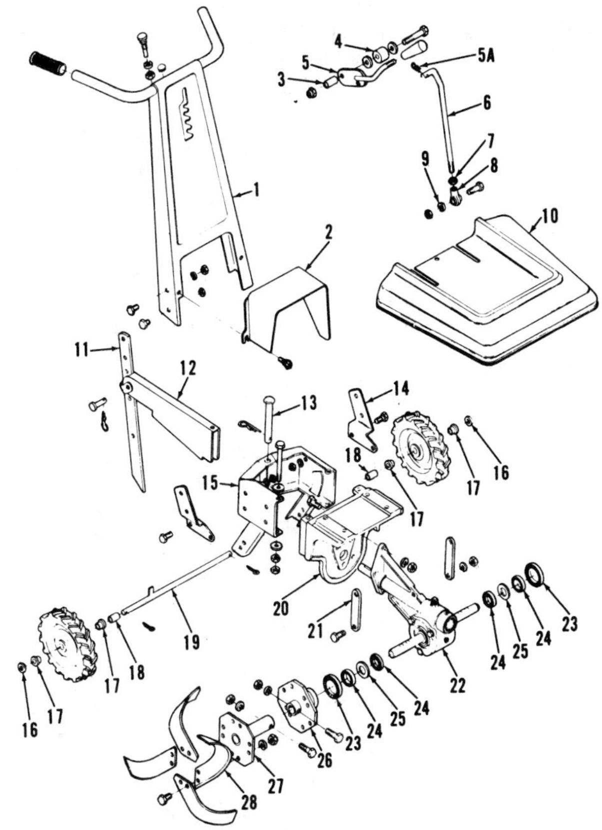

Fig. G23 – Exploded view of Model 51083 tiller assembly.

1. Handle assy.
2. Belt guard
3. Spacer
4. Rubber disc
5. Control lever assy.
5A. Spring clip
6. Control rod
7. Jam nut
8. Ball joint
9. Lockwasher
10. Tine shield
11. Depth control
12. Tail piece assy.
13. Hanger pin
14. Handle bracket
15. Main frame assy.
16. Washer
17. Bearing
18. Spacer
19. Axle
20. Engine base
21. Support strap
22. Gear case
23. Intermediate felt seal
24. Inner felt seal
25. Washer
26. Inner tine hub assy.
27. Outer tine hub assy.
28. Tine

GILSON

Model	Engine Make	Engine Series	Engine Horsepower	No. of Forward Speeds	Power Reverse?	Tilling Width (In.)	Drive Type
51094	B&S	90000	3.5	1	No	12-26	Gear
51096	B&S	130000	5	1	No	12-26	Gear
51106	B&S	130000	5	1	No	12-24	Gear

LUBRICATION

ENGINE

All Models

Refer to Briggs and Stratton engine section for engine lubrication requirements. Recommended fuel is regular or low lead gasoline.

GEAR DRIVE

Oil level in gear housing should be checked at least every 25 hours of operation. Gear housing oil level should be even with oil level plug hole (L–Fig. G31) with tiller in level position. Recommended oil is SAE 140 EP.

The worm shaft bushing (4–Fig. G32) is lubricated through a grease fitting (F–Fig. G31) with number 2 wheel bearing grease. A small amount of grease should be added after every 10 hours of operation.

MAINTENANCE

Inspect nuts and bolts periodically for looseness and retighten as necessary. Check condition of control linkage and shift yoke (13–Fig. G33) and repair or renew if excessive play or binding pro-

hibits easy, complete engagement of drive mechanism. The pivot pin (18–Fig. G33) should be lubricated annually to avoid binding and lessen wear of clutch linkage. Remove pivot pin (18) by first removing retaining ring (14) and pushing pivot pin out of the bell housing (8) with a wooden dowel rod the same size or slightly smaller in diameter than the pivot pin. Once the pivot pin is removed clean thoroughly and lubricate with SAE 30 oil. To install pivot pin, push dowel through bell housing with pivot pin (18), then reinstall retaining ring. Periodically lubricate wheel bushings with SAE 30 oil.

ADJUSTMENT

CLUTCH CONTROL ROD ADJUSTMENT-NEUTRAL. Clutch control rod may be adjusted to compensate for normal wear of clutch cone assembly. With clutch control rod (1–Fig. G34) in neutral position, tines should not turn. Check by disconnecting

spark plug wire and pulling recoil starter. If tines turn, move control rod out of neutral, then remove cotter pin (3) and clevis pin (4) making note of previous holes used. Relocate clutch yoke (2) to next higher set of holes in control rod (1). Reinstall clevis pin (4) and cotter pin (3), then recheck adjustment.

GEAR CASE BEARING ADJUSTMENT. After many hours of operation, end play may develop in the worm shaft bearings (10–Fig. G32). To adjust, remove cotter pin (7) from gear housing and turn adjustment plug (17) in as far as possible, then back off one notch and reinstall cotter pin.

OVERHAUL

ENGINE

All Models

Engine model no. is stamped on

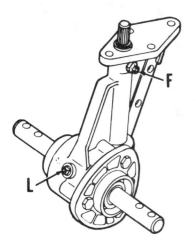

Fig. G31 – Drawing of gear box oil level plug (L) and worm shaft bushing grease fitting (F).

Fig. G32 – Exploded view of gear box assembly. Shaft 23 is substituted for 21 on Models 51094 and 51096.

1. Snap ring
2. Alignment bushing
3. Felt wick
4. Bushing
5. Grease fitting
6. Gear case
7. Cotter pin
8. Oil level plug
9. Bearing cup
10. Bearing cone
11. Spacer
12. Worm shaft
13. Hypro key
14. Worm gear
15. Snap ring
16. "O" Ring
17. Adjustment plug
18. Seal
19. Bushing
20. Washer
21. Tine shaft
22. Hypro key
23. Tine shaft
24. Worm wheel
25. Snap ring
26. Gasket
27. Gasket
28. Cover
29. Lock tab

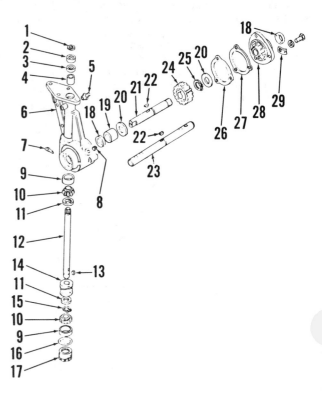

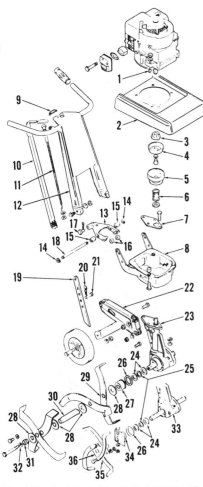

Fig. G33 — Exploded view of Model 51106 tiller. Parts 33, 34, 35 and 36 are substituted for parts 23, 27, 28, 29, 30, 31 and 32 on Models 51094 and 51096.

1. Hypro key	19. Depth control
2. Engine base	20. Spring clip
3. Cone clutch hub	21. Clevis pin
4. Upper cone	22. Tailpiece assy.
5. Clutch cone assy.	23. Gear case assy.
6. Clutch spring	24. Felt seal
7. Reinforcement plate	25. Washer
8. Bell housing assy.	26. Seal
9. Spring	27. Seal collar
10. Clutch rod	28. Tine washer
11. Throttle control	29. Tine
12. Handle assy.	30. Tine extension
13. Clutch yoke	31. Bushing
14. Retaining ring	32. Lockwasher
15. Pivot pin spacer	33. Gear case assy.
16. Clutch roller	34. Inner tine hub assy.
17. Clevis pin	35. Tine
18. Pivot pin	36. Outer tine hub assy.

blower housing. Refer to appropriate Briggs and Stratton engine section for overhaul procedures.

CLUTCH CONE ASSEMBLY

To renew clutch assembly, engine must be removed from engine base (2 – Fig. G33) and bell housing assembly (8). Disconnect throttle control (11) and three 5/16 x 1⁷⁄₈ bolts securing the engine to base and bell housing, then remove engine. Inspect upper cone (4) and clutch cone assembly (5) for gouging and excessive wear, renew as necessary. The upper cone (4) and clutch assembly (5) should be renewed as a set. Check condition of spring (6) and renew if stretched or broken. Clean and lubricate splines of worm shaft and clutch cone assembly (5) with SAE 30 oil. Check condition of clutch yoke assembly (13) including rollers (16) and renew if worn or damaged. Clean and lubricate clutch yoke and rollers with SAE 30 oil before assembling.

GEAR CASE

All Models

OIL SEAL INSTALLATION. Remove tines from output shaft. Remove bolts securing side cover (28 – Fig. G32) to gear case and remove cover. Remove old seal (18), install new oil seal, then reinstall side cover and bolts. On opposite side of gear case hub, pry seal from hub and drive new seal in until bottomed in bore of case hub.

INSPECTION. Refer to Fig. G32 for gear case parts breakdown and identification. Inspect all components and renew all that are worn or damaged. Install new gaskets and seals. Lubricate gears and bearings with a light film of oil during reassembly. Refer to **GEAR CASE ADJUSTMENT** section for end play adjusting procedure. Refer to **LUBRICATION** section for lubrication requirements.

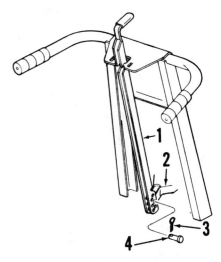

Fig. G34 — Drawing of clutch control. Refer to text for adjustment procedures.

1. Clutch rod	3. Cotter pin
2. Clutch yoke	4. Clevis pin

GILSON

Model	Engine Make	Engine Series	Engine Horsepower	No. of Forward Speeds	Power Reverse?	Tilling Width (In.)	Drive Type
51080	B&S	90000	3.5	1	No	12-26	Gear
51084	B&S	90000	3.5	1	Yes	12-26	Gear

LUBRICATION

ENGINE

All Models

Refer to Briggs and Stratton engine section for engine lubrication requirements. Recommended fuel is regular or low lead gasoline.

GEAR DRIVE

Oil level in gear housing should be checked at least every 25 hours of operation. Gear housing oil level should be even with oil level plug hole (L – Fig. G41) with tiller in level position. It may be necessary to place boards under the tiller wheels to level the unit. Recommended oil is SAE 140 EP.

The worm shaft bushing (3 – Fig. G42) is lubricated through a grease fitting (F – Fig. G41) with number 2 wheel bearing grease. A small amount of grease should be added at least every 10 hours of operation.

MAINTENANCE

Inspect belt pulleys and reverse disc (if so equipped) and renew if damaged or worn excessively. Check condition of control levers and linkage and renew if

excessive play or binding prohibits easy, complete engagement of drive mechanism. The success of the slide type pulley engagement system is dependent upon the ability of the engine base slides (33 and 35 – Fig. G44) to move freely over the slide blocks (32) thus allowing the pulleys and belt to engage and disengage properly. Periodically clean and lubricate the slide blocks (32) with a lithium type grease. Periodically lubricate wheel bushings with SAE 30 oil.

ADJUSTMENT

CLUTCH CONTROL

With the clutch control lever in neutral position, tiller should not creep either forward or reverse (if so equipped). Check by disconnecting spark plug wire and pulling recoil starter. If tiller moves backward (Model 51084 only) loosen lock nut (2 – Fig. G43) remove

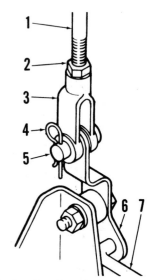

Fig. G43 – Drawing of clutch control rod adjustment. Refer to text for procedures.

1. Control rod
2. Lock nut
3. Clevis
4. Spring clip
5. Clevis pin
6. Bell crank
7. Clutch link

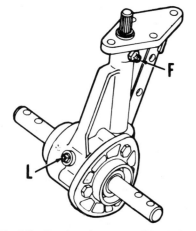

Fig. G41 – Drawing of gear box oil level plug (L) and worm shaft bushing grease fitting (F).

Fig. G42 – Exploded view of gear box assembly.

1. Alignment bushing
2. Felt wick
3. Worm shaft bushing
4. Grease fitting
5. Gear case
6. Oil level plug
7. Worm shaft bearing cup
8. Bearing cone
9. Spacer
10. Worm gear
11. Snap ring
12. Worm shaft
13. Hypro key
14. "O" ring
15. Cotter pin
16. Adjustment plug
17. Gear case cover
18. Cover gasket
19. Cover gasket
20. Tine shaft seal
21. Bushing
22. Washer
23. Snap ring
24. Tine shaft
25. Woodruff key
26. Worm wheel
27. Intermediate felt seal
28. Inner felt seal
29. Washer
30. Inner tine hub assy.
31. Outer tine hub assy.
32. Tine

spring clip (4) and clevis pin (5). Turn clevis (3) counter-clockwise off of the control rod (1) one to two turns. If the tiller moves forward follow above procedures except turn the clevis (3) clockwise one to two turns. Recheck for improper engagement in neutral, then retighten jam nut (2) against clevis (3) when proper adjustment is attained.

GEAR CASE BEARING

After many hours of operation end play may develop in the worm shaft bearings (8 – Fig. G42). To adjust, remove cotter pin (15) from gear housing and turn adjustment plug (16) in as far as possible then back off one notch and reinstall cotter pin.

OVERHAUL

ENGINE

All Models

Engine model no. is stamped on blower housing. Refer to appropriate Briggs and Stratton engine section for overhaul procedures.

GEAR CASE

All Models

OIL SEAL INSTALLATION. Remove tines from output shaft. Remove bolts securing side cover (17 – Fig. G42) to gear case and remove cover. Remove old seal (20), install new seal, then reinstall side cover and bolts. On opposite side of gear case hub, pry seal from hub and drive new seal in until bottomed in bore of case hub.

INSPECTION. Refer to Fig. G42 for gear case parts breakdown and identification. Inspect all components and renew all that are worn or damaged. Install new gaskets and seals. Lubricate gears and bearings with a light film of oil

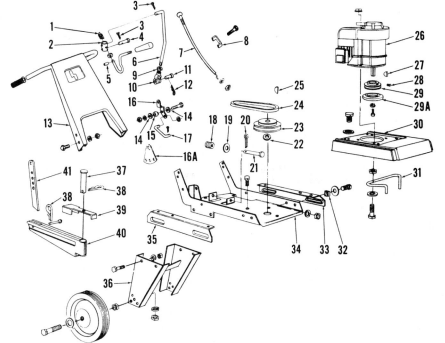

Fig. G44 – Exploded view of typical tiller assembly. Parts 16A and 29A are used only on Model 51084.

1. Spring	13. Handle assy.	22. Washer
2. Control tube	14. Washer	23. Input pulley
3. Cotter pin	15. Control bushing	24. Drive belt
4. Control pin	16. Bellcrank, Model	25. Hypro key
5. Roll pin	51080	26. Engine˙
6. Control rod	16A. Bellcrank, Model	27. Hypro key
7. Throttle control	51084	28. Set screw
8. Throttle clamp	17. Connecting link	29. Engine pulley
9. Jam nut	18. Spring	29A. Reverse disc
10. Clevis	19. Washer	30. Engine base
11. Clevis pin	20. Cotter pin	31. Belt guide
12. Spring clip	21. Spring retainer pin	32. Slide block

33. Engine base slide, L.H.
34. Frame
35. Engine base slide, R.H.
36. Wheel frame assy.
37. Tailpiece pin
38. Spring clip
39. Tailpiece lock
40. Tailpiece assy.
41. Depth control

during reassembly. Refer to **GEAR CASE ADJUSTMENT** section for end play adjusting procedure. Refer to **LUBRICATION** section for lubrication requirements.

DRIVE BELT

All Models

Refer to Fig. G44 for parts breakdown and identification. Remove cotter pin from connecting link (17), then remove link from bell crank (16 or 16A). Remove engine securing bolts, then lift engine assembly from tiller frame. Slip drive belt off engine pulley and install new belt. Manufacturer recommends Gilson drive belt No. 28673. Reinstall engine assembly on tiller frame. Reach under front of tiller frame and slip belt on gear case drive pulley. Complete reassembly in reverse order of disassembly. Refer to **CLUTCH CONTROL** section for adjusting procedure.

GILSON

Model	Engine Make	Engine Series	Engine Horsepower	No. of Forward Speeds	Power Reverse?	Tilling Width (In.)	Drive Type
51095	B&S	60000	2	1	No	12-26	Gear
51170	B&S	60000	2	1	No	6-18	Gear
51105	B&S	90000	3.5	1	Yes	12-26	Gear

LUBRICATION

ENGINE

All Models

Refer to Briggs and Stratton engine section for engine lubrication requirements. Recommended fuel is regular or low lead gasoline.

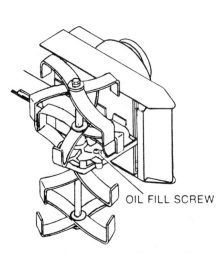

Fig. G51 — View showing oil fill screw of Model 51105. Refer to text for lubrication procedures.

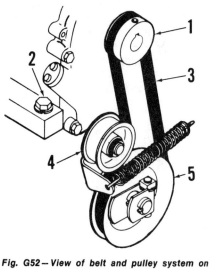

Fig. G52 — View of belt and pulley system on Models 51095 and 51170.

1. Engine pulley
2. Engine bolt
3. Drive belt
4. Idler pulley
5. Input pulley

WHEELS AND CONTROLS

All Models

Periodically lubricate wheel bushings and check for loose bolts. Idler pulley

shaft (14 – Fig. G53) on Models 51095 and 51170 should be lubricated with SAE 30 oil after each 10 hours of opera-

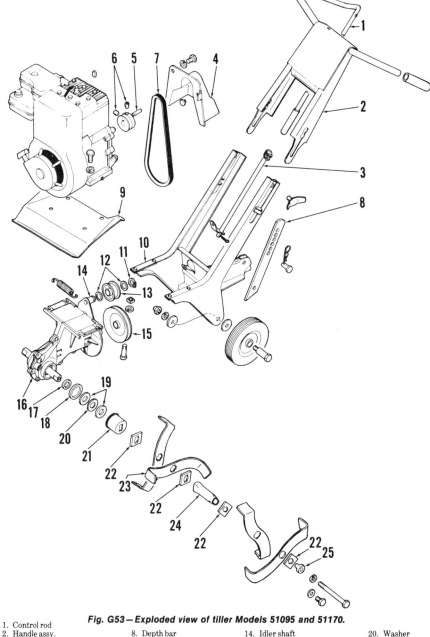

Fig. G53 — Exploded view of tiller Models 51095 and 51170.

1. Control rod
2. Handle assy.
3. Clutch arm assy.
4. Belt guard
5. Square key
6. Set screw
7. Drive belt
8. Depth bar
9. Tine shield
10. Support assy.
11. Snap ring
12. Washer
13. Idler pulley
14. Idler shaft
15. Input pulley
16. Gear case assy.
17. Seal
18. Felt seal
19. Felt seal
20. Washer
21. Seal collar
22. Tine washer
23. Tine
24. Tine extension
25. Bushing

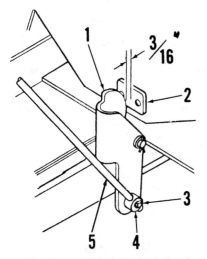

Fig. G54—Drawing of clutch control rod and cam adjustment. Refer to text for adjusting procedures.

1. Cam
2. Pad
3. Set screw
4. Pivot pin
5. Control rod

tion. Caution should be taken in not getting oil on drive belt.

The success of the slide type pulley engagement system on Model 51105 is de-

pendent upon the ability of the engine base (7–Fig. G55) to move freely over the slides (8), thus allowing the pulleys and belt to engage and disengage properly. Periodically clean and lubricate slide points with a lithium type grease.

GEAR DRIVE

The gear box on Models 51095 and 51170 is lubricated for the life of the unit and there is no plug for adding oil. Model 51105 is also lubricated for the life of the unit; however, oil may be added should leakage occur. To add oil, turn tiller on side as shown in Fig. G51, remove oil fill screw and completely fill unit with SAE 140 EP oil. When no air bubbles are evident, reinstall screw.

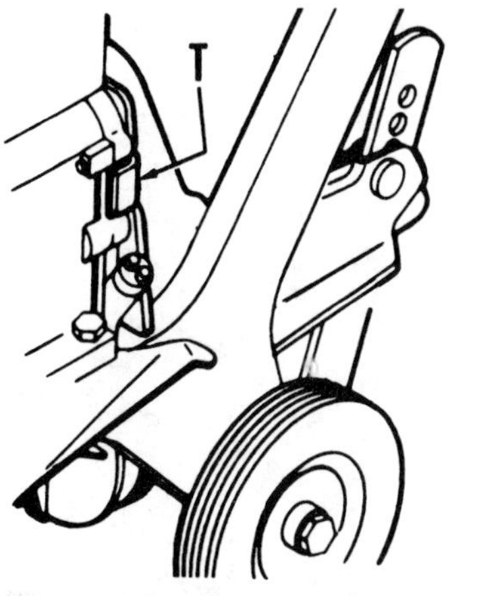

MAINTENANCE

Check condition of control levers and linkage and renew if excessive play or binding prohibits easy, complete en-

Fig. G56—Drawing showing belt guard tab (T) properly secured against side of engine.

gagement of drive mechanism. Inspect drive belt and renew if frayed, cracked, burnt or otherwise damaged. Inspect belt pulleys and renew if damaged or worn excessively.

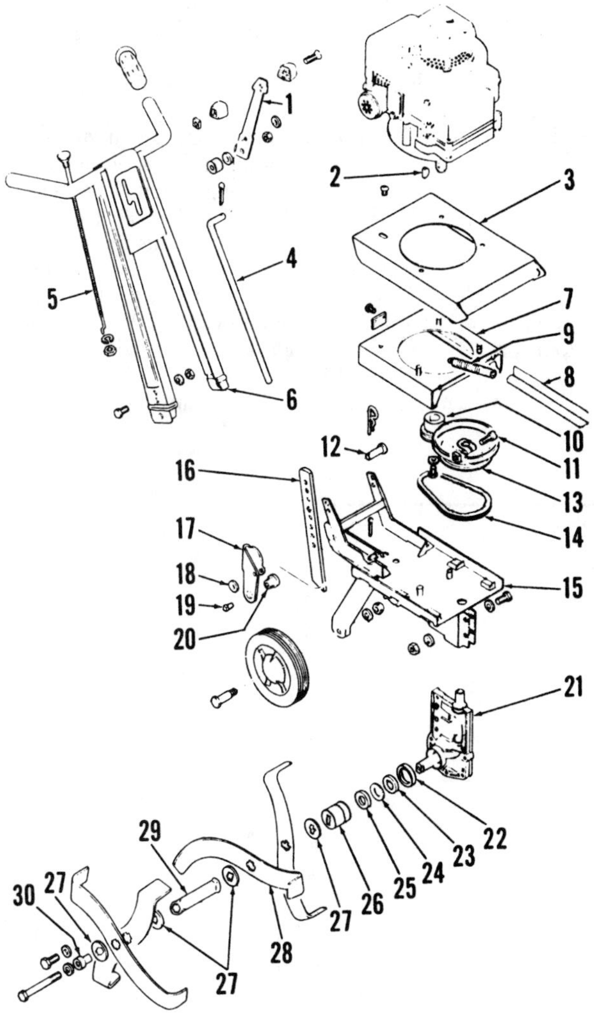

ADJUSTMENT

CLUTCH CONTROL ROD

Model 51105

With clutch control lever in forward position initial adjustment should be 3/16-inch (4.8 mm) gap between cam (1–Fig. G54) and pad (2). Adjustment is made by loosening set screw (3) and sliding pivot pin (4) over rod (5) until proper gap is attained, then retighten set screw. With control rod in neutral, tiller should not creep either forward or reverse. Check by disconnecting spark plug wire and pulling recoil starter. If tiller moves backward, gap between the cam (1) and pad (2) will have to be increased slightly with control rod in forward position. If tiller moves forward in neutral, gap between cam (1) and pad (2)

Fig. G55—Exploded view of tiller Model 51105.

1. Control handle
2. Woodruff key
3. Shroud
4. Control rod
5. Throttle control
6. Handle assy.
7. Engine base assy.
8. Slide
9. Spring
10. Engine pulley
11. Screw
12. Pin
13. Input pulley
14. Drive belt
15. Frame assy.
16. Depth bar
17. Cam
18. Washer
19. Set screw
20. Pivot pin
21. Gear case assy.
22. Seal
23. Felt seal
24. Felt seal
25. Washer
26. Seal collar assy.
27. Tine washer
28. Tine
29. Tine extension
30. Bushing

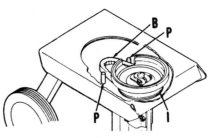

Fig. G57—Drawing of proper belt arrangement.

P. Belt guide pin
I. Input pulley
B. Drive belt

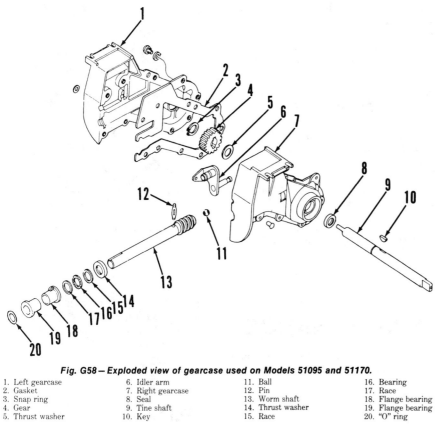

Fig. G58 — Exploded view of gearcase used on Models 51095 and 51170.

1. Left gearcase	6. Idler arm	11. Ball	16. Bearing
2. Gasket	7. Right gearcase	12. Pin	17. Race
3. Snap ring	8. Seal	13. Worm shaft	18. Flange bearing
4. Gear	9. Tine shaft	14. Thrust washer	19. Flange bearing
5. Thrust washer	10. Key	15. Race	20. "O" ring

GEAR BOX

Models 51095 and 51170

Overhaul of gear box assembly is evident after inspection of unit and referral to Fig. G58. Note that gear box housing is riveted together and will require special tools to overhaul.

Model 51105

Gear box assemblies on these models cannot be serviced and individual repair parts are not available. Gear box is renewed as a unit.

DRIVE BELT

Models 51095 and 51170

To renew belt, remove belt guard (4 – Fig. G53) from engine and pull up on belt (3 – Fig. G52) sliding it off engine pulley (1). If belt will not come off engine pulley, then loosen engine-to-gear case assembly bolts and tilt engine back until belt slides off. Install belt by reversing removal procedure. Manufacturer recommends Gilson drive belt 33622. Belt guard tab (T – Fig. G56) must be pushed down securely against side of engine.

Model 51105

To remove belt, place control lever (1 – Fig. G55) in neutral position and remove bolts securing engine to tiller. Detach throttle control cable (5) from engine and remove engine from tiller. Remove belt by slipping over input pulley (I – Fig. G57). Install belt by reversing removal procedure. Manufacturer recommends the use of Gilson drive belt 36019. Be certain belt is installed inside pins (P) as shown in Fig. G57.

will have to be decreased slightly with control rod in forward position.

Models 51095 and 51170

There is no clutch adjustment provided. If drive belt slippage is encountered, drive belt and/or other worn parts will need to be renewed. Refer to **DRIVE BELT** section for belt removal procedures.

OVERHAUL

ENGINE

All Models

Engine model number is stamped on blower housing. Refer to appropriate Briggs and Stratton engine section for overhaul procedures.

GILSON

Model	Engine Make	Engine Series	Engine Horsepower	No. of Forward Speeds	Power Reverse?	Tilling Width (In.)	Drive Type
51114	B&S	130000	5	1	Yes	18	Chain
51134	B&S	130000	5	1	Yes	18	Chain
51159	B&S	130000	5	1	Yes	18	Chain
51175	B&S	130000	5	1	Yes	18	Chain
51175A	B&S	130000	5	1	Yes	18	Chain
51176A	B&S	130000	5	1	Yes	18	Chain
51135	B&S	190000	8	5	Yes	26	Chain
51179	B&S	190000	8	5	Yes	26	Chain
51179A	B&S	190000	8	5	Yes	26	Chain

LUBRICATION

ENGINE

All Models

Refer to Briggs and Stratton engine section for engine lubrication requirements. Recommended fuel is regular or low lead gasoline.

DRIVE CONTROLS

All Models

Clean and lubricate friction points with SAE 30 oil after each eight hours of operation. Caution should be taken in not getting oil on belts.

Inner flange of variable speed pulley mounted on engine must slide freely in and out. Clutch control lever may be difficult to move into forward drive position if pulley flange does not move free-ly. To clean, drive roll pin (2 – Fig. G73) from outer pulley half (22) and engine pulley (1), then remove ouer pulley half. While removing roll pin hold pulley securely because internal spring (19) should force pulley apart. Remove inner pulley half (20), then clean pulley half and shaft portion of engine pulley (1). Reassemble cleaned parts dry. Do not apply oil or grease to pulley parts.

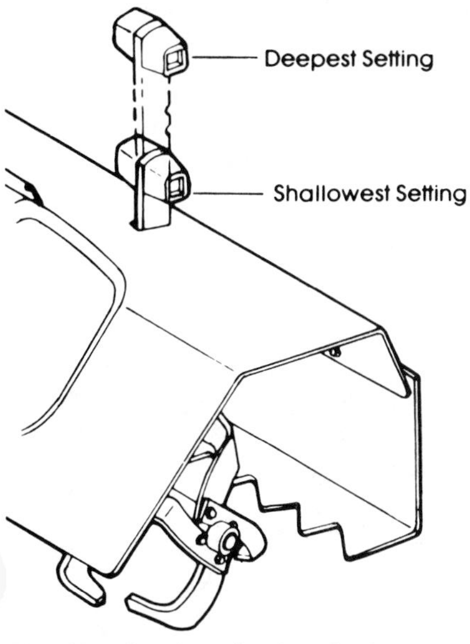

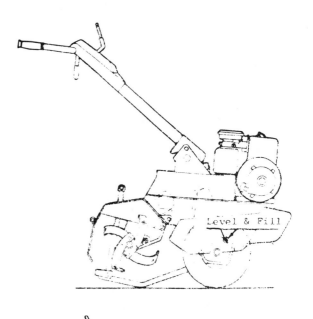

Fig. G62—Oil level and fill plug location on wheel drive case. Note depth control lever is on shallowest set-ting.

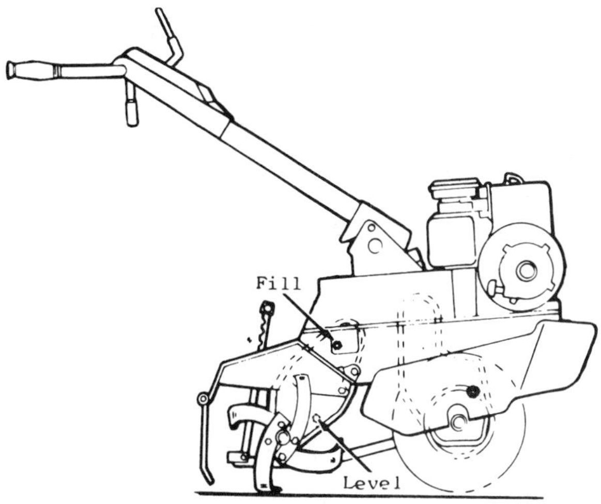

Deepest Setting

Shallowest Setting

Fig. G61—Drawing showing depth control lever.

Fig. G63—Oil level plug and oil fill plug location. Oil level plug is on the left side of tine drive case.

WHEEL DRIVE CASE

To check oil level, place tiller depth control lever at shallowest setting as shown in Fig. G61. Unbolt and remove right wheel from output shaft. Clean dirt from around oil level and fill plug (Fig. G62), then remove plug. Oil level should be at bottom of plug hole. Recommended oil is SAE 140 EP and capacity

is 16 ounces. Oil level should be checked at least every 25 hours of operation and added as needed.

TINE DRIVE CASE

All Models Except 51114

To check oil level, locate tiller on level ground, then set tilling depth control

lever at shallowest setting (Fig. G61). Clean dirt from around oil level plug (Fig. G63) and remove plug. Oil level should be at bottom of plug hole. If oil level is low, clean dirt from around fill plug and remove plug. Add oil slowly until it runs out level plug hole, then reinstall both plugs.

Model 51114

To check oil level, set tilling depth control lever Fig. G61 to deepest setting and raise front drive wheels six inches off ground by placing boards under wheels. Clean dirt from around oil level and fill plug Fig. G64, then remove plug. Oil level should be at bottom of plug hole. Recommended oil is SAE 140 EP gear lube and capacity is one pound. Check gear oil at least every 25 hours and add as needed.

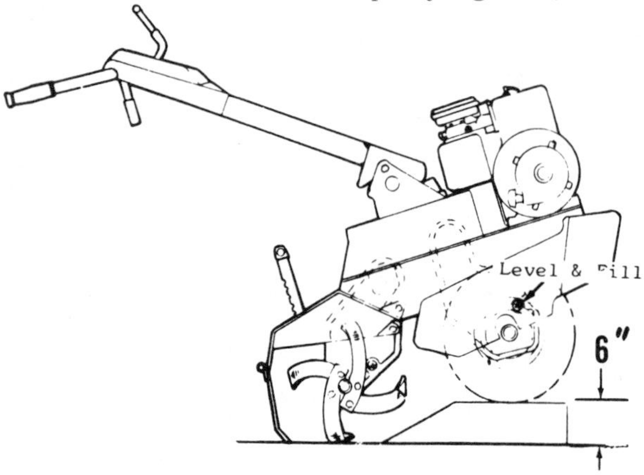

Fig. G64 — Tiller Model 51114 must have its tires raised six inches before oil level may be accurately checked. Note depth control lever set on deepest setting.

MAINTENANCE

Inspect nuts and bolts for looseness and retighten as needed. Check condition of control linkage and idler arm assemblies (10 – Fig. G65). Renew if excessive play or binding prohibits easy, complete engagement of drive mechanism. Inspect drive belts and renew if frayed, cracked, burnt or otherwise damaged. Inspect pulleys and renew if damaged or worn excessively.

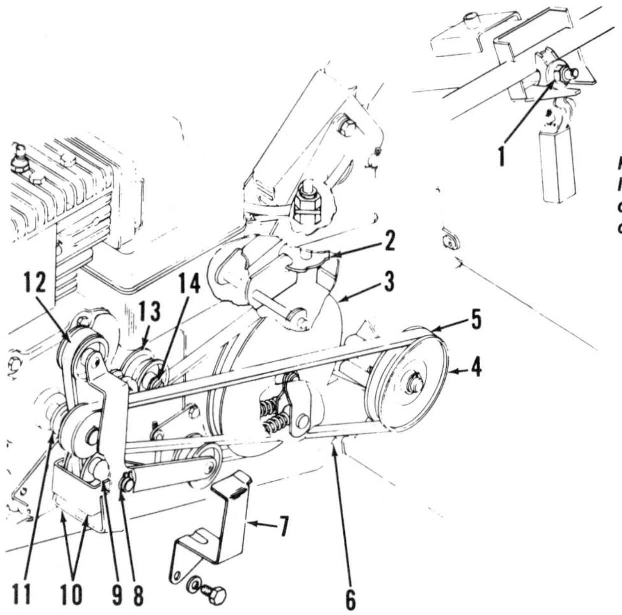

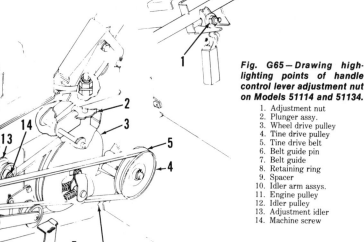

Fig. G65 — Drawing highlighting points of handle control lever adjustment nut on Models 51114 and 51134.

1. Adjustment nut
2. Plunger assy.
3. Wheel drive pulley
4. Tine drive pulley
5. Tine drive belt
6. Belt guide pin
7. Belt guide
8. Retaining ring
9. Spacer
10. Idler arm assys.
11. Engine pulley
12. Idler pulley
13. Adjustment idler
14. Machine screw

ADJUSTMENT

CLUTCH CONTROL LEVER

Models 51114, 51134 and 51135

Adjustment is provided to center clutch control lever in slot at handle, if necessary, due to wear. To adjust, locate

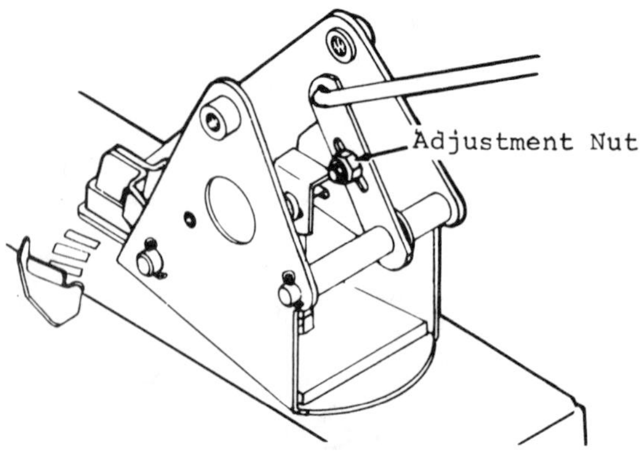

Fig. G66 — Adjustment nut is provided to center the clutch control lever in the slot on the handle.

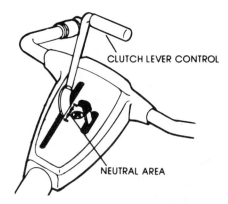

Fig. G67 — Clutch control lever shown in neutral position.

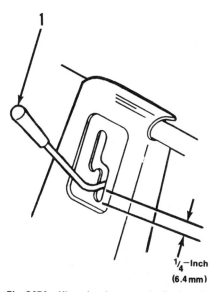

Fig. G67A — View showing correct adjustment of clutch lever (1) in forward position on Models 51159, 51175 and 51175A.

DRIVE BELTS

Models 51114, 51134, 51159, 51175, 51175A, and 51176A

TINE DRIVE BELT. With clutch control lever in forward drive position, distance between inside of belt (A – Fig. G69) should be ⅞-inch (22.2 mm) on Model 51114 and ¾-inch (19 mm) on Models 51134, 51159, 51175, 51175A and 51176A. Adjustment is accomplished by loosening bolts securing tine chain case (11 – Fig. G71) to frame slots (9). Rotate case forward to loosen belt and back to tighten belt. Tighten clamp bolts securely after adjustment. Move

Fig. G69 — Drawing showing adjustment distance (A) on Models 51114, 51134, 51159, 51175, 51175A, and 51176A. Refer to text for specific model requirement on the tine drive belt adjustment.

handle bar straight to rear and in lowest position. Loosen adjustment nut shown in Fig. G66, center clutch lever in neutral area (Fig. G67), then retighten adjustment nut.

Models 51159, 51175 and 51175A

Refer to Fig. G67B and position stop collar (5) 2¾ inches (69.9 mm) from end of tine drive link (4). To check adjustment, refer to Fig. G67A. With clutch lever (1) in forward gear position and all slack taken up in linkage, specified clearance between lever and bottom of slot is ¼-inch (6.4 mm).

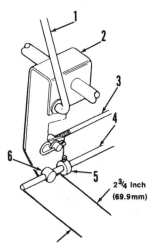

Fig. G67B — View showing control linkage adjustment on Models 51159, 51175 and 51175A.

1. Control link	4. Tine drive link
2. Pivot	5. Stop collar
3. Wheel drive link	6. Lower trunnion

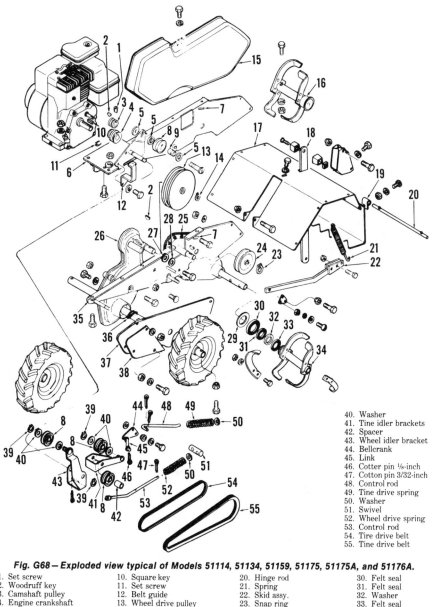

Fig. G68 — Exploded view typical of Models 51114, 51134, 51159, 51175, 51175A, and 51176A.

1. Set screw	10. Square key	20. Hinge rod	30. Felt seal
2. Woodruff key	11. Set screw	21. Spring	31. Felt seal
3. Camshaft pulley	12. Belt guide	22. Skid assy.	32. Washer
4. Engine crankshaft pulley	13. Wheel drive pulley	23. Snap ring	33. Felt seal
5. Washer	14. Snap ring	24. Tine drive pulley	34. Left tine assy.
6. Right frame assy.	15. Belt guard	25. Tine case assy.	35. Left frame assy.
7. Adjusting slot	16. Right tine assy.	26. Wheel case assy.	36. Oil seal
8. Idler pulley	17. Tine shield	27. "O" ring	37. Counterweight
9. Spacer	18. Depth control assy.	28. Cup	38. Counterweight
	19. Hinge	29. Washer	39. Snap ring

40. Washer
41. Tine idler brackets
42. Spacer
43. Wheel idler bracket
44. Bellcrank
45. Link
46. Cotter pin ⅛-inch
47. Cotton pin 3/32-inch
48. Control rod
49. Tine drive spring
50. Washer
51. Swivel
52. Wheel drive spring
53. Control rod
54. Tire drive belt
55. Tine drive belt

depth control lever to shallowest setting Fig. G61 and start engine. With clutch control lever in neutral position, tines should not rotate. If tines rotate, readjust to increase belt slack until tines do not drive in neutral.

WHEEL DRIVE BELT. Traction belt should have approximately ¼-inch (6.4 mm) clearance between upper idler and belt (Fig. G70), with control lever in neutral position. Adjustment is accomplished by removing screw (14–Fig. G65), then moving pulley (13) to another of four locations.

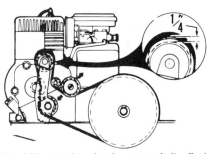

Fig. G70 — Drawing showing proper belt adjustment of wheel drive belt on Models 51114, 51134, 51175, 51175A and 51176A. Refer to text for adjustment procedures.

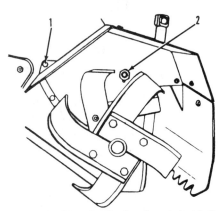

Fig. G70A — View showing location of pivot bolt (1) and clamp bolt (2) on Models 51179 and 51179A. Refer to text for tine drive belt adjustment.

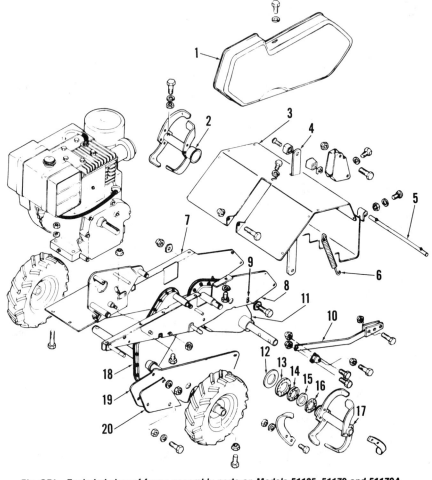

Fig. G71 — Exploded view of frame assembly parts on Models 51135, 51179 and 51179A.

1. Belt cover	6. Spring	11. Tine case assy.	16. Felt seal
2. Right tine assy.	7. Right frame assy.	12. Washer	17. Left tine assy.
3. Tine shield	8. Left frame assy.	13. Felt seal	18. Wheel case assy.
4. Depth control assy.	9. Adjusting slot	14. Felt seal	19. Counterweight
5. Hinge rod	10. Skid assy.	15. Washer	20. Counterweight

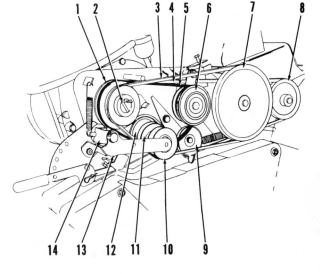

Fig. G70B — View showing tine drive belt pulley spring compressed to proper length when tine clutch is in forward position on Models 51179 and 51179A.

½-inch (12.7mm) to ¾-inch (19 mm)

Fig. G72 — View of belt and pulley system on Model 51135.

1. Engine pulley
2. Roll pin
3. Wheel drive belt
4. Tine drive belt
5. Reverse belt
6. Reverse drive pulley
7. Wheel drive pulley
8. Tine drive pulley
9. Tine idler pulley
10. Forward idler pulley
11. Reverse idler pulley
12. Flat idler
13. Forward idler arm
14. Reverse idler arm

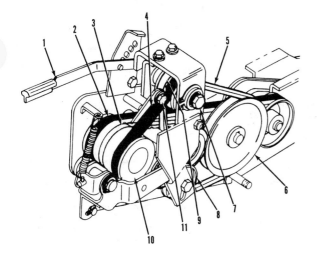

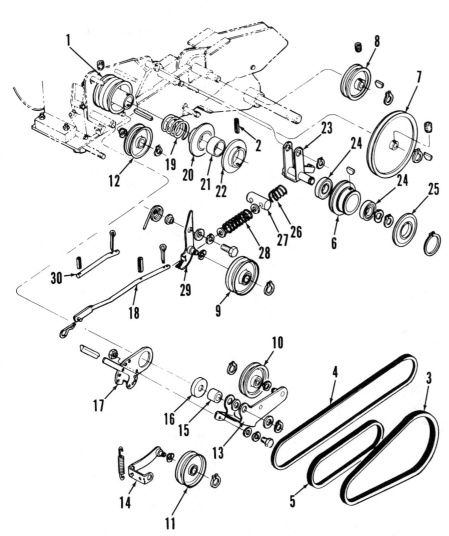

Fig. G72A – View of belt and pulley system used on Models 51179 and 51179A.

1. Ground speed lever
2. Tine drive belt
3. Reverse drive belt
4. Primary drive belt
5. Secondary drive belt
6. Wheel drive pulley
7. Pivot bracket cap screw
8. Secondary idler pulley
9. Middle pulley
10. Engine pulley
11. Shoulder bolt

Fig. G73 – Exploded view of drive assembly belt and pulley system used on Model 51135.

1. Engine pulley	9. Tine idler pulley	16. Spacer cup	23. Reverse arm assy.
2. Roll pin	10. Forward idler pulley	17. Adjuster	24. Bearing
3. Wheel drive belt	11. Reverse idler pulley	18. Clutch rod	25. Drive ring
4. Tine drive belt	12. Flat idler	19. Compression spring	26. Spring
5. Reverse belt	13. Forward idler arm	20. Inner pulley half	27. Swivel
6. Reverse drive pulley	14. Reverse idler arm	21. Bushing	28. Compression spring
7. Wheel drive pulley	15. Spacer	22. Outer pulley half	29. Idler arm assy.
8. Tine drive pulley			30. Reverse rod

Model 51135

TINE DRIVE BELT. With clutch lever in drive, idler arm compression spring (28 – Fig. G73) should be compressed ½ to ¾-inch (12.7-19 mm) from roll pin (C – Fig. G75).

Adjustment is accomplished by loosening bolts securing tine chain case (11 – Fig. G71) to frame assembly, then rotating entire chain case in slots (9). Rotate chain case up and forward to slacken belt and down and back to tighten. With clutch control lever in neutral (Fig. G67) drive belt should slip on drive pulleys. Check for proper adjustment by disconnecting plug wire and pulling recoil starter with control lever in neutral. If tines turn, then drive belt tension will need to be lowered.

WHEEL DRIVE BELT. With handle bar clutch control in neutral, drive belt should be loose enough to keep tines from rotating. With clutch control lever in forward drive and ground speed lever in fast or up position, drive belt should be tight enough to propel tiller.

The forward wheel drive belt (3 – Fig. G72) is adjusted by relocating adjustment end of traction and tine control rod (16 – Fig. G73) in one of the various holes in adjustment lever (17). Insert rod in hole closer to rear of lever (17) to increase belt tension.

Models 51179 and 51179A

TINE DRIVE BELT. Adjustment is made by pivoting entire chain case and tine assembly. Refer to Fig. 70A and loosen pivot bolt (1) and clamp bolt (2). Rotate case forward to loosen belt and back to tighten belt. Tighten pivot and clamp bolts securely after adjustment. With clutch control lever in neutral position, tines should not rotate. If tines rotate, readjust to increase belt slack until tines do not drive in neutral. When adjustment is correct, tine belt idler spring should be compressed ½-inch (12.7 mm) to ¾-inch (19 mm) as shown in Fig. 70B.

PRIMARY FORWARD DRIVE BELT. Belt is self-adjusted by spring-loaded idler pulley.

SECONDARY FORWARD DRIVE BELT. Place ground speed lever in lowest forward speed, then slide middle pulley (9 – Fig. G72A) towards outside as far as it will go. Move clutch control lever all the way forward. If belt slips after moving middle pulley, slide secondary idler pulley (8) down until belt is tight.

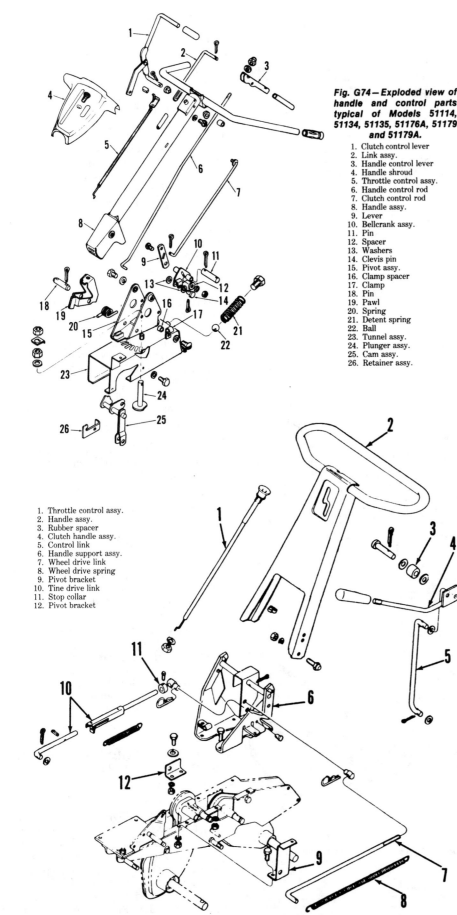

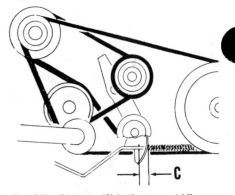

Fig. G74 — Exploded view of handle and control parts typical of Models 51114, 51134, 51135, 51176A, 51179 and 51179A.

1. Clutch control lever
2. Link assy.
3. Handle control lever
4. Handle shroud
5. Throttle control assy.
6. Handle control rod
7. Clutch control rod
8. Handle assy.
9. Lever
10. Bellcrank assy.
11. Pin
12. Spacer
13. Washers
14. Clevis pin
15. Pivot assy.
16. Clamp spacer
17. Clamp
18. Pin
19. Pawl
20. Spring
21. Detent spring
22. Ball
23. Tunnel assy.
24. Plunger assy.
25. Cam assy.
26. Retainer assy.

Fig. G75 — Distance (C) is the amount idler arm spring is compressed from roll pin on 51135 model only. Refer to text for adjustment procedures.

REVERSE DRIVE BELT. Belt is self-adjusted by spring-loaded idler pulley.

OVERHAUL

ENGINE

All Models

Engine model number is stamped on blower housing. Refer to appropriate Briggs and Stratton engine section for overhaul procedures.

CHAIN CASE

All Models

INSPECTION. Refer to Figs. G76, G77 and G78 for parts breakdown and identification for all models.

Inspect and renew all parts that are worn or damaged. Install new gasket and seals. Lubricate chains, sprockets and bearings with a light film of oil during reassembly. Keep all dirt and foreign matter out of chain case during reassembly. Refer to **LUBRICATION** section for lubrication requirements after reassembly and installation.

DRIVE BELTS

Models 51114, 51134, 51159, 51175, 51175A and 51176A

TINE DRIVE BELT. To remove belt, place clutch control lever in neutral position. Remove belt guard (15 — Fig. G68) and belt guide (7 — Fig. G65). Slide belt (5) off tine drive case pulley (4). Remove belt from engine pulley (11) and slip from between pulley and idler arm (10). Reverse removal procedure to install belt. Gilson recommends using Gilson drive belt 200554. Be sure belt is installed over guide pin (6). Check tine

1. Throttle control assy.
2. Handle assy.
3. Rubber spacer
4. Clutch handle assy.
5. Control link
6. Handle support assy.
7. Wheel drive link
8. Wheel drive spring
9. Pivot bracket
10. Tine drive link
11. Stop collar
12. Pivot bracket

Fig. G74A — Exploded view of handle and control parts typical of Models 51159, 51175 and 51175A.

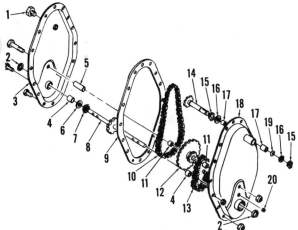

Fig. G76 – Exploded view of tine drive chain case parts on Models 51134, 51135, 51159, 51175, 51175A, 51176A, 51179 and 51179A.

1. Fill plug
2. Seals
3. Right chain case
4. Needle bearings
5. Idler sleeve
6. Shim
7. Spacer cup
8. Tine shaft assy.
9. Gasket
10. Upper chain
11. Bearing
12. Sprocket assy.
13. Lower chain
14. Input shaft assy.
15. Snap ring
16. Washer
17. Bearing
18. Left chain case
19. Seal
20. Oil level plug

drive belt adjustment as previously outlined.

WHEEL DRIVE BELT. Remove tine drive belt as previously outlined. Remove snap ring (14 – Fig. G68) securing wheel drive pulley (13) to case shaft, then remove pulley taking care not to lose Woodruff key (2). Remove cotter pin (46) from link (45). Slide idler arm assemblies (10 – Fig. G65) out until spacer (9) can be slid out from between idler arms. Remove belt (12). To reinstall, reverse removal procedure. Gilson recommends using Gilson belt 200555. Be sure belt is installed with flat side against engine drive pulley. Check for proper belt adjustment as previously outlined.

Model 51135

FORWARD WHEEL DRIVE BELT. Place clutch control lever in neutral position as shown in Fig. G67. Remove belt guard and slide belt off engine pulley (1 – Fig. G72), then remove belt from wheel drive pulley (7). Belt may now be removed from tiller after slipping between forward pulley (7) and reverse pulley (6). Reverse removal procedure to install belt. Gilson recommends using Gilson drive belt 208526. Be sure belt is installed under upper belt guide pin and on top of tractor arm guide pin. Check drive belt adjustment as previously outlined.

REVERSE WHEEL DRIVE BELT. Remove forward wheel drive belt as outlined in previous paragraph. Move clutch control lever to forward position. Raise reverse idler arm (14 – Fig. G73) and remove belt (5 – Fig. G72) from reverse idler pulley (11). Belt may be removed from between wheel drive pulley and rubber reverse drive wheel. Reverse removal procedure to install belt. Gilson recommends using Gilson belt 208525. Be sure belt is under upper

belt guide pin. Reinstall forward belt. Check drive belt adjustment as previously outlined.

TINE DRIVE BELT. Remove forward drive belt and reverse drive belt as outlined in previous paragraphs. Move clutch control lever to neutral position as shown in Fig. G67. Slide belt (4 – Fig. G72) off tine drive pulley (8). Remove snap ring from tine driver idler pulley shaft, then slide tine drive idler pulley (9) so belt can be removed. Remove snap ring from idler pivot pin. Slide idler arm outward so belt can be removed. Unhook clutch rod (18 – Fig. G73) from adjustment lever after removing cotter pin securing them together. Remove retaining

ring from idler arm shaft, then slide both reverse idler arm (14 – Fig. G72) and traction idler arm outward until belt can be removed from engine pulley. Remove belt.

To reinstall belt, reverse removal procedure. Gilson recommends using Gilson belt 208527. Be sure belt is on top of flat idler (12 – Fig. G72), under upper guide pin and above belt guide pin at tine drive pulley. Reinstall reverse wheel drive belt and forward wheel drive belt. Check drive belt adjustments as previously outlined.

Models 51179 and 51179A

PRIMARY FORWARD DRIVE BELT. Place clutch lever in neutral position. Remove belt guard and unscrew cap screw (7 – Fig. G72A) on left side of pivot bracket approximately ¾-inch (19 mm). Remove bolt (11) from inside of pivot bracket and remove screws from top of pivot bracket. Place ground speed lever (1) in low speed position, then remove pulleys from inside of pivot bracket. Remove outside shoulder bolt, outside section of bracket and speed lever as an assembly. Move clutch control lever to forward position and slip secondary drive belt (5) off secondary idler pulley (8). Slide primary drive belt (4) off engine pulley (10) and forward idler pulley, then slide belt through space between forward idler and left

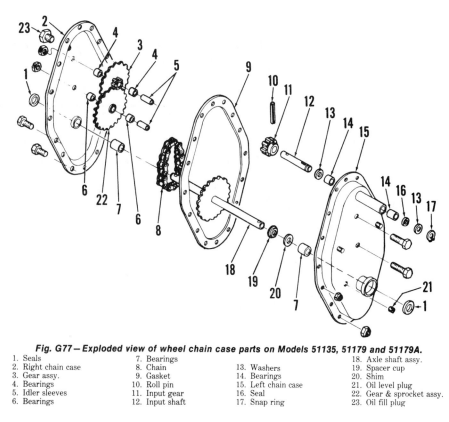

Fig. G77 – Exploded view of wheel chain case parts on Models 51135, 51179 and 51179A.

1. Seals	7. Bearings	13. Washers	18. Axle shaft assy.
2. Right chain case	8. Chain	14. Bearings	19. Spacer cup
3. Gear assy.	9. Gasket	15. Left chain case	20. Shim
4. Bearings	10. Roll pin	16. Seal	21. Oil level plug
5. Idler sleeves	11. Input gear	17. Snap ring	22. Gear & sprocket assy.
6. Bearings	12. Input shaft		23. Oil fill plug

frame assembly. Remove belt by sliding between secondary idler pulley and rubber reverse drive wheel.

Reverse removal procedure to install belt. Gilson recommends using Gilson drive belt 213926. When reassembling, be sure ground speed lever is ahead of stop tab and in lowest position. Belt is self-adjusted by spring-loaded idler pulley.

SECONDARY FORWARD DRIVE BELT.

Remove primary forward drive belt (4–Fig. G72A) as outlined i previous section. Slide secondary belt (8 off wheel drive pulley (6) and secondary idler pulley (8). Reinstall by reversing removal procedure. Gilson recommends using Gilson drive belt 208525. Check adjustment as previously outlined.

REVERSE DRIVE BELT. Remove primary forward drive belt and secondary forward drive belt as previously outlined. Unhook spring from idler arm assembly and remove cotter pin holding trunnion to idler arm assembly. Remove retaining ring from idler arm pivot and move clutch lever to neutral position. Lift up reverse idler and slide off belt (3–Fig. G72A). Slide idler arm assembly off pivot pin and slide belt off engine pulley (10). Remove belt by rolling between rubber drive wheel and drive wheel pulley. Reinstall by reversing removal procedure. Gilson recommends using Gilson belt 208525. Belt is self-adjusted by spring-loaded idler pulley.

TINE DRIVE BELT. Remove forward drive belts and reverse drive belt as outlined in previous paragraphs. Move clutch control lever to neutral position. Remove retaining ring from tine drive idler pulley shaft and slide belt (2–Fig. G72A) off tine drive pulley. Remove retaining ring from reverse drive wheel. Remove pulley hanger pivot pin. Slide hanger outward until belt can be removed and remove belt. Reinstall by reversing removal procedure. Gilson recommends using Gilson belt 208527. Check adjustment as previously outlined.

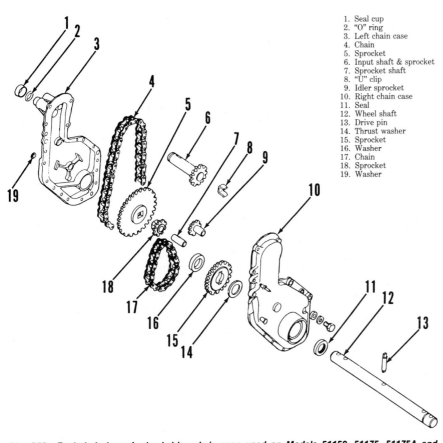

1. Seal cup
2. "O" ring
3. Left chain case
4. Chain
5. Sprocket
6. Input shaft & sprocket
7. Sprocket shaft
8. "U" clip
9. Idler sprocket
10. Right chain case
11. Seal
12. Wheel shaft
13. Drive pin
14. Thrust washer
15. Sprocket
16. Washer
17. Chain
18. Sprocket
19. Washer

Fig. G78—Exploded view of wheel drive chain case used on Models 51159, 51175, 51175A and 51176A.

GILSON

Model	Engine Make	Engine Series	Engine Horsepower	No. of Forward Speeds	Power Reverse?	Tilling Width (In.)	Drive Type
51104	B&S	60000	2	1	No	7-22	Chain
51171	B&S	80000	3	1	No	7-22	Chain
51171A	B&S	8000	3	1	No	7-22	Chain
51181	B&S	130000	5	1	No	7-22	Chain
51116	B&S	130000	5	1	No	12-26	Chain
51158	B&S	130000	5	1	No	12-26	Chain
51142	B&S	130000	5	1	No	12-26	Chain
51143	B&S	130000	5	1	Yes	12-26	Chain
51172	B&S	130000	5	1	No	12-26	Chain
51173	B&S	130000	5	1	Yes	12-26	Chain

LUBRICATION

ENGINE

All Models

Refer to Briggs and Stratton engine section for engine lubrication requirements. Recommended fuel is regular or low lead gasoline.

WHEELS AND CONTROLS

All Models

Transport wheel bushings should be lubricated occasionally with SAE 30 oil. **DO NOT** oil idler rollers as this will attract dirt and cause premature bearing failure.

CHAIN DRIVE

Oil level in chain case should be checked at least every 25 hours or more frequently if there are signs of continuous leakage. Recommended oil for all models is SAE 140 EP.

Models 51104, 51171, 51171A and 51181

To check oil level wipe dirt from around oil level and fill screw, then remove screw. Raise tiller handle to vertical position as shown in Fig. G80. Oil should be level with bottom of oil fill screw hole with tiller in raised position.

Models 51116 and 51158

To check oil level, place tiller on level surface and place the wheel hanger (17 – Fig. G83) in center hole. Clean dirt from around slotted level plug (Fig. G81) and remove. Oil should be level with bottom of level plug hole. If oil level is low clean dirt from around fill plug and remove plug. Add oil slowly until it runs out level plug hole, then reinstall plugs.

Models 51142, 51143, 51172 and 51173

To check oil level place tiller on level surface. Clean dirt from around oil level plug (Fig. G82) and remove plug. Oil should be level with bottom of level plug hole. If oil level is low, clean dirt from around fill plug and remove. Add oil slowly until it runs out level plug hole, then reinstall plugs.

MAINTENANCE

Inspect nuts and bolts for looseness and retighten as necessary. Check condition of control linkage and idler arm assemblies. Renew if excessive play or binding prohibits easy, complete engagement of drive mechanism. Inspect drive belt(s) and renew if frayed, cracked, burnt or otherwise damaged. Inspect belt pulleys and renew if damaged or worn excessively.

BELT

ADJUSTMENT

Models 51116 and 51158

Adjustment is provided to compensate for belt wear. To adjust, loosen outside

Fig. G80 – Drawing showing proper position of tiller when checking chain case oil level on Models 51104, 51171, 51171A and 51181.

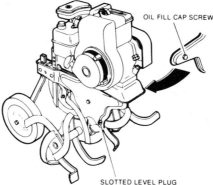

Fig. G81 – Oil level plug and oil fill plug location on Models 51116 and 51158.

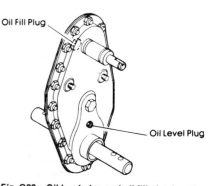

Fig. G82 – Oil level plug and oil fill plug location on Models 51142, 51143, 51172 and 51173. Oil level plug is found on the left side of tine drive case.

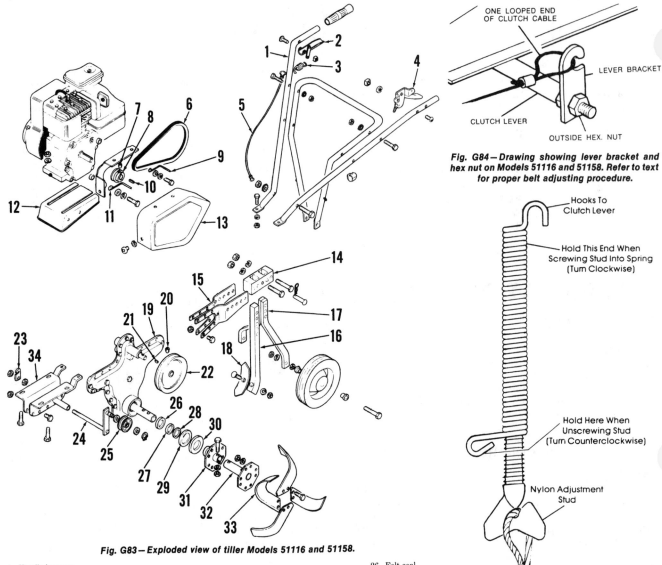

Fig. G84 — Drawing showing lever bracket and hex nut on Models 51116 and 51158. Refer to text for proper belt adjusting procedure.

ONE LOOPED END OF CLUTCH CABLE

LEVER BRACKET

CLUTCH LEVER

OUTSIDE HEX. NUT

Fig. G83 — Exploded view of tiller Models 51116 and 51158.

1. Handle bar assy.
2. Clutch handle
3. Clutch spring
4. Throttle control
5. Clutch cable
6. Drive belt
7. Set screw
8. Engine pulley
9. Belt guide
10. Square key
11. Belt guard bracket
12. Tine shield
13. Belt guard
14. Rear hitch casting
15. Rear hitch
16. Depth control bar
17. Wheel hangar
18. Spade
19. Chain case
20. Set screw
21. Woodruff key
22. Input pulley
23. Lever bracket
24. Clutch lever assy.
25. Idler pulley
26. Felt seal
27. Washer
28. Felt seal
29. Washer
30. Felt seal
31. Inner tine hub
32. Outer tine hub
33. Tine
34. Engine mount

Hooks To Clutch Lever

Hold This End When Screwing Stud Into Spring (Turn Clockwise)

Hold Here When Unscrewing Stud (Turn Counterclockwise)

Nylon Adjustment Stud

Clutch Cable

Fig. G85 — Adjuster spring and stud used for proper tensioning of clutch cable. It is important to temporarily remove cable from adjustment stud when turning stud.

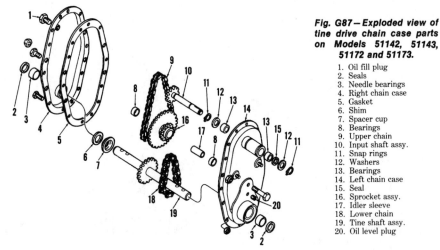

Fig. G87 — Exploded view of tine drive chain case parts on Models 51142, 51143, 51172 and 51173.

1. Oil fill plug
2. Seals
3. Needle bearings
4. Right chain case
5. Gasket
6. Shim
7. Spacer cup
8. Bearings
9. Upper chain
10. Input shaft assy.
11. Snap rings
12. Washers
13. Bearings
14. Left chain case
15. Seal
16. Sprocket assy.
17. Idler sleeve
18. Lower chain
19. Tine shaft assy.
20. Oil level plug

Jam Nut

Control Rod

Top Hex Nut

Swivel Stud

Bottom Hex Nut

Idler Arm (Right Side View)

Fig. G86 — Drawing showing parts used in adjusting clutch on Models 51143, 51172 and 51173. Refer to text for procedure.

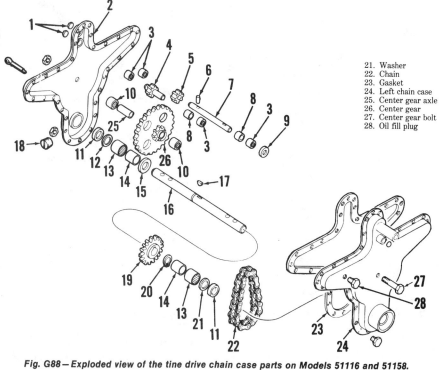

21. Washer
22. Chain
23. Gasket
24. Left chain case
25. Center gear axle
26. Center gear
27. Center gear bolt
28. Oil fill plug

Fig. G88 — Exploded view of the tine drive chain case parts on Models 51116 and 51158.

1. Shaft sleeve plugs
2. Right chain case
3. Bearings
4. Idler gear
5. Drive gear
6. Pin
7. Input shaft
8. Spacer
9. Seal
10. Bearings
11. Seals
12. Washer
13. Bearings
14. Inner races
15. Washer
16. Tine shaft
17. Woodruff key
18. Oil level plug
19. Sprocket assy.
20. Snap ring

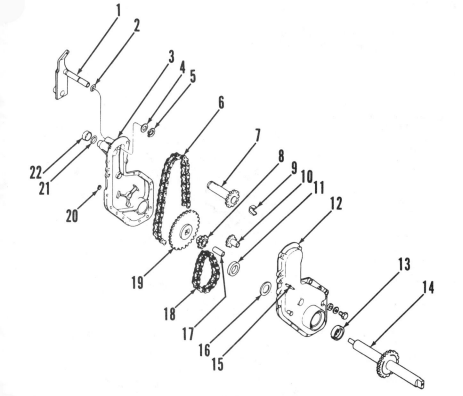

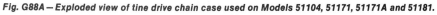

Fig. G88A — Exploded view of tine drive chain case used on Models 51104, 51171, 51171A and 51181.

1. Idler arm assy.
2. "O" ring
3. Left chain case
4. Washer
5. Snap ring
6. Chain
7. Input shaft & sprocket
8. Sprocket
9. "U" clip
10. Idler sprocket
11. Spacer
12. Right chain case
13. Seal
14. Tine shaft
15. Pop rivet
16. Thrust washer
17. Shaft
18. Chain
19. Sprocket
20. Washer
21. "O" ring
22. Cup

hex nut securing lever bracket to clutch lever (Fig. G84). Move idler arm up until idler pulley tightens belt. With idler arm held in this position move lever bracket forward until clutch cable is tight. Retighten outside hex nut. Check adjustment by disconnecting plug wire and pulling recoil starter. Belt should slip on pulleys. If belt does not slip on pulleys when clutch lever is released, follow preceding procedure to move idler further away from belt.

Model 51142

Adjustment is provided to compensate for belt wear. Adjustment is accomplished by overtightening control cable slightly, then loosening clutch control cable to just provide complete disengagement. To determine if adjustment is necessary, disconnect spark plug wire, push down on handle to raise tines off ground, then pull on recoil starter. If tines rotate, loosen clutch cable by turning nylon adjustment stud (Fig. G85) counterclockwise just enough so that tines do not rotate when recoil starter is pulled. Be certain cable still runs through "U" shaped bracket on lower left corner of handle. **NOTE:** Remove

Fig. G89 — View showing where belt guard is secured to tiller.

Fig. G90 — Drawing showing belt and pulley system typical of Models 51104, 51171, 51171A and 51181.

1. Spring
2. Drive belt
3. Input pulley
4. Idler pulley
5. Engine pulley

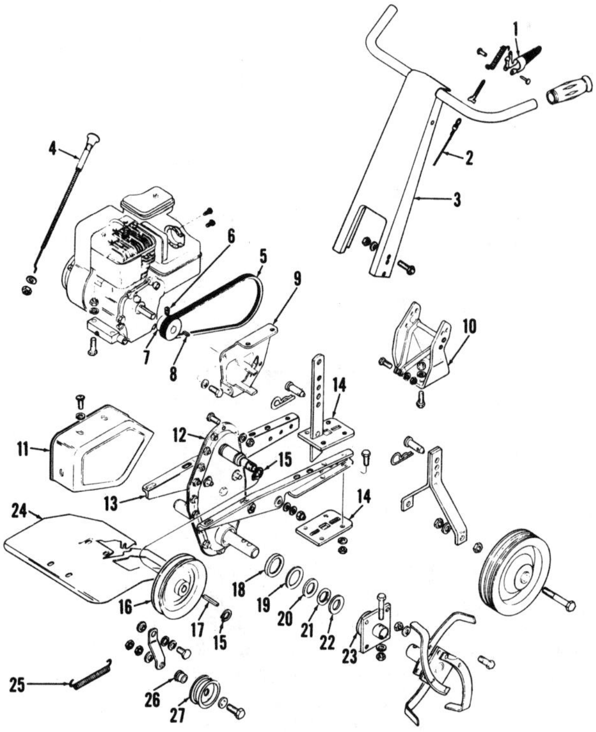

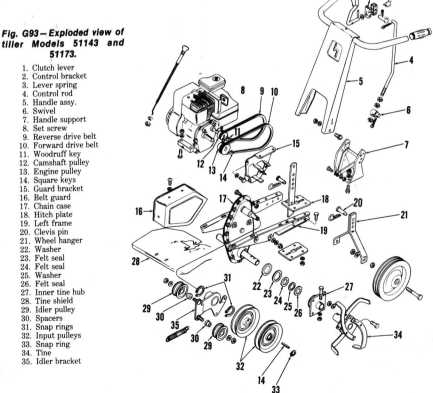

Fig. G91 — Exploded view of tiller Models 511142 and 51172.

1. Clutch lever
2. Clutch cable
3. Handle assy.
4. Throttle control
5. Drive belt
6. Set screw
7. Engine pulley
8. Square key
9. Guard bracket
10. Handle support
11. Belt guard
12. Chain case
13. Right frame
14. Hitch plate
15. Snap rings
16. Input pulley
17. Square key
18. Washer
19. Felt seal
20. Felt seal
21. Washer
22. Felt seal
23. Inner tine hub
24. Tine shield
25. Spring
26. Spacer
27. Idler pulley

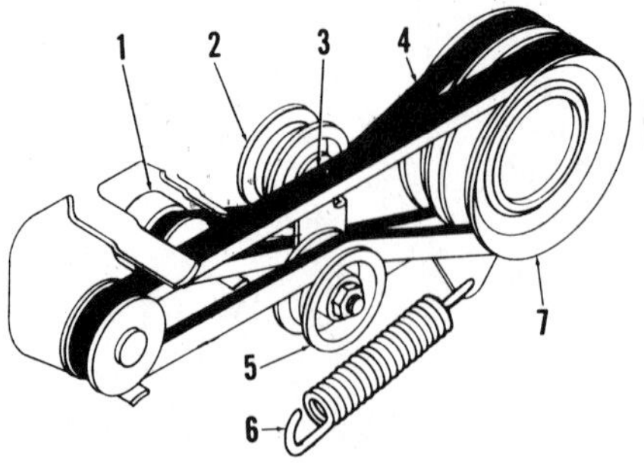

Fig. G94 — View of belt and pulley assembly on Models 51143 and 51173.

1. Camshaft pulley
2. Reverse idler pulley
3. Forward drive belt
4. Reverse drive belt
5. Forward idler pulley
6. Spring
7. Input pulley

Briggs and Stratton engine section for overhaul procedures.

CHAIN CASE

All Models

INSPECTION. Refer to Fig. G88A for an exploded view of the chain case used on Models 51116 and 51158. Refer to Fig. G87 for an exploded view of the chain case used on Models 51142, 51143, 51172 and 51173.

Inspect and renew all parts that are worn or damaged. Install new gasket

cable from nylon adjustment stud temporarily when turning adjustment stud.

If tines do not rotate with clutch lever engaged, tighten cable by turning nylon adjustment stud (Fig. G85) clockwise in increments of one full turn until tines just begin to rotate when engine is turned with recoil starter.

Models 51143, 51172 and 51173

To check adjustment, place clutch control lever in neutral position, disconnect spark plug wire, then pull recoil starter. Belt should slip on all pulleys. If tiller moves forward, loosen jam nut (Fig. G86) and top hex nut. Move bottom hex nut up slightly by turning, then retighten top hex nut and jam nut. If tiller moves backward, when clutch lever is in neutral position, then move bottom hex nut down slightly and retighten top hex nut and jam nut.

OVERHAUL

ENGINE

All Models

Engine model number is stamped on blower housing. Refer to appropriate

Fig. G93 — Exploded view of tiller Models 51143 and 51173.

1. Clutch lever
2. Control bracket
3. Lever spring
4. Control rod
5. Handle assy.
6. Swivel
7. Handle support
8. Set screw
9. Reverse drive belt
10. Forward drive belt
11. Woodruff key
12. Camshaft pulley
13. Engine pulley
14. Square keys
15. Guard bracket
16. Belt guard
17. Chain case
18. Hitch plate
19. Left frame
20. Clevis pin
21. Wheel hanger
22. Washer
23. Felt seal
24. Felt seal
25. Washer
26. Felt seal
27. Inner tine hub
28. Tine shield
29. Idler pulley
30. Spacers
31. Snap rings
32. Input pulleys
33. Snap ring
34. Tine
35. Idler bracket

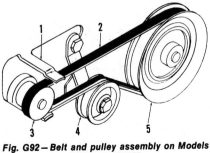

Fig. G92 — Belt and pulley assembly on Models 51142 and 51172.

1. Belt guide
2. Drive belt
3. Engine pulley
4. Idler pulley
5. Input pulley

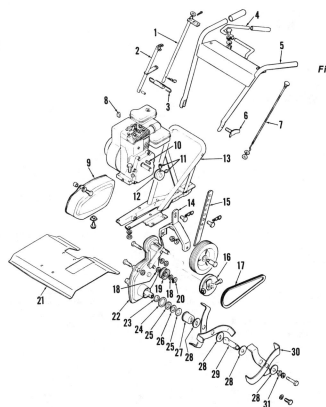

Fig. G95 – Exploded view of tiller Model 51104.

1. Upper control rod
2. Lower control rod
3. Spring
4. Handle control rod
5. Handle assy.
6. Wing screw
7. Throttle control
8. Grip
9. Belt guard
10. Square key
11. Set screws
12. Engine pulley
13. Frame assy.
14. Wheel hanger
15. Depth stick
16. Pulley assy.
17. Drive belt
18. Washer
19. Idler pulley
20. Snap ring
21. Tine shield
22. Chain case
23. Seal
24. Felt seal
25. Felt seal
26. Washer
27. Seal collar
28. Tine washers
29. Tine extension
30. Tine
31. Bushing

install belt, reverse removal procedure. Gilson recommends the use of Gilson drive belt 280301 for Model 51142 and drive belt 207159 for Model 51172. Be sure belt is installed between belt guides. Check drive belt adjustment as outlined in **ADJUSTMENT** section.

Models 51143 and 51173

FORWARD DRIVE BELT. Remove belt guard (16 – Fig. G93) and unhook spring (6 – Fig. G94) from engine mounting frame (19 – Fig. G93), then remove belt. To install, reverse removal procedure. Gilson recommends the use of Gilson drive belt 208301 for Model 51143 and drive belt 207159 for Model 51173. Be sure belt is installed between belt guides. Check drive belt adjustment as outlined in **ADJUSTMENT** section.

REVERSE DRIVE BELT. Remove forward drive belt as previously outlined, then remove reverse belt. Gilson recommends the use of Gilson drive belt 208626 for both models. Be sure belt is installed between belt guides and under reverse idler.

and seals. Lubricate chains, sprockets and bearings with a light film of oil during reassembly. Keep all dirt and foreign matter out of chain case during reassembly. Refer to **LUBRICATION** section for lubrication requirements after reassembly and installation.

DRIVE BELTS

Models 51104, 51116, 51171, 51171A, 51116 and 51158

To renew belt, remove two screws and belt guard (Fig. G89). Slip belt over edge of engine pulley (5 – Fig. G90) and turn pulley until belt slides off, then remove belt from input pulley (3). Install new belt by reversing removal procedure. Gilson recommends the use of Gilson drive belts as follows: Drive belt 35900 for Model 51104, drive belt 35901 for Models 51171 and 51171A, drive belt 237985 for Model 51181 and drive belt 9304 for Models 51116 and 51158. Check drive belt adjustment as outlined in **ADJUSTMENT** section.

Models 51142 and 51172

To renew belt, remove belt guard (11 – Fig. G91) and unhook clutch cable from nylon adjustment stud (Fig. G85). Remove belt (2 – Fig. 92) from around engine pulley (3) and input pulley (5). To

Fig. G96 – Exploded view of tiller typical of Models 51171, 51171A and 51181.

1. Clutch cable
2. Belt guard bracket
3. Handle support assy.
4. Belt guard
5. Engine spacer
6. Wheel hanger assy.
7. Frame
8. Depth stick
9. Washers
10. Pulley
11. Washers
12. Idler pulley
13. Belt
14. Tine shield
15. Chain case
16. Seal
17. Felt seal
18. Felt seal
19. Washer
20. Seal collar
21. Right tine
22. Left tine
23. Tine washer
24. Tine extension
25. Bushing

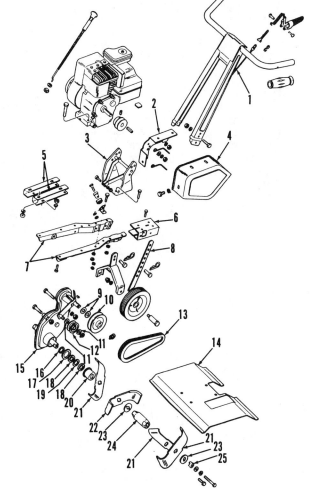

HABAN

HABAN MANUFACTURING CO.
2100 Northwestern Avenue
Racine, WI 53404

Model	Engine Make	Engine Series	Engine Horsepower	No. of Forward Speeds	Power Reverse?	Tilling Width (In.)	Drive Type
861-002	B&S	130000	5	2	Yes	12-26	Chain

LUBRICATION

ENGINE

Refer to Briggs & Stratton section for engine lubrication requirements.

CHAIN CASE

Oil level in chain case should be checked at least every 10 hours of operation. Oil level with tiller in level position should be even with oil level plug hole (6A – Fig. HB1) on lower right side of chain case. Recommended oil is SAE 140 EP. Chain case oil capacity is four ounces.

MAINTENANCE

Inspect belt pulleys and renew if damaged or worn excessively. Check condition of control levers and linkage. Renew or repair parts if excessive play or binding prohibits easy, complete engagement of drive mechanism. A few drops of oil should be placed periodically on all movable parts such as wheel bearings and idler roller arms.

ADJUSTMENT

CLUTCH

Clutch lever adjustment is accomplished by loosening locknut (N – Fig. HB2), then turning rod (R) clockwise to decrease belt tension after removing pin (P). Clutch rod should return to neutral when released.

If clutch lever does not automatically seek a neutral position the drive lever spring (S – Fig. HB3) may be stretched or otherwise incorrectly adjusted. Spring length (T) should be adjusted to approximately 2⅝ inches (66.7 mm) measured between spring loop ends. This length should not be less than 2½ inches (63.5 mm) nor more than 2¾ inches (69.8 mm). The spring may be adjusted by turning nuts (N) until proper length (T) is attained.

DRIVE BELTS

REVERSE DRIVE BELT. To check

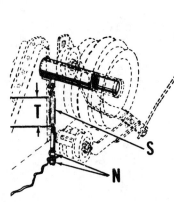

Fig. HB2 – Drawing of clutch control components. Refer to text and adjust as outlined.

Fig. HB3 – View of clutch lever spring (S). Refer to text and adjust as outlined.

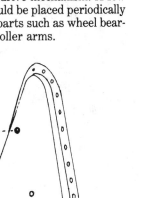

Fig. HB1 – View of transmission oil fill plug (6) and oil level plug (6A) location.

reverse belt tension, idle engine, then move drive clutch control to reverse and back to neutral. Make sure there is a positive release back to neutral. Repeat procedure with engine under full throttle. If tiller tines do not completely disengage with clutch control lever in neutral, adjust reverse belt tension.

To adjust reverse drive belt (10 – Fig. HB4), loosen nut in center of reverse idler pulley (6), then slide pulley up in slot to decrease tension or down to increase tension. Pulley should be moved in increments of ⅛-inch (3.2 mm). Retighten pulley nut then recheck belt tension.

FORWARD DRIVE BELTS. To check forward drive belt tension, idle engine then engage drive clutch control into forward and back to neutral making sure there is a positive release back to neutral. Repeat procedure with engine under full throttle. If tiller creeps forward with control lever in neutral, decrease forward belt tension.

To adjust forward drive belt (9 – Fig. HB4), loosen nut in center of idler pulleys (4 & 5), then slide pulleys up in slot to increase tension or down to decrease tension. Pulley should be moved in increments of ⅛-inch (3.2 mm). Retighten pulley nut then recheck belt tension.

FORWARD TILLER SPEED

Forward tiller speed ranges are low and high range. The forward drive belt (9 – Fig. HB4) must be relocated on pulleys to shift forward speed from low to high range or vice versa. To change belt from low to high pull up on engagement rod (1 – Fig. HB4) relieving tension on forward drive belt (9). Remove drive belt and install on appropriate pulleys. If adjustment is necessary refer to **FORWARD DRIVE BELT ADJUSTMENT** section.

OVERHAUL

ENGINE

Refer to Briggs & Stratton engine section for engine overhaul procedure. Engine model series is 130000.

CHAIN CASE

Overhaul of chain case assembly is evident after inspection of unit and referral to Fig. HB5.

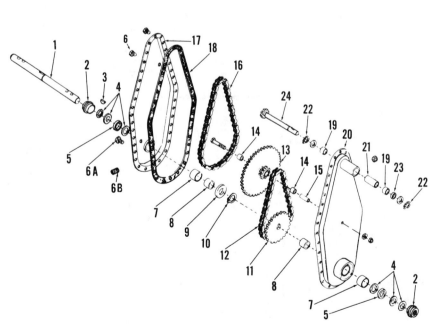

Fig. HB4 – View of belt and pulley system.

1. Clutch control rod
2. Triple groove pulley
3. Idler arm
4. High speed idler pulley
5. Low speed idler pulley
6. Reverse idler pulley
7. High speed engine pulley
8. Reverse engine pulley
9. Forward drive belt
10. Reverse drive belt
11. Low speed engine pulley

Fig. HB5 – Exploded view of chain case components.

1. Output shaft	6B. Slotted pipe plug	12. Lower chain	18. Gasket
2. Hub caps	7. Bearings	13. Idler sprocket assy.	19. Bearings
3. Woodruff key	8. Inner races	14. Bearings	20. Chain case, left
4. Washers	9. Spacer	15. Idler sleeve	21. Bearing spacer
5. Seals	10. Snap ring	16. Upper chain	22. Snap rings
6. Oil fill plug	11. Output sprocket	17. Chain case, right	23. Seal
6A. Oil level plug			24. Input shaft

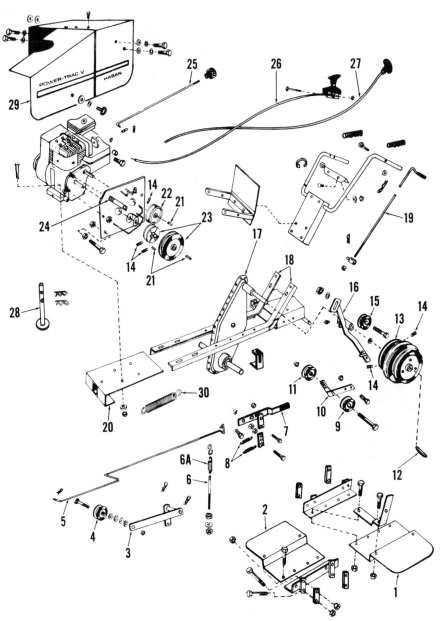

Fig. HB6 — Exploded view of Power Trac V.

1. Fender
2. Fender
3. PTO idler arm assy.
4. PTO idler pulley
5. PTO control rod
6. Spring adj. rod
6A. Drive lever spring
7. PTO control lever
8. PTO control lever springs
9. High speed idler pulley
10. Idler arm
11. Low speed idler pulley
12. Key
13. Triple groove pulley
14. Set screws
15. Reverse idler pulley
16. Idler arm assy.
17. Chain case assy.
18. Main frame assy.
19. Control rod
20. Engine mounting plate
21. Keys
22. Reverse engine pulley
23. Forward engine pulleys
24. Belt guide
25. Choke control rod
26. Throttle control cable
27. Starter cord
28. Pin
29. Shield

DRIVE BELTS

Use the following procedure to renew excessively worn or damaged drive belts. Refer to Fig. HB4. Remove hood, release tension on forward belt (9) by pulling up on engagement lever (1) and remove forward belt. Remove reverse idler pulley (6) then remove reverse belt (10). Install new belts by reversing removal procedure. Forward drive belt size is ½-inch x 53.5 inches long. Reverse drive belt size is ½-inch x 43.5 inches long. Check reverse and forward drive belt adjustment as previously outlined.

Fig. HB7 — Exploded view of tiller kit parts.

1. Inside tine mounting hub
2. Tine, right
3. Outside tine mounting hub
4. Tine, left
5. Drag bar
6. Drag bar ext. assy.
7. Chain
8. Pin tubes
9. Wheel mtg. strap
10. Wheel mtg. bracket
11. Tiller wheel pin

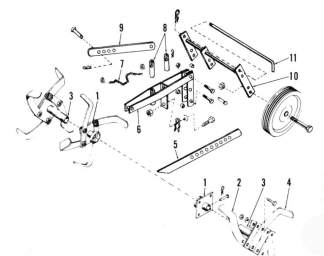

HOFFCO

HOFFCO, INC.
358 Northwest "F" Street
Richmond, IN 47374-9990

Model	Engine Make	Engine Series	Power Rating	No. of Forward Speeds	Power Reverse?	Tilling Width	Drive Type
Li'l Hoe	Tec.	TC200	1.5 hp (1.1 kW)	1	No	6-9 in. (15-23 cm)	Gear

LUBRICATION

ENGINE

The engine is lubricated by mixing oil with fuel. Recommended oil is a good quality oil designed for use in air-cooled two-stroke engines. Mix fuel and oil at a 24:1 ratio. Use a separate container when mixing fuel and oil. Refer to appropriate Tecumseh engine section.

GEARCASE

Tiller gearcase should be lubricated at beginning of each tilling season and every 25 hours of operation thereafter. Recommended lubricant is a good quality petroleum base automotive-type gun grease.

To lubricate gearcase, lay tiller on its side and remove right-hand tine assembly. If dust cap (4—Fig. H1) is plastic, remove cap by prying with two screwdrivers or suitable tools. If dust cap is metal, loosen set screw on cap and slide cap off tine shaft (7).

Remove plugs (5 and 6). Using a grease gun, pump grease into fill hole (2) until grease escapes from vent hole (3). Place a few drops of oil on tine shaft prior to reinstalling tines.

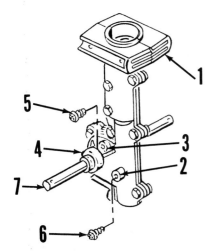

Fig. H1—Gearcase is lubricated by pumping grease into fill hole (2) until grease begins to escape from vent hole (3). Refer to text.

1. Gearcase
2. Fill hole
3. Vent hole
4. Dust cap
5. Vent plug
6. Fill plug
7. Tine shaft

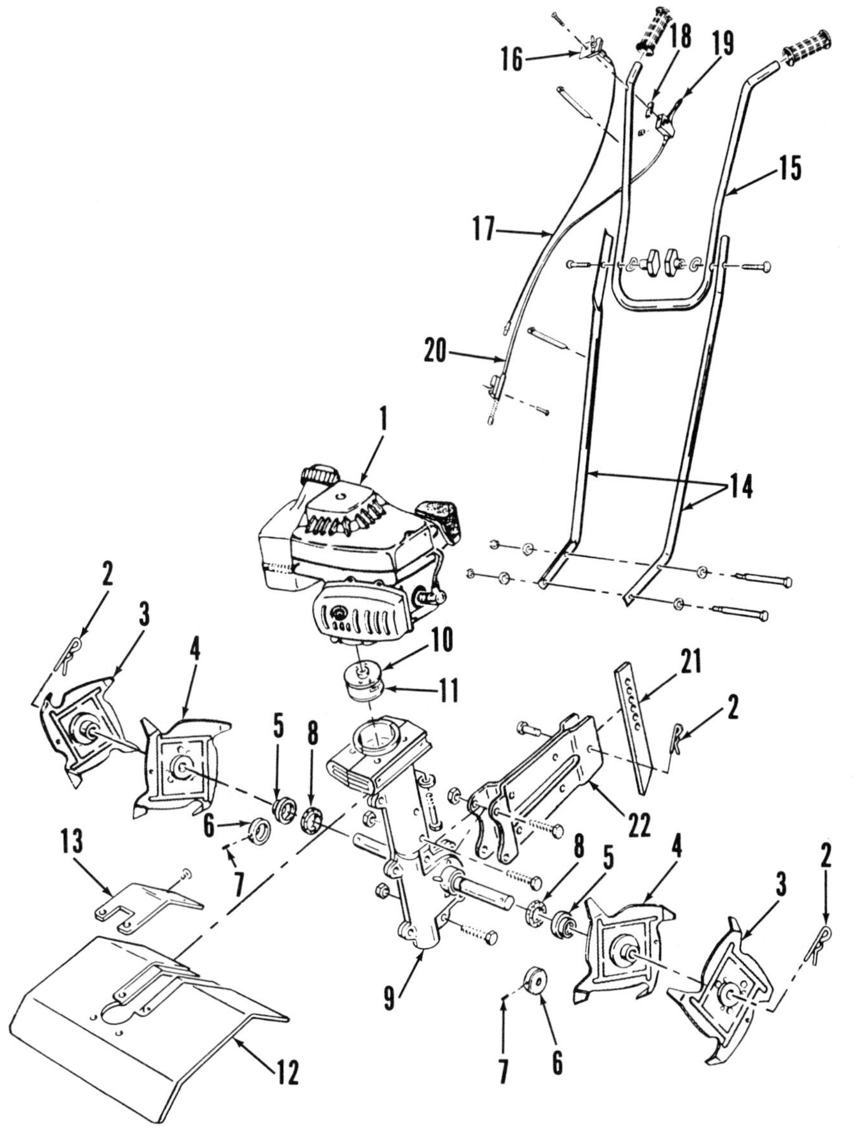

Fig. H2—Exploded view of tiller assembly. Tiller may be equipped with either plastic dust caps (5) or metal dust caps (6) with set screws (7).

1. Engine assy.
2. Hairpin clip
3. Outer tine assy.
4. Inner tine assy.
5. Dust cap (plastic)
6. Dust cap (metal)
7. Set screw
8. Felt seal
9. Gearcase assy.
10. Clutch
11. Clutch spring
12. Shield
13. Shield
14. Lower handlebar
15. Upper handlebar
16. Switch
17. Switch ground wire
18. Insulator
19. Throttle trigger
20. Throttle cable
21. Depth stake
22. Frame

MAINTENANCE

Inspect all fasteners for looseness and tighten as necessary. Renew all components that are excessively worn or show any other damage.

ADJUSTMENT

CLUTCH

Units are equipped with a centrifugal clutch. Adjust engine idle speed so tine movement is stopped when throttle trigger is released. Refer to Tecumseh TC200 engine section for carburetor adjustment procedure.

OVERHAUL

ENGINE

Refer to Tecumseh engine section for engine overhaul procedure. Engine model is TC200 and engine type is TC2026C.

GEARCASE

Overhaul of gearcase is evident after inspection of unit and referral to Fig. H3.

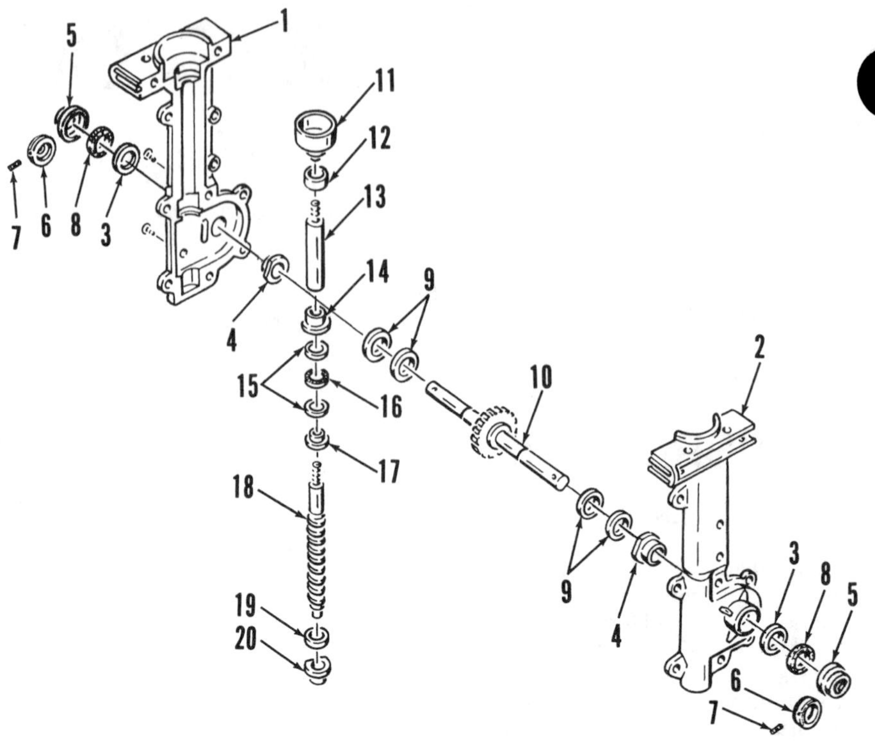

Fig. H3—Exploded view of gearcase assembly. Note that tiller may be equipped with either plastic dust caps (5) or metal dust caps (6) with set screws (7).

1. Right case half
2. Left case half
3. Seal
4. Bushing
5. Dust cap (plastic)
6. Dust cap (metal)
7. Set screw
8. Felt seal
9. Thrust washer
10. Tine shaft
11. Clutch assy.
12. Bearing
13. Shaft
14. Bushing
15. Thrust washer
16. Needle thrust bearing
17. Collar
18. Worm shaft
19. Thrust washer
20. Bushing

HOMELITE

HOMELITE DIVISION OF TEXTRON INC.
14401 Carowinds Blvd.
Charlotte, NC 28217

Model	Engine Make	Engine Series	Power Rating	No. of Forward Speeds	Power Reverse?	Tilling Width	Drive Type
MTC-12	Tec.	TC200	1.6 hp (1.2 kW)	1	No	7-10 in. (18-25 cm)	Gear
FT-5	B&S	130000	5 hp (3.7 kW)	1	No	20-26 in. (51-66 cm)	Chain
RT-5	B&S	130000	5 hp (3.7 kW)	1	No	11-24 in. (28-61 cm)	Chain

LUBRICATION

ENGINE

Model MTC-12

Engine is lubricated by mixing oil with the fuel. Recommended oil is Homelite two-stroke engine oil mixed at a 32:1 ratio. If Homelite two-stroke engine oil is not available, use a good quality SAE 30 or SAE 40 oil designed for use in air-cooled two-stroke engines mixed at a 24:1 ratio. Do not use multiviscosity oil. Recommended fuel is unleaded gasoline. Regular leaded gasoline is an acceptable substitute. Mix fuel and oil in a separate container.

Models FT-5 and RT-5

Refer to appropriate Briggs & Stratton engine section for engine lubrication specifications. Recommended oil is a good quality oil which meets or exceeds API specification SF, SE or SD with viscosity chosen according to ambient temperature. Recommended fuel is fresh, clean unleaded gasoline (leaded gasoline is an acceptable substitute), with a minimum octane rating of 77.

GEAR DRIVE

Model MTC-12

Gear drive assembly should be lubricated after every 25 hours of operation. Recommended lubricant is a good quality automotive-type multipurpose grease. To lubricate gearcase, remove right-hand tine assembly and lay tiller down on its left side. Remove vent screw and fill plug (Fig. HM1) and pump grease into gearcase until grease escapes from vent hole.

CHAIN CASE

Models FT-5 and RT-5

Recommended oil for chain case is SAE 140 gear lubricant. Remove plug marked "oil level" on right side of chain case. Remove oil fill plug on right side and fill with specified oil until lubricant level is even with bottom of oil level plug hole. Note that Max models are equipped with separate chain case assemblies for tine drive and wheel drive. Lubrication procedures for both chain case assemblies are the same.

MAINTENANCE

All Models

Inspect all fasteners for looseness and tighten as necessary. Check control levers, linkage and cables for freedom of movement and excessive play. Inspect drive belt(s) for excessive stretching, wear, cracks or other damage and renew as necessary. Inspect all pulleys and renew if excessively worn or damaged. Periodically lubricate pivot points and transport wheels with a suitable oil.

ADJUSTMENT

CLUTCH CONTROL

Model FT-5

To adjust clutch control, lengthen or shorten clutch cable at spring on clutch lever as necessary to allow proper clutch operation.

Model RT-5

Wheel drive and tine drive clutch controls are adjusted by loosening adjusting nuts (2 or 10—Fig. HM3) and moving cable housing as necessary to permit proper clutch operation. Springs (4 and 11) should stretch upon their respective clutch engagement.

Fill Hole

Vent

Fig. HM1—To lubricate gearcase on Model MTC-12, remove vent and fill plugs and pump grease into gearcase until grease escapes from vent hole.

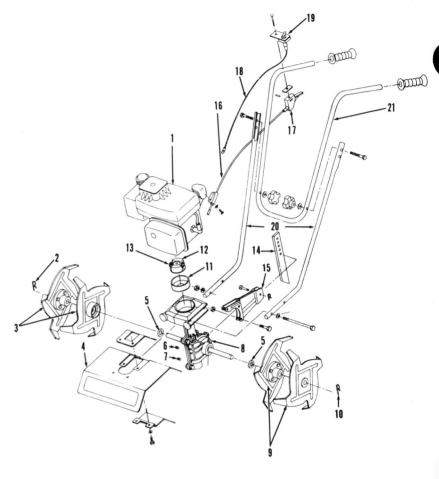

Fig. HM2—Exploded view of Model MTC-12 tiller assembly.

1. Engine assy.
2. Hairpin clip
3. Right-hand tines
4. Tine shield
5. Dust seal
6. Vent plug
7. Fill plug
8. Gearcase assy.
9. Left-hand tines
10. Hairpin clip
11. Clutch drum
12. Clutch assy.
13. Clutch spring
14. Depth stake
15. Bracket
16. Throttle cable
17. Throttle lever
18. On/off switch lead
19. On/off switch
20. Lower handlebar assy.
21. Upper handlebar assy.

OVERHAUL

ENGINE

All Models

Engine model and type number is stamped in blower housing adjacent to spark plug on Tecumseh engines, and model number is stamped in blower housing on Briggs & Stratton engines. Refer to appropriate Briggs & Stratton or Tecumseh engine section for overhaul procedures.

Fig. HM3—View of drive belt arrangement and related components used on RT-5 models.

1. Tine drive idler pulley
2. Adjusting nuts
3. Tine drive cable
4. Spring
5. Tine drive pulley
6. Tine drive belt
7. Wheel drive pulley
8. Wheel drive idler pulley
9. Primary wheel drive belt
10. Adjusting nuts
11. Spring
12. Return spring
13. Return spring
14. Wheel drive cable
15. Secondary wheel drive belt

CHAIN CASE

Models FT-5 and RT-5

TINE SHAFT OIL SEAL RENEWAL. Remove tines from tine shaft. Use a seal puller or other suitable tool to remove tine shaft seals (5—Fig. HM4). Inspect tine shaft for burrs or scratches that may damage seal during reinstallation. Clean tine shaft with emery cloth. Install seals (5) with lip facing inward. Drive seals into case until outer surface of seal is flush with case.

INSPECTION. Refer to Fig. HM4 for exploded view and component identification. Inspect and renew all components that are worn or damaged. Install new gaskets and seals. Lubricate gears, chains and bearings with a light film of oil during reassembly. Keep all dirt and foreign matter out of chain case during reassembly. Refer to LUBRICATION section for lubrication requirements after reassembly.

GEAR DRIVE

Model MTC-12

Refer to Fig. HM5 for exploded view of gear drive assembly used on Model MTC-12. Disassembly is evident after referral to exploded view and inspection of unit. Refer to LUBRICATION section for lubrication requirements.

DRIVE BELTS

Model FT-5

Remove belt guard and slip belt off pulleys. Manufacturer's part number for belt is 01212-01. Adjust clutch control as outlined in ADJUSTMENT section.

Model RT-5

Drive belt renewal is evident after referral to Fig. HM3 and inspection of unit. Manufacturer's part numbers for belts are: Tine drive belt (6) 01213-41, primary wheel drive belt (9) 01213-14 and secondary wheel drive belt (15) 01213-15.

1. Right-hand case half
2. Left-hand case half
3. Bushing (short)
4. Seal
5. Seal
6. Bearing
7. Spacer
8. Primary chain
9. Tine shaft & sprocket assy.
10. Needle bearings
11. Intermediate sprocket
12. Input shaft & sprocket assy.
13. Bearing race
14. Retainer
15. Thrust washer
16. Secondary chain
17. Gasket
18. Seal washer
19. Oil level screw
20. Oil fill plug
21. Bushing (long)
22. Cap

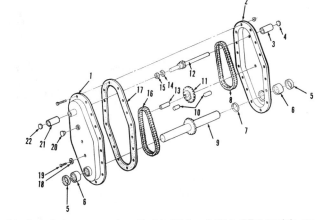

Fig. HM4—Exploded view of typical chain case used on Models FT-5 and RT-5. RT-5 models are equipped with a wheel drive chain case and a separate tine drive chain case. Both assemblies are the same.

1. Right case half
2. Left case half
3. Seal
4. Felt seal
5. Dust cap
6. Set screw
7. Clutch drum
8. Bearing
9. Shaft
10. Bushing
11. Thrust washers
12. Bushing
13. Thrust washers
14. Needle thrust bearing
15. Washer
16. Worm shaft
17. Thrust washer
18. Bushing

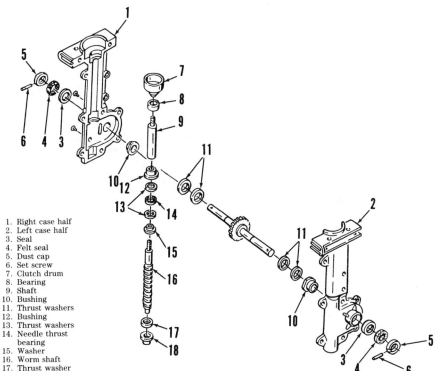

Fig. HM5—Exploded view of gear drive assembly used on Model MTC-12.

HONDA

AMERICAN HONDA MOTOR COMPANY INC.
100 West Alondra Blvd.
Gardena, CA 90247

Model	Engine Make	Engine Series	Power Rating	No. of Forward Speeds	Power Reverse?	Tilling Width	Drive Type
F210	Honda	GV100	1.79 kW (2.4 hp)	1	No	56 cm (22 in.)	Gear
F401AD	Honda	GX110	2.6 kW (3.5 hp)	1	No	61 cm (24 in.)	Chain
F401A2	Honda	GX110	2.6 kW (3.5 hp)	2	Yes	91.4 cm (36 in.)	Chain
F501A1	Honda	GX140	3.7 kW (5 hp)	1	No	61 cm (24 in.)	Chain
F501A2	Honda	GX140	3.7 kW (5 hp)	2	Yes	91.4 cm (36 in.)	Chain

LUBRICATION

ENGINE

All Models

Refer to the appropriate Honda engine section for engine lubrication requirements. Recommended fuel is unleaded gasoline.

TRANSMISSION

All Models

Check oil level in transmission before each use of tiller. Tiller must be on a level surface when checking oil level. To check transmission oil level on F210 models, remove level plug (1—Fig. HD1). Oil level should be even with bottom of level plug hole. To add oil, remove plug (2) and add oil until oil reaches bottom of level plug (1) hole. Recommended oil is SAE 10W-40 engine oil. To check transmission oil level on F401 and F501 models, place tiller on a level surface and remove fill plug (Fig. HD2). Oil should be even with bottom of fill plug hole. Recommended oil is SAE 10W-30 engine oil. Transmission oil capacity on F401 and F501 models is 0.95 liter (1.0 qt.).

ADJUSTMENT

DRIVE BELT

Models F401 and F501

To check drive belt adjustment, engage clutch and measure distance be-tween upper and lower surfaces of belt in location shown in Fig. HD3. Loosen engine mounting bolts (B) and slide engine as necessary to obtain distance of 60-65 mm (2.36-2.56 in.). Make sure engine pulley (1) is aligned with transmission pulley (3) after retightening engine mounting bolts (B). Adjust clutch control lever free play after adjusting belt tension. After adjusting drive belt, engage clutch and measure distance between belt and belt guides (4—Fig. HD4) in location shown. Clearance between belt and guides should be 3 mm (0.12 in.). Loosen screws (5) and move guides (4) to adjust. After adjustment, disengage clutch and start engine. Make sure

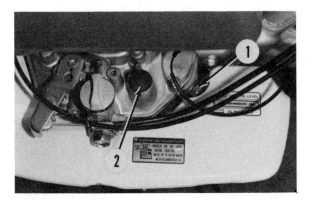

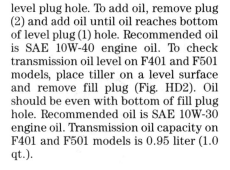

Fig. HD1—View of transmission oil level plug (1) and transmission fill plug (2) on Model F210. With tiller on level surface, oil level should be even with bottom of level plug (1) hole.

Fig. HD2—View of transmission oil fill plug on Models F401 and F501. With tiller on level surface, oil level should be even with bottom of fill plug hole.

belt guides are not too close to belt causing belt to drag on pulleys.

CLUTCH CONTROL LEVER

All Models

To adjust clutch control lever (3-Fig. HD5), loosen locknut (2) and turn adjusting nut (1) to obtain 2-6 mm (0.08-0.24 in.) free play (P) on Model F210 and zero free play (P) on all other models. On Models F401 and F501, make sure drive belt is properly adjusted before adjusting clutch control.

OVERHAUL

ENGINE

All Models

Engine model and serial numbers are located on the left-hand side of engine crankcase on F210 models and on the front of crankcase on F401 and F501 models. Refer to appropriate Honda engine section for overhaul procedures.

TRANSMISSION

All Models

TINE SHAFT OIL SEAL RENEWAL. Remove tines from tine shaft. Pry out seal with screwdriver or other suitable tool. Clean tine shaft with emery cloth and inspect tine shaft for nicks or scratches that would cut new seal during installation. Repair any nicks or scratches found with a fine file and emery cloth. On Model F210, lubricate seal lip and drive into transmission housing until outer surface of seal is flush with transmission housing. On F401 and F501 models, use special Honda tool 07945-7140000 to drive seal into transmission housing until seal is fully seated. Check transmission oil level after repair. Refer to LUBRICATION section.

OVERHAUL. Overhaul information was not available at the time of publication. Contact your nearest Honda power equipment dealer if transmission service is required.

Fig. HD3—With clutch engaged, distance between upper and lower drive belt surfaces should be as specified for Models F401 and F501. Refer to text for adjustment procedure.
　B. Engine mounting bolts
　1. Engine pulley
　2. Idler pulley
　3. Transmission pulley

Fig. HD4—Clearance between belt and belt guides (4) should be 3 mm (0.012 in.). Loosen screws (5) and move guides (4) to adjust.
　1. Engine pulley
　2. Idler pulley
　3. Transmission pulley
　4. Belt guides
　5. Adjustment screws

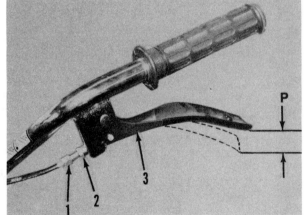

Fig. HD5—View of clutch lever (3) adjusting point for all models. Refer to text.
　1. Adjusting nut
　2. Locknut
　3. Clutch lever
　P. Free play

INTERNATIONAL

INTERNATIONAL HARVESTER COMPANY
401 North Michigan Avenue
Chicago, Illinois 60611

Model	Engine Make	Engine Series	Engine Horsepower	No. of Forward Speeds	Power Reverse?	Tilling Width (In.)	Drive Type
526	B&S	130000	5	1	Yes	26	Gear
526A	B&S	130000	5	1	Yes	11-26	Gear

LUBRICATION

ENGINE

All Models

Refer to appropriate Briggs and Stratton engine section for engine lubrication specifications. Recommended oil grade is SAE 30 or equivalent. Recommended fuel is either regular or low-lead gasoline having an octane rating of 90 or higher. The use of non-leaded gasolines reduces cylinder head deposits, but could shorten engine valve life if carburetor is adjusted too lean.

WHEELS AND CONTROLS

All Models

Lubricate transport wheels, pivot points and idler pulley hub at least every

15 hours of operation with SAE 30 oil. Caution should be taken in not getting oil on drive belts.

GEAR DRIVE

Oil level in gear case should be checked at least every 10 hours of operation. Gear case oil should be changed at beginning of each year. Recommended gear case oil is (EP) SAE 90 gear oil.

To check oil level in gear case place tiller on a level surface. Clean front of gear case housing. Remove level plug on front of case. Oil level should be at bottom of plug hole. If oil level is low on earlier 526 model, remove fill plug at top of gear case and add oil through fill hole until oil begins to run out level hole. Reinstall and tighten plugs. On later 526A model add oil through level hole until oil is flush with bottom of plug hole, then reinstall plug.

MAINTENANCE

Inspect all fasteners for looseness and retighten as needed. Check control levers, linkage and cables for freedom of movement and excessive play. Inspect

drive belts for excessive stretching, wear, cracks, or any other damage. Install new belts if needed. Inspect all belt pulleys and renew if damaged or excessively worn.

ADJUSTMENT

CLUTCH CONTROL AND DRIVE BELT

Model 526

FORWARD DRIVE BELT. If tines turn when clutch lever is in neutral position, belt tension will need to be decreased. If drive belt slips on pulleys with clutch lever engaged, belt tension will need to be increased. Adjust belt by loosening idler pulley (8–Fig. I1) bolt and nut and sliding pulley in idler bracket slot. Slide pulley towards belt to increase tension and away from belt to decrease tension.

REVERSE DRIVE BELT. Place clutch control lever in forward running position. Lift reverse belt out of reverse idler pulley (3–Fig. I1) groove and place it on lip of idler pulley. Loosen idler

Fig. I1 – View of drive belt(s) and pulley arrangement for Model 526.

1. Engine pulley
2. Reverse belt restrictor
3. Reverse idler pulley
4. Reverse belt
5. Reverse arm
6. Forward belt
7. Belt guide bracket
8. Forward idler pulley
9. Forward belt restrictor

Fig. I2 – View of forward clutch control components for Model 526A. Similar parts are used for reverse clutch control.

1. Cable pulley
2. Idler spring
3. Loop

Fig. I3 – View showing forward belt adjustment procedure for Model 526A. Reverse belt is similarly adjusted.

D. Direction to decrease tension
N. Nut
I. Direction to increase tension

pulley bolt and move pulley up until belt is tight, then retighten idler pulley bolt. Reinstall belt back in pulley groove.

Model 526A

FORWARD DRIVE BELT AND REVERSE DRIVE BELT. Fig. I2 shows location of clutch control components for forward drive belt. Reverse belt clutch components are similar to forward and are adjusted in same manner as forward. To adjust belt tension refer to Fig. I3. If belt slips on pulleys when clutch lever is engaged, then loosen nut (N) and swing cable pulley (1 – Fig. I2) out to increase tension. If tines do not disengage with lever released, then loosen nut and swing pulley in slightly to decrease tension.

OVERHAUL

ENGINE

All Models

Engine model no. is stamped on blower housing. Refer to appropriate Briggs and Stratton engine section for overhaul procedures.

GEAR CASE

Model 526 and 526A

INSPECTION. On Model 526 refer to Fig. I4 for gear case parts breakdown and identification. On Model 526A refer to Fig. I5 for gear case parts breakdown and identification. Inspect and renew all components that are worn or damaged. Install new gaskets and seals. Lubricate gears and bearings with a light film of oil during reassembly. Keep all dirt and foreign matter out of gear case during reassembly. Refer to **LUBRICATION** section for lubricating requirements after reassembly and installation.

DRIVE BELTS

Model 526

Remove drive belt(s) cover. Place

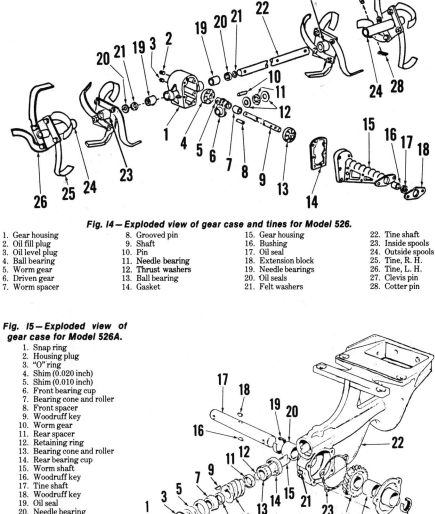

Fig. I4 — Exploded view of gear case and tines for Model 526.

1. Gear housing	8. Grooved pin	15. Gear housing	22. Tine shaft
2. Oil fill plug	9. Shaft	16. Bushing	23. Inside spools
3. Oil level plug	10. Pin	17. Oil seal	24. Outside spools
4. Ball bearing	11. Needle bearing	18. Extension block	25. Tine, R. H.
5. Worm gear	12. Thrust washers	19. Needle bearings	26. Tine, L. H.
6. Driven gear	13. Ball bearing	20. Oil seals	27. Clevis pin
7. Worm spacer	14. Gasket	21. Felt washers	28. Cotter pin

Fig. I5 — Exploded view of gear case for Model 526A.

1. Snap ring
2. Housing plug
3. "O" ring
4. Shim (0.020 inch)
5. Shim (0.010 inch)
6. Front bearing cup
7. Bearing cone and roller
8. Front spacer
9. Woodruff key
10. Worm gear
11. Rear spacer
12. Retaining ring
13. Bearing cone and roller
14. Rear bearing cup
15. Worm shaft
16. Woodruff key
17. Tine shaft
18. Woodruff key
19. Oil seal
20. Needle bearing
21. Oil level plug
22. Gear housing
23. Cover gasket
24. Worm wheel gear
25. Needle bearing
26. Side cover
27. Oil seal

clutch control lever in neutral position. Loosen nut retaining forward drive belt restrictor (9 – Fig. I1) sufficiently enough to withdraw belt from idler pulley groove, then remove belt. To remove reverse belt, loosen nut retaining reverse belt restrictor (2), then remove belt. Install new belts in reverse order of disassembly. Forward drive belt size is ½-inch x 40 inches long. Reverse drive belt size is ½-inch x 45 inches long. Refer to **ADJUSTMENT** section for adjusting procedure.

Model 526A

Remove drive belt(s) cover. Unhook clutch engagement cable loop (3 – Fig. I2) from idler pulley spring (2), then remove forward drive belt. Use similar procedure on reverse drive belt and idler. Install new belts in reverse order of disassembly. Forward drive belt size is ½-inch x 34 inches long. Reverse drive belt size is ⅜-inch x 35 inches long. Refer to **ADJUSTMENT** section for adjusting procedure.

KUBOTA

KUBOTA TRACTOR CORPORATION
550 West Artesia Boulevard
P.O. Box 7020
Compton, CA 90224

Model	Engine Make	Engine Series	Power Rating	No. of Forward Speeds	Power Revers?	Tilling Width	Drive Type
AT25	Kubota	GS90V-2TS	1.64 kW (2.2 hp)	1	No	58 cm (23 in.)	Gear
AT55	Kubota	GS200-2T	3.82 kW (5.2 hp)	4	Yes	66-92 cm (26-36 in.)	Chain

LUBRICATION

ENGINE

All Models

Refer to Kubota engine section. Recommended oil is a good quality engine oil which meets or exceeds API specification SC. Choose oil viscosity according to anticipated ambient temperatures. Recommended fuel is leaded or unleaded gasoline.

TRANSMISSION

All Models

Recommended oil for all models is a good quality SAE 80W-90 gear lubricant. Check transmission oil level every eight hours of operation. To check oil level, place tiller on a level surface. On Model AT25, remove dipstick (1—Fig. KB1). Oil level should be within lines (2 and 3). On Model AT55, remove level plug (1—Fig. KB2). If oil is not even with bottom of level plug hole, top off through fill plug (2). Do not mix oil of different viscosity ranges or of different manufacturer.

Change transmission oil yearly. On Model AT25, place tiller on a level surface and remove transmission bottom cover (3—Fig. KB3). On Model AT55, lean tiller back as far as possible and remove drain plug (1—Fig. KB4). Allow all oil to drain, reinstall cover (3—Fig. KB3) or plug (1—Fig. KB4) and refill transmission with specified lubricant. Transmission oil capacity is 0.95 liter (1.0 qt.) on Model AT25 and 2.4 liter (2.5 qts.) on Model AT55.

Fig. KB1—To check transmission oil level on Model AT25, place tiller on a level surface and remove dipstick (1). Oil level should be within lines (2 and 3).
1. Dipstick
2. Oil level (Max.)
3. Oil level (Min.)

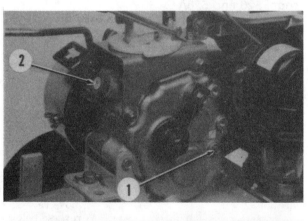

Fig. KB2—On Model AT55, transmission oil level should be even with bottom of level plug (1) hole. Add oil through fill plug (2) opening.

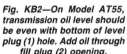

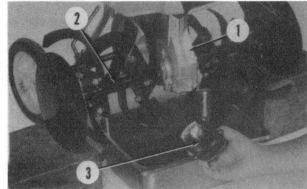

Fig. KB3—To drain transmission oil on Model AT25, place tiller on level surface and remove cover (3).
1. Transmission case
2. Tine shaft
3. Cover

Fig. KB4—To drain transmission oil on Model AT55, tilt tiller backward as far as possible and remove plug (1).

1. Plug
2. Tine shaft
3. Transmission case

Model AT55

With clutch engaged, drive belt deflection (D—Fig. KB8) should be 10-15 mm (0.4-0.6 in.) under a pressure of approximately 14.7 N (3.3 lbs.). Loosen locknut (6) and turn adjusting nut (5) to obtain specified deflection (D). If the

MAINTENANCE

Inspect all fasteners for looseness and tighten as necessary. Check control levers, linkage and cables for freedom of movement and excessive play.

On Model AT55, periodically lubricate control cables (Fig. KB5) and idler pulley shaft (4—Fig. KB6) with SAE 30 engine oil.

Inspect drive belt for excessive stretching, wear, cracks or any other damage. Renew belt as necessary. Inspect all belt pulleys and renew if damaged or excessively worn. Transport wheels should be lubricated occasionally with SAE 30 oil.

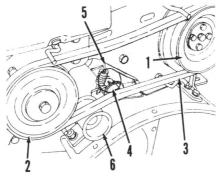

Fig. KB6—On Model AT55, periodically lubricate idler pulley shaft (4) at point shown with SAE 30 oil.

1. Transmission pulley	4. Shaft
2. Engine pulley	5. Spring
3. Drive belt	6. Idler pulley

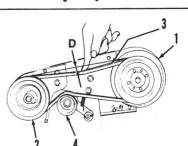

Fig. KB8—On Model AT55, loosen locknut (6) and turn adjusting nut (5) to obtain drive belt (3) deflection of 10-15 mm (0.4-0.6 in.). Engage clutch before measuring deflection (D).

1. Transmission pulley	5. Adjusting nut
2. Engine pulley	6. Locknut
3. Drive belt	7. Clutch cable
4. Idler pulley	8. Clutch lever

ADJUSTMENT

CLUTCH CONTROL

Model AT25

Free play at clutch lever (1—Fig. KB7) should be 0-3 mm (0-0.118 in.). Loosen nuts (3) and move clutch cable (2) to set specified lever free play.

Fig. KB7—Free play in clutch lever (1) should be 0-3 mm (0-0.118 in.) on Model AT25. Loosen nuts (3) and move cable (2) to adjust free play.

1. Clutch lever
2. Cable
3. Nuts

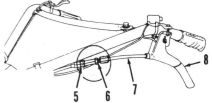

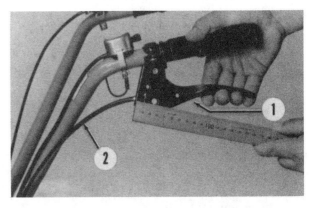

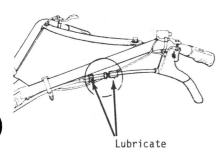

Lubricate

Fig. KB5—Lubricate control cables on Model AT55 at points shown with SAE 30 oil.

proper deflection can not be obtained by adjusting clutch cable, loosen four engine bolts and fuel tank setbolts and slide engine as necessary to obtain correct deflection.

DRIVE BELT RETAINERS

Model AT55

Drive belt retainers at engine pulley should be adjusted to length shown (View A—Fig. KB9). Engage clutch and check clearance of retainers (R—View B). Adjust retainers as necessary.

OVERHAUL

ENGINE

All Models

Engine serial number is located on engine shroud above air filter on Model AT25 and on crankcase below drive pulley on Model AT55. Refer to appropriate Kubota engine section for overhaul procedure.

TRANSMISSION

Model AT25

OIL SEAL RENEWAL. Tine shaft oil seals (16—Fig. KB10) can be renewed with transmission installed on tiller. Remove tines and pry off seal cover (17). Using a seal puller or other suitable tool, remove tine shaft seal (16). Clean rust or burrs from tine shaft (20) with emery cloth. Lubricate lip of new seal prior to installation. Install seal with lip facing inward.

R&R AND OVERHAUL. Drain oil from transmission. Refer to LUBRICATION section. Remove engine, separate handlebar assembly from transmission and remove tines.

Remove four screws (S—Fig. KB11), springs (23) and steel balls (24). Remove ring gear (6). Remove "E" rings (5), washers (4) and lift off planetary gears (3). Remove washers under planetary gears (3). Remove snap ring (8—Fig. KB10) and remove carrier (7), clutch balls (21), clutch spring (9) and clutch ball retainer (10). Refer to Fig. KB12 and remove screw (S) and clutch shaft (12). Pry seal covers (17—Fig. KB10) and seals (16) from case (1). Remove snap ring (22) and tap tine shaft (20) out of case. Pull pinion shaft (13) with bearing (14) from case to complete disassembly.

Check all components for excessive wear or damage and renew as necessary. Check bearings for roughness and

gears for broken teeth or other damage. Renew clutch spring (9) if free length is less than 29.5 mm (1.16 in.).

Reassembly is the reverse of disassembly procedure while noting the following: Renew all seals and gaskets. Lubricate internal components with SAE 80W-90 gear lube during reassembly. Install ring gear (6) with side marked "TMA 20" facing upward. Using a suitable dial indicator set up as shown in Fig. KB13, check bevel gear (18) backlash. Backlash should be within 0.1-0.4 mm (0.004-0.016 in.). Vary thickness of shim (23—Fig. KB10) to adjust backlash. Shims are available in thicknesses of 0.1 mm (0.004 in.) and 0.3 mm (0.012 in.). Refer to LUBRICATION section for lubrication requirements after reassembly.

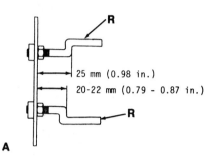

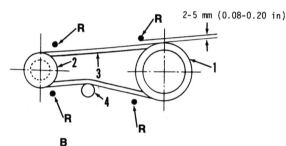

Fig. KB9—Adjust drive belt (3) retainers to dimensions shown. View "A" is side view of retainers at engine pulley (2).

1. Transmission pulley
2. Engine pulley
3. Drive belt
4. Idler pulley
R. Retainer

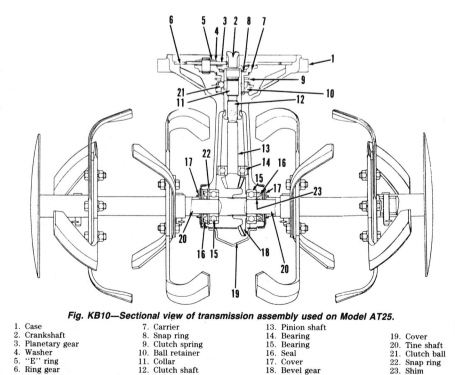

Fig. KB10—Sectional view of transmission assembly used on Model AT25.

1. Case	7. Carrier	13. Pinion shaft
2. Crankshaft	8. Snap ring	14. Bearing
3. Planetary gear	9. Clutch spring	15. Bearing
4. Washer	10. Ball retainer	16. Seal
5. "E" ring	11. Collar	17. Cover
6. Ring gear	12. Clutch shaft	18. Bevel gear

19. Cover	
20. Tine shaft	
21. Clutch ball	
22. Snap ring	
23. Shim	

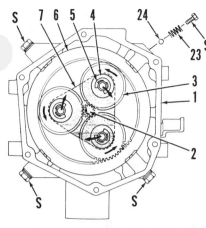

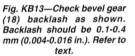

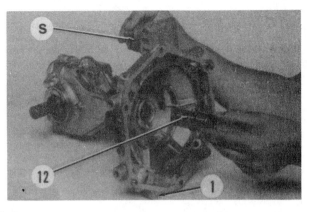

Fig. KB12—On Model AT25, take out screw (S) to remove clutch shaft (12) from case (1).

Fig. KB11—View of ring gear (6) and planetary (3) arrangement used on Model AT25. Refer to legend in Fig. KB10 for component identification except spring (23), ball (24) and screws (S).

Model AT55

TINE SHAFT OIL SEAL RENEWAL.
Tine shaft oil seals (12 and 35—Fig. KB14) can be renewed with transmission installed on tiller. Drain transmission oil, remove covers (11 and 36) and pry out seals (12 and 35) using a suitable tool. Clean shaft (3) with emery cloth and inspect shaft (3) for scratches or burrs. Lubricate sealing lip of seal and drive into case until bottomed with a suitable seal driver. Refer to LUBRICATION section for lubrication requirements.

Fig. KB13—Check bevel gear (18) backlash as shown. Backlash should be 0.1-0.4 mm (0.004-0.016 in.). Refer to text.

1. Right case half
2. Bearing
3. Tine shaft
4. Chain
5. Bearing
6. Bearing
7. Gear
8. Bearing
9. Gasket
10. Left case half
11. Cover
12. Seal
13. Shift link
14. Shift link
15. Seals
16. Screw
17. Washer
18. Spring
19. Steel ball
20. Seal
21. Bearing
22. Shaft
23. Washer
24. Needle bearing
25. Spacer
26. Gear
27. Gear
28. Needle bearing
29. Thrust washer
30. Spacer
31. Washer
32. Bearing
33. "O" ring
34. Seal
35. Seal
36. Cover
37. Cover
38. Shift fork
39. Bearing
40. Spacer
41. Gear
42. Gear & shaft
43. Bearing
44. Shaft
45. Cotter pin
46. Shift fork
47. Pin

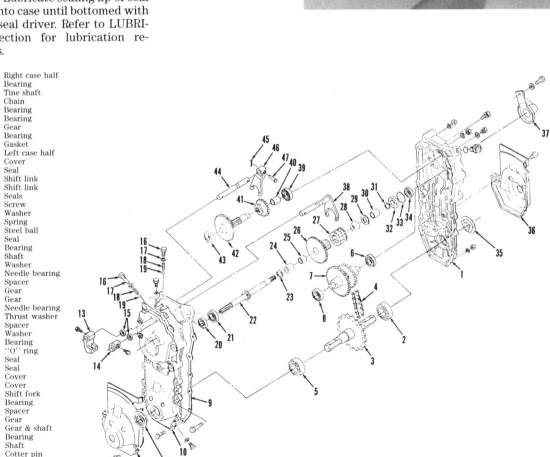

Fig. KB14—Exploded view of transmission assembly used on Model AT55.

R&R AND OVERHAUL. Remove engine from tiller. Drain oil from transmission. Remove clutch cable at transmission. Remove snap ring at top of handlebar mounting post and remove handlebar. Remove transmission drive pulley, drive belt idler pulley, engine mounting frame and tiller tines. Remove handlebar mounting post assembly.

Remove all attaching screws and split case halves (1 and 10—Fig. KB14). Lay transmission on left side so all internal components remain in left case half (10). Remove screws (16) and take out springs (18) and steel balls (19). Pull tine shaft (3) and gear (7) along with chain (4) and bearings (2, 5, 6 and 8) from left case half (10). Remove shaft (42) with gear (41), spacer (40) and bearings (39 and 43) attached. Pull shift fork assembly (44 and 46) from case half (10). Slide shift fork (38) from case along with entire shaft assembly (21 through 32).

Inspect all components for excessive wear or damage and renew as necessary. Check bearings for roughness and gears and shafts for broken teeth or other damage. Renew springs (18) if free length is less than 22 mm (0.866 in.). Place shift fork (38) into position in gear (27) and check fork-to-gear clearance with a feeler gage as shown in Fig. KB15. Clearance between fork (46) and gear (41) should be 0.2-0.4 mm (0.008-0.016 in.) or 0.1-0.3 mm (0.004-0.012 in.) between fork (38) and gear (27). Renew fork and gear as a unit if clearance exceeds 0.5 mm (0.020 in.) on either assembly. Running clearance of gear (26-Fig. KB14) and bearings (24 and 28) on shaft (22) should be 0.007-0.040 mm (0.0003-0.0015 in.). Renew gear (26), shaft (22) and bearings (24 and 28) if running clearance exceeds 0.1 mm (0.004 in.). Reassembly is the reverse of the disassembly procedure. Renew all seals and gaskets. Refer to LUBRICATION section for lubrication requirements after reassembly.

DRIVE BELT

Model AT55

Belt size is 37 inches x 5/8 inch. Manufacturer's part number is 53761-43170. Remove belt cover. Loosen bolts (B—Fig. KB16) and slide engine to allow belt to be removed. If necessary, loosen drive belt retainers to allow belt to be removed. After reinstalling belt, make sure engine pulley is aligned with transmission pulley. Adjust engine so engine pulley centerline is approximately 294 mm (11.6 in.) from transmission pulley centerline. Refer to CLUTCH CONTROL under ADJUSTMENT section for adjustment procedure. Reinstall belt cover.

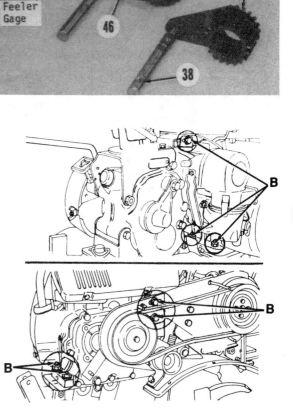

Fig. KB15—Measure shift fork-to-gear clearance as shown. Renew fork and gear as a unit if clearance is not within specified limits. Refer to text. Refer to legend in Fig. KB14 for component identification.

Fig. KB16—Loosen seven bolts (B) and slide engine to loosen or tighten drive belt tension on Model AT55.

KUBOTA

Model	Engine Make	Engine Series	Forward Rating	No. of Power Speeds	Tilling Reverse	Drive Width	Type
AT60	Kubota	GS230-2T	4.1 kW (5.5 hp)	2	Yes	50 cm (20 in.)	Chain
AT70S	Kubota	GS280-TE	5.2 kW (7 hp)	2	Yes	50 cm (20 in.)	Chain
AT70S-E	Kubota	GS280-TES	5.2 kW (7 hp)	2	Yes	50 cm (20 in.)	Chain

LUBRICATION

ENGINE

All Models

Refer to appropriate Kubota engine section for engine lubrication specifications. Recommended oil is a good quality SAE 30 oil which meets or exceeds API specification SC. SAE 20 oil may be used during cold weather operation. Recommended fuel is leaded or unleaded gasoline.

CONTROLS

All Models

Control cables are equipped with oil holes located at adjustment screws. Refer to ADJUSTMENT section. After every eight hours of operation, lubricate control cables and all other moving or sliding components with engine oil.

TRANSMISSION

All Models

Recommended oil is a good quality SAE 80W-90 gear lubricant which meets or exceeds API specification GL-3 or GL-4. Transmission oil level should be checked after every eight hours of operation. To check transmission oil level, place tiller on a level surface and remove level plug (1—Fig. KB20). Oil should be even with bottom of level plug (1) hole. Fill transmission at fill plug (1). Do not use oil of a different viscosity or manufacturer than oil currently in transmission.

Change transmission oil after each year of operation. Refer to Fig. KB21 and remove drain plug and allow all oil to drain. Refill transmission with 2.3 liters (2.5 qts.) of SAE 80W-90 gear lube which meets API specification GL-3 or GL-4. Refer to Fig. KB20.

TINE GEARCASE

All Models

Recommended oil is SAE 80W-90 gear lube meeting or exceeding API specification GL-3 or GL-4. Periodically check oil level in tine gearcase by removing level plug (4—Fig. KB22). Oil should be even with bottom of level plug hole. If not, add oil through fill plug (3) hole. Do not mix oil of different viscosity or of different manufacturer.

Change oil in tine gearcase after every year of operation. Remove drain plug (Fig. KB23) and allow all oil to drain. Reinstall drain plug and fill case with 1.2 liters (1.25 qts.) of SAE 80W-90 gear lube or until oil begins to run out level plug (4—Fig. KB22).

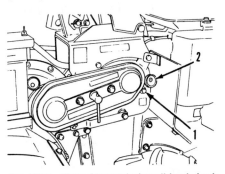

Fig. KB20—View of transmission oil level check plug (1) and fill plug (2) typical of all models. Oil level should be even with bottom of level plug (1) hole with tiller on level surface.

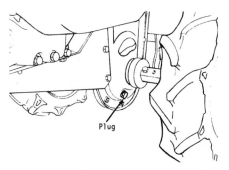

Fig. KB21—To drain transmission oil, remove plug shown.

AUXILIARY CHAIN CASE

All Models

Auxiliary chain case (7—Fig. KB22) should be removed and packed with a good quality multipurpose grease after every 50 hours of operation. Remove screw (6) and remove case assembly (7) from tiller. Remove nuts (8), split case and pack with 100-200 grams (3.53-7.05 oz.) of multipurpose grease.

MAINTENANCE

Inspect all fasteners for looseness and tighten as necessary. Check control

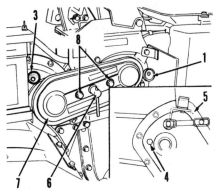

Fig. KB22—Oil level in tine gearcase (5) should be even with bottom of level plug (4) hole.

1. Transmission fill plug
3. Tine case fill plug
4. Level plug
5. Tine gearcase
6. Screw
7. Auxiliary chain case
8. Nuts

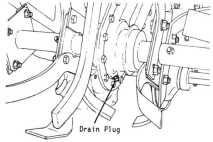

Fig. KB23—To drain tine gearcase oil, remove plug shown. Refer to text.

levers, linkage and cables for freedom of movement and excessive play. Inspect drive belts for excessive stretching, wear, cracks or any other damage. Renew belts if necessary. Inspect all belt pulleys and renew if damaged or excessively worn. Periodically check tire pressure and maintain at 1.2 kg/cm (17 psi). On Model AT70S-E, check electrical connections and wiring on a frequent basis. Repair or renew loose or corroded connecters or damaged wiring. Electrical system is protected by a fusible link located in wiring harness near starter motor. If fusible link is blown, locate and repair short circuit or other cause and renew fusible link with one of the same amperage rating. Refer to appropriate engine section for wiring diagram.

ADJUSTMENT

CLUTCH CONTROL AND DRIVE BELTS

All Models

To adjust clutch cable, loosen locknut (4—Fig. KB24) and turn adjusting nut (3). To check adjustment, engage clutch and check drive belt deflection at center of belt. If clutch is properly adjusted, deflection will be 1.0-1.5 cm (0.4-0.6 in.) at center of belt span. Make sure tiller drive wheels stop movement when clutch is disengaged. If the proper belt deflection cannot be obtained with clutch cable adjustment, it will be

necessary to adjust belt tension by moving engine assembly. Loosen clutch cable adjustment (Fig. KB24) until at least 5 mm (0.2 in.) of threaded portion of cable is exposed. Loosen all engine mounting bolts and bolts attaching fuel tank to engine. Loosen bolt below engine drive pulley attaching plate to engine. Drive belt will have approximately 3 cm (1.2 in.) deflection in center of belt when engine is properly positioned. Make sure engine pulley and transmission pulley are aligned prior to tightening mounting bolts. Adjust clutch cable as outlined above.

STEERING CLUTCH

Models AT70S and AT70S-E

Steering clutch lever (6—Fig. KB25) should be within 1-3 mm (0.04-0.12 in.) for correct steering clutch operation. To adjust, loosen locknut (9) and turn adjusting nut (8) to obtain specified free play.

OVERHAUL

ENGINE

All Models

On Model AT60, engine model number is located on the bottom of the left side engine crankcase below engine drive pulley, or on the front of engine crankcase adjacent to engine oil drain plug on Models AT70S and AT70S-E.

Refer to appropriate engine section for overhaul procedures.

TRANSMISSION

All Models

WHEEL SHAFT SEAL RENEWAL. Remove wheel and axle tube assemblies. If necessary, drain transmission oil to prevent spillage. Refer to LUBRICATION. Use a seal puller or other suitable tool to remove seal. Clean wheel shaft with emery cloth and inspect seal surface on shaft for burrs, scratches or other damage. Clean seal cavity in case. Apply a film of multipurpose grease on lip of seal and drive seal into case until shoulder of seal bottoms on case.

OPERATION. All models are equipped with a gear-type wheel drive transmission with a chain linking input and output mechanisms.

Models AT70S and AT70S-E are equipped with a steering clutch system permitting tiller to be steered easily. In the engaged position (view A—Fig. KB26), ball retainers (8) are pushed outward by spring (7) pressure forcing clutch balls (9) into holes in sprocket (6), delivering power output from chain (5) to both wheel shafts (2 and 10). In the disengaged position (view B), fork (3) pushes ball retainer (8) inward against spring (7), allowing clutch balls (9) to move out of holes in sprocket (6), cutting power output to right wheel shaft (2).

R&R AND OVERHAUL. Drain transmission oil. Remove belt cover and drive belts. Remove screw (6—Fig. KB22) and auxiliary chain case (7). Remove steering clutch cables at transmission. Complete disassembly as necessary to remove transmission from tiller and separate transmission case halves.

Mark special screws (S—Fig. KB28) for reinstallation in the same location. Remove case half retaining screws and separate case halves. Lay transmission down so gears and shafts will remain in case half (18—Fig. KB27). Remove screw attaching block (61). Lift out wheel shaft assembly, chain (20) and gear (31) as a unit (Fig. KB29). Lift out remainder of components as a unit as shown in Fig. KB30.

To disassemble shift fork block (61—Fig. KB27), hold down spring (59) with a suitable tool and remove cotter pin (58).

CAUTION: Do not allow spring (59) to fly out uncontrolled.

Remove springs (59), balls (60) and slide out shift forks (37 and 47).

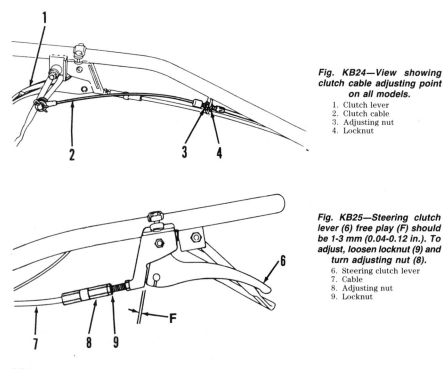

Fig. KB24—View showing clutch cable adjusting point on all models.

1. Clutch lever
2. Clutch cable
3. Adjusting nut
4. Locknut

Fig. KB25—Steering clutch lever (6) free play (F) should be 1-3 mm (0.04-0.12 in.). To adjust, loosen locknut (9) and turn adjusting nut (8).

6. Steering clutch lever
7. Cable
8. Adjusting nut
9. Locknut

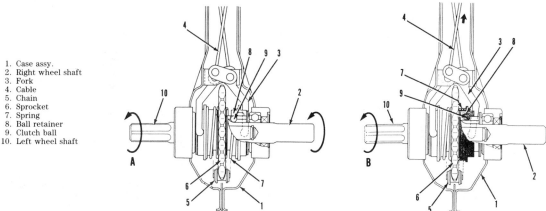

1. Case assy.
2. Right wheel shaft
3. Fork
4. Cable
5. Chain
6. Sprocket
7. Spring
8. Ball retainer
9. Clutch ball
10. Left wheel shaft

Fig. KB26—Sectional view of steering clutch used on Models AT70S and AT70S-E. In View "A," steering clutch is engaged on both sides delivering power output to left (10) and right (2) wheel shafts equally. In View "B," right-hand clutch is applied, disengaging power output to right wheel shaft (2), allowing shaft (2) to turn free while power output is transmitted to left wheel shaft (10). Refer to text.

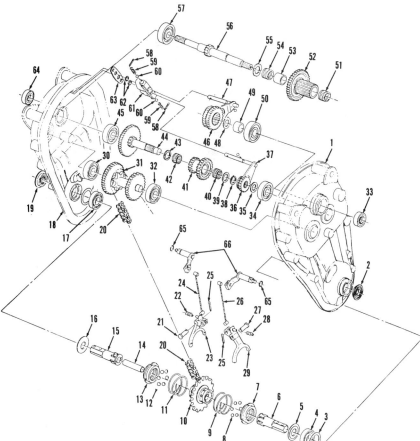

Inspect all components for excessive wear or damage and renew as necessary. Renew springs (59) if free length is less than 21.5 mm (0.85 in.). Renew steering clutch springs (9 and 11) if free length is less than 28.5 mm (1.12 in.). Using a feeler gage, check clearance between shift fork (37) and gear (36), and shift fork (47) and gear (46). Clearance should be 0.1-0.3 mm (0.004-0.012 in.) on both assemblies. Renew gear and fork if clearance exceeds 0.5 mm (0.020 in.) on either assembly. Running clearance of gear (52) and bearings (51 and 54) on shaft (56) should be 0.007-0.041 mm (0.0003-0.0015 in.). Renew gear (52), bearings (51 and 54) and shaft (56) if clearance exceeds 0.1 mm (0.0039 in.). Running clearance of gear (41) and bearings (40 and 42) on shaft (44) should be 0.007-0.040 mm (0.0003-0.0015 in.). Renew gear (41), bearings (40 and 42) and shaft (44) if clearance exceeds 0.01 mm (0.0039 in.).

Fig. KB27—Exploded view of transmission assembly used on Models AT70S and AT70S-E. Transmission used on Model AT60 is similar except steering clutch is not used.

1. Case half	18. Case half	34. Bearing	51. Needle bearing
2. Seal	19. Seal	35. Thrust washer	52. Gear
3. Shim	20. Chain	36. Gear	53. Spacer
4. Bearing	21. Pin	37. Shift fork	54. Needle bearing
5. Collar	22. Spring	38. Snap ring	55. Thrust washer
6. Wheel shaft	23. Fork	39. Thrust washer	56. Shaft
7. Ball retainer	24. Cable	40. Needle bearing	57. Bearing
8. Clutch balls	25. Cotter pin	41. Gear	58. Cotter pin
9. Spring	26. Cable	42. Needle bearing	59. Spring
10. Sprocket	27. Pin	43. Thrust washer	60. Ball
11. Spring	28. Spring	44. Gear & shaft assy.	61. Block
12. Clutch balls	29. Fork	45. Bearing	62. Seals
13. Ball retainer	30. Bearing	46. Gear	63. Gasket
14. Shaft	31. Gear & sprocket assy.	47. Shift fork	64. Bearing
15. Wheel shaft	32. Bearing	48. Thrust washer	65. "O" ring
16. Collar	33. Seal	49. Spacer	66. Steering clutch levers
17. Bearing		50. Bearing	

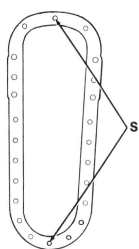

Fig. KB28—Mark special screws (S) located at top and bottom of case where shown for reinstallation in original location.

Reassembly is the reverse of disassembly procedure. Renew all seals and gaskets. Apply a film of SAE 80W-90 gear lube during reassembly. Install thrust washers (48 and 55) with grooved side of washers facing gear (52). Install thrust washers (39 and 43) with grooved side facing gear (41). Use a suitable multipurpose grease to hold balls (8 and 12) in sprocket (10). Refer to LUBRICATION section for lubrication requirements after reassembly.

TINE GEARCASE

All Models

TINE SHAFT OIL SEAL RENEWAL. Remove tiller tines. If necessary, drain oil from gearcase. Use a seal puller or other appropriate tool to remove seals (3 and 7—Fig. KB31). Clean tine shaft with emery cloth and inspect shaft for burrs or scratches. Lubricate lip of seal and drive seal into case until bottomed on seal shoulder. Refer to LUBRICATION section for lubrication requirements.

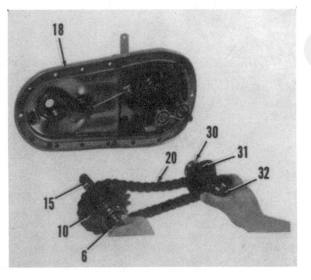

Fig. KB29—Remove and install gear (31), chain (20) and wheel shaft assembly (6, 10 and 15) as shown. Refer to legend in Fig. KB27 for component identification.

Fig. KB30—Remove and reinstall gears and shafts as a unit assembly as shown. Refer to legend in Fig. KB27 for component identification.

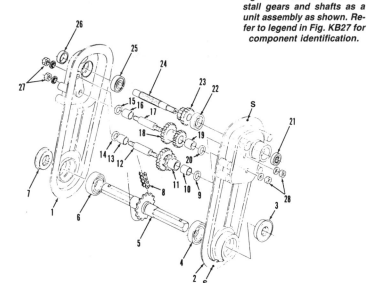

Fig. KB31—Exploded view of tine gearcase used on all models.

1. Case half	11. Gear & sprocket	20. Thrust washer
2. Case half	assy.	21. Seal
3. Seal	12. Idler shaft	22. Bearing
4. Bearing	13. Bushing	23. Gear
5. Tine shaft	14. Thrust washer	24. Input shaft
6. Bearing	15. Thrust washer	25. Bearing
7. Seal	16. Bushing	26. Plug
8. Chain	17. Idler shaft	27. Nuts
9. Thrust washer	18. Gear	28. Nuts
10. Bushing	19. Bushing	S. Special screw

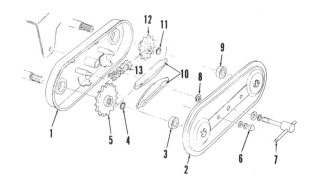

Fig. KB32—Exploded view of auxiliary chain case used on all models.

1. Case		
2. Cover	6. Nut	10. Chain guide
3. Thrust bearing	7. Attaching screw	11. Snap ring
4. Snap ring	8. Clip	12. Sprocket
5. Sprocket	9. Thrust bearing	13. Chain

LAZY BOY

PARMI TOOL COMPANY
P.O. Box 326
Lynn, IN 47355

Model	Engine Make	Engine Series	Power Rating	No. Forward Speeds	Power Reverse?	Tilling Width	Drive Type
T5500	Tec.	TC200	1.6 hp (1.2 kW)	1	No	9 in. (22.8 cm)	Gear
LB200GT	Tec.	TC200	1.6 hp (1.2 kW)	1	No	12 in. (30.5 cm)	Chain
3LBCT	B&S	80000	3 hp (2.2 kW)	1	No	11-18 in. (27.9-45.7 cm)	Chain
S265	B&S	130000	5 hp (3.7 kW)	1	No	20-26 in. (50.8-66 cm)	Chain
756T	B&S	130000	5 hp (3.7 kW)	1	Yes	20-26 in. (50.8-66 cm)	Chain
LB5RT	B&S	130000	5 hp (3.7 kW)	3	Yes	20-26 in. (50.8-66 cm)	Gear
LB8RT	B&S	190000	8 hp (6 kW)	3	Yes	20-26 in. (50.8-66 cm)	Gear
Max	B&S	130000	5 hp (3.7 kW)	1	No	11-24 in. (27.9-61 cm)	Chain

LUBRICATION

ENGINE

Models T5500 and LB200GT

Engine is lubricated by mixing oil with the fuel. Recommended oil is a good quality SAE 30 or SAE 40 oil designed for use in air-cooled two-stroke engines. Do not use multiviscosity oil. Recommended fuel is unleaded gasoline. Regular leaded gasoline is an acceptable substitute. Fuel:oil ratio is 24:1. Mix fuel and oil in a separate container.

Models 3LBCT, S265, 756T, LB5RT and Max

Refer to appropriate Briggs & Stratton engine section for engine lubrication specifications. Recommended oil is a good quality oil which meets or exceeds API specification SF, SE or SD with viscosity chosen according to ambient temperature. Recommended fuel is fresh, clean unleaded gasoline (leaded gasoline is an acceptable substitute), with a minimum octane rating of 77.

GEAR DRIVE

Model T5500

Gear drive assembly should be lubricated after every 25 hours of operation.

Recommended lubricant is a good quality automotive-type multipurpose grease. To lubricate gearcase, remove right-hand tine assembly and lay tiller down on left side. Remove vent screw and fill plug (Fig. LB1) and pump grease into gearcase through fill plug hole until grease escapes from vent hole.

CHAIN CASE

All Models So Equipped

Recommended oil for chain case is SAE 140 gear lubricant. Remove plug

Fig. LB1—To lubricate gearcase on Model T5500, remove vent and fill plugs and pump grease into case through fill plug hole until grease escapes from vent hole.

marked "oil level" on right side of chain case. Remove oil fill plug on right side and fill with specified oil until lubricant level is even with bottom of oil level plug hole. Note that Max models are equipped with separate chain case assemblies for tine drive and wheel drive.

TRANSMISSION

Model LB5RT

Model LB5RT is equipped with a Peerless 700 series transmission. Transmission does not normally require lubrication unless disassembled for repair or component renewal. If unit is disassembled, pack transmission case with 12 ounces (355 mL) of Bentonite grease or an EP lithium base grease.

MAINTENANCE

All Models

Inspect all fasteners for looseness and tighten as necessary. Check control levers, linkage and cables for freedom of movement and excessive play. Inspect drive belt(s) for excessive stretching, wear, cracks or other damage and renew as necessary. Inspect all pulleys and renew if excessively worn or damaged. Periodically lubricate pivot points and transport wheels with a suitable oil.

Fig. LB2—Exploded view of Model T5500 tiller assembly.

1. Engine assy.
2. Hairpin clip
3. Right-hand tines
4. Tine shield
5. Dust seal
6. Vent plug
7. Fill plug
8. Gearcase assy.
9. Left-hand tines
10. Hairpin clip
11. Clutch drum
12. Clutch assy.
13. Clutch spring
14. Depth stake
15. Bracket
16. Throttle cable
17. Throttle lever
18. On/off switch lead
19. On/off switch
20. Lower handlebar assy.
21. Upper handlebar assy.

ADJUSTMENT

DRIVE BELT

Model LB200GT

If drive belt becomes loose on Model LB200GT, remove belt cover and hook idler pulley tension spring in a lower notch in backing plate thus causing spring to exert more tension on idler pulley.

CLUTCH CONTROL

Models 3LBCT, S265, 756T and LB5RT

To adjust clutch control, loosen or tighten clutch cable at spring on clutch lever as necessary to allow proper clutch operation.

Model Max

Wheel drive and tine drive clutch controls are adjusted by loosening adjusting nuts (2 or 10—Fig. LB3) and moving

Fig. LB3—View of drive belt arrangement and related components used on Max models.

1. Tine drive idler pulley	4. Spring	8. Wheel drive idler pulley	11. Spring
2. Adjusting nuts	5. Tine drive pulley	9. Wheel drive belt	12. Return spring
3. Tine drive cable	6. Tine drive belt	10. Adjusting nuts	13. Return spring
	7. Wheel drive pulley		14. Wheel drive cable

cable as necessary to permit proper clutch operation. If belt slips upon clutch engagement, increase length of cable, or if clutch fails to disengage, decrease length of cable.

OVERHAUL

ENGINE

All Models

Engine model and type number is stamped in blower housing adjacent to spark plug on Tecumseh engines, and model number is stamped in blower housing on Briggs & Stratton engines. Refer to appropriate Briggs & Stratton or Tecumseh engine section for overhaul procedures.

CHAIN CASE

All Models

TINE SHAFT OIL SEAL RENEWAL. Remove tines from tine shaft. Use a seal puller or other suitable tool to remove tine shaft seals (5—Fig. LB4). Inspect tine shaft for burrs or scratches that may damage seal during installation. Clean tine shaft with emery cloth. Install seals (5) with lip facing inward. Drive seals into case until outer surface of seal is flush with case.

INSPECTION. Refer to Fig. LB4 for exploded view and component identification. Inspect and renew all components that are worn or damaged. Install new gaskets and seals. Lubricate gears, chains and bearings with a light film of oil during reassembly. Keep all dirt and foreign matter out of chain case during reassembly. Refer to LUBRICATION section for lubrication requirements after reassembly.

TRANSMISSION

Model LB5RT

OVERHAUL. Model LB5RT is equipped with a 3 speed 700 series Peerless transmission. To disassemble the transmission, place shift lever in neutral position, then remove shift lever. Refer to Fig. LB5 and remove set screw (5), spring (4) and detent ball (3). Remove the six cap screws (1) and lift off cover (2). Pull shifter assembly (27) upward and remove from case. See Fig. LB6. Lift both gear and shaft assemblies straight upward out of case (23—Fig. LB5). Move reverse sprockets (18 and 22) together until bushing (7), thrust washer (8) and reverse drive sprocket (22) can be removed from countershaft (28) and chain

(21). Remove chain and separate shaft assemblies. Remove bushing, thrust washer, spur gears (33, 32, 31 and 30)

and beveled spur gear (29) from countershaft (28). Remove bushing (7), thrust washer (8), spur gears (9, 11, 12, 13 and

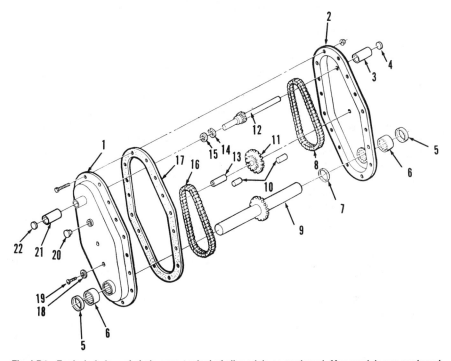

Fig. LB4—Exploded view of chain case typical of all models so equipped. Max models are equipped with two separate chain case assemblies.

1. Right-hand case half	8. Primary chain	12. Input shaft &
2. Left-hand case half	9. Tine shaft &	sprocket assy.
3. Bushing (short)	sprocket assy.	13. Bearing race
4. Seal	10. Needle bearings	14. Retainer
5. Seal	11. Intermediate	15. Thrust washer
6. Bearing	sprocket	16. Secondary chain
7. Spacer		

17. Gasket
18. Seal washer
19. Oil level screw
20. Oil fill plug
21. Bushing (long)
22. Cap

Fig. LB5—Exploded view of 700 series Peerless 5 speed transmission. Model LB5RT is equipped with a 700 series Peerless 3 speed transmission which is similar to 5 speed shown, except fourth speed gear (11), fourth drive gear (32), fifth speed gear (9) and fifth drive gear (33) are absent and replaced with spacers.

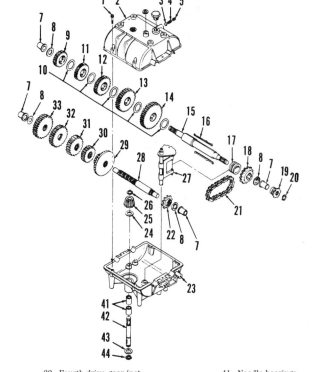

1. Cap screw
2. Cover
3. Detent ball
4. Spring
5. Set screw
7. Flanged bushing
8. Thrust washer
9. Fifth speed gear (not used on Model LB5RT)
10. Thrust washers
11. Fourth speed gear (not used on Model LB5RT)
12. Third speed gear
13. Second speed gear
14. First speed gear
15. Output shaft
16. Shifter keys
17. Shifter collar
18. Reverse driven sprocket
19. Output sprocket
20. Snap ring
21. Chain
22. Reverse drive sprocket
23. Case
24. Thrust washer
25. Input bevel gear
26. Snap ring
27. Shifter assy.
28. Countershaft
29. Beveled spur gear
30. Second drive gear
31. Third speed gear

32. Fourth drive gear (not used on Model LB5RT)
33. Fifth drive gear (not used on Model LB5RT)

41. Needle bearings
42. Input shaft
43. Thrust washer
44. Snap ring

14) and thrust washers (10) from output shaft (15). Then, remove snap ring (20), output sprocket (19), bushing (7), thrust washer (8) and reverse driven sprocket (18) from opposite end of shaft. Slide shifter collar (17) and shifter keys (16) from shaft. Remove snap ring (26), input bevel gear (25) and thrust washer (24), then withdraw input shaft (42) from bottom of case.

Clean and inspect all parts and renew any components showing excessive wear or other damage. If needle bearings (41) are being renewed, press bearings in until they are flush to 0.005 inch (0.13 mm) below case surfaces. Refer to Fig. LB7. Apply a light coat of Bentonite or a good quality EP lithium base grease to bearings, shafts and gears, then reassemble by reversing the disassembly procedure. Refer to Fig. LB8 and install shifter collar and shifter keys on output shaft. Thick side of collar must face shoulder on shaft. When installing gears and thrust washers (9 through 14—Fig. LB5), flat side of gears and the 45 degree inside chamfer on thrust washers must face the shoulder on shaft. Refer

to Fig. LB9. Reverse drive sprocket (22—Fig. LB5) must be installed with large hub side of sprocket facing toward beveled spur gear (29).

Make certain that thrust washers are installed in positions shown in Fig. LB10 and that bearing locator tangs are seated in notches in case. Install shifter assembly, then cover gears, shafts, reverse sprocket and chain with 12 ounces (355 mL) of Bentonite grease. EP lithium base grease is a suitable substitute. Install cover (2—Fig. LB5) and tighten cap screws (1) to 90-100 in.-lbs. (10.2-11.3 N·m). Install detent ball (3), spring (4) and set screw (5) and tighten set screw two full turns below flush.

DRIVE BELTS

Front Tine Models

On Models LB200GT, S265 and 3LBCT, remove belt guard and slip belt off pulleys. Manufacturer's part number for belts are as follows: Model LB200GT—PT50036-00, Model 3LBCT—PT10228-00, Model S265—PT10244-00.

On Model 756T, forward drive belt is in the outer position. Remove belt guard and slip forward belt off chain case pulley, then engine pulley. Remove two nuts securing reverse belt retainer to engine block, and remove reverse belt from engine pulley, then chain case pulley. Reverse procedure to reinstall belts. Manufacturer's part numbers for Model 756T are as follows: Forward belt—PT10244-00, Reverse belt—PT01246-00.

Rear Tine Models

Manufacturer's part numbers for Model LB5RT are as follows: Engine drive belt—PT01254-00, Tine belt—PT01257-00 and Transmission drive belt—PT01256-00. Manufacturer's part number for Max models are as follows: Primary wheel drive belt—PT60017-00, Secondary wheel drive belt—PT60018-00 and Tine drive belt—PT60016-00.

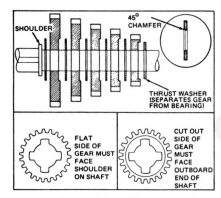

Fig. LB9—View showing correct installation of thrust washers and gears on output shaft. The 45 degree inside chamfer on thrust washers must face the shoulder on the shaft.

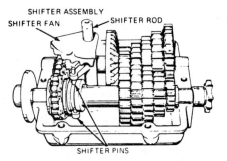

Fig. LB6—View of 700 series transmission with cover removed. Shifter rod, fan, fork, and pins are removed as an assembly.

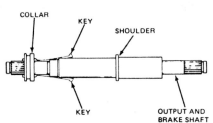

Fig. LB8—Install shifter collar and shifter keys on output shaft as shown. Thick side of collar must face shoulder on shaft.

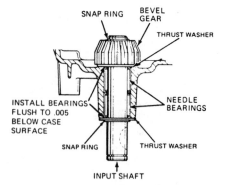

Fig. LB7—Input shaft needle bearings must be installed flush to 0.005 inch (0.13 mm) below case surfaces.

Fig. LB10—Make certain that thrust washers are in positions shown and that bearing locator tangs on bushings (7—Fig. LB5) are seated in notches in case.

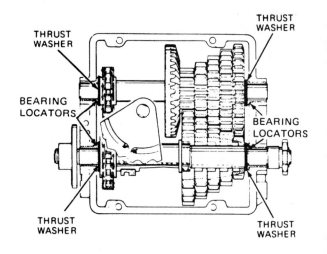

MERRY

MERRY TILLER, INC.
4500 5th Avenue South,
Birmingham, AL 35222

Model	Engine Make	Engine Series	Power Rating	No. of Forward Speeds	Power Reverse?	Tilling Width	Drive Type
Scotsman G-76	B&S	80000	3 hp (2.2 kW)	1	No	26 in. (66 cm)	Chain
Custom G-77	Tec.	H40	4 hp (3.0 kW)	1	No	26 in. (66 cm)	Chain
Custom G-78	B&S	110000	4 hp (3.0 kW)	1	No	26 in. (66 cm)	Chain
Suburban G-80	B&S	130000	5 hp (3.7 kW)	1	No	26 in. (66 cm)	Chain
Suburban G-82	B&S	130000	5 hp (3.7 kW)	1	Yes	26 in. (66 cm)	Chain
Professional G-83	B&S	130000	5 hp (3.7 kW)	1	No	37 in. (94 cm)	Chain
Professional G-84	Wisc.	EY-18-3W	4.6 hp (3.4 kW)	1	No	37 in. (94 cm)	Chain
Professional G-87	Kohler	K91	4 hp (3.0 kW)	1	No	37 in. (94 cm)	Chain
Professional G-88	B&S	130000	5 hp (3.7 kW)	1	Yes	37 in. (94 cm)	Chain
Exporter G-90	Kohler	K91	4 hp (3.0 kW)	1	No	48 in. (122 cm)	Chain
Exporter G-91	B&S	130000	5 hp (3.7 kW)	1	No	48 in. (122 cm)	Chain
Exporter G-92	Wisc.	EY-18-3W	4.6 hp (3.4 kW)	1	No	48 in. (122 cm)	Chain
Minnie MM-1	B&S	60000	2 hp (1.5 kW)	1	No	18 in. (46 cm)	Chain
Minnie 2000	B&S	60000	2 hp (1.5 kW)	1	No	18 in. (46 cm)	Chain
Minnie 2001	B&S	60000	2 hp (1.5 kW)	1	No	18 in. (46 cm)	Chain
Minnie 3200	B&S	60000	2 hp (1.5 kW)	1	No	18 in. (46 cm)	Chain
Minnie 7100	B&S	60000	2 hp (1.5 kW)	1	No	18 in. (46 cm)	Chain
Scotsman 7200	B&S	80000	3 hp (2.2 kW)	1	No	26 in. (66 cm)	Chain
Custom 7300	B&S	110000	4 hp (3.0 kW)	1	No	26 in. (66 cm)	Chain
Suburban 7400	B&S	130000	5 hp (3.7 kW)	1	No	26 in. (66 cm)	Chain
Suburban 7402	B&S	130000	5 hp (3.7 kW)	1	No	26 in. (66 cm)	Chain
Suburban 7480	B&S IC	130000	5 hp (3.7 kW)	1	No	26 in. (66 cm)	Chain
Suburban Rev. 7401	B&S	130000	5 hp (3.7 kW)	1	Yes	26 in. (66 cm)	Chain
Suburban Rev. 7403	B&S	130000	5 hp (3.7 kW)	1	Yes	26 in. (66 cm)	Chain
Professional 7500	B&S	130000	5 hp (3.7 kW)	1	No	37 in. (94 cm)	Chain
Professional 7501	Wisc.	EY-18-3W	4.6 hp (3.4 kW)	1	No	37 in. (94 cm)	Chain
Professional 7502	Kohler	K91	4 hp (3.0 kW)	1	No	37 in. (94 cm)	Chain
Exporter 7600	B&S	130000	5 hp (3.7 kW)	1	No	48 in. (122 cm)	Chain

Model	Engine Make	Engine Series	Power Rating	No. of Forward Speeds	Power Reverse?	Tilling Width	Drive Type
Exporter 7601	Wisc.	EY-18-3W	4.6 hp (3.4 kW)	1	No	48 in. (122 cm)	Chain
Exporter 7602	Kohler	K91	4 hp (3.0 kW)	1	No	48 in. (122 cm)	Chain
International 7600	B&S IC	130000	5 hp (3.7 kW)	1	No	24 in. (61 cm)	Chain
International 7601	Wisc.	EY-18-3W	4.6 hp (3.4 kW)	1	No	24 in. (61 cm)	Chain

LUBRICATION

ENGINE

All Models

Refer to appropriate Briggs & Stratton, Tecumseh, Wisconsin or Kohler engine section for engine lubrication specifications. Recommended oil grade is SAE 30. Recommended fuel is either regular or low-lead gasoline having an octane rating of 90 or higher. The use of unleaded gasoline reduces cylinder head deposits, but could shorten engine valve life if carburetor is adjusted too lean.

CHAIN DRIVE

All Models

Chain case oil should be checked at least every 25 hours of operation. Recommended lubricant is SAE 90 gear oil.

To check oil level in chain case, place tiller on a level surface. Clean dirt from chain case housing and remove oil level plug on bottom of left-hand housing. Oil level should be at bottom of plug hole. If oil level is low, remove fill plug on upper right-hand side of chain case. Add oil slowly until it starts to run out of level plug hole, then reinstall plugs.

MAINTENANCE

Inspect all fasteners for looseness and retighten as needed. Check control levers, linkage and cables for freedom of movement and excessive play. Inspect drive belt(s) for excessive stretching, wear, cracks, or other damage. Install new belt(s) if needed. Inspect all belt pulleys and renew if damaged or excessively worn. Lubricate transport wheels occasionally with SAE 30 oil.

ADJUSTMENT

CLUTCH CONTROL AND DRIVE BELT

All Models

On Minnie 2000 and 2001 models, adjust clutch by engaging clutch spring in the correct chain link. Clutch spring should stretch when clutch is applied. Adjust belt by loosening four engine mounting bolts and sliding engine as required to obtain proper belt adjustment.

On all other models, loosen hex nut on each side of idler link (3—Fig. ME1). Raise idler pulley to take slack out of belt. Hold idler pulley and pull down on idler link to take slack out of clutch cable, then retighten hex nuts. If clutch spring does not stretch when clutch lever is engaged, then clutch adjustment is too loose. Small adjustments may be made by adjusting chain links attached to clutch cable and cable spring. Reverse clutch control and belt are adjusted in

the same fashion, on models so equipped.

OVERHAUL

ENGINE

All Models

Engine model number is stamped on blower housing for Briggs & Stratton en-

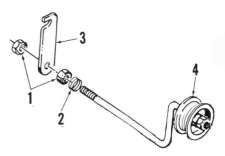

Fig. ME1—View of drive belt idler assembly.
1. Hex nuts
2. Spring
3. Idler link
4. Idler pulley

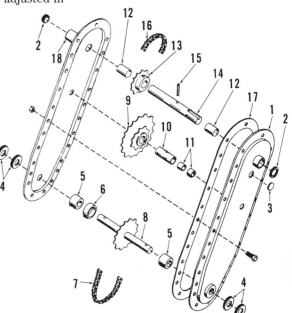

Fig. ME2—Exploded view of chain case Model 1275.
1. Right case half
2. Drive shaft seals
3. Oil fill plug
4. Tine shaft seals
5. Tine shaft needle bearings
6. Spacer
7. Chain
8. Tine shaft assy.
9. Idler sprocket
10. Idler sprocket bearing race
11. Idler sprocket bearings
12. Drive shaft bearings
13. Drive shaft sprocket
14. Drive shaft
15. Roll pin
16. Chain
17. Gasket
18. Left case half

gines. Engine make and series number is marked on data plate attached to engine for Tecumseh, Wisconsin and Kohler engines. Refer to appropriate engine section for overhaul procedures.

CHAIN CASE

Three different chain case models are used. The Model 1275 chain case is used on Models: Scotsman G-76; Custom G-77 and G-78; Suburban G-80 and G-82; Professional G-83, G-84, G-87 and G-88; Scotsman 7200; Custom 7300; Suburban 7400, 7402 and 7480; Suburban Rev. 7401 and 7403; Professional 7500, 7501 and 7502. The Model 2281 chain case is used on Models: Exporter G-90, G-91, G-92, 7600, 7601 and 7602; International 7600 and 7601. The Model 3260 chain case is used on Models: Minnie MM-1, 2000, 2001, 3200 and 7100.

All Models

OIL SEAL INSTALLATION. Remove tines from tine shaft. Use a seal puller or other appropriate tool to pull outer and inner seals out of case hub. Clean tine shaft with emery cloth. Install inner seal with lip facing toward inside and outer seal with lip facing toward outside. Drive new seals in until outer seal is flush with case hub.

INSPECTION. Chain case Model 1275 parts breakdown and identification is shown in Fig. ME2. For chain case Model 2281 refer to Fig. ME3. Refer to Fig. ME4 for parts breakdown and identification of Model 3260 chain case.

Inspect and renew all components that are worn or damaged. Install new gasket and seals. Lubricate chains, sprockets and bearings with a light film of oil during reassembly. Keep all dirt and foreign matter out of chain case during reassembly. Refer to LUBRICATION section for lubrication requirements after reassembly and installation.

DRIVE BELTS

All Models Except Power Reverse

Remove drive belt cover. Remove belt from pulleys and install new belt. Models G-76, G-77, G-78, G-80, G-83, G-84, G-87, 7200, 7300, 7400, 7402, 7480, 7500, 7501 and 7502 drive belt size is ½ inch x 50 inches long. Models G-90, G-91, G-92, 7600, 7601 and 7602 drive belt size is ½ inch x 41 inches long. International 7600 and 7601 models are equipped with a double drive belt arrangement. Double drive belts should be renewed as a set. Double belt size is ½ inch x 41 inches long. Models MM-1, 2000, 2001, 3200 and 7100 drive belt size

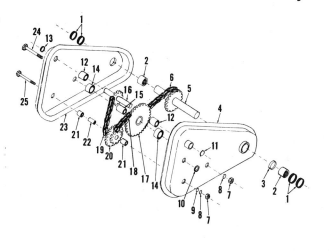

Fig. ME3—Exploded view of chain case Model 2281.
1. Tine shaft seals
2. Tine shaft needle bearings
3. Spacer
4. Right case half
5. Tine shaft
6. Chain
7. Nuts
8. Lockwashers
9. Flat washer
10. Oil fill plug
11. Soft plug
12. Drive shaft bearings
13. Drive shaft seal
14. Idler sprocket bearings
15. Inner race
16. Drive shaft assy.
17. Idler sprocket
18. Chain
19. Chain
20. Idler sprocket
21. Idler sprocket bearings
22. Inner race
23. Left case half
24. Bolt, 2-7/8 inches (73 mm)
25. Bolt, 2-1/2 inches (63.5 mm)

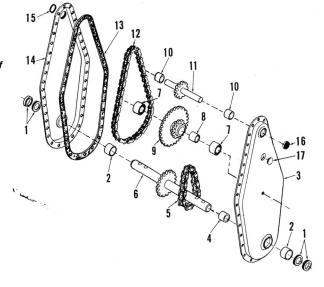

Fig. ME4—Exploded view of chain case Model 3260.
1. Tine shaft oil seals
2. Tine shaft needle bearings
3. Right case half
4. Spacer
5. Chain
6. Tine shaft
7. Idler sprocket bearings
8. Idler sprocket bearing race
9. Idler sprocket
10. Drive shaft bearings
11. Drive shaft
12. Chain
13. Gasket
14. Left case half
15. Drive shaft oil seal
16. Soft plug
17. Oil fill plug

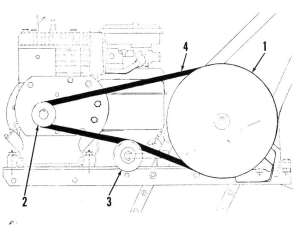

Fig. ME5—View of drive belt routing and parts identification on models without power reverse. International 7600 and 7601 models are equipped with a double drive belt arrangement.
1. Chain case drive pulley
2. Engine pulley
3. Idler pulley assy.
4. Drive belt

is ½ inch x 34 inches long. Refer to Fig. ME5 for belt routing and parts identification. Refer to ADJUSTMENT section for adjusting procedure. Reinstall drive belt cover.

Power Reverse Models

Remove drive belt cover. Remove forward drive belt from pulleys, then remove reverse drive belt from pulleys. Install new belts. Forward drive belt size is ½ inch x 50 inches long. Reverse drive belt size is 3/8 inch x 45 inches long. Refer to Fig. ME6 for belt routing and parts identification. Refer to ADJUSTMENT section for adjusting procedure. Reinstall drive belt cover.

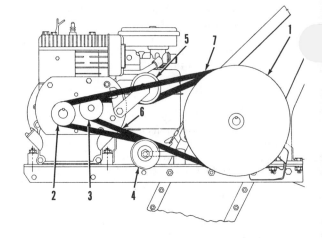

Fig. ME6—View of forward and reverse drive belt routing and parts identification.

1. Chain case drive pulley
2. Forward drive engine pulley
3. Reverse drive engine pulley
4. Forward drive belt idler assy.
5. Reverse drive belt idler assy.
6. Reverse drive belt
7. Forward drive belt

MIGHTY MAC

AMERIND-MACKISSIC, INC.
P.O. Box 111
Parker Ford, PA 19457

Model	Engine Make	Engine Series	Engine Horsepower	No. of Forward Speeds	Power Reverse?	Tilling Width (In.)	Drive Type
324	B&S	80000	3	1	No	24	Chain
524	B&S	130000	5	1	No	24	Chain
524R	B&S	13000	5	1	Yes	24	Chain
822RT	B&S	190000	8	1	Yes	24	Chain

LUBRICATION

ENGINE

All Models

Refer to Briggs and Stratton engine section for engine lubrication requirements. Recommended fuel is regular or low-lead gasoline having an octane rating of 90 or higher. Recommended oil is SAE 30.

CHAIN DRIVE

Models 324, 524 and 524R

Chain case oil should be checked at least every 25 hours of operation. Recommended lubricant is SAE 90 gear oil.

To check oil in chain case, place tiller on a level surface. Clean dirt from chain case housing and remove oil level plug (2–Fig. MM1) on top or right side of housing. Oil level should be at bottom of plug hole. If oil is needed, add slowly until it starts to run out of plug hole, then reinstall plug.

Model 822RT

Chain case oil should be checked at least every 25 hours of operation. Recommended lubricant is SAE 90 gear oil or SAE 50 engine oil.

To check oil level in chain case, place tiller on a level surface. Clean dirt from chain case housing and remove oil level plug on right side. Oil should be at bottom of plug hole. If oil is needed, add slowly until it starts to run out of plug hole, then reinstall plug.

MAINTENANCE

Inspect all fasteners for looseness and retighten as needed. Check control levers, linkage and cables for freedom of movement and excessive play. Inspect drive belt(s) for excessive stretching, wear, cracks or any other damage. Install new belt(s) if needed. Inspect all belt pulleys and renew if damaged or excessively worn. Lubricate transport wheels occasionally with SAE 30 oil.

ADJUSTMENT

CLUTCH CONTROL AND DRIVE BELT

Models 324, 524 and 524R

FORWARD BELT. Loosen nuts holding idler shaft to frame, then slide idler arm up slightly to increase tension on belt. Retighten nuts. If necessary, adjust slack in control cable leading to clutch lever on handle bar by taking up a link in chain connecting cable to spring.

Model 524R

REVERSE BELT. To increase belt tension, loosen locknut and slide idler pulley further out on idler arm. If necessary, adjust slack in control cable leading to clutch lever on handle bar by taking up a link in chain connecting cable to spring.

Model 822RT

To check for proper engine belt tension, remove belt cover and press down on both belts so they touch the horizontal round bar on belt engagement lever. Forward idler pulley should move 1/4-1/2 inch (6.4-12.7 mm). If more movement is observed, loosen engine base plate and move engine to the rear 1/16-1/8 inch (1.6-3.2 mm). After moving engine, readjust linkage at bellcrank on forward belt idler and at collar under handle.

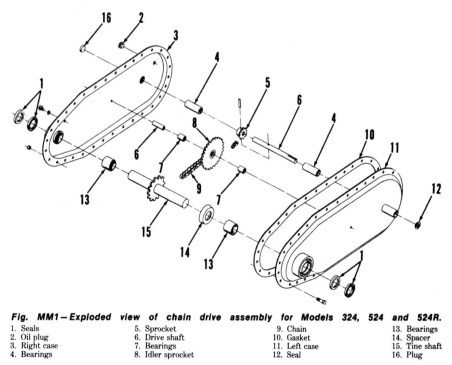

Fig. MM1—Exploded view of chain drive assembly for Models 324, 524 and 524R.

1. Seals	5. Sprocket	9. Chain	13. Bearings
2. Oil plug	6. Drive shaft	10. Gasket	14. Spacer
3. Right case	7. Bearings	11. Left case	15. Tine shaft
4. Bearings	8. Idler sprocket	12. Seal	16. Plug

MTD

MTD PRODUCTS
5965 Grafton Road,
Cleveland, Ohio 44136

Model	Engine Make	Engine Series	Engine Horsepower	No. of Forward Speeds	Power Reverse?	Tilling Width (In.)	Drive Type
030	B&S	80000	3	1	No	18	Chain
320	B&S	130000	5	1	No	20	Chain
355	B&S	130000	5	1	No	26	Gear
385	B&S	130000	5	1	Yes	26	Chain
386	B&S	130000	5	4	Yes	26	Chain
405	B&S	130000	5	5	Yes	21	Chain
408	B&S	190000	8	5	Yes	21	Chain
409	B&S	190000	8	5	Yes	21	Chain

LUBRICATION
ENGINE

All Models

Refer to appropriate Briggs and Stratton engine section for engine lubrication specification.

Recommended oil grade is SAE 30 or equivalent. Recommended fuel is either regular or low-lead gasoline having an octane rating of 90 or higher. The use of non-leaded gasolines reduces cylinder head deposits, but could shorten engine valve life if carburetor is adjusted too lean.

CHAIN DRIVE

All Models

Chain case is factory sealed and must be removed and disassembled in order to add or change grease in case. Refer to **OVERHAUL** section for servicing grease.

GEAR CASE

Model 355

Gear case oil should be checked at least every 10 hours of operation.

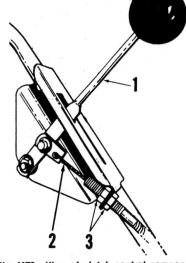

Fig. MT2 – View of clutch control components for Model 030.
1. Clutch lever
2. Clutch cable
3. Hex nuts

Recommended lubricant is Pennant oil EP#35000 or suitable equivalent.

To check gear case oil place tiller on a level surface. Clean dirt from around front of gear case and remove oil level plug (1–Fig. MT1). Oil level should be at bottom of plug hole. If oil level is low remove fill plug (2), then add oil through fill hole until it begins to run out level hole. Reinstall and tighten plugs.

MAINTENANCE

Inspect all fasteners for looseness and retighten as needed. Check control levers, linkage and cables for freedom of movement and excessive play. Inspect drive belt(s) for excessive stretching, wear, cracks or any other damage. Install new belt(s) if needed. Inspect all belt pulleys and renew if damaged or excessively worn. Transport wheels on Models 030, 320, 355, 385 and 386

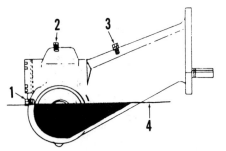

Fig. MT1 – View of gear case oil level and plugs for Model 355.
1. Oil level plug
2. Fill plug
3. Breather plug
4. Oil level

Fig. MT3 – View of clutch adjusting components for Model 320.
1. Hex nuts
2. Clutch cable
3. Bracket

Fig. MT4 – View of clutch control components for Models 355, 385, 386, 405, 408 and 409.
1. Clutch lever
2. Threaded control rod
3. Adjustment ferrule
4. Bracket

should be lubricated occasionally with SAE 30 oil.

ADJUSTMENT
CLUTCH CONTROL AND DRIVE BELT

Models 030 and 320

For Model 030 refer to Fig. MT2 for clutch components identification. For Model 320 refer to Fig. MT3 for clutch components identification.

Loosen and turn hex nuts to adjust clutch, then check for correct adjustment. For Model 030 place clutch lever in neutral position. For Model 320 make sure clutch engagement lever is in released position. Unhook spark plug lead and pull on starter rope handle. If tines do not turn, then adjustment is correct. If tines do turn, then clutch cable will need to be adjusted.

Models 355, 385 and 386

Remove hair pin clip from ferrule (3 – Fig. MT4), then remove ferrule from bracket (4). Turn ferrule on control rod (2) to adjust clutch. Reinstall ferrule in bracket and install hair pin clip. To check for correct clutch adjustment place clutch lever (1) in neutral position. Unhook spark plug lead and pull on starter rope handle. If tines do not turn, then adjustment is correct. If tines do turn, then clutch rod will need to be adjusted.

GEAR CASE

Model 355

Gear case bearings should be adjusted approximately every five hours of operation. Adjust by removing cotter pin (17 – Fig. MT10), then turning adjustment cap (16) in until snug. Do not overtighten. Reinstall cotter pin, then check adjustment by starting tiller and engaging tines. If engine stalls out, then bearing adjustment is too tight and adjustment cap should be loosened slightly.

ENGINE POSITION

Model 386

Loosen engine securing hex bolts and slide engine in slots to adjust position. If there is no reverse or a slippage in reverse, then engine assembly will need to be slid back until engine disc and friction disc on variable speed pulley make contact. If neutral cannot be obtained, then engine assembly will need to be slid forward. Refer to **CLUTCH CONTROL AND DRIVE BELT AD-**

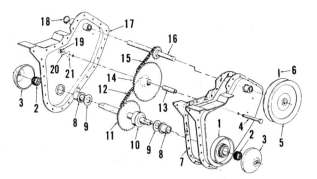

Fig. MT5 – Exploded view of chain case for Model 030.
1. Chain case, L.H.
2. Oil seal
3. Dust cover
4. Bolt 2½ inches long
5. Input pulley
6. Roll pin
7. Gasket
8. Flange bearings
9. Washers
10. Spacer
11. Tine shaft assy.
12. Chain, 0.375 inch pitch x 50 links
13. Inner race
14. Hub and sprocket assy.
15. Chain, ½-inch pitch x 38 links
16. Input shaft assy.
17. Chain case, R.H.
18. Expansion ring
19. Hex nut
20. Lockwasher
21. Flat washer

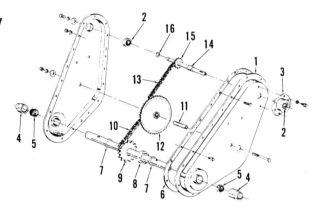

Fig. MT6 – Exploded view of chain case for Model 320.
1. Chain case, L.H.
2. Bearings
3. Bearing housing
4. Dust caps
5. V-Ring seals
6. Gasket
7. Thrust washers
8. Step spacer
9. Tine shaft and sprocket
10. Chain, ⅝-inch pitch x 38 links
11. Inner race
12. Sprocket
13. Chain, ⅜-inch pitch x 70 links
14. Spacer
15. Input shaft and sprocket
16. Snap ring

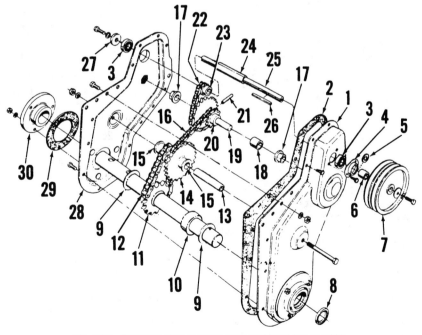

Fig. MT7 – Exploded view of chain case for Model 385 and 386.

1. Chain case, L.H.	10. Spacer	17. Hex flanged bearings	24. Spacer
2. Gasket	11. Tine shaft assy.	18. Spacer	25. Input shaft
3. Bearings	12. Chain, ⅝-inch pitch x 28 links	19. Sprocket shaft	26. Square key
4. Bearing housing	13. Sprocket shaft	20. Sprocket sleeve assy.	27. Flat washer
5. Flat washer	14. Sprocket	21. Roll pin	28. Chain case, R.H.
6. Spacer	15. Flange bearings	22. Chain, ½-inch pitch x 34 links	29. Gasket
7. Input pulley	16. Chain, ½-inch pitch x 48 links	23. Sprocket	30. Bearing housing assy.
8. Oil seal			
9. Flat washer			

JUSTMENT section for clutch rod adjusting procedure.

OVERHAUL
ENGINE

All Models

Engine model no. is stamped on
blower housing. Refer to appropriate
Briggs and Stratton engine section for
overhaul procedures.

CHAIN CASE

All Models

OIL SEAL INSTALLATION. The
chain case is factory sealed and no provision is made for checking or adding
lubricant. Chain case must be separated
as described in following **INSPECTION**
paragraph to accurately add specific
amount of lubricant. Seals may be renewed as follows:

Remove tines from tine shaft. Use a
seal puller or other appropriate tools to
remove seal(s) from case hub. Clean tine
shaft with emery cloth. Drive new seal(s)
in until outside face is flush with case
hub. On models with two seals on each
side install inner seal with lip facing
toward inside and outer seal with lip facing toward outside. On Models 405, 408
and 409 remove wheels to install axle
shaft seals.

INSPECTION. For Model 030 refer
to Fig. MT5 for parts breakdown and
identification. For Model 320 refer to
Fig. MT6 for parts breakdown and identification. For Models 385 and 386 refer
to Fig. MT7 for parts breakdown and
identification. For Model 405 refer to
Fig. MT8 for parts breakdown and identification. For Models 408 and 409 refer
to Fig. MT9 for parts breakdown and
identification.

Inspect and renew all components that
are worn or damaged. Install new
gasket(s) and seals. Lubricate chains,
sprockets and bearings with a light film
of grease during reassembly. Keep all
dirt and foreign matter out of chain case
during reassembly.

Recommended lubricant for all models
is Plastilube #0 grease or suitable
equivalent. Capacity for Model 030 is 16
ounces. Capacity for Model 320 is 12
ounces. Capacity for Models 385 and 386
is 14 ounces. Capacity for Models 405,
408 and 409 is 28 ounces. To fill chain
case with grease, lay right half of case
on its side, add grease and assemble left
half to right. Complete reassembly and
reinstall in tiller frame.

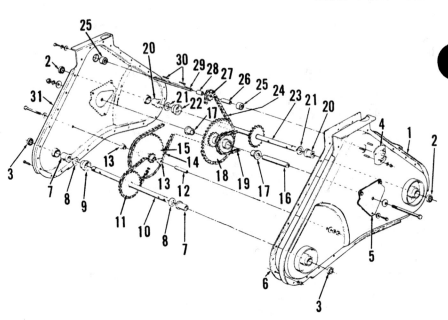

Fig. MT8 — Exploded view of chain case for Model 405.

1. Chain case, L.H.	9. Spacer	16. Inner race	24. Chain, ½-inch pitch x 58 links
2. Seals	10. Axle shaft assy.	17. Flange bearings	25. Ball bearings
3. Seals	11. Chain, ½-inch pitch x 42 links	18. Sprocket	26. Spacer
4. Bearing housing	12. Inner race	19. Chain, ⅝-inch pitch x 52 links	27. Sprocket
5. Side plate, L.H. and R.H.	13. Flange bearings	20. Flange bearings	28. Spacer
6. Gasket	14. Chain, ½-inch pitch x 58 links	21. Flat washers	29. Input shaft
7. Flange bearings	15. Sprocket	22. Spacer	30. Square keys
8. Flat washers		23. Tine shaft assy.	31. Chain case, R.H.

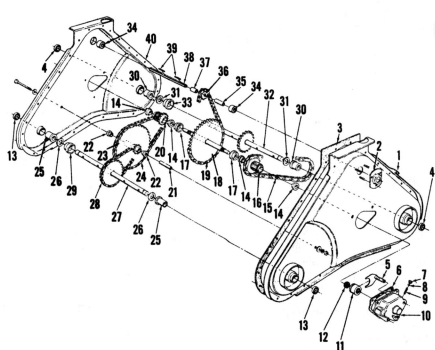

Fig. MT9 — Exploded view of chain case for Models 408 and 409. Shift parts (5 through 12) are used on both right hand wheel drive engagement and left hand tine engagement.

1. Chain case, L.H.	13. Oil seals	20. Sprocket bearing sleeve assy.	29. Spacer
2. Bearing housing	14. Flange bearings	21. Hub sleeve	30. Flange bearings
3. Gasket	15. Chain, ⅝-inch pitch x 52 links	22. Flange bearings	31. Flat washers
4. Oil seals	16. Sprocket bearing sleeve assy.	23. Sprocket assy.	32. Tine shaft assy.
5. Shift yoke	17. Stepped spacer	24. Chain, ½-inch pitch x 58 links	33. Spacer
6. Gasket	18. Clutch shaft assy.	25. Flange bearings	34. Ball bearings
7. Cap plug	19. Chain, ½-inch pitch x 58 links	26. Flat washers	35. Spacer
8. Detent ball		27. Axle shaft assy.	36. Sprocket
9. Spring		28. Chain, ½-inch pitch x 42 links	37. Spacer
10. Shift housing			38. Input shaft
11. Clutch dog			39. Square keys
12. Clutch dog driver			40. Chain case, R.H.

GEAR CASE

Model 355

OIL SEAL INSTALLATION. Remove tines from tine shaft. Use a seal puller to remove seals from case hub. Clean tine shaft with emery cloth. Drive new seals in until outside face is flush with case hub.

REMOVE AND DISASSEMBLE. Refer to Fig. MT10 for parts breakdown and identification. Inspect and renew all components that are worn or damaged. Install new gaskets and seals. Lubricate gears and bearings with a light film of oil during reassembly. Keep all dirt and foreign matter out of gear case during reassembly. Refer to **LUBRICATION** section for lubricating requirements after reassembly and installation. Refer to **GEAR CASE ADJUSTMENT** section for bearing preload adjusting procedure.

DRIVE BELTS

Model 030

Refer to Fig. MT11 for belt routing and parts identification. Place clutch lever in forward position, then unhook extension spring (3) from drive belt cover. Remove drive belt cover. Remove belt from pulleys and install new belt. Drive belt size is ⅜-inch x 29 inches long. Reinstall drive belt cover, then rehook extension spring in cover. Refer to **CLUTCH CONTROL AND DRIVE BELT ADJUSTMENT** section for adjusting procedure.

Model 320

Refer to Fig. MT12 for belt routing and parts identification. Remove drive belt cover. Remove drive belt from chain case pulley (2), then remove belt from idler pulley (3) and engine pulley (1). Install new drive belt, making sure belt is positioned inside two pins at engine pulley. Drive belt size is ½-inch x 39 inches long. Reinstall drive belt cover. Refer to **CLUTCH CONTROL AND DRIVE BELT ADJUSTMENT** section for adjusting procedure.

Model 355

Refer to Fig. MT13 for belt(s) routing and parts identification. Remove drive belt cover, then remove wire belt retainer at front of gear case pulley. Remove forward drive belt from engine pulley (1) and gear case pulley (2). Remove retaining nut from reverse idler pulley (3), then pull pulley out away from idler bracket. Slip reverse belt off idler pulley and gear case pulley. Install new drive belt(s). Reassemble in reverse order of disassembly. Forward drive belt size is ½-inch x 37 inches long. Reverse drive belt size is ½-inch x 44 inches long. Refer to **CLUTCH CONTROL AND DRIVE BELT ADJUSTMENT** section for adjusting procedure.

Model 385

Refer to Fig. MT14 for belt(s) routing and parts identification. Remove drive belt cover. Loosen belt wire finger (2) retaining bolt and nut. Place clutch lever in reverse position, then remove forward drive belt from pulleys. Place clutch lever in neutral position, then remove reverse drive belt from chain case pulley. Place clutch lever in reverse position. Remove reverse idler pulley (5) retaining nut, then slip pulley and belt off idler bracket together. Install new belts, then reassemble in reverse order

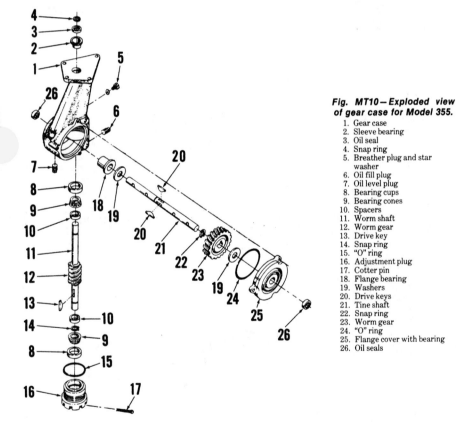

Fig. MT10 — Exploded view of gear case for Model 355.

1. Gear case
2. Sleeve bearing
3. Oil seal
4. Snap ring
5. Breather plug and star washer
6. Oil fill plug
7. Oil level plug
8. Bearing cups
9. Bearing cones
10. Spacers
11. Worm shaft
12. Worm gear
13. Drive key
14. Snap ring
15. "O" ring
16. Adjustment plug
17. Cotter pin
18. Flange bearing
19. Washers
20. Drive keys
21. Tine shaft
22. Snap ring
23. Worm gear
24. "O" ring
25. Flange cover with bearing
26. Oil seals

Fig. MT11 — View of drive belt routing and parts identification for Model 030.

1. Engine pulley
2. Idler pulley
3. Extension spring
4. Chain case pulley
5. Clutch cable
6. Drive belt

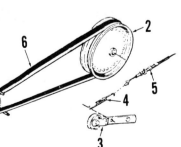

Fig. MT12 — View of drive belt routing and parts identification for Model 320.

1. Engine pulley	4. Extension spring
2. Chain case pulley	5. Clutch cable assy.
3. Idler assy.	6. Drive belt

of disassembly. Forward drive belt size is ½-inch x 37 inches long. Reverse drive belt size is ½-inch x 41 inches long. Refer to **CLUTCH CONTROL AND DRIVE BELT ADJUSTMENT** section for adjusting procedure.

Model 386

Refer to Fig. MT15 for belt(s) routing and parts identification. Remove drive belt cover. Push idler pulley (8) forward, then slip reverse belt off chain case pulley, idler pulley and variable speed pulley. Place shift lever in forward speed position, then lift forward drive belt from engine pulley and variable speed pulley. Install new belts, make sure forward drive belt is positioned inside two pins at engine pulley. Forward drive belt size is ½-inch x 19 inches long. Rear

drive belt size is ½-inch x 28 inches long. Reassemble in reverse order of disassembly. Refer to **ENGINE POSITION ADJUSTMENT** section and **CLUTCH CONTROL AND DRIVE BELT ADJUSTMENT** section for adjusting procedure.

Models 405, 408 and 409

Refer to Fig. MT16 for belt(s) routing and parts identification. Remove drive belt cover. Place clutch lever in reverse position, then remove forward belt (13)

from engine pulley towards engine. Slip belt off variable speed pulley (4) and remove belt. Place clutch lever in second speed position, then remove rear drive belt (14) from chain case pulley (11) and variable speed pulley. Model 405 forward drive belt size is ⅝-inch x 26 inches long. Rear drive belt size is ⅝-inch x 52 inches long. Models 408 and 409 forward drive belt size is ⅝-inch x 27 inches long. Rear drive belt size is ⅝-inch x 52 inches long. Install new belts, then reassemble in reverse order of disassembly.

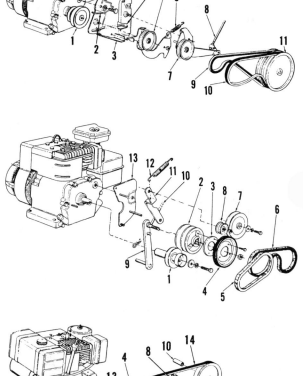

Fig. MT14 — View of drive belt(s) routing and parts identification for Model 385.

1. Engine pulley
2. Belt wire finger
3. Clutch plate
4. Control rod
5. Reverse idler assy.
6. Spring
7. Forward idler assy.
8. Clutch control rod assy.
9. Reverse belt
10. Forward belt
11. Chain case pulley

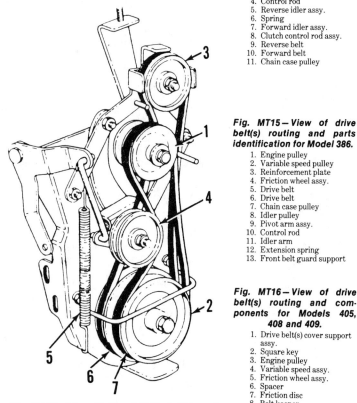

Fig. MT13 — View of drive belt(s) routing and parts identification for Model 355.

1. Engine pulley
2. Gear case pulley
3. Reverse idler assy.
4. Forward idler assy.
5. Extension spring
6. Reverse drive belt
7. Forward drive belt

Fig. MT15 — View of drive belt(s) routing and parts identification for Model 386.

1. Engine pulley
2. Variable speed pulley
3. Reinforcement plate
4. Friction wheel assy.
5. Drive belt
6. Drive belt
7. Chain case pulley
8. Idler pulley
9. Pivot arm assy.
10. Control rod
11. Idler arm
12. Extension spring
13. Front belt guard support

Fig. MT16 — View of drive belt(s) routing and components for Models 405, 408 and 409.

1. Drive belt(s) cover support assy.
2. Square key
3. Engine pulley
4. Variable speed assy.
5. Friction wheel assy.
6. Spacer
7. Friction disc
8. Belt keeper
9. Idler pulley
10. Spacer
11. Chain case input pulley
12. Drive belt(s) cover
13. Drive belt
14. Drive belt

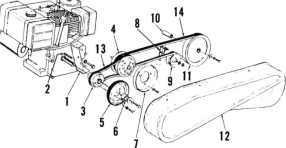

MTD

Model	Engine Make	Engine Series	Engine Horsepower	No. of Forward Speeds	Power Reverse?	Tilling Width (In.)	Drive Type
410A	B&S	130000	5	5	Yes	21	Chain
412A	B&S	190000	8	5	Yes	21	Chain
418A	B&S	190000	8	5	Yes	21	Chain

LUBRICATION

ENGINE

All Models

Refer to appropriate Briggs and Stratton engine section for engine lubrication specification.

Recommended oil grade is SAE 30 or equivalent. Recommended fuel is either regular or low-lead gasoline having an octane rating of 90 or higher. The use of non-leaded gasolines reduces cylinder head deposits, but could shorten engine valve life if carburetor is adjusted too lean.

CHAIN DRIVE

All Models

Chain case is factory sealed and must be removed and disassembled in order to add or change grease in case. Refer to **OVERHAUL** section for servicing grease.

MAINTENANCE

Inspect all fasteners for looseness and retighten as needed. Check control levers, linkage and cables for freedom of movement and excessive play. Inspect drive belt(s) for excessive stretching, wear, cracks or any other damage. Install new belt(s) if needed. Inspect all belt pulleys and renew if damaged or excessively worn.

ADJUSTMENT

GEAR SHIFT LEVER

All Models

Place tiller drive wheels in freewheeling position. Put tine depth bar all the way down to raise tines off ground. Start tiller engine, then move gear shift lever to each of five forward speed positions. Return lever to neutral position and turn engine off. Remove hair pin clip from ferrule, then remove ferrule

from gear shift lever. Place shift lever in first (1) forward speed position and pull lever to rear of position slot. Thread ferrule on control rod to align with shift lever hole, then reinstall ferrule in lever and install hair pin clip.

OVERHAUL

ENGINE

All Models

Engine model no. is stamped on blower housing. Refer to appropriate Briggs and Stratton engine section for overhaul procedures.

CHAIN CASE

All Models

OIL SEAL INSTALLATION. Remove tines from tine shaft. Use a seal puller to remove seal(s) from case hub. Clean tine shaft with emery cloth. Drive new seal in until outside face is flush with case hub. Remove drive wheels to install axle shaft seals.

INSPECTION. Refer to Fig. MT21 for parts breakdown and identification. Inspect and renew all components that are worn or damaged. Install new gaskets and seals. Lubricate chains,

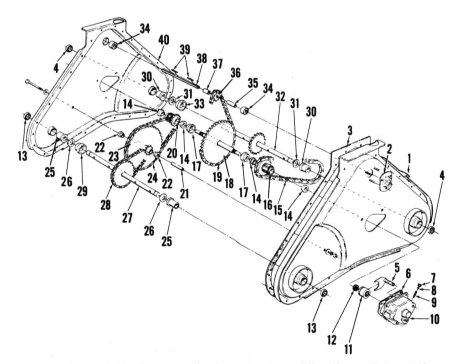

Fig. MT21 — Exploded view of chain case for Models 410, 412 and 418. Shift parts (5 through 12) are used on both right hand wheel drive engagement and left hand tine engagement.

1. Chain case, L.H.
2. Bearing housing
3. Gasket
4. Oil seals
5. Shift yoke
6. Gasket
7. Cap plug
8. Detent ball
9. Spring
10. Shift housing
11. Clutch dog
12. Clutch dog driver
13. Oil seals
14. Flange bearing
15. Chain, ⅝-inch pitch x 52 links
16. Sprocket bearing sleeve assy.
17. Stepped spacer
18. Clutch shaft assy.
19. Chain, ½-inch pitch x 58 links
20. Sprocket bearing sleeve assy.
21. Hub sleeve
22. Flange bearings
23. Sprocket assy.
24. Chain, ½-inch pitch x 58 links
25. Flange bearings
26. Flat washers
27. Axle shaft assy.
28. Chain, ½-inch pitch x 42 links
29. Spacer
30. Flange bearings
31. Flat washers
32. Tine shaft assy.
33. Spacer
34. Ball bearings
35. Spacer
36. Sprocket
37. Spacer
38. Input shaft
39. Square keys
40. Chain case, R.H.

sprockets and bearings with a light film of grease during reassembly. Keep all dirt and foreign matter out of chain case during reassembly. Recommended lubricant is Plastilube #0 grease or suitable equivalent. Capacity is 28 ounces. To fill chain case with grease, lay right half of case on its side, add grease and assemble left half to right. Complete reassembly and reinstall in tiller frame.

DRIVE BELTS

All Models

Refer to Fig. MT22 for belt(s) routing and parts identification. Remove drive belt cover and engine brace. Place gear shift lever in neutral position. Remove three cap screws securing friction disc (4) on variable speed assembly (3). Slip belt off variable speed pulley, then remove two cap screws and washers securing belt guard (11) on engine. Remove belt guard, then remove belt off

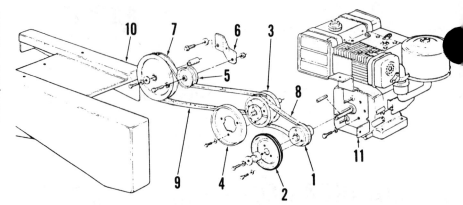

Fig. MT22 — View of drive belt(s) routing and parts identification for Models 410, 412 and 418.

1. Engine pulley	4. Friction disc	7. Chain case input pulley	9. Drive belt
2. Friction wheel	5. Idler pulley	8. Drive belt	10. Drive belt cover
3. Variable speed assy.	6. Idler bracket		11. Drive belt guard

engine pulley. Place gear shift lever in a forward speed position. Lift up on idler pulley (5) and remove belt from under pulley. Slip belt off chain case input pulley (7) and variable speed pulley (3).

Install new drive belts. Forward drive belt size is ⅝-inch x 27 inches long. Rear drive belt size is ⅝-inch x 51 inches long. Reassemble in reverse order of disassembly.

MURRAY

THE MURRAY OHIO MANUFACTURING COMPANY
Box 268
Brentwood, Tennessee 37027

Model	Engine Make	Engine Series	Engine Horsepower	No. of Forward Speeds	Power Reverse?	Tilling Width (In.)	Drive Type
1000	B&S	60000	2	1	No	11-24	Chain
1190	B&S	130000	5	1	No	14-28	Chain
1202	B&S	130000	5	1	Yes	14-28	Chain
1203	B&S	130000	5	1	Yes	14-28	Chain
1290	B&S	130000	5	1	No	14-28	Chain
1302	B&S	130000	5	1	Yes	14-28	Chain
1303	B&S	130000	5	1	Yes	14-28	Chain

LUBRICATION

ENGINE

All Models

Refer to appropriate Briggs and Stratton engine section for engine lubrication specifications. Recommended oil grade is SAE 30 or equivalent. Recommended fuel is either regular or low-lead gasoline having an octane rating of 90 or higher. The use of non-leaded gasolines reduces cylinder head deposits, but could shorten engine valve life if carburetor is adjusted too lean.

CHAIN DRIVE

All Models

Chain case oil should be checked at least every 25 hours of operation. Recommended oil is SAE 30 API SE engine oil.

To check oil level, clean case and remove oil level plug on right hand side of case. Raise transport wheels to their highest position. Oil level should be at bottom of plug hole. If oil level is low add oil until level is flush with bottom of plug hole, then reinstall oil level plug.

MAINTENANCE

Inspect all fasteners for looseness and

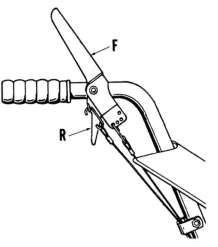

Fig. MU2 — View of clutch control linkage for Models 1202, 1203, 1302 and 1303.
F. Forward drive lever   R. Reverse drive lever

retighten as needed. Check control levers, linkage and cables for freedom of movement and excessive play. Inspect drive belt(s) for excessive stretching, wear, cracks or any other damage. Install new belt(s) if needed. Inspect all belt pulleys and renew if damaged or excessively worn. Lubricate transport wheels occasionally with SAE 30 oil.

ADJUSTMENT

CLUTCH CONTROL

All Models

FORWARD DRIVE. Refer to Fig. MU1 for Models 1000, 1190 and 1290 and Fig. MU2 for Models 1202, 1203, 1302 and 1303 for clutch control parts and identification. With drive lever disengaged tines should not turn. If tines continue to turn, then reposition clutch cable in cable guide. If drive belt slips when lever is engaged, then reposition clutch spring in drive lever.

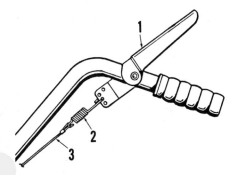

Fig. MU1 — View of clutch control linkage for Models 1000, 1190 and 1290.
1. Drive lever
2. Spring   3. Clutch cable

Fig. MU3 — View of reverse clutch idler adjustment for Models 1202, 1203, 1302 and 1303.
1. Reverse drive cable
2. Cable hook
3. Reverse drive idler

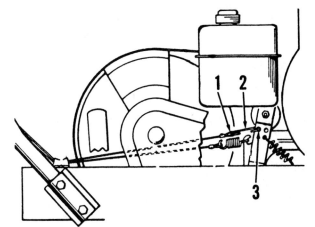

Models 1202, 1203, 1302 and 1303

REVERSE DRIVE. Refer to Fig. MU3 for clutch control parts and identification. If belt slippage occurs when reverse clutch lever is engaged, then reposition cable hook in forward most hole in reverse idler lever.

OVERHAUL

ENGINE

All Models

Engine model no. is stamped on blower housing. Refer to appropriate Briggs and Stratton engine section for overhaul procedures.

CHAIN CASE

All Models

INSPECTION. For Model 1000 refer to Fig. MU4 for parts breakdown and identification. For other models refer to Fig. MU5 for parts breakdown and identification. Inspect and renew all components that are worn or damaged. Install new gaskets and seals. Lubricate gears, chains and bearings with a light film of oil during reassembly. Keep all dirt and foreign matter out of chain case during reassembly. Refer to **LUBRICATION** section for lubricating requirements after reassembly and installation.

DRIVE BELTS

Model 1000

Refer to Fig. MU6 for drive belt parts and identification. Remove drive belt guard, then loosen engine pulley set screw and remove pulley. Remove idler pulley retaining nut, then remove pulley and drive belt. Drive belt size is ½-inch x 26 inches long. Install new belt and reassemble in reverse order of disassembly.

Model 1190 and 1290

Refer to Fig. MU7 for drive belt parts and identification. Remove drive belt guard, then remove hex nut securing belt guide (2) and remove guide from around engine pulley. Remove idler pulley (1) hex nut and remove idler pulley from idler bracket (4). Slide belt off of pulleys and install a new belt. Drive belt size is ½-inch x 48 inches long. Complete reassembly in reverse order of disassembly.

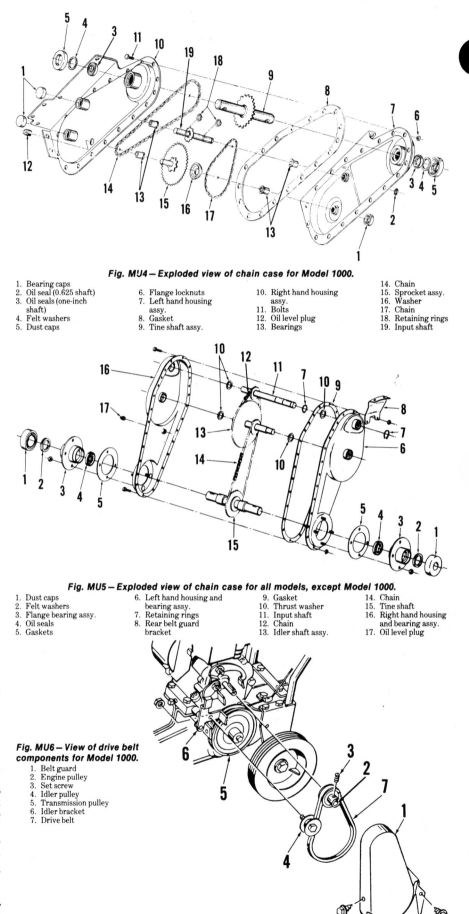

Fig. MU4 — Exploded view of chain case for Model 1000.

1. Bearing caps	6. Flange locknuts	14. Chain
2. Oil seal (0.625 shaft)	7. Left hand housing assy.	15. Sprocket assy.
3. Oil seals (one-inch shaft)	8. Gasket	16. Washer
4. Felt washers	9. Tine shaft assy.	17. Chain
5. Dust caps	10. Right hand housing assy.	18. Retaining rings
	11. Bolts	19. Input shaft
	12. Oil level plug	
	13. Bearings	

Fig. MU5 — Exploded view of chain case for all models, except Model 1000.

1. Dust caps	6. Left hand housing and bearing assy.	9. Gasket	14. Chain
2. Felt washers	7. Retaining rings	10. Thrust washer	15. Tine shaft
3. Flange bearing assy.	8. Rear belt guard bracket	11. Input shaft	16. Right hand housing and bearing assy.
4. Oil seals		12. Chain	17. Oil level plug
5. Gaskets		13. Idler shaft assy.	

Fig. MU6 — View of drive belt components for Model 1000.

1. Belt guard
2. Engine pulley
3. Set screw
4. Idler pulley
5. Transmission pulley
6. Idler bracket
7. Drive belt

Model 1202, 1203, 1302 and 1303

Refer to Fig. MU8 for drive belt parts and identification. Remove drive belt guard. On Models 1203 and 1303 remove tin shield (8) on front of tiller. Remove belt guide (4) from around engine pulley. Remove reverse belt from reverse idler and input pulley (6). Drive belt size is ½-inch x 39 inches long. Remove idler pulley (3) retaining nut and remove pulley from idler bracket. Remove forward drive belt from engine pulley (5) and transmission pulley (7). Drive belt size is ½-inch x 48 inches long. Install new belts and reassemble in reverse order of disassembly.

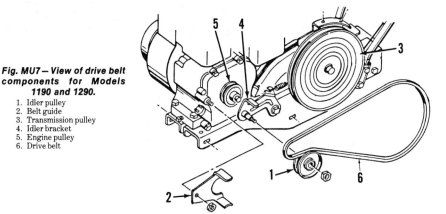

Fig. MU7 — View of drive belt components for Models 1190 and 1290.

1. Idler pulley
2. Belt guide
3. Transmission pulley
4. Idler bracket
5. Engine pulley
6. Drive belt

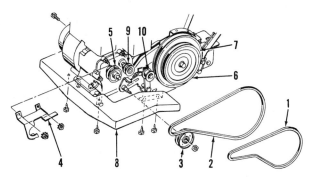

Fig. MU8 — View of drive belt components for Models 1202, 1203, 1302 and 1303.

1. Reverse drive belt
2. Forward drive belt
3. Forward idler pulley
4. Belt guide
5. Crankshaft (forward) pulley
6. Reverse drive pulley
7. Forward drive pulley
8. Shield
9. Camshaft (reverse) pulley
10. Reverse idler pulley

J.C. PENNEY

J.C. PENNEY CO., INC.
11800 West Burleigh Street,
Milwaukee, Wisconsin 53201

The following J.C. Penney tillers were manufactured for J.C. Penney Co., Inc., by MTD Products, Cleveland, Ohio and by Atlas Tool & Manufacturing Co., St. Louis, Missouri. Service procedures for these J.C. Penney models will not differ greatly from those given for similar MTD and Atlas models. However, parts are not necessarily interchangeable and should be obtained from J.C. Penney Co., Inc.

J.C. Penney Model	J.C. Penney Catalog No.	Atlas Section	MTD Section
3040	812-0628	12-5100	....
3041	812-0313	....	405
3046	812-0644	....	408

ROPER

ROPER OUTDOOR POWER EQUIPMENT
P.O. Box 1687
Orangeburg, SC 29116

Model	Engine Make	Engine Series	Power Rating	No. of Forward Speeds	Power Reverse?	Tilling Width	Drive Type
RF300	B&S	80000	3 hp (2.2 kW)	1	No	17 in. (43.2 cm)	Chain
RF500	B&S	130000	5 hp (3.7 kW)	1	No	26 in. (66 cm)	Chain
RF550	B&S	130000	5 hp (3.7 kW)	1	Yes	26 in. (66 cm)	Chain
RT130	B&S	80000	3 hp (2.2 kW)	1	Yes	14 in. (35.6 cm)	Chain
RT150	B&S	130000	5 hp (3.7 kW)	1	Yes	17 in. (43.2 cm)	Chain
RT180	B&S	190000	8 hp (6.0 kW)	1	Yes	21 in. (53.3 cm)	Chain

LUBRICATION

ENGINE

All Models

Refer to appropriate Briggs & Stratton engine section for engine lubrication specifications. Recommended oil is SAE 30 oil meeting API specification SD, SE or SF. Use SAE 10W-30 oil during cold weather operation. Recommended fuel is unleaded gasoline with regular leaded gasoline an acceptable substitute. Manufacturer does not recommended using gasoline containing alcohol additives.

TRANSMISSION

Models RF300, RF500 and RF550

Transmission on front tine tillers is a sealed unit and does not require lubrication. If repair of transmission becomes necessary, the transmission must be renewed as a unit assembly.

Models RT130, RT150 and RT180

Transmission on rear tine tillers does not require routine lubrication unless disassembled for repair or component renewal. Recommended lubricant is Plastilub number 1 grease available from the manufacturer. Minimum capacity of transmission on Models RT130 and RT150 is 8 ounces (237 mL) or 14 ounces (414 mL) on Model RT180.

MAINTENANCE

All Models

Inspect all fasteners for looseness and tighten as necessary. Check control linkage and cables for freedom of movement and excessive play. Inspect drive belt(s) for excessive stretching, wear, cracks or other damage and renew as necessary. Inspect belt pulleys and renew if excessively worn or damaged. After every five hours of operation, lubricate all pivot points with a suitable oil.

Fig. R1—On front tine models, adjust clutch by loosening screw (2) and sliding cable (4) as necessary to provide correct clutch operation.
1. Clutch lever
2. Screw
3. Clip
4. Clutch cable

ADJUSTMENT

CLUTCH CONTROL

Models RF300, RF500 and RF550

Check clutch cable adjustment by starting engine and depressing clutch lever (1—Fig. R1). Tines should engage when lever (1) is depressed and stop movement when lever is released. To ad-

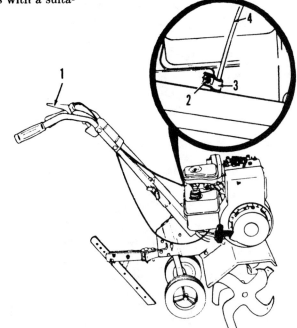

just, loosen screw (2) and slide cable (4) up or down as necessary to provide correct tine operation.

Models RT130, RT150 and RT180

To check clutch cable adjustment, measure distance (D—Fig. R2) of clutch spring (5) with clutch lever disengaged. Engage clutch lever and remeasure distance (D). Spring (5) should stretch 5/8 inch (3.4 mm) with clutch engaged. Loosen clip securing clutch cable and move cable to adjust.

OVERHAUL

ENGINE

All Models

Engine model is stamped on engine blower housing. Refer to appropriate

Briggs & Stratton engine section for overhaul procedures.

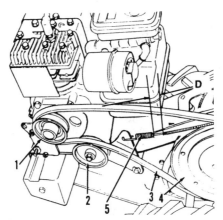

Fig. R2—On rear tine models, clutch spring (5) should stretch a distance (D) of 5/8 inch (3.4 mm) when clutch is applied. Loosen clutch cable retaining clip and slide cable as necessary to adjust.

1. Engine pulley
2. Idler pulley
3. Drive belt
4. Transmission pulley
5. Clutch spring

TRANSMISSION

Models RF300, RF500 and RF550

No provision for repair is made for transmission used on front tine models. If transmission malfunction is noted, complete transmission must be renewed as a unit assembly.

Models RT130, RT150 and RT180

Refer to Figs. R3 and R4 for exploded views of transmission assemblies used on rear tine models. Disassembly for repair or component renewal is evident after inspection of unit and referral to appropriate exploded view. Inspect all components for excessive wear or damage and renew as necessary. Inspect bearings for roughness and gears for broken teeth or other damage. Renew all seals and gaskets. Refer to LUBRICATION section for lubrication requirements after reassembly.

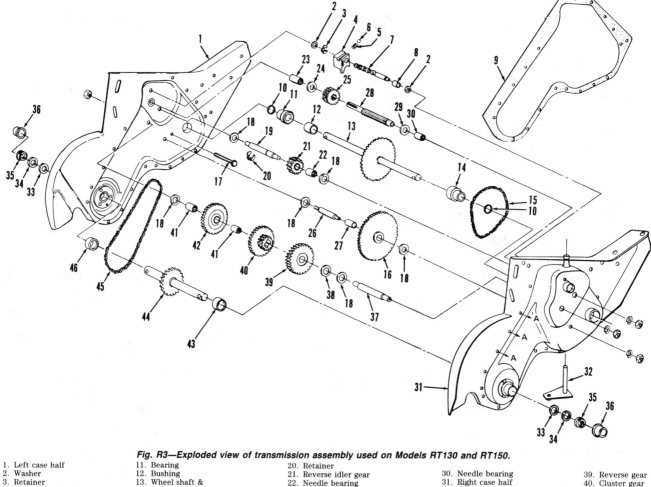

Fig. R3—Exploded view of transmission assembly used on Models RT130 and RT150.

1. Left case half	11. Bearing	20. Retainer
2. Washer	12. Bushing	21. Reverse idler gear
3. Retainer	13. Wheel shaft &	22. Needle bearing
4. Shift fork	sprocket assy.	23. Needle bearing
5. Spring	14. Bearing	24. Thrust washer
6. Steel ball	15. Chain	25. Input pinion gear
7. Shift shaft	16. Sprocket	26. Reduction shaft
8. Spacer	17. Screw	27. Spacer
9. Gasket	18. Washer	28. Input shaft
10. "O" ring	19. Reverse idler shaft	29. Thrust washer

30. Needle bearing	39. Reverse gear
31. Right case half	40. Cluster gear
32. Shift lever	41. Needle bearing
33. Seal	42. Sprocket
34. Seal	43. Spacer
35. Ring	44. Tine shaft &
36. Cup	sprocket assy.
37. Reduction shaft	45. Chain
38. Thrust washer	46. Spacer

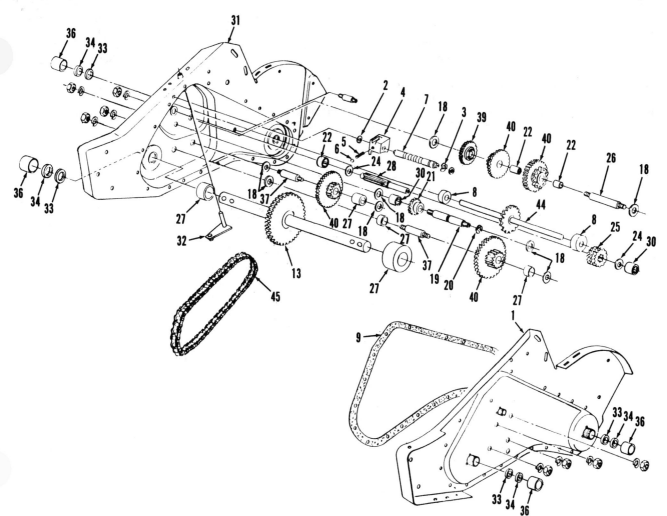

Fig. R4—Exploded view of transmission assembly used on Model RT180. Refer to legend in Fig. R3 for component identification.

DRIVE BELTS

Model RF550

Remove belt guard. Remove reverse idler pulley (1—Fig. R5) and reverse belt (6). Work forward belt (5) off transmission pulley (4), then engine pulley (2).

Install forward belt (5) around engine pulley (2) and over top of forward idler pulley (3), then work over transmission pulley (4). Turn reverse belt inside out and place into reverse idler pulley (1) and reinstall pulley (1) on arm (8). Make sure belt (6) is located on top of belt guide (7) and work belt over transmission pulley (4).

Forward belt is ½ inch wide x 41 inches long and manufacturer's part number is 4833H. Reverse belt is 3/8 inch wide x 44 inches long and manufacturer's part number is 2614J. Refer to ADJUSTMENT section to adjust clutch control.

Fig. R5—View of drive belt arrangement and related components on Model RF550.

1. Reverse idler pulley
2. Engine pulley
3. Forward idler pulley
4. Transmission pulley
5. Forward belt (inside position)
6. Reverse belt (outside position)
7. Belt guide
8. Reverse idler arm

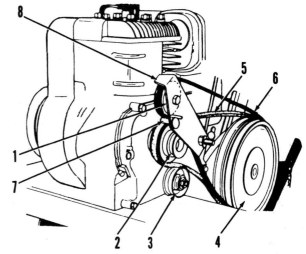

Models RF300 and RF500

Drive belt for Model RF300 is 3/8 inch wide x 40 inches long and manufacturer's part number is 9179R. Belt for Model RF500 is 17/32 inch wide x 41-5/16 inches long and part number is 9180R. To renew belt, remove belt guard and work belt off transmission pulley, then off engine pulley. Reinstall belt on engine pulley first, then over idler pulley and onto transmission pulley. Refer to

ADJUSTMENT section to adjust clutch control.

Models RT130, RT150 and RT180

Manufacturer's part number and belt size for rear tine models are as follows: Models RT130 and RT150, part 102143, ½ inch wide x 52-3/4 inches long; Model RT180, part 8377J, ½ inch wide x 59 inches long.

Remove hairpin clip and pin from left drive wheel and slide wheel away from tiller approximately 1-1/2 inches (38.1 mm). Remove belt guard and loosen two belt guides near transmission pulley. Remove belt from idler pulley, then from engine and transmission pulleys.

Reinstall belt on transmission pulley, then onto engine pulley and idler pulley. Make sure belt is properly positioned on top of idler pulley and that transmission and engine pulleys are aligned. Loosen set screws in pulleys to align.

ROTO-HOE

The ROTO-HOE Co.
100 Auburn Rd.
Newbury, OH 44065

Model	Engine Make	Engine Series	Engine Horsepower	No. of Forward Speeds	Power Reverse?	Tilling Width (In.)	Drive Type
SP	Tec.	H35	3.5	2	No	12-24	Chain
SP	Tec.	H50	5	2	No	12-24	Chain
220	Tec.	H35	3.5	1	No	12-24	Chain
220	Tec.	HS50	5	1	No	12-24	Chain
904	B&S	110000	4	1	Yes	15.25	Chain
910	Tec.	H50	5	4	Yes	16.5	Chain
910	B&S	110000	4	5	Yes	18	Chain
910	B&S	130000	5	5	Yes	18	Chain
990	B&S	130000	5	5	Yes	18-24	Chain
990	Tec.	H60	6	4	Yes	18-24	Chain
990	Tec.	HM80	8	4	Yes	18-24	Chain
990	Kohler	K-181	8	5	Yes	18-24	Chain
990	Kohler	M8	8	5	Yes	18-24	Chain

LUBRICATION

ENGINE

Refer to appropriate Briggs & Stratton, Tecumseh or Kohler engine section for engine lubrication specification.

Recommended oil grade is SAE 30 or equivalent. Recommended fuel is either regular or low-lead gasoline having an octane rating of 90 or higher.

CHAIN AND WHEEL DRIVE

All Models

Lubricate grease fittings every 25 hours of operation with a good grade multi-purpose grease. Chains and transmissions are packed with grease at the time of manufacture and should not require additional lubrication.

Oil transport wheel bearings on front tine models every 25 hours of operation.

MAINTENANCE

Inspect all fasteners for looseness and retighten as needed. Check control levers, linkage and cables for freedom of movement and excessive play. Inspect drive belt(s) for excessive stretching, wear, cracks, or any other damage. Install new belt(s) if needed. Inspect all belt pulleys and renew if damaged or excessively worn.

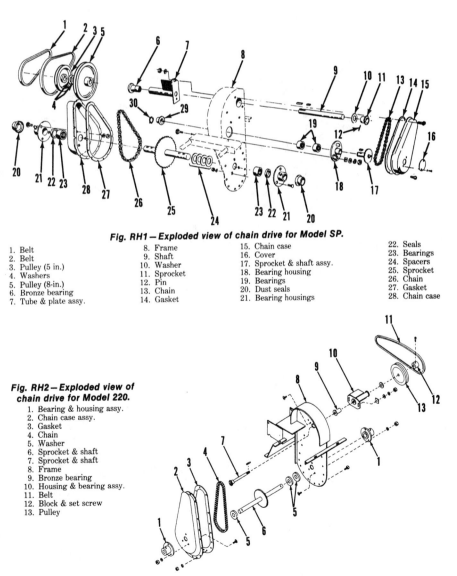

Fig. RH1 — Exploded view of chain drive for Model SP.

1. Belt	8. Frame	15. Chain case	22. Seals
2. Belt	9. Shaft	16. Cover	23. Bearings
3. Pulley (5 in.)	10. Washer	17. Sprocket & shaft assy.	24. Spacers
4. Washers	11. Sprocket	18. Bearing housing	25. Sprocket
5. Pulley (8-in.)	12. Pin	19. Bearings	26. Chain
6. Bronze bearing	13. Chain	20. Dust seals	27. Gasket
7. Tube & plate assy.	14. Gasket	21. Bearing housings	28. Chain case

Fig. RH2 — Exploded view of chain drive for Model 220.

1. Bearing & housing assy.
2. Chain case assy.
3. Gasket
4. Chain
5. Washer
6. Sprocket & shaft
7. Sprocket & shaft
8. Frame
9. Bronze bearing
10. Housing & bearing assy.
11. Belt
12. Block & set screw
13. Pulley

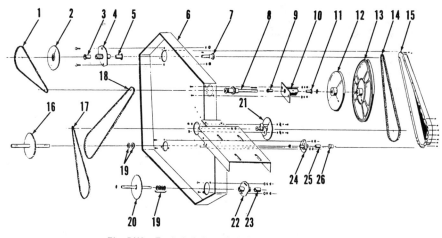

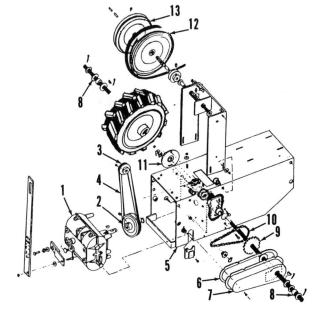

Fig. RH3 — *Exploded view of chain drive for Model 904.*

1. Intermediate chain
2. Sprocket
3. Bearing
4. Bearing housing assy.
5. Bearing
6. Frame
7. Shaft
8. Shaft & sprocket

9. Bronze bearing
10. Bearing housing assy.
11. Bronze bearing
12. Pulley (5 in.)
13. Pulley (8 in.)
14. Chain
15. Chain case assy.

16. Sprocket & shaft, tiller drive
17. Chain, wheel drive
18. Chain, tiller drive
19. Washers
20. Sprocket & shaft, wheel drive

21. Sprocket
22. Bearing housing
23. Bearing
24. Bearing housing
25. Bearing
26. Dust cap

Fig. RH4 — *Exploded view of wheel drive components for Models 910 and 990.*

1. Transmission
2. Pulley
3. Pulley
4. Belt
5. Frame
6. Gasket
7. Chain case
8. Wheel drive shaft
9. Sprocket
10. Chain
11. Bearing carrier
12. Pulley (to engine)
13. Pulley (to tiller)

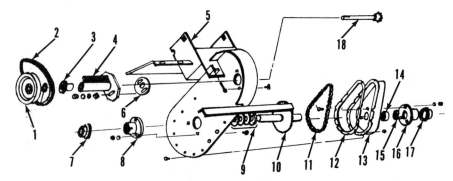

Fig. RH5 — *Exploded view of chain drive for tiller used on Models 910 and 990.*

1. Pulley (6 in.)
2. Belt
3. Bronze bearing
4. Bearing housing
5. Frame

6. Gasket
7. Dust shield
8. Bearing housing
9. Washers

10. Sprocket & shaft
11. Chain
12. Gasket
13. Chain case

14. Bearing
15. Wiper bearing
16. Bearing housing
17. Bearing
18. Shaft & sprocket

ADJUSTMENT

CHAIN

Model 904

Remove chain guard cover (15 – Fig. RH3) from left hand side and adjust bearing equally on both sides of unit. Slots for adjustment are provided on bearing housing (22); note that a similar bearing is located on opposite side of frame. Align square serrated washers with serrations on bearing housing before tightening bolts.

SHIFT CONTROL AND DRIVE BELT

Model 904

Shift control adjustments are provided at both top and bottom of shift control handle near idler arm assembly.

To adjust drive belt tension, remove cotter pins at either end or both ends of shift control rod and reengage in next position.

OVERHAUL

ENGINE

All Models

Engine model number is stamped on blower housing for Briggs & Stratton engines and on an attached data plate for Kohler and Tecumseh engines. Refer to appropriate Briggs & Stratton, Kohler or Tecumseh engine section for overhaul procedures.

TRANSMISSION

Models 910 and 990

Transmission is a Peerless 700 series with four or five forward speeds and one reverse speed.

Thoroughly clean outside of transmission and remove screw (5 – Fig. RH6), spring (4) and detent ball (3) from upper case half (1). Remove six cap screws and separate case halves (1 and 41). Remove shifter shaft and fork assembly (26). Lift chain, shaft and gear assemblies (8 through 37) out of lower case half (41). Remove snap rings (38 and 46) from input shaft (44) and remove input shaft and pinion gear (39) assembly.

Check chain (25) for stretching and check gears for broken teeth or other damage. Inspect shafts, bushings and thrust washers for excessive wear or scoring. Inspect keys (19) for excessive wear in shaft slots. Replace all components that are excessively worn or damaged.

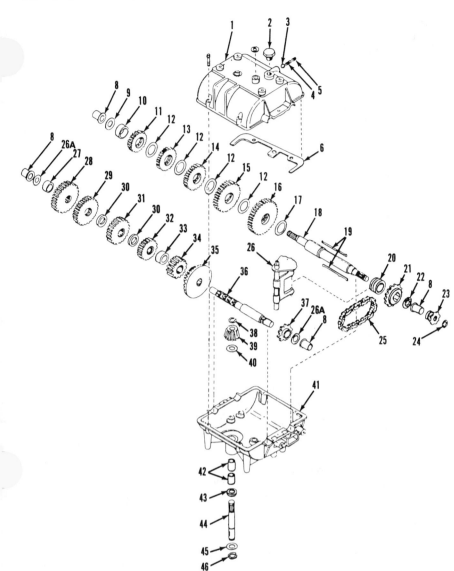

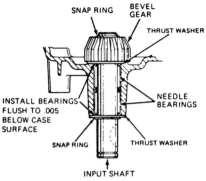

Fig. RH7—Input shaft needle bearings must be installed flush to 0.005-inch (0.13 mm) below case surface.

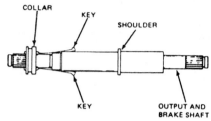

Fig. RH8—Install shifter collar and shifter (drive) keys on output shaft as shown. Thick side of collar must face shoulder on shaft.

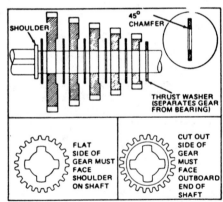

Fig. RH9—View showing correct installation of thrust washers and gears on output shaft. The 45° inside chamfer on thrust washers must face the shoulder on the shaft.

Fig. RH6—Exploded view of Peerless 700 series gearbox used on late Models 910 and 990. Note that transmission shown has 5 speeds; transmission used in early Model 910 and 990 tillers is similar but has 4 speeds.

1. Case, upper half	13. Gear, 22T	25. Chain	35. Gear, 42T
2. Filler plug	14. Gear, 25T	26. Shift rod & fork	36. Countershaft
3. Ball	15. Gear, 30T	assy.	37. Sprocket
4. Spring	16. Gear, 37T	26A. Thrust race	38. Snap ring
5. Screw	17. Thrust washer	27. Spacer	39. Pinion gear
6. Gasket	18. Shaft	28. Gear, 30T	40. Thrust race
8. Bushing	19. Key	29. Gear, 28T	41. Case, lower half
9. Washer	20. Collar	30. Washer	42. Needle bearings
10. Spacer	21. Sprocket, 18T	31. Gear, 25T	43. "O" ring
11. Gear, 20T	22. Thrust race	32. Gear, 15T	44. Input shaft
12. Thrust washer	23. Sprocket	33. Spacer	45. Thrust race
	24. Snap ring	34. Gear, 12T	46. Snap ring

Reassemble by reversing disassembly procedure. Install a new gasket (6). When installing shift collar (20) and keys (19) on shaft (18), the thin side of collar must face towards outer end of shaft. Refer to Fig. RH8. When assembling gears on shaft, note that the 45 degree chamfer on thrust washers (12–Fig. RH6) must face shoulder on shaft (18) and that flat side of gears must also face shoulder of shaft as shown in Fig. RH9. Input shaft needle bearings (42–Fig. RH6) must be installed flush or 0.005-inch (0.13 mm) below inside and outside surfaces of case (41) as shown in Fig. RH7.

SEARS

SEARS, ROEBUCK & COMPANY
Sears Tower
Chicago, Illinois 60684

Model	Engine Make	Engine Series	Engine Horsepower	No. of Forward Speeds	Power Reverse?	Tilling Width (In.)	Drive Type
29852	B&S	60000	2	1	No	15	Chain
29943	B&S	80000	3	1	No	17	Chain
29945	B&S	130000	5	1	Yes	24	Chain
29936	Craftsman	.....	6	1	Yes	24	Chain
29937	Craftsman	.....	6	1	No	24	Chain
29966	Craftsman	.....	6	2	Yes	21	Gear & Chain
29968	Craftsman	.....	8	2	Yes	21	Gear & Chain
29958	B&S	190000	8	2	No	28	Gear
299130	Craftsman	744012	3.5	1	Yes	14	Chain
299150	B&S	130000	5	1	Yes	17	Chain
299382	Craftsman	736062	6	1	Yes	24	Chain

LUBRICATION

ENGINE

All Models

Refer to appropriate Briggs and Stratton engine section for Briggs and Stratton engine lubrication specifications. Refer to appropriate Tecumseh engine section for Craftsman engine lubrication specifications.

Recommended oil grade is SAE 30 or equivalent. Recommended fuel is either regular or low-lead gasoline having an octane rating of 90 or higher. The use of non-leaded gasolines reduces cylinder head deposits, but could shorten engine valve life if carburetor is adjusted too lean.

CHAIN DRIVE

All Models

Chain case lubricant cannot be added on any models except Models 29966 and 29968. Chain case on other models is factory sealed and must be removed and disassembled in order to add or change grease in case.

GEAR CASE

Model 29958

Gear case oil should be checked at least every 10 hours of operation. Recommended lubricant is SAE 30 heavy duty detergent oil or suitable equivalent.

To check gear case oil place tiller on a level surface. Clean dirt from around gear case housing and remove oil level plug (1–Fig. SE1). Oil level should be at bottom of plug hole. If oil level is low add oil through level hole until it begins to run out hole. Reinstall and tighten plug.

Models 29966, 29968, 299130, 299150 and 299382

Gear case is factory sealed and must be removed and disassembled in order to add or change grease in case. Refer to **OVERHAUL** section for servicing grease.

MAINTENANCE

Inspect all fasteners for looseness and retighten as needed. Check control levers, linkage and cables for freedom of movement and excessive play. Inspect drive belt(s) for excessive stretching, wear, cracks or any other damage. In-stall new belt(s) if needed. Inspect all belt pulleys and renew if damaged or excessively worn. Transport wheels on Models 29852, 29943, 29945, 29937,

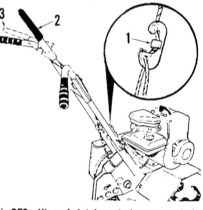

Fig SE2 – View of clutch control components for Model 29852.
1. Adjusting clip
2. Clutch lever in released position
3. Clutch lever in engaged position

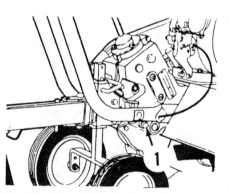

Fig. SE1 – View of oil level plug for Model 29958. Oil level plug is shown at (1).

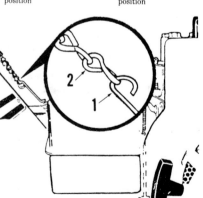

Fig. SE3 – View of clutch adjusting components for Models 29937 and 29943.
1. Idler spring
2. Chain

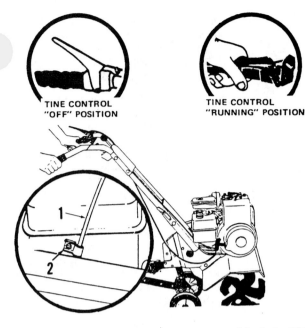

TINE CONTROL "OFF" POSITION

TINE CONTROL "RUNNING" POSITION

29958 and 299382 should be lubricated occasionally with SAE 30 oil.

ADJUSTMENT

CLUTCH CONTROL

Model 29852

Refer to Fig. SE2 for view of clutch control components. Adjustment is achieved by repositioning clutch cable in adjusting clip (1). With clutch lever in released position idler pulley arm should just touch drive belt cover. To check for correct adjustment, make sure clutch lever is in released position and pull on starter rope handle. If tines do not turn, then adjustment is correct. If tines do turn, then clutch cable will need to be adjusted.

Fig. SE4—View of clutch operation and adjusting components for Models 29936 and 29945.

1. Clutch control cable
2. Retaining clip screw

Models 29937 and 29943

Refer to Fig. SE3 for view of clutch adjustment components. Adjustment is achieved by repositioning chain (2) in idler spring loop (1). To check for correct adjustment, make sure clutch lever is in released position and pull on starter rope handle. If tines do not turn, then

adjustment is correct. If tines do turn, then chain will need to be adjusted.

Models 29936 and 29945

Refer to Fig. SE4 for view of clutch adjustment components. Adjustment is achieved by sliding clutch cable (1) in retaining clip (2). To check for correct adjustment, make sure clutch lever is in released position and pull on starter rope handle. If tines do not turn, then adjustment is correct. If tines do turn, then clutch cable will need to be adjusted.

Model 29958

Refer to Fig. SE5 for view of clutch adjustment components. Adjustment is achieved by loosening wing nut (4) and turning turnbuckle (2) on clutch rod (1). To check for correct adjustment, make sure clutch lever is in released position and pull on starter rope handle. If drive belt does not turn, then adjustment is correct. If drive belt does turn, then turnbuckle will need to be adjusted.

Models 29966 and 29968

TINE DRIVE BELT. Refer to Fig. SE6 for view of belt adjustment com-

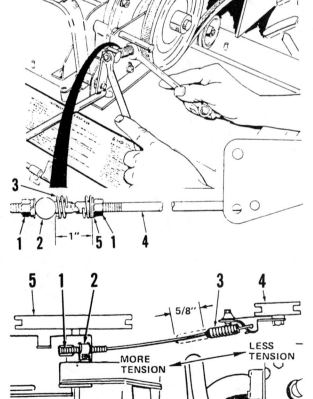

Fig. SE6—View of tine drive belt adjusting components for Models 29966 and 29968.

1. Adjustment nuts
2. Idler arm swivel
3. Tine control spring
4. Adjustment rod
5. Washer

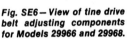

Fig. SE5—View of clutch operation and adjusting components for Model 29958.

1. Clutch rod
2. Turnbuckle
3. Lockwasher
4. Wing nut
5. Clutch lever in released position
6. Clutch lever in engaged position

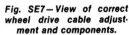

Fig. SE7—View of correct wheel drive cable adjustment and components.

1. Control cable
2. Clip & screw
3. Extension spring
4. Idler pulley assy.
5. Ground drive input pulley

MORE TENSION   LESS TENSION

5/8"

ponents. Place tine engagement lever in disengaged position, then remove drive belt cover. Place engagement lever in engaged position. Turn adjustment nuts (1) until there is a one-inch distance be-

tween idler arm swivel (2) and washer (5). Reinstall drive belt cover.

GROUND DRIVE BELT. Refer to Fig. SE7 for view of clutch adjustment

components. Adjustment is achieved by sliding control cable (1) in retaining clip (2). There should be a 5/8 inch (15.9 mm) stretch in extension spring (3) when clutch lever is completely engaged.

Models 299130 and 299150

Refer to Fig. SE7A. Extension spring (1) should stretch (A) 5/8 inch (15.9 mm) when clutch control handle is held down. Adjustment is made by loosening clip (2) and sliding cable in or out as needed.

Model 299382

Refer to Fig. SE15. Adjust belt guide (7) position so there is 3/16-inch (4.8 mm) clearance between belt guide and belt when clutch control lever is held down. Align engine and transmission pulleys as shown in Figs. SE17 and SE18.

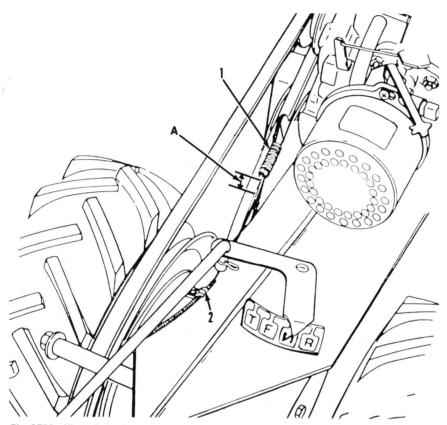

Fig. SE7A — View of clutch control extension spring (1) showing 5/8-inch (15.88 mm) stretch (A) on Models 299130 and 299150.

OVERHAUL

ENGINE

All Models

Engine model number is stamped on blower housing for Briggs and Stratton engines. Engine make and series number is marked on data plate attached to engine for Craftsman engines. Refer to appropriate Briggs and Stratton engine section for overhaul procedures. Refer to appropriate Tecumsech engine section for Craftsman engine overhaul procedures.

CHAIN CASE

All Models

On all models except Models 29966, 29968, 299130 and 299150, chain case is factory sealed and must be replaced as a complete unit if service is required. Chain case parts breakdown and identification is shown in Fig. SE8 for Models 29966 and 29968 or in Fig. SE10A for Models 299130 and 299150.

OIL SEAL INSTALLATION. Remove tines from tine shaft. Use a seal puller to remove seals out of case hub. Clean tine shaft with emery cloth. Drive new seals in until outside face is flush with case hub.

INSPECTION. Inspect and renew all components that are worn or damaged. Install new gasket and seals. Lubricate chains, sprockets and bearings with a light film of grease during reassembly. Keep all dirt and foreign matter out of chain case during reassembly. Recom-

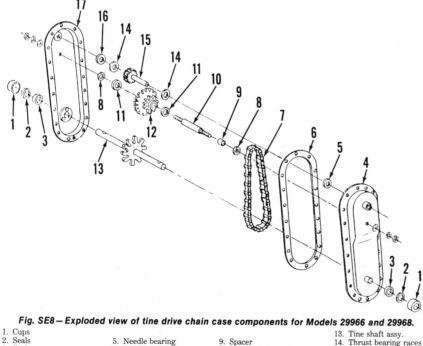

Fig. SE8 — Exploded view of tine drive chain case components for Models 29966 and 29968.

1. Cups	5. Needle bearing	9. Spacer	13. Tine shaft assy.
2. Seals	6. Gasket	10. Intermediate shaft	14. Thrust bearing races
3. Seals	7. Chain	11. Needle bearings	15. Input shaft assy.
4. Chain case cover,	8. Washers	12. Sprocket	16. Needle bearing
R.H.			17. Chain case cover, L.H.

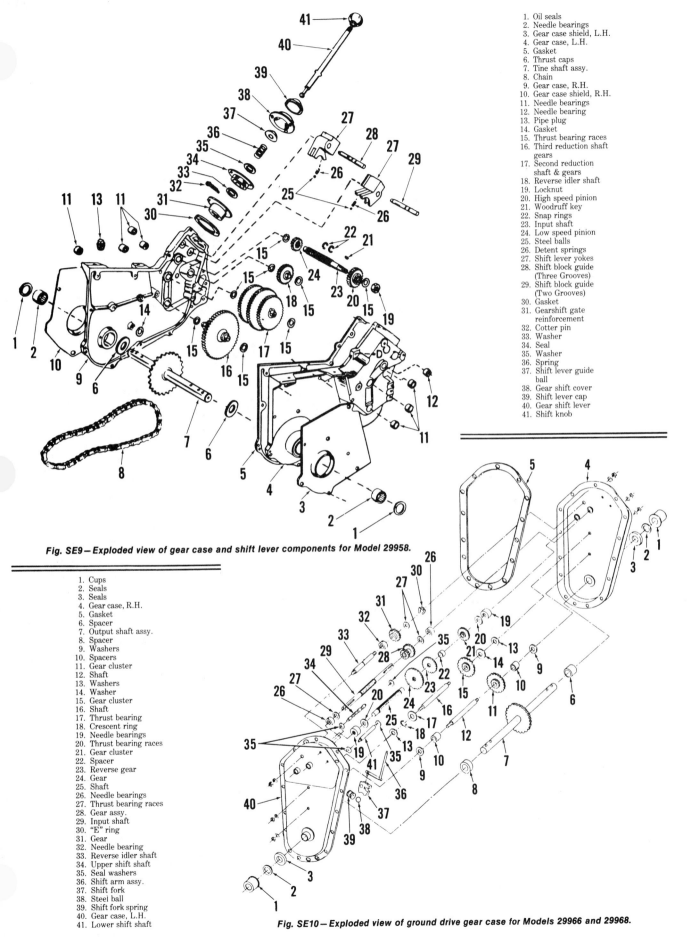

1. Oil seals
2. Needle bearings
3. Gear case shield, L.H.
4. Gear case, L.H.
5. Gasket
6. Thrust caps
7. Tine shaft assy.
8. Chain
9. Gear case, R.H.
10. Gear case shield, R.H.
11. Needle bearings
12. Needle bearing
13. Pipe plug
14. Gasket
15. Thrust bearing races
16. Third reduction shaft gears
17. Second reduction shaft & gears
18. Reverse idler shaft
19. Locknut
20. High speed pinion
21. Woodruff key
22. Snap rings
23. Input shaft
24. Low speed pinion
25. Steel balls
26. Detent springs
27. Shift lever yokes
28. Shift block guide (Three Grooves)
29. Shift block guide (Two Grooves)
30. Gasket
31. Gearshift gate reinforcement
32. Cotter pin
33. Washer
34. Seal
35. Washer
36. Spring
37. Shift lever guide ball
38. Gear shift cover
39. Shift lever cap
40. Gear shift lever
41. Shift knob

Fig. SE9 — *Exploded view of gear case and shift lever components for Model 29958.*

1. Cups
2. Seals
3. Seals
4. Gear case, R.H.
5. Gasket
6. Spacer
7. Output shaft assy.
8. Spacer
9. Washers
10. Spacers
11. Gear cluster
12. Shaft
13. Washers
14. Washer
15. Gear cluster
16. Shaft
17. Thrust bearing
18. Crescent ring
19. Needle bearings
20. Thrust bearing races
21. Gear cluster
22. Spacer
23. Reverse gear
24. Gear
25. Shaft
26. Needle bearings
27. Thrust bearing races
28. Gear assy.
29. Input shaft
30. "E" ring
31. Gear
32. Needle bearing
33. Reverse idler shaft
34. Upper shift shaft
35. Seal washers
36. Shift arm assy.
37. Shift fork
38. Steel ball
39. Shift fork spring
40. Gear case, L.H.
41. Lower shift shaft

Fig. SE10 — *Exploded view of ground drive gear case for Models 29966 and 29968.*

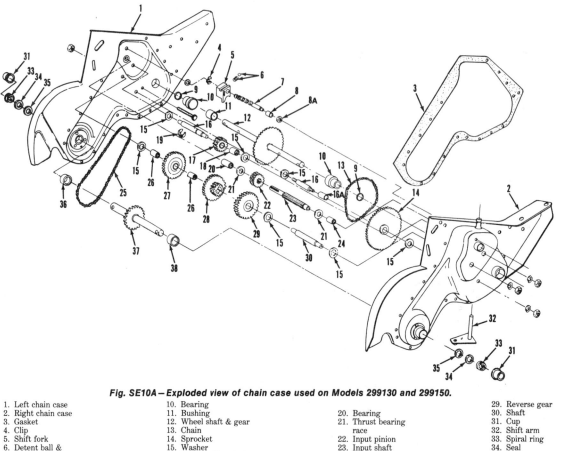

Fig. SE10A — Exploded view of chain case used on Models 299130 and 299150.

1. Left chain case	10. Bearing	20. Bearing	29. Reverse gear
2. Right chain case	11. Bushing	21. Thrust bearing	30. Shaft
3. Gasket	12. Wheel shaft & gear	race	31. Cup
4. Clip	13. Chain	22. Input pinion	32. Shift arm
5. Shift fork	14. Sprocket	23. Input shaft	33. Spiral ring
6. Detent ball &	15. Washer	24. Bearing	34. Seal
spring	16. Reverse idler shaft	25. Chain	35. Seal
7. Shift shaft	16A. Spacer	26. Bearing	36. Spacer
8. Spacer	17. Reverse idler gear	27. Sprocket	37. Tine shaft &
8A. Seal	18. Needle bearing	28. Gear	sprocket
9. "O" Ring	19. Clip		38. Spacer

mended lubricant for all models except Models 299130 and 299150 is six ounces of Plastilube #1 grease or suitable equivalent. Recommended lubricant for Models 299130 and 299150 is eight ounces of Plastilube #1 grease or suitable equivalent. To fill chain case with grease, lay right half of case on its side, add grease and assemble left half to right half. Complete reassembly and reinstall in tiller frame.

Fig. SE11 — View of single drive belt and components for Models 29852, 29943, 29937 and 29958.

1. Engine pulley
2. Idler pulley
3. Transmission pulley
4. Drive belt

GEAR CASE

Model 29958

OIL SEAL INSTALLATION. Remove tines from tine shaft. Use a seal puller to remove seals from case hub. Clean tine shaft with emery cloth. Drive new seals in until outside face is flush with case hub.

INSPECTION. Refer to Fig. SE9 for parts breakdown and identification. Inspect and renew all components that are worn or damaged. Install new gasket and seals. Lubricate gears and bearings with a light film of oil during reassembly. Keep all dirt and foreign matter out

Fig. SE12 — View of drive belt arrangement and components for Models 29936 and 29945.

1. Engine pulley
2. Idler pulley
3. Transmission pulley
4. Reverse isler pulley
5. Reverse drive belt
6. Forward drive belt
7. Reverse idler arm

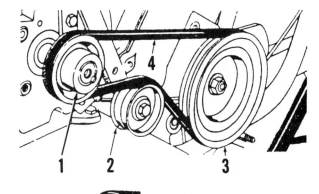

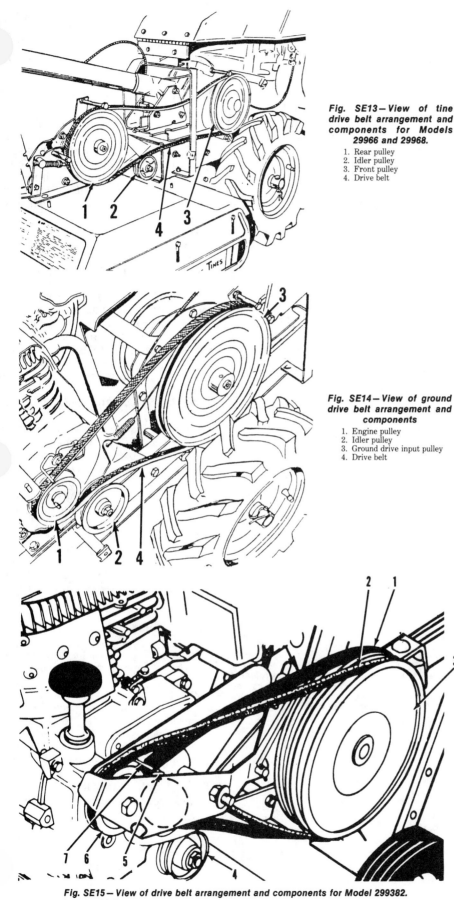

Fig. SE13 – View of tine drive belt arrangement and components for Models 29966 and 29968.
1. Rear pulley
2. Idler pulley
3. Front pulley
4. Drive belt

Fig. SE14 – View of ground drive belt arrangement and components
1. Engine pulley
2. Idler pulley
3. Ground drive input pulley
4. Drive belt

Fig. SE15 – View of drive belt arrangement and components for Model 299382.
1. Forward belt
2. Reverse belt
3. Transmission pulley
4. Idler pulley
5. Engine pulley
6. Reverse idler pulley
7. Belt guide

of gear case during reassembly. Refer to **LUBRICATION** section for lubrication requirements after reassembly and installation.

Models 29966, 29968, 299130 and 299150

OIL SEAL INSTALLATION. Remove drive wheels from output shaft. Using a seal puller pull seals out of case hub. If seal puller is not available use an awl and screwdriver to pry seals out. Clean tine shaft with emery cloth. Drive new seals in until outside face is flush with case hub.

INSPECTION. Refer to Fig. SE10 for parts breakdown and identification for Models 29966 and 29968. Refer to Fig. SE10A for parts breakdown and identification for Models 299130 and 299150. Inspect and renew all components that are worn or damaged. Install new gasket and seals. Lubricate gears and bearings with a light film of grease during reassembly. Keep all dirt and foreign matter out of gear case during reassembly. Recommended lubricant is Plastilube #1 grease or equivalent. Lubricant capacity is six ounces for Models 29966 & 29968 and eight ounces for Models 299130 & 299150. To fill gear case with grease, lay right half of case on its side, add grease and assemble left half to right half. Complete reassembly and reinstall in tiller frame.

DRIVE BELTS

Models 29852, 29943, 29937 and 29958

Refer to Fig. SE11 for belt routing and parts identification. Remove drive belt cover, then slip drive belt off engine pulley and chain case input pulley. Install new drive belt. Drive belt size for Models 29852 and 29943 is ⅜-inch x 39 inches long. Drive belt size for Model 29937 is ½-inch x 42 inches long. Drive belt size for Model 29958 is ½-inch x 37 inches long. Reinstall drive belt cover. Refer to appropriate **CLUTCH CONTROL ADJUSTMENT** section for readjustment of clutch linkage.

Models 29936 and 29945

Refer to Fig. SE12 for belt(s) arrangement and parts identification. Remove drive belt cover, then remove bolt and nut securing reverse idler pulley (4) to idler arm (7). Remove reverse drive belt from pulleys. To remove forward drive belt, loosen drive belt guide nut and swing belt guide away from belt. Slip drive belt from transmission pulley, then from engine pulley. Install new drive

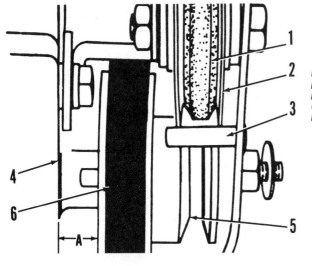

Fig. SE16 — View showing
proper alignment of belt
pulleys on Model 299382.
Distance (A) between engine
pulley and crankcase should
be 5/16-inch (7.9 mm).

1. Reverse belt
2. Reverse idler pulley
3. Idler arm pin
4. Forward belt
5. Engine pulley
6. Crankcase face

belts. Forward drive belt size is ½-inch x
41 inches long. Reassemble in reverse
order of disassembly. Refer to **CLUTCH
CONTROL ADJUSTMENT** section for
adjusting procedures.

Models 29966 and 29968

TINE DRIVE. Refer to Fig. SE13 for
belt routing and parts identification.
Place tine engagement lever in disengaged position. Place control handle to
highest position, then remove drive belt
cover. Loosen drive belt guides, then
slip drive belt off pulleys. Install new
drive belt. Refer to **CLUTCH CONTROL ADJUSTMENT** section for belt
adjusting procedures. Reassemble in
reverse order of disassembly.

GROUND DRIVE. Refer to Fig.
SE14 for belt routing and parts identification. Remove drive belt cover, then
loosen belt guides. Slip belt off engine
pulley and ground drive input pulley. Install new drive belt. Refer to **CLUTCH
CONTROL ADJUSTMENT** section for
adjusting procedures. Reassemble in
reverse order of disassembly.

Models 299130 and 299150

Refer to Fig. SE14 for belt routing
and parts identification. Remove hairpin
clip and rivet from left-hand side wheel
and slide wheel assembly out approximately 1½ inch (38.1 mm). Remove
drive belt cover, then loosen belt guides.
Slip belt away from idler pulley (2) and
remove belt from engine pulley (1) and
input shaft pulley (3). Install new drive
belt and retighten belt guides. Reassemble in reverse order of disassembly.
Refer to **CLUTCH CONTROL
ADJUSTMENT** section for adjusting
procedures.

Model 299382

Refer to Fig. SE15 for belt routing
and parts identification. Remove belt
guard. Unbolt and remove reverse idler
pulley (6) and remove reverse belt (2).
Loosen and move belt guide (7) away
from forward belt (1). Roll belt off
transmission pulley (3), then remove
from engine pulley (5). Reassemble in reverse order of disassembly. Note that
reverse belt is installed inside out. Refer
to **CLUTCH CONTROL ADJUSTMENT** section for adjusting procedures.

Fig. SE17 — View showing
specified clearance (CA) of 1
9/16-inch (39.7 mm) between
transmission input hub (1)
and transmission pulley hub
(2) on Model 299382.

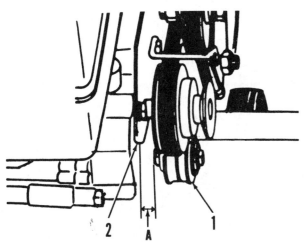

Fig. SE18 — View showing
specified clearance (A) of
5/16-inch (7.9 mm) between
engine pulley (1) and reverse
idler arm assembly (2) on
Model 299382.

SNAPPER

SNAPPER POWER EQUIPMENT
McDonough, GA 30253

(Front Tine Models)

Model	Engine Make	Engine Series	Power Rating	No. of Forward Speeds	Power Reverse?	Tilling Width	Drive Type
300T	B&S	80000	3 hp (2.2 kW)	1	No	26 in. (66 cm)	Chain
300T	Tec.	H30	3 hp (2.2 kW)	1	No	26 in. (66 cm)	Chain
500T	B&S	130000	5 hp (3.7 kW)	1	No	26 in. (66 cm)	Chain
500T	Tec.	H50	5 hp (3.7 kW)	1	No	26 in. (66 cm)	Chain
301T	B&S	80000	3 hp (2.2 kW)	1	No	26 in. (66 cm)	Chain
301TR	B&S	80000	3 hp (2.2 kW)	1	No	26 in. (66 cm)	Chain
401T	B&S	110000	4 hp (3.0 kW)	1	No	26 in. (66 cm)	Chain
401TR	B&S	110000	4 hp (3.0 kW)	1	No	26 in. (66 cm)	Chain
401TCR	Wisc. Robin	W1-145V	4 hp (3.0 kW)	1	No	26 in. (66 cm)	Chain
501T	Tec.	H50	5 hp (3.7 kW)	1	No	26 in. (66 cm)	Chain
501TR	Tec.	H50	5 hp (3.7 kW)	1	No	26 in. (66 cm)	Chain
501TC	B&S	130000	5 hp (3.7 kW)	1	No	26 in. (66 cm)	Chain
501TCR	B&S	130000	5 hp (3.7 kW)	1	No	26 in. (66 cm)	Chain

* On some models, extension tines may be added to extend tilling width to 36 inches (91.4 cm).

LUBRICATION

ENGINE

All Models

Refer to appropriate Briggs & Stratton, Tecumseh or Wisconsin Robin engine section for engine lubrication specifications. Recommended oil grade is SAE 30 or a suitable equivalent. Recommended fuel is either regular or low-lead gasoline having an octane rating of 90 or higher. The use of unleaded gasoline reduces cylinder head deposits, but could shorten engine valve life if carburetor is adjusted too lean.

CHAIN DRIVE

All Models

Chain case oil should be checked at least every time engine oil is changed. SAE 90 gear oil is recommended.

To check chain case oil, place tiller on a level surface. Clean case housing and remove oil level plug and washer (24—Fig. S4). Oil level should be at bottom of plug hole. If oil level is low, remove plastic oil fill plug (4). Add oil through fill hole until oil begins to run out oil level hole, then replace plugs.

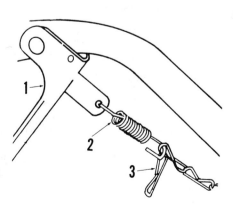

Fig. S1—View of clutch lever (1), spring (2) and chain links (3) for clutch control and adjustment.

MAINTENANCE

Inspect all fasteners for looseness and retighten as needed. Check control levers, linkage and cables for freedom of movement and excessive play. Inspect drive belt(s) for excessive stretching, wear, cracks, or any other damage. Install new belt(s) if needed. Inspect all belt pulleys and renew if damaged or excessively worn. Transport wheels should be lubricated occasionally with SAE 30 oil.

ADJUSTMENT

CLUTCH CONTROL

All Models

Small clutch adjustment may be done by repositioning spring (2—Fig. S1) in chain links (3). If clutch spring does not stretch when clutch lever is engaged, then chain will need to be shortened. If correct clutch engagement and disengagement cannot be obtained by adjusting chain links, then adjustment of idler link (2—Fig. S2 and S3) will need to be done. For single belt models, refer to Fig. S2 and for two belt models, refer to Fig. S3 for idler assembly breakdown and identification. To adjust: loosen two hex nuts (1—Fig. S2 and S3) on each side of idler link (2). Raise idler pulley to take slack out of belt. Hold idler pulley and pull down on idler link to take slack out of clutch cable, then retighten hex nuts. Adjust spring (2—Fig. S1) and chain (3) if clutch is too tight or too loose.

BELT ADJUSTMENT

Single Belt Models

Remove drive belt cover. Loosen engine mounting bolts. Slide engine forward or backward to adjust belt tension. Belt should slip on pulleys when clutch is not engaged. Retighten engine mounting bolts, then reinstall drive belt cover.

Two Belt Models

Remove drive belt cover. Loosen engine and speed reducer mounting bolts. Slide engine or reducer forward or backward to adjust belt(s) tension. Belt from engine to reducer should be adjusted tight. Belt from reducer to chain drive should slip on pulleys when clutch is not engaged. Retighten mounting bolts, then reinstall drive belt cover.

OVERHAUL

ENGINE

All Models

Engine model number is stamped on blower housing for Briggs & Stratton and Wisconsin Robin engines. Engine

make and series number is marked on data plate attached to engine for Tecumseh engines. Refer to appropriate Briggs & Stratton, Tecumseh or Wisconsin Robin engine section for overhaul procedures.

CHAIN CASE

All Models

OIL SEAL INSTALLATION. Remove tines from tine shaft. Tiller may be tilted back and allowed to rest on handlebars to prevent spillage when seals are removed. Use a seal puller to remove outer and inner seals (7—Fig. S4) from case hub. Clean tine shaft with emery cloth. Install inner seal with lip facing toward inside and outer seal with lip facing toward outside. Drive new seals in until outer seal is flush with case hub.

REMOVE AND DISASSEMBLE. Unbolt handlebar tie bars from chain case. Remove two lower handlebar bolts and nuts. Lift handlebar assembly from chain case and place to the side. Tip tiller forward until engine is resting on ground. Remove chain case to side rail bolts and nuts. Remove side rail to hitch assembly bolts. Remove transport

wheels, skid arm and hitch from tiller as a unit. Remove drive belt cover, then remove belt from input pulley. Withdraw chain case from frame. Remove tines from tine shaft. Loosen set screw in drive pulley hub and remove pulley and Woodruff key. Drain chain case oil. Split chain case in half and withdraw chain sprocket assembly as a unit. Refer to Fig. S4 for chain case parts breakdown and identification. Inspect and renew all components that are worn or damaged. Install nylon spacer (10) on tine shaft (16) with concave side of spacer facing toward sprocket. Reassemble chains and sprockets and install into case as a unit. Install new gasket and seals. Lubricate chains, sprockets and bearings with a light film of oil during reassembly.

NOTE: Needle bearings (9) are hardened on numbered side to allow pressing or driving without damage to bearings. Bearings (9) may be installed into case halves from either direction, but should only be pressed or driven from numbered side of bearing.

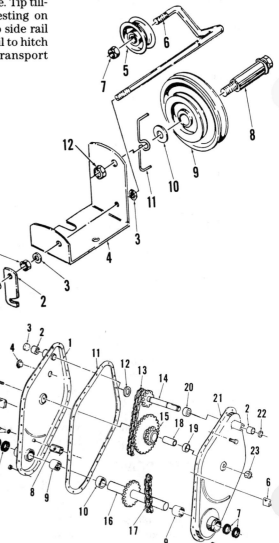

Fig. S3—Exploded view of drive belt idler assembly for two belt models.

1. Hex nut
2. Idler link
3. Washer
4. Mounting bracket
5. Idler pulley
6. Idler pulley arm
7. Locknut
8. Bolt, washer & race assy.
9. Reduction pulley
10. Washer
11. Belt guide
12. Hex nut

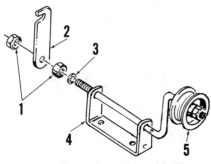

Fig. S2—Exploded view of drive belt idler assembly for single belt models.

1. Hex nut
2. Idler link
3. Washer
4. Mounting bracket
5. Idler pulley

Fig. S4—Exploded view of chain case assembly.

1. Right case half
2. Bronze bushings
3. Welch plug
4. Oil fill plug
5. Cap screw
6. Spacer clips
7. Oil seals
8. Case half spacer
9. Needle bearings
10. Nylon spacer
11. Gasket
12. Shim washer
13. Primary drive chain
14. Drive shaft
15. Sprocket
16. Tine shaft
17. Final drive chain
18. Race
19. Roller bearing
20. Spacer
21. Left case half
22. Oil seal
23. Locknut
24. Oil level check plug & washer

Keep all dirt and foreign matter out of chain case during reassembly. Refer to LUBRICATION section for lubricating requirements after reassembly and installation.

DRIVE BELTS

Single Belt Models

Remove drive belt cover. Remove belt from pulleys and install new belt. Drive belt is ½ inch wide x 51 inches long. Loosen engine mounting bolts and slide engine. Belt should slip on pulleys when clutch is not engaged. Retighten engine mounting bolts. Refer to CLUTCH CONTROL under ADJUSTMENT section for adjusting procedure. Reinstall drive belt cover.

Two Belt Models

Loosen engine mounting bolts. Slide engine backward to lower tension on belt. Remove engine to reducer belt, then remove reducer to chain drive belt. Install new belts. Reducer to chain drive belt is ½ inch wide x 37 inches long. Reducer to engine belt is ½ inch wide x 26.5 inches long. Belt from reducer to chain drive should slip on pulleys when clutch is not engaged. Reposition speed reducer mounting bracket to adjust belt tension. Belt from engine to reducer should be adjusted tight. Retighten mounting bolts. Refer to CLUTCH CONTROL under ADJUSTMENT section for adjusting procedure. Reinstall drive belt cover.

SNAPPER

(Rear Tine Models)

Model	Engine Make	Engine Series	Power Rating	No. of Forward Speeds	Power Reverse?	Tilling Width	Drive Type
RT5	B&S	130000	5 hp (3.7 kW)	4	Yes	20 in. (50.8 cm)	Chain
RT5X	Wisc. Robin	W1-185V	5 hp (3.7 kW)	4	Yes	20 in. (50.8 cm)	Chain
RT8	B&S	190000	8 hp (6.0 kW)	4	Yes	20 in. (50.8 cm)	Chain
RT8S	B&S	190000	8 hp (6.0 kW)	4	Yes	20 in. (50.8 cm)	Chain
R5000	B&S	130000	5 hp (3.7 kW)	4	Yes	20 in. (50.8 cm)	Chain
R5001	B&S	130000	5 hp (3.7 kW)	4	Yes	20 in. (50.8 cm)	Chain
R5002	B&S	130000	5 hp (3.7 kW)	4	Yes	20 in. (50.8 cm)	Chain
R5002R	B&S	130000	5 hp (3.7 kW)	4	Yes	20 in. (50.8 cm)	Chain
R8000	B&S	190000	8 hp (6.0 kW)	4	Yes	20 in. (50.8 cm)	Chain
R8001	B&S	190000	8 hp (6.0 kW)	4	Yes	20 in. (50.8 cm)	Chain
R8001S	B&S	190000	8 hp (6.0 kW)	4	Yes	20 in. (50.8 cm)	Chain
R8002	B&S	190000	8 hp (6.0 kW)	4	Yes	20 in. (50.8 cm)	Chain
R8002S	B&S	190000	8 hp (6.0 kW)	4	Yes	20 in. (50.8 cm)	Chain

LUBRICATION

CAUTION: Frequently, the performance of maintenance, adjustment or repair operations on a rotary tiller is more convenient if tiller is standing on end. This procedure can be considered a recommended practice providing the following safety recommendations are performed:

1. Drain fuel tank or make certain that fuel level is low enough so that fuel will not drain out.
2. Close fuel shut-off valve if so equipped.
3. Remove battery on models so equipped.
4. Disconnect spark plug wire and tie out of way.
5. Although not absolutely essential, it is recommended that crankcase oil be drained to avoid flooding the combustion chamber with oil when engine is tilted.
6. Secure tiller from tipping by lashing unit to a nearby post or overhead beam.

ENGINE

All Models

Refer to appropriate Briggs & Stratton or Wisconsin Robin engine section for engine lubrication specifications. Recommended oil is a good quality SAE 30 engine oil. Recommended fuel is either regular or unleaded gasoline having an octane rating of 90 or higher.

CONTROL MECHANISM

Apply a suitable grease at least twice a year to sliding surfaces of shift mechanism and drive components.

TINE CHAIN DRIVE

The oil level in the chain drive should be checked at least each time engine oil is changed. Oil level should be even with bottom edge of oil plug hole (P—Fig. S10). To add oil, remove plastic plug (G—Fig. S11) on side of chain case. Do

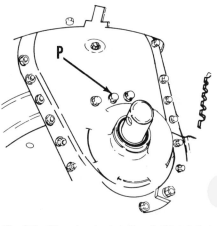

Fig. S10—View showing location of oil level plug (P) on the tine chain case.

not overfill. Approximate capacity of chain case is one quart (0.95 L). Recommended oil is Snapper 00 or a suitable equivalent.

PRIMARY CHAIN DRIVE

The primary chain drive is lubricated during assembly with Snapper 00 oil and does not normally require new lubricant.

GEAR DRIVE

The gear drive is lubricated during assembly with Snapper 00 oil and does not normally require new lubricant.

MAINTENANCE

Inspect all fasteners for looseness and retighten as needed. Check control levers, linkage and cables for freedom of movement and excessive play. Inspect drive belt(s) for excessive stretching, wear, cracks, or any other damage. Install new belt(s) if needed. Inspect all belt pulleys and renew if damaged or excessively worn.

ADJUSTMENT

CLUTCH CONTROL

To check adjustment, position tiller on front end. Measure lengths of both springs at end of each control cable with clutch disengaged. Pull clutch control to engaged position (toward handlebar) and remeasure lengths of springs. The springs should be ¼ to ½ inch (6.4-12.7 mm) longer when extended from the clutch disengaged to the clutch engaged positions. Adjust clutch spring length by rotating adjusting nuts located at upper and lower ends of cables. If wheels or tines turn when clutch control is in dis-

engaged position, clutch spring length is too great and should be readjusted. If clutch springs will not adjust properly, check drive belt adjustment and drive disc.

TINE DRIVE BELT

To adjust drive belt, position tiller on front end. Move belt cover away so belt is accessible. Pull clutch control toward handlebar so clutch is engaged. Note position of idler arm attached to idler bracket assembly (19—Fig. S12). The idler arm should be nearly parallel with

the idler bracket when the belt is tight. If not parallel, loosen cap screw securing idler pulley (L—Fig. S13) adjacent to chain case pulley. Move idler pulley (L) so idler arm is parallel with idler bracket (19—Fig. S12) when the belt is tight, then tighten pulley cap screw.

WHEEL DRIVE DISC

Power for the tiller's wheels is transmitted through two discs, a drive disc and a driven disc. The drive disc is attached to the engine's crankshaft while the driven disc is attached to the prima-

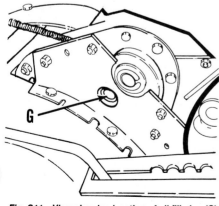

Fig. S11—View showing location of oil fill plug (G) on tine chain case.

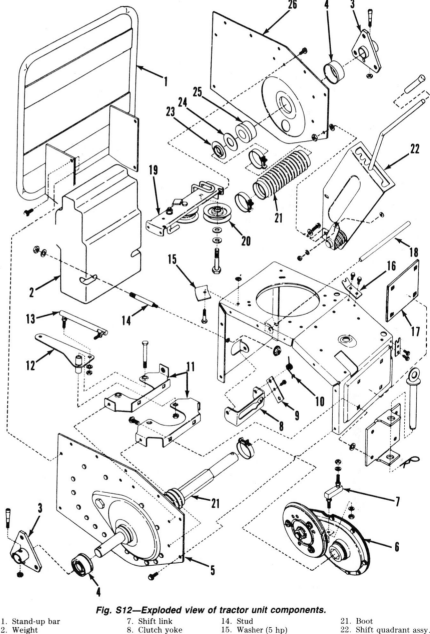

Fig. S12—Exploded view of tractor unit components.

1. Stand-up bar	7. Shift link	14. Stud	21. Boot
2. Weight	8. Clutch yoke	15. Washer (5 hp)	22. Shift quadrant assy.
3. Wheel hub	9. Lever	16. Cable clip	23. Thrust washer
4. Dust cap	10. Spring	17. Spacer (5 hp)	24. Nylon thrust
5. Transmission & left	11. Braces	18. Rod	washer
frame	12. Bellcrank	19. Idler bracket assy.	25. Bearing
6. Primary chain case	13. Shift link	20. Idler	26. Right frame

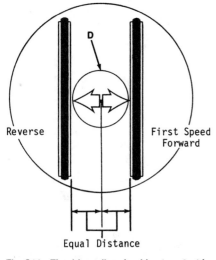

Fig. S13—View showing location of idler pulley (L) which may be relocated to adjust the drive belt as outlined in text.

ry chain case input shaft. As the primary chain case is moved from side to side through the shift mechanism, the driven friction disc contacts a different spot on the drive disc to change ground speed. Moving the driven disc to the opposite side of the drive disc reverses direction.

To check friction disc adjustment, position tiller on front end. Shift speed lever to first speed and then to reverse speed. The driven disc should be equidistant from the center of the drive disc in first and reverse positions (see Fig. S14). The driven disc must also be outside the indentation in the center of the drive disc. To position disc away from indentation, loosen screws securing shift quadrant (22—Fig. S12) to the frame, move the quadrant forward then retighten screws. Recheck disc movement and position.

OVERHAUL

ENGINE

The engine model number is stamped on the engine's blower housing on Briggs & Stratton engines and on cooling shroud above rewind starter on Wisconsin Robin engines. Refer to the appropriate Briggs & Stratton or Wisconsin Robin engine section for overhaul information.

TINE CHAIN CASE

OIL SEAL INSTALLATION. Position tiller on front end. Remove tines from tine shaft. Use a seal puller to remove outer and inner seals (20—Fig. S15) from case hub. Clean tine shaft with emery cloth. Install inner seal with lip facing toward inside and outer seal with lip facing toward outside. Drive new seals into case until outer seal is flush with case hub.

R&R AND OVERHAUL. Position tiller on front end. Remove tines from tine shaft. Remove spring and grip from depth bar. Detach drive belt from chain case pulley. Unscrew retaining bolt and remove depth bar. Unscrew chain case pulley retaining nut (1—Fig. S15) and re-

move pulley (3). Remove screws securing chain case mounting brackets to tine cover. Remove nuts securing front bracket to chain case and note position of spacers. Remove pulley shield and cover attaching pin. Remove chain case along with mounting brackets then detach brackets from chain case.

Drain lubricant from chain case. Separate chain case halves and remove chain sprocket assembly as a unit. Refer to Fig. S15 for an exploded view of chain case assembly. Inspect all components for damage and excessive wear.

Reassemble and reinstall chain case by reversing disassembly and removal procedure while noting the following: Install needle bearings (19) by driving against numbered end of bearing; numbered end of bearing must be to inside of case half. Install ball bearings (5) so numbered end of bearing is to inside of case half. Install nylon spacer (17) so cupped side is toward sprocket (16). Install new gasket and seals. Lubricate chains, sprockets and bearings with oil during assembly. Alternate from side to side when tightening the case screws. Tighten case screws to 8-10 ft.-lbs. (10.8-13.5 N·m). Tighten center through-bolt to 18-26 ft.-lbs. (24.4-35.2 N·m). Install Belleville washers (2) with concave side toward pulley. Refill with oil as outlined in LUBRICATION section.

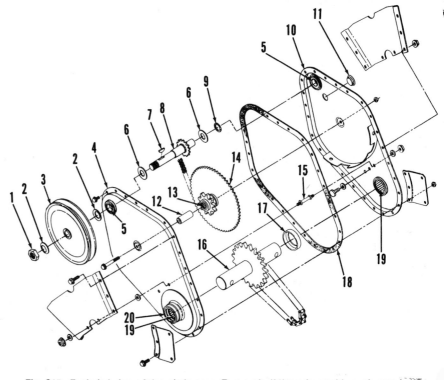

Fig. S14—The driven disc should not contact indentation (D) in first or reverse speed. Refer to text for adjustment. The driven disc should be approximately equidistant from drive disc center in first and reverse speeds.

Fig. S15—Exploded view of tine chain case. Two seals (20) are located in each case half.

1. Nut	7. Key	11. Oil fill plug	16. Tine shaft &
2. Belleville washers	8. Input shaft &	12. Shaft	sprocket
3. Pulley	sprocket	13. Bearing (2)	17. Spacer
4. Left chain case half	9. "O" ring	14. Intermediate	18. Gasket
5. Ball bearing	10. Right chain case	sprocket	19. Needle bearing
6. Washer	half	15. Spacer stud	20. Seals (2)

TRANSMISSION

R&R AND OVERHAUL. Although not necessary, the tiller unit should be separated from the tractor unit to ease disassembly.

The transmission is located on the left frame and may be removed for overhaul as follows: Remove the front stand-up bar and both wheels and hubs. Loosen clamps securing left boot. Remove bolts and screws securing left frame (5—Fig. S16) to tractor unit components then separate left frame from tractor.

To disassemble transmission, remove through-bolt (20) and screws retaining cover (2) to frame. Refer to Fig. S16 and disassemble transmission while noting location of components.

Reassemble and reinstall transmission by reversing disassembly and removal sequences. Note that split washers may be installed at right end of hex shaft adjacent to bearing (25—Fig. S12) so shaft end play does not exceed 1/16 inch (1.6 mm). Fill transmission with 4 ounces (118 mL) of Snapper 00 oil or equivalent after installation.

PRIMARY CHAIN CASE

R&R AND OVERHAUL. To remove the primary chain case, remove the transmission as previously outlined. Detach shift link (7—Fig. S12), twist unit sideways and remove primary chain case. Drain grease from case. Refer to Fig. S17 and disassemble chain case.

Press bearings or bushings (4, 14 or 20) toward inside of case half if they must be removed. Press bearings or bushings toward outside of case half when installing. Early models may be equipped with bushings (20) which should be discarded and replaced with needle bearings (14). Note that different thrust washers (15 and 21) must also be installed if bushings are replaced with bearings. Install spacers (15) so cupped side is toward sprocket (16). Two shims (6) are located on each side of input sprocket (5).

Reinstall primary chain case by reversing disassembly procedure. Fill chain case with 2 ounces (59.1 mL) of Snapper 00 oil or equivalent.

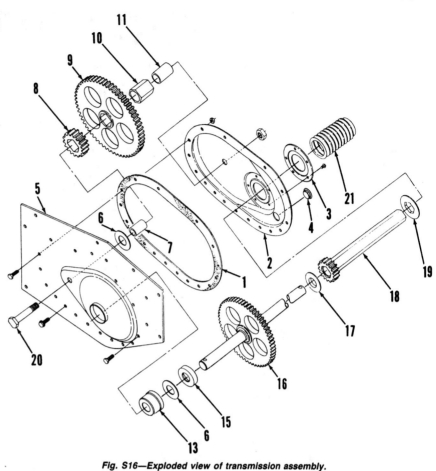

Fig. S16—Exploded view of transmission assembly.

1. Gasket	5. Left frame	9. Gear	15. Spacer
2. Cover	6. Thrust washer	10. Hex tube	16. Wheel shaft assy.
3. Boot retainer	7. Shaft	11. Bearing	17. Thrust washer	19. Washer
4. Oil fill plug	8. Gear	13. Bearing	18. Drive tube	20. Through-bolt
				21. Boot

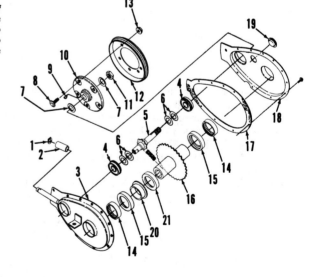

Fig. S17—Exploded view of primary chain case. Bushings (20) and spacers (21) are used on early models in place of bearings (14) and spacers (15).

1. Snap ring
2. Roller
3. Case half
4. Ball bearing
5. Input shaft & sprocket
6. Shims
7. Belleville washer
8. Bolt
9. Key
10. Hub
11. Locknut
12. Driven disc
13. Locknut
14. Needle bearing
15. Spacer
16. Sprocket & shaft
17. Gasket
18. Case half
19. Oil fill plug
20. Bushing (early models)
21. Spacer (early models)

TROY-BILT

GARDEN WAY MFG. CO.
102nd St. & 9th Ave.
Troy, NY 12180

Model	Engine Make	Engine Series	Power Rating	No. of Forward Speeds	Power Reverse?	Tilling Width	Drive Type
Tuffy	Tec.	H30	3 hp (2.2 kW)	1	No	14 in. (35.5 cm)	Gear
Junior	Tec.	H35	3.5 hp (2.6 kW)	2	Yes	14 in. (35.5 cm)	Gear
Pony	B&S	130000	5 hp (3.7 kW)	1	Yes	16 in. (40.6 cm)	Gear
Horse	Clinton	498-0301-280	4.5 hp (3.4 kW)	4	Yes	20 in. (50.8 cm)	Gear
Econo-Horse	Tec.	H60	6 hp (4.5 kW)	2	Yes	18 in. (45.7 cm)	Gear
Horse	Kohler	K-161	7 hp (5.2 kW)	4	Yes	20 in. (50.8 cm)	Gear
Horse	B&S	190000	8 hp (6.0 kW)	4	Yes	20 in. (50.8 cm)	Gear
Horse	Kohler	K-181	8 hp (6.0 kW)	4	Yes	20 in. (50.8 cm)	Gear
PTO Horse	Tec.	HMXL-70	7 hp (5.2 kW)	4	Yes	20 in. (50.8 cm)	Gear
PTO Horse	Kohler	M8T	8 hp (6.0 kW)	4	Yes	20 in. (50.8 cm)	Gear

LUBRICATION

ENGINE

All Models

Refer to Briggs & Stratton, Tecumseh, Kohler or Clinton engine section for engine lubrication specifications. Recommended oil grade is SAE 30 with a SF or SE classification. SAE 10W-30 oil may be used during cold weather operation. The manufacturer does not recommend using 10W-40 engine oil in Tuffy, Junior or Econo-Horse models. Recommended fuel is either regular or unleaded gasoline.

WHEELS AND CONTROLS

All Models

At least every 10 hours of operation, lubricate wheel shafts, control cables and pivot points with SAE 30 oil and apply a thin coat of grease to engine mounting bars and belt adjustment block. Do not get oil or grease on drive belts.

GEAR DRIVE

All Models Except Tuffy

Oil level in gear housing should be checked at least every 30 hours of operation. With tiller in a level position, gear housing oil level should be even with oil level plug hole on left side of transmission above wheel shaft. If oil level is low, add oil through fill plug hole at top of transmission case until oil flows out of oil level plug hole. Recommended gear oil is SAE 90 or SAE 140. Gear drive oil does not normally require changing unless contamination is noted. Gear drive housing capacity is approximately 3-1/4 pints (1.5 L) on Junior, Pony, Econo-Horse and Horse models. On PTO Horse models, measure distance from top of wheel shaft to center of oil level check plug. On models with check plug located 1-3/4 inches (44.4 mm) above wheel shaft, gear drive housing capacity is approximately 3-3/4 pints (1.8 L), or if level plug is located 3-7/8 inches above wheel shaft, capacity is approximately 5.4 pints (2.5 L).

Tuffy Models

Recommended oil is SAE 90W-140 gear lubricant. Oil level in gear drive should be checked every 30 hours of operation. With tiller in a level position, remove plug located in gear housing top cover. Using a suitable light, look into plug hole and note worm shaft below plug hole. Oil will cover one-half of worm shaft if gear drive housing is properly filled. Gear drive oil does not normally require changing unless contamination is noted.

TINE GEARCASE

PTO Horse Models

Check oil level in tine gearcase after every 30 hours of operation. Recommended oil is SAE 90W-140 gear lubricant. To check oil, place tiller on a level surface and engage tiller depth bar in highest position causing tiller to rest on drag bar located in center of tines. Block up drag bar so bar is approximately 3-

1/2 inches (88.9 mm) above ground. Tiller is now in the proper position to check gearcase oil level. Allow tiller to set in this position for at least two minutes, or longer if ambient temperature is below 40° F (4.5° C), then remove dipstick (D—Fig. TB1). Note "cold" and "hot" markings on dipstick. With "hot" and "cold" markings on dipstick facing toward rear of tiller, insert dipstick straight down into hole as shown in Fig. TB1 until dipstick contacts shaft inside gearcase. Remove dipstick and note oil level. Oil level should be within the "cold" to "hot" markings. To add oil, insert a clean funnel into dipstick hole and add oil slowly. Check level frequently to prevent overfilling.

Oil in tine gearcase does not normally require changing unless contamination is noted. Gearcase capacity is approximately 1 pint (0.47 L).

MAINTENANCE

All Models

Inspect drive belt(s) and renew if frayed or stretched to the point where adjustment is no longer effective.

On Horse and PTO Horse models, reverse disc should be inspected at least every 30 hours of operation. Replace disc if there are any chunks of rubber missing from outside diameter or if there are any flat spots if the disc is made of fiber material. Periodically check tires for a specified pressure of 10-20 psi (68.9-137.9 kPa).

Inspect all fasteners for looseness and tighten as necessary. Inspect control cables and levers for looseness and excessive play. On electric start models, check battery electrolyte level after every 10 hours of operation. Inspect all wiring for loose or corroded connections or other damage and repair or renew as necessary.

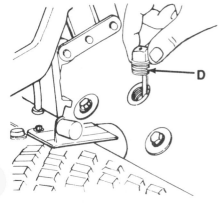

Fig. TB1—View of tine gearcase dipstick (D) on PTO Horse models. Refer to text for proper oil checking procedure.

ADJUSTMENT

DRIVE BELTS

Horse Models

BELT TENSION. To adjust belt tension, push forward/reverse shift lever all the way down and lock in forward position, then loosen mounting bolt for the adjustment block (2—Fig. TB2). Press

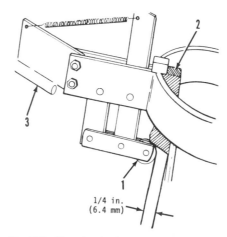

1/4 in. (6.4 mm)

Fig. TB2—View showing belt tension adjustment block (2) and related components typical of Horse and PTO Horse models. Refer to text for adjustment procedure.

1. Roller
2. Adjustment block
3. Forward/reverse lever

Fig. TB3—On early Pony and Junior models, turn screw (4) to adjust forward belt (1) tension. Refer to text.

1. Forward belt
2. Forward idler
3. Idler pivot
4. Screw

Fig. TB4—Before attempting to adjust forward belt tension on Econo-Horse or late Pony and Junior models, make sure clutch rod is located in the corresponding hole with handlebar height adjustment. Be sure to change clutch rod location after changing handlebar height.

down hard on shift lever until roller (1) moves down onto lower surface of adjustment block. In this position, roller (1) should be ¼ inch (6.4 mm) from adjustment block mounting bracket. Slide adjusting block up or down to obtain proper adjustment. Retighten mounting bolt.

REVERSE DISC. With shift lever in neutral position, tab on motor mount should be resting on top of reverse plunger adjusting bolt and reverse disc should be at least 3/16 inch (4.8 mm) above flat surface of transmission drive pulley. Move plunger up or down as needed to obtain specified clearance between reverse disc and transmission drive pulley.

Pony, Junior and Econo-Horse Models

FORWARD BELT TENSION. Tension is applied to forward belt by a forward idler pulley which on early Junior and Pony models, is adjusted by screw (4—Fig. TB3) at the idler pivot (3). Screw head must always be 1/8 to ¼ inch (3.2-6.4 mm) above pivot when shift lever is in "forward" position. Adjust as needed.

To check forward belt tension on Econo-Horse and late Pony and Junior models, first make sure lower end of clutch rod is in the correct hole (Fig. TB4). Next, fully apply forward clutch

1/8 - 1/4 in. (3.2 - 6.3 mm)

Lever   Clutch Rod

and measure gap between "E" ring (3—Fig. TB5) and adjuster bracket (5). Gap should be 3/16 to 5/16 inch (4.8-7.9 mm). Disconnect lower end of clutch rod (4) and turn rod to adjust.

All models can be set up for additional adjustment if belt is overly stretched. This can be accomplished by placing shift lever in neutral and loosening clutch adjustment all the way, then remove belt from top pulley. Remove retainer pin and washer from idler on left side. Remove pin from outside hole in adjustable link and reinstall in inside hole. Reinstall washer, retainer pin and belt, and make adjustment with adjusting screw as previously outlined.

REVERSE BELT TENSION. Tension is applied to reverse belt by the reverse idler pulley. To adjust, remove reverse belt from engine pulley, then remove retainer pin and washer from idler on right side. Remove pin from outside hole in adjustable link and reinstall through inside hole. Reinstall retainer pin and washer, then reinstall reverse belt.

Tuffy Models

FORWARD BELT TENSION. To check belt tension adjustment, lift clutch handle up to bottom of handlebar and measure length of spring attached to clutch handle. Spring should be 1-7/8 inch (47.6 mm) long with clutch applied. Turn adjuster located below spring to adjust.

OVERHAUL

ENGINE

All Models

Engine model number is stamped on blower housing or on a plate which is attached to blower housing on Briggs & Stratton, Tecumseh or Kohler engines. On Clinton engines, model number is stamped on air baffle at rear of cylinder. Refer to appropriate Briggs & Stratton, Tecumseh, Kohler or Clinton engine sections for overhaul procedures.

TRANSMISSION

All Models

WHEEL SHAFT OIL SEAL INSTALLATION. Support gearcase and remove wheel. Drive a screwdriver or chisel into seal at an angle and pry seal out of casting bore. Polish wheel shaft with emery cloth to remove rust or burrs. Check to be sure there is at least one wheel shaft shim 0.062 inch (1.57 mm) thick or two

0.030 inch (0.76 mm) thick shims inside seal bore. Apply nonhardening gasket sealer to outside surface of seal and coat lip of seal with a light coat of grease. Drive new seal into casting bore until it is almost flush with outside edge of bore. Repeat procedure for opposite side if necessary.

TINE SHAFT SEAL RENEWAL. Remove tine hood and tine assemblies. On all models except Tuffy, remove five housing cover screws on left side of

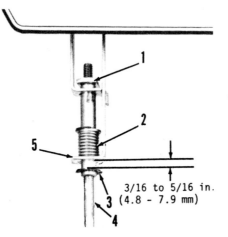

Fig. TB5—To check forward belt tension on Econo-Horse and late Pony and Junior models, engage forward clutch and measure gap where indicated. Make sure lower end of clutch rod (4) is in the proper hole (Fig. TB4). Remove lower end of clutch rod (4) and turn rod to adjust.

1. Nut
2. Spring
3. "E" ring
4. Clutch rod
5. Adjuster bracket

3/16 to 5/16 in. (4.8 - 7.9 mm)

housing. With cover removed, tap seal out from inside of cover. If right-hand seal requires renewal, remove housing cover and tap tine shaft and gear assembly out of housing with a soft-faced mallet, then drive out right-hand seal from inside housing.

On Tuffy models, drive a chisel or other suitable tool into seal and pry seal out of housing bore. Use care not to damage tine shaft or seal bore in housing.

Carefully inspect tine shaft for scratches or burrs that may cut seal during reassembly. Make sure bronze gear is centered over Woodruff key on tine shaft. Clean rust or burrs from shaft with a fine file or sandpaper.

After reassembly, check tine shaft for a slight amount of end play. On all models except Tuffy, end play is adjusted by varying thickness of gasket between cover and housing. Gasket is available in 0.010 inch (0.25 mm) thickness on Pony, Junior and Econo-Horse models, and 0.010 inch (0.25 mm) and 0.030 inch (0.76 mm) thickness on Horse and PTO Horse models.

On Tuffy models, tine shaft end play is adjusted by shims (27—Fig. TB7). Shims (27) are available in 0.005 inch (0.13 mm), 0.010 inch (0.25 mm), 0.15 inch (0.38 mm), 0.030 inch (0.76 mm) and 0.062 inch (1.57 mm) thicknesses.

When proper end play is determined coat housing cover cap screws with nonhardening sealer and reinstall. When installing new seals, coat outside diameter of seal with nonhardening gasket seal-

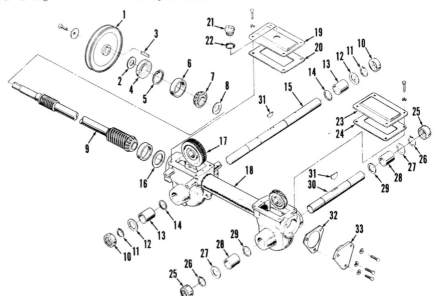

Fig. TB7—Exploded view of transmission assembly used on Tuffy models. Note that taper bearing and race at rear of drive shaft (9) is a press fit on shaft (9) and not available separately.

1. Pulley	10. Seal	18. Housing	26. Snap ring
2. Washer	11. Snap ring	19. Cover	27. Shim
3. Key	12. Shim	20. Gasket	28. Bushing
4. Seal	13. Bushing	21. Fill plug	29. Washer
5. Snap ring	14. Washer	22. Seal	30. Tine shaft
6. Bearing race	15. Wheel shaft	23. Cover	31. Woodruff key
7. Taper bearing	16. Shim	24. Gasket	32. Gasket
8. Washer	17. Bronze gear	25. Seal	33. End cap
9. Drive shaft			

er and coat inside lip of seal with a light coat of grease. Tap seals into casting bores until seal is almost flush with outside edge of bore.

FRONT TRANSMISSION OIL SEAL.

Remove engine assembly along with transmission drive pulley and pulley shim. On all models except Tuffy, remove the three cap screws and bearing cap. With cap removed, push out oil seal from inside. Using an emery cloth, clean any rust or burrs off shaft. Using a new gasket, reinstall bearing cap without seal. Coat cap screw threads with nonhardening gasket sealer before installation. Coat outside diameter of seal with nonhardening gasket sealer and coat sealing lip of seal with a light coat of grease. Tap seal into cap and align front edge of seal with front edge of bearing cap.

To renew front transmission seal on Tuffy models, remove pulley (1—Fig. TB7), washer (2) and key (3) and pry seal

(4) from case (18). Clean rust or burrs off shaft (9) with emery cloth. Coat outer diameter of seal with nonhardening gasket sealer, lubricate seal lip with a suitable grease and reassemble in reverse of disassembly.

Horse Models

NOTE: The following overhaul section is intended specifically for Horse models. Overhaul information for other models was not available at the time of publication, although the procedures are similar and specifications are the same. Refer to Figs. TB11, TB13 and TB14 for exploded view of transmission assemblies used on other models and Fig. TB12 for exploded view of tine gearcase used on PTO Horse models.

Transmission assembly consists of a main gearbox at the front and a tine drive gearbox at the rear which are connected by a drive shaft tube. PTO Horse

models have a clutch in between the two gearboxes which can be disconnected.

REMOVE AND REINSTALL. Remove throttle cable, belt(s), and reverse disc. If equipped with an electric starter, disconnect key switch wiring, charging system wire and battery cables, then remove battery. Disconnect positive cable at starter and remove the two battery bracket screws on top of the transmission cover, then remove battery bracket and starter solenoid as an assembly. Remove control yoke bolts from engine mount and engine mount bar lock bolts. Support engine with blocks of wood and tap engine mount bars down and out of housing. Engine may now be lifted away from transmission.

Remove "T" bar handlebar mounting bolt and remove handlebars as an assembly. Remove control yoke pivot point bolts from each side of transmission and remove yoke as an assembly. Disconnect

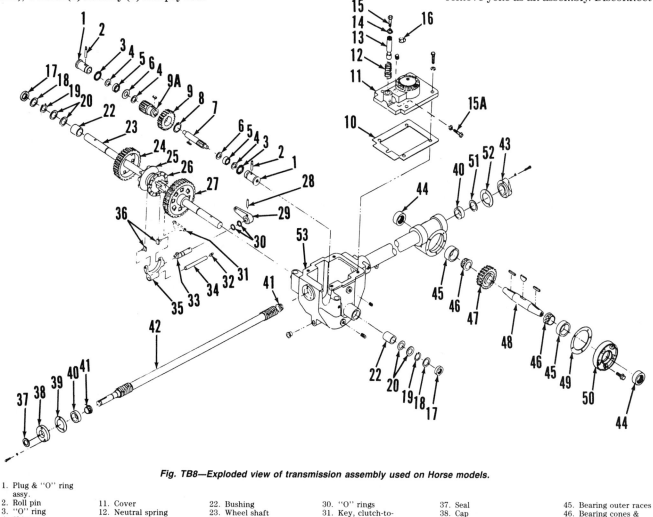

Fig. TB8—Exploded view of transmission assembly used on Horse models.

1. Plug & "O" ring assy.	11. Cover	22. Bushing	30. "O" rings	37. Seal	45. Bearing outer races
2. Roll pin	12. Neutral spring	23. Wheel shaft	31. Key, clutch-to-wheel shaft	38. Cap	46. Bearing cones & rollers
3. "O" ring	13. Neutral plunger	24. High speed gear	32. Plug	39. Gasket	47. Gear (bronze)
4. Shims	14. Nut	25. Dog clutch, high speed	33. Shifter shaft eccentric	40. Bearing outer race	48. Tine shaft
5. Bearings	15. Bolt	26. Dog clutch, low speed	34. Shifter shaft fork pivot	41. Bearing cone & roller	49. Gasket
6. Washers	16. Clip	27. Low speed gear	35. Shift fork	42. Drive shaft, welded type	50. Housing cover
7. Shaft	17. Seal	28. Roll pin	36. Shift fork shoes	43. Cap	51. Shims
8. Snap ring	18. Shim	29. Lever		44. Seals	52. Gasket
9. Gear (bronze)	19. Snap ring				53. Housing
9A. Pinion gear	20. Shims				
10. Gasket					

depth regulator bar from transmission and remove the two bolts from rear of tine transmission end cap (43—Fig. TB8). Remove the two rear transmission bolts which hold the tine hood front bracket in place. Disconnect wheel shift linkage from transmission shift lever. Lift tine hood assembly away from transmission. Remove tine retaining stud in each side and using a soft hammer, tap tine assemblies off shaft. To remove wheels, tap roll pins out of wheel shafts, then remove wheels.

Reassemble tiller by reversing disassembly procedure.

OVERHAUL. Remove outer snap ring and pull transmission pulley off drive shaft, then remove inner snap ring from drive shaft. Drain gear oil from transmission. Remove the two remaining bolts and remove the top cover (11—Fig. TB8). Remove front bearing cap (38) and rear bearing cap (43). When removing rear bearing cap, note the number and thickness of the bearing adjusting shims (51). Place shift lever (29) in neutral position. Using a soft-faced mallet, tap drive shaft (42) and rear bearing race (40) out toward the rear.

Remove roll pins (2). Using pliers, remove pinion shaft plugs (1). Remove shims (4) and keep in order for left and right sides. Using a hammer and brass drift, carefully tap pinion shaft (7) out through left side plug hole, then remove bronze gear (9) and pinion gear (9A) as an assembly. Left pinion bearing (5) will be removed as the pinion shaft is removed. The right side bearing may be tapped out with a hammer handle.

Remove left side wheel shaft oil seal (17), shims (18 and 20) and snap ring (19). Align keyway on high speed gear (24) with key on wheel shaft (23). Note that high speed gear and high speed gear dog clutch (25) may be marked on outside edge to show keyway position.

With keyways aligned, use a soft hammer and tap wheel shaft (23) out through right side of transmission case (53). As shaft moves out, shims (18 and 20), seal (17), snap ring (19) and bushing (22) will also be removed from right side. As wheel shaft is removed, lift low speed gear (27), low speed dog clutch (26), high speed dog clutch (25) and high speed gear (24) out of transmission case. If necessary, bushing (22) on left side of housing may be tapped out with a pipe or brass drift of the proper diameter. Remove shift fork shoes (36) from shift fork (35). Remove plug (32) at rear of case under shift lever (29). Thread a rear bearing cap retaining screw into threaded hole in shift fork shaft (34) and pull shaft out of case, then lift shift fork (35) out of case. Drive roll pin (28) out of shift lever and remove lever from ec-

centric shaft (33), then using a soft hammer, tap eccentric shaft into case and remove.

Remove the five screws from tine shaft housing cover (50) and remove cover and gasket (49). Using a soft hammer, tap tine shaft (48), bronze gear (47) and bearings (46) out of housing as an assembly.

Inspect gears and dog clutches for broken teeth or other obvious damage. Inspect shafts for scoring or damage around keyways. Inspect bearings for roughness. Renew components as necessary.

Reassemble by reversing disassembly procedure. During reassembly, replace all seals, gaskets and "O" rings. Reinstall wheel shaft bushings (22—Fig. TB8) flush with outside edge of bores and with oil pickup grooves facing toward inside of housing. Specified wheel shaft (23) side play is 0.005-0.010 inch (0.13-0.25 mm). During initial assembly, manufacturer recommends using any combination of shims (20) equaling 0.030 inch (0.76 mm) on the right side. Install shims for end play adjustment on the left side. Install wheel shaft snap rings (19) with flat side facing away from housing. When installing shims (18) between snap ring and outer wheel shaft seal (17), manufacturer recommends using one 0.062 inch (1.57 mm) shim or two 0.030 inch (0.76 mm) shims on each side. Refer to WHEEL SHAFT OIL SEAL INSTALLATION paragraph for oil seal installation procedure.

Bronze gear (9) must be centered in housing when pinion shaft (7) and pinion gear (9A) are installed. Centering and side play of pinion shaft is adjusted with shims (4). Shims are available in thicknesses of 0.010 inch (1.57 mm).

Specified drive shaft end play is 0.002-0.010 inch (0.05-0.25 mm). Drive shaft end play is adjusted with shims (51) which are available in thicknesses of 0.005 inch (0.13 mm), 0.010 inch (0.25

mm) and 0.030 inch (0.76 mm). Refer to FRONT TRANSMISSION OIL SEAL paragraph for seal installation procedure.

Tine shaft (48) should be installed so there is a very slight amount of side play. Adjustment is controlled by thickness of gasket (49). Gaskets are available in thicknesses of 0.010 inch (0.25 mm) and 0.030 inch (0.76 mm). Adjust by trial and error using the thinnest gasket first. Maximum thickness of gasket(s) should be a combination of the thin and thick gaskets totaling 0.040 inch (1.02 mm). If proper tine shaft side play is not attainable by using gaskets, shims are available for installation between bearing cone (46) and bronze gear (47). These shims are available in thicknesses of 0.005 inch (0.13 mm), 0.010 inch (0.25 mm) and 0.015 inch (0.38 mm). Refer to TINE SHAFT SEAL RENEWAL paragraph for seal installation procedure.

ASSEMBLED ADJUSTABLE DRIVE SHAFT. Some models are equipped with an assembled drive shaft as shown in Fig. TB9. To remove the assembled drive shaft, remove front and rear bearing caps. Bend up tabs on lockwasher (10). Using a soft hammer, tap shaft rearward until rear bearing outer race falls out. Tap rear bearing cone (2), spacer (14) and worm gear (13) off end of shaft. With shaft moved rearward, use a brass drift and hammer to tap front bearing outer race out of transmission housing. Shaft may now be removed through front of housing. Unthread spacer (12) from nut (11) and slide spacer off shaft (8). Remove front bearing cone (2), shim (3) and snap ring (4), then slide spacer (5) and worm gear (6) off shaft.

Reassemble by reversing disassembly procedure. Specified drive shaft end play is 0.002-0.010 inch (0.05-0.25 mm). Adjust end play by turning adjusting nut (11). After adjustment, bend over two or three tabs on lockwasher (10).

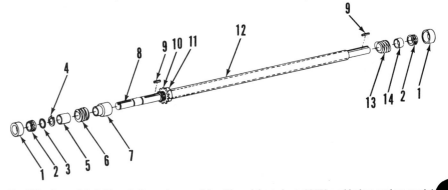

Fig. TB9—Assembled drive shaft used on models with serial numbers 14158 and below and on models with serial numbers 14518 through 14717.

1. Bearing outer races	4. Snap ring	8. Shaft
2. Bearing cones & rollers	5. Spacer	9. Woodruff keys
3. Shim	6. Worm gear, front	10. Washer, locking tab
	7. Thrust bushing	11. Adjustment nut
		12. Spacer
		13. Worm gear, rear
		14. Spacer

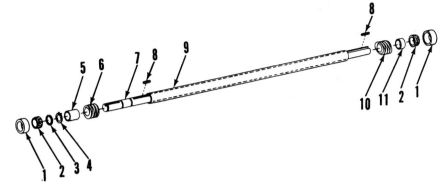

Fig. TB10—Assembled drive shaft first used on tiller serial number 14159 and occasionally used on later models.

1. Bearing outer races
2. Bearing cones & rollers
3. Shim
4. Snap ring
5. Spacer
6. Worm gear, front
7. Shaft
8. Woodruff keys
9. Spacer
10. Worm gear, rear
11. Spacer

Fig. TB11—Exploded view of transmission assembly used on PTO Horse models.

1. Plug	12. Neutral spring	25. High speed dog clutch	51. Shims	64. Lockwasher
2. Roll pin	13. Neutral plunger	26. Low speed dog clutch	53. Housing	65. Screw
3. "O" ring	14. Nut	27. Low speed gear	54. Spring	66. Roll pin
4. Shims	15. Bolt	29. Lever	55. Washer	67. Lever
5. Bearing	15A. Screw	37. Seal	56. Pulley	68. Seal
6. Washer	16. "E" ring	38. Cap	57. Key	69. Snap ring
7. Shaft	17. Seal	39. Gasket	58. Washer	70. Seal
8. Snap ring	18. Shims	40. Bearing race	59. Lever	71. Key
9. Bronze gear	19. Snap ring	41. Taper bearing	60. Snap ring	72. PTO dog clutch
9A. Pinion gear	22. Bushing	42. Drive shaft	61. Bushing	73. Snap ring
10. Gasket	23. Wheel shaft		62. Snap ring	74. Pin
11. Cover	24. High speed gear		63. Lever	

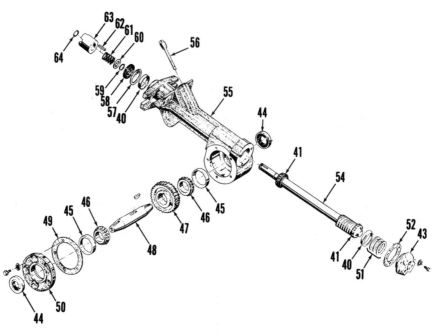

Fig. TB12—Exploded view of tine gearcase used on PTO Horse models. Refer to Fig. TB8 for component identification except tine shaft (54), case (55), dipstick (56), snap ring (57), seal (58), snap ring (59), shim (60), spring (61), key (62), dog clutch (63) and snap ring (64).

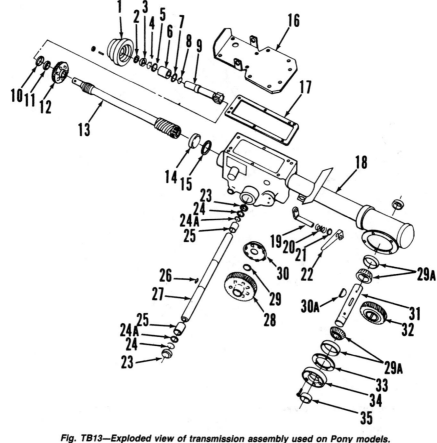

Fig. TB13—Exploded view of transmission assembly used on Pony models.

1. Pulley	9. Input pinion		29A. Bearings
2. Washer	10. Bearing race		30. Clutch hu…
3. Seal	11. Bearing roller	17. Gasket	24. Snap rings	30A. Key
4. Snap ring	12. Gear	18. Housing	24A. Shims	31. Tine shaft
5. Thrust washer	13. Drive shaft	19. Shift shaft	25. Bushings	32. Worm gear
6. Bushing	14. Bearing race	20. Spring	26. Key	33. Gasket
7. Thrust washer	15. Shim	21. Seal	27. Wheel shaft	34. Cover
8. Snap ring	16. Cover	22. Lever	28. Gear	35. Seal
		23. Oil seals	29. Shim	

REVERSE DISC

orse and PTO Horse Models

Loosen disc mounting bolt as far as possible, then pry disc away from engine pulley. Slide disc backward and angle enough to remove bolt past reverse plunger, then remove disc. Reinstall by reversing removal procedure.

DRIVE BELTS

Horse and PTO Horse Models

FORWARD DRIVE BELT. To replace drive belt, first place shift lever in neu-tral position, then work belt away from lower and upper pulleys. Place shift lever in forward position and work belt out between reverse disc and lower pulley assembly. Reinstall by reversing removal procedure. Replacement belt 9245 is available only from Troy-Bilt.

Pony, Junior and Econo-Horse Models

FORWARD AND REVERSE BELT. Remove belt cover and refer to Fig. TB15 for component identification. Place forward/reverse lever in neutral position and remove reverse belt (1) from engine pulley (3) and idler pulley. Remove for-ward belt (7) from forward engine pulley (4 and 5). Remove reverse belt from transmission pulley and remove from tiller. Remove forward belt from transmission pulley and remove from tiller. Reinstall belts by reversing removal procedure. Replacement belts are available only from Troy-Bilt. Stock numbers for Pony models are: forward belt—20565, reverse belt—50134, set of forward and revese belts—4922. Stock numbers for Junior models are: forward belt—20565, reverse belt—9095, set of forward and reverse belts—11018. Stock numbers for Econo-Horse models are: forward belt—20565, reverse belt—9022, set of forward and reverse belts—11019.

Tuffy Models

FORWARD DRIVE BELT. Unbolt and remove belt guard. Push down on top of belt to create slack and reach under tiller and remove belt from transmission pulley, then slide belt off engine pulley.

To reinstall belt, position belt behind engine pulley and install over transmis-sion pulley. Making sure belt is proper-ly located between belt guides, work belt on engine pulley. Refer to ADJUST-MENT section for clutch adjustment procedure.

The manufacturer recommends using belts only produced by Troy-Bilt. Man-ufacturer part number for belt is 55037.

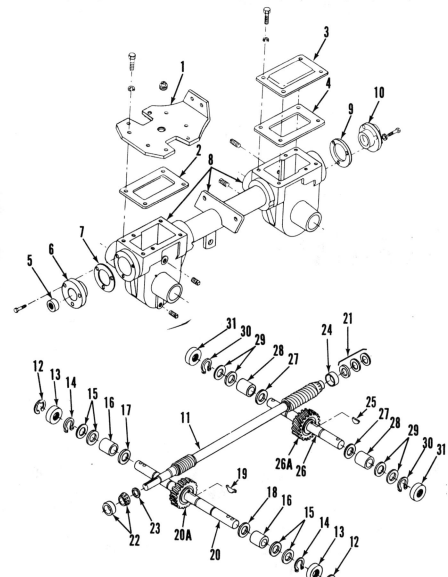

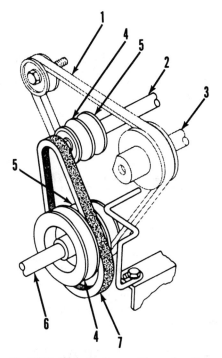

Fig. TB15—View of belt assembly used on Pony, Junior and Econo-Horse models.

1. Reverse belt
2. Forward engine shaft
3. Reverse engine shaft
4. Low speed sheaves
5. High speed sheaves
6. Input shaft
7. Forward belt

Fig. TB14—Exploded view of transmission assembly used on Junior models.

1. Cover	10. Cap, rear bearing	18. Spacer	25. Key
2. Gasket	11. Drive shaft	19. Key	26. Tine shaft
3. Cover	12. Retainers	20. Wheel shaft	26A. Worm gear
4. Gasket	13. Seals	20A. Worm gear	27. Spacers
5. Seal	14. Snap rings	21. Shims	28. Bushings
6. Cap, front bearing	15. Shims	22. Bearing	29. Shims
7. Gasket	16. Bushings	23. Washer	30. Snap rings
8. Housing assy.	17. Spacer	24. Bearing race	31. Seals
9. Gasket			

WARDS

MONTGOMERY WARD
Montgomery Ward Plaza
Chicago, Illinois 60671

The following Wards tillers were manufactured for Montgomery Ward by the Gilson Brothers Company, Plymouth, Wisconsin and by MTD Products, Cleveland, Ohio. Service procedures for these models will not differ greatly from those given for similar Gilson and MTD models. However, parts are not necessarily interchangeable and should be obtained from Montgomery Ward.

Wards Model	Gilson Section	MTD Section
39000	51095	.....
39011	51143	.....
39023	.....	320
39025	.....	385
39031	51142	.....
1580	51097	.....
39032	51134	.....
39008	51135	.....
39095	.....	410A
39098	.....	412A
39103	.....	412A

WARDS

Model	Engine Make	Engine Series	Engine Horsepower	No. of Forward Speeds	Power Reverse?	Tilling Width (In.)	Drive Type
39083	B&S	110000	4	1	Yes	14	Chain
39084	B&S	130000	5	1	Yes	18	Chain
39096	B&S	130000	5	1	No	18	Chain
39097	B&S	130000	5	1	No	18	Chain

LUBRICATION

ENGINE

All Models

Refer to Briggs and Stratton engine section for lubrication specifications. Recommended oil grade is SAE 30 or equivalent. Recommended fuel is either regular or low-lead gasoline having an octane rating of 90 or higher.

DRIVE CONTROLS AND WHEELS

All Models

Clean and lubricate friction points with SAE 30 oil after each eight to fifteen

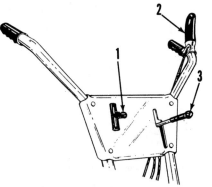

Fig. MW1 — View of control components for Models 39083 and 39084.
1. Throttle lever
2. Tine clutch lever
3. Drive clutch lever

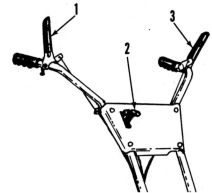

Fig. MW2 — View of control components for Model 39097.
1. Drive clutch lever
2. Throttle lever
3. Tine clutch lever

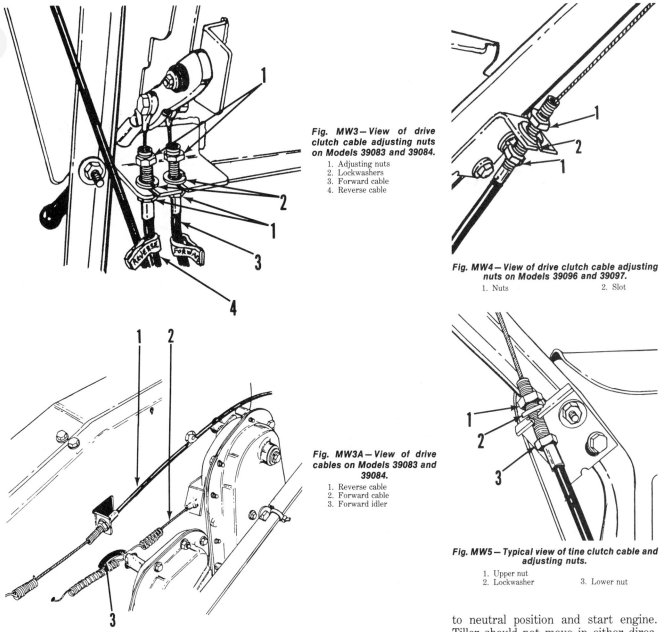

Fig. MW3 – View of drive clutch cable adjusting nuts on Models 39083 and 39084.
1. Adjusting nuts
2. Lockwashers
3. Forward cable
4. Reverse cable

Fig. MW4 – View of drive clutch cable adjusting nuts on Models 39096 and 39097.
1. Nuts   2. Slot

Fig. MW3A – View of drive cables on Models 39083 and 39084.
1. Reverse cable
2. Forward cable
3. Forward idler

Fig. MW5 – Typical view of tine clutch cable and adjusting nuts.
1. Upper nut
2. Lockwasher   3. Lower nut

hours of operation. Do not get oil on belts.

Models 39096 and 39097

Lubricate wheel pawl and ratchet drive at least twice a season with a silicone type lubricant.

CHAIN CASES

Chain cases are factory sealed and must be removed and disassembled in order to add or change lubricant. Refer to **OVERHAUL** section.

MAINTENANCE

Inspect all fasteners for looseness and retighten as needed. Check control levers, linkage and cables for freedom of movement or excessive play. Inspect drive belt(s) for excessive stretching, wear, cracks or any other damage. Install new belt(s) if needed. Inspect all pulleys and renew if damaged or excessively worn.

ADJUSTMENT

DRIVE CLUTCH

Models 39083 and 39084

PRIMARY ADJUSTMENT. Move lever (3 – Fig. MW1) to forward position, then adjust hex nuts (1 – Fig. MW3) so cables are tight.

To check adjustment, place tiller against a solid object, move control lever to neutral position and start engine. Tiller should not move in either direction. If tiller moves forward, adjust forward cable (3 – Fig. MW3) by loosening hex nut on top and tightening hex nut on bottom. If tiller moves in reverse, adjust reverse cable (4) by loosening hex nut on bottom and tightening hex nut on top. If tiller has no movement in neutral position, check clutch operation in the forward and reverse positions. If there is no movement in the forward position, adjust forward cable by loosening bottom hex nut and tightening upper hex nut. If there is no movement in the reverse position, adjust reverse cable by loosening upper hex nut and tightening lower hex nut.

SECONDARY ADJUSTMENT. If there is no adjustment left at upper ends of cables, the lower ends may be adjusted as follows: If tiller will not move

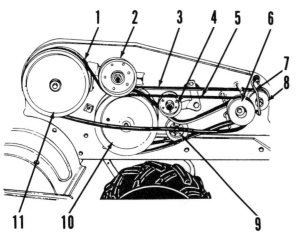

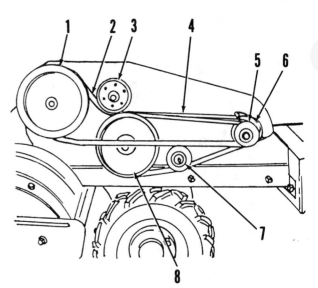

Fig. MW6—View of belt and pulley system on Models 39083 and 39084.

1. Tine belt
2. Idler pulley
3. Forward drive belt
4. Idler pulley
5. Reverse drive belt
6. Two-step engine pulley
7. Wire belt keeper
8. Forward engine pulley
9. Idler pulley
10. Wheel chain case pulley
11. Tine chain case pulley

Fig. MW7—View of belt and pulley system on Models 39096 and 39097.

1. Tine chain case pulley
2. Tine belt
3. Idler pulley
4. Wheel drive belt
5. Engine pulley, rear
6. Engine pulley, front
7. Idler pulley
8. Wheel chain case pulley

forward, refer to Fig. MW3A and loosen hex nut in back of forward cable bracket and tighten hex nut at front. If tiller will not move in reverse, loosen hex nut in front of reverse cable bracket and tighten nut at rear.

When making secondary adjustments on either forward or reverse cable, recheck neutral adjustment at upper end of cable.

Models 39096 and 39097

Refer to Fig. MW4 and with clutch lever in "up" position, adjust bottom hex nut at cable bracket so there is only a slight amount of slack in control cable. Tighten upper hex nut. With lever held down, control cable should be straight.

TINE CLUTCH

All Models

Refer to Fig. MW5. With tine clutch control lever in released position, adjust bottom hex nut (3) at cable bracket so that there is a slight amount of slack in control cable, then tighten upper hex nut (1). With control lever held down, control cable should be straight.

OVERHAUL

ENGINE

All Models

Engine model number is stamped on blower housing. Refer to appropriate Briggs and Stratton engine section for overhaul procedure.

CHAIN CASE

All Models

OIL SEAL INSTALLATION. Chain cases are factory sealed and no provision is made for checking or adding lubricant. Chain case must be separated as described in the following **INSPEC-**

TION paragraph to accurately add specific amounts of lubricant. Seals may be renewed as follows:

Remove tines or wheels from shaft. Use a seal puller or other appropriate tool to remove seal(s) from case hub. Clean tine/wheel shaft with emery cloth. Drive new seal(s) in until outside face is flush with case hub. Install inner seal

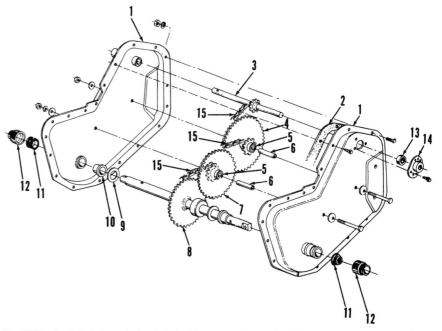

Fig. MW8—Exploded view of wheel chain drive assembly used on Models 39083, 39084, 39096 and 39097.

1. Chain case
2. Gasket
3. Input shaft & sprocket
4. Sprocket
5. Bearings
6. Sleeves
7. Sprocket
8. Wheel shaft & sprocket assy.
9. Washer
10. Flange bearing
11. Seals
12. Dust caps
13. Bearing
14. Bearing housing
15. Chain

DRIVE BELTS

Models 39083 and 39084

Refer to Fig. MW6 for belt routing and parts identification. Remove drive belt cover. Lift up idler pulley (2) and slip tine (belt(s) off chain case pulley (11) and two-step engine pulley (6). Lift up small idler pulley (4) and slip reverse drive belt (5) off outside sheave of wheel chain case pulley (10). Loosen and rotate wire keeper (7) away from forward engine pulley (8). Lift forward drive belt (3) off forward engine pulley and lift away from inside groove of wheel chain case pulley. Reverse procedure to install new belts. Tine drive belt size is ½-inch x 54 inches long. Forward drive belt size is ½-inch x 43 inches long. Reverse drive belt size is ½-inch x 39 inches long. Manufacturer recommends that only belts constructed with Kevlar Tensile be used.

Models 39096 and 39097

Refer to Fig. MW7 for belt routing and parts identification. Remove drive belt cover. Lift tine drive belt (2) out from under idler pulley (3). Loosen hex bolt on rear engine pulley (5) and slide pulley out far enough to remove belt, then slide belt off tine case pulley (1). To remove wheel drive belt (4), remove hex bolt, lockwasher and flat washer from rear engine pulley (5). Slide rear pulley off shaft. Loosen the two set screws on front engine pulley (6). Remove locknut on idler pulley (7). Slide idler and front engine pulleys out on their respective shafts and remove. Remove belt from wheel chain case pulley (8). Reverse procedure to install new belts. Tine drive belt size is ½-inch x 54 inches along. Wheel drive belt size is ½-inch x 43 inches long. Manufacturer recommends that only belts constructed with Kevlar Tensile be used.

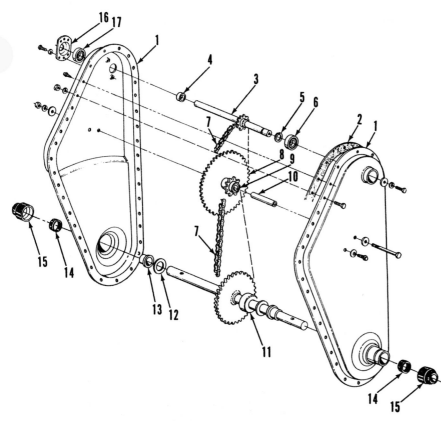

Fig. MW9—Exploded view of the chain drive assembly used on Models 39083, 39084, 39096 and 39097.

1. Chain case	6. Bearing	
2. Gasket	7. Chain	11. Tine shaft &
3. Input shaft & sprocket	8. Sprocket	sprocket assy.
4. Spacer	9. Bearing	12. Washer
5. Snap ring	10. Sleeve	13. Flange bearing
		14. Seal
		15. Dust cap
		16. Bearing housing
		17. Bearing

with lip facing towards inside and outer seal with lip facing towards outside.

INSPECTION. For wheel chain case, refer to Fig. MW8 for parts breakdown and identification. For tine chain case, refer to Fig. MW9 for parts breakdown and identification.

Inspect and renew all components that are worn or damaged. Install new gasket(s) and seals. Lubricate chains, sprockets and bearings with a light film of grease during reassembly. Keep all dirt and foreign matter out of chain case during reassembly.

Recommended lubricant for all models is Plastilube #0 grease or suitable equivalent. Wheel chain case capacity for all models is 10 ounces. Tine chain case capacity for all models is 12 ounces. To fill chain case with lubricant, lay left half of case on its side, add lubricant and assemble right half to left. Complete reassembly and reinstall in tiller frame.

WHEEL HORSE

WHEEL HORSE PRODUCTS INC.
P.O. Box 2649
515 West Ireland Road
South Bend, IN 46680-9988

Model	Engine Make	Engine Series	Power Rating	No. of Forward Speeds	Power Reverse?	Tilling Width	Drive Type
. . . .	B&S	80000	3 hp (2.2 kW)	1	No	15 in. (38 cm)	Gear
. . . .	Kawasaki	FA130	3.1 hp (2.3 kW)	1	No	15 in. (38 cm)	Gear

LUBRICATION

ENGINE

Refer to appropriate Briggs & Stratton or Kawasaki engine section for engine lubrication specifications. Recommended oil is a good quality oil which meets or exceeds API specification SC, SD, SE or SF, with viscosity chosen according to anticipated ambient temperature.

Recommended fuel is either regular or unleaded gasoline having an octane rating of 85 or higher. Use of fuel with alcohol additives is not recommended.

TINE GEARCASE

Check tine gearcase oil level after every 10 hours of operation. Place tiller on level surface and remove plug (1—Fig. WH1). Oil level should be at bottom of oil level plug hole. Recommended oil is a good quality SAE 90 or SAE 140 gear lubricant. Change tine gearcase oil after every 25 hours of operation, or sooner if contamination is noted.

WHEEL DRIVE GEARCASE

Check oil level in wheel drive gearcase after every 10 hours of operation. With tiller on level surface, oil should run out oil level plug (1—Fig. WH2) hole. Recommended oil is SAE 90 or SAE 140 gear lubricant. Wheel drive gearcase oil should be changed after every 25 hours of operation, or sooner if contamination is noted. To fill gearcase, remove tiller attachment and lean tiller backward so handlebars are sitting on the ground. Remove plug (1) and fill to bottom of plug hole.

GEAR REDUCTION HOUSING

Check oil level in gear reduction housing after every 10 hours of operation.

With tiller on level surface, oil level should be at bottom of oil level plug (2—Fig. WH3) hole. Change reduction housing oil after every 100 hours of op-

eration, or sooner if contamination is noted. To fill housing, remove oil fill plug (1) and add SAE 30 oil until oil runs out level plug (2) hole.

Fig. WH1—View of tine gearcase oil level plug (1).

Fig. WH2—View of wheel drive gearcase oil level plug (1).

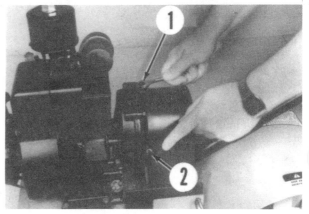

Fig. WH3—View of gear reduction oil fill plug (1) and oil level check plug (2).

MAINTENANCE

Periodically inspect all bolts and fasteners for looseness and tighten as necessary. Check control levers, linkage and cables for freedom of movement and excessive play. Inspect drive belt for excessive stretching, wear, cracks or any other damage. Renew belt as necessary. Inspect all belt pulleys and renew if damaged or excessively worn.

ADJUSTMENT

If drive belt slips when belt clutch is applied, position washers or shims under engine at engine mounting bolts to compensate for belt wear. Make certain tine movement stops when belt clutch is disengaged.

OVERHAUL

ENGINE

Engine identification numbers are located on engine shroud. Refer to appropriate Briggs & Stratton or Kawasaki engine section for overhaul procedure.

TINE GEARCASE

Refer to tiller identification number on plate (Fig. WH4) when ordering parts. Overhaul of tine gearcase is evident after referral to Fig. WH5 and inspection of unit. Inspect and renew all components that are excessively worn or damaged. Install new gaskets and seals. Lubricate gears and bearings with a light film of gear lube during reassembly. Refer to LUBRICATION section for lubrication requirements after reassembly.

WHEEL DRIVE GEARCASE

Refer to tiller identification number on plate (Fig. WH4) when ordering parts. Overhaul of wheel drive gearcase is evident after referral to Fig. WH6 and inspection of unit. Inspect and renew all components that are excessively worn or damaged. Renew all gaskets and seals. Lubricate gears and bearings during reassembly. Refer to LUBRICATION section for lubrication requirements after reassembly.

DRIVE BELT

To renew belt, remove tiller attachment and belt guard from unit. Push looped end of belt retainer (4—Fig. WH7) toward belt until retainer snaps free. Disengage wheel clutch lever (5) from clutch hook (6) and work belt off pulleys. Make sure clutch lever (5) properly engages hook (6) upon reassembly. Reinstall belt retainer (4) and check operation of unit.

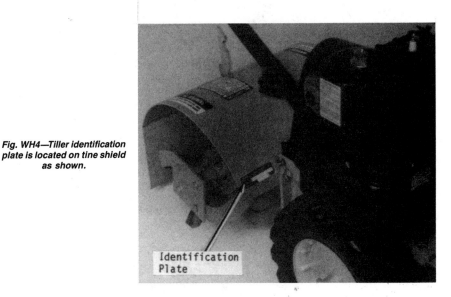

Fig. WH4—Tiller identification plate is located on tine shield as shown.

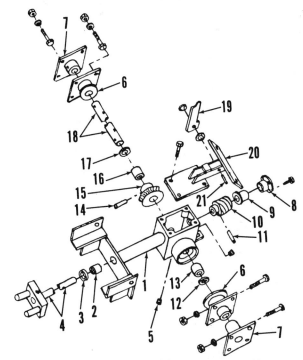

Fig. WH5—Exploded view of tine gearcase assembly.

1. Case & frame assy.		12. Seal	17. Seal
2. Bearing	7. Outer tine hub	13. Bearing	18. Tine shaft
3. Seal	8. Bearing retainer	14. Roll pin	19. Lever
4. Yoke	9. Bearing	15. Gear	20. Bracket
5. Plug	10. Worm gear	16. Bearing	21. Roll pin
6. Inner tine hub	11. Roll pin		

Fig. WH6—Exploded view of wheel drive gearcase assembly.

1. Case		20. Bearing
2. Bearing		21. Pulley
3. Seal		22. Roll pin
4. Bearing		23. Spacer
5. Plug		24. Worm gear
6. Wheel shaft		25. Clutch lever
7. Sleeve		26. Worm shaft
8. Ring		27. Seal
9. Roll pin		28. Bearing
10. Collar		29. Clutch engage
11. Clutch pin		actuator
12. Gear		30. Clutch disengage
13. Collar		actuator
14. Roll pin		31. Belt
15. Spring		32. Engine pulley
16. Roll pin		33. Spring
17. Idler lever		34. Cover
18. Idler		35. Pin
19. Lever		

Fig. WH7—Push looped end of belt retainer (4) toward belt (1) to remove retainer (4).

1. Belt	4. Retainer
2. Pulley	5. Lever
3. Spring	6. Hook

WHITE

WHITE MOTOR CORPORATION
1830 White Boulevard
Libertyville, IL 60048

Model	Engine Make	Engine Series	Engine Horsepower	No. of Forward Speeds	Power Reverse?	Tilling Width (In.)	Drive Type
Roto Boss 200	B&S	60000	2	1	No	6½-18	Chain
Roto Boss 300	B&S	80000	3	1	No	10-18	Chain
Roto Boss 350	B&S	90000	3.5	1	Yes	12-26	Gear
Roto Boss 500	B&S	130000	5	1	Yes	14-26	Chain
Roto Boss 800	B&S	190000	8	4	Yes	12-26	Chain
Roto Boss 802	B&S	190000	8	5	Yes	20	Chain

LUBRICATION

ENGINE

All Models

Refer to appropriate Briggs and Stratton engine section for engine lubrication specifications.

Recommended oil grade is SAE 30 or equivalent. Recommended fuel is either regular or low-lead gasoline having an octane rating of 90 or higher. The use of non-leaded gasolines reduces cylinder head deposits, but could shorten engine valve life if carburetor is adjusted too lean.

CHAIN DRIVE

All Models

Chain case is factory sealed and must be removed and disassembled in order to add or change lubricant in case. Refer to **OVERHAUL** section.

GEAR CASE

Model 350

Gear case oil should be checked at least every 10 hours of operation. Recommended lubricant is Pennant oil EP#35000 or suitable equivalent.

To check gear case oil place tiller on a level surface. Clean dirt from around front of gear case and remove oil level plug (1 – Fig. W1). Oil level should be at bottom of plug hole. If oil level is low add oil through plug hole until it begins to run out, then replace and tighten plug.

MAINTENANCE

Inspect all fasteners for looseness and retighten as needed. Check control levers, linkage and cables for freedom of movement and excessive play. Inspect drive belt(s) for excessive stretching, wear, cracks, or any other damage. Install new belt(s) if needed. Inspect all belt pulleys and renew if damaged or excessively worn. Transport wheels on Models 200, 300, 350, 500 and 800 should be lubricated occasionally with SAE 30 oil.

ADJUSTMENT

CLUTCH CONTROL AND DRIVE BELT

Models 200 and 300

Loosen and turn hex nuts (3 – Fig. W2) to adjust clutch. To check for correct clutch adjustment place clutch lever (1) in neutral position. Unhook spark plug lead and pull on starter rope handle. If tines do not turn, then adjustment is correct. If tines do turn, then clutch cable should be adjusted.

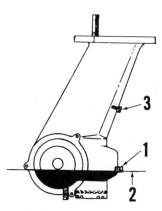

Fig. W1 — View of oil plugs and oil level for Model 350 gear case.
1. Oil level plug
2. Oil level
3. Breather plug

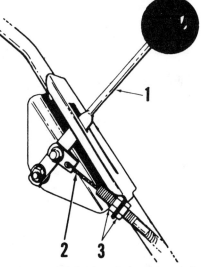

Fig. W2 — View of clutch control components for Models 200 and 300.
1. Clutch lever
2. Clutch cable
3. Cable adjusting nuts

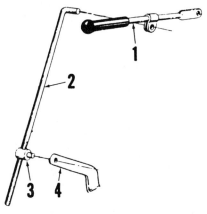

Fig. W3 — View of clutch control components for Models 350, 500, 800 and 802.
1. Clutch lever
2. Threaded control rod
3. Adjustment ferrule
4. Bracket

Models 350, 500, 800 and 802

Remove hair pin clip from ferrule (3 – Fig. W3), then remove ferrule from bracket (4). Turn ferrule up or down control rod (2) to adjust clutch. Reinstall ferrule in bracket and install hair pin clip. To check for correct clutch adjustment place clutch lever (1) in neutral position. Unhook spark plug lead and pull on starter rope handle. If tines do not turn, then adjustment is correct. If tines do turn, then clutch rod will need to be adjusted.

GEAR CASE

Model 350

Gear case bearing adjustment should be accomplished approximately every five hours of operation. Adjust by removing cotter pin (17 – Fig. W8), then turning adjustment cap (16) in until snug. Do not over-tighten. Reinstall cotter pin, then check adjustment by starting tiller and engaging tines. If engine stalls, then bearing adjustment is too tight and adjustment cap should be loosened slightly.

OVERHAUL

ENGINE

All Models

Engine model no. is stamped on blower housing. Refer to appropriate Briggs and Stratton engine section for overhaul procedures.

CHAIN CASE

All Models

OIL SEAL INSTALLATION. Remove tines from tine shaft. Using a seal puller pull seal(s) out of case hub. If seal puller is not available use an awl and screwdriver to pry seals out. Clean tine shaft with emery cloth. Drive new seal(s) in until outside face is flush with case hub. On models with two seals on each side install inner seal with lip facing toward inside and outer seal with lip facing toward outside. On Model 802 remove wheels to install axle shaft seals.

INSPECTION. On Models 200 and 300 refer to Fig. W4 for parts breakdown and identification. For Model 500 refer to Fig. W5, for Model 800 refer to Fig. W6 and for Model 802 refer to Fig. W7.

Inspect and renew all components that are worn or damaged. Install new gasket and seals. Lubricate chains, sprockets and bearings with a light film

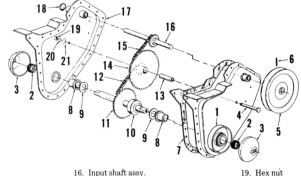

Fig. W4 — Exploded view of chain case for Models 200 and 300.

1. Chain case, L.H.
2. Oil seals
3. Dust covers
4. Bolt, 2½ inches long
5. Input pulley
6. Roll pin
7. Gasket
8. Flange bearings
9. Washers
10. Spacer
11. Tine shaft assy.
12. Chain, 0.375 inch pitch x 50 links
13. Inner race
14. Hub and sprocket assy.
15. Chain, 0.50 inch pitch x 38 links
16. Input shaft assy.
17. Chain case, R.H.
18. Expansion ring
19. Hex nut
20. Lockwasher
21. Flat washer

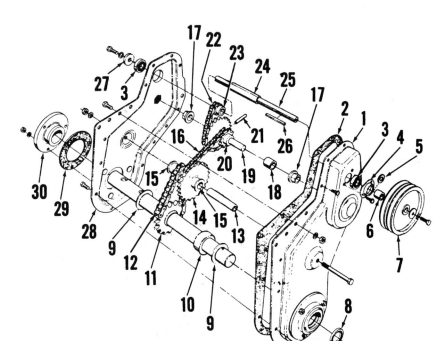

Fig. W5 — Exploded view of chain case for Model 500.

1. Chain case, L.H.
2. Gasket
3. Bearings
4. Bearing housing
5. Flat washer
6. Spacer
7. Input pulley
8. Oil seal
9. Flat washer
10. Spacer
11. Tine shaft assy.
12. Chain, ⅝-inch pitch x 28 links
13. Sprocket shaft
14. Sprocket
15. Flange bearing
16. Chain, ½-inch pitch x 48 links
17. Hex flanged bearing
18. Spacer
19. Sprocket shaft
20. Sprocket sleeve assy.
21. Roll pin
22. Chain, ½-inch pitch x 34 links
23. Sprocket
24. Spacer
25. Input shaft
26. Square key
27. Flat washer
28. Chain case, R.H.
29. Gasket
30. Bearing housing assy.

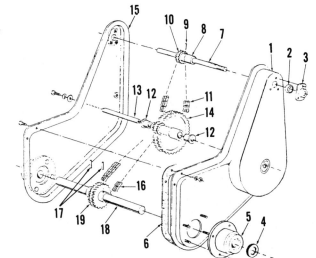

Fig. W6 — Exploded view of chain case for Model 800.

1. Chain case, L.H.
2. Ball bearing, L.H and R.H.
3. Bearing housing, L.H. and R.H.
4. Oil seal, L.H. and R.H.
5. Bearing housing with bearing, L.H. and R.H.
6. Gasket
7. Input shaft
8. Spacer
9. Roll pin
10. Spacer
11. Chain, #35-2 x 36-¾ inches long
12. Flange bearings
13. Sprocket shaft
14. Sprocket
15. Chain case, R.H.
16. Chain, #40-2 x 34 inches long
17. Roll pins
18. Tine shaft
19. Sprocket

of grease during reassembly. Keep all dirt and foreign matter out of chain case during reassembly.

Recommended lubricant for Models 200 and 300 is 16 ounces of Plastilube #0 grease or suitable equivalent. Recommended lubricant for Model 500 is 14 ounces of Plastilube #0 grease or suitable equivalent. Recommended lubricant for Model 800 is Lubriplate No. 310 or suitable equivalent. Adequately lubricate chains and gears during reassembly. Recommended lubricant for Model 802 is 28 ounces of Plastilube #1 grease or suitable equivalent. To fill chain case with grease, lay right half of case on its side, add grease and assemble left half to right. Complete reassembly and reinstall in tiller frame.

GEAR CASE

Model 350

OIL SEAL INSTALLATION. Remove tines from tine shaft. Use a seal puller to remove seal(s) from case hub. Clean tine shaft with emery cloth. Drive new seal(s) in until outside face is flush with case hub.

REMOVE AND DISASSEMBLE. Refer to Fig. W8 for parts breakdown and identification. Inspect and renew all components that are worn or damaged. Install new gaskets and seals. Lubricate gears and bearings with a light film of oil during reassembly. Keep all dirt and foreign matter out of gear case during reassembly. Refer to **LUBRICATION** section for lubricating requirements after reassembly and installation. Refer to **GEAR CASE ADJUSTMENT** section for bearing preload adjusting procedure.

DRIVE BELTS

Models 200 and 300

Refer to Fig. W9 for belt routing and parts identification. Place clutch lever in forward position, then unhook extension spring (3) from drive belt cover. Remove drive belt cover. Remove belt from pulleys and install new belt. Drive belt size is 3/8-inch x 29 inches long. Reinstall drive belt cover, then rehook extension spring in cover. Refer to **CLUTCH CONTROL AND DRIVE BELT ADJUSTMENT** section for adjusting procedure.

Model 350

Refer to Fig. W10 for belt(s) routing and parts identification. Place clutch lever in neutral position. Remove four cap screws securing engine bed to mounting plate assembly, then remove

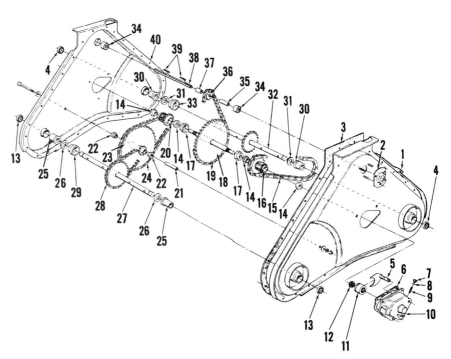

Fig. W7 — Exploded view of chain case for Model 802. Shift parts (5 through 12) are used on both sides.

1. Chain case, L.H.	13. Oil seals	21. Hub sleeve
2. Bearing housing	14. Flange bearings	22. Flange bearings
3. Gasket	15. Chain, 5/8-inch pitch	23. Sprocket assy.
4. Oil seals	x 52 links	24. Chain, 1/2-inch pitch x
5. Shift yoke	16. Sprocket bearing	58 links
6. Gasket	sleeve assy.	25. Flange bearings
7. Cap plug	17. Stepped spacer	26. Flat washers
8. Detent ball	18. Clutch shaft assy.	27. Axle shaft assy.
9. Spring	19. Chain, 1/2-inch pitch	28. Chain, 1/2-inch pitch x
10. Shift housing	x 58 links	42 links
11. Clutch dog	20. Sprocket bearing	29. Spacer
12. Clutch dog driver	sleeve assy.	30. Flange bearings

31. Flat washers
32. Tine shaft assy.
33. Spacer
34. Ball bearings
35. Spacer
36. Sprocket
37. Spacer
38. Input shaft
39. Square keys
40. Chain case, R.H.

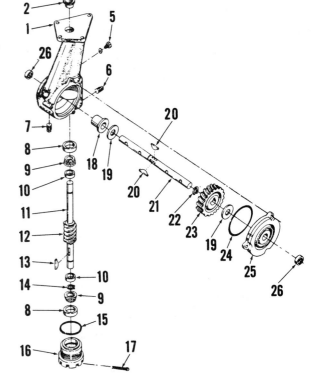

Fig. W8 — Exploded view of gear case for Model 350.

1. Gear case
2. Sleeve bearing
3. Oil seal
4. Snap ring
5. Breaker plug and star washer
6. Oil fill plug
7. Oil level plug
8. Bearing cups
9. Bearing cones
10. Spacers
11. Worm shaft
12. Worm gear
13. Drive key
14. Snap ring
15. "O" ring
16. Adjustment plug
17. Cotter pin
18. Flange bearing
19. Washers
20. Drive keys
21. Tine shaft
22. Snap ring
23. Worm gear
24. "O" ring
25. Flange cover with bearing
26. Oil seals

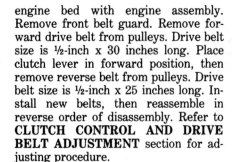

Fig. W9 — View of drive belt routing and components for Model 200 and 300.
1. Engine pulley
2. Idler pulley
3. Extension spring
4. Chain case pulley
5. Clutch cable
6. Drive belt

engine bed with engine assembly. Remove front belt guard. Remove forward drive belt from pulleys. Drive belt size is ½-inch x 30 inches long. Place clutch lever in forward position, then remove reverse belt from pulleys. Drive belt size is ½-inch x 25 inches long. Install new belts, then reassemble in reverse order of disassembly. Refer to **CLUTCH CONTROL AND DRIVE BELT ADJUSTMENT** section for adjusting procedure.

Model 500

Refer to Fig. W11 for belt(s) routing and parts identification. Remove drive belt cover. Loosen belt wire finger (2) retaining bolt and nut. Place clutch lever in reverse position, then remove forward drive belt from pulleys. Drive belt size is ½-inch x 37 inches long. Place clutch lever in neutral position, then remove reverse drive belt from chain case pulley. Place clutch lever in reverse position. Remove reverse idler pulley (5) retaining nut, then slip pulley and belt off of idler bracket together. Drive belt size is ½-inch x 41 inches long. Install new belts, then reassemble in reverse order of disassembly. Refer to **CLUTCH CONTROL AND DRIVE BELT ADJUSTMENT** section for adjusting procedure.

Model 800

Refer to Fig. W12 for belt(s) routing and parts identification. Remove drive belt cover. Place tine depth bar across top of transport wheel hanger, then place tip of bar under variable speed bracket assembly (8). Stand on back of bar, using wheel hanger as a fulcrum apply upward pressure on bracket. Slack should be present in belts if enough pressure is applied. Remove rear drive belt (6) first, then remove forward drive

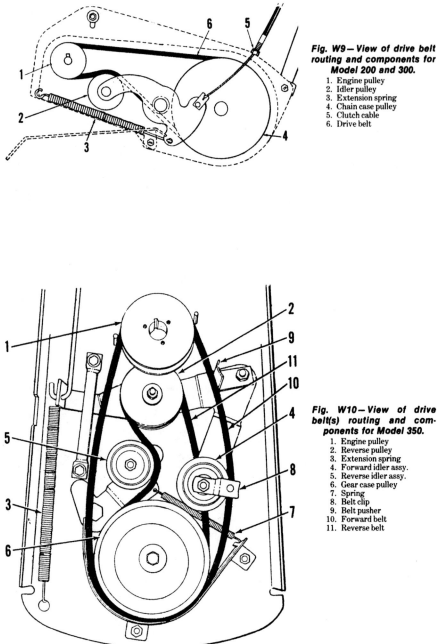

Fig. W10 — View of drive belt(s) routing and components for Model 350.
1. Engine pulley
2. Reverse pulley
3. Extension spring
4. Forward idler assy.
5. Reverse idler assy.
6. Gear case pulley
7. Spring
8. Belt clip
9. Belt pusher
10. Forward belt
11. Reverse belt

Fig. W11 — View of drive belt(s) routing and components for Model 500.
1. Engine pulley
2. Belt wire finger
3. Clutch plate
4. Control rod
5. Reverse idler assy.
6. Spring
7. Forward idler assy.
8. Clutch control rod assy.
9. Reverse belt
10. Forward belt
11. Chain case pulley

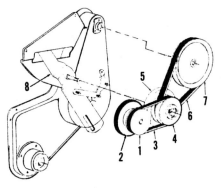

Fig. W12 — View of drive belt(s) routing and components for Model 800.
1. Engine pulley
2. Friction wheel assy.
3. Drive belt
4. Variable speed pulley assy.
5. Friction disc
6. Drive belt
7. Chain case pulley
8. Variable speed bracket assy.

belt (3). Rear drive belt size is ⅝-inch x 35 inches long. Forward drive belt size is ⅝-inch x 28 inches long. Install new belts, then reassemble in reverse order of disassembly. Refer to **CLUTCH CONTROL AND DRIVE BELT ADJUSTMENT** section for adjusting procedure.

Model 802

Refer to Fig. W13 for belt routing and parts identification. Remove drive belt cover. Place clutch lever in reverse position, then remove forward belt (13) from engine pulley towards engine. Slip belt off variable speed pulley (4) and remove belt. Drive belt size is ⅝-inch x 27 inches long. Place clutch lever in second (2) speed position, then remove rear drive belt (14) from chain case pulley (11) and variable speed pulley. Drive belt size is ⅝-inch x 52 inches long. Install new belts, then reassemble in reverse order of disassembly. Refer to **CLUTCH CONTROL AND DRIVE BELT ADJUSTMENT** section for adjusting procedure.

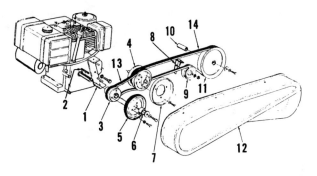

Fig. W13—View of drive belt routing and components for Model 802.
1. Drive belt(s) cover support assy.
2. Square key
3. Engine pulley
4. Variable speed assy.
5. Friction wheel assy.
6. Spacer
7. Friction disc
8. Belt keeper
9. Idler pulley
10. Spacer
11. Chain case input pulley
12. Drive belt(s) cover
13. Drive belt
14. Drive belt

DRIVE BELTS

Make & Model	Mfg. Part No.	Dayco No.	Gates No.	Size*
ARIENS				
RT214	72109	L432	6832	1/2X32
RT320	72109	L432	6832	1/2X32
RT324	72109	L432	6832	1/2X32
RT424				
Fwd.	72056	L432	6832	1/2X32
Rev.	72099	L331	6731	3/8X31-1/16
RT424X				
Fwd.	72056	L432	6832	1/2X32
Rev.	72099	L331	6731	3/8X31-1/16
RT424CI				
Fwd.	72056	L432	6832	1/2X32
Rev.	72099	L331	6731	3/8X31-1/16
RT524				
Fwd.	72056	L432	6832	1/2X32
Rev.	72085	L332	6732	3/8X32
RT524C	72073	L450	6831	1/2X31
RT524S				
Fwd.	72056	L432	6832	1/2X32
Rev.	72043	L332	6732	3/8X32
RT5020				
Fwd.	72119	L4305	6830	1/2X30.5
Rev.	72106	L337	6731	3/8X37
SRT5020				
Fwd.	72119	L4305	6830	1/2X30.5
Rev.	72106	L337	6737	3/8X37
RT7020				
Fwd.	72046†	L331†	6731†	3/8X31
Rev.	72106	L337	6737	3/8X37
RT8020				
Fwd.	72126†	L336†	6736†	7/16X36
Rev.	72127	L3415	6742	3/8X41.75
RT8028				
Fwd.	72126†	L336†	6736†	7/16X36
Rev.	72127	L3415	6742	3/8X41.75
ATLAS				
2100	107-38	L436	6836	1/2X36
3010	107-37	L431	6831	1/2X31
3011	107-37	L431	6831	1/2X31
3100	107-38	L436	6836	1/2X36
3150	107-38	L436	6836	1/2X36
5012	107-37	L431	6831	1/2X31
5013	107-37	L431	6831	1/2X31
5015				
Fwd.	107-37	L431	6831	1/2X31
Rev.	107-37	L431	6831	1/2X31
5016				
Fwd.	107-37	L431	6831	1/2X31
Rev.	107-37	L431	6831	1/2X31
5021				
Fwd.	107-37	L431	6831	1/2X31
Rev.	107-37	L431	6831	1/2X31
5022				
Fwd.	107-37	L431	6831	1/2X31
Rev.	107-37	L431	6831	1/2X31
5100				
Fwd.	107-38	L436	6836	1/2X36
Rev.	107-39	L432	6832	1/2X32
5300	107-38	L436	6836	1/2X36
CLINTON				
500-T-14	10228‡	L327	6727	3/8X27

Make & Model	Mfg. Part No.	Dayco No.	Gates No.	Size*
JOHN DEERE				
216	M81805			17/32X49
324				
Fwd.	M45680	L433	6833	1/2X33
Rev.	M46030	L433	6833	1/2X33
524				
Fwd.	M45680	L433	6833	1/2X33
Rev.	M45681	L432	6832	1/2X32
624				
Fwd.	M45680	L433	6833	1/2X33
Rev.	M45681	L432	6832	1/2X32
FORD				
1005				
Fwd.	2435	L437	6837	1/2X37
Rev.	6184	L339	6739	3/8X39
1013	9304	L429	6829	1/2X29
1023				
Fwd.	1110	L435	6835	1/2X35
Rev.	6163	L337	6737	3/8X37
1105 & 1200	36019	L320	6720	3/8X20
1114 & 1134				
Trac	200555	L346	6746	3/8X46
Tine	200554	L338	6738	3/8X38
GILSON				
51080	28673			
51081				
Fwd.	1110			
Rev.	6163			
51082				
Fwd.	1110			
Rev.	6163			
51083				
Upper	26344			
Lower	26345			
51084	28673			
51085				
Fwd.	1110			
Rev.	6163			
51088				
Fwd.	1110			
Rev.	6163			
51095	33622			
51097				
Fwd.	1110			
Rev.	6163			
51104	35900			
51105	36019			
51114				
Trac	200555			
Tine	200554			
51116	9304			
51134				
Trac	200555			
Tine	200554			
51135				
Fwd.	208526			
Rev.	208525			
Tine	208527			
51142	208301			

Make & Model	Mfg. Part No.	Dayco No.	Gates No.	Size*
GILSON (Cont.)				
51143				
Fwd.	208301			
Rev.	208626			
HABAN				
861-002				
Fwd.	10467	L452	6852	1/2X53.5
Rev.	10371	L443	6843	1/2X43.5
HOMELITE				
FT-5	01212-01			
RT-5				
Tine	01213-41			
Pri. wheel drive	01213-14			
Sec. wheel drive	01213-15			
HONDA				
F401	047765	L536	6936	5/8X36
F501	047765	L536	6936	5/8X36
INTERNATIONAL				
526				
Fwd.	59-004	L440	6840	1/2X40
Rev.	59-003	L445	6845	1/2X45
526A				
Fwd.	73-692	L434	6834	1/2X34
Rev.	73-691	L335	6735	3/8X35
KUBOTA				
AT55	53761-43170			5/8X37
AT60	62421-62310			1/2X40
AT70	62421-62310			1/2X40
LAZY BOY				
LB200GT	50036			
3LBCT	01228			
S265	10244			
756T				
Fwd.	01244			
Rev.	01246			
LB5RT				
Eng.-to-jackshaft	011256			
Tine	01254			
Wheel	01257			
Max				
Pri. wheel	60017			
Sec. wheel	60018			
Tine	60016			
MERRY				
G-76	2059	L450	6850	1/2X50
G-77	2059	L450	6850	1/2X50
G-78	2059	L450	6850	1/2X50
G-80	2059	L450	6850	1/2X50

Make & Model	Mfg. Part No.	Dayco No.	Gates No.	Size*
MERRY (Cont.)				
G-82				
Fwd.	2059	L450	6850	1/2X50
Rev.	2313	L345	6745	3/8X45
G-83	2059	L450	6850	1/2X50
G-84	2059	L450	6850	1/2X50
G-87	2059	L450	6850	1/2X50
G-88				
Fwd.	2059	L450	6850	1/2X50
Rev.	2313	L345	6745	3/8X45
G-90	2278	L441	6841	1/2X41
G-91	2278	L441	6841	1/2X41
G-92	2278	L441	6841	1/2X41
MM-1	3292	L434	6834	1/2X34
2000	3292	L434	6834	1/2X34
2001	3292	L434	6834	1/2X34
3200	3292	L434	6834	1/2X34
7100	3292	L434	6834	1/2X34
7200	2059	L450	6850	1/2X50
7300	2059	L450	6850	1/2X50
7400	2059	L450	6850	1/2X50
7401				
Fwd.	2059	L450	6850	1/2X50
Rev.	2313	L345	6745	3/8X45
7402	2059	L450	6850	1/2X50
7403				
Fwd.	2059	L450	6850	1/2X50
Rev.	2313	L345	6745	3/8X45
7480	2059	L450	6850	1/2X50
7500	2059	L450	6850	1/2X50
7501	2059	L450	6850	1/2X50
7502	2059	L450	6850	1/2X50
7600	2278	L441	6841	1/2X41
7601	2278	L441	6841	1/2X41
7602	2278	L441	6841	1/2X41
MTD				
030	754-216	L329	6729	3/8X29
320	754-190	L439	6839	1/2X39
355				
Fwd.	754-154	L437	6837	1/2X37
Rev.	754-189	L444	6844	1/2X44
385				
Fwd.	754-154	L437	6837	1/2X37
Rev.	754-201	L441	6841	1/2X41
386				
Fwd.	754-254	L419	6819	1/2X19
Rear	754-231	L428	6828	1/2X28
405				
Fwd.	754-224	L526	6926	5/8X26
Rear	754-221	L552	6952	5/8X52
408				
Fwd.	754-220	L527	6927	5/8X27
Rear	754-221	L552	6952	5/8X52
409				
Fwd.	754-220	L527	6927	5/8X27
Rear	754-221	L552	6952	5/8X52
410				
Fwd.	754-220	L527	6927	5/8X27
Rear	754-268	L551	6951	5/8X51
412				
Fwd.	754-220	L527	6927	5/8X27
Rear	754-268	L551	6951	5/8X51
418				
Fwd.	754-220	L527	6927	5/8X27
Rear	754-268	L551	6951	5/8X51

Make & Model	Mfg. Part No.	Dayco No.	Gates No.	Size*
MURRAY				
1000	75370	L426	6826	1/2X26
1190	75121	L448	6848	1/2X48
1202				
Fwd.	75121	L448	6848	1/2X48
Rev.	75147	L339	6739	3/8X39
1203				
Fwd.	75121	L448	6848	1/2X48
Rev.	75147	L339	6739	3/8X39
1290	75121	L448	6848	1/2X48
1302				
Fwd.	75121	L448	6848	1/2X48
Rev.	75147	L339	6739	3/8X39
1303				
Fwd.	75121	L448	6848	1/2X48
Rev.	75147	L339	6739	3/8X39
ROPER				
RF300	9179R	L339	6739	3/8X40
RF500	9180R	L441	6841	1/2X41.3
RF550				
Fwd.	4833H	L441	6841	1/2X41
Rev.	2614J	L344	6744	3/8X44
RT130	102143X			1/2X52.75
RT150	102143X			1/2X52.75
RT180	8377J	L459	6859	1/2X59
ROTO-HOE				
SP				
Low speed	1078	L443	6843	1/2X43
High speed	1079	L437	6837	1/2X37
220				
Eng.-to-jackshaft	1543	L447	6847	1/2X47
Tine	1078	L443	6843	1/2X43
904				
Inner	3L355	L335	6735	3/8X35.5
Outer	4L460	L446	6846	1/2X46
910				
Eng.-to-jackshaft	5065	L449	6849	1/2X49
Jackshaft-to-tines	1542	L452	6852	1/2X52
Trans.	5051		6364	
990				
Eng.-to-jackshaft	5065	L449	6849	1/2X49
Jackshaft-to-tines	1542	L452	6852	1/2X52
Trans.	5051		6364	
SEARS				
29852	9179R	L339	6739	3/8X39
29936				
Fwd.	4833H	L441	6841	1/2X41
Rev.	2614J			
29937	9180R	L442	6842	1/2X42
29943	9179R	L339	6739	3/8X39
29945				
Fwd.	4833H	L441	6841	1/2X41
Rev.	2614J			
29958	4897H1	L437	6837	1/2X37

Make & Model	Mfg. Part No.	Dayco No.	Gates No.	Size*
SEARS (Cont.)				
29966				
Tine	4454J			
Trac	4376J			
29968				
Tine	4454J			
Trac	4376J			
SNAPPER				
300T	1-1969	L451	6851	1/2X51
500T	1-1969	L451	6851	1/2X51
301T	1-1969	L451	6851	1/2X51
301TR				
Fwd.	1-2248	L427	6827	1/2X26.5
Rear	1-2249	L437	6837	1/2X37
401T	1-1969	L451	6851	1/2X51
401TR				
Fwd.	1-2248	L427	6827	1/2X26.5
Rear	1-2249	L437	6837	1/2X37
401TCR				
Fwd.	1-2248	L427	6827	1/2X26.5
Rear	1-2249	L437	6837	1/2X37
501T	1-1969	L451	6851	1/2X51
501TR				
Fwd.	1-2248	L4265	68265	1/2X26.5
Rear	1-2249	L437	6837	1/2X37
501TC	1-1969	L451	6851	1/2X51
501TRC				
Fwd.	1-2248	L427	6827	1/2X26.5
Rear	1-2249	L437	6837	1/2X37
RT5	1-4353			
RT5X	1-4353			
RT8	1-4353			
RT8S	1-4353			
R5000	§			
R5001	§			
R5002	1-4353			
R5002R	1-4353			
R8000	§			
R8001	§			
R8001S	§			
R8002	1-4353			
R8002S	1-4353			
TROY-BILT				
Horse (4 spd.)				
Fwd.	9245			
Horse (2 spd.)				
Fwd.	1128†			
PTO Horse				
Fwd.	9245			
Econo-Horse				
Fwd.	20565			
Rev.	9022			
Pony				
Fwd.	20565			
Rev.	50134			
Set	4922			
Junior				
Fwd.	20565			
Rev.	9095			
Set	11018			
Tuffy	55037			

Make & Model	Mfg. Part No.	Dayco No.	Gates No.	Size*	Make & Model	Mfg. Part No.	Dayco No.	Gates No.	Size*
WHEELHORSE					**WHITE (Cont.)**				
All Models	114765				500				
					Fwd.	41327	L437	6837	1/2X37
					Rev.	41165	L441	6841	1/2X41
WHITE					800				
200	45527	L329	6729	3/8X29	Fwd.	05908	L528	6928	5/8X28
300	45527	L329	6729	3/8X29	Rear	05843	L535	6935	5/8X35
350					802				
Fwd.	05118	L430	6830	1/2X30	Fwd.	54089	L527	6927	5/8X27
Rev.	05096	L425	6825	1/2X25	Rear	54100	L552	6952	5/8X52

* All belt dimensions are in inches.
† Two required. Order in matched set.
‡ Notched belt is preferred.
§ Use belt 1-4686 on 1982 and 1983 5 hp (3.7 kW) models or belt 1-4353 on all 1984 and later models.

ACME

ACME NORTH AMERICA CORP.
5209 W. 73rd St.
Minneapolis, MN 55435

Model	No. Cyls.	Bore	Stroke	Displacement
A 220 B	1	72 mm	54 mm	220 cc
		(2.83 in.)	(2.13 in.)	(13.43 cu. in.)

ENGINE IDENTIFICATION

Model A 220 B is a four-stroke, air-cooled, single-cylinder engine.

Engine is equipped with a horizontal crankshaft with intake and exhaust valves located in the cylinder block. The suffix ''B'' indicates models are gasoline fuel engines.

Engine model number is located on a plate mounted on the right side of the shroud as viewed from flywheel side. The engine serial number is stamped into the engine block approximately 3 inches (76.2 mm) below model number plate, just above oil fill plug (Fig. AC1).

Always furnish engine model and serial number when ordering parts.

MAINTENANCE

SPARK PLUG. Recommended spark plug is a Bosch RO10846 or equivalent. Spark plug should be removed, cleaned and inspected after every 100 hours of operation. Spark plug electrode gap should be 0.6-0.8 mm (0.024-0.032 in.).

CARBURETOR. Model A 220 B is equipped with the float type carburetor shown in Fig. AC4.

Initial adjustment of idle speed mixture screw (3) from a lightly seated position is 1-1/2 turns open. Main fuel mixture is controlled by fixed main jet (13).

Fixed main jet size is #98. Idle jet (7) size is #35.

Final adjustments are made with engine at operating temperature and running. Adjust engine idle speed to 1000-1100 rpm at throttle stop screw (5). Adjust idle mixture screw (3) to obtain smoothest engine idle and smooth acceleration.

To check float level, remove carburetor float bowl (15). Invert carburetor body (1). Float height should be 15 mm (19/32 in.) measured from carburetor body gasket surface to bottom of float (12). Float weight should be 8 grams (0.29 oz.). If float is heavier than specified, it must be renewed.

Fuel filter screen (8) should be removed and cleaned after every 50 hours of operation.

AIR FILTER. Model A 220 B is equipped with a paper element type air filter. Filter should be checked daily. After removing element, clean element by gently tapping element to dislodge dust and dirt or use very low air pressure and blow from the inside of the air filter element toward the outside. Element should be renewed after 100 hours of operation when engine is operated under normal conditions. Shorten element renewal intervals when engine is operated under adverse conditions.

GOVERNOR. Model A 220 B is equipped with a flyweight type governor. Governor gear and flyweight assembly is located on the crankcase cover and is driven by the crankshaft gear. The governor regulates engine speed via external linkage.

To adjust external governor linkage, first make certain all linkage moves freely with no binding or loose connections. Place throttle control lever (8— Fig. AC7) in full throttle position. Loos-

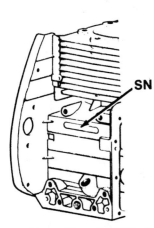

Fig. AC1—Engine serial number (SN) is stamped into engine block.

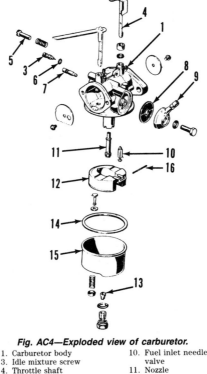

Fig. AC4—Exploded view of carburetor.

1. Carburetor body	10. Fuel inlet needle
3. Idle mixture screw	valve
4. Throttle shaft	11. Nozzle
5. Throttle stop screw	12. Float
6. Gasket	13. Main jet
7. Idle jet	14. Gasket
8. Screen (filter)	15. Float bowl
9. Filter housing	16. Float pin

Fig. AC7—View showing relative position and relationship of external governor linkage and throttle parts.

1. Clamp bolt	
2. Governor shaft	6. Throttle lever
3. Governor lever	7. Spring
4. Spring	8. Throttle control
5. Governor lever-to-	lever
carburetor rod	9. Throttle stop screw

en clamp bolt (1). Insert screwdriver into slot of governor shaft (2) and rotate shaft clockwise as far as possible. Tighten clamp bolt (1). Place throttle control lever (8) in idle position, then start and run engine. Engine idle should be adjusted to 1000-1100 rpm. Place throttle control lever (8) in full throttle position and adjust throttle stop screw (9) to obtain 2400, 3000 or 3600 rpm. Do not exceed maximum engine speed of 3600 rpm.

IGNITION SYSTEM. A solid-state electronic ignition system is standard on Model A 220 B.

The solid-state electronic ignition system requires no regular maintenance. Use the correct feeler gage to check clearance between ignition coil and flywheel. Clearance should be 0.40-0.45 mm (0.016-0.018 in.).

LUBRICATION. Check engine oil level after every 8 hours of operation. Maintain oil level at lower edge of fill plug opening.

Change oil after every 50 hours of operation. Manufacturer recommends oil with an API service classification SC or CC. Use SAE 40 oil for ambient temperatures above 10° C (50° F); SAE 30 oil for a temperature range of 0° to 10° C (32° to 50° F); SAE 20W-20 oil for a temperature range of -10° to 0° C (14° to 32° F) and SAE 10W oil for temperatures below -10° C (14°F). Crankcase oil capacity is 0.6 L (0.634 qt.).

VALVE ADJUSTMENT. Valves should be adjusted after every 200 hours of operation. Valve stem-to-tappet clearance (cold) should be 0.10-0.15 mm

(0.004-0.006 in.) for intake and exhaust valves. If clearance is not as specified, remove or install shims (7 and 8—Fig. AC9) in shim holder (9) as necessary. Shims are available in 0.1 mm (0.004 in.) and 0.2 mm (0.008 in.) thicknesses.

CRANKCASE BREATHER. A crankcase breather which is an integral part of the valve chamber cover is used. No regular maintenance is required.

GENERAL MAINTENANCE. Check and tighten all loose bolts, nuts or clamps prior to each day of operation. Check for fuel or oil leakage and repair if necessary.

Clean dust, dirt, grease or any foreign material from cylinder head and cylinder block cooling fins after every 100 hours of operation. Inspect fins for damage and repair if necessary.

REPAIRS

TIGHTENING TORQUES. Recommended tightening torque specifications are as follows:

Cylinder head . . . . .24.5 N·m
(18 ft.-lbs.)
Connecting rod . . . . .11.8 N·m
(9 ft.-lbs.)
Crankcase cover. . . . . .11.8 N·m
(9 ft.-lbs.)
Flywheel . . . . .157 N·m
(116 ft.-lbs.)

CYLINDER HEAD. Engine is equipped with an aluminum alloy cylinder head which should not be removed when engine is hot.

To remove the cylinder head, first allow engine to cool, then remove fuel tank and cooling shrouds. Loosen head bolts evenly following sequence shown in Fig. AC11. Remove cylinder head.

Check cylinder head for warpage by placing head on a flat surface and using a feeler gage to determine warpage. Warpage should not exceed 0.3-0.5 mm (0.012-0.020 in.).

Always install a new head gasket. Tighten cylinder head bolts to specifi-

cation listed under TIGHTENING TORQUES following sequence shown in Fig. AC11. Note that two longer head bolts are present and must be installed in positions 1 and 3 shown in Fig. AC11.

CONNECTING ROD. An aluminum alloy connecting rod rides directly on the crankpin journal.

To remove connecting rod, remove cylinder head and crankcase cover. Remove connecting rod cap and push connecting rod and piston assembly out of cylinder head end of block. Remove piston pin retaining rings and separate piston from connecting rod. Camshaft and lifters may be removed at this time if required.

Clearance between piston pin and connecting rod pin bore should be 0.006-0.022 mm (0.0002-0.0009 in.).

Clearance between crankpin and connecting rod bearing bore should be 0.030-0.049 mm (0.0012-0.0019 in.). If clearance exceeds specified dimension, renew connecting rod and/or crankshaft.

Connecting rod side play on crankpin should be 0.150-0.250 mm (0.0060-0.0100 in.).

Renew connecting rod if crankpin bearing bore is excessively worn or out-of-round more than 0.10 mm (0.004 in.).

Piston should be installed on the connecting rod with arrow (1—Fig. AC12),

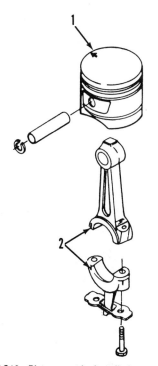

Fig. AC12—Piston must be installed on connecting rod so arrow (1) on top of piston faces toward side of connecting rod with mark (2). Connecting rod and connecting rod cap match marks (2) must align when components are assembled.

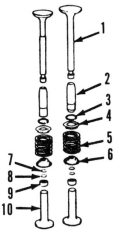

Fig. AC9—View of valve system components.

1. Valves	7. Shims (valve
2. Guides	adjustment)
3. Seals	8. Shims (valve
4. Seats	adjustment)
5. Springs	9. Shim holder (cap)
6. Retainers	10. Tappets

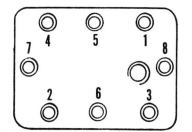

Fig. AC11—Loosen or tighten cylinder head bolts following sequence shown. The two longer head bolts must be installed in positions 1 and 3.

on top of piston, facing toward side of connecting rod with mark (2). Connecting rod and connecting rod cap marks (2) must align when components are assembled.

When installing piston assembly in cylinder block, connecting rod and cap match marks must be toward crankcase cover side of engine and arrow on top of piston must be on side opposite the valves on engines with clockwise rotation. On engines with counterclockwise rotation, arrow on top of piston must be toward valve side of engine and connecting rod and cap match marks will face toward flywheel side of engine. Tighten connecting rod bolts to specification listed under TIGHTENING TORQUES. Crankcase cover has two longer bolts which should be installed in the upper right and lower left positions. Tighten crankcase cover bolts to specification listed under TIGHTENING TORQUES.

CYLINDER AND CRANKCASE. Cylinder and crankcase are an integral casting of aluminum alloy on all models. A high density perlite cylinder sleeve is cast as an integral part of the cylinder block.

Standard cylinder bore diameter is 72.000-72.013 mm (2.8300-2.8305 in.). If cylinder bore is 0.06 mm (0.0024 in.) or more out-of-round or tapered, cylinder should be bored to nearest oversize for which piston and rings are available.

Crankshaft ball type main bearings should be a slight press fit in crankcase and crankcase cover. It may be necessary to slightly heat crankcase cover or crankcase assembly to remove or install main bearings. Renew bearings if they are loose, rough or damaged.

PISTON, PIN AND RINGS. Refer to previous CONNECTING ROD paragraphs for piston removal and installation procedure.

Standard piston diameter is 71.987-72.000 mm (2.8295-2.8300 in.) and is a select fit at the factory. Piston should be renewed and/or cylinder reconditioned if there is 0.013 mm (0.0005 in.) or more clearance between piston and cylinder bore. Clearance between piston and piston rings in ring grooves should be 0.05 mm (0.002 in.) on all models.

Compression ring end gap should be 0.25-0.45 mm (0.010-0.018 in.). Oil control ring end gap should be 0.20-0.35 mm (0.008-0.014 in.).

Piston pin should be a 0.004-0.012 mm (0.0002-0.0005 in.) interference fit in piston pin bore. It may be necessary to slightly heat piston to aid in pin removal and installation.

CRANKSHAFT. Crankshaft is supported at each end in ball bearing type main bearings (11 and 16—Fig. AC14) and crankshaft timing gear (15) is a press fit on crankshaft (13). Refer to previous CONNECTING ROD paragraphs for crankshaft removal procedure and crankpin-to-connecting rod bearing bore clearance.

Standard crankshaft crankpin journal diameter is 25.989-26.000 mm (1.0232-1.0236 in.). Standard crankshaft main bearing journal diameter is 25.002-25.015 mm (0.98433-0.98484 in.). Main bearings should be a slight press fit on crankshaft journal. Renew bearings if they are rough, loose or damaged. To prevent crankshaft damage, crankshaft should be supported on counterweights when pressing bearings or crankshaft timing gear onto crankshaft.

When installing crankshaft, make certain crankshaft and camshaft gear timing marks are aligned.

CAMSHAFT. Camshaft and camshaft gear on all models are an integral casting which rides in bearing bores in crankcase and crankcase cover.

On some models, a compression release mechanism is mounted on back side of camshaft gear. The spring-loaded compression release mechanism should snap back against camshaft when weighted lever is pulled against spring tension and released. Spring is in the correct position when dimension (A—Fig. AC15) of pin projection is 0.5-0.6 mm (0.020-0.024 in.).

Inspect camshaft journals and lobes on all models. Renew camshaft if worn, scored or damaged.

Standard camshaft bearing journal diameter is 14.973-14.984 mm (0.589-

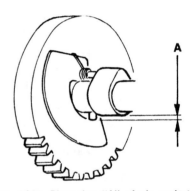

Fig. AC15—Dimension "A" of pin projection should be 0.5-0.6 mm (0.020-0.024 in.) for correct compression release mechanism operation.

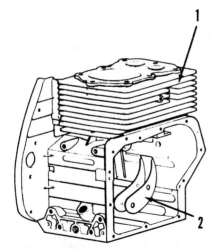

Fig. AC13—View of cylinder block (1) and oil slinger trough (2). If trough is removed, it must be securely repositioned prior to engine reassembly.

Fig. AC14—Exploded view of crankshaft, connecting rod and piston assembly.

1. Retaining rings
2. Piston pin
3. Compression rings
4. Oil control ring
5. Piston
6. Connecting rod
7. Connecting rod cap
8. Lockplate
9. Bolts
10. Seal
11. Main bearing
12. Key
13. Crankshaft
14. Crankshaft gear key
15. Crankshaft gear
16. Main bearing
17. Seal

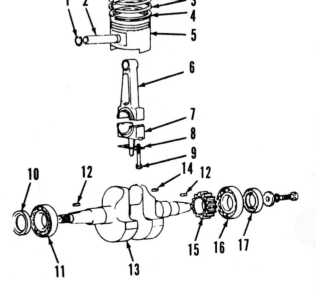

0.590 in.) at each end. Standard intake lobe height is 23.275-23.325 mm (0.916-0.918 in.). Standard exhaust lobe height is 17.575-17.625 mm (0.692-0.694 in.).

When installing camshaft, make certain camshaft and crankshaft gear timing marks are aligned.

VALVE SYSTEM. Refer to VALVE ADJUSTMENT paragraphs in MAINTE-NANCE section for valve clearance adjustment procedure.

Valve face and seat angles is 45 degrees. Standard valve seat width is 1.2-1.3 mm (0.047-0.051 in.). If seat width is 2 mm (0.079 in.) or more, seat must be narrowed. If valve face margin is 0.5 mm (0.020 in.) or less, renew valve.

Standard intake and exhaust valve stem diameter is 6.955-6.970 mm (0.2738-0.2744 in.).

Standard valve guide inside diameter is 7.015-7.025 mm (0.2762-0.2766 in.) for intake and exhaust valve guides. Worn valve guides can be renewed using puller 365109.

Standard valve spring free length is 34 mm (1.34 in.). If spring free length is 31 mm (1.22 in.) or less, renew spring.

ACME

Model	No. Cyls.	Bore	Stroke	Displacement
ALN 290 WB	1	75 mm (2.95 in.)	65 mm (2.56 in.)	290 cc (17.51 cu. in.)
ALN 330 WB	1	80 mm (3.15 in.)	65 mm (2.56 in.)	327 cc (20.00 cu. in.)

ENGINE IDENTIFICATION

All models are four-stroke, air-cooled single cylinder engines.

Models ALN 290 WB and ALN 330 WB are horizontal crankshaft models. Valves are located in cylinder block on all models.

The suffix "B" after the W indicates models are gasoline fuel engines.

Engine model number is located on a plate mounted on cooling shroud on the right-hand side of engine as viewed from flywheel side. The engine serial number is stamped in the engine block approximately 3 inches (76.2 mm) below model number plate, just above oil fill plug (Fig. AC20).

Always furnish engine model and serial numbers when ordering parts.

MAINTENANCE

SPARK PLUG. Recommended spark plug for all models is a Champion L90 or equivalent.

Spark plug should be removed, cleaned and inspected at 100 hour intervals. Spark plug electrode gap should be 0.6-0.8 mm (0.024-0.032 in.) for all models.

CARBURETOR. All models are equipped with a float type carburetor. Refer to Fig. AC21 for exploded view and parts location.

Initial adjustment of idle mixture screw (3) from a lightly seated position is 1-1/4 turns open. Main fuel mixture is controlled by a fixed main jet (13).

Final adjustments should be made with engine at operating temperature and running. Adjust engine idle speed to 1000-1100 rpm at throttle stop screw (5). Adjust idle mixture screw (3) to obtain smoothest engine idle and smooth acceleration.

When installing new fuel inlet needle and seat, install seat and measure from point (A) to edge of fuel inlet needle seat. Measurement should be 33-37 mm (1.30-1.46 in.). Vary number of fiber washers between fuel inlet seat and carburetor body to obtain correct measurement.

To check float (12) level, carefully remove float bowl (15) and measure distance from carburetor mating surface of bowl to top of fuel level in bowl (Fig. AC22). Measurement should be 32-34 mm (1.26-1.34 in.). If float level is incorrect, fuel inlet needle seat must be shimmed as outlined in previous paragraph.

Float weight should be 16.5 grams. If float is heavier than recommended weight, then float must be renewed.

Fuel filter screen (8—Fig. AC21) should be removed and cleaned at 50 hour intervals.

AIR FILTER. All models are equipped with an oil bath type air filter (Fig. AC23). Air filter element should be removed and cleaned at 8 hour intervals and old oil discarded. Replenish with new engine oil to level indicated on oil reservoir housing (5).

GOVERNOR. All models are equipped with a flyball type centrifugal governor. Governor assembly is incorporated on

Fig. AC22—Measure distance from fuel level (F) to top of bowl (E). Distance should be 32-34 mm (1.26-1.34 in.).

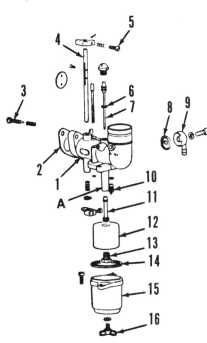

Fig. AC20—Engine serial number (SN) is stamped into crankcase on all models.

Fig. AC21—Exploded view of carburetor used on all models. Screen (8) should be cleaned after every 50 hours of operation.

1. Carburetor body
2. Gasket
3. Idle mixture screw
4. Throttle shaft
5. Throttle stop screw
6. Gasket
7. Idle jet
8. Screen (filter)
9. Filter housing
10. Fuel inlet needle valve
11. Nozzle
12. Float
13. Main jet
14. Gasket
15. Float bowl
16. Wing bolt

Fig. AC23—Oil bath air filter is used on all models.

1. Cover
2. Gasket
3. Element
4. Plate
5. Oil reservoir
6. Clamp

camshaft gear. Governor regulates engine speed via external linkage.

To adjust external linkage, first make certain all linkage moves freely with no binding or loose connections. Lock throttle control lever (5—Fig. AC24) in midposition with throttle locknut (6). Hook tension spring (3) in hole "A" for 3000 rpm engine speed, hole "B" for 3600 rpm engine speed or for special applications only, hole "C" for 4000 rpm engine speed. An alternate spring (part 551.107) is available, and when tension spring is hooked in hole "A", spring allows 2400 rpm engine speed. Place throttle lever (5) in full speed position, loosen carburetor-to-governor lever adjustment lock (7) and push throttle fully open. Tighten rod adjustment lock (7) in this position. Governor and throttle linkage should work freely and easily return to normal set position.

IGNITION SYSTEM. A breaker-point ignition system is standard on all models. Breaker-point set and condenser are located on the left-hand side of crankcase as viewed from flywheel side and ignition coil is located behind flywheel. Breaker points are actuated by plunger (1—Fig. AC25).

Point gap should be checked and adjusted at 400 hour intervals. To check point gap, remove cover (5) and use a suitable feeler gage. Point gap should be 0.4-0.5 mm (0.016-0.020 in.).

Ignition timing should be set at 21 degrees BTDC by aligning "AA" mark on flywheel with "PMS" mark on crankcase. Points should just begin to open at this position. Shift breaker-point plate (3) as necessary.

When "TDC" mark on flywheel is aligned with "PMS" mark on crankcase, piston is at top dead center.

Ignition coil, which is located behind the flywheel, should have 0.6-0.8 mm (0.024-0.031 in.) clearance between coil and flywheel magnets.

LUBRICATION. Check engine oil level at 8 hours intervals. Maintain oil level at lower edge of fill plug opening.

Change oil at 50 hour intervals. Manufacturer recommends oil with an API service classification of SC or CC. Use SAE 40 oil for ambient temperatures of 10° C (50° F); SAE 30 oil for temperatures between 10° C (50° F) and 0° C (32° F); SAE 20W-20 oil for temperatures between 0° C (32° F) and -10° C (14° F) and SAE 10W oil for temperatures below -10° C (14° F).

Crankcase oil capacity is 0.76 L (0.793 qt.) for all models.

Engines are lubricated by an oil dipper located on connecting rod cap.

VALVE ADJUSTMENT. Valves should be adjusted at 200 hour intervals. Valve stem to tappet clearance should be 0.15 mm (0.006 in.) for intake and exhaust valves on all models. If clearance is not as specified, remove or install shims (7 and 8—Fig. AC26) in shim holder (9) as necessary.

CRANKCASE BREATHER. Crankcase breather must be removed and cleaned at 50 hour intervals. Breather is located on tube mounted on valve chamber cover. Rubber valve must be installed as shown in Fig. AC27 to ensure crankcase vacuum.

GENERAL MAINTENANCE. Check and tighten all loose bolts, nuts or clamps daily. Check for fuel or oil leakage and repair as necessary.

Clean dust, dirt, grease or any foreign material from cylinder head and cylinder block cooling fins at 100 hour intervals. Inspect fins for damage and repair as necessary.

REPAIRS

TIGHTENING TORQUES. Recommended tightening torque specifications are as follows:

Cylinder head . . . . .30 N·m
(22 ft.-lbs.)
Connecting rod . . . . .19 N·m
(14 ft.-lbs.)
Crankcase cover . . . . .30 N·m
(22 ft.-lbs.)
Flywheel . . . . .157 N·m
(116 ft.-lbs.)

CYLINDER HEAD. To remove cylinder head, remove cooling shrouds and loosen head bolts evenly in sequence shown in Fig. AC28 and remove cylinder head.

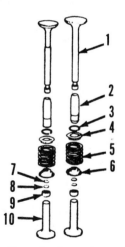

Fig. AC26—View of valve system component parts.

1. Valve
2. Guide
3. Seal
4. Seat
5. Spring
6. Retainer
7. Shim (valve adjustment)
8. Shim (Valve adjustment)
9. Shim holder (cap)
10. Tappet

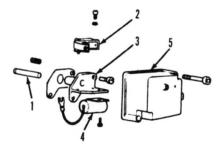

Fig. AC25—Breaker points and condenser are located on left-hand side of crankcase behind cover (5).

1. Plunger
2. Breaker points
3. Point plate
4. Condenser
5. Cover

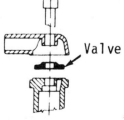

Fig. AC24—View showing relative position and relationship of external governor linkage and throttle parts.

1. Carburetor-to-governor lever rod
2. Governor lever
3. Tension spring
4. Spring
5. Throttle control lever
6. Throttle lever locknut
7. Carburetor-to-governor lever rod adjustment lock

Fig. AC27—Breather valve must be installed as shown to ensure crankcase vacuum.

CAUTION: Never remove cylinder head while engine is hot as cylinder head warpage will result.

Check cylinder head for warpage by placing on a flat surface and using a feeler gage to determine warpage. Warpage should not exceed 0.3-0.5 mm (0.012-0.020 in.).

Always install new head gasket and tighten cylinder head bolts to specified torque following sequence shown in Fig. AC28.

CONNECTING ROD. Aluminum alloy connecting rod rides directly on crankpin journal.

To remove connecting rod, remove cylinder head and crankcase cover. Use care when crankcase cover is removed as governor flyweight balls will fall out of ramps in camshaft gear. Remove connecting rod cap and push connecting rod and piston assembly out of cylinder head end of block. Remove piston pin retaining rings and separate piston from connecting rod. Camshaft and lifters may be removed at this time also.

Clearance between piston pin and connecting rod pin bore should be 0.000-0.023 mm (0.0000-0.0009 in.).

Clearance between crankpin and connecting rod crankpin bore should be 0.040-0.064 mm (0.0016-0.0025 in.). Connecting rod side play on crankpin should be 0.150-0.250 mm (0.0060-0.0100 in.).

Renew connecting rod if excessively worn or out-of-round more than 0.10 mm (0.004 in.).

Piston can be installed on connecting rod either way, however, when installing connecting rod, triangle match marks on connecting rod and cap must be aligned and facing crankcase cover side of engine for clockwise rotation engines or flywheel side of engine for counterclockwise rotation engines. Tighten connecting rod bolts to specified torque. Use heavy grease to retain governor flyweight balls in camshaft ramps to aid crankcase cover installation. Tighten crankcase cover to specified torque.

CYLINDER AND CRANKCASE. Cylinder and crankcase are an integral casting of aluminum alloy with a high density perlite cylinder sleeve cast as an integral part of the cylinder block.

Standard cylinder bore diameter is 75.000-75.013 mm (2.9528-2.9533 in.) for Model ALN 290 WB and 80.000-80.013 mm (3.1496-3.1501 in.) for Model ALN 330 WB. If cylinder bore is 0.06 mm (0.0024 in.) or more out-of-round or tapered, cylinder should be bored to nearest oversize for which piston and rings are available.

Crankshaft ball type main bearings should be a slight press fit in crankcase and crankcase cover. Renew bearings if they are loose, rough or damaged.

An oil slinger trough (2—Fig. AC30) is installed in the crankcase. And if removed, it must be securely repositioned prior to engine reassembly.

PISTON, PIN AND RINGS. Refer to CONNECTING ROD paragraphs for piston removal and installation procedure.

Standard piston diameter is 74.987-75.000 mm (2.9522-2.9528 in.) for Model ALN 290 WB and 79.987-80.000 mm (3.1102-3.1491 in.) for Model ALN 330 WB. On all models, pistons are a select fit at the factory.

Piston should be renewed and/or cylinder reconditioned if there is 0.013 mm (0.0005 in.) or more clearance between piston and cylinder bore.

Compression ring end gap should be 0.250-0.400 mm (0.0100-0.0160 in.). Oil control ring end gap should be 0.300-0.500 mm (0.0120-0.0200 in.).

Piston pin should be 0.004-0.012 mm (0.0002-0.0005 in.) interference fit in piston pin bore. It may be necessary to heat piston slightly to aid in pin removal or installation.

CRANKSHAFT. Crankshaft is supported at each end by ball bearing type main bearings (11 and 16—Fig. AC29) Crankshaft timing gear (15) is a press fit on crankshaft (13).

Refer to CONNECTING ROD paragraphs for crankshaft removal procedure.

Standard clearance between crankpin journal and connecting rod crankpin bore should be 0.040-0.064 mm (0.0016-0.0025 in.).

Standard crankshaft crankpin journal diameter is 29.985-30.000 mm (1.1805-1.1811 in.). If crankshaft crankpin journal is worn or out-of-round 0.015 mm (0.0006 in.) or more, renew crankshaft.

Standard main bearing journal diameter is 30 mm (1.18 in.) and ball type main bearings should be a slight press

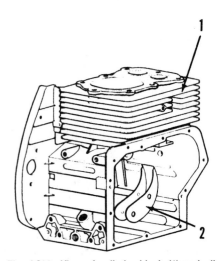

Fig. AC30—View of cylinder block (1) and oil slinger trough (2). If trough is removed, it must be securely repositioned prior to assembly of engine.

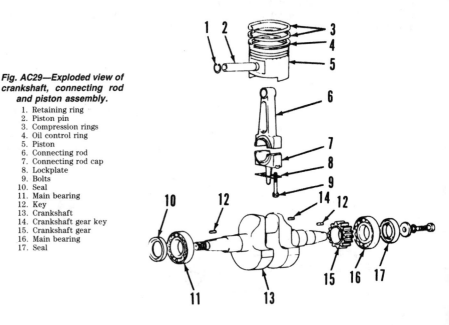

Fig. AC29—Exploded view of crankshaft, connecting rod and piston assembly.

1. Retaining ring
2. Piston pin
3. Compression rings
4. Oil control ring
5. Piston
6. Connecting rod
7. Connecting rod cap
8. Lockplate
9. Bolts
10. Seal
11. Main bearing
12. Key
13. Crankshaft
14. Crankshaft gear key
15. Crankshaft gear
16. Main bearing
17. Seal

Fig. AC28—Loosen and tighten cylinder head bolts following the sequence shown.

fit on crankshaft journal. Renew bearings if they are rough, loose or damaged and note that crankshaft should be supported on counterweights when pressing bearings or crankshaft timing gear onto or off of crankshaft to prevent bending crankshaft.

When installing crankshaft, make certain crankshaft and camshaft gear timing marks are aligned.

CAMSHAFT. Camshaft and camshaft gear are an integral casting which rides in bearing bores in crankcase and crankcase cover. A compression release mechanism is mounted on back side of camshaft gear and governor flyballs are located in ramps machined into face of gear.

Spring loaded compression release mechanism should snap back against camshaft when weighted lever is pulled against spring tension and released.

Inspect camshaft journals and lobes and renew camshaft if worn, scored or damaged. Governor flyball should move smoothly across ramp faces without catching.

When installing camshaft, retain governor flyballs in ramps with heavy grease and make certain camshaft and crankshaft gear timing marks are aligned.

VALVE SYSTEM. Refer to VALVE ADJUSTMENT paragraph in MAINTENANCE section for valve clearance adjustment procedure.

Valve face and seat angles are 45 degrees. Standard valve seat width is 1.2-1.3 mm (0.047-0.051 in.). If seat width is 2 mm (0.079 in.) or more, seat must be narrowed.

If valve face margin is 0.5 mm (0.020 in.) or less, renew valve.

Standard exhaust valve stem diameter is 6.955-6.970 mm (0.2738-0.2744 in.) and standard intake valve stem diameter is 6.965-6.987 mm (0.2742-0.2751 in.).

Valve guide inside diameter for cast iron intake valve guide or bronze exhaust valve guide should be 7.000-7.022 mm (0.2756-0.2764 in.). Guides are renewable using a suitable puller (Acme tool 365109).

Standard valve spring free length is 35 mm (1.38 in.). If valve spring free length is 32 mm (1.26 in.) or less, renew valve spring.

ACME

Model	No. Cyls.	Bore	Stroke	Displacement
VT 88 WB	1	88 mm (3.46 in.)	79 mm (3.11 in.)	480 cc (29.28 cu. in.)

ENGINE IDENTIFICATION

Model VT 88 WB is a four-stroke, air-cooled single cylinder, overhead valve engine. Cylinder and crankcase are separate assemblies.

The suffix "B" after the W indicates the model is a gasoline fuel engine.

Engine model and serial numbers for Model VT 88 WB are stamped into the crankcase just above oil filler cap and cylinder-to-crankcase mating surface (Fig. AC35).

Always furnish engine model and serial numbers when ordering parts.

MAINTENANCE

SPARK PLUG. Recommended spark plug for Model VT 88 WB is a Champion D16 or equivalent.

Spark plug should be removed, cleaned and inspected at 100 hour intervals. Spark plug electrode gap for all models should be 0.6-0.8 mm (0.024-0.032 in.).

CARBURETOR. Model VT 88 WB is equipped with a float type carburetor. Refer to Fig. AC36 for an exploded view of the carburetor used.

Initial adjustment of idle mixture screw (3—Fig. AC36) from a lightly seated position is 1-1/4 turns open. Main fuel mixture is controlled by a fixed main jet (13).

Final adjustments should be made with engine at operating temperature and running. Adjust engine idle speed to 1100 rpm at throttle stop screw (5). Adjust idle mixture screw (3) to obtain smoothest engine idle and smooth acceleration.

When installing new fuel inlet needle and seat, install seat and measure from point (A) to edge of fuel inlet needle seat. Measurement should be 33-37 mm (1.30-1.46 in.). Vary number of fiber washers between fuel inlet seat and carburetor body to obtain correct measurement.

To check float (12) level, carefully remove float bowl (15) and measure distance from top of float bowl to the top of fuel level in bowl (Fig. AC37). Measurement should be 32-34 mm (1.26-1.34 in.). If float level is incorrect, fuel inlet needle seat must be shimmed as outlined in previous paragraph.

Float weight should be 16.5 grams. If float is heavier than recommended weight, then float must be renewed.

Fuel filter screen (8—Fig. AC36) should be removed and cleaned at 50 hour intervals.

AIR FILTER. An oil bath type air filter typical to type shown in Figure AC38 is used. Air filter element should be removed and cleaned after every 8 hours of operation. Discard old oil and refill with new engine oil to level indicated on oil reservoir housing (5).

GOVERNOR. Model VT 88 WB is equipped with a flyball type centrifugal governor. The governor assembly is incorporated on the magneto gear and drive shaft (Fig. AC39). Governor lever should be adjusted to hold carburetor throttle plate in wide open position when engine is not running.

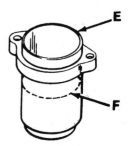

Fig. AC37—Measure distance from fuel level (F) to top of bowl (E). Distance should be 32-34 mm (1.26-1.34 in.).

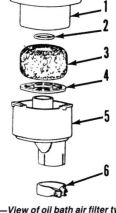

Fig. AC38—View of oil bath air filter typical of the type used.

1. Cover	4. Plate
2. Gasket	5. Oil reservoir
3. Element	6. Clamp

Fig. AC36—Exploded view of float type carburetor used.

1. Carburetor body
3. Idle mixture screw
4. Throttle shaft
5. Throttle stop screw
6. Gasket
7. Idle jet
8. Screen (filter)
9. Filter housing
10. Fuel inlet needle valve
11. Nozzle
12. Float
13. Main jet
14. Gasket
15. Float bowl
16. Wing bolt

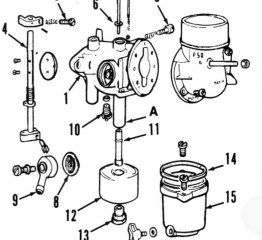

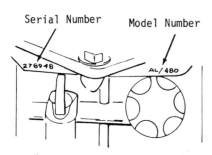

Fig. AC35—On Model VT 88 WB, model and serial numbers are stamped into crankcase as shown.

IGNITION SYSTEM. Model VT 88 WB is equipped with a self-contained magneto unit (Fig. AC40).

The self-contained magneto unit (Fig. AC40) is equipped with a breaker point set, condenser and ignition coil which are located in the magneto unit. Point gap should be checked and adjusted at 400 hour intervals. To check point gap, remove cover (3—Fig. AC40) and use a suitable feeler gage. Point gap should be 0.4-0.5 mm (0.016-0.020 in.).

Magneto should be installed so the points just begin to open when flywheel is at the 30 degree BTDC mark. This mark should be located on the flywheel 62.8 mm (2.472 in.) before the piston is at top dead center position.

LUBRICATION. Check engine oil level at 8 hour intervals. Maintain oil level at lower edge of fill plug opening. Change oil at 50 hour intervals. Manufacturer recommends oil with an API service classification SC or CC. Use SAE 40 oil for ambient temperatures above 10° C (50° F); SAE 30 oil for temperatures between 10° C (50° F) and 0° C (32° F); SAE 20W-20 oil for temperatures between 0° C (32° F) and -10° C (14° F) and SAE 10W oil for temperatures below -10° C (14° F).

Crankcase oil capacity is 1.1 L (1.16 qt.)

VALVE ADJUSTMENT. Valves should be adjusted at 200 hour intervals. Valve stem to rocker arm clearance should be 0.05 mm (0.0020 in.) for the intake valve and 0.10 mm (0.0039 in.) for the exhaust valve. Valves are adjusted with the piston at TDC. Remove the rocker arm cover and loosen jam nut (3—Fig. AC41). Turn adjusting bolt (4) in rocker arm (5) to obtain correct clearance between the rocker arm and the valve stem. When correct clearance is obtained, hold adjustment bolt (4) in position while jam nut (3) is tightened.

CRANKCASE BREATHER. Crankcase breather must be removed and cleaned at 50 hour intervals. The breather is located on the rocker arm cover (Fig. AC42). The flat face of diaphragm (3) must be installed toward rocker arm cover (4).

GENERAL MAINTENANCE. Check and tighten all loose bolts, nuts or clamps daily. Check for fuel or oil leakage and repair as necessary.

Clean dust, dirt, grease or any foreign material from cylinder head and cylinder block cooling fins at 100 hour intervals. Inspect fins for damage and repair as necessary.

REPAIRS

TIGHTENING TORQUES. Recommended tightening torque specifications are as follows:

Cylinder head . . . . .39 N·m
(29 ft.-lbs.)
Cylinder-to-
crankcase . . . . .22 N·m
(16 ft.-lbs.)
Rocker arm cover . . . . .19 N·m
(14 ft.-lbs.)
Valve adjustment
bolt jam nut . . . . .18 N·m
(13 ft.-lbs.)
Flywheel . . . . .176 N·m
(130 ft.-lbs.)
Spark plug . . . . .19 N·m
(14 ft.-lbs.)

CYLINDER HEAD AND VALVES. The cylinder head is an aluminum alloy casting with hardened steel valve seat inserts. To remove the cylinder head, remove all cooling shrouds and the rocker arm cover. Loosen and remove all head bolts in the sequence shown in Fig. AC43.

CAUTION: Never remove cylinder head while engine is hot as cylinder head warpage will result.

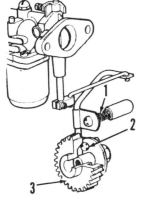

Fig. AC39—View of governor control linkage.
1. Spring
2. Flyball
3. Magneto drive gear

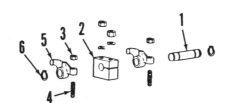

Fig. AC41—Exploded view of rocker arm assembly similar to type used.
1. Rocker arm shaft
2. Rocker arm shaft support
3. Jam nut
4. Adjustment bolt
5. Rocker arm
6. Retaining ring

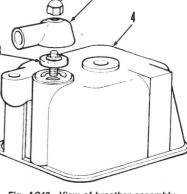

Fig. AC42—View of breather assembly.
1. Nut
2. Cap
3. Diaphragm
4. Rocker arm cover

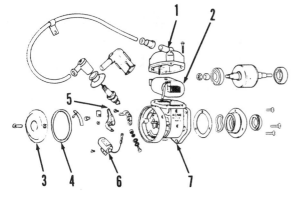

Fig. AC40—Exploded view of the magneto unit.
1. Cap
2. Coil
3. Cover
4. Seal
5. Points
6. Condenser
7. Housing

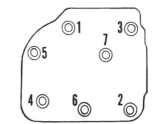

Fig. AC43—Tighten or loosen cylinder head bolts following the sequence shown.

Check cylinder head for warpage by placing on a flat surface and using a feeler gage to determine warpage. Warpage should not exceed 0.3-0.5 mm (0.012-0.020 in.). Always install a new head gasket and tighten cylinder head bolts to specified torque following sequence shown in Fig. AC43.

The intake valve guide is cast iron and the exhaust valve guide is bronze. Standard valve guide inside diameter is 8.025-8.035 mm (0.3159-0.3185 in.).

Valve faces and seats should be ground at 45 degree angles. Valve seat width should be 1.2-1.3 mm (0.0472-0.0512 in.).

Valve stem diameter should be 8.9650-8.9870 mm (0.3530-0.3538 in.) for intake and exhaust valves.

Maximum clearance between rocker arm and rocker arm shaft is 0.15 mm (0.0059 in.). If clearance exceeds specified dimension, renew rocker arm and/or rocker arm shaft.

Valve spring free length should be 54 mm (2.126 in.). It should require 45 kg (99.22 lbs.) force to compress valve spring to 30.4 mm (1.1969 in.).

CONNECTING ROD. The connecting rod is installed on the connecting rod journal which is then pressed into the crankshaft halves. The connecting rod bearing is selected together with the connecting rod and crankshaft journal in three classes, each having a tolerance of 0.004 mm (0.00016 in.) Connecting rod, bearing and crankshaft journal must be renewed as an assembly.

To remove connecting rod, remove all shrouds. Remove the cylinder head. Remove the cylinder retaining nuts and carefully pull the cast iron cylinder up off the piston assembly. Use a suitable puller (Acme tool 365111) to remove the flywheel and then the crankcase cover. Remove the crankshaft and connecting rod assembly. If the connecting rod must be removed from the crankshaft, remove the piston from the connecting rod. The crankshaft halves must be separated using a suitable puller (Acme tool 365126). To reassemble the crankshaft, use a suitable jig (Acme tool 365130) and a press capable of 7 to 8 tons pressure. Press crankshaft together until there is 0.2-0.4 mm (0.0079-0.0157 in.) clearance between connecting rod and crankshaft shoulder. Shims are available to adjust clearance between connecting rod and crankshaft shoulder. The two crankshaft halves must be concentric with the crankshaft connecting rod journal. Maximum off-

center allowance is 0.05 mm (0.0020 in.).

Clearance between the piston pin and connecting rod pin bore should be 0.02-0.05 mm (0.00079-0.00197 in.).

Piston can be installed on connecting rod either way. When installing crankcase cover on crankcase, tighten bolts to the specified torque in a crisscross pattern.

CYLINDER AND CRANKCASE. The cast iron cylinder is a separate casting and can be removed from the crankcase. Standard cylinder bore diameter is 88.000-88.013 mm (3.46-3.51 in.).

If cylinder bore is 0.06 mm (0.0024 in.) or more out-of-round or tapered, cylinder should be bored to nearest oversize for which piston and rings are available.

Crankshaft ball type main bearings should be a slight press fit in engine main bearing bores. Renew bearings if they are loose, rough or damaged.

PISTON, PIN AND RINGS. Refer to CONNECTING ROD for piston removal and installation procedure.

Standard piston diameter is 87.987-88.000 mm (3.4252-3.4641 in.). Pistons are a select fit at the factory.

Piston should be renewed and/or cylinder reconditioned if there is 0.013 mm (0.0005 in.) or more clearance between piston and cylinder bore.

Compression ring end gap should be 0.250-0.400 mm (0.010-0.016 in.). Oil control ring end gap should be 0.30-0.50 mm (0.012-0.020 in.).

Piston pin should be 0.004-0.012 mm (0.0002-0.0005 in.) interference fit in piston pin bore. It may be necessary to heat piston slightly to aid in pin removal or installation.

Refer to Fig. AC44 for correct ring installation. Stagger ring end gaps equally around piston diameter.

CRANKSHAFT. The crankshaft is supported at each end by ball bearing type main bearings. Refer to Fig. AC45 for an exploded view of the crankshaft assembly. Refer to CONNECTING ROD for crankshaft removal procedure.

The crankshaft is a three-piece assembly (Fig. AC45) wich must be pressed together using the procedure and special jig described under CONNECTING ROD. When installing crankshaft, make certain crankshaft and camshaft gear timing marks are aligned.

CAMSHAFT. The camshaft is supported at each end by renewable bushings. The camshaft gear has helical teeth to reduce noise and improve meshing. Camshaft axial thrust is controlled by a ball tensioned by a spring (Fig. AC46).

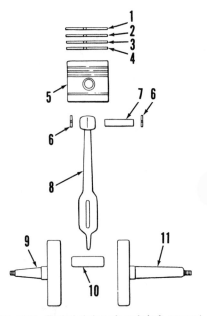

Fig. AC45—Exploded view of crankshaft, connecting rod and piston assembly.

1. Compression ring		7. Piston pin	
2. Compression ring		8. Connecting rod	
3. Oil control ring		9. Crankshaft half	
4. Oil control ring		10. Connecting rod	
5. Piston		journal	
6. Retaining ring		11. Crankshaft half	

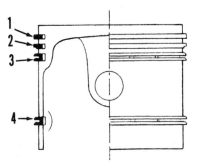

Fig. AC44—Piston rings must be installed so the step on second ring (2) faces down and the bevel on oil control rings (3 and 4) faces up.

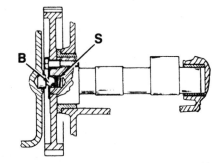

Fig. AC46—Camshaft axial thrust is controlled by ball (B) and spring (S).

ACME

SERVICING ACME ACCESSORIES

REWIND STARTER

Refer to Fig. AC50 for exploded view of rewind starter used on models so equipped. Rewind spring (5) and spring housing (4) are only serviced as an assembly.

When installing rewind starter assembly on engine, install but do not tighten the six bolts retaining assembly to cooling shroud. Pull cable handle (7) until 150 mm (6 in.) of cable has been pulled from housing and starter dogs (9) have centered assembly. Hold tension on cable while the six bolts are tightened.

ALTERNATOR

Some models are equipped with a fixed armature type alternator mounted on engine with rotor as an integral part of the flywheel.

To test alternator output, disconnect rectifier leads and connect to an AC voltmeter with at least a 30 volt capacity. Start engine and refer to the following specifications for voltage output according to engine operation.

2400 rpm . . . . .20-22 volts
2800 rpm . . . . .23-25 volts
3200 rpm . . . . .26-28 volts
3600 rpm . . . . .29-30 volts

Rectifier may be checked by connecting ammeter between positive battery

Fig. AC50—Exploded view of rewind starter assembly.
1. Snap ring
2. Starter dog housing
3. Cable pulley
4. Spring housing
5. Rewind spring
6. Housing
7. Handle
8. Cable
9. Starter dogs

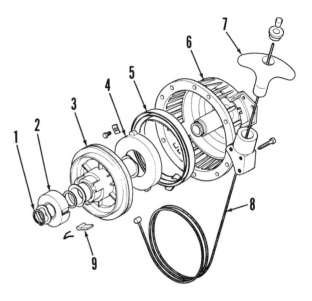

lead and the positive rectifier terminal. Connect 20 volt voltmeter to battery posts and use lights or other battery drain method to lower battery voltage below 13 volts. Start engine and refer to the following specifications for amperage output according to engine speed.

1500 rpm . . . . .0.5 amp
2400 rpm . . . . .1.5 amp

3000 rpm . . . . .2.2 amp
3600 rpm . . . . .2.7 amp

If battery charge current is 0 amp with 12.5 volt or less battery voltage, renew rectifier.

CAUTION: Never operate engine with rectifier disconnected as rectifier will be damaged.

ACME SPECIAL TOOLS

The following special tools are available from Acme Central Parts Distributors or Acme Corporation.

Tool Description	Tool Number
Valve spring extractor	365110
Ignition coil positioning tool	365168
Valve guide check tool	365048
Valve guide puller	365109
Electrical tester	365180
Oil seal installation cone	365152
Engine flywheel and timing cover puller	365113

BCS

BCS MOSA
13601 Providence Road
P. O. Box 1739
Matthews, NC 28105

Model	HP	Crankshaft (Series)	Bore	Stroke	Displacement
180	5	Horizontal 180 (3.7 kW)	65 mm (2.56 in.)	54 mm (2.13 in.)	179 cc (10.9 cu. in.)

Model 180 has an aluminum cylinder block with a cast iron cylinder integrally cast into the block.

MAINTENANCE

SPARK PLUG. Recommended spark plug is Bosch W 175 T1 or Champion L86C. Spark plug electrode gap should be 0.6-0.7 mm (0.024-0.027 in.). Spark plug should be removed and inspected and electrode gap adjusted after every 50 hours of operation. Renew spark plug after 500 hours of operation. Tighten spark plug to 29 N·m (21 ft.-lbs.).

CARBURETOR. Refer to Fig. BC1 for exploded view of carburetor used. For

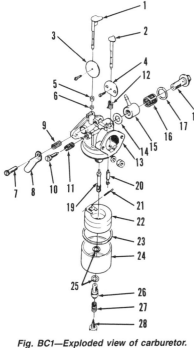

Fig. BC1—Exploded view of carburetor.

1. Throttle shaft	15. Filter housing
2. Choke shaft	16. Filter
3. Throttle valve	17. Gasket
4. Choke valve	18. Bolt
5. Seal	19. Main nozzle & jet
6. Seal	20. Inlet needle
7. Idle speed screw	21. Pin
8. Plate	22. Float
9. Spring	23. Seal
10. Idle mixture screw	24. Float bowl
11. Spring	25. Gaskets
12. Spring	26. Bowl nut
13. Body assy.	27. Spring
14. Gasket	28. High speed screw

initial adjustment, open idle mixture screw (10) ¾ turn. Start engine and allow to warm up to operating temperature. Adjust idle speed screw (7) to obtain approximately 1,000 rpm. Adjust idle mixture screw (10) to obtain best possible idle performance. Readjust idle speed to 1,000 rpm if necessary.

To check float level, remove float bowl (24) and invert carburetor assembly. There should be 2-3 mm (0.08-0.12 in.) between float and carburetor body. To adjust float level, carefully bend float tang that contacts inlet needle to obtain specified measurement.

GOVERNOR. A mechanical flyball type governor with external adjustments is used.

NOTE: Maximum no-load engine speed is 3,500-3,600 rpm.

Before adjusting governed speed, make sure governor linkage is properly adjusted. Loosen nut (5—Fig. BC2) and

Fig. BC2—View showing external governor adjustments. Refer to text. Placing spring (3) in a higher hole in governor lever (2) increases maximum rpm while placing spring (3) in a higher hole in throttle lever (4) decreases maximum rpm.

1. Governor shaft
2. Governor lever
3. Spring
4. Throttle lever
5. Nut
6. Link

rotate shaft (1) fully clockwise. Push lever (2) toward carburetor to open throttle valve completely, then tighten nut (5). Vary spring (3) tension to adjust maximum engine speed.

IGNITION. Refer to Fig. BC3 for exploded view of ignition system. Breaker-point gap should be 0.4 mm (0.016 in.). Ignition timing is 4.06-4.16 mm (0.160-0.164 in.) BTDC. Adjust ignition timing by rotating stator plate (1—Fig. BC3). Timing should be correct if reference mark (R) is aligned with reference mark on engine block. If reference marks are absent, rotate engine in normal direction (clockwise) of rotation until piston is at TDC. Make reference marks on flywheel and engine block and rotate flywheel counterclockwise 41 mm (1.61 in.). Piston should be 4.06-4.16 mm (0.160-0.164 in.) BTDC with flywheel at this position. Without turning crankshaft, remove flywheel and rotate stator plate (1) until breaker points start to open. Make certain breaker points are adjusted to specified gap prior to setting

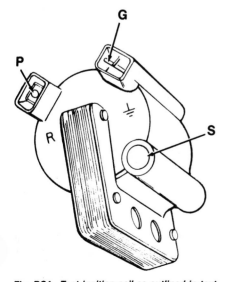

Fig. BC3—Exploded view of primary ignition system.
1. Stator plate
2. Felt wick
3. Armature
4. Breaker points assy.
5. Condenser
6. Cover
7. Rotor (magnets)
R. Reference mark

timing. Mark stator plate and engine block for future reference.

Test ignition coil with an ohmmeter. Resistance between primary terminal (P—Fig. BC4) and ground terminal (G) should be 0.8-0.9 ohm. Resistance between high tension terminal (S) and ground terminal (G) should be 4,500-5,000 ohms. Renew coil if resistance is outside specified limits.

LUBRICATION. Engine oil level should be even with fill plug hole. Change oil after every 50 hours of operation or every six months. Recommended oil is a good quality SAE 40 engine oil or SAE 20 for cold weather operation. SAE 10W-40 is an acceptable substitute for year-round operation. Internal engine components are lubricated by splash created inside crankcase.

CRANKCASE BREATHER. The crankcase breather provides a vent for crankcase pressure, preventing oil leakage at crankcase seals. The crankcase breather is attached to valve cover. Clearance between valve inside breather and valve seat should be 0.4-0.7 mm (0.016-0.027 in.). If slight crankcase vacuum is not present, inspect breather for faulty valve.

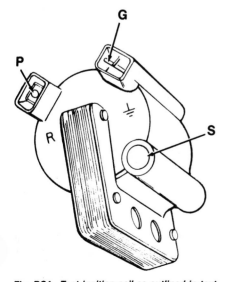

Fig. BC4—Test ignition coil as outlined in text.
G. Ground terminal
P. Primary terminal
S. High tension terminal

AIR FILTER. Air filter should be removed and cleaned each time tiller is used. Remove filter and thoroughly clean in a suitable solvent. Dry filter and saturate with SAE 20 engine oil. Squeeze excess oil from filter and reinstall.

REPAIRS

TIGHTENING TORQUES. Specified tightening torques are as follows:
Connecting rod screws . . . . . 10.4 N·m
(8 ft.-lbs.)
Crankcase cover . . . . 5.9 N·m
(4 ft.-lbs.)
Cylinder head . . . . 19.6 N·m
(15 ft.-lbs.)
Flywheel nut . . . . 98.0 N·m
(72 ft.-lbs.)
Spark plug . . . . 29.0 N·m
(22 ft.-lbs.)

CONNECTING ROD. Aluminum alloy connecting rod rides directly on crankpin. Standard rod big end diameter is 25.026-25.036 mm (0.9853-0.9857 in.). Connecting rod for reconditioned crankpin is available in 0.25 mm (0.010 in.) and 0.50 mm (0.020 in.) undersize. Preferred connecting rod-to-crankpin clearance is 0.026-0.036 mm (0.0010-0.0014 in.). Standard connecting rod small end diameter is 14.010-14.021 mm (0.5516-0.5520 in.).

Piston may be installed on rod in either direction, but rod must be installed into engine with match marks on rod cap and rod aligned and facing toward camshaft. Tighten rod cap screws to 10.4 N·m (8 ft.-lbs.).

CYLINDER, PISTON, PIN AND RINGS. Standard cylinder diameter is 65.00-65.010 mm (2.5591-2.5594 in.). Maximum allowable taper is 0.1 mm (0.004 in.). Maximum allowable out-of-round is 0.06 mm (0.002 in.).

Measure piston diameter at right angle to piston pin, 2 mm (0.08 in.) from bottom of piston skirt. Standard piston diameter is 64.945-64.955 mm (2.5569-2.5573 in.). Piston and rings are available in 0.50 mm (0.020 in.) and 1.0 mm (0.039 in.) oversize. Piston pin diameter should be 13.994-14.000 mm (0.5509-

0.5512 in.). Piston pin bore diameter in piston should be 13.992-13.996 mm (0.5509-0.5510 in.). Oversize piston pins are not available.

Piston ring in ring groove side play should not exceed 0.1 mm (0.004 in.). Ring end gap should be 0.20-0.35 mm (0.0079-0.0138 in.). Install rings on piston as shown in Fig. BC5. Stagger ring gaps approximately 120 degrees. Do not position any ring end gaps inline with piston pin.

CYLINDER HEAD. Inspect cylinder head for warpage or other damage. Head surface may be machined to correct warped or damaged gasket surface, but do not exceed minimum combustion chamber depth of 7.2 mm (0.28 in.) as shown in Fig. BC6. Renew head gasket when installing cylinder head. Tighten cylinder head cap screws following sequence shown in Fig. BC7 to 19.6 N·m (15 ft.-lbs.).

CAMSHAFT. Camshaft can be removed after separating crankcase cover from crankcase. Standard intake lobe

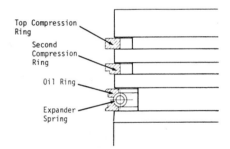

Top Compression Ring
Second Compression Ring
Oil Ring
Expander Spring

Fig. BC5—Install piston rings as shown and stagger end gaps approximately 120 degrees. Do not align any ring end gap with piston pin.

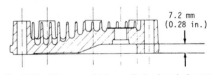

7.2 mm (0.28 in.)

Fig. BC6—When machining cylinder head, do not exceed dimension shown.

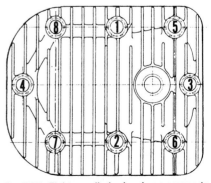

Fig. BC7—Tighten cylinder head cap screws to 19.6 N·m (15 ft.-lbs.) following sequence shown.

height is 24.725 mm (0.9734 in.). Standard exhaust lobe height is 24.030 mm (0.9461 in.). Renew camshaft if intake lobe height is less than 23.6 mm (0.93 in.) or 23.0 mm (0.905 in.) on exhaust lobe.

The camshaft is equipped with a compression release mechanism which prevents exhaust valve from fully closing during starting. Make sure compression release tab protrudes beyond back side of exhaust lobe and is not loose in camshaft. If compression release is faulty, camshaft must be renewed.

Install camshaft with timing marks on camshaft gear and crankshaft gear aligned as shown in Fig. BC9. If timing mark on crankshaft or camshaft is absent, proceed as follows: Position piston at TDC and install camshaft with exhaust lobe facing crankshaft. Temporarily install crankcase cover (2—Fig. BC8).

Rotate crankshaft one complete revolution. With piston at TDC, check that valves are open equally. If valves are not open equal distance, remove camshaft and turn one tooth as necessary to ensure that valves will open equally.

Fig. BC9—Install camshaft with timing marks aligned as shown.

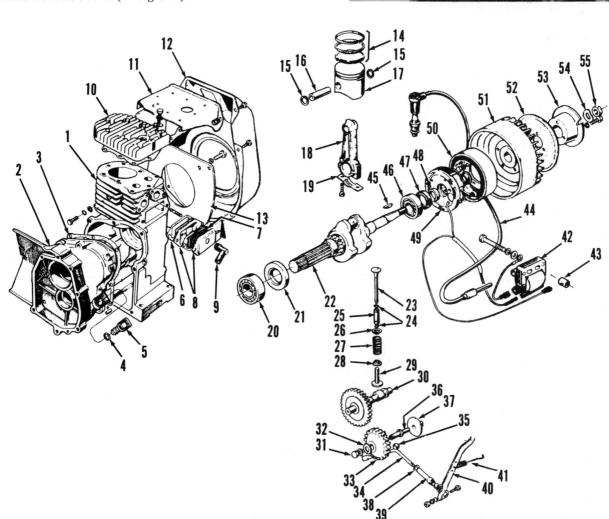

Fig. BC8—Exploded view of engine assembly.

1. Engine block	11. Shroud	20. Main bearing	29. Lifter	38. Washer	46. Main bearing
2. Crankcase cover	12. Blower housing	21. Seal	30. Camshaft	39. Governor rod	47. Seal
3. Gasket	13. Plate	22. Crankshaft	31. Screw	support	48. Gasket
4. "O" ring	14. Piston rings	23. Valve	32. Washer	40. Lever	49. Stator plate
5. Crankcase fill plug	15. Pin retainers	24. Retainer rings	33. Governor gear	41. Spring	50. Rotor
6. Gasket	16. Piston pin	25. Valve guide	34. Governor rod	42. Ignition coil	51. Flywheel
7. Breather valve	17. Piston	26. Upper valve cap	35. Governor ball	43. Spacer	52. Screen
8. Breather housing	18. Connecting rod	27. Spring	36. Governor shaft	44. High tension lead	53. Starter cup
9. Vent tube	19. Lock tab	28. Lower valve cap	37. Thrust spool	45. Woodruff key	54. Wave washer
10. Cylinder head					55. Flywheel nut

GOVERNOR. Inspect governor gear (33—Fig. BC8) for excessive wear or broken teeth. Make sure gear (33) turns freely on governor shaft (36). Make sure balls (35) are free to move in ball seats. Inspect thrust spool (37) for excessive wear or damage and make sure spool (37) moves freely on governor shaft (36).

CRANKSHAFT. The crankshaft is supported in two ball-type main bearings (20 and 46—Fig. BC8). Standard crankpin diameter is 24.990-25.000 mm (0.9839-0.9843 in.). Crankpin may be turned down to fit undersize connecting rod. Standard crankshaft main journal diameter is 24.996-25.005 mm (0.9841-0.9844 in.) on crankcase cover side and 25.002-25.011 mm (0.9843-0.9847 in.) on flywheel side. Crankshaft must be renewed if main bearing journals are excessively worn or damaged. Dress slight scratches or scoring at seal contact area with fine grit emery cloth.

Install crankshaft with timing marks aligned (Fig. BC9). Install crankshaft seals with lips facing inward. Use care not to cut or damage seal lip.

VALVE SYSTEM. Cold valve lash should be 0.25 mm (0.01 in.) for intake valve, and 0.30 mm (0.012 in.) for exhaust valve. Grind valve seat to correct excessive lash, or grind valve stem to correct insufficient lash. Renew valve guides if excessive valve stem clearance is noted. Standard valve stem diameter is 5.963-5.975 mm (0.2348-0.2352 in.). Standard valve guide inside diameter is 6.020-6.032 mm (0.2370-0.2375 in.). Heat engine block in a hot oil bath to approximately 120° C (248° F) to remove or install valve guides. Valve guides must be ground after renewing. Grind seat to a true 45 degree angle. Maximum valve seat width is 2.0 mm (0.08 in.). The manufacturer does not recommended refacing valves. Renew valves if valve face is excessively worn, pitted or damaged. Valve spring free length should be 30 mm (1.18 in.). Renew springs if free length is less than 28 mm (1.1 in.).

SERVICING BCS ACCESSORIES

REWIND STARTER

OVERHAUL. Remove starter from engine. Untie or cut knot from rope to remove handle. Carefully allow rope to rewind into starter housing. Remove nut (2—Fig. BC15), through-bolt (10), pawl (8) and spring (9). Remove screws securing cover (11) to housing (1). Remove rope pulley (6).

CAUTION: Rewind spring (5) is under load. Do not allow spring to escape uncontrolled. Wear gloves and eye protection to prevent personal injury.

Inspect all components for excessive wear or any other damage and renew as necessary.

Lubricate rewind spring (5) and wind into housing (1) in a counterclockwise direction starting with the outer coil. Wind rope around rope pulley (6) in a counterclockwise direction as viewed from flywheel side of pulley. Reverse disassembly procedure. To preload rewind spring, rotate rope pulley approximately three turns in a counterclockwise direction. Hold rope pulley from turning and pass rope through rope guide (3) and install handle (4).

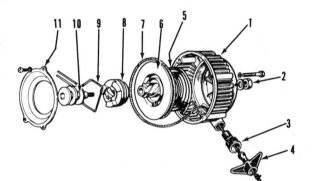

Fig. BC15—Exploded view of early type rewind starter assembly.
1. Housing
2. Nut
3. Rope guide
4. Handle
5. Rewind spring
6. Rope pulley
7. Rope
8. Pawl
9. Spring
10. Through-bolt
11. Cover

BCS SPECIAL TOOLS

The following special tools are available from the manufacturer.

590.51956.5—Puller for removing flywheel.
561.51960.4—Valve spring compressor.
590.51964.4—Valve guide removal and installation.
561.51966.3,
561.51968.3 and
561.51972.2—Seal protectors.

Fig. BC16—Exploded view of late type rewind starter assembly. Refer to legend in Fig. BC15 for component identification except washer (12), through-bolt (13) and starter cup (14).

BRIGGS & STRATTON

BRIGGS & STRATTON CORPORATION
Milwaukee, Wisconsin 53201

HP	Crankshaft	Basic Model (Series)	Bore	Stroke	Displacement
2 (1.49 kW)	Horizontal	60000	2.4 in. (60.3 mm)	1.5 in. (38.1 mm)	6.65 cu. in. (108.97 cc)
3 (2.24 kW)	Horizontal	80000	2.4 in. (60.3 mm)	1.75 in. (44.45 mm)	7.75 cu. in. (126 cc)
3.5 (2.61 kW)	Vertical	90000	2.6 in. (65.1 mm)	1.75 in. (44.45 mm)	9.02 cu. in. (147.8 cc)
4 (2.98 kW)	Horizontal	110000	2.8 in. (70.6 mm)	1.9 in. (47.6 mm)	11.39 cu. in. (186.6 cc)
5 (3.73 kW)	Vertical	130000	2.6 in. (65.1 mm)	2.4 in. (61.9 mm)	12.57 cu. in. (207.6 cc)
5 (3.73 kW)	Horizontal	130000	2.6 in. (65.1 mm)	2.4 in. (61.9 mm)	12.57 cu. in. (207.6 cc)
7 (5.22 kW)	Horizontal	170000	3.0 in. (76.2 mm)	2.4 in. (60.3 mm)	16.70 cu. in. (273.7 cc)
8 (5.97 kW)	Horizontal	190000	3.0 in. (76.2 mm)	2.75 in. (69.85 mm)	19.44 cu. in. (318.6 cc)

All engines covered in this section have aluminum cylinder blocks with either plain aluminum cylinder bore or with a cast iron sleeve integrally cast into the block.

MAINTENANCE

SPARK PLUG. On models with five horsepower or less, use AC 45, Autolite 295, Champion J-8 or equivalent plug. If resistor type plugs are necessary to decrease radio interference, use Champion RJ-8 or equivalent. Seven horsepower and eight horsepower models use AC GC46, Autolite A71, Champion J-8 or equivalent plug. If resistor type plugs are necessary to decrease radio interference, use Champion XJ-8 or equivalent. On all models, set gap to 0.030 inch (0.76 mm). Briggs & Stratton Corporation recommends that plugs not be cleaned by abrasive blasting method as this may introduce some abrasive

material into the engine which could cause extensive damage.

FLOAT TYPE (FLO-JET) CARBURETORS. Three different float type carburetors are used. They are called a "two-piece" (See Fig. B60), a small "one-piece" (See Fig. B64) or a large "one-piece" (See Fig. B66) carburetor depending upon the type of construction.

Float type carburetors are equipped with adjusting needles for both idle and power fuel mixtures. Counterclockwise rotation of the adjusting needles richens the mixture. For initial starting adjustment, open the main needle valve (power fuel mixture) 1½ turns on the two-piece carburetor and 2½ turns on the small one-piece carburetor. Open the idle needle ½ to ¾ turn on the two-piece carburetor and 1½ turns on the small one-piece carburetor. On the large one-piece carburetor, open both needle valves 1⅛ turns. Start the engine and when it is warm, make final adjustments

as follows: Set the speed control for desired operating speed, turn main needle clockwise until engine misses, and then turn it counterclockwise just past the smooth operating point until the engine begins to run unevenly. Return the speed control to idle positon and adjust the idle speed stop screw un-

Fig. B61—Checking upper body of "two-piece" carburetor for warpage.

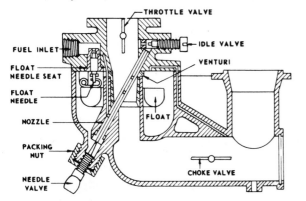

THROTTLE VALVE
IDLE VALVE
FUEL INLET
VENTURI
FLOAT NEEDLE SEAT
FLOAT NEEDLE
NOZZLE
FLOAT
PACKING NUT
NEEDLE VALVE
CHOKE VALVE

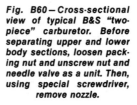

Fig. B60—Cross-sectional view of typical B&S "two-piece" carburetor. Before separating upper and lower body sections, loosen packing nut and unscrew nut and needle valve as a unit. Then, using special screwdriver, remove nozzle.

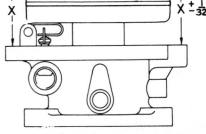

Fig. B62—Carburetor float setting should be within specifications shown. To adjust float setting, bend tang with needle nose pliers as shown in Fig. B63.

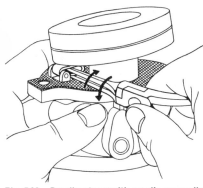

Fig. B63 — Bending tang with needle nose pliers to adjust float setting. Refer to Fig. B62 for method of checking float setting.

Fig. B65 — Disassembling the small "one-piece" float type carburetor. Pry out welch plug, remove choke butterfly (disc), remove choke shaft and needle valve; venturi can then be removed as shown in left view.

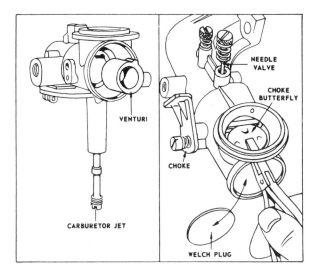

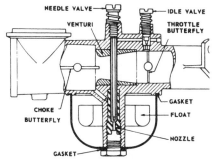

Fig. B64 — Cross-sectional view of typical B&S small "one-piece" float type carburetor. Refer to Fig. B65 for disassembly views.

Fig. B66 — Cross-sectional view of B&S large "one-piece" float type carburetor.

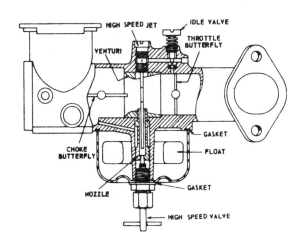

til the engine idles at 1750 rpm. Then adjust the idle needle valve until the engine runs smoothly. Reset the idle speed stop screw, if necessary. The engine should then accelerate without hesitation or sputtering. If it does not accelerate properly, turn the main needle valve counterclockwise slightly to provide a richer fuel mixture.

The float setting on all float type carburetors should be within dimensions shown in Fig. B62. If not, bend the tang on float as shown in Fig. B63 to adjust float setting. If any wear is visible on the inlet valve or the inlet valve seat, install a new valve and seat assembly. On large one-piece carburetors, the renewable inlet valve seat is pressed into the carburetor body until flush with the body.

NOTE: The upper and lower bodies of the two-piece float type careburetor are locked together by the main nozzle. Refer to cross-sectional view of carburetor in Fig. B60. Before attempting to separate the upper body from the lower body, loosen packing nut and unscrew nut and needle valve. Then, using special screwdriver (B&S tool No. 19061 or 19062), remove nozzle.

If a 0.002-inch (0.05 mm) feeler gage can be inserted between upper and

Fig. B67 — Cutaway view of typical suction type (Vacu-Jet) carburetor. Inset shows fuel metering holes which are accessible for cleaning after removing needle valve. Be careful not to enlarge the holes when cleaning them.

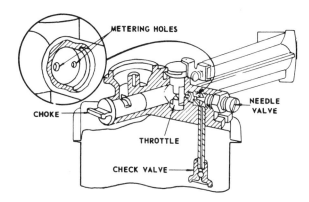

lower bodies of the two-piece carburetor as shown in Fig. B61, the upper body is warped and should be replaced.

Check throttle shaft for wear on all float type carburetors. If 0.10-inch (0.25 mm) or more free play (shaft to bushing clearance) is noted, install new throttle shaft and/or throttle shaft bushings. To remove worn bushings, turn a ¼-inch x 20 tap into bushing and pull bushing from body casting with the tap. Press new bushings into casting by using a vise and, if necessary, ream bushings with a 7/32-inch drill bit.

SUCTION TYPE (VACU-JET) CARBURETORS. A typical suction type (Vacu-Jet) carburetor is shown in Fig. B67. This type carburetor has only one fuel mixture adjusting needle. Turning the needle clockwise leans the fuel-air mixture. Adjust suction type carburetors with fuel tank approximately one-half full and with engine warm and running at approximately 3000 rpm at no load. Turn needle valve clockwise until engine begins to run unevenly from a too-lean fuel-air mixture, then turn needle valve counterclockwise, counting

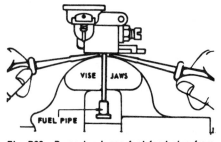

Fig. B68—Removing brass fuel feed pipe from suction type carburetor. Press new brass pipe into carburetor until it projects 2.28-2.31 inches (57.9-58.7 mm) from carburetor face. Nylon fuel feed pipe is threaded into carburetor.

Fig. B70—Exploded view of fuel pump that is incorporated in Pulsa-Jet carburetor.

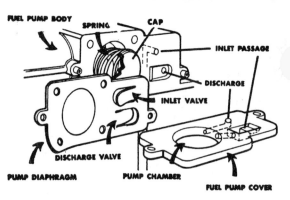

the number of turns, until engine begins to run unevenly from a too-rich fuel-air mixture. Turn needle valve back clockwise one-half the number of turns that it took to go from a too-lean to a too-rich fuel-air condition. This should result in a correct adjustment for full load operation. Adjust idle speed to 1750 rpm.

To remove the suction type carburetor, first remove carburetor and fuel tank as an assembly, then remove carburetor from fuel tank. When reinstalling carburetor on fuel tank, use a new gasket and tighten retaining screws evenly.

The suction type carburetor has a fuel feed pipe extending into fuel tank. The pipe has a check valve to allow fuel to feed up into the carburetor, but prevents fuel from flowing back into the tank. If check valve is inoperative and cleaning in alcohol or acetone will not free the check valve, renew the fuel feed pipe. If feed pipe is made of brass, remove as shown in Fig. B68. Using a vise, press new pipe into carburetor so that it ex-

tends 2.28-2.31 inches (57.9-58.7 mm) from carburetor body. If pipe is made of nylon (plastic), screw pipe out of carburetor body with wrench. When installing new nylon feel pipe, be careful not to overtighten.

NOTE: If soaking carburetor in cleaner for more than one-half hour, be sure to remove all nylon parts and "O" ring, if used, before placing the carburetor in cleaning solvent.

PUMP TYPE (PULSA-JET) CARBURETORS. The pump type (Pulsa-Jet) carburetor is basically a suction type carburetor incorporating a fuel pump to fill a constant level fuel sump in top of fuel tank. Refer to schematic view in Fig. B69. This makes a constant fuel-air mixture available to engine regardless of fuel level in tank. Adjustment of the pump type carburetor fuel mixture needle valve is the same as outlined for suction type carburetors in previous paragraph, except that fuel level in tank is not important.

To remove the pump type carburetor, first remove the carburetor and fuel tank as an assembly; then, remove carburetor from fuel tank. When reinstalling carburetor on fuel tank, use a new gasket or pump diaphragm as required and tighten retaining screws evenly.

Fig. B70 shows an exploded view of the pump unit used on some carburetors.

On other carburetors pump diaphragm is placed between the carburetor and fuel tank as shown in Fig. B71.

The pump type carburetor has two fuel feed pipes; the long pipe feeds fuel into the pump portion of the carburetor from which fuel then flows to the constant level fuel sump. The short pipe extends into the constant level sump and feeds fuel into the carburetor venturi via fuel mixture needle valve.

As check valves are incorporated in the pump diaphragm, fuel feed pipes on pump type carburetors do not have a check valve. However, if the fuel screen in lower end of pipe is broken or clogged and cannot be cleaned, the pipe or screen housing can be renewed. If pipe is made of nylon, unscrew old pipe and install new pipe with a wrench; be careful not to overtighten new pipe. If pipe is made of brass, clamp pipe lightly in a vise and drive old screen housing from pipe with screwdriver or small chisel as shown in Fig. B72. Drive a new screen housing onto pipe with a soft faced hammer.

NOTE: If soaking carburetor in cleaner for more than one-half hour, be sure to remove all nylon parts and "O" ring, if used, before placing carburetor in cleaning solvent.

NOTE: Be sure air cleaner retaining screw is in place if engine is being operated (during tests) without air cleaner installed. If screw is not in place, fuel may lift up through the screw hole and enter carburetor throat as the screw hole leads directly into the constant level fuel sump.

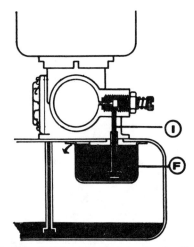

Fig. B69—Fuel flow in Pulsa-Jet carburetor. Fuel pump incorporated in carburetor fills constant level sump below carburetor (F) and excess fuel flows back into tank. Fuel is drawn from sump through inlet (1) past fuel mixture adjusting needle by vacuum in carburetor.

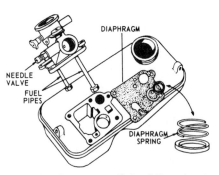

Fig. B71—Pump type (Pulsa-Jet) carburetor diaphragm is installed between carburetor and fuel tank.

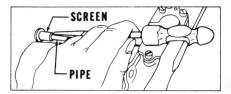

Fig. B72—To renew screen housing on pump type carburetors with brass feed pipes, drive old screen housing for pipe as shown. To hold pipe, clamp lightly in a vise.

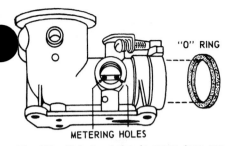

Fig. B73—Metering holes in pump type carburetors are accessible for cleaning after removing fuel mixture needle valve. On models with intake pipe, carburetor is sealed to pipe with "O" ring.

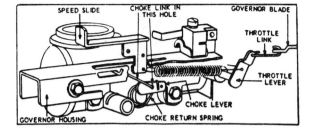

Fig. B76—Choke-A-Matic control on float type carburetor. Remote control can be attached to speed slide.

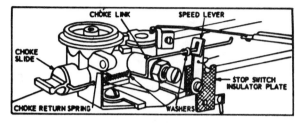

Fig. B77—Typical Choke-A-Matic control on suction type carburetor. Remote control can be attached to speed lever.

INTAKE TUBE. Intake tube is attached between carburetor and engine intake port in one of three methods. First method: Carburetor is sealed to intake tube with an "O" ring as shown in Fig. B73. Second method: Intake tube is threaded in engine intake port. A gasket is used between engine intake port cover and engine casting as shown in Fig. B74. Third method: Intake tube is bolted to engine intake port and a gasket is used between intake tube and engine casting as shown in Fig. B75.

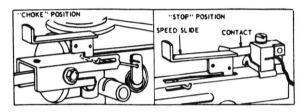

Fig. B78—Choke-A-Matic control in choke and stop positions on float carburetor.

CHOKE-A-MATIC CARBURETOR CONTROLS. Engines equipped with float, suction or pump type carburetors may be equipped with a control unit with which the carburetor choke and throttle and the magneto grounding switch are operated from a single lever (Choke-A-Matic carburetors). Refer to Figs. B76

Fig. B79—Choke-A-Matic control in choke and stop positions on suction carburetor. Bend choke link if necessary to adjust control.

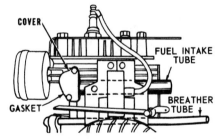

COVER

FUEL INTAKE TUBE

GASKET

BREATHER TUBE

Fig. B74—Intake tube is threaded into intake port of engine; a gasket is placed between intake port cover and intake port.

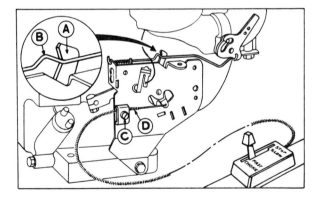

Fig. B80—On Choke-A-Matic control, choke actuating lever (A) should just contact choke link or shift (B) when control is at "FAST" position. If not, loosen screw (C) and move control wire housing (D) as required.

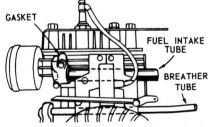

GASKET

FUEL INTAKE TUBE

BREATHER TUBE

Fig. B75—Fuel intake tube is bolted to engine intake port and a gasket is placed between tube and engine.

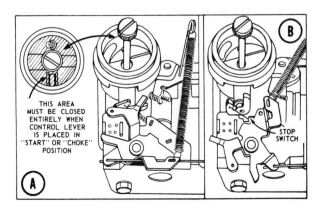

Fig. B81—When Choke-A-Matic control is in "START" or "CHOKE" position, choke must be completely closed as shown in view A. When control is in "STOP" position arm should contact stop switch (View B.)

through B82 for views showing the different types of Choke-A-Matic carburetor controls.

To check operation of Choke-A-Matic carburetor controls, move control lever to "CHOKE" position; carburetor choke slide or plate must be completely closed. Then, move control lever to "STOP" position; magneto grounding switch should be making contact. With the control lever in "RUN", "FAST", or "SLOW" position, carburetor choke should be completely open. On units with remote controls, synchronize movement of remote lever to carburetor control lever by loosening screw (C–Fig. B80 or Fig. B82) and moving control wire housing (D) as required; then, tighten screw to clamp the housing securely. Refer to Fig. B83 to check remote control wire movement.

AUTOMATIC CHOKE (THERMO-STAT TYPE). A thermostat operated choke is used on some models equipped with the two-piece carburetor. To adjust choke linkage, hold choke shaft so thermostat lever is free. At room temperature, stop screw in thermostat collar should be located midway between thermostat stops. If not, loosen stop screw, adjust the collar and tighten stop screw. Loosen set screw (S–Fig. B84) on thermostat lever. Then, slide lever on shaft to ensure free movement of choke unit. Turn thermostat shaft clockwise until stop screw contacts thermostat stop. While holding shaft in this position, move shaft lever until choke is open exactly 1/8 inch (3.2 mm) and tighten lever set screw. Turn thermostat shaft counterclockwise until stop screw contacts thermostat stop as shown in Fig. B85. Manually open choke valve until it stops against top of choke link opening. At this time, choke valve should be open at least 3/32-inch (2.4 mm), but not more than 5/32-inch (4.0 mm). Hold choke valve in wide open position and check

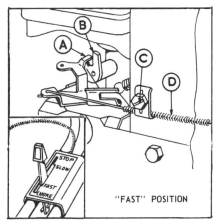

Fig. B82—On Choke-A-Matic control, lever (A) should just contact choke shaft arm (B) when control is in "FAST" position. If not, loosen screw (C) and move control wire housing (D) as required, then tighten screw.

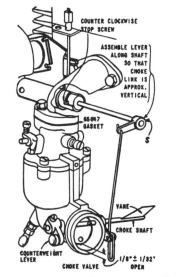

Fig. B85 — Automatic choke on two-piece Flo-Jet carburetor in "Cold" position.

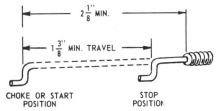

Fig. B83—For proper operation of Choke-A-Matic controls, remote control wire must extend to dimension shown and have a minimum travel at 1⅜ inches (34.9 mm).

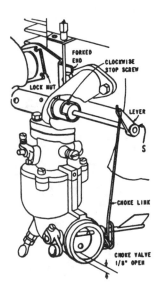

Fig. B84—Automatic choke used on some models equipped with a two-piece Flo-Jet carburetor showing unit used in "Hot" position.

Fig. B86—Diagram showing vacuum operated automatic choke used on some vertical crankshaft engines in closed (engine not running) position.

Fig. B87—Diagram showing vacuum operated automatic choke in open (engine running) position.

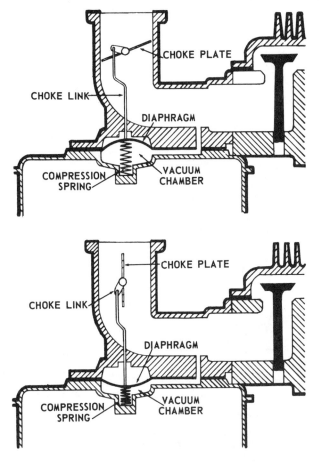

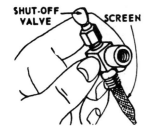

Fig. B88—Fuel tank outlet used on smaller engines with float type carburetor.

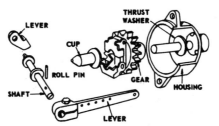

Fig. B91—Exploded view of governor unit used on two and three horsepower horizontal crankshaft models.

equipped with a fuel tank outlet as shown in Fig. B88. On larger engines, a fuel sediment bowl is incorporated with fuel tank outlet as shown in Fig. B89. Clean any lint and dirt from tank outlet screens with a brush. Varnish or other gasoline deposits may be removed by use of a suitable solvent. Tighten packing nut or remove nut and shut-off valve, then renew packing if leakage occurs around shut-off valve stem.

GOVERNOR. All models are equipped with either a mechanical (flyweight type) or an air vane (pneumatic) governor. Refer to following appropriate paragraph for service and adjustment information on the governor unit being serviced.

MECHANICAL GOVERNOR. Three different designs of mechanical governors are used.

On two and three horspower engines a governor unit as shown in Fig. B90 is used. An exploded view of this governor unit is shown in Fig. B91. The governor housing is attached to inner side of crankcase cover and the governor gear is driven from the engine camshaft gear. Use Figs. B90 and B91 as a disassembly and assembly guide. Renew any parts that bind or show excessive wear. After governor is assembled, refer to Fig. B92 and adjust linkage as follows: Loosen screw clamping governor lever to governor crank. Turn governor lever counterclockwise so that carburetor throttle is in wide open position and while holding lever, turn governor crank as far counterclockwise as possible and tighten screw clamping lever to crank. Governor crank can be turned with screwdriver. Check linkage to be sure it is free and that the carburetor throttle will move from idle to wide open position.

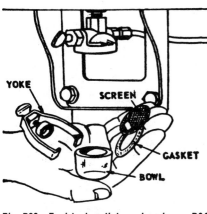

Fig. B89—Fuel tank outlet used on larger B&S engines.

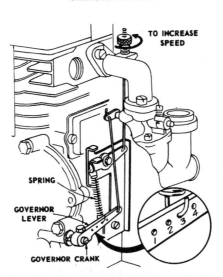

Fig. B92—View of governor linkage used on two and three horsepower horizontal crankshaft engines using a mechanical governor. Governor spring should be hooked in governor lever as shown in inset.

position of counterweight lever. Lever should be in a horizontal position with free end towards right.

AUTOMATIC CHOKE (VACUUM TYPE). A spring and vacuum operated automatic choke is used on some vertical crankshaft engines. A diaphragm under carburetor is connected to the choke shaft by a link. The compression spring works against the diaphragm, holding choke in closed position when engine is not running. See Fig. B86. As engine starts, increased vacuum works against the spring and pulls the diaphragm and choke link down holding choke in open (running) position shown in Fig. B87.

During operation, if a sudden load is applied to engine or a lugging condition develops, a drop in intake vacuum occurs, permitting choke to close partially. This provides a richer fuel mixture to

meet the condition and keeps the engine running smoothly. When the load condition has been met, increased vacuum returns choke valve to normal running (fully open) position.

FUEL TANK OUTLET. Small models with float type carburetors are

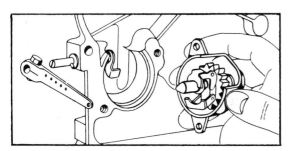

Fig. B90—Removing governor unit from inside crankcase cover on two and three horsepower horizontal crankshaft models.

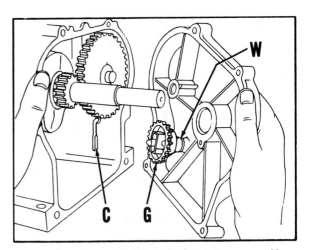

Fig. B93—Installing crankcase cover on four horsepower and larger engines with mechanical governor. Governor crank (C) must be in position shown. A thrust washer (W) is placed between governor (G) and crankcase cover.

On four horsepower and larger engines the governor gear and weight unit (G – Fig. B93) is supported on a pin in engine crankcase cover and the governor crank is installed in a bore in the engine crankcase. A thrust washer (W) is placed between governor gear and crankcase cover. When assembling crankcase cover to crankcase, be sure governor crank (C) is in position shown in Fig. B93. After governor unit and crankcase cover is installed, refer to Fig. B94 for installation of linkage. Before attempting to start engine, refer to Fig. B95 and adjust linkage as follows: Loosen bolt clamping governor lever to governor crank. Set control lever in high speed position, then, using screwdriver, turn governor crank as far clockwise as possible and tighten governor lever clamp bolt. Check to be sure carburetor throttle can be moved from idle to wide open position and that linkage is free.

On vertical crankshaft engines having a mechanical governor, the governor weight unit is integral with the lubricating oil slinger and is mounted on lower end of camshaft gear as shown in Fig. B96. With engine upside down, place governor and slinger unit on camshaft gear as shown, place spring washer on camshaft gear and assemble engine base to crankcase. Assemble linkage as shown in Fig. B97; then, refer to Fig. B98 and adjust linkage as follows: With bolt clamping governor lever to governor crank loose and control lever in high speed position, turn governor crank with screwdriver as far clockwise as possible and tighten governor lever clamping bolt.

AIR VANE (PNEUMATIC) GOVERNORS. Some models are equipped with an air vane governor; refer to Fig. B99 for schematic operational views of a typical unit.

Vane should stop 1/8-1/4 inch (3.2-6.35 mm) from magneto coil (See Fig. B100, illustration 2) when linkage is assembled and attached to carburetor throttle shaft. If necessary to adjust, spring the vane while holding the shaft. With wide open throttle, the link from the air vane arm to the carburetor throttle should be in a vertical position on horizontal crankshaft models and in a horizontal position on vertical crankshaft models. (See Fig. B100, illustration 3 and 4). Check linkage for binding; if binding

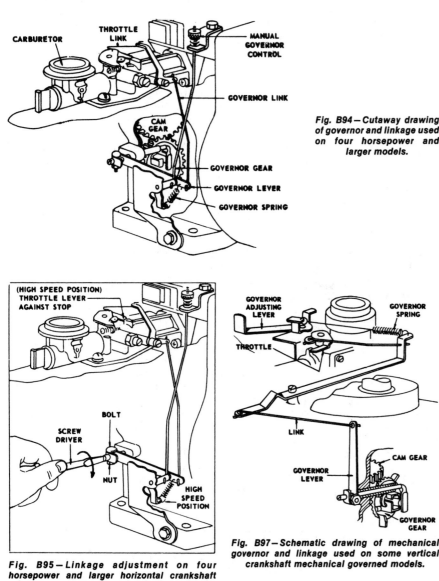

Fig. B94 – Cutaway drawing of governor and linkage used on four horsepower and larger models.

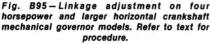

Fig. B95 – Linkage adjustment on four horsepower and larger horizontal crankshaft mechanical governor models. Refer to text for procedure.

Fig. B97 – Schematic drawing of mechanical governor and linkage used on some vertical crankshaft mechanical governed models.

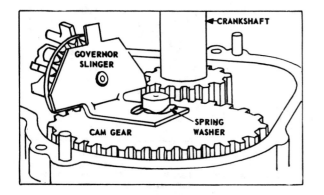

Fig. B96 – View showing vertical crankshaft mechanical governor unit. Drawing is of lower side of engine with oil sump (engine base) removed; note spring washer location.

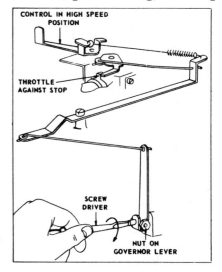

Fig. B98 – View showing adjustment of vertical crankshaft mechanical governor; refer to text for procedure.

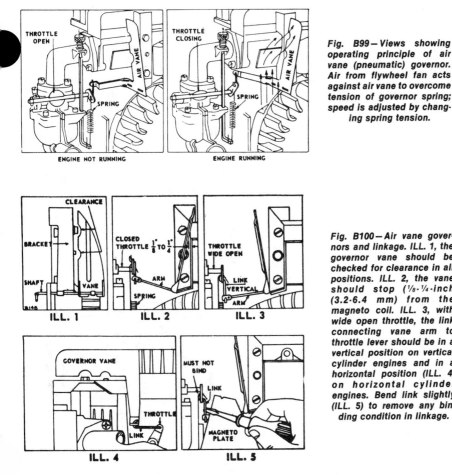

Fig. B99 — Views showing operating principle of air vane (pneumatic) governor. Air from flywheel fan acts against air vane to overcome tension of governor spring; speed is adjusted by changing spring tension.

Fig. B100 — Air vane governors and linkage. ILL. 1, the governor vane should be checked for clearance in all positions. ILL. 2, the vane should stop (1/8-1/4-inch (3.2-6.4 mm) from the magneto coil. ILL. 3, with wide open throttle, the link connecting vane arm to throttle lever should be in a vertical position on vertical cylinder engines and in a horizontal position (ILL. 4) on horizontal cylinder engines. Bend link slightly (ILL. 5) to remove any binding condition in linkage.

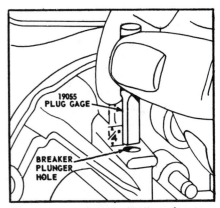

Fig. B102 — Adjustment of breaker point gap on models having breaker point separate from condenser.

condition exists, bend links slightly to correct. Refer to Fig. B100, illustration 5.

NOTE: Some engines are equipped with a nylon governor vane which does not require adjustment.

MAGNETO. The breaker contact gap is 0.020 inch (0.51 mm) on all models. Condenser capacity on all models is 0.18-0.24 mfd.

Breaker points and condenser are accessible after removing engine flywheel and breaker cover.

On some models, one breaker contact point is an integral part of the ignition condenser and the breaker arm is pivoted on a knife edge retained in a slot in pivot post. On these models, breaker contact gap is adjusted by moving the condenser as shown in Fig. B101. On other models, breaker contact gap is adjusted by relocating position of breaker contact bracket; refer to Fig. B102.

On all models, breaker contact arm is actuated by a plunger held in a bore in engine crankcase and riding against a cam on engine crankshaft. Plunger can

be removed after removing breaker points. Renew the plunger if worn to a length of 0.870 inch (22.10 mm) or less. If breaker point plunger bore in crankcase is worn, oil will leak past plunger. Check bore with B&S plug gage No. 19055; if plug gage will enter bore 1/4-inch (6.4 mm) or more, bore should be reamed and a bushing installed. Refer to Fig. B103 for method of checking bore and to Fig. B104 for steps in reaming bore and installing bushing if bore is worn. To ream bore and install bushing, it is necessary that the breaker points, armature and ignition coil and the crankshaft be removed.

Armature and ignition coil are located outside flywheel and armature to flywheel air gap should be as follows:

Series 60000 & 80000
   Two Leg Armature . . . 0.006-0.010 in.
                   (0.15-0.25 mm)
   Three Leg Armature . . 0.012-0.016 in.
                   (0.30-0.41 mm)
Series 90000
   & 110000 . . . . 0.006-0.010 in.
                   (0.15-0.25 mm)

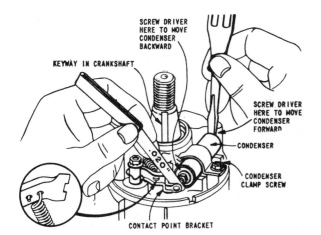

Fig. B101 — View showing breaker point adjustment on models having breaker point integral with condenser. Move condenser to adjust point gap.

Fig. B103 — If Briggs & Stratton plug gage #19055 can be inserted in breaker plunger bore a distance of 1/4-inch (6.35 mm) or more, bore is worn and must be rebushed.

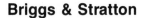

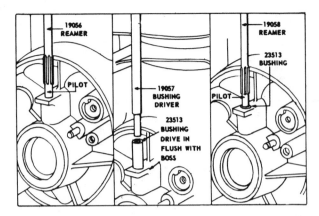

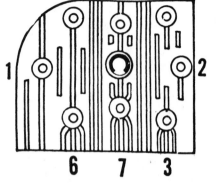

Fig. B104— Views showing reaming plunger bore to accept bushing (left view), installing bushing (center) and finish reaming bore (right) of bushing.

Fig. B106— Cylinder head screw tightening sequence. Long screws are used in positions 2, 3 and 7.

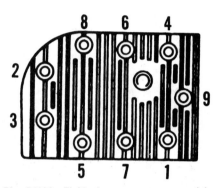

Fig. B106A— Tightening sequence on models with nine cylinder head screws. Long screws are used in positions, 1, 7 and 9.

Series 130000 . . . . 0.010-0.014 in.
(0.25-0.36 mm)
Series 170000 & 190000
Two Leg Armature . . . 0.010-0.014 in.
(0.25-0.36 mm)
Three Leg Armature . . 0.016-0.019 in.
(0.41-0.48 mm)

LUBRICATION. Vertical crankshaft engines are lubricated by an oil slinger wheel driven by the cam gear. On vertical crankshaft engines, the oil slinger wheel, pin and bracket are an integral unit with the bracket being retained by the lower end of the engine camshaft. A spring washer is placed on lower end of camshaft between bracket and oil sump boss. Renew the oil slinger assembly if teeth are worn on slinger gear or gear is loose on bracket. On horizontal crankshaft engines, a splash system (oil dipper on connecting rod) is used for engine lubrication.

Use oils labeled API classification SE or SF. SAE-30, 10W-30 or 10W-40 oil is recommended for temperatures above 40°F, SAE 10W-30 or 10W-40 recommended for temperatures above 40°F, SAE 10W-30 or 10W-40 for temperatures between 40°F and 0°F, or SAE 5W-20 or 5W-30 for below 0°F. Fill crankcase to point of overflowing or to **FULL** mark on dipstick when engine is level.

CRANKCASE BREATHER. The crankcase breather is built into the engine valve cover. The mounting holes are offset so the breather can only be installed one way. Rinse breather in solvent and allow to drain. A vent tube connects the breather to the carburetor air horn on certain model engines for extra protection against dusty conditions.

REPAIRS

NOTE: When checking compression on models with "Easy-Spin" starting, turn engine opposite the direction of normal rotation. See CAMSHAFT paragraph.

CYLINDER HEAD. When removing cylinder head, be sure to note the position from which each of the different length screws were removed. If they are not used in the same holes when installing the head, it will result in screws bottoming in some holes and not enough thread contact in others. Lubricate the cylinder head screws with graphite grease before installation. Do not use sealer on head gasket. When installing cylinder head, tighten all screws lightly and then retighten them in sequence shown in Fig. B106 and Fig. B106A to a torque of 165 in.-lbs. (18.63 N·m) on seven and eight horsepower models. On all other models, torque screws to 140 in.-lbs. (15.81 N·m). Run engine for 2 to 5 minutes to allow it to warm up and retighten the head screws again following the sequence and torque value mentioned above.

CONNECTING ROD. The connecting rod and piston are removed from cylinder head end of block as an assembly. The aluminum alloy connecting rod rides directly on the induction hardened crankpin. The rod should be rejected if the crankpin hole is scored or out-of-round over 0.0007-inch (0.018 mm) or if the piston pin hole is scored or out-of-round over 0.0005-inch (0.013 mm). Wear limit sizes are given in the following chart. Reject the connecting rod if either the crankpin or piston pin hole is worn to or larger than the sizes given in the chart.

NOTE: Piston pins of 0.005-inch (0.13 mm) oversize are available for service. Piston pin hole in rod can be reamed to this size if crankpin hole is O.K.

Torque connecting rod cap screws to 165 in.-lbs. (18.63 N·m) on seven and eight horsepower engines and 100 in.-lbs. (11.29 N·m) on all other engines.

PISTON, PIN AND RINGS. Pistons for use in engines having aluminum bore are not interchangeable with those for use in cylinders having cast-iron sleeve. Pistons may be identified as follows: Those for use in cast-iron sleeve

CONNECTING ROD REJECTION SIZES

Basic Model	Crankpin Hole	*Piston Pin Hole
60000	0.876 in. (22.25 mm)	0.492 in. (12.50 mm)
80000, 90000, 110000 & 130000	1.0013 in. (25.433 mm)	0.492 in. (12.50 mm)
170000	1.0949 in. (27.810 mm)	0.674 in. (17.12 mm)
190000	1.1265 in. (28.613 mm)	0.674 in. (17.12 mm)

*Standard Size

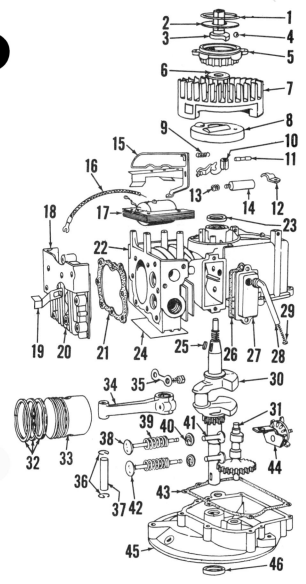

1. Snap ring
2. Washer
3. Ratchet
4. Steel balls
5. Starter clutch
6. Washer
7. Flywheel
8. Breaker cover
9. Breaker point spring
10. Breaker arm & pivot
11. Breaker plunger
12. Condenser clamp
13. Coil spring (primary wire retainer)
14. Condenser
15. Governor air vane & bracket assy.
16. Spark plug wire
17. Armature & coil assy.
18. Air baffle
19. Spark plug grounding switch
20. Cylinder head
21. Header head gasket
22. Cylinder block
23. Crankshaft oil seal
24. Cylinder shield
25. Flywheel key
26. Gasket
27. Breather & tappet chamber cover
28. Breather tube assy.
29. Coil spring
30. Crankshaft
31. Cam gear & shaft
32. Piston rings
33. Piston
34. Connecting rod
35. Rod bolt lock
36. Piston pin retaining rings
37. Piston pin
38. Intake valve
39. Valve springs
40. Valve spring keepers
41. Tappets (cam followers)
42. Exhaust valve
43. Gasket (0.005, 0.009 or 0.015 in.)
44. Oil slinger assy.
45. Oil sump (engine base)
46. Crankshaft oil seal

Fig. B107 — Exploded view of typical vertical crankshaft model with air vane (pneumatic) governor. To remove flywheel, remove blower housing and starter unit; then, unscrew starter clutch housing (5). Flywheel can then be pulled from crankshaft.

gap of 0.035-inch (0.89 mm) or more and reject oil rings having an end gap of 0.045-inch (1.14 mm) or more.

Pistons and rings are available in 0.010-inch (0.25 mm), 0.020-inch (0.51 mm) and 0.030-inch (0.76 mm) oversizes as well as standard size.

A chrome ring set is available for slightly worn standard bore cylinders. Refer to note in **CYLINDER** paragraph.

CYLINDER. If cylinder bore wear is 0.003-inch (0.08 mm) or more or is 0.0025-inch (0.06 mm) or more out-of-round, cylinder must be rebored to next larger oversize.

Standard bore sizes for each basic model series are given below:

STANDARD CYLINDER BORE SIZES

Basic Model	Standard Cylinder Bore
60000 & 80000	2.374-2.375 in.
	(60.30-60.33 mm)
90000	2.5615-2.5625 in.
	(65.062-65.088 mm)
110000	2.7802-2.7812 in.
	(70.617-70.642 mm)
130000	2.5615-2.5625 in.
	(65.062-65.088 mm)
170000 & 190000 ..	2.999-3.000 in.
	(76.17-76.2 mm)

It is recommended that a hone be used for resizing cylinders. Operate hone at 300-700 rpm with an up and down movement that will produce a 45 degree crosshatch pattern. Clean cylinder after honing with oil or soap suds. Always resize to exact 0.010-inch (0.25 mm), 0.020-inch (0.51 mm) or 0.030-inch (0.76 mm) oversize from given dimensions. Approved hones are as follows: For aluminum bore, use Ammco hone 3956 for rough and finishing or Sunnen hone AN200 for rough and Sunnen hone AN500 for finishing. For sleeved bores, use Ammco hone 4324 for rough and finishing or Sunnen hone AN100 for rough and Sunnen hone AN300 for finishing.

NOTE: A chrome piston ring set is available for slightly worn standard bore cylinders. No honing or cylinder deglazing is required for these rings. Cylinder bore can be a maximum of 0.005-inch (0.13 mm) oversize when using chrome rings.

CRANKSHAFT AND MAIN BEARINGS. Except where equipped with ball bearings, main bearings are an integral part of crankcase and cover or sump. Bearings are renewable by reaming out crankcase and cover on sump bearing bores and installing service bushings. Tools for reaming crankcase and cover

cylinders have a plain, dull aluminum finish, have an "L" stamped on top and use an oil ring expander. Those for use in aluminum bore cylinders are chrome plated (shiny finish), do not have an identifying letter and do not use an oil ring expander.

Reject pistons showing visible signs of wear, scoring or scuffing. If, after cleaning carbon from top ring groove, a new top ring has a side clearance of 0.007-inch (0.18 mm) or more, reject the piston. Reject piston or hone piston pin hole to 0.005-inch (0.13 mm) oversize if pin hole is 0.0005-inch (0.013 mm) or more out-of-round, or is worn to a diameter of 0.491-inch (12.47 mm) on 60000, 80000, 90000, 110000 or 130000 model engines. On 170000 and 190000 models, reject piston or hone piston pin

hole to 0.005-inch (0.13 mm) oversize if pin hole is 0.0005-inch (0.013 mm) or more out-of-round, or is worn to a diameter of 0.673-inch (17.09 mm).

If piston pin is 0.0005 (0.013 mm) or more out-of-round, or is worn to a diameter of 0.489-inch (12.42 mm) or smaller on 60000, 80000, 90000, 110000 and 130000 models, reject pin. On 170000 and 190000 models, reject piston pin if pin is 0.0005-inch (0.013 mm) or more out-of-round, or is worn to a diameter of 0.671-inch (17.04 mm) or smaller.

Specified piston ring gap for new rings is 0.010-0.025 inch (0.25-0.64 mm) on models with aluminum cylinder bore and 0.010-0.018 inch (0.25-0.46 mm) on models with cast-iron cylinder bore. Reject compression rings having an end or sump and for installing service bushings are available from Briggs & Stratton. If bearings are scored, out-of-round 0.0007-inch (0.018 mm) or more, or are worn to or larger than the reject sizes given at bottom of page, ream and install service bushings.

Rejection sizes for crankshaft bearing journals are given in the adjoining chart. Figures given for main bearing journals apply to plain bearing applications only.

Ball bearing mains are a press fit on crankshaft and must be removed by pressing crankshaft out of bearing. Reject ball bearing if worn or rough. Expand new bearing by heating in hot oil (325°F maximum) and install on crankshaft with seal side towards crankpin journal.

Crankshaft end play on all models is 0.002-0.008 inch (0.05-0.20 mm) with at least one 0.015-inch (0.38 mm) cover or sump gasket in place. Additional sump or cover gaskets of 0.005-inch (0.13 mm) and 0.009-inch (0.23 mm) thicknesses are available if end play is less than 0.002-inch (0.05 mm). If end play is over 0.008-inch (0.20 mm), metal shims are available for use on crankshaft between crankshaft gear and cylinder block.

CAMSHAFT. Camshaft and camshaft gear are an integral part which rides in journals at each end of the camshaft. Inspect camshaft assembly for wear on journals, cam lobes and gear teeth. Rejection sizes for journals and cam lobes are given in the chart at the bottom of the page.

On models with "Easy-Spin" starting, intake cam lobe is designed to hold intake valve slightly open on part of the compression stroke. Therefore, to check compression, engine must be turned backwards.

"Easy-Spin" camshafts (cam gears) can be identified by two holes drilled in web of gear. Where part number of an older cam gear and an "Easy-Spin" cam gear are the same (except for an "E" following the "Easy-Spin" part number), the gears are interchangeable.

VALVE SYSTEM. Intake valve tappet clearance is 0.005-0.007 inch (0.13-0.18 mm) and exhaust tappet

21. Exhaust valve
22. Intake valve
23. Valve spring retainers
24. Cylinder block
25. Muffler
26. Valve springs
27. Gasket
28. Breather & tappet chamber cover
29. Breather pipe
30. Governor lever
31. Clamping bolt
32. Governor crank

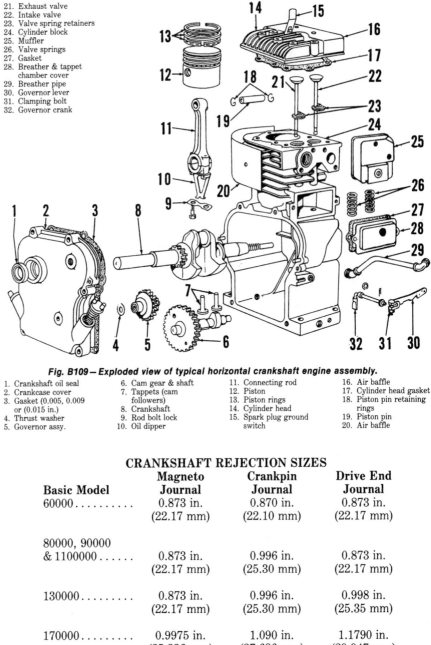

Fig. B109— Exploded view of typical horizontal crankshaft engine assembly.

1. Crankshaft oil seal
2. Crankcase cover
3. Gasket (0.005, 0.009 or (0.015 in.)
4. Thrust washer
5. Governor assy.
6. Cam gear & shaft
7. Tappets (cam followers)
8. Crankshaft
9. Rod bolt lock
10. Oil dipper
11. Connecting rod
12. Piston
13. Piston rings
14. Cylinder head
15. Spark plug ground switch
16. Air baffle
17. Cylinder head gasket
18. Piston pin retaining rings
19. Piston pin
20. Air baffle

CRANKSHAFT REJECTION SIZES

Basic Model	Magneto Journal	Crankpin Journal	Drive End Journal
60000.........	0.873 in. (22.17 mm)	0.870 in. (22.10 mm)	0.873 in. (22.17 mm)
80000, 90000 & 1100000......	0.873 in. (22.17 mm)	0.996 in. (25.30 mm)	0.873 in. (22.17 mm)
130000.........	0.873 in. (22.17 mm)	0.996 in. (25.30 mm)	0.998 in. (25.35 mm)
170000.........	0.9975 in. (25.336 mm)	1.090 in. (27.686 mm)	1.1790 in. (29.947 mm)
190000.........	0.9975 in. (25.336 mm)	1.122 in. (28.50 mm)	1.1790 in. (29.947 mm)

MAIN BEARING REJECT SIZES

Basic Model	Bearing Magneto	Bearing Drive
60000, 80000, 90000 & 110000...	0.878 in. (22.30 mm)	0.878 in. (22.30 mm)
130000.........	0.878 in. (22.30 mm)	1.003 in. (25.48 mm)
170000 & 190000	1.0036 in. (25.49 mm)	1.185 in. (30.10 mm)

CAMSHAFT REJECTION SIZES

Basic Model	Journal Reject Size	Lobe Reject Size
60000, 80000 & 90000........	0.498 in. (12.65 mm)	0.883 in. (22.43 mm)
110000.........	0.498 in. (12.65 mm)	0.870 in. (22.10 mm)
130000.........	0.498 in. (12.65 mm)	0.950 in. (24.13 mm)
170000 & 190000	0.4985 in. (12.660 mm)	0.977 in. (24.82 mm)

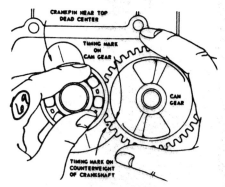

Fig. B112 – Align timing marks on cam gear with mark on crankshaft counterweight on ball bearing equipped models.

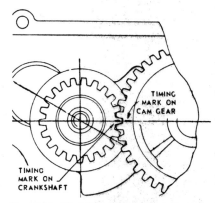

Fig. B113 – Align timing marks on cam gear and crankshaft gear on plain bearing models.

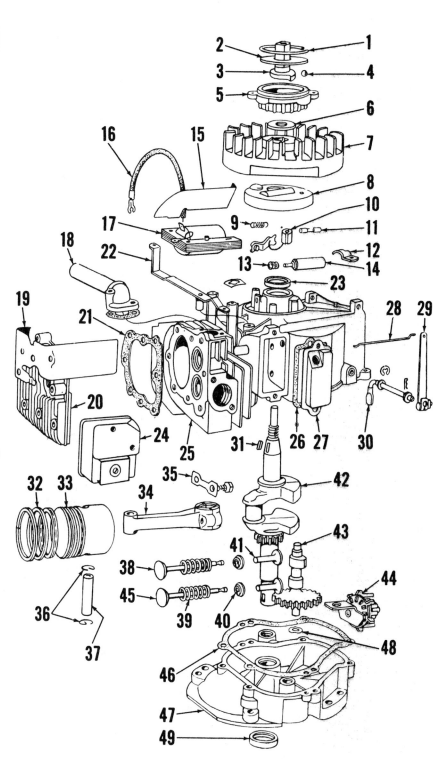

Fig. B110 – Exploded view of typical vertical engine with mechanical governor.

clearance is 0.009-0.011 inch (0.23-0.28 mm) on all models when engine is cold. Valve seat angle is 45 degrees. Regrind or renew valve seat insert if seat width is 0.078-inch (1.98 mm) or wider. Regrind to a width of 0.047-0.063 inch (1.19-1.60 mm). Obtain specified valve tappet clearance by grinding end of valve stem squarely. Replace valve if margin is 0.063-inch (1.60 mm) or less after refacing.

Valve guides on all engines with aluminum blocks are an integral part of the cylinder block. To renew valve guides, ream out old guide and install a bushing. Reamers and bushings are available from Briggs & Stratton. Part numbers are as follows:

Engine Model	Reamer Part No.	Bushing Part No.
60000, 80000 90000, 110000 & 130000......	19064, 19066 (Driver- 10965)	63709
170000 & 190000..........	19183	230655

On 60000, 80000, 90000, 110000 and 130000 models, use reamer 19064 with oil to ream worn guides and ream only

1. Snap ring
2. Washer
3. Starter ratchet
4. Steel balls
5. Starter clutch
6. Washer
7. Flywheel
8. Breaker cover
9. Breaker arm spring
10. Breaker arm & pivot
11. Breaker plunger
12. Condenser clamp
13. Primary wire retainer spring
14. Condenser
15. Air baffle
16. Spark plug wire
17. Armature & coil assy.
18. Intake pipe
19. Air baffle
20. Cylinder head
21. Cylinder head gasket
22. Linkage lever
23. Crankshaft oil seal
24. Muffler
25. Cylinder block
26. Gasket
27. Breather & tappet chamber cover
28. Governor link
29. Governor lever
30. Governor crank
31. Flywheel key
32. Piston rings
33. Piston
34. Connecting rod
35. Rod bolt lock
36. Piston pin retaining rings
37. Piston pin
38. Intake valve
39. Valve springs
40. Valve spring retainers
41. Tappets (cam followers)
42. Crankshaft
43. Camshaft & gear
44. Oil slinger assy.
45. Exhaust valve
46. Gasket (0.005, 0.009 & 0.015 in.)
47. Oil sump (engine base)
48. Thrust washer
49. Crankshaft oil seal

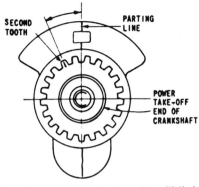

Fig. B114—Location of tooth to align with timing mark on cam gear if mark is not visible on crankshaft gear.

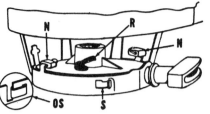

Fig. B120—View of Briggs & Stratton rewind starter assembly.

N. Nylon bumpers
OS. Old style spring

R. Starter rope
S. Rewind spring

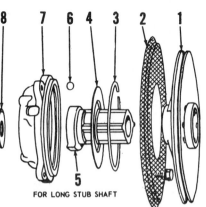

FOR LONG STUB SHAFT

Fig. B123—Exploded view of early production starter clutch unit; refer to Fig. B126 for view of "long stub shaft". A late type unit (Fig. B125) should be installed when renewing "long" crankshaft with "short" (late production) shaft.

1. Starter rope pulley
2. Rotating screen
3. Snap ring
4. Ratchet cover
5. Starter ratchet

6. Steel balls
7. Clutch housing (flywheel nut)
8. Spring washer

about 1/16-inch (1.6 mm) deeper than length of bushing. Press in bushing with driver 19065 until it is flush with top of guide bore. Finish ream bushing with reamer 19066.

On 170000 and 190000 models, use reamer 19183 to ream worn valve guides and ream only about 1/16-inch (1.6 mm) deeper than top end of flutes on reamer. Press in bushings with soft driver as bushing is finish reamed at factory.

VALVE TIMING. On engines equipped with ball bearing mains, align the timing mark on the cam gear with the timing mark on the crankshaft counterweight as shown in Fig. B112. On engines with plain bearings, align the timing marks on the camshaft gear with timing mark on the crankshaft gear (Fig. B113). If the timing mark is not visible on the crankshaft gear, align the timing mark on the camshaft gear with the second tooth to the left of the crankshaft counterweight parting line as shown in Fig. B114.

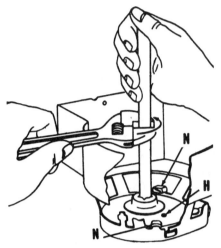

Fig. B121—Using square shaft and wrench to wind up the rewind starter spring. Refer to text.
H. Hole in starter pulley   N. Nylon bumpers

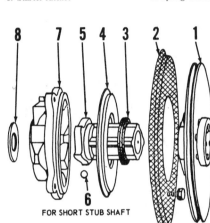

FOR SHORT STUB SHAFT

Fig. B124—View of late production sealed starter clutch unit. Late unit can be used with "short stub shaft" only; refer to Fig. B126. Refer to Fig. B125 for cutaway view of ratchet (5).

1. Starter rope pulley
2. Rotating screen
3. Rubber seal
4. Ratchet cover
5. Starter ratchet

6. Steel balls
7. Clutch housing (flywheel nut)
8. Spring washer

SERVICING BRIGGS & STRATTON ACCESSORIES

REWIND STARTERS

OVERHAUL. To renew broken rewind spring, proceed as follows: Grasp free outer end of spring (S–Fig. B120) and pull broken end from starter housing. With blower housing removed, bend nylon bumpers (N) up and out of the way and remove starter pulley from housing. Untie knot in rope (R) and remove rope and inner end of broken spring from pulley. Apply a small amount of grease on inner face of pulley, thread inner end

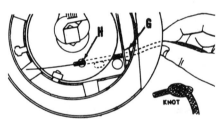

Fig. B122—Threading starter rope through guide (G) in blower housing and hole (H) in starter pulley with wire hooked in end of rope. Tie knot in end of rope as shown.

of new spring through notch in starter housing, engage inner end of spring in pulley hub (on older models, install retainer in hub with split side of retainer away from spring hook) and place pulley in housing. Renew nylon bumpers if necessary and bend bumpers down to within 1/8-inch (3.2 mm) of the pulley. Insert a 3/4-inch (19 mm) square bar in pulley hub and turn pulley approximately 13½ turns in a counterclockwise direction as shown in Fig. B121. Tie wrench to blower housing with wire to hold pulley so that hole (H) in pulley is aligned with rope guide (G) in housing as shown in Fig. B122. Hook a wire in inner end of rope and thread rope through guide and hole in pulley; then, tie a knot in rope and release the pulley allowing

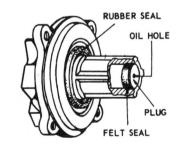

Fig. B125—Cutaway view showing felt seal and plug in end of late production starter ratchet (5—Fig. B124).

the spring to wind the rope into the pulley groove.

To renew starter rope only, it is not generally necessary to remove starter pulley and spring. Wind up the spring

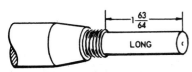

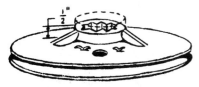

Fig. B126 — Crankshaft with short stub (top view) must be used with late production starter clutch assembly. Early crankshaft (bottom view) can be modified by cutting off stub end to the dimension shown in top view and beveling end of shaft to allow installation of late type clutch unit.

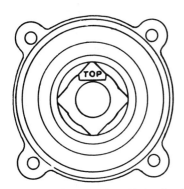

Fig. B127 — When installing a late type starter clutch unit as replacement for early type, either install new starter rope pulley or cut hub of old pulley to dimension shown.

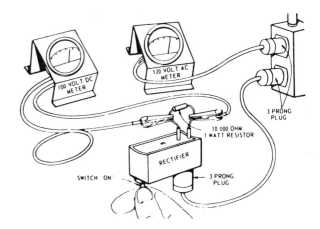

Fig. B202 — Exploded view of 12 volt 4-brush starter motor.

1. Cap
2. Roll pin
3. Retainer
4. Pinion spring
5. Spring cup
6. Starter gear
7. Clutch assy.
8. Drive end cap assy.
9. Armature
10. Housing
11. Spring
12. Brush assy.
13. Battery wire terminal
14. Commutator end cap assy.

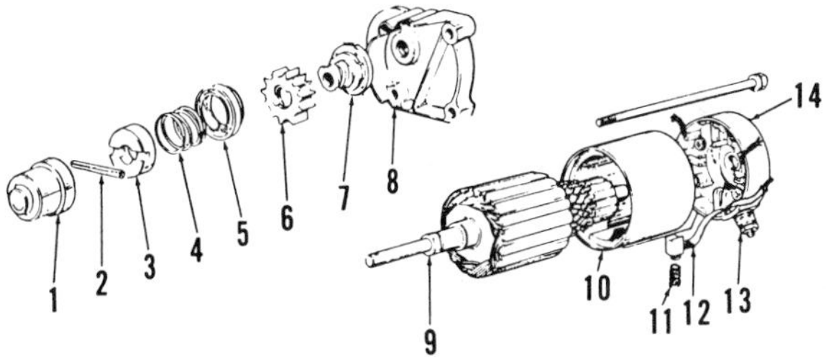

Fig. B203 — View of test connections for 110 volt rectifier. Refer to text for procedure.

Fig. B128 — When reinstalling blower housing and starter assembly, turn starter ratchet so that word "TOP" stamped on outer end of ratchet is towards engine cylinder head.

and install new rope as outlined in preceding paragraph.

Two different types of starter clutches have been used; refer to exploded view of early production unit in Fig. B123 and exploded view of late production unit in Fig. B124. The outer end of the late production ratchet (refer to cutaway view in Fig. B125) is sealed with a felt and a retaining plug and a rubber ring is used to seal ratchet to ratchet cover.

To disassemble early type starter clutch unit, refer to Fig. B123 and proceed as follows: Remove snap ring (3) and lift ratchet (5) and cover (4) from starter housing (7) and crankshaft. Be careful not to lose the steel balls (6).

Starter housing (7) is also flywheel retaining nut; to remove housing, first remove screen (2) and using Briggs & Stratton flywheel wrench 19114, unscrew housing from crankshaft in counterclockwise direction. When reinstalling housing, be sure spring washer (8) is placed on crankshaft with cup (hollow) side towards flywheel, then install starter housing and tighten securely Reinstall rotating screen. Place ratchet on crankshaft and into housing and insert the steel balls. Reinstall cover and retaining snap ring.

To disassemble late starter clutch unit, refer to Fig. B124 and proceed as follows: Remove rotating screen (2) and starter ratchet cover (4). Lift ratchet (5) from housing and crankshaft and extract the steel balls (6). If necessary to remove housing (7), hold flywheel and unscrew housing in counterclockwise direction using Briggs & Stratton flywheel wrench 19114. When installing housing, be sure spring washer (8) is in place on crankshaft with cup (hollow) side towards flywheel; then, tighten housing securely. Inspect felt seal and plug in outer end of ratchet; renew ratchet if seal or plug are damaged as these parts are not serviced separately. Lubricate the felt with oil and place ratchet on crankshaft. Insert the steel balls and install ratchet cover, rubber seal and rotating screen.

NOTE: Crankshafts used with early and late starter clutches differ; refer to Fig. B126. If renewing early (long) crankshaft

with late (short) shaft, also install late type starter clutch unit. If renewing early starter clutch with late type unit, the crankshaft must be shortened to the dimension shown for short shaft in Fig. B126; also, hub of starter rope pulley must be shortened to ½-inch (12.7 mm) dimension shown in Fig. B127. Bevel end of crankshaft after removing the approximate ⅜-inch (9.5 mm) from shaft.

When installing blower housing and starter assembly, turn starter ratchet so that word "TOP" on ratchet is toward engine cylinder head.

GEAR-DRIVE STARTERS

Two types of gear drive starters may be used, a 110 volt AC starter or a 12 volt DC starter. Refer to Fig. B202 for exploded view of starter motor. A properly grounded receptacle should be used with power cord connected to 110 volt AC starter motor. A 32 ampere hour capacity battery is recommended for use with 12 volt DC starter motor.

To renew a worn or damaged flywheel ring gear, drill out retaining rivets using a 3/16-inch drill. Attach new ring gear using screws provided with new ring gear.

To check for correct operation of starter motor, remove starter motor from engine and place motor in a vise or other holding fixture. Install a 0-5 amp ammeter in power cord to 110 volt AC starter motor. On 12 volt DC motor,

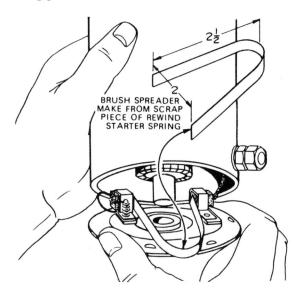

BRUSH SPREADER
MAKE FROM SCRAP
PIECE OF REWIND
STARTER SPRING

Fig. B204 — Tool shown may
be fabricated to hold
brushes when installing
motor end cap.

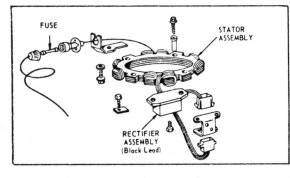

Fig. B206 — Stator and rectifier assemblies used on
the 4 ampere nonregulated
flywheel alternator. Fuse is
7½ amp AGC or 3AG.

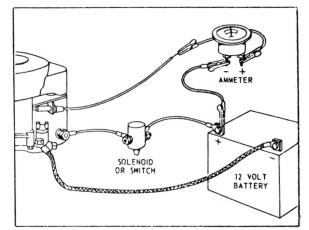

Fig. B207 — Install ammeter
as shown for output test.

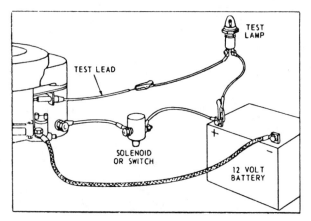

Fig. B208 — Connect a test
lamp as shown to test for
shorted stator or defective
rectifier. Refer to text.

connect a 12 volt battery to motor with a 0-50 amp ammeter in series with positive line from battery to starter motor. Connect a tachometer to drive end of starter. With starter activated on 110 volt motor, starter motor should turn at 5200 rpm minimum with a maximum current draw of 3½ amps. The 12 volt motor should turn at 6200 rpm minimum with a current draw of 16 amps maximum. If starter motor does not operate satisfactorily, check operation of rectifier or starter switch. If rectifier and starter switch are good, disassemble and inspect starter motor.

To check the rectifier used on the 110 volt AC starter motor, remove rectifier unit from starter motor. Solder a 10,000 ohm 1 watt resistor to the DC internal terminals of the rectifier as shown in Fig. B203. Connect a 0-100 range DC voltmeter to resistor leads. Measure the voltage of the AC outlet to be used. With starter switch in "OFF" position, a zero reading should be shown on DC voltmeter. With starter switch in "ON" position, the DC voltmeter should show a reading that is 0-14 volts lower than AC line voltage measured previously. If voltage drop exceeds 14 volts, renew rectifier unit

Disassembly of starter motor is self-evident after inspection of unit and referral to Fig. B202. Note position of bolts during disassembly so that they can be installed in their original positions during reassembly. When reassembling motor, lubricate end cap bearings with #20 oil. Be sure to match the drive cap keyway to the stamped key in the housing when sliding the armature into the motor housing. Brushes may be held in their holders during installation by making a brush spreader tool from a piece of metal as shown in Fig. B204.

FLYWHEEL ALTERNATORS

4 Amp. Non-Regulated Alternator

Some engines are equipped with the 4 ampere non-regulated flywheel alternator shown in Fig. B206. A solid state rectifier and 7½ amp fuse is used with this alternator.

If battery is run down and no output from alternator is suspected, first check the 7½ amp fuse. If fuse is good, clean and tighten all connections. Disconnect charging lead and connect an ammeter as shown in Fig. B207. Start engine and check for alternator output. If ammeter shows no charge, stop engine, remove ammeter and install a test lamp as shown in Fig. B208. Test lamp should not light. If it does light, stator or rectifier is defective. Unplug rectifier plug

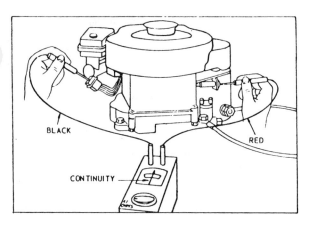

Fig. B209—Use an ohmmeter to check condition of stator. Refer to text.

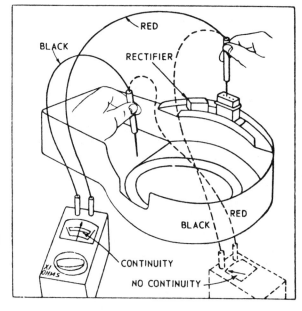

Fig. B210—If ohmmeter shows continuity in both directions or in neither direction, rectifier is defective.

under blower housing. If test lamp does not go out, stator is shorted.

If shorted stator is indicated, use an ohmmeter and check continuity as follows: Touch one test lead to lead inside of fuse holder as shown in Fig. B209. Touch the other test lead to each of the four pins in rectifier connector. Unless the ohmmeter shows continuity at each of the four pins, stator winding is open and stator must be renewed.

If defective rectifier is indicated, unbolt and remove the flywheel blower housing with rectifier. Connect one ohmmeter test lead to blower housing and other test lead to the single pin connector in rectifier connector. See Fig. B210. Check for continuity, then reverse leads and again test for continuity. If tests show no continuity in either direction or continuity in both directions, rectifier is faulty and must be renewed.

BRIGGS & STRATTON SPECIAL TOOLS

The following special tools are available from Briggs & Stratton Central Service Distributors.

TOOL KITS

19158—Main bearing service kit for engine Models 60000, 80000, 90000, 110000 and 130000. Includes tool numbers 19094, 19095, 19096, 19097, 19099, 19100, 19101, 19123, 19124 and 19166.

19184—Main bearing service kit for Series 170000 and 190000. Includes tool numbers 19096, 19168, 19169, 19170, 19171, 19172, 19173, 19174, 19175, 19178, 19179 and 19201.

291661—Dealer service tool kit. Includes tool numbers 19051, 19055, 19056, 19057, 19058, 19061, 19062, 19063, 19064, 19065, 19066, 19068, 19069, 19070, 19114, 19122, 19151, 19165, 19167, 19191 and 19203.

PLUG GAGES

19055—Check breaker plunger hole on all models.

19122—Check valve guide bore on Models 60000, 80000, 90000, 110000 and 130000.

19151—Check valve guide bore on Models 170000 and 190000.

19164—Check camshaft bearings on all models.

19166—Check main bearing bore on Models 60000, 80000, 90000, 110000 and 130000.

19178—Check main bearing bore on engine Series 170000 and 190000.

REAMERS

19056—Ream hole to install breaker plunger bushing on all models.

19058—Finish ream breaker plunger bushing on same models as 19056 Reamer.

19064—Ream valve guide bore to install bushing on Models 60000, 80000, 90000, 110000 and 130000.

19066—Finish ream valve guide bushing on same models as listed for 19064 Reamer.

19095—Finish ream main bushings on same models as listed for 19064 Reamer.

19099—Ream counterbore for main bearings on Models 60000, 80000, 90000 and 110000.

19172—Ream counterbore for main bearing on Model 130000.

19173—Finish reamer for main bearing on Model 130000.

19174—Ream counterbore for main bearing on Series 170000 and 190000.

19175—Finish ream main bearing on Series 170000 and 190000.

GUIDE BUSHINGS FOR VALVE GUIDE REAMERS

19191—For Models 60000, 80000, 90000, 110000 and 130000.

19192—For Models 170000 and 190000.

PILOTS

19096—Pilot for main bearing reamer on all models.

19126—Expansion pilot for valve seat counterbore cutter on Models 60000, 80000, 90000, 110000 and 130000.

19127—Expansion pilot for valve seat counterbore cutter on Models 170000 and 190000.

DRIVERS

19057—To install breaker plunger bushing on all models.

19065—To install valve guide bushings on Models 60000, 80000, 90000, 110000 and 130000.

19124—To install main bearing bushings on Models 60000, 80000, 90000, 110000 and 130000.

19136 — To install valve seat inserts on all models.

19179 — Install main bearing on Models 170000 and 190000.

GUIDE BUSHINGS FOR MAIN BEARING REAMERS

19094 — For Models 60000, 80000, 90000, 110000 and 130000.

19100 — For Models 60000, 80000, 90000 and 110000.

19101 — For Models 60000, 80000, 90000, 110000 and 130000.

19168 — For Models 130000, 170000 and 190000.

19169 — For Models 170000 and 190000.

19170 — For Models 130000, 170000 and 190000.

19171 — For Models 170000 and 190000.

19186 — For Model 130000.

COUNTERBORE CUTTERS

19131 — To install intake valve seat on Model 190000.

CRANKCASE SUPPORT JACK

19123 — To support crankcase when removing and installing main bearing bushings on all models.

FLYWHEEL PULLERS

19069 — For Models 60000, 80000, 90000, 110000 and 130000.

19165 — For Models 170000 and 190000.

FLYWHEEL HOLDER

19167 — For Models 60000, 80000, 90000, 110000 and 130000.

VALVE SPRING COMPRESSOR

19063 — For all models.

PISTON RING COMPRESSOR

19070 — For all models.

STARTER WRENCH

19114 — All models with rewind starters.

19161 — All models with rewind starters.

IGNITION SPARK TESTER

19051 — For all models.

VALVE SEAT REPAIR TOOLS

19129 — Planer shank-driver for counterbore cutter on all models.

19130 — T-handle for planer shank 19129 on all models.

19135 — Knockout pin to remove counterbore cutter from planer shank.

19137 — T-handle for expansion pilots

19138 — Insert puller to remove valve seats on all models (when puller nut 19140, included with 19138, is ground to 1/32-inch (0.8 mm) thick for pulling insert on aluminum alloy models).

19141 — Puller nut to remove valve seats for Models 170000 and 190000.

19182 — Puller nut to adapt 19138 puller to aluminum alloy models.

CLINTON

CLINTON ENGINES
CORPORATION
Maquoketa, Iowa

HP	Crankshaft	Basic Model (Series)	Bore	Stroke	Displacement
3 (2.24 kW)	Horizontal	500-0100-000	2⅛ in. (54 mm)	1⅝ in. (41.3 mm)	5.76 cu. in. (94.39 cc)

Clinton two-stroke engines are of aluminum alloy die-cast construction with an integral cast-in cast iron cylinder sleeve. Reed type inlet valves are used on all models.

MAINTENANCE

SPARK PLUG. Recommended spark plug is Champion J-12J or equivalent. Set electrode gap to 0.030 inch (0.76 mm). Use graphite on threads when installing spark plug and tighten spark plug to a torque of 275-300 in.-lbs. (31.05-33.88 N·m).

CARBURETOR. Clinton (Walbro designed) "LMB" and "LMG" float type carburetors are used. Refer to Fig. CL5 for exploded view of typical model.

For initial adjustment, open both of the fuel adjustment needles approximatley 1¼ turns. Make final adjustments with engine running at operating temperature. Move speed control to "fast" position and turn main fuel needle in or out to obtain maximum power under load. If load cannot be applied, turn main fuel needle in or out for smoothest engine operation; then, turn needle out (counterclockwise) approximately ⅛ to ¼-turn to provide a richer fuel mixture.

Move engine speed control to "slow" or idle position and adjust idle fuel needle and stop screw for best performance and correct idle speed. Check acceleration from slow to fast idle and open idle needle approximately ⅛-turn (counterclockwise) if necessary for proper acceleration.

When overhauling "LMB" and "LMG"

carburetors and main fuel nozzle is removed, it must be discarded and a service type nozzle installed (See Fig. CL6). Do not reinstall old nozzle.

Float setting on "LMB" and "LMG" carburetors should be 5/32-inch (4.0 mm) clearance between outer rim of carburetor casting and top of free side of float. Bend tabs on float hinge to adjust float setting and to limit float travel to approximately 3/16-inch (4.8 mm) at free side of float.

GOVERNOR. Speed control is maintained by an air-vane type governor. Renew bent or worn governor vane or linkage and be sure that linkage does not bind in any position when moved through fulll range of travel.

Renew or re-tension governor spring to limit maximum speed to 3600 rpm. Be sure that blower housing is clean and free of dents that would cause binding of air vane.

MAGNETO AND TIMING. Ignition timing is 27 degrees BTDC and is nonadjustable. Specified armature air gap is 0.007-0.017 inch (0.18-0.43 mm). Adjust breaker contact gap to 0.018-0.021 inch (0.46-0.53 mm).

Fig. CL5—Exploded view of typical "LMG" series carburetor. "LMV" and "LMB" series are similar.

1. Throttle shaft	13. Main nozzle
2. Choke shaft	14. Float
3. Spring	14A. Float pin
4. Throttle disc	15. Gasket
5. Spring	16. Gaskets
6. Carburetor body	17. Float bowl
7. Idle stop screw	18. Drain valve
8. Springs	19. Retainer
9. Idle fuel needle	20. Seal
10. Spring	21. Spring
11. Choke disc	22. Main fuel needle
12. Inlet needle & seat	23. Lever (optional)

Fig. CL6—When original main fuel nozzle is removed from "LM" series carburetor, it must be discarded and service type nozzle shown must be installed.

Fig. CL16—Magneto can be considered in satisfactory condition if it will fire an 18 mm spark plug with electrode gap set at 0.156-0.187 inch (3.96-4.75 mm).

Magneto may be considered satisfactory if it will fire an 18 mm spark plug with gap set at 0.156-0.187 inch (3.96-4.75 mm). Refer to Fig. CL16.

LUBRICATION. Use a high-quality outboard motor or two-stroke engine oil, SAE 30 weight. There are no precise API ratings for two-stroke engine oils; consequently, the safest course is to use oil identified by the refiner as designed for two-cycle or outboard motor use. Because of the high level of additives used in four-stroke (automotive) oils, their use should be avoided. Never use oils marked ML (light duty), DG (diesel) or SA (light duty). If an improper oil is used to meet an emergency, change to correct two-stroke oil as soon as possible and discard the improper fuel-oil mix.

Oil to gasoline mixing ratio is determined by type of bearings installed in a particular two-stroke engine. Plain sleeve main and connecting rod bearings require ¾-pint of oil for each gallon of gasoline. Engines equipped with needle bearings call for a mixing ratio of ½-pint of oil per gallon of gasoline. During break-in (first five hours of operation) a 50% increase of oil portion is advisable, especially if engine will be operated at or near maximum load or rpm.

CARBON. Power loss on two-stroke engines can often be corrected by cleaning the exhaust ports and muffler. To clean the exhaust ports, remove the muffler and turn engine until piston is below ports. Use a dull tool to scrape carbon from the ports; take care not to damage top of piston or cylinder walls.

REPAIRS

NOTE: Graphite should be applied to the threads of all screws which thread into die cast parts.

TIGHTENING TORQUES. Engine tightening torques are as follows:

Bearing plate to block . . . . . 75-95 in.-lbs.
(8.47-10.73 N·m)

Blower housing . . . . .65-70 in.-lbs.
(7.34-7.90 N·m)
Carburetor mounting . . . . .60-65 in.-lbs.
(6.77-7.90 N·m)
Connecting rod . . . . .35-45 in.-lbs.
(3.95-5.08 N·m)
Engine base . . . . .125-150 in.-lbs.
(14.11-16.94 N·m)
Flywheel . . . . .375-400 in.lbs.
(42.34-45.17 N·m)
Muffler . . . . .40-60 in.-lbs.
(2.46-6.75 N·m)
Spark plug . . . . .275-300 in.-lbs.
(31.05-33.87 N·m)
Stator to bearing plate . . . .50-60 in.-lbs.
(5.65-7.90 N·m)

BEARING PLATE. Because of the pressure and vacuum pulsations in crankcase, bearing plate and gasket must form an air-tight seal when installed. Make sure gasket surfaces are not cracked, nicked or warped, that oil passages in crankcase, gasket and plate are aligned and that correct number and thickness of thrust washers are used. Also check to be sure the right cap screws are installed when engine is reassembled.

CAUTION: Cap screws (1 – Fig. C17) may bottom in threaded holes (2) if incorrect screws are used. When long screws are tightened, damage to cylinder walls can result.

CONNECTING ROD. Connecting rod and piston unit can be removed after removing the reed plate and crankshaft.

An aluminum connecting rod with bronze bearing surfaces is used. Recommended clearances are as follows:
Connecting rod to
crankshaft . . . . .0.0026-0.004 in.
(0.635-0.10 mm)
Renew rod and/or crankshaft if
clearance exceeds . . . . .0.0055 in.
(0.140 mm)
Connecting rod to
piston pin . . . . .0.0004-0.0011 in.
(0.010-0.028 mm)
Renew rod and/or piston pin
if clearance exceeds . . . . .0.002 in.
(0.05 mm)

Reinstall cap to connecting rod with embossments (A – Fig. CL18) aligned and carefully tighten screws to recommended torque value; bend the locking tabs against screw heads as shown in Fig. CL19.

PISTON, PIN AND RINGS. Pistons may be equipped with either two or three compression rings. On three-ring pistons, a locking wire is fitted in a small groove behind each piston ring to prevent ring rotation on the piston. To install the three locking wires, refer to Fig. CL20 and proceed as follows: Hold piston with top up and intake side of piston to right. Install top and bottom locking wires with locking tab (end of wire ring bent outward) to right of locating hole in ring groove and install center locking wire with locking tab to left of locating hole.

Piston and rings are available in oversizes of 0.010-inch (0.25 mm) and 0.020-inch (0.51 mm) as well as standard size. Piston pin is available in standard size only.

When installing pistons with ring locating pins or locking wires, be sure that end gaps of rings are properly located over the pins or the locking tabs and install piston using a ring compressor. Refer to Fig. CL20.

Be sure to reinstall piston and rod assembly with exhaust side of piston (long sloping side of piston dome) towards exhaust ports in cylinder.

Check piston, pin and rings against the following specifications:

Two-Ring Piston
Ring End Gap:
Desired . . . . .0.007-0.017 in.
(0.18-0.43 mm)
Max. Allowable . . . . .0.025 in.
(0.64 mm)

Ring Side Clearance:
Desired . . . . .0.0015-0.004 in.
(0.038-0.10 mm)
Max. Allowable . . . . .0.006 in.
(0.15 mm)

(See Next Page)

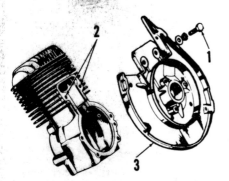

Fig. CL17—If cap screws (1) which thread into holes (2) are too long, they may bottom and damage cylinder walls.

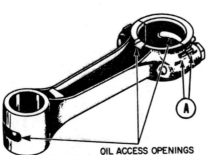

OIL ACCESS OPENINGS

Fig. CL18—Be sure that embossments (A) are aligned when assembling cap to connecting rod.

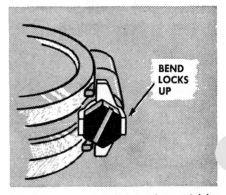

BEND LOCKS UP

Fig. CL19—Bend connecting rod cap retaining screw locks up as shown.

Fig. CL20—View showing method of installing ring locking wires on 3-ring pistons and placement of rings on two and three-ring pistons. Some two-ring pistons do not have ring locking pins.

CRANKSHAFT. To remove crankshaft, proceed as follows: Remove blower housing and nut retaining flywheel to crankshaft. Thread an impact nut to within ⅛-inch (3.20 mm) of flywheel, pull on flywheel and tap impact nut with hammer. After flywheel is removed, remove magneto assembly. Remove the engine base and inlet reed valve plate from crankcase and detach connecting rod from crankshaft. Push connecting rod and piston unit up against top of cylinder. On models with ball bearing main on output end of crankshaft, remove the snap ring retaining ball bearing in crankcase. Remove the magneto stator plate and withdraw crankshaft from engine taking care not to damage connecting rod.

Skirt Clearance:
Desired ....0.005-0.007 in.
(0.13-0.18 mm)
Max. Allowable ....0.008 in.
(0.20 mm)

Three-Ring Piston
Ring End Gap:
Desired ....0.010-0.015 in.
(0.25-0.38 mm)
Max. Allowable ....0.017 in.
(0.43 mm)

Ring Side Clearance:
Desired ....0.002-0.004 in.
(0.05-0.10 mm)
Max. Allowable ....0.0055 in.
(0.140 mm)

Skirt Clearance:
Desired ....0.0045-0.005 in.
(0.114-0.13 mm)
Max. Allowable ....0.007 in.
(0.18 mm)

All Models
Piston pin diameter ...0.4999-0.5001 in.
(12.697-12.702 mm)
Pin bore in piston.....0.5000-0.5003 in.
(12.700-12.708 mm)
Piston pin-to-rod clearance:
Desired ....0.0004-0.0011 in.
(0.010-0.028 mm)
Max. Allowable..........0.002 in.
(0.05 mm)

Cylinder can be honed to 0.010-inch (0.25 mm) or 0.020-inch (0.51 mm) oversize for oversize piston and rings. Standard cylinder bore size is 2.125-2.126 inches (53.98-54.00 mm).

CYLINDER AND CRANKCASE.
The one-piece aluminum alloy cylinder and crankcase unit is integrally die-cast around a cast iron sleeve (cylinder liner).

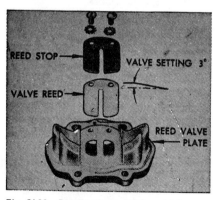

Fig. CL22—Details of two-petal reed inlet valve used on some models.

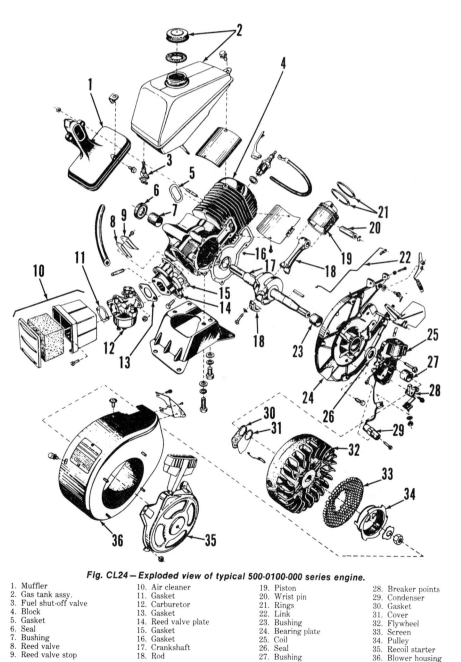

Fig. CL24—Exploded view of typical 500-0100-000 series engine.

1. Muffler	10. Air cleaner	19. Piston	28. Breaker points
2. Gas tank assy.	11. Gasket	20. Wrist pin	29. Condenser
3. Fuel shut-off valve	12. Carburetor	21. Rings	30. Gasket
4. Block	13. Gasket	22. Link	31. Cover
5. Gasket	14. Reed valve plate	23. Bushing	32. Flywheel
6. Seal	15. Gasket	24. Bearing plate	33. Screen
7. Bushing	16. Gasket	25. Coil	34. Pulley
8. Reed valve	17. Crankshaft	26. Seal	35. Recoil starter
9. Reed valve stop	18. Rod	27. Bushing	36. Blower housing

On crankshafts used with plain bushing mains and/or cast-in crankpin bearing, check crankshaft against the following values:

Crankpin diameter ...0.7788-0.7795 in.
(19.782-19.799 mm)
Main journal diameter,
flywheel end ......0.7495-0.7502 in.
(19.037-19.055 mm)
Main journal diameter,
output end ....0.8745-0.8752 in
(22.212-22.230 mm)
or.................0.995-1.002 in.
(25.387-25.405 mm)
Rod, crankpin end I.D .0.7829-0.7827 in.
(19.860-19.881 mm)
Main bearing bushing I.D.,
flywheel end ......0.7517-0.7525 in.
(19.093-19.114 mm)
Main bearing bushing I.D.,
output end ....0.8770-0.8780 in.
(22.276-22.301 mm)
or...............1.0020-1.0030 in.
(25.451-25.476 mm)
Main bearing clearance,
desired ....0.0015-0.0030 in.
(0.038-0.076 mm)
Max. allowable clearance ...0.0055 in.
(0.140 mm)

Renew crankshaft if either main bearing journal or crankpin journal is out-of-round 0.0015-inch (0.038 mm) or more.

Main bearing bushings, bushing remover and driver, reamers and reamer alignment plate are available through Clinton parts sources for renewing bushings in crankcase and bearing plate. On vertical crankshaft engines having two bushings in crankcase, the outer bushing must be removed towards outside of crankcase and the inner bushing towards inside of crankcase. Bushings must be recessed 0.031-inch (0.79 mm) from insider surface of bearing plate or crankcase except when thrust washer is used between crankcase or plate and thrust surface of crankshaft.

Renew ball bearing type mains if bearing is rough or is worn. Renew needle type main bearings if one or more needles show any defect or if needles can be separated the width of one roller.

When reinstalling crankshaft with bushing or needle roller mains, crankshaft end play should be 0.005-0.020 inch (0.13-0.51 mm). The gasket used between bearing (stator) plate and crankcase is available in thicknesses of 0.025-inch (0.64 mm), 0.030-inch (0.76 mm) and 0.035-inch (0.90 mm) for adjusting crankshaft end play. It may also be necessary to renew crankshaft thrust washer.

There is no specification covering end play where ball type main bearing is used, however, crankshaft should turn freely after installation.

CRANKSHAFT OIL SEALS. As on all two-stroke engines, crankshaft oil seals must be maintained in good condition to hold crankcase compression on the downward stroke of the piston. It is usually good service procedure, therefore, to renew seals when overhauling an engine. apply a small amount of gasket sealer to outer rim of seal and install with lip towards inside of crankcase. Outer surface of seal should be flush with outer face of crankcase or bearing plate.

REED VALVE. The 3 degree setting of the dual reed shown in Fig. CL22 is the design of the reed as stamped in the manufacturing process. The 3 degree bend should be towards the reed seating surface. Reed stop should be adjusted to approximately 0.280-inch (7.11 mm) from tip of stop to reed seating surface.

Renew reed if any petal is cracked, rusted or does not lay flat against the reed plate. Renew reed plate if rusted, pitted or shows any signs of wear.

CLINTON SPECIAL TOOLS

(500 SERIES ENGINES)

Bearing Tools

951-18 and 951-39 BEARING DRIVER. Used to remove and reinstall bearings in engine block.
951-48 REAMER GUIDE. Three bushings included with the following inside diameters: 0.878-inch (22.301 mm), 1.0003-inch (25.408 mm) and 1.030-inch (26.162 mm). Used to line ream bearing in engine block.
951-29 REAMER. Diameter, 0.877-inch (22.283 mm). Used to ream bearing in engine block.
951-30 REAMER. Diameter, 0.7518-0.7523 inch (19.096-19.108 mm). Used to ream bearing in bearing plates.

Flywheel and Crankshaft Tools

IMPACT NUTS. Impact or knock-off nuts are available for removing flywheels as follows:
951-23, for crankshafts having 7/16-inch threads.
951-36, for crankshafts having 7/8-inch threads.
951-66, for crankshafts having 1/2-inch threads.
951-133 FLYWHEEL PULLER
951-42 FLYWHEEL HOLDER
951-45 HAND CRANK. Used for turning engine when adjusting breaker point gap, checking timing etc.
951-64 CRANKSHAFT RUNOUT GAGE. Used for checking for bent crankshafts.

Oil Seal Pullers and Drivers

951-62 OIL SEAL DRIVER. Inside diameter, 0.760-inch (19.30 mm): outside diameter, 1-inch (25.40 mm).

Piston Ring Tools

951-153 SLEEVE FOR 2.125-inch (53.975 mm) BORE. Used for installing standard size and 0.020-inch (0.51 mm) oversize piston assemblies.

CLINTON

HP	Crankshaft	Basic Model (Series)	Bore	Stroke	Displacement
4½ (3.36 kW)	Horizontal	498-0301-000	2 15/32 in. 62.7 mm	2⅛ in. 54 mm	10.2 cu. in. 167 cc

MAINTENANCE

SPARK PLUG. All models use a 14 mm, ⅜-inch reach spark plug. Recommended plug is a Champion J-8 or equivalent. Set electrode gap to

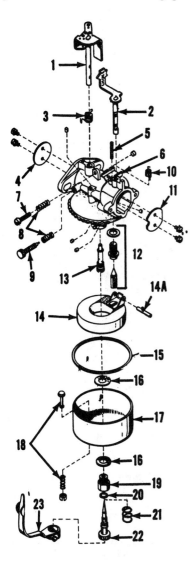

Fig. CL46 – Exploded view of typical "LMG" series carburetor. "LMV" and "LMB" series are similar.

1. Throttle shaft	13. Main nozzle
2. Choke shaft	14. Float
3. Spring	14A. Float pin
4. Throttle disc	15. Gasket
5. Spring	16. Gaskets
6. Carburetor body	17. Float bowl
7. Idle stop screw	18. Drain valve
8. Springs	19. Retainer
9. Idle fuel needle	20. Seal
10. Spring	21. Spring
11. Choke disc	22. Main fuel needle
12. Inlet needle & seat	23. Lever (optional)

0.025-0.028 inch (0.64-071 mm). When installing, apply graphite to threads and tighten to a torque of 275-300 in.-lbs. (31.05-33.88 N·m).

CARBURETOR. Several different carburetors, both suction lift and float type, have been used on this series of Clinton engines. Refer to the following paragraphs for information on each carburetor model.

NOTE: The throttle shaft on some carburetors may have several holes in which the throttle link and governor backlash spring (if used) may be installed. On these carburetors, be sure to mark the holes in which spring and linkage were installed so that they may be reinstalled correctly.

CLINTON FLOAT CARBURETORS. Several different Clinton "LMG" and "LMV" series float type carburetors have been used. To identify a particular carburetor, look for the identification number on carburetor body as shown in Fig. CL47.

Refer to the exploded view shown in Fig. CL46 for typical "LM" series carburetor. When overhauling or cleaning carburetor, do not remove main fuel nozzle (13) unless necessary. If nozzle is removed, it must be discarded and a service type nozzle (Fig. CL48) installed.

Install choke plate (11 – Fig. CL46) with the "W" or part number to the outside. Install throttle plate with the side marked "W" facing towards mounting flange and with part number toward idle needle side of carburetor bore when plate by gently tapping with a small ing throttle plate, back idle speed adjustment screw out, turn plate and throttle shaft to closed position and seat plate by gently tapping with a small screwdriver before tightening plate retaining screws.

If either float or seat is damaged, install a new matched valve and seat assembly (12) and tighten seat to a torque of 40-50 in.-lbs. (4.52-5.65 N·m).

Fig. CL47 – View showing locations of identification numbers on "LMB", "LMG" and "LMV" carburetors. Identification number must be used when ordering service parts.

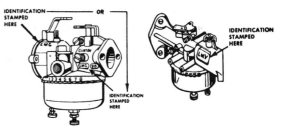

When carburetor body (6) and float (14) assembly are inverted, there should be 5/32-inch (4.0 mm) clearance between body casting and free side of float.

Adjust float level by bending tab that contacts float valve. When carburetor body and float assembly are returned to normal position, float should not drop more than 3/16-inch (4.8 mm) at free side. Adjust by bending tab that contacts carburetor body.

Reassemble carburetor using new gaskets.

Initial adjustment for both idle needle and high speed is 1¼ turns open. Make final adjustment with engine at operating temperature. If engine does not accelerate properly, open high speed adjustment needle slightly.

CARTER FLOAT TYPE CARBURETORS. Refer to Fig. CL49 for exploded view typical of the Carter "N" series carburetors used on this group of Clinton engines. Some carburetors may differ as to shape of float and bowl.

Refer to the following chart for float setting and for initial adjustment (turns open) of idle and high speed fuel adjustment needles:

Carburetor Model	Float Setting	Initial Mixture Setting Idle	High Speed
N-705S	13/64 in. (5.16 mm)	1½	1½
N-707S, SA	13/64 in. (5.16 mm)	1½	1½

(See Next Page)

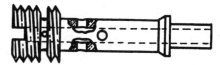

Fig. CL48 – When original main fuel nozzle is removed from "LM" series carburetor, it must be discarded and service type nozzle shown installed.

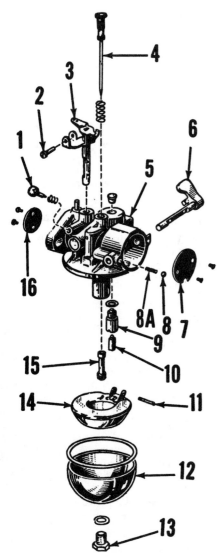

Fig. CL49 — Exploded view of typical Carter Model "N" carburetor. Design of float and float bowl may vary from that shown.

1. Idle fuel needle	9. Inlet valve seat
2. Idle stop screw	10. Inlet needle
3. Throttle shaft	11. Float pin
4. Main fuel needle	12. Float bowl
5. Carburetor body	13. Retainer
6. Choke shaft	14. Float
7. Choke disc	15. Main nozzle
8. Detent ball	16. Throttle disc
8A. Spring	

Carburetor Model	Float Setting	Initial Mixture, Setting Idle	High Speed
N-2020S	11/64 in. (4.37 mm)	1½	1½
N-2147S	11/64 in. (4.37 mm)	1½	1½
N-2236S	11/64 in. (4.37 mm)	1	2
N-2246S	11/64 in. (4.37 mm)	1	1½
N-2399S	11/64 in. (4.37 mm)	1½	2

Carburetor Model	Float Setting	Initial Mixture, Setting Idle	High Speed
N-2449S	13/64 in. (5.16 mm)	1½	1½
N-2456S	13/64 in. (5.16 mm)	1½	1½
N-2459S	11/64 in. (4.37 mm)	1	1½
N-2466S	11/64 in. (4.37 mm)	1½	2

Float setting is measured by inverting carburetor casting and float assembly and gaging distance between casting and free side of float. Adjust by bending tab that contacts float valve.

Make final idle and high speed fuel mixture adjustments after engine is at operating temperature.

TILLOTSON FLOAT CARBURETOR. Some early models were equipped with Tillotson "ML" series carburetors. Float setting on ML carburetors is 1 5/64-1 3/32 inch (27.4-27.8 mm) from edge of carburetor casting to farthest side of float when carburetor body and float assembly is held in inverted position.

Initial adjustment for idle fuel adjustment needle is 1 turn open; initial adjustment for high speed needle is 1½ turns open. Make final adjustment with engine running at operating temperature.

ZENITH FLOAT TYPE CARBURETORS. Zenith float type carburetors 10390, 10658 and 10665 were used on some early model engines:

The 10390 model carburetor has only one fuel mixture adjustment needle. Adjust mixture screw so maximum high idle speed is obtained then set fuel mixture ¼-turn rich (counterclockwise). On Models 10658 and 10665, turning idle fuel mixture needle clockwise will enrichen the fuel mixture and turning the main fuel needle clockwise will lean the fuel mixture. Float setting is nonadjustable on this series of Zenith carburetors.

GOVERNOR. The mechanical governor is shown in the exploded view in Fig. CL56.

NOTE: The carburetor throttle shaft, governor arm and speed control devices may have several different holes in which springs and linkage can be installed. Before removing carburetor, governor arm, springs, linkage or controls, be sure to mark location of holes in which springs and linkage were installed so that they may be reassembled correctly.

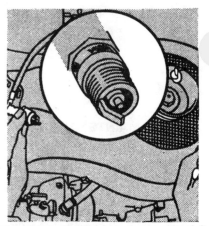

Fig. CL49A — Magneto can be considered in satisfactory condition if it will fire an 18 mm spark plug with electrode gap set at 0.156-0.187 inch (3.96-4.75 mm).

TIMING. Condenser, breaker points and armature coil are located under flywheel on all models. Condenser capacity is 0.15-0.19 mfd. Adjust breaker point gap to 0.018-0.021 inch (0.46-0.53 mm). Specified armature air gap is 0.007-0.017 inch (0.18-0.43 mm). Timing is fixed and nonadjustable at 21 degrees BTDC.

Ignition system can be assumed to be in satisfactory condition if it will fire an 18 mm spark plug with the electrode gap set at 0.156-0.187 inch (3.96-4.75 mm). See Fig. CL49A.

LUBRICATION. Oil of "SE" or "SF" grade should be used. Use SAE 30 above 32°F (0°C), SAE 10W from −10°F (−23°C) and SAE 5W below −10°F (1−23°C)

Use SAE 30 oil in reduction gearbox if so equipped.

CRANKCASE BREATHER. Crankcase breather assembly (37A − Fig. CL56) should be removed and cleaned if difficulty is experienced with oil loss through hole in valve cover or whenever engine is being overhauled. Be sure that breather is correctly reassembled and reinstalled.

MECHANICAL GOVERNOR. The governor weight unit (26 − Fig. CL56) is driven by the cam gear and is retained to the gear by a pin (27A) driven into the gear. Governor collar (27) has a notch in the inner flange of the collar which fits around weight unit retaining pin. Governor shaft (38A) is fitted with a square crosssection weight that contacts outer flange of governor collar and shaft is supported in a renewable bushing.

It is very important that travel of governor and carburetor throttle be synchronized. With engine not running,

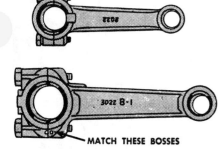

Fig. CL52 — When assembling cap to connecting rod, be sure that embossments on rod and cap are aligned as shown.

Fig. CL54 — On early models, connecting rod bearing was lubricated by oil spray from hole in oil line as shown. Be sure the squared-off end of the oil line fits into the recess in oil pump adapter when reassembling engine.

move governor throttle arm (38) so that governor shaft holds governor weight unit in the fully closed position. At this time, there should be 1/32-1/16 inch (0.8-1.6 mm) clearance between high speed stop on carburetor throttle arm and carburetor casting. To obtain this adjustment, loosen adjustment screw (38B) and reposition arm (38) on adjuster (38C) and tighten adjustment screw (38B).

Adjust desired maximum speed (do not exceed 3600 rpm) by adjusting tension of govern spring (39).

CAUTION: Do not use any spring other than correct Clinton part specified for a particular engine as spring must be balanced to governor weight unit for proper speed control.

On most models, a backlash spring is used to hold any free play out of governor to carburetor linkage and thereby reduce any tendency for engine to surge.

REPAIRS

TIGHTENING TORQUES. Recommended torque values are as follows:

Adapter flange . . . . 120-150 in.lbs.
(13.55-16.94 N·m)
Base bolts . . . . 325-375 in.lbs.
(36.70-42.34 N·m)
Carburetor to manifold . . . . 35-50 in.lbs.
(3.95-4.17 N·m)
Carburetor (or manifold) to
block . . . . 60-65 in.lbs.
(6.78-7.34 N·m)
Connecting rod . . . . 70-80 in.lbs.
(7.90-9.03 N·m)
Cylinder head . . . . 200-220 in.lbs.
(22.58-24.84 N·m)
End cover . . . . 120-150 in.lbs.
(13.55-16.94 N·m)
Flywheel . . . . 400-450 in.lbs.
(45.17-50.81 N·m)*
Spark plug . . . . 275-300 in.lbs.
(31.05-33.88 N·m)
Stator plate . . . . 50-60 in.lbs.
(4.17-6.78 N·m)
*350 in.lbs. (39.52 N·m) maximum on 7/16-inch (11.1 mm) crankshaft.

CONNECTING ROD. Rod and piston assembly can be removed from engine after cylinder head and crankshaft rear cover are removed.

Recommended clearances are as follows:
Connecting rod to
crankshaft . . . . 0.0018-0.0035 in.
(0.046-0.089 mm)
Maximum allowable . . . . 0.0045 in.
(0.114 mm)
Connecting rod to piston
pin . . . . 0.0004-0.0011 in.
(0.010-0.028 mm)
Maximum allowable . . . . 0.002 in.
(0.05 mm)
Rod side play . . . . 0.005-0.020 in.
(0.13-0.51 mm)
Connecting rod is available in standard size only. When reassembling, be sure that embossments on connecting rod and cap are aligned as shown in Fig. CL52. Oil hole or oil access slot in connecting rod should face flywheel side of engine. On some models, the connecting rod has a "clearance side" which must be towards the camshaft. Be sure that rod locks and oil distributor (on horizontal crankshaft models) clears the camshaft after assembly.

PISTON, PIN AND RINGS. Piston is fitted with two compression rings and one oil control ring. Recommended piston ring end gap is 0.007-0.017 inch (0.18-0.43 mm). Renew rings if end gap of top ring is 0.025 inch (0.64 mm) or more. Specified ring side clearance in groove is 0.002-0.005 inch (0.05-0.13 mm). Maximum allowable side clearance is 0.006 inch (0.15 mm). Rings are available in oversizes of 0.010 inch (0.25 mm) and 0.020 inch (0.51 mm) as well as standard size.

Piston pin is retained in piston with a snap ring at each end of pin. Piston pin is available in standard size only and should be a "hand push fit" in piston. Specifications are as follows:

Piston pin diameter . . . 0.5624-0.5626 in.
(14.285-14.290 mm)
Pin bore in piston . . . . . 0.5625-0.5628 in.
(14.287-14.295 mm)

Pin bore in rod . . . . 0.5630-0.5635 in.
(14.300-14.313 mm)
Max. pin to rod clearance . . . . . 0.002 in.
(0.05 mm)

Specified piston skirt clearance is 0.005-0.007 inch (0.13-0.18 mm). Maximum skirt clearance for all models is 0.008 inch (0.20 mm). Piston is available in oversizes of 0.010 inch (0.25 mm) and 0.020 inch (0.51 mm) as well as standard size.

CYLINDER. Standard cylinder bore diameter is 2.4685-2.4695 inches (62.700-62.725 mm).

If piston skirt clearance is 0.008 inch (0.20 mm) or more with new piston or ring gap is 0.025 inch (0.64 mm) or more with new rings, cylinder must be rebored or honed and oversize piston and rings installed or cylinder and crankcase assembly must be renewed. Piston and rings are available in oversizes of 0.010 inch (0.25 mm) and 0.020 inch (0.51 mm) as well as standard size.

CRANKSHAFT. Specified connecting rod to crankpin clearance is 0.0018-0.0035 inch (0.046-0.089 mm). Renew rod and/or crankshaft if clearance exceeds 0.0045 inch (0.114 mm). Standard crankpin diameter is either 0.8745-0.8752 inch (22.212-22.230 mm) or 0.9114-0.9120 inch (23.150-23.165 mm). Specified maximum out-of-round is 0.001 inch (0.03 mm). Renew crankshaft if crankpin is out-of-round 0.0015 inch (0.038 mm). Connecting rod is available in standard size only.

Specified main bearing clearance is 0.0018-0.0035 inch (0.046-0.089 mm) on all plain bushing models. Renew crankshaft and/or bushings if clearance exceeds 0.005 inch (0.13 mm). Flywheel end journal diameter is 0.8745-0.8752 inch (22.212-22.230 mm). Pto end journal diameter is either 0.8745-0.8752 inch (22.212-22.230 mm) or 0.9995-1.0002 inch (25.387-25.405 mm). Bushings are available in standard size only and must be reamed after installation for proper size. Bushing driving tools, reamers and reamer alignment plates are available through Clinton parts sources.

Inspect tapered roller main bearings and renew bearing cones and cups if roller or cup is scored or rough.

Specified crankshaft end play is 0.001-0.006 inch (0.03-0.15 mm) with a maximum allowable end play of 0.008 inch (0.20 mm). Bearing plate gaskets are available in thicknesses of 0.005 inch (0.13 mm), 0.010 inch (0.25 mm), 0.015 inch (0.38 mm) and 0.020 inch (0.51 mm) for adjustment of end play.

CAMSHAFT AND GEAR. The hollow camshaft and cam gear unit rotates on an axle that is pressed into the engine crankcase. Camshaft can be removed after removing engine crankshaft and pressing camshaft axle from crankcase. On models with mechanical governor, governor weight unit is attached to cam gear by a pin that is pressed into the gear.

Specified operating clearance between camshaft axle and camshaft is 0.001-0.003 inch (0.03-0.08 mm). Renew axle and/or camshaft if clearance exceeds 0.005 inch (0.13 mm).

Specified camshaft end play is 0.003-0.010 inch (0.08-0.25 mm). Maximum allowable camshaft end play is 0.015 inch (0.38 mm).

VALVE SYSTEM. Recommended valve tappet gap for both intake and exhaust valves is 0.009-0.011 inch (0.23-0.28 mm). Adjust clearance by grinding end of valve stem. A 45 degree bevel should be maintained on ends of stems. Specified valve face angle is 45 degrees and valve seat angle is between 43½ and 44½ degrees. Specified seat width is 0.030-0.045 inch (0.76-1.14 mm). Recut seat width with combination tool 951-37 which has cutters of 44 and 30 degrees. Do not allow seat width to exceed 0.060 inch (1.52 mm).

Valve head margin for a new valve is 1/32-inch (0.8 mm). When margin is reduced by regrinding and wear to 1/64-inch (0.4 mm), valve should be renewed.

Recommended valve stem-to-guide clearance is 0.002-0.0045 inch (0.05-0.114 mm). If clearance is 0.006 inch (0.15 mm) or more, guides may be reamed to 0.260 inch (6.60 mm) or 0.2812 inch (7.142 mm) for valves with 0.010 inch (0.25 mm) or 0.031 inch (0.79 mm) oversize stem. Also, valve guide may be knurled and reamed to 0.250 inch (6.35 mm) for standard size stem.

Stellite exhaust valves and seats are available; also, stellite exhaust valves with roto-caps are available for service. Install regular exhaust valve in place of intake valve if installing a stellite ex-

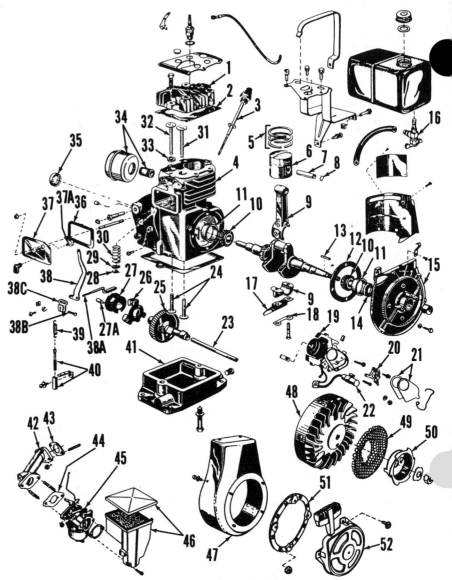

Fig. CL56 — Exploded view of Model 498-0000-000 series engine.

1. Cylinder head	16. Fuel shut-off valve	29. Retainer	39. Governor spring
2. Head gasket	17. Oil dipper	30. Spring	40. Adjustable link
3. Oil filler cap	18. Lock tab	31. Intake valve	41. Base
4. Block	19. Coil	32. Exhaust valve	42. Intake manifold
5. Rings	20. Contacts	33. Valve seat	43. Gasket
6. Piston	21. Cover & gasket	34. Muffler	44. Gasket
7. Wrist pin	22. Condenser	35. Seal	45. Carburetor
8. Retainer	23. Camshaft axle	36. Gasket	46. Air cleaner
9. Rod	24. Tappets	37. Valve cover	47. Blower housing
10. Bearing	25. Camshaft	37A. Breather	48. Flywheel
11. Bearing race	26. Weight assy.	38. Governor lever	49. Screen
12. Gasket	27. Collar	38A. A governor shaft	50. Starter pulley
13. Woodruff key	27A. Pin	38B. Screw	51. Adapter
14. Seal	28. Valve keeper	38C. Adjuster	52. Recoil starter
15. Bearing plate			

haust valve with seat. Stellite valves are available with standard and 0.010 inch (0.25 mm) oversize stems only.

Intake and exhaust valves are actuated by mushroom type tappets that ride directly in unbushed bores in engine crankcase. Tappet stem diameter is 0.2475-0.2485 inch (6.287-6.312 mm). Tappet guide bore diameter is 0.2495-0.2510 inch (6.337-6.375 mm). Tappets are available in standard size only. If guides are worn excessively, they may be knurled and reamed with same tools as used to knurl and ream

valve guides. Tappets may be removed from engine block after removing camshaft.

CAUTION: If ends of valve stems or ends of tappet stems have become enlarged or burred, do not force stems through bores in block. Remove burrs with emery cloth before attempting to remove valves and tappets.

Valve seat inserts are available for service; also, tools for cutting counterbore and installing valve seat inserts are available through Clinton parts sources.

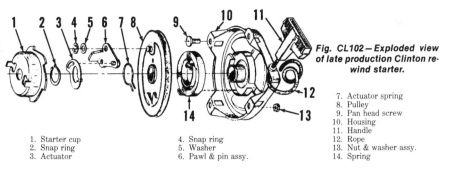

Fig. CL102 — Exploded view of late production Clinton rewind starter.

1. Starter cup
2. Snap ring
3. Actuator
4. Snap ring
5. Washer
6. Pawl & pin assy.
7. Actuator spring
8. Pulley
9. Pan head screw
10. Housing
11. Handle
12. Rope
13. Nut & washer assy.
14. Spring

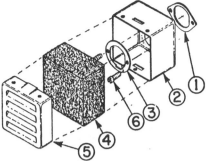

Fig. CL119 — Exploded view of polyurethane air cleaner.

1. Gasket
2. Body
3. Retainer
4. Element
5. Cover
6. Screws

SERVICING CLINTON ACCESSORIES

REWIND STARTERS

Exploded view of rewind starter currently used on most Clinton engines is shown in Fig. CL102. Care should be taken when reassembling all starters to be sure the recoil spring is not wound too tightly. The spring should be wound tight enough to rewind the rope, but so the spring will not be fully wound when the rope is pulled out to full length. Coat spring and all internal parts with Lubriplate or equivalent grease when reassembling. Be sure that spring, pulley and related parts are assembled for correct rotation.

MAINTENANCE

POLYURETHANE AIR CLEANER. Some Clinton models are equipped with a polyurethane air filter element. After each 10 hours of use, the element should be removed and washed in solvent or kerosene. (Element may be washed in detergent soap and water.) Re-oil the element with 10 weight or 10-30 weight motor oil and wring out to remove excess oil. Insert the element evenly into air cleaner housing and snap cover in place. See Fig. CL119 for exploded view of this type air cleaner.

CLINTON SPECIAL TOOLS

(498 SERIES ENGINES)

Oil Seal Loaders (Installation Sleeves)

951-12, 951-57, 951-145. Diameter, 0.750-inch (19.050 mm) OD. For installing oil seals over shafts.

Flywheel and Crankshaft Tools

IMPACT NUTS. Impact or knock-off nuts are available for removing flywheels as follows:

951-23, for crankshafts having 7/16-inch threads.

951-36, for crankshafts having 7/8-inch threads.

951-66, for crankshafts having 1/2-inch threads.

951-133 FLYWHEEL PULLER

951-42 FLYWHEEL HOLDER

951-45 HAND CRANK. Used for turning engine when adjusting breaker point gap, checking timing etc.

951-64 CRANKSHAFT RUNOUT GAGE. Used for checking for bent crankshafts.

Valve Tools

951-22 VALVE GUIDE REAMER. Diameter, 0.281-inch (7.14 mm). Used to enlarge valve guide holes so oversize stemmed valves can be used.

951-58 VALVE GUIDE PILOT ASSEMBLY. Used in conjunction with 951-37 valve seat cutter and 951-41 & 951-61 counter cutters.

951-37 VALVE SEAT CUTTER. Used to reface valve seats.

951-53 ROLLING TOOL. Used to peen or roll metal around outside diameter of valve seat insert after installation.

Camshaft Tool

951-46 CAMSHAFT AXLE DRIVER. Used to drive camshaft axle from block.

HONDA

AMERICAN HONDA MOTOR CO., INC.
100 W. Alondra Blvd.
Gardena, CA 90247

Model	No. Cyls.	Bore	Stroke	Displacement
GV100	1	50 mm	46 mm	90 cc
		(1.97 in.)	(1.81 in.)	(5.5 cu. in.)

ENGINE IDENTIFICATION

Model GV100 is a four-stroke, air-cooled, single-cylinder engine. Valves are located in cylinder block and crankcase casting. Model GV100 is rated at 1.8 kW (2.4 hp). The "GV" prefix indicates vertical crankshaft model.

Engine serial number is located on crankcase or crankcase cover near oil filler and dipstick opening. See Fig. HN1.

Always furnish engine model and serial number when ordering parts.

MAINTENANCE

SPARK PLUG. Recommended spark plug is a NGK BMR-4A or equivalent. Spark plug should be removed and cleaned after every 100 hours of operation. Set electrode gap at 0.6-0.7 mm (0.024-0.028 in.).

NOTE: Caution should be exercised if abrasive type spark plug cleaner is used. Inadequate cleaning procedure may allow the abrasive cleaner to be deposited in engine cylinder causing rapid wear and part failure.

CARBURETOR. A float type side draft carburetor is used. Carburetor is equipped with idle fuel mixture screw. High speed fuel mixture is controlled by a fixed jet.

Engine idle speed should be 1850-2150 rpm. Idle speed is adjusted by turning

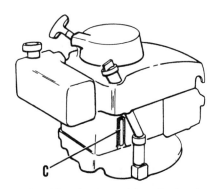

Fig. HN1—View showing serial number location.

throttle stop screw (3—Fig. HN2). Initial adjustment of idle fuel mixture screw (2) from a lightly seated position is 1-1/2 turns open. Final adjustment is made with engine at operating temperature and running. Adjust idle mixture screw to attain smoothest engine operation. Recheck engine idle speed and adjust if necessary.

Main jet (5) controls fuel mixture for high speed operation. Standard main jet size is #60.

Float level should be 10.7-13.3 mm (0.42-0.52 in.). To measure float level, invert carburetor throttle body and float assembly. Measure distance from top of float to float bowl mating surface. If dimension is not as specified, renew float.

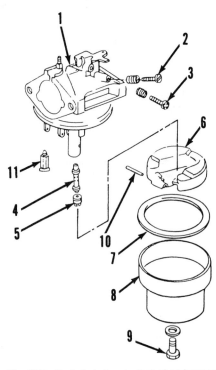

Fig. HN2—Exploded view typical of carburetor used.

1. Carburetor throttle body	6. Float
2. Idle mixture screw	7. Gasket
3. Throttle stop screw	8. Float bowl
4. Nozzle	9. Bolt
5. Main jet	10. Float pin
	11. Fuel inlet needle

FUEL FILTER. A fuel filter screen is located in fuel line at sediment bowl below fuel shut-off valve. To clean filter screen, shut off fuel and remove sediment bowl. Empty sediment bowl and clean bowl and filter screen.

AIR FILTER. Engines are equipped with a dual element type foam and paper element air filter.

Filter should be checked prior to each use and removed and serviced after every 50 hours of operation. Remove wing nut, cover and elements. Separate foam outer element from paper element. Wash foam element in warm soapy water and thoroughly rinse. Allow element to air dry. Dip dry foam element in clean engine oil and gently squeeze out excess oil.

Direct low pressure air from inside paper element toward the outside to remove all loose dirt and foreign material. Reassemble elements and reinstall.

GOVERNOR. The internal centrifugal flyweight governor assembly is located inside crankcase and is gear driven.

To adjust governor, first stop engine and make certain all linkage is in good condition and tension spring (2—Fig. HN4) is not stretched or damaged. Spring (4) must pull governor lever (3) toward throttle pivot (6).

Loosen clamp bolt (8) and turn governor shaft clockwise as far as it will go and move governor lever as far to the right as it will go. Tighten retaining bolt. Start and run engine until it reaches operating temperature. Adjust stop screw (9) to obtain maximum engine speed of 3800-4000 rpm.

IGNITION SYSTEM. Engines are equipped with a breakerless, transistorized ignition system. No regular ignition system maintenance is required. Ignition timing is fixed at 20 degrees BTDC. Air gap between transistorized ignition coil and flywheel magnets should be 0.2-0.6 mm (0.008-0.024 in.).

To check transistorized ignition coil, connect positive ohmmeter lead to black wire and remaining lead to coil

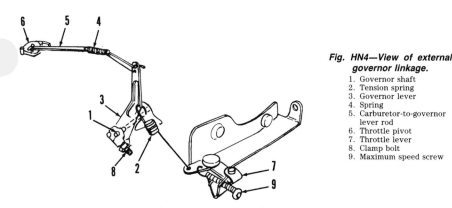

Fig. HN4—View of external governor linkage.
1. Governor shaft
2. Tension spring
3. Governor lever
4. Spring
5. Carburetor-to-governor lever rod
6. Throttle pivot
7. Throttle lever
8. Clamp bolt
9. Maximum speed screw

laminations. Ohmmeter should register 0.7-0.9 ohm. Disconnect positive lead and reconnect lead to spark plug wire. Ohmmeter should register 6.3-7.7 ohms.

VALVE ADJUSTMENT. Valves and seats should be refaced and stem clearance adjusted after every 300 hours of operation. Refer to REPAIRS section for service procedures and sepcifications.

CYLINDER HEAD AND COMBUSTION CHAMBER. Cylinder head, combustion chamber and piston should be cleaned and carbon and other deposits removed after every 300 hours of operation. Refer to REPAIRS section for service procedure.

LUBRICATION. Engine oil should be checked prior to each operating interval. Oil level should be maintained between reference marks on dipstick with dipstick just touching first threads. Do not screw dipstick in to check oil level.

Manufacturer recommends SAE 10W-40 oil with an API service classification SE or SF.

Oil should be changed after the first 20 hours of operation and after every 100 hours of operation thereafter. Crankcase capacity is 0.4 L (0.4 qt.).

GENERAL MAINTENANCE. Check and tighten all loose bolts, nuts and clamps prior to each operating interval. Check for fuel and oil leakage and repair if necessary.

Clean dust, dirt, grease and any foreign material from cylinder head and cylinder block cooling fins after every 100 hours of operation. Inspect fins for damage and repair if necessary.

REPAIRS

TIGHTENING TORQUES. Recommended tightening torque specifications are as follows:
Flywheel nut . . . . .45-54 N·m
(33-40 ft.-lbs.)
Crankcase cover . . . . 7.8-11.7 N·m
(6-9 ft.-lbs.)

Cylinder head bolts . . . . .7.8-11.7 N·m
(6-9 ft.-lbs.)
Connecting rod bolts . . . . .4-6 N·m
(3-4 ft.-lbs.)

CYLINDER HEAD. To remove cylinder head, first remove cooling shrouds. Clean engine to prevent entrance of foreign material. Remove spark plug. Loosen cylinder head bolts following the sequence shown in Fig. HN8. Remove cylinder head. Clean carbon and deposits from cylinder head.

Reinstall cylinder head and new gasket. Tighten head bolts to specified torque using the correct sequence shown (Fig. HN8).

CONNECTING ROD. Connecting rod rides directly on crankshaft crankpin journal. Piston and connecting rod are accessible after cylinder head removal and oil pan is separated from crankcase. Remove the two connecting rod bolts, lockplate and connecting rod cap. Push piston and connecting rod assembly out through the top of cylinder block. Remove snap rings and piston pin to separate piston from connecting rod.

Standard diameter for piston pin bore in connecting rod small end is 10.006 mm (0.3939 in.). If dimension exceeds 10.05 mm (0.396 in.), renew connecting rod.

Standard clearance between connecting rod bearing surface and crankpin journal is 0.016-0.038 mm (0.0006-

0.0015 in.). If clearance exceeds 0.1 mm (0.0004 in.), renew connecting rod and/or recondition crankshaft.

Standard connecting rod side play on crankpin journal is 0.20-0.90 mm (0.008-0.035 in.). If side play exceeds 1.1 mm (0.043 in.), renew connecting rod.

Install piston on connecting rod so the mark "ZG1" stamped on top of piston is toward long side of connecting rod (Fig. HN10).

PISTON, PIN AND RINGS. Piston and connecting rod are removed as an assembly. Refer to CONNECTING ROD section for removal and installation procedure.

After separating piston and connecting rod, carefully remove rings. Clean carbon and deposits from piston surface and ring lands.

CAUTION: Extreme care should be exercised when cleaning ring lands. Do not damage squared edges or widen ring grooves. If ring lands are damaged, piston must be renewed.

Measure piston diameter at piston thrust surfaces, 90 degrees from piston pin. Standard piston diameter is 49.995 mm (1.968 in.). If piston diameter is less than 49.92 mm (1.96 in.), renew piston.

Before installing rings, install piston in cylinder bore and use a suitable feeler gage to measure clearance between piston and cylinder bore. Standard clearance is 0.005-0.035 mm (0.0002-0.0014 in.). If clearance exceeds 0.13 mm (0.005 in.), renew piston and/or recondition cylinder bore.

Standard piston pin outside diameter is 10.000 mm (0.3937 in.). Service limit for piston pin outside diameter is 9.950 mm (0.3917 in.). If diameter is less than service limit, renew piston pin.

Standard piston ring-to-piston groove side clearance is 0.025-0.055 mm (0.0009-0.0022 in.) for top ring and second ring. If ring side clearance exceeds 0.10 mm (0.0039 in.), renew rings and/or piston.

If piston ring end gap exceeds 1.0 mm (0.039 in.) with ring squarely installed

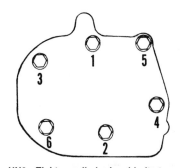

Fig. HN8—Tighten cylinder head bolts to specified torque following sequence shown.

Fig. HN10—Install piston so "ZG1" on piston is toward long side of rod.

in cylinder bore, renew ring and/or recondition cylinder bore.

Install piston rings with marked side toward top of piston. Stagger ring end gaps equally around circumference of piston.

CYLINDER AND CRANKCASE. Cylinder and crankcase are an integral casting. Standard cylinder bore is 50.0 mm (1.968 in.). If cylinder bore diameter at any point in cylinder bore exceeds 50.05 mm (1.97 in.), recondition cylinder bore.

CRANKSHAFT, MAIN BEARINGS AND SEALS. Crankshaft is supported by ball bearing type main bearings at each end. To remove crankshaft, remove all cooling shrouds, flywheel, cylinder head and oil pan. Remove piston and connecting rod assembly. Carefully remove crankshaft and camshaft. Remove main bearings and crankshaft oil seals if necessary.

Standard crankpin diameter is 17.984 mm (0.7080 in.). If crankpin diameter is less than 17.940 mm (0.7063 in.), renew or recondition crankshaft.

Main bearings are a light press fit on crankshaft and in bearing bores of crankcase and crankcase cover. It may be necessary to slightly heat crankcase or crankcase cover to reinstall bearings.

Inspect main bearings for roughness and looseness. Also check bearings for a loose fit on crankshaft journals or in crankcase and crankcase cover. Renew bearings if any of the previously described conditions are evident.

If crankshaft oil seals have been removed, use suitable seal driver to install new seals.

Make certain crankshaft gear (sprocket) and camshaft gear (sprocket) timing marks are aligned (Fig. HN11) during crankshaft installation.

CAMSHAFT. Standard camshaft lobe height is 20.82 mm (0.820 in.) for intake and exhaust lobes. If intake or exhaust lobe is less than 20.45 mm (0.805 in.), renew camshaft.

Make certain camshaft gear (sprocket) and crankshaft gear sprocket timing marks are aligned during installation.

GOVERNOR. The internal centrifugal governor is gear driven off of the camshaft gear. Refer to GOVERNOR paragraphs in MAINTENANCE section for external governor adjustments.

To remove governor assembly, remove external linkage, metal cooling shrouds and crankcase oil pan. Remove "E" clip (Fig. HN13) and slide governor assembly off of shaft.

When reassembling, make certain governor sliding sleeve and internal governor linkage is correctly positioned.

VALVE SYSTEM. Clearance between valve stem and valve tappet (cold) should be 0.08-0.16 mm (0.003-0.006 in.) for intake and exhaust valves.

Check valve clearance with engine cold. Valve clearance is adjusted by varying thickness of valve adjuster located under valve stem. Use a suitable valve spring compressor to lift valve spring and spring retainer to remove and reinstall valve adjuster. Valve adjuster is available in 3.15 mm (0.124 in.), 3.25 mm (0.128 in.), 3.34 mm (0.131 in.), 3.43 mm (0.135 in.), 3.52 mm (0.139 in.), 3.61 mm (0.142 in.), 3.72 mm (0.146 in.) and 3.82 mm (0.150 in.) thicknesses. If the proper valve clearance cannot be obtained by changing thickness of valve adjuster, the bottom of adjuster can be

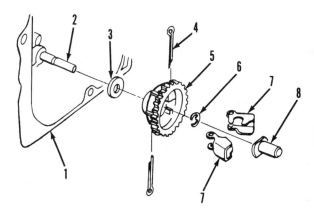

Fig. HN13—Exploded view of governor assembly.

1. Crankcase cover
2. Governor stud
3. Thrust washer
4. Pin
5. Gear
6. "E" clip
7. Weights
8. Sleeve

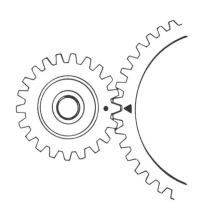

Fig. HN11—When installing crankshaft or camshaft, make certain timing marks on gears are aligned as shown.

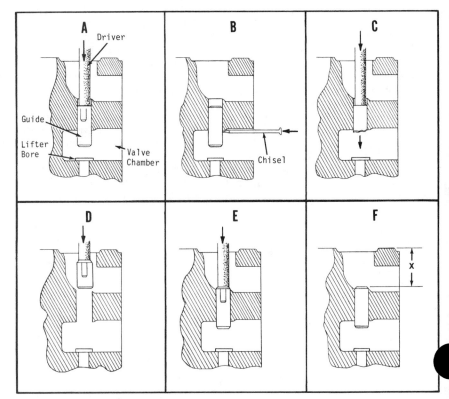

Fig. HN14—View showing valve guide removal and installation sequence.

lapped using a suitable oil stone and Honda Valve Lapping Guide 07975-8920000.

Valve face and seat angles are 45 degrees. Standard valve seat width is 0.7 mm (0.03 in.). If valve seat width exceeds 1.0 mm (0.039 in.), seats must be narrowed.

Standard valve stem diameters are 5.490 mm (0.2161 in.) for intake valve stem and 5.445 mm (0.2144 in.) for exhaust valve stem. If intake valve stem diameter is less than 5.450 mm (0.2146 in.) or exhaust valve stem diameter is less than 5.400 mm (0.2126 in.), renew valve.

Standard valve guide inside diameter for both intake and exhaust valve guides is 5.500 mm (0.216 in.). If inside diameter of guide exceeds 5.560 mm (0.2189 in.), guides must be renewed.

To remove and install valve guides, use the following procedure and refer to the sequence of illustrations in Fig. HN14. Use driver 07942-8920000 and drive valve guide down into valve chamber 15 mm (0.59 in.). Refer to view (A). Use a suitable cold chisel and sever guide adjacent to guide bore (B). Cover tappet opening to prevent fragments from entering crankcase. Drive remaining piece of guide into valve chamber (C) and remove from chamber. Place new guide on driver and start guide into guide bore (D). Alternate between driving guide into bore and measuring guide depth below cylinder head surface (E). Guide is driven in to a depth of 18.5 mm (0.73 in.) measured from end of guide to cylinder head surface as shown in view (F) at (X). Finish ream guide after installation with reamer 07984-2000000.

HONDA

Model	No. Cyls.	Bore	Stroke	Displacement
GX110	1	57 mm	42 mm	107 cc
		(2.2 in.)	(1.7 in.)	(6.6 cu. in.)
GX140	1	64 mm	45 mm	144 cc
		(2.5 in.)	(1.8 in.)	(8.8 cu. in.)

ENGINE INFORMATION

All models are four-stroke, overhead valve, single-cylinder, air-cooled engines.

Model GX110 is rated at 2.6 kW (3.5 hp) at 3600 rpm and Model GX140 is rated at 3.8 kW (5.0 hp) at 3600 rpm.

Engine model number is cast into side of crankcase (Fig. HN30) and engine serial number is stamped into crankcase (Fig. HN31). Always furnish engine model and serial number when ordering parts.

MAINTENANCE

SPARK PLUG. Spark plug should be removed, cleaned and inspected at 100 hour intervals.

Recommended spark plug is a Champion N9YC or equivalent. Recommended spark plug electrode gap is 0.7-0.8 mm (0.028-0.031 in.).

Fig. HN30—Engine model number (MN) is cast into side of engine crankcase.

Fig. HN31—Engine serial number (SN) is stamped on raised portion of crankcase.

When installing spark plug, manufacturer recommends installing spark plug fingertight, then for a new plug, tighten an additional ½ turn and for a used plug, tighten an additional ¼ turn.

CARBURETOR. All models are equipped with a Keihin float type carburetor with a fixed main fuel jet and an adjustable low speed fuel mixture needle.

Initial adjustment of low speed fuel mixture screw (LS—Fig. HN32) from a lightly seated position is 3 turns open for Model GX110 and 1-5/8 turns open for Model GX140.

For final adjustment, engine must be at operating temperature and running. Operate engine at idle speed (1400 rpm) and adjust low speed mixture screw (LS) to obtain a smooth idle and satisfactory acceleration. Adjust idle speed to 1400 rpm by turning throttle stop screw (TS).

To check float level, remove float bowl and invert carburetor throttle body and float assembly. Measure from top edge of float to float bowl mating edge of carburetor throttle body. Measurement should be 12.2-15.2 mm (0.48-0.60 in.). Renew float if float height is incorrect.

Standard main jet for Model GX110 is a #65 and standard main jet for Model GX140 is a #68.

Fig. HN32—View of Keihin float type carburetor used on all models showing location of low speed mixture screw (LS) and throttle stop screw (TS).

AIR CLEANER. Engine may be equipped with either a dry type, semi-dry type or oil bath air filter which should be cleaned and inspected after every 50 hours of operation. Refer to appropriate paragraph for type being serviced.

Dry Type Air Cleaner. Remove foam and paper air filter elements from air filter housing. Foam element should be washed in a mild detergent and water solution, rinsed in clean water and allowed to air dry. Soak foam element in clean engine oil. Squeeze out excess oil.

Paper element may be cleaned by directing a low pressure compressed air stream from inside filter toward the outside. Reinstall elements.

Semi-Dry Type Air Cleaner. Remove element and clean in solvent. Wring out excess solvent and allow element to air dry. Dip element in clean engine oil and wring out excess oil. Reinstall element.

Oil Bath Type Air Cleaner. Remove elements and clean in suitable solvent. Foam element should be washed in mild detergent and water solution and allowed to air dry. Discard old oil and clean oil reservoir with solvent. Refill oil reservoir with 60 mL (1.3 pt.) clean engine oil. Soak foam element in clean engine oil and wring out excess oil. Reassemble air cleaner.

GOVERNOR. The mechanical flyweight type governor is located inside engine crankcase. To adjust external linkage, stop engine and make certain all linkage is in good condition and tension spring (5—Fig. HN33) is not stretched or damaged. Spring (2) must pull governor lever (3) and throttle pivot toward each other. Loosen clamp bolt (7) and move governor lever (3) so throttle is completely open. Hold governor lever in this position and rotate governor shaft (6) in the same direction until it stops. Tighten clamp bolt.

Start engine and operate at an idle until operating temperature has been reached. Attach a tachometer to engine

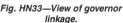

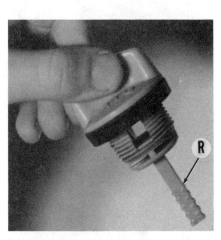

Fig. HN33—View of governor linkage.

1. Governor-to-carburetor rod
2. Spring
3. Governor lever
4. Choke rod
5. Tension spring (behind plate & lever)
6. Governor shaft
7. Clamp bolt
8. Throttle stop screw

and move throttle so engine is operating at maximum speed (3800-4000 rpm). Adjust throttle stop screw (8) so throttle movement is limited to correct maximum engine rpm.

IGNITION SYSTEM. Breakerless ignition system requires no regular maintenance. Ignition coil unit is mounted outside the flywheel and air gap between flywheel and coil should be 0.2-0.6 mm (0.008-0.024 in.).

To check ignition coil primary side, connect one ohmmeter lead to primary (block) coil lead and touch iron coil laminations with remaining lead. Ohmmeter should register 0.7-0.9 ohm.

To check ignition coil secondary side, connect one ohmmeter lead to the spark plug lead wire and remaining lead to the iron coil laminations. Ohmmeter should register 6.3-7.7 ohms. If ohmmeter readings are not as specified, renew ignition coil.

VALVE ADJUSTMENT. Valve stem clearance should be checked and adjusted at 300 hour intervals.

To adjust valve stem clearance, refer to Fig. HN34 and remove rocker arm

cover. Rotate engine so piston is at top dead center (TDC) on compression stroke. Insert a feeler gage between rocker arm (3) and end of valve stem. As necessary, loosen rocker arm jam nut (1) and turn adjusting nut (2) to obtain 0.15 mm (0.006 in.) clearance on intake valve and 0.20 mm (0.008 in.) clearance on exhaust valve. Tighten jam nut and recheck clearance. Install rocker arm cover.

CYLINDER HEAD AND COMBUSTION CHAMBER. It is recommended that cylinder head be removed and carbon and lead deposits be cleaned from head and combustion chamber and valves and seats be refaced at 300 hour intervals. Refer to CYLINDER HEAD paragraphs in REPAIRS section for service procedure.

LUBRICATION. Engine oil level should be checked prior to each operating interval. Maintain oil level at top of reference marks (Fig. HN35) when checked with cap not screwed in, but just touching first threads.

Oil should be changed after the first 20 hours of engine operation and at 100 hour intervals thereafter.

Manufacturer recommends oil with an API service classification SE or SF. Use SAE 10W-30 or 10W-40 oil.

Crankcase capacity is 0.6 L (0.63 qt.).

GENERAL MAINTENANCE. Check and tighten all loose bolts, nuts or clamps daily. Check for fuel or oil leakage and repair as necessary.

Clean dust, dirt, grease or any foreign material from cylinder head and cylinder block cooling fins at 100 hour intervals. Inspect fins for damage and repair as necessary.

REPAIRS

TIGHTENING TORQUES. Recommended tightening torque specifications are as follows:

Rocker arm cover	8-12 N·m (6-9 ft.-lbs.)
Cylinder head	22-26 N·m (16-19 ft.-lbs.)
Oil pan	10-14 N·m (7-10 ft.-lbs.)
Crankcase cover	22-26 N·m (16-19 ft.-lbs.)
Connecting rod bolts	10-14 N·m (7-10 ft.-lbs.)
Oil drain plug	15-20 N·m (11-15 ft.-lbs.)
Rocker arm jam nut	8-12 N·m (6-9 ft.-lbs.)
Flywheel nut	70-80 N·m (51-58 ft.-lbs.)

CYLINDER HEAD. To remove cylinder head, remove cooling shroud, disconnect and remove carburetor linkage and carburetor. Remove muffler. Remove rocker arm cover and the four head bolts. Remove cylinder head. Use care not to lose push rods.

Remove rocker arms, compress valve springs and remove valve retainers. Note exhaust valve is equipped with a valve rotator on valve stem. Remove

Fig. HN34—View of rocker arm and related parts.

1. Jam nut
2. Adjustment nut
3. Rocker arm
4. Valve stem clearance
5. Push rod

Fig. HN35—Do not screw in oil plug and gage when checking oil level. Maintain oil level at top edge of reference marks (R) on dipstick.

valves and springs. Remove push rod guide plate if necessary.

Valve face and seat angle is 45 degrees. Standard valve seat width is 0.8 mm (0.032 in.). Narrow seat if seat width is 2.0 mm (0.079 in.) or more.

Standard valve spring free length is 34.0 mm (1.339 in.). Renew valve spring if free length is 32.5 mm (1.280 in.) or less.

Standard valve guide inside diameter is 5.50-5.51 mm (0.2165-0.2170 in.). Renew guide if inside diameter is 5.562 mm (0.219 in.) or more.

Valve stem-to-guide clearance should be 0.02-0.04 mm (0.001-0.002 in.) for intake valve and 0.06-0.09 mm (0.002-0.003 in.) for exhaust valve. Renew valve and/or guide if clearance is 0.10 mm (0.004 in.) or more for intake valve or 0.12 mm (0.005 in.) or more for exhaust valve.

To renew valve guide, heat entire cylinder head to 150° F (300° C) and use valve guide driver 07942-8920000 to remove and install guides. Drive guides into cylinder head until top of guide is 23.0 mm (0.905 in.) below cylinder head surface (cylinder head-to-cylinder bore mating surface) for Model GX110 or 25.5 mm (1.004 in.) below cylinder head surface for Model GX140. New valve guides must be reamed after installation using reamer 07984-4600000 or 07984-2000000.

When installing cylinder head, tighten head bolts to specified torque following sequence shown in Fig. HN36. Ad-

just valves as outlined under VALVE ADJUSTMENT paragraphs in MAINTENANCE section.

CONNECTING ROD. The aluminum alloy connecting rod rides directly on crankpin journal on all models. Connecting rod cap is equipped with an oil dipper (Fig. HN38).

To remove connecting rod, remove cylinder head and crankcase cover or oil pan. Remove connecting rod cap screws and cap. Push connecting rod and piston assembly out of cylinder. Crankshaft and camshaft may also be removed if required. Remove piston pin retaining rings and separate piston from connecting rod.

Standard piston pin bore diameter in connecting rod is 13.005-13.020 mm (0.512-0.513 in.) for Model GX110 and 18.005-18.020 mm (0.7089-0.7094 in.) for Model GX140. Renew connecting rod if diameter is 13.07 mm (0.5 in.) or more for Model GX110 or 18.07 mm (0.711 in.) or more for Model GX140.

Standard piston pin-to-connecting rod pin bore clearance is 0.005-0.026 mm (0.0002-0.001 in.). Renew connecting rod and/or pin if clearance is 0.08 mm (0.0031 in.) or more.

Standard connecting rod bearing bore-to-crankpin clearance is 0.040-0.063 mm (0.0015-0.0025 in.). Renew connecting rod and/or crankshaft if clearance is 0.12 mm (0.0047 in.) or more.

Connecting rod side play on crankpin should be 0.1-0.7 mm (0.004-0.028 in.). Renew connecting rod if side play is 1.1 mm (0.043 in.) or more.

When reassembling piston on connecting rod, long side of connecting rod and arrowhead on piston top (Fig. HN39) must be on the same side.

When reinstalling piston and connecting rod assembly in cylinder, arrowhead on piston top must be on push rod side of engine. Align connecting rod cap and connecting rod match marks and install connecting rod bolts and tighten to specified torque.

PISTON, PIN AND RINGS. Piston and connecting rod are removed as an assembly. Refer to previous CONNECTING ROD paragraphs for removal and installation procedure.

Standard piston diameter measured at lower edge of skirt and 90 degrees from piston pin bore is 56.965-56.985 mm (2.242-2.243 in.) for Model GX110 and 63.965-63.985 mm (2.518-2.519 in. for Model GX140. Renew piston if diameter is 56.55 mm (2.226 in.) or less for Model GX110 or 63.55 mm (2.502 in.) or less for Model GX140. Standard piston-to-cylinder clearance is 0.015-0.050 mm (0.0006-0.0020 in.). Renew piston and/or cylinder if clearance is 0.12 mm (0.0047 in.) or more.

Standard piston pin bore diameter is 13.002-13.008 mm (0.5118-0.5120 in.) for Model GX110 and 18.002-18.048 mm (0.709-0.711 in.) for Model GX140. Standard piston pin diameter is 12.994-13.000 mm (0.5115-0.5118 in.) for Model GX110 and 17.994-18.000 mm (0.7084-0.7087 in.) for Model GX140. If pin diameter is 12.954 mm (0.510 in.) or less for Model GX110 or 17.954 mm (0.707 in.) or less for Model GX140, renew piston pin. Standard clearance between piston pin and pin bore in piston is 0.002-0.014 mm (0.0001-0.0006 in.). If clearance is 0.08 mm (0.0031 in.) or more, renew piston and/or pin.

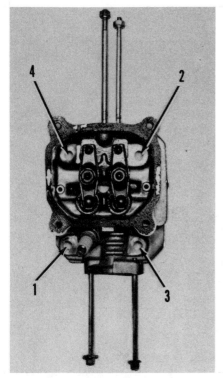

Fig. HN36—Tighten cylinder head bolts in sequence shown.

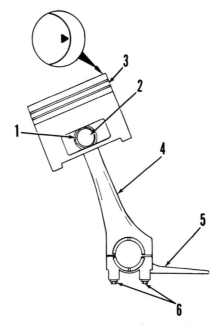

Fig. HN38—Exploded view of rod and piston assembly. Note location of oil dipper on connecting rod cap.

1. Retaining rings
2. Piston pin
3. Piston
4. Connecting rod
5. Rod cap & dipper
6. Bolts

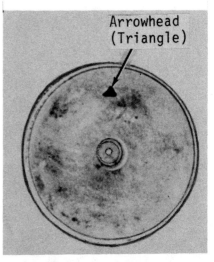

Fig. HN39—Arrowhead (triangle) on top of piston must be on push rod side of engine after installation. Refer to text.

Ring side clearance should be 0.015-0.045 mm (0.0006-0.0018 in.). Ring end gap for compression rings should be 0.2-0.4 mm (0.008-0.016 in.). Ring end gap for oil control ring should be 0.15-0.35 mm (0.006-0.014 in.). If ring end gap for any ring is 1.0 mm (0.039 in.) or more, renew ring and/or cylinder.

Install marked piston rings with marked side toward top of piston and stagger ring end gaps equally around circumference of piston.

CYLINDER AND CRANKCASE. Cylinder and crankcase are an integral casting. Standard cylinder bore diameter is 57.000-57.015 mm (2.244-2.245 in.) for Model GX110 and 64.000-64.015 mm (2.519-2.520 in.) for Model GX140.

If cylinder diameter is 57.165 mm (2.251 in.) or more for Model GX110 or 64.165 mm (2.526 in.) or more for Model GX140, renew cylinder.

CRANKSHAFT, MAIN BEARINGS AND SEALS. Crankshaft is supported at each end in ball bearing type main bearings. To remove crankshaft, refer to previous CONNECTING ROD paragraphs.

Standard crankpin journal diameter is 26.0 mm (1.024 in.) for Model GX110 and 30.0 mm (1.181 in.) for Model GX140. If crankpin diameter is 25.92 mm (1.020 in.) or less for Model GX110 or 29.92 mm (1.178 in.) or less for Model GX140, renew crankshaft.

Ball bearing type main bearings are a press fit on crankshaft journals and in bearing bores of crankcase and cover. Renew bearings if loose, rough or loose fit on crankshaft or in bearing bores.

Seals should be pressed into seal bores until outer edge of seal is flush with seal bore.

When installing crankshaft, make certain crankshaft gear and camshaft gear timing marks are aligned as shown in Fig. HN41.

CAMSHAFT. Camshaft and camshaft gear are an integral casting equipped with a compression release mechanism (Fig. HN43). To remove camshaft, refer to previous CONNECTING ROD paragraphs.

Standard camshaft bearing journal diameter is 13.984 mm (0.551 in.). Renew camshaft if journal diameter is 13.916 mm (0.548 in.) or less.

Standard camshaft lobe height is 27.7 mm (1.091 in.) for intake lobe and 27.75 mm (1.093 in.) for exhaust lobe (Fig. HN44). If intake lobe measures 27.45 mm (1.081 in.) or less or exhaust lobe measures 27.50 mm (1.083 in.) or less, renew camshaft.

Inspect compression release mechanism for damage. Spring must pull

Fig. HN41—Align crankshaft gear and camshaft gear timing marks (F) during installation.

weight tightly against camshaft so decompressor lobe holds exhaust valve slightly open. Weight overcomes spring tension at 1000 rpm and moves decom-

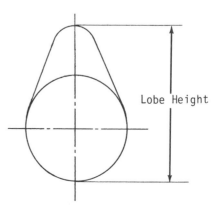

Fig. HN43—Compression release mechanism spring (1) and weight (2) installed on camshaft gear.

Fig. HN44—Drawing showing camshaft lobe height measurement.

pressor lobe away from cam lobe to release exhaust valve.

When installing camshaft, make certain camshaft and crankshaft gear timing marks are aligned as shown in Fig. HN41.

GOVERNOR. Centrifugal flyweight type governor controls engine rpm via external linkage. Governor is located on flywheel side of crankcase. Refer to GOVERNOR paragraphs in MAINTENANCE section for adjustment procedure.

To remove governor assembly, refer to previous CONNECTING ROD paragraphs and remove crankshaft and camshaft. Remove governor sleeve and washer. Remove retaining clip from governor gear shaft, then remove gear and weight assembly and remaining thrust washer.

Reinstall governor assemblies by reversing removal procedure. Adjust external linkage as outlined under GOVERNOR in MAINTENANCE section.

Lobe Height

HONDA

SERVICING HONDA ACCESSORIES

REWIND STARTER

Refer to Fig. HN60 for exploded view of the rewind starter assembly used on some models. Starter can be disassembled as follows: Pull rope out slightly and untie knot at handle end while holding the rope pulley (6) from turning. Remove handle from rope and allow spring to unwind slowly. Remove special bolt (1), friction plate (2), spring (3) and friction disc (5). Remove ratchets (4) from pulley and remove pulley and spring from housing. Reassemble by reversing disassembly procedure and check action of starter before reinstalling.

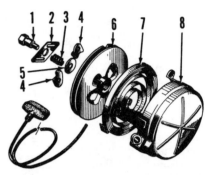

Fig. HN60—Exploded view of rewind starter assembly. Starter cup (attached to engine crankshaft) is not shown.

1. Special bolt
2. Friction plate
3. Friction spring
4. Ratchets
5. Friction disc
6. Rope pulley
7. Rewind spring
8. Housing

KAWASAKI

KAWASAKI MOTORS CORP. USA
P. O. Box 504
Shakopee, MN 55379

Model	No. Cyls.	Bore	Stroke	Displacement
FA130	1	62 mm	43 mm	129 cc
		(2.44 in.)	(1.69 in.)	(7.9 cu. in.)

ENGINE IDENTIFICATION

Kawasaki FA130 engine is a four-stroke, single-cylinder, air-cooled, horizontal crankshaft engine. Model FA130 develops 2.3 kW (3.1 hp) at 4000 rpm. Engine model number is located on the cooling shroud just above the rewind starter. Engine model number and serial number are both stamped on crankcase cover (Fig. KW1). Always furnish engine model and serial numbers when ordering parts or service information.

MAINTENANCE

SPARK PLUG. Recommended spark plug is a NGK BM-6A, or equivalent.

Spark plug should be removed and cleaned and electrode gap set at 0.6-0.7 mm (0.024-0.027 in.) after every 100 hours of operation. Renew spark plug if electrode is severely burnt or damaged. Tighten spark plug to 27 N·m (20 ft.-lbs.).

NOTE: Caution should be exercised if abrasive type spark plug cleaner is used. Inadequate cleaning procedure may allow the abrasive cleaner to be deposited in engine cylinder accelerating wear and part failures.

CARBURETOR. Engine may be equipped with either a pulse type (Fig. KW2) or a float type (Fig. KW3) carburetor. Engine idle speed should first be adjusted to 1500 rpm using idle stop screw (IS—Fig. KW2 or Fig. KW3) on carburetor, then adjust idle limit screw (IL—Fig. KW4) on throttle plate assembly so engine idles at 1600 rpm. Adjust maximum speed limit screw (ML) so maximum engine speed is 4000 rpm.

CAUTION: Maximum engine speed must not exceed 4000 rpm even during adjustment procedure. Running engine at speeds in excess of 4000 rpm may result in engine damage and possible injury to operator.

For initial carburetor adjustment of pulse type carburetor, lightly seat pilot air screw (P—Fig. KW2) and then open pilot screw 1-1/4 turns. Make final adjustments with engine at operating temperature and running. Back out idle limit screw (IL—Fig. KW4) so it does not limit idle speed, then adjust idle stop screw (IS—Fig. KW2) on carburetor so engine runs at lowest speed possible. Adjust pilot air screw (P) to obtain highest engine idle speed. Readjust idle stop screw (IS) and idle limit screw (IL—Fig. KW4) for correct speeds.

For initial carburetor adjustment of float type carburetor, lightly seat pilot air screw (P—Fig. KW3) and fuel mix-

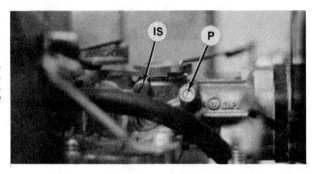

Fig. KW2—View of pulse type carburetor showing location of idle stop screw (IS) and pilot air screw (P). Refer to text for adjustment procedure.

Fig. KW1—View showing location of engine model and serial number stamped on engine crankcase cover.

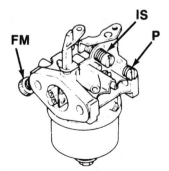

Fig. KW3—View of float type carburetor.
P. Pilot air screw
IS. Throttle stop screw
FM. Main fuel mixture screw

ture needle (FM). Open pilot air screw (P) 1-1/2 turns. Open fuel mixture screw (FM) 1-1/2 turns. Make final adjustments with engine at operating temperature and running. Back out idle limit screw (IL—Fig. KW4) so it does not limit idle speed, then adjust idle stop screw (IS—Fig. KW3) on carburetor so engine runs at lowest speed possible. Adjust pilot air screw (P) to obtain highest engine idle speed. Readjust idle stop screw and idle limit screw for correct speeds. Operate engine under a load at maximum engine speed (4000 rpm) and readjust fuel mixture needle (FM) to obtain smoothest engine operation.

To check float level, invert carburetor throttle body and float assembly. Float surface should be parallel to carburetor throttle body. If float is equipped with metal tang which contacts inlet needle, carefully bend tang to adjust float. If float is a plastic assembly, float level is nonadjustable and float must be renewed if float level is incorrect.

AIR FILTER. Engine may be equipped with either a foam type (Fig. KW7) or a paper (dry) type (Fig. KW8) air cleaner. Refer to appropriate paragraph for model being serviced.

Foam Type Air Cleaner. Foam type air cleaner (Fig. KW7) should be removed and cleaned after every 25 hours of operation under normal operating

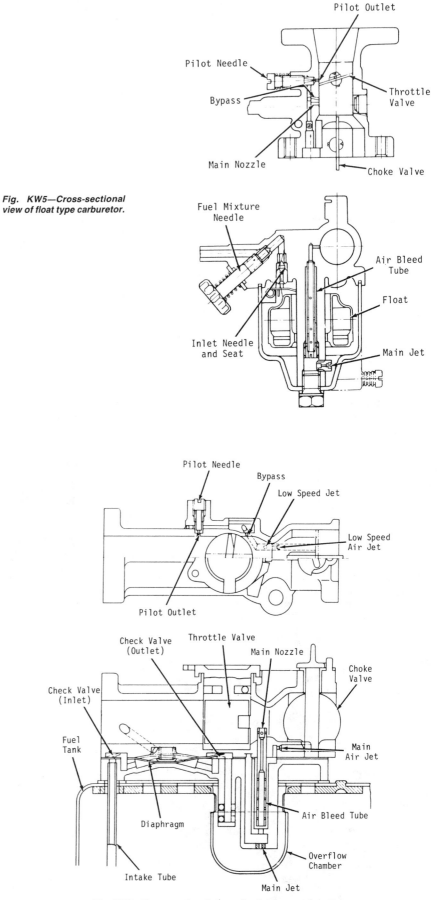

Fig. KW5—Cross-sectional view of float type carburetor.

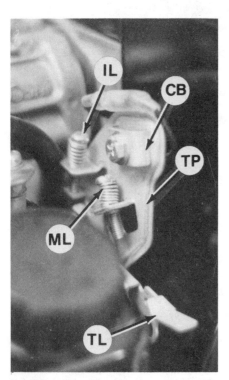

Fig. KW4—View of throttle plate assembly (TP) showing idle limit screw (IL) and maximum speed limit screw (ML). Throttle lever (TL) and remote throttle cable clamp (CB) are also shown.

Fig. KW6—Cross-sectional view of pulse type carburetor.

conditions. Remove foam element and clean in a suitable nonflammable solvent. Carefully squeeze out solvent and allow element to air dry. Soak element in clean engine oil and squeeze out the excess. Reinstall element making certain filament (hair like protrusions) side is toward cover (Fig. KW7).

Paper (Dry) Type Air Cleaner. Paper type air cleaner (Fig. KW8) should be removed and cleaned after every 100 hours of operation under normal operating conditions. Remove foam and paper element, separate foam precleaner from paper element, wash element and foam precleaner in water and detergent and rinse in clean water. Allow to air dry. Soak foam precleaner in clean engine oil and carefully squeeze out excess oil. Slide precleaner over paper element and reinstall elements in air cleaner case.

GOVERNOR. A gear driven flyweight governor assembly is located inside engine crankcase on crankcase cover. To adjust external linkage, place engine throttle control in idle position. Make certain all linkage is in good condition and tension spring (4—Fig. KW9) is not stretched. Spring (2—Fig. KW10) around governor-to-carburetor rod must pull governor lever (3) and throttle pivot (4) toward each other. Loosen clamp bolt (5—Fig. KW9) and rotate governor shaft (6) clockwise as far as possible. Hold shaft in this position and pull governor lever (3) as far right as possible. Tighten clamp bolt (5). Install tension spring (4) in correct hole for speed desired.

IGNITION SYSTEM. Ignition coil (1—Fig. KW11) is located just above flywheel and breaker point set and condenser are located behind flywheel. Ignition timing should be set at 23 degrees BTDC in the following manner. Remove flywheel and then reinstall it loosely on crankshaft. Rotate flywheel until edge of coil laminations are aligned with edge of notch in flywheel as shown in Fig. KW12. Remove flywheel making certain crankshaft does not turn. Slowly move breaker-point plate assembly until points just begin to open. Tighten breaker-point plate screw. Turn crankshaft clockwise until point gap is at widest open position and adjust gap to 0.3-0.5 mm (0.012-0.020 in.). Place a small amount of point cam lube on lubricating felt (4—Fig. KW11) and reinstall flywheel. Coil edge gap should be 0.05 mm (0.020 in.).

VALVE ADJUSTMENT. Valves and seats should be refaced and stem clearance adjusted after every 300 hours of operation. Refer to REPAIRS section for service procedure and specifications.

Fig. KW10—Spring (2) around governor-to-carburetor rod (1) must pull governor lever (3) toward throttle pivot (4).

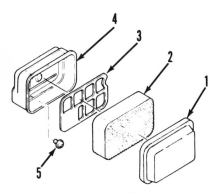

Fig. KW7—Exploded view of foam type air cleaner. Element (2) is installed with filament (hair like protrusions) away from carburetor.

1. Cover
2. Element
3. Plate
4. Element case
5. Screw

Fig. KW9—View of external governor linkage. Refer to text for adjustment procedure.

1. Governor-to-carburetor rod
2. Spring
3. Governor lever
4. Tension spring
5. Clamp bolt & nut
6. Governor shaft

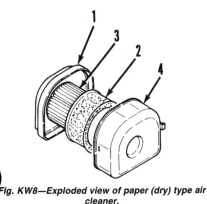

Fig. KW8—Exploded view of paper (dry) type air cleaner.

1. Cover
2. Precleaner (foam)
3. Paper element (filter)
4. Element case

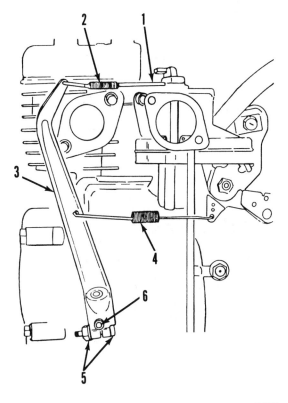

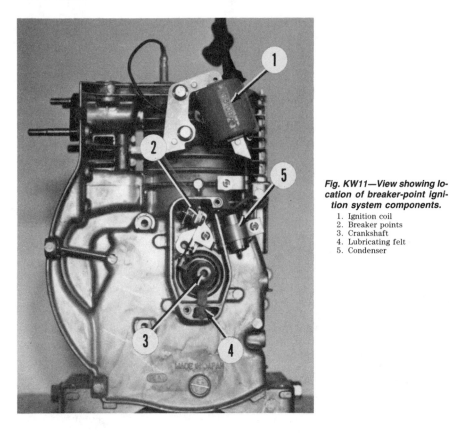

Fig. KW11—View showing location of breaker-point ignition system components.

1. Ignition coil
2. Breaker points
3. Crankshaft
4. Lubricating felt
5. Condenser

GENERAL MAINTENANCE. Check and tighten all loose bolts, nuts or clamps prior to each day of operation. Check for fuel or oil leakage and repair if necessary.

Clean dirt, dust, grease or any foreign material from cylinder head and cylinder block cooling fins after every 100 hours of operation. Inspect fins for damage and repair if necessary.

REPAIRS

TIGHTENING TORQUES. Recommended tightening torques are as follows:

Spark plug . . . . .16 N·m
(12 ft.-lbs.)
Head bolts . . . . .19 N·m
(14 ft.-lbs.)
Connecting rod bolts . . . . .11 N·m
(8 ft.-lbs.)
Crankcase cover bolts . . . . .5 N·m
(4 ft.-lbs.)
Flywheel nut . . . . .60 N·m
(44 ft.-lbs.)
Drain plug . . . . .13 N·m
(10 ft.-lbs.)

CYLINDER HEAD. To remove cylinder head, first remove cylinder head shroud. Clean engine to prevent entrance of foreign material. Loosen cylinder bolts in ¼ turn increments in sequence shown in Fig. KW14 until all bolts are loose enough to remove by hand.

Remove spark plug and clean carbon and other deposits from cylinder head. Place cylinder head on a flat surface and check entire sealing surface for warpage. If warpage exceeds 0.25 mm (0.010 in.), cylinder head must be renewed. Slight warpage may be repaired by lapping cylinder head. In a figure eight pattern, lap head against 200 grit

CYLINDER HEAD AND COMBUSTION CHAMBER. Cylinder head, combustion chamber and piston should be cleaned and carbon and other deposits removed after every 300 hours of operation. Refer to REPAIRS section for service procedure.

LUBRICATION. All models are splash lubricated. Engine oil level should be checked prior to each operation interval. Oil level should be maintained between reference marks on gage with oil fill plug just touching first threads. Do not screw oil fill plug in to check oil level (Fig. KW13).

Manufacturer recommends oil with an API service classification SC, SD or SE. Use SAE 20 oil in winter and SAE 30 oil in summer.

Oil should be changed after the first 20 hours of operation and every 100 hours of operation thereafter. Crankcase capacity is 500 cc (1.06 pt.).

Align Coil and Flywheel Edge

Fig. KW12—Align edge of flywheel notch with coil core laminations as shown to adjust timing. Refer to text.

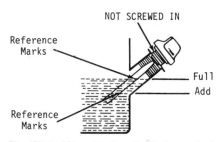

Fig. KW13—View showing oil fill plug and oil gage. Plug is not screwed in, but is just touching threads when checking oil level.

Fig. KW14—Loosen or tighten cylinder head bolts using the sequence shown.

and then 400 grit emery paper on a flat surface.

Reinstall cylinder head and tighten bolts evenly to specified torque in sequence shown in Fig. KW14.

CONNECTING ROD. Connecting rod rides directly on crankshaft journal. Piston and connecting rod are removed as an assembly after cylinder head and crankcase cover have been removed. Bend lock plate up to release connecting rod bolts and remove the two bolts, lockplate, oil dipper and connecting rod cap. Rotate crankshaft so piston can be pushed out of cylinder and remove piston and rod assembly. Carefully remove piston rings (1 and 2—Fig. KW15). Remove the two wire retaining rings (4) and push pin (5) out to separate piston (3) from connecting rod (6).

Inspect connecting rod and renew if piston pin bore or crankpin bearing bore are scored or damaged. If clearance between piston and connecting rod piston pin bore exceeds 0.05 mm (0.002 in.), renew connecting rod.

If clearance between crankpin journal and connecting rod bearing bore exceeds 0.10 mm (0.004 in.), renew connecting rod and/or crankshaft. Correct connecting rod side play on crankpin is 0.70 mm (0.028 in.).

Install piston on connecting rod so the side of connecting rod which is marked "MADE IN JAPAN" (Fig. KW16) is toward "M" stamped on piston pin boss (Fig. KW17). Secure piston pin with wire retaining rings. Install piston and connecting rod assembly so side of connecting rod marked "MADE IN JAPAN" is toward flywheel side of engine. Lubricate crankpin journal and install connecting rod cap and oil dipper as shown in Fig. KW18. Install new lockplate and bolts. Tighten bolts to specified torque and lock by bending lockplate.

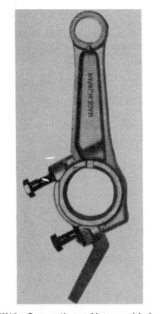

Fig. KW16—Connecting rod is assembled on piston so the side marked "MADE IN JAPAN" is toward "M" stamped on piston pin boss (Fig. KW17).

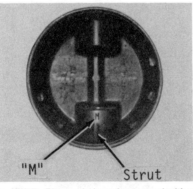

Fig. KW17—Piston pin boss is stamped with an "M". Note "M" is on boss with the strengthening strut.

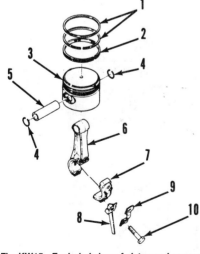

Fig. KW15—Exploded view of piston and connecting rod assembly.

1. Compression rings
2. Oil control ring
3. Piston
4. Retaining rings
5. Pin
6. Connecting rod
7. Connecting rod cap
8. Oil dipper
9. Lockplate
10. Bolts (2)

PISTON, PIN AND RINGS. Piston and connecting rod are removed as an assembly. Refer to CONNECTING ROD section for removal and installation procedure.

After carefully removing piston rings and separating piston and connecting rod, carefully clean carbon and other deposits from piston surface and ring lands.

CAUTION: Extreme care should be exercised when cleaning ring lands. Do not damage squared edges or widen ring grooves. If ring lands are damaged, piston must be renewed.

Before installing rings on piston, install piston in cylinder and use a suitable feeler gage to measure clearance between piston and cylinder bore. If clearance exceeds 0.25 mm (0.010 in.), renew piston and/or renew cylinder bore.

If ring side clearance between new ring and piston groove exceeds 0.15 mm (0.006 in.), renew piston. If ring end gap on new rings exceeds 0.10 mm (0.004 in.) when installed, renew cylinder. If clearance between piston pin and piston pin bore exceeds 0.05 mm (0.002 in.), renew piston.

Refer to CONNECTING ROD section to properly assemble piston to rod. Piston is marked "M" on piston pin boss (Fig. KW17) and on top of piston (Fig. KW19).

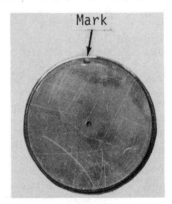

Fig. KW19—On some models, piston top has a mark which must be toward flywheel side of engine after installation.

Fig. KW18—Install connecting rod and piston assembly with oil dipper in position shown.

Mark on top of piston must be toward flywheel side of engine after piston installation.

CYLINDER AND CRANKCASE. Cylinder and crankcase are an integral casting. Standard cylinder bore diameter is 62 mm (2.44 in.). If cylinder bore diameter exceeds standard diameter by 0.07 mm (0.003 in.), renew cylinder and crankcase assembly.

Because of the high silicone content of the die-cast aluminum block, special honing procedures, stones and conditioning compounds are required to hone engine cylinder. Procedures outlined and material prescribed are recommended to produce a cylinder bore finish comparable to the factory finish.

The following procedures outlined are designed to remove 0.258 mm (0.0102 in.) total material from cylinder bore diameter upon completion. Use 38.1 mm (1-1/2 in.) strokes throughout the honing process. Honing time should be varied to remove only the amount of material specified to obtain desired bore size.

The cylinder bore is silicone impregnated. Refacing a cylinder bore removes the thin silicone contact surface and exposes both aluminum and silicone particles. If the aluminum particles are not removed, damage to the cylinder and piston may result. To erode the aluminum particles so only a silicone surface is present in bore, the last honing procedure must be performed exactly as outlined.

Use a Sunnen JN-95 hone with a spindle speed of approximately 150 rpm. Equip hone with four V24-J85-85xxx stones and hone cylinder until 0.229 mm (0.009 in.) of material is removed. Hone should remove specified amount of material in 1-1/2 minutes.

Equip hone with four V24-J85-85xxx stones and hone cylinder until 0.025 mm (0.001 in.) of material is removed. Hone should remove specified amount of material in 20 seconds.

Alter V24-J85-85xxx felt set as shown in Fig. KW20. Saturate altered felt set with MB-30 honing oil. Mix AN-30 conditioning compounds thoroughly and coat felts and entire cylinder wall surface with compound. Equip hone with

altered felt set and insert hone into cylinder. Tighten wing nut fingertight. Hone cylinder, periodically tightening feed pinion, until 0.004 mm (0.0002 in.) of material is removed. Hone should remove specified amount of material in approximately 1-1/2 minutes.

CAUTION: Do not use additional honing oil as it will wash away the AN-30 conditioning compound.

Thoroughly clean cylinder and block after honing procedure. Lightly oil and assemble engine.

If crankcase cover has been removed, refer to CRANKSHAFT, MAIN BEARINGS AND SEALS section for bearing, bushing and seal installation. Tighten crankcase cover bolts to specified torque in sequence shown in Fig. KW21.

CRANKSHAFT, MAIN BEARINGS AND SEALS. Crankshaft is supported in a ball bearing at crankcase cover (pto) end and in a bushing type main bearing which is pressed into crankcase at flywheel end.

To remove crankshaft, remove all metal shrouds, flywheel, cylinder head and crankcase cover. Remove connecting rod and piston assembly and remove crank-

Fig. KW21—Loosen or tighten crankcase cover bolts in sequence shown. Refer to text for torque specifications.

shaft and camshaft. Remove valve tappets.

Minimum crankpin diameter is 23.92 mm (0.942 in.). If dimension is not as specified, renew crankshaft.

Maximum clearance between bushing type main bearing and crankshaft journal is 0.13 mm (0.005 in.). When renewing bushing type main bearing, make sure oil hole in bushing is aligned with oil hole in crankcase. Press bushing in 1 mm (0.039 in.) below inside edge of bushing bore. See Fig. KW22.

Ball bearing type main bearing is a light press fit on crankshaft and maximum bearing play is 0.30 mm (0.001 in.). It may be necessary to slightly heat crankcase cover to remove or install ball bearing.

Crankcase cover oil seal should be pressed into seal bore until seal is 4 mm (0.158 in.) below outer edge of seal bore. Crankcase crankshaft seal should be pressed into seal bore until flush with outer edge of seal bore.

To reinstall crankshaft, reverse removal procedure making sure crankshaft and camshaft gear timing marks are aligned during installation. Refer to Fig. KW23.

CAMSHAFT AND BEARINGS. Camshaft is supported at each end in bushing type bearings which are an integral part of crankcase and crankcase cover. To remove camshaft, refer to CRANKSHAFT, MAIN BEARINGS AND SEALS section.

Maximum clearance between camshaft and bushing type bearings is 0.10 mm (0.004 in.). If clearance exceeds specifications, renew camshaft and/or crankcase cover or crankcase.

Make certain camshaft lobes are smooth and free of scoring, scratches

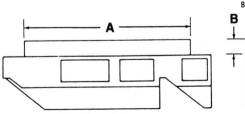

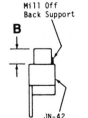

Fig. KW20—Felt strips must be altered as shown. Dimension A is 76.251 mm (3.0 in.). Dimension B is 5.207 mm (0.205 in.).

Fig. KW22—View of crankcase bushing. Oil holes must be aligned during installation. Refer to text.

and other damage. Make certain cam-shaft and crankshaft gear timing marks are aligned during installation. Refer to Fig. KW23.

GOVERNOR. The internal centrifugal flyweight governor is gear driven off of the camshaft gear. Refer to GOVERNOR paragraph in MAINTENANCE section for external governor adjustments.

To remove governor assembly, remove external linkage, metal cooling shrouds and crankcase cover. Governor gear and flyweights are attached to crankcase cover. Remove governor sleeve (S—Fig. KW24), gear (G) and flyweight assembly only if renewal is necessary. Use a screwdriver to press lock tabs (LT) in to remove sleeve. Flyweights are pinned to gear. Remove thrust washer located between gear and crankcase cover.

Reverse removal procedure for rein-stallation. Adjust external linkage as outlined in MAINTENANCE section.

VALVE SYSTEM. Clearance between valve stem and valve tappet (cold) should be 0.12-0.18 mm (0.005-0.007 in.) for intake valve and 0.10-0.34 mm (0.004-0.013 in.) for exhaust valve. If

clearance is not as specified, valves must be removed and end of stems ground off to increase clearance or seats ground deeper to reduce clearance.

Valve seats are ground directly into crankcase casting and valve face and seat angles are 45 degrees. Correct valve

seat width is 1.0-1.6 mm (0.039-0.063 in.).

Fig. KW23—Align crankshaft and camshaft gear timing marks as shown during assembly.

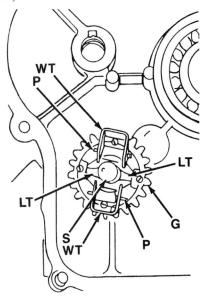

Fig. KW24—View of governor assembly. Lock tabs (LT) must be pressed in to remove sleeve and governor assembly. Renew sleeve prior to reassembly to ensure lock tabs will retain sleeve and governor assembly.

G. Gear
P. Pins
S. Sleeve

LT. Lock tabs
WT. Flyweights

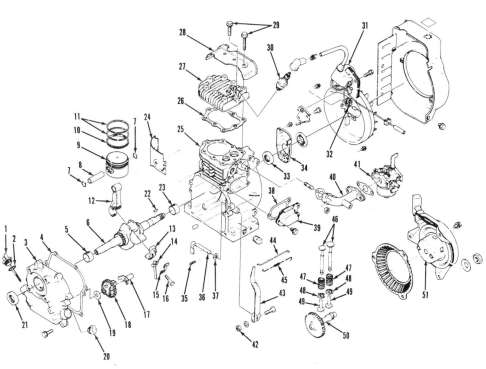

Fig. KW25—Exploded view typical of Model FA130 engine.

1. Oil plug & gage
2. "O" ring
3. Crankcase cover
4. Gasket
5. Main bearing
6. Crankshaft
7. Retaining ring
8. Piston pin
9. Piston
10. Oil control ring
11. Compression rings
12. Compression rod
13. Connecting rod cap
14. Oil plate
15. Lockplate
16. Connecting rod bolts
17. Governor sleeve
18. Governor gear & weight assy.
19. Thrust washer
20. Oil fill plug
21. Crankcase cover seal
22. Crankshaft key
23. Ball bearing
24. Cooling shroud
25. Cylinder block (crankcase)
26. Gasket
27. Cylinder head
28. Cooling shroud
29. Cylinder head cap screws
30. Spark plug
31. Ignition coil
32. Points & condenser
33. Seal
34. Point & condenser cover
35. Retaining clip
36. Governor crank
37. Washer
38. Gasket
39. Valve chamber cover
40. Manifold
41. Carburetor
42. Clamp bolt nut
43. Governor lever
44. Governor-to-carburetor rod
45. Spring
46. Valves
47. Valve springs
48. Valve spring retainers
49. Valve lifters
50. Camshaft & gear assy.
51. Rewind starter assy.

KOHLER

KOHLER COMPANY
444 Highland Drive
Kohler, WI 53044

HP	Crankshaft	Basic Model (Series)	Bore	Stroke	Displacement
4 (2.98 kW)	Horizontal	K91	2⅜-in. (60.3 mm)	2 in. (50.8 mm)	8.86 in. (145 cc)

MAINTENANCE

SPARK PLUG. Recommended plug is Champion J-8, AC-C45, Autolite A7 or Prestolite 14-7. Electrode gap is 0.025-inch (0.64 mm).

CARBURETOR. Engines are equipped with the Kohler carburetor shown in Fig. KO2.

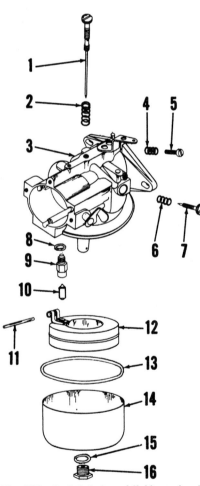

Fig. KO2 — Exploded view of Kohler carburetor used on late production engines.

1. Main fuel needle
2. Spring
3. Carburetor body assy.
4. Spring
5. Idle speed stop screw
6. Spring
7. Idle fuel needle
8. Sealing washer
9. Inlet valve seat
10. Inlet valve
11. Float pin
12. Float
13. Gasket
14. Float bowl
15. Sealing washer
16. Bowl retainer

For initial adjustment, open idle fuel needle 1½ turns and open main fuel needle 2 turns. Make final adjustment with engine warm and running. Place engine under load and adjust main fuel needle for leanest setting that will allow satisfactory acceleration and steady governor operation. Adjust idle speed stop screw to maintain an idle speed of 1000 rpm, then adjust idle needle for smoothest idle operation. As adjustments affect each other, the adjustment sequence may have to be repeated.

To check float level, invert carburetor casting and float assembly. There should be 13/64-inch (5.2 mm) between free side of float and machined surface of body casting. If not, carefully bend float lever tang that contacts inlet valve as necessary to provide correct measurement.

GOVERNOR. A mechanical flyball type governor with external adjustments is used. The governor flyball unit is attached to and rotates with the camshaft gear. Refer to Fig. KO4 for exploded view of governor flyball unit. Engine speed is controlled by tension on governor spring (B–Fig. KO5).

NOTE: Maximum (no load) engine speed is 4000 rpm.

Before attempting to adjust governed speed, synchronize linkage as follows: Loosen clamp bolt nut (N) and using a pair of pliers, turn shaft (H) counterclockwise as far as possible. Pull arm (L) completely to the left (away

Fig. KO4 — Exploded view of camshaft and flyball governor assembly.

1. Snap ring
2. Thrust cone
3. Steel balls
4. Flyball retainer
5. Camshaft
6. Camshaft pin

from carburetor) and tighten clamp bolt nut. To increase or decrease maximum engine speed, vary tension of governor spring (B). On engine with remote throttle control, this is accomplished by moving bracket (F) up or down; on engines without remote throttle control, by rotating disc (D) after loosening bushing (C).

MAGNETO AND TIMING. Bendix Scintilla K1-300 or Phelon Model F2100 (now called Repco) is used. Recommended spark timing is 20 degrees BTDC.

A timing port is provided in left side of bearing plate and there are two timing marks on the flywheel. (See Fig. KO6.) Satisfactory timing is obtained by adjusting breaker contact gap to 0.020 inch (0.51 mm). For precision timing, use timing light and adjust breaker gap until the first or "SP" timing mark is centered in timing port, engine running. On Bendix-Scintilla (Fig. KO7) equipped engines, a wave washer is installed on crankshaft between magneto rotor and flywheel; on Phelon (Fig. KO6) equipped engines, the wave washer is omitted.

LUBRICATION. Crankcase capacity is approximately 1½ pints. Use SAE 30 oil when operating in temperatures above 30°F (−1°C), SAE 10W-30 in temperatures between 0°F (−18°C) and 30°F (−1°C) and SAE 5W-20 in

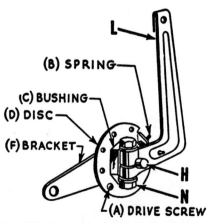

Fig. KO5 — Points of adjustment of governor.

temperatures below 0°F (−18°C). Use high quality motor oil having API classification SE or SF. An oil dipper which is attached to the connecting rod cap provides for splash type lubrication. On engines with reduction gear power take-off, use same grade oil in reduction gear housing as used in crankcase.

CRANKCASE BREATHER. The crankcase breather, which serves to eliminate oil leaks at crankcase seals, is attached to valve cover plate. There should be 1/64-1/32 inch (0.4-0.8 mm) clearance between flapper valve and its seat. If a slight amount of crankcase vacuum is not present, breather valve is faulty or engine has excessive blow-by past rings and/or valves.

AIR CLEANER. Engines may be equipped with either an oil bath type air cleaner shown in Fig. KO8 or a dry element type shown in Fig. KO9.

Oil bath air cleaner should be serviced every 25 hours of operation or more often if operating in extremely dusty conditions. To service the oil bath type, remove complete cleaner assembly from engine. Remove cover and element from

Fig. KO8 — View of oil bath type air cleaner.

FILL TO LEVEL MARK
WITH SAME OIL AS ENGINE

bowl. Empty used oil from bowl, then clean cover and bowl in solvent. Clean element in solvent and allow to drip dry. Lightly re-oil element. Fill bowl to oil level marked on bowl using same grade and weight oil as used in engine crankcase. Renew gaskets as necessary when reassembling and reinstalling unit.

Dry element type air cleaner should be cleaned every 100 hours of operation or more frequently if operating in dusty conditions. Remove dry element and tap element lightly on a flat surface to remove surface dirt. Do not wash ele-

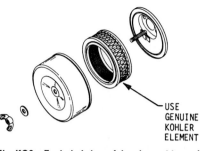

USE GENUINE KOHLER ELEMENT

Fig. KO9 — Exploded view of dry element type air cleaner.

ment or attempt to clean element with compressed air. Renew element if extremely dirty or if it is bent, crushed or otherwise damaged. Make certain the sealing surfaces of element seal effectively against the back plate and cover.

REPAIRS

TIGHTENING TORQUES. Specified tightening torques are as follows:

Spark plug . . . . .325 in.-lbs.
(36.70 N·m)
Connecting rod cap screws *140 in.-lbs.
(15.81 N·m)
Cylinder head cap screws . .200 in.-lbs.*
(22.58 N·m)
Flywheel retaining nut . . . . .540 in.-lbs.
(60.98 N·m)

*With threads lubricated.

CONNECTING ROD. Connecting rod assembly is removed from above after removing cylinder head and oil pan (engine base). The aluminum alloy connecting rod rides directly on the crankpin. A connecting rod with 0.010-inch (0.25 mm) undersize crankpin bore is available for reground crankshaft. Oversize piston pins are also available. Desired running clearances are as follows:

Connecting rod to
crankpin . . . . .0.001-0.0025 in.
(0.3-0.064 mm)
Connecting rod to
piston pin . . . . .0.0005-0.001 in.
(0.013-0.3 mm)
Connecting rod side
play on crankpin . . . . . .0.005-0.016 in.
(0.13-0.41 mm)

Fig. KO6 — Phelon (Repco)
magneto installation.
A. Magnets
B. Timing marks
C. Coil
D. Condenser

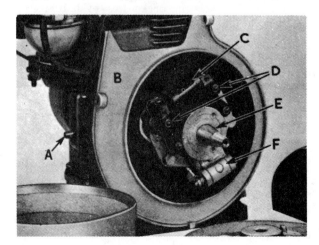

Fig. KO7 — Bendix-Scintilla
magneto installation. Rotating magnet (E) is pressed on crankshaft.
A. Ground button
B. Bearing plate
C. Magneto coil
D. Pole shoes
E. Rotating magnet
F. Condenser

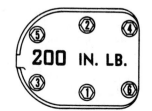

200 IN. LB.

Fig. KO10 — Tighten cylinder head cap screws to a torque of 200 in.-lbs. in sequence shown.

Standard crankpin diameter is 0.9355-0.936 inch (23.762-23.77 mm). Standard piston pin diameter is 0.563-inch (14.27 mm).

When reinstalling connecting rod and piston assembly, piston can be installed either way on rod, but make certain the match marks on connecting rod and cap are aligned and are towards flywheel side of engine. Tighten connecting rod cap screws to a torque of 140 in.-lbs. (15.81 N·m) (with threads lubricated).

PISTON, PIN AND RINGS. The aluminum alloy piston is fitted with two 0.093-inch (2.34 mm) wide compression rings and one 0.187-inch (4.75 mm) wide oil control ring. Renew piston if scored or if side clearance of new ring in piston top groove exceeds 0.005-inch (0.13 mm). Pistons and rings are available in oversizes of 0.010-inch (0.25 mm), 0.020-inch (0.51 mm) and 0.030-inch (0.76 mm) as well as standard. Piston pin fit in piston bore should be from 0.0002-inch (0.005 mm) interference to 0.0002-inch (0.005 mm) loose. Piston pins are available in oversizes of 0.005-inch (0.13 mm) and 0.010-inch (0.25 mm). Always renew piston pin retaining rings.

Recommended piston-to-cylinder bore clearance (measured at thrust face of piston) is 0.003-0.004 inch (0.08-0.10 mm).

Piston ring specifications are as follows:

Ring end gap . . . . 0.007-0.017 inch
(0.18-0.43 mm)

Ring side clearance:

Compression rings . . 0.003-0.004 inch
(0.08-0.10 mm)

Oil control ring . . . . 0.0015-0.0035 inch
(0.04-0.09 mm)

If compression ring has a groove or bevel on outside surface, install ring with groove or bevel down. If groove or bevel is on inside surface of compression ring, install ring or bevel up. Oil control ring can be installed either side up.

CYLINDER HEAD. Always use a new head gasket when installing cylinder head. Tighten cylinder head cap screws evenly and in steps using the sequence shown in Fig. KO10 until a tightening torque of 200 in.-lbs. (22.58 N·m) is reached.

CYLINDER BLOCK. If cylinder wall is scored or bore is tapered or out-of-round more than 0.005 inch (0.13 mm), hone cylinder to nearest suitable oversize of either 0.010-inch (0.25 mm), 0.020-inch (0.51 mm) or 0.030-inch (0.76 mm). Standard cylinder bore diameter is 2.375 inches (60.33 mm).

CAMSHAFT. The hollow camshaft

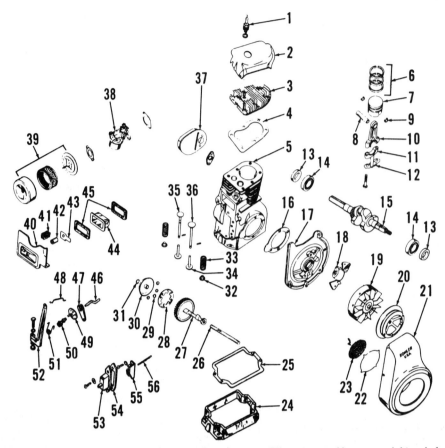

Fig. KO11 — Exploded view of typical engine. Breaker points (55) are actuated by cam on right end of camshaft (27) through push rod (56).

1. Spark plug	15. Crankshaft	29. Steel balls	43. Breather reed
2. Air baffle	16. Gasket	30. Thrust cone	44. Breather plate
3. Cylinder head	17. Bearing plate	31. Snap ring	45. Gaskets
4. Head gasket	18. Magneto	32. Spring retainer	46. Governor shaft
5. Cylinder block	19. Flywheel	33. Valve spring	47. Bracket
6. Piston rings	20. Pulley	34. Valve tappets	48. Link
7. Piston	21. Shroud	35. Exhaust valve	49. Speed disc
8. Piston pin	22. Screen retainer	36. Intake valve	50. Bushing
9. Retaining rings	23. Screen	37. Muffler	51. Governor spring
10. Connecting rod	24. Oil pan	38. Carburetor	52. Governor lever
11. Rod cap	25. Gasket	39. Air cleaner assy.	53. Breaker cover
12. Rod bolt lock	26. Camshaft pin	40. Valve cover	54. Gasket
13. Oil seal	27. Camshaft	41. Filter	55. Breaker points
14. Ball bearing	28. Flyball retainer	42. Breather seal	56. Push rod

and integral cam gear (27 – Fig. KO11) rotate on a pin (26). To remove camshaft, first remove bearing plate (17) and crankshaft, then drive pin out towards bearing plate side of crankcase. Camshaft pin is a press fit in closed (pto) side of crankcase and a slip fit in bearing plate side. Specified slip fit clearance of camshaft pin in bearing plate side is 0.0005-0.0012 inch (0.013-0.030 mm). Specified camshaft-to-camshaft pin clearance is 0.001-0.0025 inch (0.03-0.064 mm). Desired camshaft end play is 0.005-0.020 inch (0.13-0.51 mm) and is adjusted by installing shim washers between camshaft and bearing plate side of crankcase. Shim washers are available in thicknesses of 0.005-inch (0.13 mm) and 0.010-inch (0.25 mm). Flyball retainer (28), flyballs (29), thrust cone (30) and snap ring (31) are attached to and rotate with camshaft assembly.

CRANKSHAFT. The crankshaft is

supported in two ball bearing mains. Renew ball bearings (14 – Fig. KO11) if excessively loose or rough. Desired crankshaft end play of 0.0038-0.0228 inch (0.096-0.579 mm) is controlled by thickness of bearing plate gaskets (16). Gaskets in thicknesses of 0.010-inch (0.25 mm) and 0.020-inch (0.51 mm) are available.

Standard crankpin journal diameter is 0.9355-0.9360 inch (23.762-23.774 mm). Specified connecting rod to crankpin journal running clearance is 0.001-0.0025 inch (0.03-0.064 mm). Crankpin journal may be ground to 0.010-inch (0.25 mm) undersize for use of undersize connecting rod if journal is scored or out-of-round.

When installing crankshaft, align timing marks on crankshaft gear and camshaft gear. Install seals (13) in crankcase and bearing plate after crankshaft and bearing plate are installed. Carefully work seals over crankshaft with lips to inside and drive seals into place with hollow driver that contacts outer edge of seals.

VALVE SYSTEM. Valve tappet gap (cold) is 0.005-0.009 inch (0.13-0.23 mm) for intake valve and 0.011-0.015 inch (0.28-0.38 mm) for exhaust valve. Correct tappet gap is obtained by grinding end of valve stems squarely. Be sure to remove all burrs from end of stem after grinding.

The exhaust valve seats on a renewable seat insert and intake valve seats directly on machined seat in cylinder block. Intake and exhaust valve seats are available for service. Valve face and seat angle is 45 degrees. Desired seat width is 0.037-0.045 inch (0.94-1.14 mm).

Specified valve stem clearance in guide is 0.0005-0.002 inch (0.013-0.05 mm) for intake valve and 0.002-0.0035 inch (0.01-0.089 mm) for exhaust valve. Valve guides are not renewable. Excessive valve stem-to-guide clearance is corrected by reaming guides and installing new valves with 0.005-inch (0.13 mm) oversize stems. Standard valve stem diameter is 0.248-0.2485 inch (6.30-6.312 mm) for intake valve and 0.246-0.2465 inch (6.25-6.261 mm) for exhaust valve.

KOHLER

HP	Crankshaft	Basic Model (Series)	Bore	Stroke	Displacement
6.25 (4.66 kW)	Horizontal	K-141	2.94 in. (74.7 mm)	2.50 in. (63.5 mm)	16.9 cu. in. (276.9 cc)
7 (5.22 kW)	Horizontal	K-161	2.94 in. (74.7 mm)	2.50 in. (63.5 mm)	16.9 cu. in. (276.9 cc)
8 (5.97 kW)	Horizontal	K-181	2.94 in. (74.7 mm)	2.75 in. (69.8 mm)	18.6 cu. in. (304.8 cc)
10 (7.46 kW)	Horizontal	K-241	3.25 in. (82.5 mm)	2.88 in. (73 mm)	23.9 cu. in. (391.6 cc)

Model K-141 engine has a ball bearing main at pto end of crankshaft, a bushing type main bearing at flywheel end of crankshaft and is equipped with an up- draft carburetor. All other engines of this series have ball bearing mains at each end of crankshaft and are equipped with a side draft carburetor.

All models are horizontal crankshaft engines and are splash lubricated.

MAINTENANCE

SPARK PLUG. Recommended plug for Model K-241 engine is Champion H-10; all other standard engines in series use a Champion J-8 spark plug. For renewal of radio shielded spark plugs, use Champion EH-10 in Model K-241 engine and Champion EJ-8 in other models. Set electrode gap to 0.020 inch (0.51 mm) on radio shielded plug and to 0.025 inch (0.635 mm) on stan- dard plug.

CARBURETOR. Model K-141 engines are equipped with a Tillotson "E" series updraft carburetor. Models K-161, K-181 and K-241 engines are equipped with Kohler side draft car- buretors. Refer to appropriate following paragraph for carburetor service infor- mation.

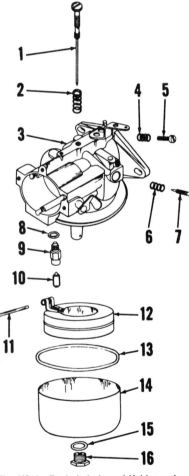

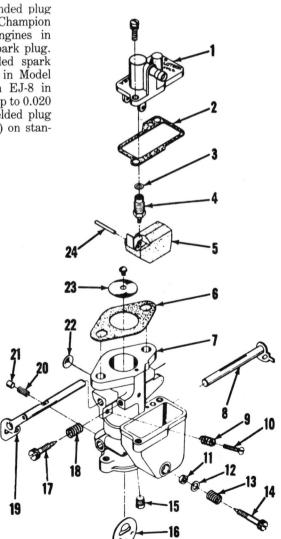

Fig. KO13—Exploded view of Tillotson "E" series car- buretor used on Model K-141 engine. Refer to Fig. KO14 for method checking float level.

1. Float bowl cover
2. Gasket
3. Gasket
4. Inlet valve assy.
5. Float
6. Gasket
7. Carburetor body
8. Choke shaft
9. Spring
10. Idle speed stop screw
11. Packing
12. Washer
13. Spring
14. Main fuel needle
15. Screw plug
16. Choke disc
17. Idle fuel needle
18. Spring
19. Throttle shaft
20. Spring
21. Choke shaft detent
22. Plug
23. Throttle disc
24. Float pin

Fig. KO12—Exploded view of Kohler carburetor used on Models K-161, K-181 and K-241.

1. Main fuel needle
2. Spring
3. Carburetor body assy.
4. Spring
5. Idle speed stop screw
6. Spring
7. Idle fuel needle
8. Sealing washer
9. Inlet valve seat
10. Inlet valve
11. Float pin
12. Float
13. Gasket
14. Float bowl
15. Sealing washer
16. Bowl retainer

KOHLER CARBURETOR. Refer to Fig. KO12 for exploded view of Kohler carburetor. For initial adjustment, open main fuel needle 2 turns and open idle fuel needle 1¼ turns. Make final adjustment with engine warm and running. Place engine under load and adjust main fuel needle (1) to the leanest mixture that will allow satisfactory acceleration and steady governor operation. If engine misses and backfires under load,

mixture is too lean. If engine shows a sooty exhaust and is sluggish under load, mixture is too rich.

Adjust idle speed stop screw (5) to maintain an idle speed of 1000 rpm.

Then, adjust idle fuel needle (7) for smoothest idle operation.

Since main fuel and idle fuel adjustments have some effect on each other, recheck engine operation and readjust fuel needles as necessary for smoothest operation.

To check float level, invert carburetor body and float assembly. There should be 11/64-inch (4.4 mm) clearance between machined surface of body casting and free end of float. Adjust as necessary by bending float lever tang that contacts inlet valve.

TILLOTSON CARBURETOR. Refer to Fig. KO13 for exploded view of Tillotson E series carburetor similar to that used on Model K-141 engine. The design of choke shaft lever will differ from that shown in the exploded view.

For initial adjustment, open the idle fuel needle (17) about ¾-turn and open main fuel needle (14) one turn. Make final adjustment with engine running at operating temperature. Adjust main fuel needle so that engine will accelerate smoothly without misfiring or smoky exhaust. Then, adjust idle fuel needle for smoothest idle performance. Recheck for smooth acceleration and readjust main fuel needle, if necessary.

Check float level as shown in Fig. KO14. If measurement is not 1 5/64 inches (27.4 mm) as shown, remove float and carefully bend float lever tang as necessary to provide correct level measurement.

AUTOMATIC CHOKE. Some models equipped with Kohler carburetors are also equipped with an automatic choke. The "Thermostatic" type shown in Fig. KO15 is used on manual start models.

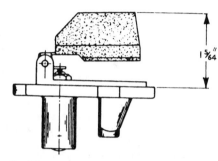

Fig. KO14—Check float setting on Tillotson carburetor by inverting float bowl cover and float assembly and measuring distance from free end of float to edge of cover as shown. Float setting is correct if distance is 1 5/64 inches (27.4 mm).

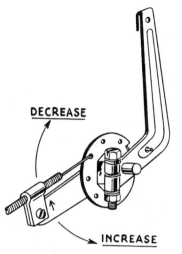

Fig. KO18—On Models K-141, K-161 and K-181, loosen bushing nut (C—Fig. KO17) and move throttle bracket as shown to change governed speed of engine.

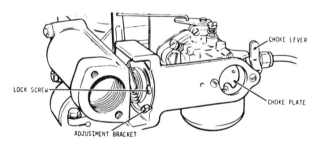

Fig. KO15—View showing "Thermostatic" automatic choke used on some engines equipped with Kohler carburetors.

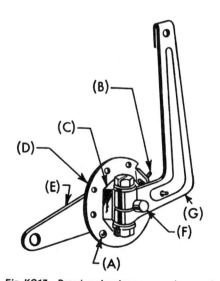

Fig. KO17—Drawing showing governor lever and related parts on Models K-141, K-161 and K-181.

A. Drive pin
B. Governor spring
C. Bushing nut
D. Speed control disc
E. Throttle bracket
F. Governor shaft
G. Governor lever

Fig. KO20—View showing governor adjusting points on K-241. Governor sensitivity is adjusted by moving governor spring to alternate holes.

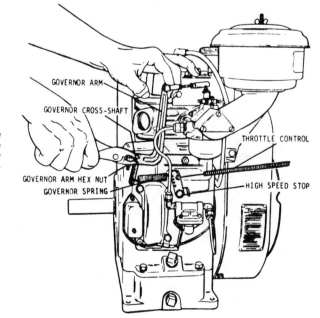

THERMOSTATIC TYPE. To adjust the "Thermostatic" type, loosen lock screw (Fig. KO15) and rotate adjustment bracket as necessary to obtain correct amount of choking. Tighten lock screw. In cold temperature, choke should be closed. At a temperature of 70°-75° F (21°-24° C), choke should be partially open and choke lever should be in vertical position. Start engine and allow it to run until normal operating temperature is obtained. Choke should be fully open when engine is at normal operating temperature.

GOVERNOR. All models are equipped with a gear driven flyweight governor that is located inside engine crankcase. Maximum recommended governed engine speed is 3600 rpm on all engines. Recommended idle speed of 1000 rpm is controlled by adjustment of throttle stop screw on carburetor.

Before attempting to adjust engine governed speed, synchronize the governor linkage on all models as follows: On Models K-141, K-161 and K-181, loosen the bolt clamping governor arm (G – Fig. KO17) to governor cross shaft (F) and turn governor cross shaft counterclockwise as far as possible. While holding cross shaft in this position, move governor arm away from carburetor to limit of linkage travel and tighten clamping bolt.

On Model K-241 refer to Fig. KO20 and loosen governor arm hex nut. Rotate governor cross shaft counterclockwise as far as possible, move governor arm away from carburetor to limit of linkage travel, then tighten hex nut on arm.

To adjust the maximum governed speed on Model K-241, adjust position of stop so that speed control lever contacts stop at desired engine speed. On Models K-141, K-161 and K-181, loosen governor shaft bushing nut (C – Fig. KO17) and move throttle bracket (E) to increase or decrease governed speed. See Fig. KO18 for direction of movement.

On Model K-241, governor sensitivity is adjusted by moving governor spring to alternate holes in governor arm and speed lever.

Governor unit is accessible after removing engine crankshaft and camshaft. The governor gear and flyweight assembly turns on a stub shaft pressed into engine crankcase. Renew gear and weight assembly if gear teeth or any part of assembly is excessively worn. Desired clearance of governor gear to stud shaft is 0.0025-0.0055 inch (0.064-0.140 mm) for Models K-141, K-161 and K-181 and 0.0005-0.002 inch (0.013-0.05 mm) for Model K-241.

MAGNETO IGNITION. The breaker points are located externally on engine crankcase as shown in Fig. KO21. The breaker points are actuated by a cam through a push rod.

Models K-141, K-161, K-181 and K-241 engines are equipped with an automatic compression release (see CAMSHAFT paragraph) and do not have an automatic timing advance; ignition occurs at 20 degrees BTDC at all engine speeds.

Nominal breaker point gap on all models is 0.020 inch (0.51 mm); however, breaker point gap should be varied to obtain exact ignition timing as follows:

With a static timing light, disconnect coil and condenser leads from breaker point terminal and attach one timing light lead to terminal and ground the other lead. Remove button plug from timing sight hole and turn engine so that piston has just completed its compression stroke and the "DC" mark (models with automatic timing advance) or "SP" mark (models with automatic compression release) on flywheel appears in the sight hole. Loosen breaker point adjustment screw and adjust points to closed position (timing light will be on); then, slowly move breaker point base towards engine until timing light goes out. Tighten the adjustment screw and check

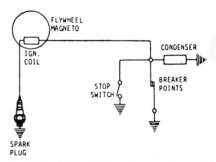

Fig. KO22 – Typical wiring diagram of magneto ignition system used on manual start engines.

point setting by turning engine in normal direction of rotation until timing light goes on. Then, continue to turn engine very slowly until timing light goes out. The "DC" mark (models with automatic time advance) or "SP" mark (models with automatic compression release) should now be in register with the sight hole. Disconnect timing light leads, connect leads from coil and condenser to breaker point terminal and install breaker cover.

If a power timing light is available, more accurate timing can be obtained by adjusting the points with engine running. Breaker point gap should be adjusted so that the light flash causes the "SP" timing mark (20 degrees BTDC) to appear in the sight hole. Engine should be running above 1500 rpm when checking breaker point setting with a power timing light on models with automatic timing advance.

A typical wiring diagram of a magneto ignition system is shown in Fig. KO22.

LUBRICATION. All models are splash lubricated. Maintain crankcase oil level at full mark on dipstick, but do not overfill. High quality detergent oil having API classification SE or SF is recommended.

Use SAE 30 oil in temperatures above 32° F (0° C), SAE 10W-30 oil in temperatures between 32° F (0° C) and 0° F (–18°C). Use SAE 5W-20 oil in subzero temperatures.

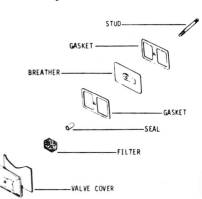

Fig. KO21 – Ignition breaker points are located externally on engine crankcase on all models equipped with magneto or battery ignition systems.

Fig. KO23 – Exploded view of crankcase breather assembly used on Models K-141, K-161 and K-181.

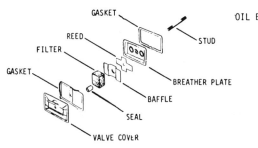

Fig. KO24—Exploded view of crankcase breather assembly used on Model K-241.

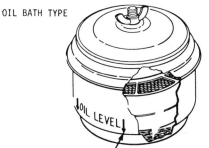

FILL TO LEVEL MARK
WITH SAME OIL AS ENGINE

Fig. KO25 — View of oil bath type air cleaner.

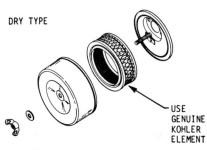

USE GENUINE KOHLER ELEMENT

Fig. KO26—Exploded view of dry element type air cleaner.

CRANKCASE BREATHER. Refer to Figs. KO23 and KO24. A reed valve assembly is located in the valve spring compartment to maintain a partial vacuum in the crankcase and thus reduce leakage of oil at bearing seals. If a slight amount of crankcase vacuum (5-10 inches water or ½-1 inch mercury) is not present, the reed valve is faulty or the engine has excessive blow-by past rings and/or valves or worn oil seals.

AIR CLEANER. Engines may be equipped with either an oil bath type air cleaner shown in Fig. KO25 or a dry element type shown in Fig. KO26.

Oil bath air cleaner should be serviced every 25 hours of operation or more often if operating in extremely dusty conditions. To service oil bath type, remove complete cleaner assembly from engine. Remove cover and element from bowl. Empty used oil from bowl, then clean cover and bowl in solvent. Clean element in solvent and allow to drip dry. Lightly re-oil element. Fill bowl to oil level marked on bowl using same grade and weight oil as used in engine crankcase. Renew gaskets as necessary when reassembling and reinstalling unit.

Dry element type air cleaner should be cleaned every 100 hours of operation or more frequently if operating in dusty conditions. Remove dry element and tap element lightly on a flat surface to remove surface dirt. Do not wash element or attempt to clean element with compressed air. Renew element if extremely dirty or if it is bent, crushed or otherwise damaged. Make certain the sealing surfaces of element seal effectively against back plate and cover.

REPAIRS

TIGHTENING TORQUES. Recommended tightening torques are as follows:

Spark plug . . . . 22 ft.-lbs.
(29.81 N·m)

Connecting rod cap screws,
K-141, K-161 and
K-181 . . . . 200 in.-lbs.*
(22.58 N·m)
K-241 . . . . 300 in.-lbs.*
(33.88 N·m)
Cylinder head cap screws,
K141-K-161 and
K-181 . . . . 240 in.-lbs.*
(27.10 N·m)
K-241 . . . . 360 in.-lbs.*
(40.65 N·m)
Flywheel retaining nut,
Models with ⅝-inch
nut . . . . 60 ft.-lbs.
(81.30 N·m)
Models with ¾-inch
nut . . . . 100 ft.-lbs.
(135.50 N·m)

*With threads lubricated.

CONNECTING ROD. Connecting rod and piston unit is removed after removing oil pan and cylinder head. The aluminum alloy connecting rod rides directly on the crankpin. Connecting rod with 0.010-inch (0.25 mm) undersize crankpin bore is available for reground crankshaft. Oversize piston pins are available on some models. Desired running clearances are as follows:
Connecting rod to crank-
pin . . . . 0.001-0.002 in.
(0.03-0.05 mm)
Connecting rod to piston pin,
K-141, K-161 &
K-181 . . . . 0.0006-0.0011 in.
(0.015-0.028 m)
K-241 . . . . 0-0003-0.008 in.
(0.008-0.020 mm)
Rod side play on crankpin,
K-141, K-161 and
K-181 . . . . 0.005-0.016 in.
(0.13-0.41 mm)
K-241 . . . . 0.007-0.016 mm
(0.18-0.041 mm)
Standard crankpin diameter is 1.1855-1.1860 inches (30.112-30.124 mm) on Models K-141, K-161 and K-181 and 1.4995-1.5000 (38.087-38.100 mm) on Model K-241.

When reinstalling connecting rod and piston assembly, piston can be installed either way on rod, but make certain the match marks (Fig. KO27) on rod and cap are aligned and are towards flywheel side of engine. Kohler recommends that connecting rod cap screws be tightened, then loosened and retightened to prevent the possibility of screws tightening in threads instead of tightening cap to rod. Tighten connecting rod cap screws to a torque of 200 in.-lbs. (22.58 N·m) on Models K-141, K-161 and K-181. On Model K-241, tighten cap screws to 300 in.-lbs. (33.86 N·m).

NOTE: Torque values for connecting rod cap screws are with lubricated threads.

PISTON, PIN AND RINGS. The aluminum alloy piston is fitted with two 0.093-inch (2.36 mm) wide compression rings and one 0.187-inch (4.75 mm) wide oil control ring. Renew piston if scored or if side clearance of new ring in piston top groove exceeds 0.006-inch (0.15 mm). Pistons and rings are available in oversizes of 0.010-inch (0.25 mm), 0.020-inch (0.51 mm) and 0.030-inch (0.76 mm) as well as standard size. Specified piston pin fit in piston bore is 0.0001-inch (0.003 mm) interference to

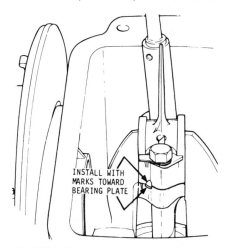

INSTALL WITH MARKS TOWARD BEARING PLATE

Fig. KO27—When installing connecting rod and piston unit, be sure that marks on rod and cap are aligned and are facing toward flywheel side of engine.

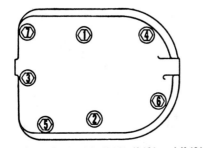

Fig. KO28—On Models K-141, K-161 and K-181 tighten cylinder head cap screws evenly, in sequence shown, to a torque of 240 in.lbs. (27.10 N·m).

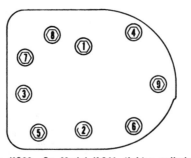

Fig. KO29—On Model K-241, tighten cylinder head cap screws evenly, in sequence shown, to a torque of 360 in.lbs. (40.65 N·m).

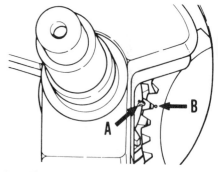

Fig. KO30—When installing crankshaft, make certain that timing mark (A) on crankshaft is aligned with timing mark (B) on camshaft gear.

0.0003-inch (0.008 mm) loose on Models K-141, K-161 and K-181. On Model K-241, specified clearance between piston pin and piston bore should be no more than 0.0002-0.0003 inch (0.005-0.008 mm). Standard piston pin diameter is 0.6248-inch (15.870 mm) on Models K-141, K-161 and K-181. On Model K-241, piston pin diameter is 0.8592-inch (21.824 mm).

Piston pins are available in oversize of 0.005-inch (0.13 mm) on some models. Always renew piston pin retaining rings.

Recommended piston-to-cylinder bore clearances are as follows:

K-141, K-161, and
   K-181 ....0.0045-0.007 in.*
           (0.114-0.18mm)
K-241 ....0.003-0.004 in.*
           (0.08-0.10 mm)
K-141, K-161 and
   K-181 ....0.006-0.008 in.**
           (0.15-0.20 mm)
K-241 ....0.0075-0.0085 in.**
           (0.191-0.216 mm)

*Measure at **bottom** of piston skirt on thrust side.
Measure just **below oil ring on thrust side.

Kohler recommends that rings be renewed whenever pistons are removed. Piston ring specifications are as follows:

Ring end gap—
  K-141, K-161 &
   K-181 ....0.007-0.017 in.
           (0.18-0.43 mm)
  K-241 ....0.010-0.020 in.
           (0.25-0.51 mm)
Ring side clearance (comp. rings)—
  K-141, K-161 &
   K-181 ....0.0025-0.004 in.
           (0.064-0.102 mm)
  K-241 ....0.002-0.004 in.
           (0.05-0.10 mm)
Ring side clearance (oil control ring)—
  K-141, K-161 &
   K-181 ....0.001-0.0025 in.
           (0.03-0.064 mm)
  K-241 ....0.001-0.003 in.
           (0.03-0.08 mm)

If compression ring has a groove or bevel on outside surface, install ring with groove or bevel down. If groove or bevel is on inside surface of compression ring, install ring with groove or bevel up. Oil control ring can be installed either side up.

CYLINDER BLOCK. Rebore cylinder to nearest suitable oversize of 0.010-inch (0.25 mm), 0.020-inch (0.51 mm) or 0.030-inch (0.76 mm) if bore is: (1) out-of-round more than 0.005-inch (0.13 mm); (2) cylinder wall is scored or bore is tapered more than 0.0025-inch (0.064 mm) on Models K-141, K-161 and K-181 or 0.0015-inch (0.038 mm) on Model K-241. Standard cylinder bore is 2.9375 inches (74.610 mm) on Models K-141, K-161 and K-181. On Model K-241, standard cylinder bore is 3.251 inches (82.58 mm).

CYLINDER HEAD. Always use a new head gasket when installing cylinder head. Tighten cylinder head cap screws evenly and in steps using correct sequence shown in Fig. KO28 or KO29.

CRANKSHAFT. Crankshaft on standard K-141 engine is supported by a ball bearing in crankcase at pto end of shaft and a bushing type bearing in bearing plate at flywheel end.

Crankshaft on all other models is supported in two ball bearings.

On Model K-141 engine with bushing type main bearing, renew crankshaft and/or bearing plate if crankshaft journal and bearing are excessively worn or scored. Recommended crankshaft journal-to-bushing running clearance is 0.001-0.0025 inch (0.03-0.064 mm).

On all models, renew ball bearing type main bearings if excessively loose or rough. Specified crankshaft end play is 0.003-0.020 inch (0.08-0.051 mm) on Model K-241 and 0.002-0.023 inch (0.05-0.58 mm) on other models. End play is controlled by thickness of bearing plate gaskets. Gaskets are available in thicknesses of 0.010-inch (0.25 mm) and 0.020-inch (0.51 mm). Install ball bearing mains with sealed side toward crankpin.

Crankpin journal may be reground to 0.010-inch (0.25 mm) undersize for use of undersize connecting rod if journal is scored or out-of-round. Standard crankpin diameter is 1.1855-1.1860 inches (30.112-30.124 mm) on Models K-141, K-161 and K-181. On Model K-241, standard crankpin diameter is 1.4995-1.500 inches (38.087-38.100 mm).

When installing crankshaft, align timing marks on crankshaft and camshaft gear as shown in Fig. KO30. On Model K-241 equipped with dynamic balancer, refer to DYNAMIC BALANCER para-

Fig. KO31—Views showing operation of camshaft with automatic compression release. In view 1, spring (C) has moved control lever (D) which moves cam lever (B) upward so that tang (T) is above exhaust cam lobe. This tang holds exhaust valve open slightly on a portion of the compression stroke to relieve compression while cranking engine. At engine speeds of 650 rpm or more, centrifugal force moves control lever (D) outward allowing tang (T) to move below lobe surface as shown in view 2.

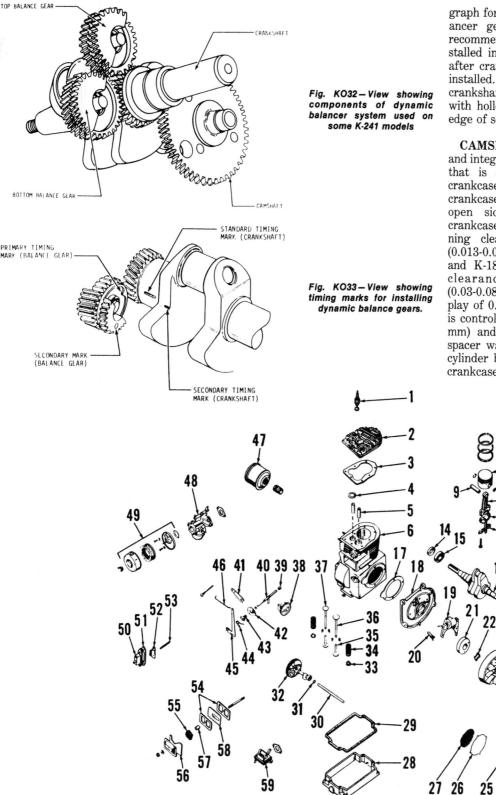

Fig. KO32—View showing components of dynamic balancer system used on some K-241 models

Fig. KO33—View showing timing marks for installing dynamic balance gears.

graph for installation and timing of balancer gears. On all models, Kohler recommends that crankshaft seals be installed in crankcase and bearing plate after crankshaft and bearing plate are installed. Carefully work oil seals over crankshaft and drive seals into place with hollow driver that contacts outer edge of seals.

CAMSHAFT. The hollow camshaft and integral camshaft gear turn on a pin that is slip fit in flywheel side of crankcase and a drive fit in closed side of crankcase. Remove and install pin from open side (bearing plate side) of crankcase. Desired camshaft to pin running clearance is 0.0005-0.003 inch (0.013-0.08 mm) on Models K-141, K-161 and K-181. On Model K-241, desired clearance is 0.001-0.0035 inch (0.03-0.089 mm). Desired camshaft end play of 0.005-0.010 inch (0.13-0.25 mm) is controlled by use of 0.005 inch (0.13 mm) and 0.010 inch (0.25 mm) thick spacer washers between camshaft and cylinder block at bearing plate side of crankcase.

Fig. KO34—Exploded view of Model K-181 basic engine assembly. Models K-141, and K-161 are similar. Standard Model K-141 engine is equipped with a bushing type main bearing in bearing plate (18).

1. Spark plug	11. Connecting rod	21. Magneto rotor	31. Shim washer	40. Governor shaft	50. Breaker cover
2. Cylinder head	12. Rod cap	22. Wave washer	32. Camshaft	41. Bracket	51. Gasket
3. Head gasket	13. Rod bolt lock	23. Flywheel	33. Spring retainer	42. Speed disc	52. Breaker points
4. Exhaust valve seat	14. Oil seal	24. Pulley	34. Valve spring	43. Bushing	53. Push rod
5. Valve guide	15. Ball bearing	25. Shroud	35. Valve tappet	44. Governor spring	54. Gaskets
6. Cylinder block	16. Crankshaft	26. Screen retainer	36. Intake valve	45. Governor lever	55. Filter
7. Piston rings	17. Gasket	27. Screen	37. Exhaust valve	46. Link	56. Valve cover
8. Piston	18. Bearing plate	28. Oil pan	38. Governor gear &	47. Muffler	57. Breather seal
9. Piston pin	19. Magneto	29. Gasket	weight assy.	48. Carburetor	58. Reed plate
10. Retaining rings	20. Condenser	30. Camshaft pin	39. Needle bearing	49. Air cleaner assy.	59. Fuel pump

Camshafts are equipped with an automatic compression release mechanism shown in Fig. KO31. The automatic compression release mechanism holds the exhaust valve slightly open during the first part of compression stroke, reducing compression pressure and allowing easier cranking of engine. Refer to Fig. KO31 for operational details. At speeds above 650 engine rpm, compression release mechanism is inactive. Service procedures remain the same as for early production camshaft units, except for the difference in timing advance and compression release mechanisms.

To check compression on engine equipped with automatic compression release, engine must be cranked at 650 rpm or higher to overcome compression release action. A reading can also be obtained by rotating flywheel in reverse direction with throttle wide open. Compression reading should be 110-120 psi on an engine in top mechanical condition. When compression reading falls below 100 psi, it indicates leaking rings or valves.

VALVE SYSTEM. Valve tappet gap (cold) is as follows:

Models K-141, K-161 and K-181
Intake . . . . 0.006-0.008 in.
(0.15-0.20 mm)
Exhaust . . . . 0.015-0.017 in.
(0.38-0.43 mm)

Model K-241
Intake . . . . 0.008-0.010 in.
(0.20-0.25 mm)
Exhaust . . . . 0.017-0.020 in.
(0.43-0.51 mm)

Correct valve tappet gap is obtained by grinding ends of valve stems on Models K-141, K-161 and K-181. Be sure to grind end square and remove all burrs from end of stem after grinding. Model K-241 has adjustable tappets.

Exhaust valve seats are renewable and intake valve seats are machined in cylinder block on most models. Valve face and seat angle is 45 degrees. Desired seat width is 1/32-1/16 inch (0.8-1.6 mm).

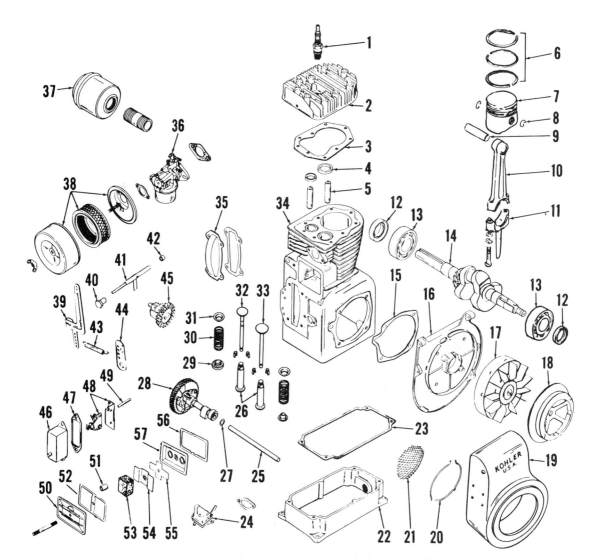

Fig. KO35 — Exploded view of Model K-241 basic engine assembly.

1. Spark plug	11. Rod cap	21. Screen	31. Spring retainer	41. Governor shaft	49. Push rod
2. Cylinder head	12. Oil seal	22. Oil pan	32. Exhaust valve	42. Needle bearing	50. Valve cover
3. Head gasket	13. Ball bearing	23. Gasket	33. Intake valve	43. Governor spring	51. Breather seal
4. Valve seat insert	14. Crankshaft	24. Fuel pump	34. Cylinder block	44. Speed lever	52. Gasket
5. Valve guide	15. Gasket	25. Camshaft pin	35. Camshaft cover	45. Governor gear &	53. Filter
6. Piston rings	16. Bearing plate	26. Valve tappets	36. Carburetor	weight unit	54. Baffle
7. Piston	17. Flywheel	27. Shim washer	37. Muffler	46. Breaker cover	55. Reed
8. Retaining rings	18. Pulley	28. Camshaft	38. Air cleaner assy.	47. Gasket	56. Gasket
9. Piston pin	19. Shroud	29. Valve rotator	39. Governor lever	48. Breaker point assy.	57. Breather plate
10. Connecting rod	20. Screen retainer	30. Valve spring	40. Bushing		

Valve guides are renewable on all models. Specified intake valve stem-to-guide clearance is 0.001-0.0025 inch (0.03-0.064 mm) and specified exhaust valve-to-guide clearance is 0.0025-0.004 inch (0.064-0.10 mm) on all models. Ream valve guides, after installation, to obtain correct inside diameter of 0.312-0.313 inch (7.93-7.95 mm).

DYNAMIC BALANCER. Refer to Fig. KO32 for view of dynamic balancer system used on some K-241 engines. The two balance gears, equipped with needle bearings, rotate on two stub shafts which are pressed into bosses on pto side of crankcase. Snap rings secure gears on stub shafts and shim spacers are used to control gear end play. Balance gears are driven by crankshaft in opposite direction of crankshaft rotation. Use the following procedure to install and time dynamic balancer components.

To install new stub shafts, press shafts into special bosses in crankcase until they protrude 0.691-inch (17.55 mm)

above thrust surface of bosses.

To install top balance gear-bearing assembly, first place one 0.010-inch (0.25 mm) thick shim spacer on stub shaft, then slide top gear assembly on shaft. Timing marks must face flywheel side of crankcase. Install one 0.005-inch (0.13 mm), one 0.010-inch (0.25 mm) and one 0.020-inch (0.51 mm) thick shim spacers in this order, then install snap ring. Using a feeler gage, check gear end play. Proper end play of balance gear is 0.005-0.010 inch (0.13-0.25 mm). Add or remove 0.005-inch (0.13 mm) thick spacers as necessary to obtain correct end play.

NOTE: Always install the 0.020-inch (0.51 mm) thick spacer next to snap ring.

Refer to Fig. KO33 and install crankshaft in crankcase. Align primary timing mark on top balance gear with standard timing mark on crankshaft. With primary timing marks aligned, engage crankshaft gear 1/16-inch (1.6

mm) into narrow section of top balance gear, then rotate crankshaft to align timing marks on camshaft gear and crankshaft as shown in Fig. KO30. Press crankshaft into crankcase until it is seated firmly into ball bearing main. Rotate crankshaft until crankpin is approximately 15 degrees past bottom dead center. Install one 0.010-inch (0.25 mm) thick shim spacer on stub shaft. Align secondary timing mark on bottom balance gear with secondary timing mark on crankshaft. Slide gear assembly into position on stub shaft. If properly timed, secondary timing mark on bottom balance gear will be aligned with standard timing mark on crankshaft after gear is fully on stub shaft. Install one 0.005-inch (0.13 mm) thick and one 0.020-inch (0.51 mm) thick shim spacer, then install snap ring. Check bottom balance gear end play and add or remove 0.005-inch (0.13 mm) thick spacers as required to obtain proper end play of 0.005-0.010 inch (0.13-0.25 mm). Make certain 0.020-inch (0.51 mm) spacer is used against snap ring.

KOHLER

Model	No. Cyls.	Bore	Stroke	Displacement	Power Rating
M8	1	2.94 in. (74.6 mm)	2.75 in. (69.9 mm)	18.64 cu. in. (305 cc)	8 hp (6.0 kW)
M14	1	3.50 in. (88.9 mm)	3.25 in. (82.5 mm)	31.27 cu. in. (512 cc)	14 hp (10.4 kW)

ENGINE IDENTIFICATION

All models are four-stroke, single-cylinder, horizontal crankshaft type engines. All engines are equipped with ball bearing mains at each end of crankshaft and are splash lubricated. A side draft carburetor is used on all engines. Engine model, specification and serial numbers are located on a tag on carburetor side of the rewind starter and cooling fan housing. Always furnish engine model, specification and serial number when ordering parts.

An automotive diaphragm type fuel pump is used on some models. This pump is equipped with a priming lever. A fuel pump repair kit is available.

MAINTENANCE

SPARK PLUG. Recommended spark plug for Model M8 is a Champion J-8. Recommended spark plug for Model M14 is a Champion H-10. Recommended electrode gap is 0.25 inch (6.35 mm) for all models.

CARBURETOR. All models are equipped with a Kohler side-draft carburetor. For initial adjustment, open idle mixture screw (7—Fig. KO40) 1-1/4 turns and main mixture screw (1) 2 turns from a lightly seated position on Model M8. For Model M14, open idle and main mixture screws 2-1/2 turns from a lightly seated position.

Make final adjustments on all models with engine at operating temperature and running. Place engine under load and adjust main mixture screw (1) to leanest mixture that will allow satisfactory acceleration and steady governor operation. If engine misses and backfires under load, mixture is too lean. If engine shows a sooty exhaust and is sluggish under load, mixture is too rich. Adjust idle speed stop screw (5) to maintain an idle speed of 1200 rpm. Then, adjust idle mixture screw (7) for smoothest idle operation.

Main and idle mixture adjustments have some effect on each other. Recheck engine operation and readjust mixture screws as necessary for smoothest operation.

To check float level, invert carburetor body and float assembly. There should be 11/64 inch (4 mm) clearance between machined surface of body casting and free end of float as shown in upper view of Fig. KO41. Adjust as necessary by bending float lever tang that contacts inlet valve. Turn carburetor over and measure float drop. Float drop should be 1-1/32 inches (26 mm) between the machined surface of body and the bottom of the free end of float as shown in middle view of Fig. KO41. Bend the float tab to adjust. Float-to-float hinge tower clearance should be 0.010 inch (0.25 mm) as shown in lower view of Fig. KO41. File float hinge tower as needed to obtain recommended clearance.

AIR FILTER. All models are equipped with a foam type precleaner and a paper air filter element. Foam precleaner should be serviced after every 25 hours of operation and paper element should be cleaned after every 100 hours of operation and renewed after every 300 hours of operation.

To service foam precleaner, remove precleaner and wash in a solution of warm water and detergent. Rinse thoroughly with clean water until all traces of detergent are eliminated.

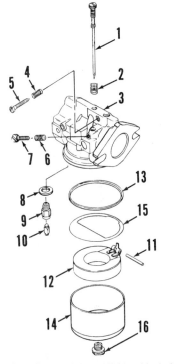

Fig. KO40—Exploded view of Kohler side draft carburetor.

1. Main mixture screw
2. Spring
3. Carburetor body
4. Spring
5. Idle speed stop screw
6. Spring
7. Idle mixture screw
8. Sealing washer
9. Inlet valve seat
10. Inlet valve
11. Float pin
12. Float
13. Gasket
14. Float bowl
15. Baffle gasket
16. Bowl retainer

Fig. KO41—View showing float adjustment procedure. Refer to text.

Squeeze out excess water and allow foam element to air dry. Saturate foam element in clean engine oil and squeeze out excess oil.

To clean paper element, remove foam precleaner and paper element. Remove foam precleaner element from paper element and gently tap paper element to dislodge dirt. Do not wash paper element or use compressed air to clean.

GOVERNOR. All models are equipped with a gear driven flyweight governor that is located inside engine crankcase. Maximum recommended governed engine speed is 3600 rpm. Recommended idle speed of 1200 rpm is controlled by adjustment of throttle stop screw on carburetor.

For initial adjustment of governor linkage, loosen governor lever clamp bolt nut and pull governor lever away from carburetor as far as it will go. Then, turn governor shaft counterclockwise as far as it will go while holding governor lever. Tighten clamp bolt nut. On Model M8, make certain there is at least 1/16 inch (1.6 mm) clearance between governor lever and cross shaft bushing nut (Fig. KO42). On Model M14, make certain there is at least 1/16 inch (1.6 mm) clearance between governor lever and upper left cam gear cover bolt (Fig. KO43).

High speed setting depends on engine application. Maximum allowable speed is 3600 rpm. Maximum speed is adjusted by loosening jam nut on high speed adjusting screw and turning screw until desired speed is obtained. Governor sensitivity is adjusted by repositioning governor spring in the holes in governor lever (Fig. KO44). Standard spring position on Model M8 is the third hole from the cross shaft. Standard spring position on Model M14 is the sixth hole from the cross shaft. To increase sensitivity, move spring toward cross shaft and to decrease sensitivity, move spring away from cross shaft.

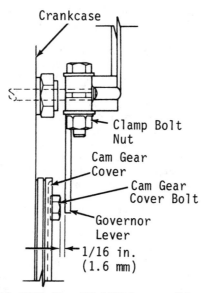

Fig. KO43—View of Model M14 governor linkage. Refer to text for adjustment procedure.

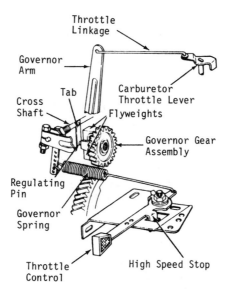

Fig. KO44—View showing typical governor linkage arrangement used on most models.

IGNITION SYSTEM. All models are equipped with an electronic magneto ignition system consisting of a magnet cast into the flywheel, an electronic magneto ignition module mounted on the engine bearing plate outside of flywheel and an ignition switch which grounds ignition module to stop engine.

Air gap between flywheel and ignition module should be 0.012-0.016 inch (0.30-0.41 mm).

Ignition system is considered satisfactory if system will produce a spark that will jump a test plug gap of 0.035 inch (0.91 mm). To test the primary side of ignition module using an ohmmeter, connect the positive ohmmeter lead to ignition module laminations (A—Fig. KO45) and the negative ohmmeter lead to kill terminal (B). Ohmmeter reading should be 1.0-1.3 ohms. To test the secondary side of ignition module using an ohmmeter, connect the positive ohmmeter lead to ignition module laminations (A) and the negative ohmmeter lead to high tension lead (C). Ohmmeter reading should be 7,900-10,850 ohms. If ohmmeter readings are not as specified, renew ignition module.

VALVE ADJUSTMENT. Valve stem clearance should be checked after every 500 hours of operation. Valve stem clearance for Model M8 should be 0.006-0.008 inch (0.15-0.20 mm) for intake valve and 0.017-0.019 inch (0.43-0.48 mm) for exhaust valve. Valve stem clearance for Model M14 should be 0.008-0.010 inch (0.20-0.25 mm) for intake valve and 0.017-0.019 inch (0.43-0.48 mm) for exhaust valve. If clearance is not as specified, refer to VALVE SYSTEM under REPAIR section for valve service procedure.

CYLINDER HEAD AND COMBUSTION CHAMBER. Cylinder head should be removed and carbon and lead deposits cleaned after every 500 hours of operation. Refer to CYLINDER HEAD

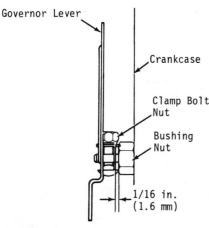

Fig. KO42—View of Model M8 governor linkage. Refer to text for adjustment procedure.

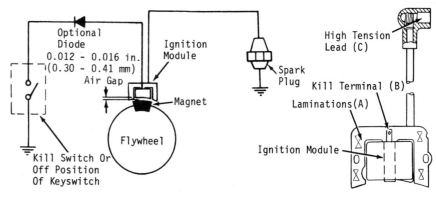

Fig. KO45—Typical wiring diagram for all models.

under REPAIR section for cylinder head removal procedure.

LUBRICATION. Engine oil should be checked daily and oil level maintained between the "F" and "L" mark on dipstick. Push dipstick all the way down in tube to obtain reading.

Manufacturer recommends oil having API service classification of SC, SD, SE or SF. Use SAE 5W-30 oil for temperatures below 32° F (0° C) and SAE 30 oil for temperatures above 32° F (0° C).

Oil should be changed after the first 5 hours of operation and at 25 hour intervals thereafter. Crankcase oil capacity is 1 quart (0.95 L) for Model M8 and 2 quarts (1.9 L) for Model M14.

GENERAL MAINTENANCE. Check and tighten all loose bolts, nuts and clamps daily. Check for fuel and oil leakage and repair if necessary. Clean cooling fins and external surfaces at 50 hour intervals.

REPAIRS

TIGHTENING TORQUES. Recommended tightening torque specifications are as follows:

Spark plug . . . . .18-22 ft.-lbs.
(24-29 N·m)
Cylinder head:
Model M8. . . . . .15-20 ft.-lbs.
(20-27 N·m)
Model M14 . . . . .25-30 ft.-lbs
(34-40 N·m)
Flywheel:
Model M8 . . . . .85-90 ft.-lbs.
(115-122 N·m)
Model M14
(plastic fan) . . . . .35-40 ft.-lbs.
(48-54 N·m)
Model M14
(iron fins) . . . . .22-27 ft.-lbs.
(29-37 N·m)
Connecting rod:
Model M8 (New) . . . . . . .12 ft.-lbs.
(16 N·m.)
Model M8 (Used) . . . . .8 ft.-lbs.
(11 N·m)
Model M14 (New). . . . . . .22 ft.-lbs.
(29 N·m)
Model M14 (Used) . . . . . .17 ft.-lbs.
(23 N·m)
Engine base . . . . .7 ft.-lbs.
(10 N·m)

CYLINDER HEAD. To remove cylinder head, first remove all necessary metal shrouds. Clean engine to prevent entrance of foreign material and remove cylinder head retaining bolts.

Always use a new head gasket when installing cylinder head. Tighten cylinder head bolts evenly and in graduated steps using the sequence shown in Fig.

KO46 for the model being serviced. Tighten bolts to specified torque.

CONNECTING ROD. The aluminum alloy connecting rod rides directly on the crankpin journal. Connecting rod and piston are removed as an assembly after cylinder head and engine base have been removed. Remove the two connecting rod bolts and connecting rod cap and push piston and rod assembly out top of block. Remove snap rings retaining piston pin and push pin out of piston and connecting rod.

Inside diameter for piston pin hole in connecting rod should be 0.6255-0.6258 inch (15.888-15.895 mm) for Model M8 and 0.8757-0.8760 inch (22.243-22.250 mm) for Model M14. Piston pin-to-connecting rod running clearance should be 0.0006-0.0011 inch (0.015-0.028 mm) for Model M8 and 0.0003-0.0008 inch (0.008-0.020 mm) for Model M14.

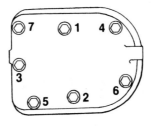

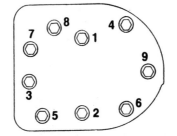

Fig. KO46—Cylinder head bolts must be tightened in the sequence shown. Upper view is for Model M8 and lower view is for Model M14.

Fig. KO47—View shows location of drilled hole used to identify connecting rod used on 0.010 inch (0.25 mm) undersize crankpin journal.

Connecting rod side play on crankpin should be 0.005-0.016 inch (0.13-0.41 mm) for Model M8 and 0.007-0.016 inch (0.18-0.41 mm) for Model M14.

Connecting rod-to-crankpin running clearance should be 0.001-0.002 inch (0.025-0.050 mm) for all models. If running clearance is 0.0025 inch (0.064 mm) or greater, renew connecting rod and/or recondition crankshaft journal. A 0.010 inch (0.25 mm) undersize connecting rod is available. Undersize connecting rod is identified by a drilled hole in connecting rod just above crankpin bearing end as shown in lower view of Fig. KO47.

Reinstall connecting rod and piston assembly with match marks on connecting rod and cap and the word "FLY" stamped on piston top toward flywheel side of engine. Tighten connecting rod nuts to specified torque.

PISTON, PIN AND RINGS. The aluminum alloy piston is fitted with two compression rings and one oil control ring. Piston pin outside diameter should be 0.6247-0.6249 inch (15.867-15.873 mm) for Model M8 and 0.8752-0.8754 inch (22.230-22.235 mm) for Model M14. Model M8 can be equipped with either a style "A" or "C" piston (Fig. KO48) and Model M14 will be equipped with a style "A" piston. Refer to the following paragraphs for style "A" and "C" piston specifications.

On all models, piston must be installed on connecting rod so the match marks on connecting rod and cap and the word "FLY" stamped on piston top are toward flywheel side of engine after installation.

Style "A" Piston. Diameter of piston is measured just below oil control ring groove as shown in upper view of Fig. KO48.

Piston diameter should be 2.9281-2.9297 inches (74.374-74.414 mm) for Model M8 and 3.4925-3.4941 inches

(88.710-88.754 mm) for Model M14. If piston diameter is 2.925 inches (74.295 mm) or less for Model M8 or 3.491 inches (88.671 mm) or less for Model M14, renew piston. Piston-to-cylinder clearance should be 0.007-0.010 inch(0.18-0.25 mm). Piston ring side clearance should be 0.006 inch (0.15 mm). Piston ring end gap for new rings should be 0.007-0.017 inch (0.18-0.37 mm) for Model M8 and 0.010-0.020 inch (0.25-0.51 mm) for Model M14. Piston ring end gap for used rings should be 0.027 inch (0.69 mm) for Model M8 and 0.030 inch (0.76 mm) for Model M14. If dimensions are not as specified, renew piston.

Style "C" Piston. Diameter of piston is measured ½ inch (12.7 mm) up from bottom of skirt as shown in lower view of Fig. KO48. Piston diameter should be 2.9329-2.9336 inches (74.496-74.513 mm) for Model M8. If piston diameter is 2.9312 inches (74.453 mm) or less, renew piston. Piston-to-cylinder clearance should be 0.0034-0.0051 inch (0.086-0.130 mm).

Piston ring side clearance should be 0.006 inch (0.15 mm). Piston ring end gap for new rings should be 0.010-0.023 inch (0.25-0.58 mm). Piston ring end gap for used rings should be 0.032 inch (0.81 mm). If dimensions are not as specified, renew piston.

CYLINDER AND CRANKCASE. Cylinder and crankcase are integral castings. Cylinder bore diameter should be 2.9370-2.9380 inches (74.5998-74.6252 mm) for Model M8 and 3.4995-3.5005 inches (88.8873-88.9127 mm) for Model M14. If cylinder bore diameter is 2.941 inches (74.679 mm) or more for Model

M8 or 3.503 inches (88.976 mm) or more for Model M14, recondition cylinder bore.

If cylinder bore is out-of-round more than 0.005 inch (0.13 mm), recondition cylinder bore. If cylinder bore taper exceeds 0.003 inch (0.08 mm) for Model M8 or 0.002 inch (0.05 mm) for Model M14, recondition cylinder bore.

CRANKSHAFT, MAIN BEARINGS AND SEALS. The crankshaft is supported at each end by a ball bearing type main bearing. Renew bearings (13—Fig. KO49) if excessively rough or loose. Crankshaft end play should be 0.002-0.023 inch (0.05-0.58 mm) for Model M8 and 0.003-0.020 inch (0.08-0.51 mm) for Model M14.

Standard crankpin journal diameter is 1.1855-1.1860 inches (30.112-30.124 mm)

for Model M8 and 1.5745-1.5749 inches (39.99-40.00 mm) for Model M14. If crankpin journal is out-of-round 0.0005 inch (0.013 mm) or more, recondition crankpin journal. If crankpin journal taper is 0.001 inch (0.025 mm) or more, recondition crankpin journal.

Main bearings should be a light press fit on crankshaft journals and in crankcase and bearing plate bores. If not, renew bearings and/or crankshaft or crankcase and bearing plate.

Front oil seal should be pressed into bearing plate seal bore so seal is 1/32 inch (0.8 mm) below seal bore surface. Rear oil seal should be pressed into crankcase bearing bore so seal is 1/8 inch (3 mm) below seal bore surface.

When installing crankshaft, align timing marks on crankshaft and camshaft gears as shown in Fig. KO50.

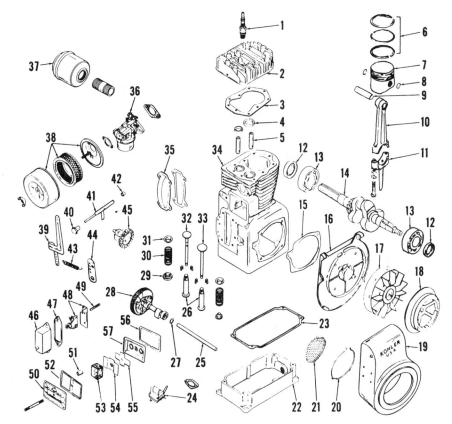

Fig. KO49—Exploded view of engine similar to Magnum series engine. Shroud (19) has been replaced with a new design and cooling fins may be cast with flywheel (17) on some models or be a bolt-on plastic assembly on others.

1. Spark plug	16. Bearing plate	45. Governor gear & weight unit
2. Cylinder head	17. Flywheel	46. Breaker cover (not used on M series)
3. Head gasket	18. Pulley	47. Gasket
4. Valve seat insert	19. Shroud	48. Breaker assy. (not used on M series)
5. Valve guide	20. Screen retainer	49. Push rod
6. Piston rings	21. Screen	50. Valve cover
7. Piston	22. Oil pan	51. Breather seal
8. Retaining ring	23. Gasket	52. Gasket
9. Piston pin	24. Fuel pump	53. Filter
10. Connecting rod	25. Camshaft pin	54. Baffle
11. Rod cap	26. Valve tappets	55. Reed
12. Oil seal	27. Shim washer	56. Gasket
13. Ball bearing	28. Camshaft	57. Breather plate
14. Crankshaft	29. Valve rotator	
15. Gasket	30. Valve spring	
	31. Spring retainer	
	32. Exhaust valve	
	33. Intake valve	
	34. Cylinder block	
	35. Camshaft cover	
	36. Carburetor	
	37. Muffler	
	38. Air cleaner assy.	
	39. Governor lever	
	40. Bushing	
	41. Governor shaft	
	42. Needle bearing	
	43. Governor spring	
	44. Speed lever	

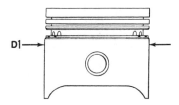

STYLE "A"

STYLE "C"

Fig. KO48—View showing differences between style "A" and "C" pistons. Measure diameter of piston at location identified by (D1 or D2). Dimension (M) is ½ inch (12.7 mm). Refer to text.

NOTE: On models equipped with dynamic balancer, refer to the following DYNAMIC BALANCER for installation and timing of balancer gears.

CAMSHAFT. The hollow camshaft and integral camshaft gear turn on a pin that is a slip fit in flywheel side of crankcase and a drive fit in closed side of crankcase. Remove and install pin from open side (bearing plate side) of crankcase. Drive camshaft pin into pto side of crankcase until pin is 0.275-0.285 inch (6.99-7.24 mm) from machined bearing plate gasket surface (Fig. KO51). Apply chemical locking compound on cup plug and install into bore in bearing plate mounting surface to a depth of 0.055-0.065 inch (1.4-1.7 mm) (Fig. KO51). Camshaft end play should be 0.005-0.010 inch (0.127-0.254 mm) and is controlled by use of 0.005 and 0.010 inch thick spacer washers between camshaft and cylinder block at bearing plate side of crankcase.

All models are equipped with automatic compression release mechanism. The automatic compression release mechanism holds exhaust valve slightly open during first part of compression stroke, reducing compression pressure and allowing easier cranking of engine. At engine speeds above 650 rpm, compression release mechanism is inactive. To check cylinder compression, engine must be cranked at 650 rpm or higher to overcome compression release action. A reading can also be obtained by rotating flywheel in reverse direction with

throttle in wide open position. Compression reading should be 110-120 psi (758-827 kPa) for an engine in top mechanical condition. When compression reading falls below 100 psi (689 kPa), engine should be disassembled as needed and worn or damaged component or components renewed.

VALVE SYSTEM. Valve tappet gap (cold) should be 0.006-0.008 inch (0.15-0.20 mm) for intake valve and 0.017-0.019 inch (0.43-0.48 mm) for exhaust valve on Model M8 and 0.008-0.010 inch (0.20-0.25 mm) for intake valve and 0.017-0.019 inch (0.43-0.48 mm) for exhaust valve on Model M14.

Correct valve tappet gap is obtained on Model M8 by grinding ends of valve stem to increase clearance or by grinding seat or face of valve to decrease clearance. Model M14 is equipped with adjustable tappets.

Valve face and seat should be ground at a 45 degree angle for intake and exhaust valves. Standard seat width should be 1/32 to 1/16 inch (0.794-1.588 mm).

Renewable valve guides are used on all models. Intake valve stem to guide clearance should be 0.001-0.0025 inch (0.025-0.064 mm) and exhaust valve stem-to-guide clearance should be 0.0025-0.004 inch (0.064-0.102 mm) on all models. Ream valve guides after installation to obtain correct inside diameter of 0.312-0.313 inch (7.93-7.95 mm). Diameter of intake valve stem should be 0.3103 inch (7.88 mm) for all models. Exhaust valve stem on all models is slightly tapered. Exhaust valve stem diameter should be 0.3074 inch (7.81 mm) at upper valve stem area which enters valve guide.

DYNAMIC BALANCER. Some models may be equipped with a dynamic balancer system (Fig. KO52). The two balancer gears, equipped with needle bearings, rotate on two stub shafts which are pressed into bosses on pto side of crankcase. Snap rings secure gears on stub shafts and shim spacers are used to control gear end play. Balancer gears are driven by crankshaft

in opposite direction of crankshaft rotation.

To renew stub shafts, press old shafts out and discard. Press new shaft in until it is 1.087-1.097 inches (25.598-25.60 mm) above stub shaft boss and use the 3/8 inch (9.525 mm) spacer between block and gear (Fig. KO53).

To install top balancer gear and bearing assembly, first place one 0.010 inch shim on stub shaft, install top gear assembly on shaft making certain timing marks are facing flywheel side of crankcase. In the following order, install one 0.005 inch shim, one 0.010 inch shim and one 0.020 inch shim on stub shaft and retain with snap ring. Using a feeler gage, check gear end play. Correct end play of balancer gear is 0.005-0.010 inch (0.13-0.25 mm). Add or remove shims in 0.005 inch increments as necessary to obtain correct end play.

NOTE: Always install the 0.020 inch thick shim next to snap ring.

Install crankshaft in crankcase and align primary timing mark on top balance gear with standard timing mark on crankshaft. See Fig. KO54. With primary timing marks aligned, engage crankshaft gear 1/16 inch (1.59 mm) into narrow section of top balancer gear and rotate crankshaft to align timing marks on camshaft gear and crankshaft as shown in Fig. KO50. Press crankshaft into crankcase until it is seated firmly in ball type main bearing.

Rotate crankshaft until crankpin is approximately 15 degrees past bottom dead center. Install one 0.010 inch shim on stub shaft, align secondary timing mark on bottom balancer gear with secondary timing mark on crankshaft

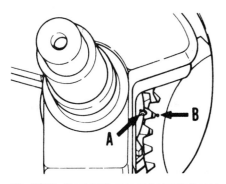

Fig. KO50—Crankshaft gear and camshaft gear timing marks (A & B) must be aligned as shown during installation.

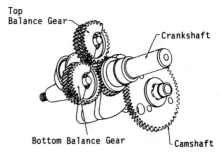

Fig. KO52—View showing components of dynamic balancer system used on all models equipped with dynamic balancer.

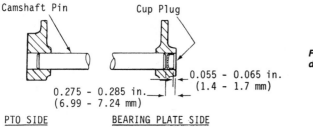

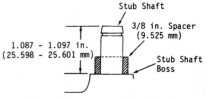

Fig. KO51—View showing dimensions for camshaft pin installation.

Fig. KO53—View showing balancer gear stub shaft installation. Refer to text.

counterweight. See Fig. KO54. Install gear assembly onto stub shaft. If properly timed, secondary timing mark on bottom balancer gear will be aligned with standard timing mark on crankshaft after gear is fully on stub shaft. Install one 0.005 inch shim and one 0.020 inch shim, then install snap ring. Check bottom balancer gear end play and add or remove shims in 0.005 inch increments as required to obtain proper end play of 0.005-0.010 inch (0.13-0.25 mm). Make certain the 0.020 inch shim is positioned against the snap ring.

Fig. KO54—View showing timing marks for installing dynamic balancer gears.

KOHLER

SERVICING KOHLER ACCESSORIES

RETRACTABLE STARTERS

Fairbanks-Morse or Eaton retractable starters are used on some Kohler engines. When servicing the starters, refer to appropriate following paragraphs.

Fairbanks-Morse

OVERHAUL. To disassemble the starter, remove retainer ring, retainer washer, brake spring, friction washer, friction shoe assembly and second friction washer as shown in Fig. KO100. Hold the rope handle in one hand and the cover in the other and allow rotor to rotate to unwind the recoil spring preload. Lift rotor from cover, shaft and recoil spring. Check the winding direction of recoil spring and rope for aid in reassembly. Remove recoil spring from cover and unwind rope from rotor.

When reassembling the unit, lubricate recoil spring, cover shaft and its bore in rotor with Lubriplate or equivalent. Install the rope on rotor and the rotor to the shaft and engage the recoil spring inner end hook. Preload the recoil spring four turns and install middle flange and mounting flange. Check friction shoe sharp ends and renew if necessary. Install friction washers, friction shoe assembly, brake spring, retainer washer and retainer ring. Make certain that friction shoe assembly is installed properly for correct starter rotation. If properly installed, sharp ends of friction shoe plates will extend when rope is pulled.

Starter operation can be reversed by winding rope and recoil spring in opposite direction and turning the friction shoe assembly upside down. See Fig. KO101 for counterclockwise assembly.

Eaton

OVERHAUL. To disassemble the starter, first release tension of rewind spring as follows: Hold starter assembly with pulley facing up. Pull starter rope until notch in pulley is aligned with rope hole in cover. Use thumb pressure to prevent pulley from rotating. Engage rope in notch of pulley and slowly release thumb pressure to allow spring to unwind until all tension is released.

After securing the pulley assembly in

housing, align notch in pulley with rope bushing in housing. Engage rope in notch and rotate pulley at least two full turns in same direction it is pulled, to properly preload starter spring. Pull rope to fully extended position. Release

Fig. KO100 — Fairbanks-Morse retractable starter with friction shoe assembly removed.

Fig. KO101 — View showing recoil spring and rope installed for counterclockwise starter operation.

handle and if spring is properly preloaded, the rope will fully rewind.

Before installing starter on engine, check teeth in starter driven hub (165 – Fig. KO103) for wear and renew hub if necessary.

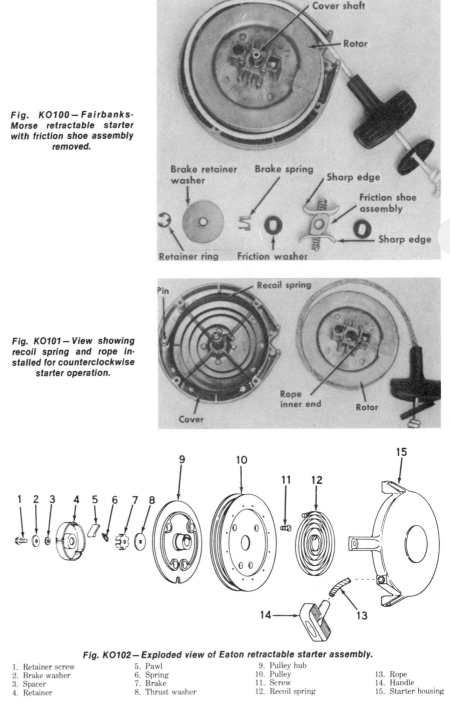

Fig. KO102 — Exploded view of Eaton retractable starter assembly.

1. Retainer screw
2. Brake washer
3. Spacer
4. Retainer
5. Pawl
6. Spring
7. Brake
8. Thrust washer
9. Pulley hub
10. Pulley
11. Screw
12. Recoil spring
13. Rope
14. Handle
15. Starter housing

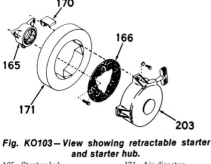

Fig. KO103 — View showing retractable starter and starter hub.

165. Starter hub
166. Screen
170. Bracket
171. Air director
203. Retractable starter assy.

Fig. KO105 — Exploded view of 2-brush compact gear drive starting motor.

A. Frame & field coil assy.
B. Armature
C. Spacer
D. Thrust washer
E. Bendix drive assy.
F. Drive end plate & mounting bracket
G. Lockwasher
H. Through-bolt
J. Commutator end plate
K. Ground brush
L. Terminal nuts
M. Lockwashers
N. Flat washer
O. Insulating washer
P. Field brush

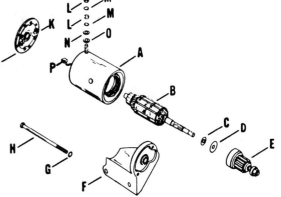

12-VOLT GEAR DRIVE STARTERS

TWO BRUSH COMPACT TYPE. To disassemble starting motor, clamp mounting bracket in a vise. Remove through-bolts (H – Fig. KO105) and slide commutator end plate (J) and frame assembly (A) off the armature. Then, clamp steel armature core in vise and remove Bendix drive retaining nut. Remove Bendix drive (E), drive end plate (F), thrust washer (D) and spacer (C) from armature (B).

Renew brushes if unevenly worn or worn to a length of 5/16-inch (7.9 mm) or less. To renew ground brush (K), drill out rivet, then rivet new brush lead to end plate. Field brush (P) is soldered to field coil lead.

Reassemble by reversing disassembly procedure. Lubricate bushings with a light coat of SAE 10 oil. Inspect Bendix drive pinion and splined sleeve for damage. If Bendix is in good condition, wipe clean and install completely dry. Tighten Bendix drive retaining nut to a torque of 130-150 in.-lbs. (14.68-16.94 N·m). Tighten through-bolts (H) to a torque of 40-55 in.-lbs. (4.52-6.21 N·m).

KUBOTA

KUBOTA TRACTOR CORPORATION
550 West Artesia Boulevard
P.O. Box 7020
Compton, CA 90224

Basic Model (Series)	Crankshaft	Bore	Stroke	Displacement	Power Rating
GS90V	Vertical	52 mm (2.05 in.)	40 mm (1.57 in.)	84 cc (5.13 cu.in.)	1.65 kW (2.2 hp)
GS200	Horizontal	69 mm (2.72 in.)	54 mm (2.13 in.)	201 cc (12.3 cu. in.)	3.82 kW (5.2 hp)
GS230	Horizontal	73 mm (2.87 in.)	54 mm (2.13 in.)	226 cc (13.8 cu. in.)	4.05 kW (5.5 hp)
GS280	Horizontal	73 mm (2.87 in.)	66 mm (2.60 in.)	276 cc (16.8 cu. in.)	5.14 kW (7.0 hp)

MAINTENANCE

All Models

SPARK PLUG. Recommended spark plug for all models is Nippondenso W14FR-U or NKG BR4HS. Electrode gap should be 6-7 mm (0.024-0.028 in.). Clean and check spark plug electrode gap after every 100 hours of operation.

CARBURETOR. A horizontal draft butterfly-type carburetor is used on all models. Refer to Figs. KU1, KU2 and KU3 for exploded views of carburetors used.

To adjust carburetor, start engine and allow to warm up to operating temperature, then shut off engine. Back out idle speed screw (7—Fig. KU4 or Fig. KU5). Turn pilot screw (18—Figs. KU1, KU2 or KU3) in until lightly seated, then back out 1 to 1-1/2 turns. Restart engine and adjust throttle stopper screw (19) to obtain lowest possible idle rpm. Turn pilot screw (18) as necessary to obtain highest possible idle rpm, then adjust throttle stopper (19) to obtain approximately 1,650 rpm on GS90V engines or 700 rpm on all other models. Adjust idle speed screw (7—Fig. KU4 or Fig. KU5) so engine idles at 1,800 rpm on GS90V models or 825 rpm on all other models.

To adjust float level, remove float bowl and invert carburetor. Float should

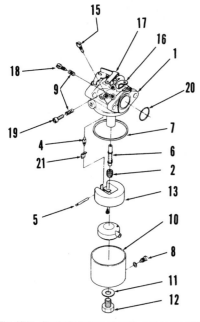

Fig. KU1—Exploded view of carburetor assembly used on Model GS90V engines. Refer to legend in Fig. KU2 for component identification except "O" ring (20) and clip (21).

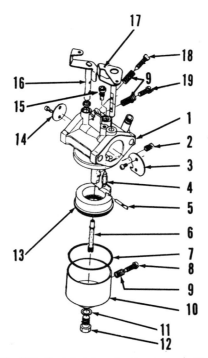

Fig. KU2—Exploded view of carburetor assembly used on Model GS200 engines.

1. Body
2. Main jet
3. Choke valve
4. Needle valve
5. Pin
6. Main nozzle
7. Gasket
8. Drain screw
9. Spring
10. Float bowl
11. Gasket
12. Screw
13. Float
14. Throttle valve
15. Pilot jet
16. Throttle lever & shaft assy.
17. Choke lever & shaft assy.
18. Pilot screw
19. Throttle stopper adjusting screw

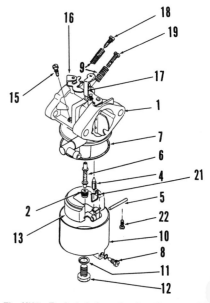

Fig. KU3—Exploded view of carburetor assembly used on Models GS230 and GS280. Refer to legend in Fig. KU2 for component identification except clip (21) and screw (22).

be level with carburetor body. Bend float arm to adjust.

GOVERNOR. A centrifugal flyweight type governor with an external adjustment is used on all models. Refer to Figs. KU4 and KU5 for views of governor external linkage. To adjust governor, first loosen nut (4). Completely open throttle valve by pushing or pulling governor lever (2). Using a suitable screwdriver, turn governor shaft (3) fully clockwise, then retighten nut (4). Start engine and accelerate to full throttle. Adjust maximum speed screw (6) so maximum no-load speed is 4,000 rpm on GS90V models, 2,000 rpm on GS200 models and 3,600 rpm on GS230 and GS280 models.

IGNITION. All models are equipped with a breakerless, transistorized ignition system. Ignition timing is fixed at 23 degrees BTDC and is not adjustable. On GS90V models, ignition coil and all electronic circuitry is contained in a one-piece ignition module mounted at outer periphery of flywheel. Air gap between module core legs and flywheel magnets should be 0.5 mm (0.020 in.). Loosen module mounting screws and move module to adjust air gap. Remove flywheel nut and tap around periphery of flywheel to loosen flywheel on crankshaft. To test ignition system, first remove spark plug, then install high tension lead on spark plug. Ground threads of spark plug and crank engine. Ignition system can be considered acceptable if proper spark is delivered to spark plug. If not, disconnect ignition kill switch lead and connect an ohmmeter between kill switch lead and engine ground. Pri-

mary resistance should be approximately 0.64 ohm. Test secondary resistance by connecting an ohmmeter between spark plug end of high tension lead and engine ground. Secondary resistance should be approximately 9,500 ohms. Renew ignition coil if resistance measurements vary greatly from specified values. If module resistance is as specified, but spark is absent at spark plug, ignition module must be renewed.

Models GS200, GS230 and GS280 are equipped with separate ignition module and coil assemblies. Ignition coil is mounted under the flywheel and ignition module is mounted adjacent to outer periphery of flywheel or on outside

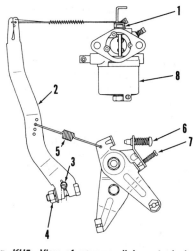

Fig. KU5—View of governor linkage typical of Models GS200, GS230 and GS280.

1. Throttle lever	5. Spring
2. Governor lever	6. Max. speed screw
3. Governor shaft	7. Idle speed screw
4. Nut	8. Carburetor assy.

of blower housing. No air gap adjustment is necessary on models with ignition coil mounted under the flywheel. Use a suitable flywheel puller to remove flywheel. Refer to SPECIAL TOOLS section. To test ignition system, remove spark plug and check for proper spark as outlined above. If proper spark is not present, disconnect connectors (3, 4 and 5—Fig. KU6) and high tension lead (1). Connect an ohmmeter between coil primary lead (4) and engine ground. Primary resistance should be approximately 0.6 ohm. Secondary resistance measured between spark plug end of high tension lead (1) and ground should be approximately 6,500 ohms on GS200 or 7,500 ohms on GS230 and GS280 engines. Pickup coil resistance between lead (3) and engine ground should be approximately 50 ohms. Renew coil assembly if resistance values vary greatly from specified values. If resistance values are as specified and spark is absent at spark plug, renew ignition module (6).

LUBRICATION. All models are splash lubricated. Maintain oil level at full mark on dipstick. Recommended oil is a good quality oil meeting API specification SC. Use SAE 30 oil during warm weather and SAE 20 during cold weather operation.

Change engine oil after every 50 hours of operation. Crankcase capacity is 0.37 L (0.39 qt.) on GS90V models, 0.6 L (0.6 qt.) on GS200 and GS230 models and 0.9 L (0.95 qt.) on GS280 models.

CRANKCASE BREATHER. Refer to Fig. KU7 for exploded view of crankcase

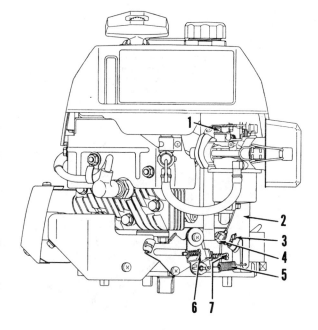

Fig. KU4—View of governor linkage used on Model GS90V. Refer to legend in Fig. KU5 for component identification.

Fig. KU6—View of ignition system used on Models GS200, GS230 and GS280.

1. High tension lead	4. Primary lead (black/yellow)
2. Ignition coil	5. Primary lead (to kill switch)
3. Pickup lead (red/white)	6. Ignition module

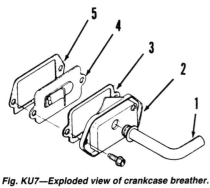

Fig. KU7—Exploded view of crankcase breather.
1. Tube
2. Cover
3. Gasket
4. Reed valve
5. Gasket

breather assembly. A reed valve is located in the valve spring compartment to maintain a slight vacuum in the crankcase preventing oil leakage around crankcase seals. If a slight vacuum is not present in crankcase, inspect crankcase breather for a faulty reed valve, or inspect engine for worn piston rings, valves or seals.

AIR CLEANER. Remove air filter and clean at least every 25 hours of operation. Models GS90V and GS200 are equipped with a paper element filter enclosed in a foam precleaner. Clean paper and foam filters in a suitable solvent and allow to thoroughly dry. Soak paper element in a 2:1 mixture of kerosene and engine oil and shake excess from element. Soak foam element in clean engine oil and squeeze excess oil from element.

On Models GS230 and GS280, remove filter element and tap on a hard surface to remove dust.

On all models, renew air filter on a yearly basis, or after cleaning the filter six times.

REPAIRS

TORQUE SPECIFICATIONS. Recommended tightening torques are as follows:
Connecting rod screws:
GS90V . . . . .3.9-5.9 N·m
(3-4 ft.-lbs.)
GS200 and GS230 . . . .13.7-19.6 N·m
(10-14 ft.-lbs.)
GS280 . . . . .16.7-22.6 N·m
(12-17 ft.-lbs.)
Crankcase screws:
GS90V . . . . .3.4-4.9 N·m
(2-4 ft.-lbs.)
All other models . . . .13.7-19.6 N·m
(10-14 ft.-lbs.)

Cylinder head:
GS90V . . . . .10.8-13.7 N·m
(8-10 ft.-lbs.)
All other models . . . .34.3-46.1 N·m
(25-34 ft.-lbs.)
Flywheel nut:
GS90V . . . . .19.6-24.5 N·m
(14-18 ft.-lbs.)
GS200 and GS230 . . .58.8-68.6 N·m
(43-50 ft.-lbs.)
GS280 . . . . .63.7-73.5 N·m
(47-54 ft.-lbs.)
Spark plug:
All models . . . . .9.8-24.5 N·m
(7-18 ft.-lbs.)

CONNECTING ROD. Piston and rod assembly is removed from cylinder head end of engine. Prior to separating rod from piston on GS90V models, mark piston and rod assemblies so piston can be reassembled on rod in same direction as removed.

On all other models, make a mark on piston crown aligned with machined side of connecting rod (Fig. KU8). When reassembling piston and rod assemblies, make sure previously made mark is on same side as machined surface on rod.

The connecting rod rides directly on crankpin. Crankpin diameter should be 19.467-19.480 mm (0.7664-0.7669 in.) on GS90V models, 25.467-25.482 mm (1.0027-1.0032 in.) on GS200 and GS230 models and 29.967-29.982 mm (1.1798-1.1804 in.) on GS280 models. Inside diameter of connecting rod big end bore should be 19.500-19.521 mm (0.7678-0.7685 in.) on Model GS90V, 25.500-25.521 mm (1.0040-1.0047 in.) on GS200 and GS230 models and 30.000-30.021 mm (1.1811-1.1819 in.) on GS280 models. Connecting rod-to-crankpin clearance should be 0.020-0.054 mm (0.0008-0.0021 in.) on Model GS90V and 0.018-0.054 mm (0.0007-0.0021 in.) on all other models. Connecting rod side clearance on crankpin should be 0.2-0.9 mm (0.008-0.035 in.) on Model GS90V and 0.4-1.1 mm (0.016-0.043 in.) on all other models. Maximum allowable rod side play is 1.5 mm (0.059 in.) on all models.

Connecting rod small end inside diameter should be 12.015-12.025 mm (0.4731-0.4734 in.) on GS90V models, 15.015-15.025 mm (0.5912-0.5915 in.) on GS200 and GS230 models and 18.015-18.025 (0.7093-0.7096 in.) on GS280 models. Piston pin diameter should be 12.000-12.005 mm (0.4724-0.4726 in.) on GS90V models, 15.000-15.005 mm (0.5906-0.5908 in.) on GS200 and GS230 models and 18.000-18.005 mm (0.7087-0.7089 in.) on GS280 models. Piston pin-to-rod small end clearance should be 0.010-0.025 mm (0.0004-0.0010 in.) on all models. Maximum allowable pin-to-rod clearance on all models is 0.10 mm (0.004 in.).

On GS90V models, install rod and piston assembly into engine with "90" casting mark facing toward pto end of crankshaft (KU9). Install rod cap with oil dipper facing direction shown in Fig. KU9. On all other models, install rod and piston assembly with Japanese casting mark (Fig. KU10) facing flywheel and install rod cap with smooth machined surfaces on rod and rod cap aligned.

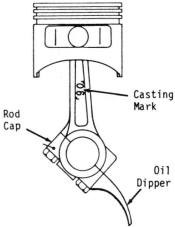

Fig. KU9—On GS90V models, install rod into engine with "90" casting mark facing toward pto side of engine. Install rod cap with oil dipper positioned as shown.

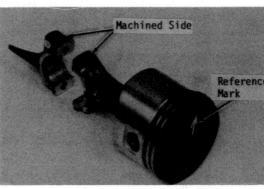

Fig. KU8—On GS200, GS230 and GS280 models, make a mark on piston crown on same side as machined surface of connecting rod prior to separating piston from rod to ensure reinstallation in same direction as removed.

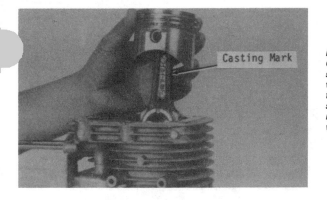

Fig. KU10—On GS200, GS230 and GS280 models, install piston and rod assembly with Japanese casting mark facing toward flywheel. Install rod cap with smooth machined surface aligned with machined surface of connecting rod.

PISTON, PIN, RINGS AND CYLINDER. Pistons on all models are equipped with two compression rings and one oil control ring. Compression pressure should be at least 490 kPa (71 psi) on all models.

Mark piston before removing from connecting rod to ensure piston reassembly in same direction as removed. Measure piston skirt diameter 18 mm (0.70 in.) up from bottom of skirt at a right angle to piston pin.

On Model GS90V, piston skirt diameter should be 51.95-51.98 mm (2.0453-2.0465 in.) with a maximum wear limit of 51.84 mm (2.0409 in.). Standard cylinder bore diameter is 52.00-52.02 mm (2.0472-2.0480 in.). Maximum cylinder bore wear limit is 52.12 mm (2.0520 in.). Oversize piston is not available for Model GS90V.

On Model GS200, piston skirt diameter should be 68.92-68.94 mm (2.7134-2.7142 in.) with a maximum wear limit of 68.84 mm (2.7102 in.). Piston and rings are available in 0.5 mm (0.020 in.) oversize. Standard cylinder bore diameter is 69.00-69.02 mm (2.7165-2.7173 in.) with a maximum wear limit of 69.12 mm (2.7213 in.).

On Models GS230 and GS280, piston skirt diameter should be 72.94-72.96 mm (2.8713-2.8724 in.) with maximum wear limit of 72.85 mm (2.8681 in.). Piston and rings are available in 0.5 mm (0.020 in.) oversize. Standard cylinder bore diameter is 73.00-73.02 mm (2.8740-2.8748 in.) with a maximum wear limit of 73.12 mm (2.8787 in.).

Piston pin outside diameter should be 12.000-12.005 mm (0.4725-0.4726 in.) on Model GS90V, 15.000-15.005 mm (0.5906-0.5908 in.) on Models GS200 and GS230, and 18.000-18.005 mm (0.7087-0.7089 in.) on Model GS280. Oversize piston pin is not available. Renew piston and pin if pin bore diameter exceeds 12.04 mm (0.4740 in.) on Model GS90V, 15.04 mm (0.5921 in.) on Models GS200 and GS230 and 18.04 mm (0.7102 in.) on Model GS280. Piston pin is a press fit in piston on all models. Heat piston in a hot oil bath to 100° C (212° F) to ease installation of pin.

NOTE: Do not use an open flame to heat piston.

Top and second compression ring end gap should be 0.1-0.3 mm (0.004-0.012 in.) on GS90V and GS230 models and 0.2-0.4 mm (0.008-0.016 in.) on GS200 and GS280 models. Maximum allowable compression ring end gap on all models is 0.9 mm (0.035 in.).

Oil ring end gap should be 0.3-0.9 mm (0.012-0.035 in.) on Model GS90V, 0.2-0.7 mm (0.008-0.028 in.) on Model GS200, 0.1-0.3 mm (0.004-0.012 in.) on Model GS230 and 0.2-0.9 mm (0.008-0.035 in.) on Model GS280.

Top compression ring-to-ring groove side clearance should be as follows: Model GS90V, 0.015-0.050 mm (0.0006-0.0020 in.); Models GS200 and GS230, 0.02-0.06 mm (0.0008-0.0024 in.); Model GS280, 0.05-0.09 mm (0.0020-0.0035 in.). Maximum allowable top compression ring side clearance is 0.13 mm (0.005 in.) on Model GS280 and 0.1 mm (0.004 in.) on all other models.

Second compression ring-to-ring groove side clearance should be as follows: Model GS90V, 0.010-0.045 mm (0.0004-0.0018 in.); All other models, 0.02-0.06 mm (0.0008-0.0024 in.). Maximum allowable side clearance on second compression ring is 0.1 mm (0.004 in.) on all models.

Install piston rings on piston with manufacturer's mark (adjacent to end gap) facing toward top of piston. Refer to Fig. KU11 when installing piston rings. Position top compression ring end gap (A) on opposite side of engine intake and exhaust valves and second compression ring end gap (B) 120 degrees from top ring gap. Position oil ring expander end gap (C) 120 degrees from top ring gap and oil ring rail end gaps (D) 90 degrees from expander gap (C).

CYLINDER HEAD. Renew head gasket when installing cylinder head. Clean head mating surface and check flatness with straight edge and feeler gage. Renew cylinder head if warpage exceeds 0.4 mm (0.016 in.). Install cylinder head gasket with gasket liner facing up as

shown in Fig. KU12. On Model GS90V, tighten all cylinder head screws to an initial tightness of 9.8 N·m (7 ft.-lbs.). Then following sequence shown in Fig. KU13, tighten head screws to 10.8-13.7 N·m (8-10 ft.-lbs.). On all other models, initial tightness is 19.6 N·m (14 ft.-lbs.). Then following sequence shown in Fig. KU13, tighten head screws to 34.3-46.1 N·m (25-34 ft.-lbs.).

CRANKSHAFT. Crankshaft is supported by two ball type main bearings on all models except GS90V. Crankshaft on Model GS90V rides in a ball type main bearing on the flywheel end and directly in bore of cover casting on pto end. Crankcase cover is secured to crankcase with two dowel pins. Tap crankcase with a soft-faced mallet to separate cover and crankcase. Do not pry crankcase between crankcase and cover. The preferred crankshaft end play is 0.2 mm (0.008 in.). Vary thickness of shim(s) located on cover end of crankshaft to adjust crankshaft end play.

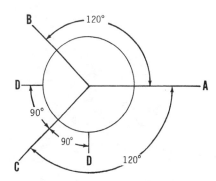

Fig. KU11—Position top compression ring gap (A) opposite of engine valves and second compression ring gap (B) 120 degrees away from top ring gap. Oil ring expander gap (C) should be 120 degrees from top ring gap with oil ring rails (D) 90 degrees from expander gap (C).

A. Top compression ring gap (opposite valves)
B. Second compression ring gap
C. Oil ring expander gap
D. Oil ring rails gap

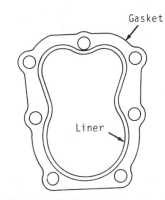

Fig. KU12—Install cylinder head gasket with liner facing up.

Crankpin diameter should be 19.467-19.480 mm (0.7664-0.7669 in.) on Model GS90V, 25.467-25.482 mm (1.0027-1.0032 in.) on Models GS200 and GS230 and 29.967-29.982 mm (1.1798-1.1804 in.) on Model GS280. Preferred connecting rod-to-crankpin clearance is 0.020-0.054 mm (0.0008-0.0021 in.) on Model GS90V and 0.018-0.054 mm (0.0007-0.0021 in.) on all other models. Maximum allowable connecting rod-to-crankpin clearance is 0.10 mm (0.0039 in.) on all models. Undersize connecting rod is not available.

When installing crankshaft, make sure camshaft and crankshaft timing marks are aligned as shown in Figs. KU14 and KU15.

CAMSHAFT. Remove crankcase cover to remove camshaft. Mark cam followers for installation in same location as removed. Intake and exhaust lobe height on Model GS90V should be 16.82 mm (0.6622 in.) with a wear limit of 16.72 mm (0.6583 in.).

Fig. KU13—Tighten cylinder head screws in sequence shown. Refer to text.

Intake and exhaust lobe height on Models GS200 and GS230 should be 27.125-27.275 mm (1.0679-1.0738 in.) with a wear limit of 27.0 mm (1.063 in.).

Intake and exhaust lobe height on Model GS280 should be 30.200-30.215 mm (1.1890-1.1895 in.) with a wear limit of 30.1 mm (1.185 in.).

Renew camshaft if wear limit is exceeded on either lobe. When installing camshaft, make sure timing marks are

Fig. KU14—View of timing marks and related components on Model GS90V.

Fig. KU15—View of timing marks and related components on Models GS200, GS230 and GS280.

aligned as shown in Figs. KU14 and KU15. Camshaft end play should not exceed 0.2 mm (0.008 in.). Vary thickness of shim(s) on camshaft at crankcase cover side on all models except GS90V to adjust camshaft end play. Shims on Model GS90V are located on crankcase side of camshaft to adjust camshaft end play.

VALVE SYSTEM. Valve lash for intake and exhaust valves on Models GS90V and GS200 should be 0.08-0.13 mm (0.003-0.005 in.), 0.10-0.15 mm (0.004-0.006 in.) on Model GS230 and 0.07-0.13 mm (0.003-0.005 in.) on Model GS280. Grind tip of valve stem to increase valve lash. If valve lash is excessive, renew valve and/or cam follower.

Maximum allowable valve stem-to-valve guide clearance is 0.1 mm (0.004 in.). Oversize valves are not available. Valve guides are renewable on all models except GS90V. If excessive valve stem-to-guide wear is noted on Model GS90V, valve and/or engine block must be renewed. Valve seats must be reconditioned if valve guides are renewed. Cut seats to a true 45 degree angle. Valve seat should contact valve at approximate center of valve face. Use a 15 degree cutter to lower valve seat. Maximum allowable valve seat width is 1.5 mm (0.060 in.) on Model GS90V and 1.7 mm (0.067 in.) on all other models. Renew valve springs if free length is less than 21.0 mm (0.827 in.) on Model GS90V, 29.2 mm (1.15 in.) on Models GS200 and GS230 and 32.5 mm (1.28 in.) on Model GS280.

SERVICING KUBOTA ACCESSORIES

REWIND STARTERS

OVERHAUL. To disassemble starter, remove starter housing from engine. Pull out rope until notch (N—Figs. KU25, KU26 and KU27) aligns with recessed area adjacent to rope guide in

housing (1). Using a screwdriver or other suitable tool, pull up rope from inside housing (1) and insert rope into notch (N) in pulley (3). With rope in this position, carefully allow rope pulley to unwind, releasing tension on rewind spring. Remainder of disassembly is evi-

dent after inspection of unit and referral to exploded views. Use caution when removing rewind spring. Do not allow rewind spring to uncoil uncontrolled. Rewind spring is wound in rope pulley on Models GS200 and GS230, and in starter housing on all other models.

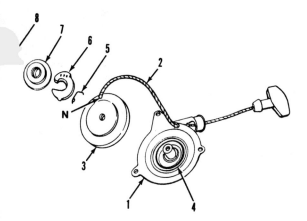

Fig. KU25—Exploded view of rewind starter used on Model GS90V. Starter used on GS200 models is similar.

1. Housing
2. Rope
3. Rope pulley
4. Rewind spring
5. Spring
6. Pawl
7. Pressure plate
8. Screw
N. Notch

KU28). On Models GS90V and GS280, wind rewind spring into starter housing in a clockwise direction, as viewed from flywheel side of housing, starting with outer coil of rewind spring. Make sure hook in outer coil of rewind spring properly engages notch in housing. Complete remainder of reassembly by reversing disassembly. To preload rewind spring, place rope into notch (N—Figs. KU25, KU26 and KU27) in rope pulley (3), and use rope to rotate rope pulley five turns in a clockwise direction on all models except Model GS280. Rotate pulley six to eight turns clockwise on Model GS280 starter. Hold pulley from turning, pull rope from notch (N), then allow rewind spring to slowly wind rope into starter housing.

With rope fully extended, rope pulley should be able to rotate further without becoming spring bound. When rope is retracted, rope handle should be pulled snug against housing. Increase or decrease rewind spring tension as necessary to obtain proper starter operation.

Inspect all components for excessive wear or damage and renew as necessary.

Lubricate rewind spring with a suitable grease. On Models GS200 and GS230, starting with outer coil, wind rewind spring into rope pulley in a clockwise direction as viewed from side opposite of flywheel. Make sure outer hook of rewind spring properly engages notch in rope pulley. On Model GS230, bend inner hook of rewind spring to obtain 0-2 mm (0-0.08 in.) clearance between hook and rope pulley center bushing (Fig.

ELECTRIC GEAR-DRIVE STARTER

To test starter motor, remove starter from engine and disconnect lead to motor from the "C" terminal of starter solenoid. Using jumper leads, connect positive (+) terminal of a fully charged 12-volt battery to disconnected starter motor lead. Connect battery negative (-) terminal to starter housing. If starter motor does not engage, disassemble motor and inspect for faulty components. To test starter solenoid, move jumper lead attached to positive (+) battery terminal to "ST" terminal of solenoid. Renew solenoid if solenoid does not activate.

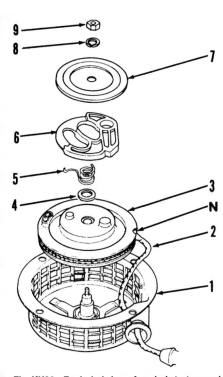

Fig. KU26—Exploded view of rewind starter used on GS230 models. Note that rewind spring (not shown) is located between rope pulley (3) and housing (1).

1. Housing
2. Rope
3. Rope pulley
4. Thrust washer
5. Spring
6. Pawl
7. Friction plate
8. Spring washer
9. Nut
N. Notch

Fig. KU27—Exploded view of rewind starter used on Model GS280.

1. Housing
2. Rope
3. Rope pulley
4. Rewind spring
5. Spring
6. Pawls
7. Friction plate
8. Spring washer
9. Nut
10. Washer
11. Pressure plate
12. Plate
13. Spring
N. Notch

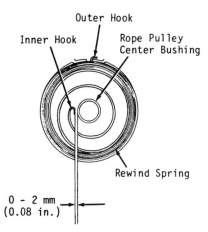

Fig. KU28—On Model GS230, bend inner hook of rewind spring as necessary to obtain 0-2 mm (0-0.08 in.) clearance between hook and center bushing of rope pulley.

To disassemble starter, remove solenoid (7—Fig. KU29) and through-bolts (15). Remove end frame (17) along with brush holder assembly (13). Slide frame and field coil assembly (12) off armature (10). Carefully tap collar (2) toward drive assembly (4) and pry off snap ring (1). Slide collar (2), spring (3) and drive (4) off armature (10) and pull armature (10) from housing (5).

Inspect starter drive assembly (4) for excessive wear, broken teeth or other damage. Make sure drive gear will turn in one direction only. Turn commutator on a suitable lathe if commutator runout exceeds 0.4 mm (0.016 in.). Renew armature if commutator diameter is less than 26.4 mm (1.039 in.). Mica between commutator segments should be undercut to 0.5-0.8 mm (0.020-0.031 in.) below outer surface of segments. Renew brushes if brush length is less than 9.3 mm (0.36 in.).

Lubricate bearings and inner diame-

ter of drive assembly with a suitable high temperature grease. Renew snap ring (1) and collar (2) when reassembling. Push snap ring (1) on armature shaft with a 12 mm socket. Make sure collar (2) is properly seated over snap ring (1) after reassembly.

CHARGING SYSTEM

Electric start models are equipped with a nonregulated charging system to maintain the proper battery charge. The charging coil (6—Fig. KU30) produces AC current which is rectified to DC current by rectifier (7).

To test charging system, connect a voltmeter to the battery and note battery voltage with engine not running. Start engine and check for voltage increase. If a voltage increase is not noted, stop the engine and disconnect charging coil (6) and connect an ohmmeter between the two green wires. Charging coil (6) resistance should be approximately 0.35 ohm. Renew charging coil (6) if ohmmeter reading is not as specified. To test rectifier (7) disconnect the four one-pin connectors lead-

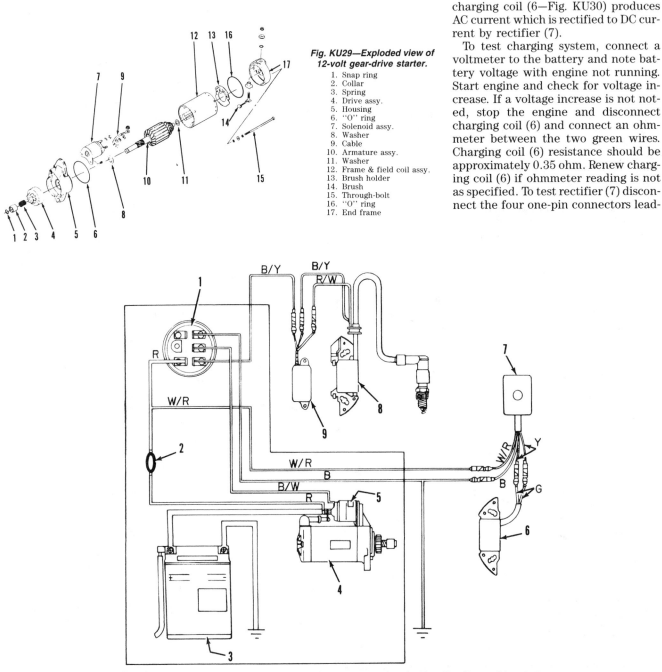

Fig. KU29—Exploded view of 12-volt gear-drive starter.

1. Snap ring
2. Collar
3. Spring
4. Drive assy.
5. Housing
6. "O" ring
7. Solenoid assy.
8. Washer
9. Cable
10. Armature assy.
11. Washer
12. Frame & field coil assy.
13. Brush holder
14. Brush
15. Through-bolt
16. "O" ring
17. End frame

Fig. KU30—Drawing of electrical system used on engines equipped with a 12-volt gear-drive starter.

1. Ignition switch	6. Charging coil	G. Green	B/Y. Black with yellow tracer
2. Fusible	7. Rectifier	R. Red	R/W. Red with white tracer
3. Battery	8. Ignition coil	Y. Yellow	W/R. White with red tracer
4. Starter motor	9. Ignition module	B/W. Black with white tracer	
5. Starter solenoid	B. Black		

ing to rectifier (7). Connect the positive (+) lead of an ohmmeter to the black (B) lead of rectifier (7) and the negative (-) ohmmeter lead to either yellow lead of rectifier. Refer to Fig. KU31. Note reading and reverse ohmmeter leads. Ohmmeter should show continuity in one direction and infinity in the other. Repeat procedure between black (B) lead and the other yellow lead and between the white/red lead and each yellow lead in turn. Renew rectifier (7) if ohmmeter does not show continuity in one direction and infinity in other direction during each test.

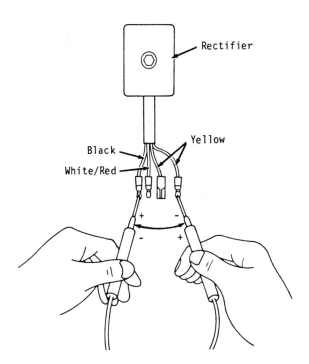

Fig. KU31—To test rectifier assembly, connect positive ohmmeter lead to black lead and negative ohmmeter lead to one yellow lead. Note reading and reverse ohmmeter leads (negative to black lead and positive to yellow lead). Reading should show continuity in one direction and infinity in other direction. Repeat procedure between black lead and other yellow lead and between white/red lead and each yellow lead. Ohmmeter should show continuity in one direction and infinity in other direction.

KUBOTA SPECIAL TOOLS

The following special tools are available from the manufacturer.

FLYWHEEL PULLER

07916-30160 — For all models except Model GS90V.

VALVE SPRING COMPRESSOR

07916-32001—For all models.

COMPRESSION TESTER

07909-30251—For all models.

PISTON RING COMPRESSOR

07909-32111—For all models.

PISTON RING TOOL

07909-32121—To remove and replace piston rings on all models.

VALVE SEAT REPAIR

07909-33102—Valve seat cutters and guides for all models.

LOMBARDINI

**BRIGGS & STRATTON
LOMBARDINI DIESEL, INC.
3402 Oakcliff Road B2
Doraville, GA 30340**

Model	No. Cyls.	Bore	Stroke	Displacement
3LD510	1	85 mm (3.35 in.)	90 mm (3.54 in.)	501 cc (30.6 cu. in.)

Model 3LD510 is a four-stroke, single-cylinder, air-cooled diesel engine. Crankshaft rotation is counterclockwise at pto end.

Metric fasteners are used throughout engine.

MAINTENANCE

LUBRICATION

Recommended engine oil is SAE 10W for temperatures below 0° C (32° F), SAE 20W for temperatures between 0° C (32° F) and 20° C (68° F) and SAE 40 for temperatures above 20° C (68° F). API classification for oil should be CD. Oil sump capacity is 1.75 liters (1.85 qts.). Manufacturer recommends changing oil after every 300 hours of operation.

A renewable oil filter is mounted on side of engine crankcase. Manufacturer recommends renewing filter after every 300 hours of operation.

Model 3LD510 is equipped with a pressurized oil system. Minimum allowable oil pressure is 100 kPa (15 psi).

ENGINE SPEED ADJUSTMENT

Low idle speed is adjusted by turning idle speed screw (I—Fig. L1-1). Idle speed should be 1000-1100 rpm. Maximum governed speed is adjusted by turning high speed screw (H). Set high idle (no-load) speed 180 rpm above specified governed full-load speed to compensate for governor droop. Normally, full-load speed should be 3000 rpm.

Maximum fuel delivery is adjusted by loosening screws (S) and moving adjusting plate (41). Set plate so satisfactory engine acceleration and power are obtained without excessive smoke. Moving plate to the left increases fuel delivery.

FUEL SYSTEM

FUEL FILTER. The fuel filter is located in bottom of fuel tank as shown in Fig. L1-2. Manufacturer recommends renewing fuel filter after every 300 hours of operation. However, fuel filter renewal interval is more dependent upon fuel quality and cleanliness than length of service or operating conditions. If engine indicates signs of fuel starvation (loss of power or surging), renew filter regardless of hours of operation. After renewing filter, air must be bled from system as outlined in following paragraph.

BLEED FUEL SYSTEM. To bleed air from fuel system, loosen bleed screw or fuel supply line fitting on injection pump. On gravity feed system, allow fuel to flow from fitting until free of air. On models equipped with fuel transfer pump, manually operate hand primer lever to purge air from fuel supply line. Retighten or bleed screw.

NOTE: If cam which drives transfer pump is at full lift, priming lever cannot be operated. Turn crankshaft one revolution to reposition camshaft.

If engine fails to start, loosen high pressure fuel line at injector. Rotate engine crankshaft until fuel is discharged from injector line. Retighten injection line fitting and start engine.

INJECTION PUMP TIMING

Injection pump timing is adjusted using shim gaskets (G—Fig. L1-2) between pump body and mounting surface on crankcase. To check injection pump timing, unscrew high pressure delivery line (D) fitting from delivery valve holder (1—Fig. L1-3). Unscrew delivery valve holder and remove spring (3) and delivery valve (4), then screw delivery valve

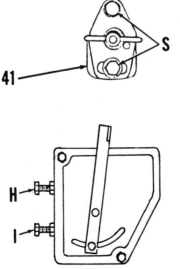

Fig. L1-1—Engine speed adjustment points. Refer to text for adjustment procedure.

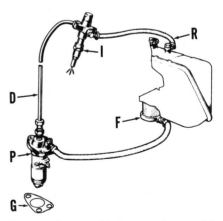

Fig. L1-2—Diagram of fuel system. Some models are also equipped with a fuel transfer pump (not shown), located between fuel tank and injection pump, which ensures constant fuel delivery to injection pump.

D. High pressure delivery line	
F. Fuel filter	I. Injector
G. Shim gasket	P. Injection pump
	R. Return line

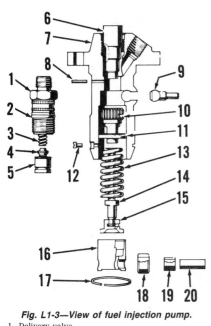

Fig. L1-3—View of fuel injection pump.

1. Delivery valve	11. Spring seat
holder	12. Pin
2. "O" ring	13. Spring
3. Spring	14. Plunger
4. Delivery valve	15. Spring retainer
5. Delivery valve seat	16. Tappet
6. Barrel	17. Snap ring
7. Pump body	18. Outer roller
8. Pin	19. Inner roller
9. Control rack	20. Pin
10. Pinion	

holder (1) into pump body. Move throttle control to full speed position. Rotate crankshaft in normal direction (counterclockwise at pto) so piston is on compression stroke. Note fuel in delivery valve holder will spill out. Stop crankshaft rotation at moment fuel ceases to flow out. At this point, beginning of injection occurs and timing dot (R—Fig. L1-4) on fan plate should be aligned with timing dot (I) on fan shroud. Injection timing should be 24-26 degrees BTDC.

Reduce pump mounting shim gasket thickness to advance timing or increase gasket thickness to retard timing. Reinstall delivery valve and spring and tighten holder to a torque of 35 N·m (26 ft.-lbs.). Tighten injection pump retaining screws to 25 N·m (18 ft.-lbs.).

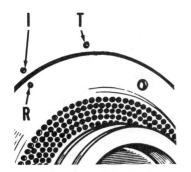

Fig. L1-4—View of timing marks located on air shroud. Refer to text for injection timing.

REPAIRS

TIGHTENING TORQUES

Refer to the following table for tightening torques.

Connecting rod	30 N·m (22 ft.-lbs.)
Cylinder head	50 N·m (37 ft.-lbs.)
Flywheel	170 N·m (125 ft.-lbs.)
Injection pump	25 N·m (18 ft.-lbs.)
Injector	25 N·m (18 ft.-lbs.)
Main bearing support:	
Flywheel side	30 N·m (22 ft.-lbs.)
Gear train side	25 N·m (18 ft.-lbs.)
Oil pan	25 N·m (18 ft.-lbs.)
Oil pump	40 N·m (30 ft.-lbs.)
Oil pump gear	20 N·m (15 ft.-lbs.)
Rocker arm cover	20 N·m (15 ft.-lbs.)
Timing gear cover	25 N·m (18 ft.-lbs.)

VALVE CLEARANCE ADJUSTMENT

Valve clearance should be 0.20 mm (0.008 inch) for intake and exhaust valve with engine cold. To adjust clearance, remove rocker arm cover and rotate crankshaft until piston is at TDC on compression stroke. Loosen rocker arm adjusting screw jam nut, then turn adjusting screw until proper thickness feeler gage can be inserted between valve stem end and rocker arm. Hold adjusting screw and tighten jam nut.

COMPRESSION RELEASE

A manual compression release is located in the rocker arm cover so the exhaust valve can be held open to aid starting. Exhaust valve should be lowered approximately 1 mm (0.040 inch) from valve seat when compression release is operated.

CYLINDER HEAD AND VALVE SYSTEM

Do not remove cylinder head when hot as head may warp. To remove rocker arms, unscrew rocker shaft locating pin (21—Fig. L1-5). Withdraw rocker shaft using a suitable puller. Maximum allowable rocker arm to shaft clearance is 0.1 mm (0.004 inch).

Valve face angle is 45 degrees for intake and exhaust. If valve head margin is less than 0.4 mm (0.016 inch), renew valve. Valve seat angle is 45 degrees and recommended seat width is 1.4-1.6 mm (0.055-0.065 inch). Renewable valve seat inserts are used on intake and exhaust. When installing new inserts, cylinder head should first be heated in an oven to 160°-180° C (320°-355° F).

With valves installed, measure distance valve head is recessed from cylinder head mounting surface. Intake valve should be recessed 0.60-0.80 mm (0.024-0.031 inch). Exhaust valve (except models with decompression should be recessed 0.55-1.05 mm (0.022-0.041 inch). On engines equipped with compression release, exhaust valve recession should be 0.55-0.95 mm (0.022-0.037 inch). If recession is less than specified, regrind valve seats. If valve recession exceeds specified limits, renew valve seat insert.

Valve stem diameter should be 6.98-7.00 mm (0.2748-0.2756 inch). Desired valve stem clearance in guides is 0.03-0.08 mm (0.001-0.003 inch). Valve guides are renewable and oversize guide must be machined to provide a 0.05-0.06 mm (0.0020-0.0023 inch) interference fit in cylinder head bore. The cylinder head should be heated to 160°-180° C (320°-355° F) prior to installing guides. Note locating ring (12—Fig. L1-5) around top of each guide. After installation, inside diameter of guides must be reamed or honed to provide desired valve stem clearance.

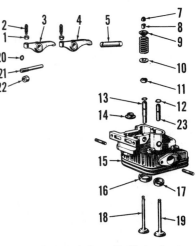

Fig. L1-5—Exploded view of cylinder head assembly.

1. Locknut	
2. Adjuster	14. Spring seat
3. Intake rocker arm	15. Cylinder head
4. Exhaust rocker arm	16. Intake valve seat
5. Rocker arm shaft	17. Exhaust valve seat
7. Cap	18. Intake valve
8. Keys	19. Exhaust valve
9. Spring retainer	20. "O" ring
10. Washer	21. Rocker shaft
11. Oil seal	locating pin
12. Snap ring	22. Locknut
13. Intake valve guide	23. Exhaust valve guide

Intake and exhaust valve springs are identical. Spring free length should be 45.6 mm (1.795 inches). Spring pressure should be 160-170 N (36-38 pounds) at a length of 34.2 mm (1.346 inches).

Cylinder head mounting surface must not be warped more than 0.3 mm (0.012 inch). Cylinder head and block mating surfaces may be lapped to improve fit.

When reinstalling cylinder head, be sure to examine push rod tube seals for damage and renew if needed. Tighten cylinder head nuts evenly using tightening sequence shown in Fig. L1-6. It is recommended that nuts be tightened in steps to a final torque of 50 N·m (37 ft.-lbs.).

INJECTOR

REMOVE AND REINSTALL. To remove injector, first clean dirt from injector, injection line, return line and cylinder head. Disconnect return and injection lines from injector and immediately cap or plug all openings. Unscrew injector retaining nuts and carefully remove injector from head being careful not to lose shims between injector and head.

Tighten injector retainer nuts to a torque of 25 N·m (18 ft.-lbs.). If accessible, measure protrusion of nozzle into combustion chamber. Nozzle tip should extend 3.0-3.5 mm (0.118-0.138 inch). Adjust position of nozzle by installing 0.5 mm (0.020 inch) shims between injector and cylinder head.

TESTING. A suitable test stand is required to check injector operation. Only clean, approved testing oil should be used to test injector. When operating properly, injector nozzle will emit a buzzing sound and should cut off quickly with no fluid leakage at nozzle valve seat.

WARNING: Fuel leaves the injector nozzle with sufficient force to penetrate the skin. When testing, keep yourself clear of nozzle spray.

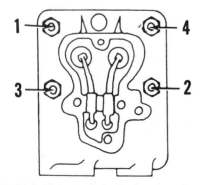

Fig. L1-6—Tighten cylinder head stud nuts in sequence shown.

Nozzle opening pressure should be 18,635-19,615 kPa (2705-2845 psi). Opening pressure is adjusted by turning adjuster screw (3—Fig. L1-7). Nozzle valve should not show leakage at orifice spray holes for 10 seconds with pressure maintained at 2100 kPa (300 psi) below opening pressure. Spray pattern should be even and well atomized. If pattern is wet, ragged or intermittent, nozzle must be overhauled or renewed.

OVERHAUL. Refer to exploded view of Fig. L1-7. When disassembling injector, protect polished parts from damage. Thoroughly clean parts in a suitable solvent. Clean inside orifice end of nozzle valve with wooden cleaning stick. The orifice spray holes may be cleaned by inserting a cleaning wire slightly smaller than the 0.28 mm (0.011 inch) diameter holes.

When reassembling injector, make certain all parts are clean and wet with diesel fuel. Nozzle valve needle (8) must slide freely in valve body (9). If needle valve sticks, reclean or renew nozzle valve assembly.

INJECTION PUMP

Refer to Fig. L1-3 for an exploded view of injection pump. To remove pump, disconnect fuel lines. Plug all openings to prevent entry of dirt. Remove retaining screws and lift out pump. Be sure to retain pump mounting gaskets for use in

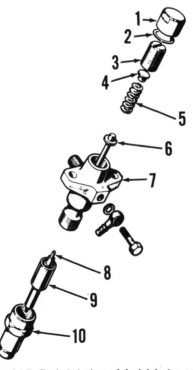

Fig. L1-7—Exploded view of fuel injector assembly.

1. Nut	6. Push rod
2. Gasket	7. Body
3. Adjuster	8. Needle
4. Spring seat	9. Nozzle valve
5. Spring	10. Nozzle nut

reassembly. Pump timing is adjusted by changing gasket thickness.

The injection pump should be tested and serviced only by a shop qualified in diesel fuel injection repair.

When reinstalling pump, assemble correct thickness of mounting shim gaskets and be sure to engage control rack pin with governor arm. Tighten retaining screws to a torque of 25 N·m (18 ft.-lbs.). Refer to MAINTENANCE section to check injection timing.

PISTON AND ROD UNIT

REMOVE AND REINSTALL. Piston and connecting rod may be removed after removing cylinder head and oil pan.

When reinstalling piston and rod, note that depression in piston crown is closer to one side of piston. Install piston so depression side of piston is nearer injector side of engine. Some pistons also have an arrow embossed in top of piston so arrow is pointing toward intake side of engine.

Install cap on connecting rod so bearing tang grooves are on the same side. Tighten rod bolts to a torque of 30 N·m (22 ft.-lbs.).

PISTON, PIN AND RINGS

The piston is equipped with three compression rings and one oil control ring. The top compression ring is chrome plated.

Ring end gap should be measured with ring positioned squarely in cylinder. Compression ring end gap should be 0.30-0.50 mm (0.011-0.020 inch). Oil control ring end gap should be 0.25-0.50 mm (0.010-0.020 inch).

To check piston ring groove wear, install new rings onto piston and check clearance between top of ring and top of groove. Renew piston if ring side clearance exceeds specified values as follows: 0.11-0.15 mm (0.004-0.006 inch) for top ring, 0.06-0.10 mm (0.002-0.004 inch) for second and third rings and 0.05-0.10 mm (0.002-0.004 inch) for oil control ring.

Refer to table in Fig. L1-9 for standard piston diameter and desired piston clearance in cylinder bore. Piston diameter is measured at bottom of skirt perpendicular to piston pin bore. Renew piston if wear exceeds 0.05 mm (0.002 inch). Pistons and rings are available in standard size and oversizes of 0.5 mm (0.020 inch) and 1.0 mm (0.040 inch).

Piston diameter is 22.995-23.000 mm (0.9053-0.9055 inch). Piston pin clearance in rod bushing should be 0.020-0.035 mm (0.0008-0.0014 inch). Maximum allowable clearance is 0.07 mm (0.003 inch). Pin is a thumb push fit in piston.

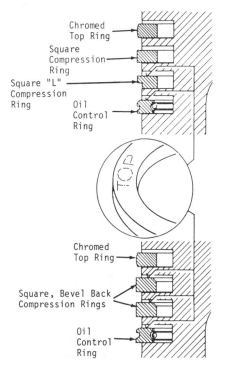

Fig. L1-8—Exploded view of crankshaft, governor and camshaft assemblies. Some models use flyweights instead of flyballs as shown.

1. Compression piston rings (3)
2. Oil control ring
3. Piston
4. Snap rings
5. Piston pin
6. Bushing
7. Connecting rod
8. Rod cap
9. Rod bearing
10. Lockplate
11. Screw
12. Lockplate
13. Plate
14. Key
15. Crankshaft
16. Key
17. Push rods
18. Exhaust cam follower
19. Intake cam follower
20. Camshaft
21. Screw
22. Snap ring
23. Rocker arm
24. Stud
27. Plate
28. Gear
29. Governor balls (6)
30. Snap ring
31. Cup
32. Washer
33. Governor shaft
34. Washer
35. Nut

Fig. L1-9—Refer to chart for standard piston diameter and desired piston clearance in cylinder bore.

CYLINDER

Model 3LD510 is equipped with a removable cylinder (1—Fig. L1-11). Standard cylinder diameter is 85.00-85.02 mm (3.346-3.347 inches). If taper or wear exceeds 0.1 mm (0.004 inch), rebore cylinder to an appropriate oversize.

With piston at top dead center, top of piston should be 0.75-0.90 mm (0.030-0.035 inch) below top surface of cylinder. Cylinder height is adjusted by varying cylinder mounting shim gaskets (2—Fig. L1-11).

TIMING GEARS

Gears are accessible after removing pto bearing support (5—Fig. L1-11). Crankshaft and camshaft gears are embossed with marks (M—Fig. L1-12) which should be aligned as shown. If crankshaft and camshaft gears are not marked, proceed as follows: If not previously removed, remove cylinder head, push rod tube and push rods. Position crankshaft so piston is at top dead center. Intake valve cam follower (nearer cylinder) should be opening (rising) and exhaust valve cam follower should be

MODEL	PISTON O.D.	PISTON CLEARANCE
3LD510	84.87 - 84.90 mm (3.341 - 3.342 in.)	0.10 - 0.15 mm (0.004 - 0.006 in.)

When installing rings onto piston, stagger ring end gaps 180 degrees apart. Be sure no end gaps are in line with piston pin bore. Refer to Fig. L1-10 for correct installation of rings on piston.

CONNECTING ROD

The connecting rod small end is fitted with a renewable bushing. Clearance between piston pin and connecting rod bushing should be 0.020-0.035 mm (0.0008-0.0014 inch). Maximum allowable clearance is 0.07 mm (0.003 inch).

A precision, insert type bearing is used in big end of connecting rod. Desired rod bearing clearance is 0.030-0.065 mm (0.0012-0.0025 inch). Bearings are available in standard and undersizes.

Fig. L1-12—View showing location of timing marks (M) on crankshaft and camshaft gears.

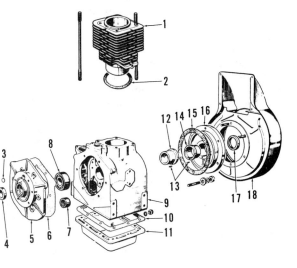

Fig. L1-11—Exploded view of typical crankcase.

1. Cylinder
2. Shim gasket
3. Plug
4. Seal
5. Pto bearing support
6. Gasket
7. Bearing
8. Bearing
9. Crankcase
10. Gasket
11. Oil pan
12. Main bearing
13. Dowel pins
14. Main bearing
15. Shim gasket
16. Main bearing support
17. Seal
18. Air shroud

Fig. L1-10—Cross section view showing correct installation of different styles of piston rings.

- Chromed Top Ring
- Square Compression Ring
- Square "L" Compression Ring
- Oil Control Ring
- Chromed Top Ring
- Square, Bevel Back Compression Rings
- Oil Control Ring

closing (going down). Both cam followers should be same height above crankcase when piston is at top dead center. If not, refer to CAMSHAFT section and remove camshaft, then reinstall camshaft so it is correctly timed with crankshaft. Mark crankshaft and camshaft gears for future reference.

CAMSHAFT, CAM FOLLOWERS AND PUSH RODS

To remove camshaft, first remove cylinder head, push rod tubes, push rods, cam followers and fuel injection pump. Remove pto bearing support (5—Fig. L1-11) and withdraw camshaft.

Inspect camshaft for excessive wear or other damage. Diameter of camshaft bearing journals is 17.96-17.98 mm (0.707-0.708 inch). Height of injection pump lobe should be 31.51 mm (1.240 inches). Height of intake lobe should be 33.95-34.05 mm (1.337-1.340 inches) on early models while intake lobe on late models is 33.68-33.78 mm (1.326-1.330 inches). Exhaust lobe height should be 33.45-33.55 (1.317-1.320 inches) on all models. If wear exceeds 0.1 mm (0.004 inch) on camshaft journals or lobes, renew camshaft.

Reassembly is the reverse of disassembly. Be certain timing marks (Fig. L1-12) on camshaft gear are aligned with mark on crankshaft gear. Camshaft end play should be 0.20-0.40 mm (0.008-0.016 inch). End play is adjusted by changing thickness of pto bearing support mounting gasket (6—Fig. L1-11). Note that cam follower rollers are offset to one side of holder and notched sliding surface is on opposite side of holder. Install cam followers so notched surfaces are together and intake cam follower is closer to cylinder barrel.

GOVERNOR

Model 3LD510 is equipped with a flyball type governor or a flyweight type governor. The governor shaft is shown in Fig. L1-8 while governor linkage is shown in Fig. L1-13. The crankshaft rotates flyball assembly (G—Fig. L1-14) which bears against fork (65—Fig. L1-13). As the flyballs move, the shaft attached to the fork is rotated thereby moving governor arm (55). Arm (55) mates with fuel injection control rack pin to regulate fuel flow. Throttle lever (45) operates through governor spring plates (64) to control engine speed.

To stop engine, stop knob (40) is turned counterclockwise which forces governor arm to move fuel injection pump control rack to no-fuel position. Model 3LD510 is equipped with a torque control rod (57) and spring (56) which allows the governor arm (59) additional

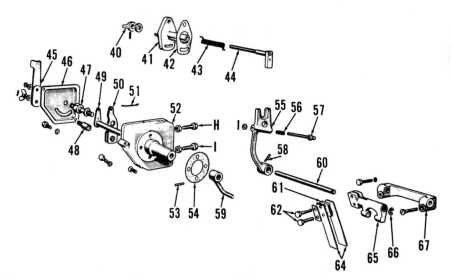

Fig. L1-13—Exploded view of governor and control linkage. Governor fork (65) contacts governor cup (31—Fig. L1-8).

40. Stop knob		62. Screws
41. Plate	48. Pivot screw	55. Arm	64. Spring plates
42. Gasket	49. Arm	56. Spring	65. Fork
43. Spring	50. Lever	57. Torque control rod	66. "E" ring
44. Stop arm	51. Link	58. Pin	67. Bracket
45. Throttle lever	52. Housing	59. Arm	I. Low idle speed
46. Cover	53. Pin	60. Shaft	screw
47. Stud	54. Gasket	61. Spacer	H. High speed screw

movement for additional fuel usage under high torque load. By pulling stop knob (40) away from engine, stop arm (44) will slide off tip of torque control rod (57) and allow governor arm to move forward so maximum fuel is delivered during starting.

Governor mechanism is accessible after removing pto bearing support (5—Fig. L1-11), however, the oil pan must be removed for access to nut (35—Fig. L1-8) so governor shaft can be withdrawn from crankcase. Inspect governor components and renew any which are damaged or excessively worn. Mechanism must move freely for proper governor operation. Tighten governor shaft nut to a torque of 40 N·m (30 ft.-lbs.).

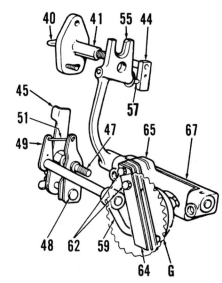

Fig. L1-14—Diagram of governor mechanism. Refer to text and Fig. L1-13 for parts identification.

To adjust governor, pto bearing support (5—Fig. L1-11) and gasket must be removed. Move throttle lever (45—Fig. L1-13) to full throttle position. Loosen spring plate screws (62), then move governor arm (55) toward crankcase opening and measure distance (G—Fig. L1-15) from pto bearing support mating surface of crankcase to upper part of governor arm. Distance between crankcase surface and governor arm should be 22 mm (0.866 inch). Retighten spring plate screws (62—Fig. L1-13).

OIL PUMP AND RELIEF VALVE

R&R AND OVERHAUL. To remove oil pump, remove pto bearing support (5—Fig. L1-11) and using a suitable puller re-

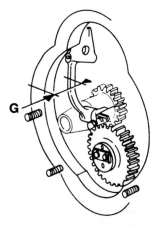

Fig. L1-15—With throttle lever in wide open position, distance (G) from pto bearing support mounting surface to upper part of governor arm should be 22 mm (0.866 inch).

move pump gear (3—Fig. L1-16). Unscrew pump mounting screws and remove pump from crankcase bulkhead. Maximum clearance between gears and pump body should not exceed 0.15 mm (0.006 inch). Maximum clearance between ends of gears and mounting surface of pump body is 0.15 mm (0.006 inch).

Apply a thin coating of sealer to mounting surface of pump body. Install pump and tighten mounting screws to 40 N·m (30 ft.-lbs.). Tighten oil pump gear nut to 20 N·m (15 ft.-lbs.). Install timing gear cover.

The oil pressure relief valve is located on inner face of main bearing support (16—Fig. L1-17). To remove main bearing support, remove crankshaft pulley or crank starter, flywheel and shroud. Unscrew retaining nuts and remove main bearing support. Inspect pressure relief valve components and renew if damaged or excessively worn. Reinstall relief valve by reversing disassembly procedure. With warm oil, minimum oil pressure should be 75 kPa (11 psi) at idle and 200 kPa (29 psi) at full throttle.

CRANKSHAFT AND BEARINGS

To remove crankshaft, remove crankshaft pulley or crank starter, then remove flywheel. Remove cylinder head,

oil pan, piston and connecting rod as previously outlined. Remove pto bearing support (5—Fig. L1-11) and air shroud (18). Remove main bearing support (16) and withdraw crankshaft from crankcase.

Thoroughly clean crankshaft making sure oil galleries are clear. Inspect for excessive wear and other damage.

Crankshaft main bearing journal standard diameter is 41.99-42.00 mm (1.6531-1.6535 inches) on pto end and 39.99-40.00 mm (1.5744-1.5748 inches) on flywheel end. Main bearings (12 and 14) are available in standard and 1.0 mm (0.040 inch) undersize. New bearings should be installed using a suitable installing tool such as part 7271.3595.047. After installation, check bearing ID and

ream bearing to obtain recommended clearance of 0.04-0.06 mm (0.0016-0.0023 inch). Maximum allowable bearing clearance is 0.10 mm (0.004 inch).

To reinstall crankshaft, reverse the removal procedure. A special installing tool, part 7271.3595.047, is available from manufacturer to install bearing in support (16—Fig. L1-11). Make certain lubrication oil holes in bearing and support are aligned. Renew oil seals (4 and 17) and lubricate lip of seals before reinstalling. Crankshaft end play should be 0.10-0.30 mm (0.004-0.012 inch) and is adjusted by varying thickness of bearing support gasket (15). Tighten nuts on flywheel side bearing support to 30 N·m (22 ft.-lbs.) and gear train side bearing support to 25 N·m (18 ft.-lbs.).

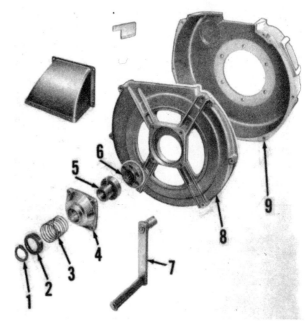

Fig. L1-18—Exploded view of manual crank starter used on some models.

1. Snap ring
2. Cap
3. Spring
4. Flange
5. Ring gear
6. Pinion
7. Crank
8. Cover
9. Case

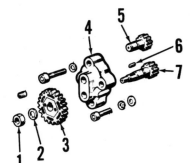

Fig. L1-16—Exploded view of oil pump.

1. Nut
2. Lockwasher
3. Gear
4. Pump body
5. Driven gear
6. Key
7. Drive gear

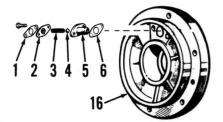

Fig. L1-17—Exploded view of typical oil pressure relief valve. Some models use a poppet type valve instead of ball (4) and body (5).

1. Lockplate
2. Cover
3. Spring
4. Ball
5. Body
6. Gasket
16. Main bearing support

Fig. L1-19—Wiring schematic for models equipped with internal alternator and electric starter.

1. Alternator
2. Regulator
3. Starter motor
4. Oil pressure switch
5. Oil pressure light

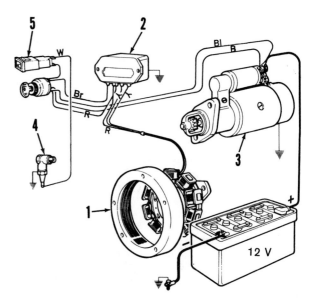

MANUAL CRANK STARTER

Some engines are equipped with a crank type manual starter as shown in Fig. L1-18. Starter repair is evident after inspection of unit.

ALTERNATOR AND REGULATOR

Refer to Fig. L1-19 or Fig. L1-20 for wiring schematic typical of models equipped with internal alternator and electric starter motor. Note that circuit illustrated in Fig. L1-20 is for models equipped with an alternator warning light and Fig. L1-19 is for models not equipped with a warning light. Voltage regulator is different for the two circuits.

The internal alternator is contained in the flywheel. Rated output is 13.5 amperes. Stator and rotor are available only as a unit assembly.

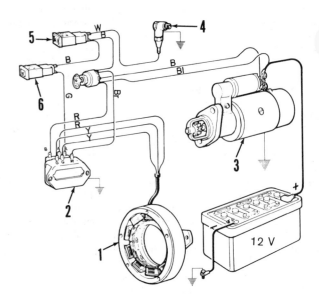

Fig. L1-20—Wiring schematic for models equipped with internal alternator and electric starter using an alternator warning light (6). Refer to L1-19 legend.

LOMBARDINI

Model	No. Cyls.	Bore	Stroke	Displacement
6LD360	1	82 mm	68 mm	359 cc
		(3.228 in.)	(2.677 in.)	(21.9 cu. in.)

Model 6LD360 is a four-stroke, air-cooled diesel engine. The cylinder head and cylinder block are aluminum while the cylinder is cast iron.

MAINTENANCE

LUBRICATION

Recommended engine oil is SAE 10W for temperatures below 0° C (32° F), SAE 20W for temperatures between 0° C (32° F) and 20° C (68° F) and SAE 40 for temperatures above 20° C (68° F). API classification for oil should be CD. Oil sump capacity is 1.0 liter (2.1 pints).

A renewable oil filter is located on side of engine block (Fig. L2-1). Manufacturer recommends renewing engine oil and filter after every 300 hours of operation.

ENGINE SPEED ADJUSTMENT

Idle speed is adjusted by turning idle speed screw (I—Fig. L2-2). Idle speed should be 1100-1400 rpm.

Maximum governed speed is adjusted by turning high speed screw (H). Set maximum (no-load) speed 180 rpm above engine rated load speed to com-pensate for governor droop during operation. Maximum speed under load is normally 3600 rpm.

FUEL SYSTEM

FUEL FILTER. The fuel filter may be located inside the fuel tank as shown in Fig. L2-3, or a cartridge type filter as shown in Fig. L2-4 may be used. Fuel filter should be renewed after every 300 hours of operation or sooner if required. After renewing filter, air must be bled from system as outlined in the following paragraph.

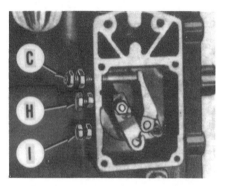

Fig. L2-2—Turn screw (I) to adjust low idle speed and screw (H) to adjust high idle speed. Refer to text for adjustment of torque control screw (C).

BLEED FUEL SYSTEM. On gravity flow fuel systems (Fig. L2-3), loosen fuel line fitting on injection pump and allow fuel to flow until free of air, then retighten fitting.

On models equipped with cartridge type filter (Fig. L2-4), unscrew bleed screw on filter housing and allow fuel to flow until free of air.

On models equipped with a fuel transfer pump (L—Fig. L2-4), loosen fuel supply line fitting on injection pump. Manually operate fuel pump primer lever until fuel flows from fitting, then retighten fitting.

If engine fails to start after bleeding air from filter and fuel line, loosen high pressure line at injector. Rotate crankshaft to operate injection pump until fuel is discharged at injector line fitting. Retighten injector line and start engine.

INJECTION PUMP TIMING

Injection pump timing is adjusted using shim gaskets (G—Fig. L2-3 and Fig. L2-4) between pump body and mounting surface of crankcase. To check pump timing, unscrew injector line (D) fitting from pump delivery union (1—Fig. L2-5). Unscrew delivery union and remove spring (3), washer (4) and delivery valve (5). Do not remove valve seat (7). Reinstall delivery union into pump body. Move throttle control lever to full speed position. Rotate crankshaft in normal

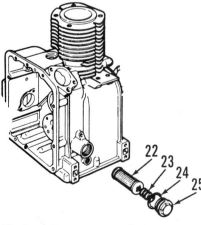

Fig. L2-1—Engine oil filter is located in side of crankcase.

22. Oil filter
23. Spring
24. "O" ring
25. Plug

Fig. L2-3—Diagram of fuel system with filter located in tank.

D. High pressure line
F. Fuel filter
G. Shim gasket
I. Injector
P. Injection pump
R. Return line

Fig. L2-4—Diagram of fuel system equipped with fuel filter cartridge and fuel transfer pump used on some models.

D. High pressure line
F. Fuel filter
G. Shim gasket
I. Injector
L. Fuel pump
P. Injection pump
R. Return line

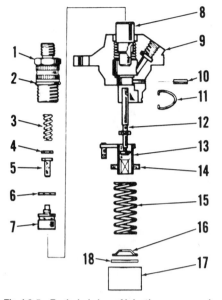

Fig. L2-5—Exploded view of injection pump used on all models. Pump is actuated by engine camshaft.

1. Delivery union
2. "O" ring
3. Spring
4. Washer
5. Delivery valve
6. Gasket
7. Delivery valve seat
8. Barrel
9. Pump body
10. Pin
11. Clip
12. Plunger
13. Control sleeve
14. Spring seat
15. Spring
16. Spring retainer
17. Tappet
18. Spacer

direction of rotation so piston is on compression stroke. Note that fuel should flow from delivery union. Stop crankshaft rotation at moment fuel ceases to spill out of union. This is beginning of injection and timing dot (R—Fig. L2-6) on crankshaft pulley should be aligned with injection timing dot (I) on fan shroud.

If fuel stops flowing before timing dots are aligned (timing advanced), add shims under pump. If fuel stops flowing late (timing retarded), reduce thickness of shim gaskets.

Fig. L2-6—Injection should occur when timing dot (R) of crankshaft pulley is aligned with timing dot (I) on fan shroud. Piston is at TDC when timing dot (R) and mark (T) are aligned.

After pump timing is properly adjusted, tighten pump mounting cap screws to a torque of 30 N·m (22 ft.-lbs.). Bleed air from system as previously outlined.

REPAIRS

TIGHTENING TORQUES

Refer to the following table for tightening torques.

Connecting rod	34 N·m (25 ft.-lbs.)
Cylinder head	34 N·m (25 ft.-lbs.)
Flywheel	145 N·m (110 ft.-lbs.)
Injection pump	30 N·m (22 ft.-lbs.)
Injector	12 N·m (9 ft.-lbs.)
Main bearing support:	
Flywheel end	30 N·m (22 ft.-lbs.)
Gear train end	44 N·m (33 ft.-lbs.)
Oil pan	25 N·m (18 ft.-lbs.)
Oil pump	12 N·m (9 ft.-lbs.)
Oil pump gear	25 N·m (18 ft.-lbs.)
Rocker arm cover	20 N·m (15 ft.-lbs.)
Timing gear cover	44 N·m (33 ft.-lbs.)

VALVE CLEARANCE ADJUSTMENT

To adjust valve clearance, first remove rocker arm cover and rotate crankshaft until piston is at TDC on compression stroke. Clearance between valve stem end and rocker arm should be 0.15 mm (0.006 inch) for both intake and exhaust with engine cold. Note that there are two adjusting screws (Fig. L2-7) in exhaust rocker arm on models equipped with compression release mechanism.

Fig. L2-7—With compression release lever (L) in released position, turn outer adjusting screw (C) so clearance is 0.9-1.1 mm (0.035-0.043 inch) between screw and shaft. Adjusting inner screw (V) on rocker arm determines valve clearance.

Inner adjusting screw (V) is used to adjust valve clearance while outer screw (C) is used to adjust compression release gap.

COMPRESSION RELEASE

Some models are equipped with a manual compression release so the exhaust valve may be held open to aid starting. Compression release components (24 through 29—Fig. L2-8) are mounted in the cylinder head. Rotating shaft (26) will force the exhaust rocker arm (10) to slightly open the exhaust valve.

The compression release is adjusted by turning outer adjusting screw (C—Fig. L2-7) in exhaust valve rocker arm. Adjust compression release gap AFTER adjusting exhaust valve clearance. With compression lever (L) in off position, clearance between adjusting screw and shaft should be 0.9-1.1 mm (0.035-0.043 inch).

Diameter of compression release shaft (26—Fig. L2-8) is 9.37-10.00 mm (0.369-0.393 inch) while lobe height is 8.45-8.50 mm (0.333-0.334 inch).

CYLINDER HEAD AND VALVE SYSTEM

Cylinder head should not be removed while hot as it may warp as a result. If cylinder head mounting surface is warped or pitted, up to 0.3 mm (0.012 inch) of material may be lapped from head to true surface.

Valve face angle is 45 degrees for both valves. Renew valve if head margin is less than 0.5 mm (0.002 inch). Valve seat angle is 45 degrees and recommended seat width is 1.4-1.6 mm (0.055-0.065 inch). Renewable valve seat inserts are used on intake and exhaust. Before installing new inserts, cylinder head should first be heated to 160°-189° C (320°-355° F).

With valves installed, measure distance valve head is recessed from cylinder head surface. Intake valve should be recessed 0.70-0.90 mm (0.028-0.035

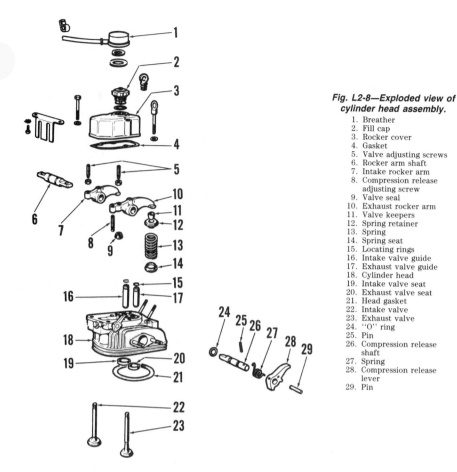

Fig. L2-8—Exploded view of cylinder head assembly.

1. Breather
2. Fill cap
3. Rocker cover
4. Gasket
5. Valve adjusting screws
6. Rocker arm shaft
7. Intake rocker arm
8. Compression release adjusting screw
9. Valve seal
10. Exhaust rocker arm
11. Valve keepers
12. Spring retainer
13. Spring
14. Spring seat
15. Locating rings
16. Intake valve guide
17. Exhaust valve guide
18. Cylinder head
19. Intake valve seat
20. Exhaust valve seat
21. Head gasket
22. Intake valve
23. Exhaust valve
24. "O" ring
25. Pin
26. Compression release shaft
27. Spring
28. Compression release lever
29. Pin

thickness. Gaskets are available in thicknesses of 0.5 mm (0.020 inch), 0.6 mm (0.023 inch), 0.7 mm (0.027 inch) and 0.8 mm (0.031 inch).

Tighten cylinder head nuts in steps using a crossing pattern as shown in Fig. L2-10. Final torque should be 34 N·m (25 ft.-lbs.).

INJECTOR

REMOVE AND REINSTALL. To remove injector, first clean dirt from injector, injection line, return line and cylinder head. Disconnect fuel return line and injection line and immediately cap or plug all openings. Unscrew retainer plate nuts and lift off retainer plate (1—Fig. L2-11) being careful not to lose dowel pin (2). Injector may now be carefully removed from cylinder head. Do

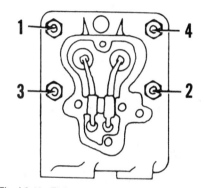

Fig. L2-10—Tighten cylinder head nuts in steps using a crossing pattern.

inch) and exhaust valve (except models with compression release) should be recessed 0.25-0.75 mm (0.010-0.030 inch). With compression release, exhaust valve recession should be 0.55-0.95 mm (0.022-0.037 inch). If recession is less than specified, regrind valve seat. If valve recession exceeds specified limit, renew valve seat insert.

Valve stem diameter is 6.98-7.00 mm (0.2748-0.2756 inch). Desired valve stem clearance in guide is 0.03-0.08 mm (0.001-0.003 inch) for both valves and maximum allowable clearance is 0.15 mm (0.006 inch). Valve guides are renewable and oversize guides available. Outer diameter of oversize guide must be machined to provide a 0.05-0.06 mm (0.0020-0.0023 inch) interference fit in cylinder head bore. Cylinder head should be heated to 160°-180° C (320°-355° F) prior to installing new guides. A locating ring around top of guide determines distance guide is pressed into head. After installation, check guide inside diameter and ream as necessary to provide desired valve stem clearance.

Intake and exhaust valve springs are identical. Spring free length should be 42 mm (1.653 inches). Valve spring pressure should be 219-233 N (49-52 pounds) at 32 mm (1.260 inches).

The cylinder head gasket is available in varying thicknesses to adjust clearance between cylinder head surface and top of piston. Clearance must be 0.6-0.7 mm (0.024-0.027 inch) with piston at TDC. To determine required gasket thickness, measure from piston crown to gasket seating surface of cylinder as shown in Fig. L2-9. Subtract measurement (if piston is below sealing surface) or add measurement (if piston is above sealing surface) to 0.6-0.7 mm (0.024-0.027 inch) to obtain required gasket

Fig. L2-9—Measure piston height in cylinder and refer to text to determine cylinder head gasket thickness.

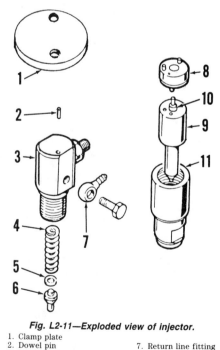

Fig. L2-11—Exploded view of injector.

1. Clamp plate
2. Dowel pin
3. Nozzle body
4. Spring
5. Shim
6. Spring seat
7. Return line fitting
8. Spacer
9. Nozzle valve
10. Nozzle needle
11. Nozzle holder nut

not lose shims between injector and cylinder head.

Tighten injector retaining plate nuts to 12 N·m (9 ft.-lbs). If accessible, measure protrusion of nozzle into combustion chamber. Nozzle tip should extend 2.5-3.0 mm (0.100-0.118 inch) above adjacent combustion chamber surface. Adjust position of nozzle by installing shims between injector and cylinder head. Shims are available in thicknesses of 0.5 mm (0.020 inch) and 1.0 mm (0.040 inch).

TESTING. A suitable test stand is required to check injector operation. Only clean, approved testing oil should be used to test injector.

Connect injector to tester and operate tester lever to purge air from nozzle and to make sure nozzle valve is not stuck. When operating properly, injector nozzle will emit a buzzing sound and cut off quickly with no leakage at the tip.

Opening pressure should be 18,630-19,610 kPa (2700-2845 psi). If a new spring (4—Fig. L2-11) is being used, set opening pressure 1000 kPa (145 psi) higher than specified pressure settings to compensate for spring seating during initial operation. On all models, opening pressure is adjusted by varying thickness of shims (5).

To check for leakage past nozzle valve, operate tester lever slowly to maintain pressure at 2100 kPa (300 psi) below opening pressure. If a drop of fuel forms on nozzle tip within a 10 second period, nozzle valve must be overhauled or renewed. Slight wetness at the tip is permissible.

Operate tester lever briskly and check for an even and well atomized spray pattern. If pattern is wet, ragged or intermittent nozzle must be overhauled or renewed.

OVERHAUL. Clamp nozzle body (3—Fig. L2-11) in a vise with nozzle tip facing upward. Remove nozzle holder nut (11). Remove nozzle valve (9) and spacer (8). Invert nozzle body and remove spring seat (6), shims (5) and spring (4).

Thoroughly clean all parts in a suitable solvent. Do not use steel wire brush or sharp metal tools to clean injector components. Clean inside orifice end of nozzle valve with wooden cleaning stick. The orifice spray holes may be cleaned by inserting a cleaning wire slightly smaller in diameter than the spray holes. Spray hole diameter is 0.24 mm (0.009 inch). Make certain nozzle needle (10) slides freely in bore of nozzle valve set (9). If needle sticks, reclean or renew nozzle assembly.

When reassembling injector, be sure all components are clean and wet with

diesel fuel. Recheck injector operation as outlined in TESTING paragraph.

INJECTION PUMP

Refer to Fig. L2-5 for an exploded view of injection pump. To remove pump, disconnect fuel lines and immediately plug all openings to prevent entry of dirt. Remove retaining screws and lift out pump assembly. Be sure to retain pump mounting gaskets for use in reassembly. Pump timing is adjusted by changing gasket thickness.

It is recommended that injection pump be tested and serviced only by a shop qualified in diesel fuel injection repair.

When reinstalling pump, assemble correct thickness of mounting shim gaskets and be sure to engage control rack pin with governor arm. Tighten pump mounting screws to a torque of 25 N·m (18 ft.-lbs.). Loosen clamp nut (N—Fig. L2-12), then move throttle lever (T) to full speed position. Push governor lever (L) in until it stops thus moving injection pump control sleeve to maximum delivery. Tighten clamp nut (N).

Torque control screw (C—Fig. L2-13) serves as the full-load stop for governor linkage (L). Control screw is equipped with a spring-loaded tip which allows

additional fuel delivery under high torque load. To adjust torque control screw, run engine at high idle with no load. Turn screw so there is a gap (G) between tip (T) and lever (L) of 2.1-2.3 mm (0.083-0.090 inch).

GOVERNOR

Model 6LD360 is equipped with a flyweight or ball type centrifugal governor which is attached to the back of oil pump drive gear as shown in Fig. L2-14. The oil pump drive gear (1) is driven by the crankshaft and rotates governor flyweights or balls. Movement of flyweights or balls causes sleeve (5) to move against fork (7) which rotates attached governor shaft (8). As governor shaft rotates, the governor lever (L—Fig. L2-12) forces arm (F) against a pin in the injection pump control sleeve thereby controlling fuel delivery to cylinder. Throttle lever (T) operates through governor spring (S) to control engine speed.

Governor components must move freely for proper governor operation. Governor spring (S—Fig. L2-12) free length should be 56.9-57.0 mm (2.240-2.244 inches). Spindle (8—Fig. L2-14) diameter should be 7.95-7.96 mm (0.3130-0.3134 inch). Desired clearance between spindle and bore in oil pump housing (13) is 0.06-0.10 mm (0.002-0.004 inch) with a maximum allowable clearance of 0.15 mm (0.006 inch).

OIL PUMP

Refer to Fig. L2-14 for an exploded view of oil pump. The oil pump is accessible after removing crankcase cover (3—Fig. L2-15). Clearance between gears and pump body walls must not exceed 0.15 mm (0.006 inch). Renew oil pump if components are excessively worn or damaged. Tighten pump mounting screws evenly to 12 N·m (9 ft.-lbs.).

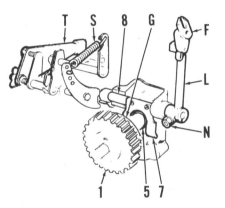

Fig. L2-12—View of governor mechanism. Refer to text for operation.

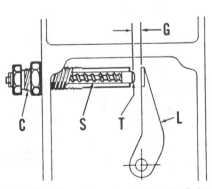

Fig. L2-13—View of torque control screw. Refer to text for adjustment.

Fig. L2-14—Exploded view of governor and oil pump assembly.

1. Drive gear	
2. Governor frame	
3. Pins	8. Spindle
4. Weights	9. Gear
5. Sleeve	10. Key
6. Stop	11. Gear & shaft
7. Fork	12. Cover
	13. Oil pump body

CAMSHAFT, CAM FOLLOWERS AND PUSH RODS

The camshaft rides directly in crankcase cover and crankcase bulkhead and is accessible after removing crankcase cover (3—Fig. L2-15). Cam followers (7 and 8) pivot on stud (9) and transfer motion to push rods (26) which pass through tube (28) to rocker arms. In addition to valve actuating lobes, a lobe is ground on the camshaft to operate the fuel injection pump.

Camshaft bearing journal diameters are 19.937-19.970 mm (0.7849-0.7862 inch) and 25.937-25.950 mm (1.0211-1.0216 inches). If wear exceeds 0.10 mm (0.004 inch), renew camshaft.

Cam follower pivot stud (9) diameter should be 9.4-9.6 mm (0.370-0.378 inch). Maximum allowable clearance between pivot stud and cam followers is 0.10 mm (0.004 inch).

Install camshaft so timing marks (M—Fig. L2-16) are aligned. If timing marks are absent from gears, proceed as follows: Position piston at top dead center (TDC) then install camshaft so intake cam follower is on opening side of cam lobe and exhaust cam follower is on closing side of cam lobe. If necessary, remesh gears so cam followers are at same height. Mark gears for future reference.

Depth of camshaft in crankcase must not be greater than 0.10 mm (0.004 inch) as measured from thrust face (TF—Fig. L2-16) to crankcase gasket surface (G). Camshaft end play should be 0.10-0.30 mm (0.004-0.012 inch) and is adjusted by varying thickness of crankcase cover gasket (4—Fig. L2-15). Apply Loctite to crankcase cover (3) screws and tighten to 45 N·m (33 ft.-lbs.).

The push rods are contained in tube (28) and must cross between cam followers and rocker arms. Push rod nearer

Fig. L2-16—View of camshaft and crankshaft gear timing marks (M). Measure depth of camshaft thrust face (TF) from crankcase gasket surface (G) as outlined in text.

cylinder connects intake cam follower and rocker arm while outer push rod connects exhaust cam follower and rocker arm.

PISTON AND ROD UNIT

Piston and connecting rod may be removed after removing cylinder head and oil pan.

When reinstalling piston and rod, note that depression (D—Fig. L2-17) in piston crown is closer to one side of piston. Install piston so depression side of piston is aligned with injector. Some pistons also have an arrow embossed in piston crown as shown in Fig. L2-17. Properly installed, arrow on piston crown will point toward flywheel.

The connecting rod and cap have machined serrations which must mate during assembly. Match marks on rod and cap must be on same side. Tighten connecting rod screws to 34 N·m (25 ft.-lbs.).

PISTON, PIN, RINGS AND CYLINDER

The piston on early models (before engine number 1098888) is equipped with two compression rings and one oil control ring. Late model engines are equipped with three compression rings and one oil control ring.

Ring end gap should be 0.25-0.45 mm (0.010-0.018 inch) for top compression ring, 0.30-0.45 mm (0.012-0.018 inch) for second and third compression rings and 0.25-0.40 mm (0.010-0.015 inch) for oil ring. Be sure rings are positioned squarely in cylinder when checking end gap.

To check piston ring groove wear, install rings onto piston and measure side clearance between top of ring and top of groove. Side clearance should be 0.11-0.15 mm (0.005-0.006 inch) for top

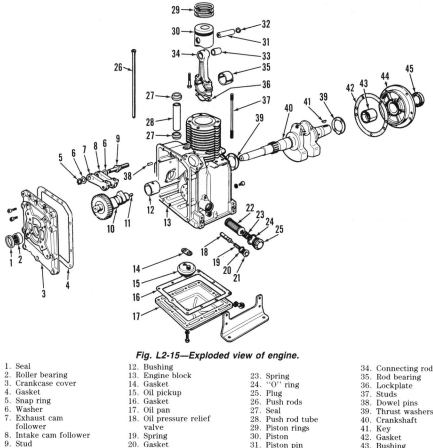

Fig. L2-15—Exploded view of engine.

1. Seal	12. Bushing	
2. Roller bearing	13. Engine block	
3. Crankcase cover	14. Gasket	
4. Gasket	15. Oil pickup	23. Spring
5. Snap ring	16. Gasket	24. "O" ring
6. Washer	17. Oil pan	25. Plug
7. Exhaust cam	18. Oil pressure relief	26. Push rods
follower	valve	27. Seal
8. Intake cam follower	19. Spring	28. Push rod tube
9. Stud	20. Gasket	29. Piston rings
10. Camshaft	21. Plug	30. Piston
11. Plug	22. Oil filter	31. Piston pin
		32. Snap ring
		33. Bushing

34. Connecting rod
35. Rod bearing
36. Lockplate
37. Studs
38. Dowel pins
39. Thrust washers
40. Crankshaft
41. Key
42. Gasket
43. Bushing
44. Support
45. Seal

Fig. L2-17—Install piston so depression (D) is nearer flywheel side of engine. Some pistons may have an arrow on crown and arrow must point toward flywheel.

groove, 0.06-0.10 mm (0.002-0.004 inch) for second and third compression ring grooves and 0.05-0.10 mm (0.002-0.004 inch) for oil ring groove. Renew piston if side clearance is excessive.

Clearance between piston pin and connecting rod bushing should be 0.01-0.03 mm (0.0004-0.0012 inch). If clearance exceeds 0.07 mm (0.0027 inch), renew pin and bushing. Pin should be a thumb push fit in piston.

Standard piston diameter, measured at bottom of skirt perpendicular to pin bore, is 81.88-81.89 mm (3.2236-3.2240 inches). Renew piston if skirt wear exceeds 0.05 mm (0.002 inch). Piston and rings are available in standard size and oversizes of 0.5 mm (0.020 inch) and 1.0 mm (0.040 inch).

Cylinder standard inside diameter is 82.00-82.02 mm (3.2283-3.2291 inches). If cylinder taper or out-of-round exceeds 0.1 mm (0.004 inch), rebore cylinder to appropriate oversize.

When reinstalling rings onto piston, stagger ring end gaps 180 degrees apart. Be sure no end gaps are in line with piston pin bore. Lubricate piston, rings and cylinder with clean engine oil prior to reassembly.

CONNECTING ROD

The connecting rod small end is fitted with a renewable bushing. Clearance between piston pin and bushing should be 0.01-0.03 mm (0.0004-0.0012 inch). An insert type bearing is used in connecting rod big end. Crankshaft crankpin diameter should be 39.99-40.00 mm (1.5744-1.5748 inches) and desired clearance in bearing is 0.03-0.06 mm (0.0012-0.0024 inch). Maximum allowable clearance is 0.10 mm (0.004 inch). Bearings are available in undersizes of 0.25 mm (0.010 inch) and 0.50 mm (0.020 inch) as well as standard size.

CRANKSHAFT AND CRANKCASE

The crankshaft is supported by bushing (12—Fig. L2-15) in the crankcase bulkhead, bushing (43) in support (44) on flywheel side and by a roller bearing (2) in the crankcase cover (3).

Desired bearing clearance for center and flywheel end main bearings is 0.03-0.06 mm (0.0012-0.0024 inch). Crankshaft journal diameter for center and flywheel end bearings is 39.99-40.00 mm (1.5744-1.5748 inches). Special bearing installing tool 7271.3595.047 is available from Lombardini to properly install main bearings. Be sure oil hole in center bearing is aligned with hole in crankcase.

Crankshaft end thrust is taken by thrust washers (39—Fig. L2-15). Thrust washer thickness should be 2.31-2.36 mm (0.090-0.092 inch). Desired crankshaft end play is 0.10-0.30 mm (0.004-0.012 inch). End play is adjusted by removing or adding gaskets (42) between support (44) and crankcase.

Inspect oil seals (1 and 45) and renew if necessary. Be sure to lubricate lip of seals before reassembling. Tighten flywheel side support plate cap screws to a torque of 30 N·m (22 ft.-lbs.) and crankcase cover cap screws to 45 N·m (33 ft.-lbs.).

ALTERNATOR

The internal alternator is mounted on the flywheel end of engine. The stator is secured to the engine crankcase while a ring of permanent magnets is carried by the flywheel. Note wiring schematic in Fig. L2-18.

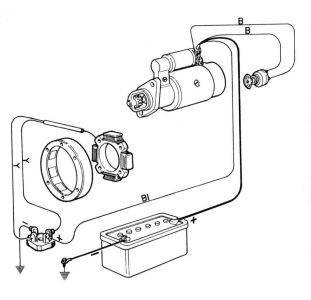

Fig. L2-18—Typical wiring schematic for engines equipped with alternator and electric starter.

TECUMSEH
2-STROKE

TECUMSEH PRODUCTS COMPANY
900 North Street
Grafton, WI 53024

Model	Bore	Stroke	Displacement
TC200	1.4375 in. (36.51 mm)	2.250 in. (57.15 mm)	2.0 cu. in. (32.8 cc)

ENGINE INFORMATION

Engine type and model numbers are stamped into blower housing base as indicated in Fig. TP3-1. Always furnish engine model and type number when ordering parts.

MAINTENANCE

SPARK PLUG. Recommended spark plug is a Champion RCJ-8Y, or equivalent. Specified electrode gap is 0.030 inch (0.76 mm).

AIR CLEANER. Air cleaner element should be removed and cleaned at eight hour intervals of use. Polyurethane element may be washed in a mild detergent and water solution and squeezed until all dirt is removed. Rinse thoroughly. Wrap in clean dry cloth and squeeze until completely dry. Apply engine oil to element and squeeze out excess. Clean air cleaner body and cover and dry thoroughly.

CARBURETOR. Tecumseh TC200 engines are equipped with a diaphragm type carburetor with a single idle mixture needle. Initial adjustment of idle mixture needle is one turn open from a lightly seated position.

Final carburetor adjustment is made with engine at operating temperature

and running. Operate engine at idle speed and turn idle mixture needle slowly clockwise until engine falters. Note this position and turn idle mixture needle counterclockwise until engine begins to run unevenly. Note this position and turn adjustment screw until it is halfway between first (lean) and last (rich) positions.

To disassemble carburetor, refer to Fig. TP3-2. Remove idle speed stop screw (9) and spring. Remove pump cover (10), gasket (11) and diaphragm (12). Remove cover (1), diaphragm (2)

and gasket (3). Carefully remove pin (15), metering lever (4), inlet needle valve (5) and spring (6). Remove screws retaining throttle plate to throttle shaft (8). Remove screws retaining choke plate to choke shaft (14). Remove "E" clip from throttle shaft and choke shaft and remove shafts. Remove all non-metallic parts, idle mixture needle, fuel inlet screen and fuel inlet (13). Remove all Welch plugs.

Clean and inspect all parts. Do not allow parts to soak in cleaning solvent longer than 30 minutes.

To reassemble, install fuel inlet needle, metering lever spring and pin. Metering lever hooks onto the inlet needle and rests on the metering spring. Entire assembly is held in place by metering lever pin screw. Tip of metering lever must be 0.060-0.070 inch (1.52-1.78 mm) from the face of carburetor body (Fig. TP3-3).

Install diaphragm gasket so tabs of gaskets align with the bosses on the carburetor body. After gasket is in place, install the diaphragm again aligning tabs to bosses. The head of the rivet in the diaphragm must be toward the carburetor body. Check the atmospheric vent hole in the diaphragm cover to make certain it is clean. Install cover on carburetor.

Install pump diaphragm with the corner holes aligning with the same holes in the carburetor body. Align pump gasket in the same manner and place pump cover onto carburetor.

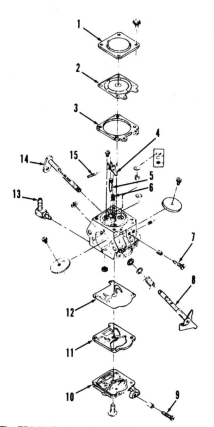

Fig. TP3-2—Exploded view of diaphragm type carburetor used on TC200 engine.
1. Cover
2. Diaphragm
3. Gasket
4. Metering lever
5. Inlet needle valve
6. Spring
7. Idle mixture needle
8. Throttle shaft
9. Idle speed screw
10. Cover
11. Gasket
12. Diaphragm
13. Fuel inlet
14. Choke shaft
15. Pin

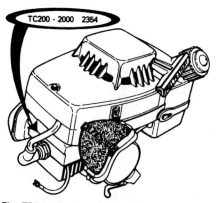

Fig. TP3-1—Engine model and type number is stamped into blower housing base.

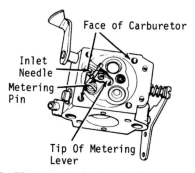

Fig. TP3-3—Tip of metering valve lever should be 0.060-0.070 inch (1.52-1.78 mm) from the face of carburetor body.

Numbers on throttle plate should face to the outside when throttle is closed. Apply a small amount of Loctite grade "A" to fuel inlet before installation.

IGNITION SYSTEM. All Model TC200 engines are equipped with a solid state ignition module located outside the flywheel. Correct air gap between laminations of module and magnets of flywheel is 0.012 inch (0.30 mm). Use Tecumseh gage part number 670297.

GOVERNOR ADJUSTMENT. Model TC200 engine is equipped with an air vane type governor. Refer to CRANK-SHAFT under REPAIRS section for adjustment procedure.

LUBRICATION. Engine is lubricated by mixing gasoline with a good quality two-stroke, air-cooled engine oil. Manufacturer recommends a fuel:oil ratio of 24:1.

CARBON. Muffler and exhaust ports should be cleaned after every 50 hours of operation if engine is operated continuously at full load. If operated at light or medium load, the cleaning interval can be extended to 100 hours.

REPAIRS

TIGHTENING TORQUES. Recommended tightening torque specifications are as follows:

Crankcase cover
to crankcase . . . . 70-100 in.-lbs.
(8-11 N · m)
Cylinder to crankcase . . 60-75 in.-lbs.
(7-8 N · m)
Carburetor . . . . 20-32 in.-lbs.
(2.3-3.6 N · m)
Flywheel nut . . . . 180-240 in.-lbs.
(20-27 N · m)
Ignition module . . . . 30-40 in.-lbs.
(3.4-4.5 N · m)
Starter retainer screw . . . . 45-55 in.-lbs.
(5.1-6.2 N · m)

CRANKSHAFT. To remove crankshaft, drain fuel tank, remove tank strap and disconnect fuel line at carburetor. Disconnect and remove spark plug. Remove the three screws retaining blower housing and rewind starter assembly and remove housing. Remove the two screws retaining ignition module. Use strap wrench to hold flywheel. Use flywheel puller tool (670299) to remove flywheel. Remove air cleaner assembly with carburetor, spacer, gaskets and screen. Mark and remove governor link from carburetor throttle lever. Remove the three 5/16 inch cap screws, then separate blower housing base from crankcase. Attach engine holder tool (670300) with the three blower housing base screws. Place tool in a bench vise. Remove muffler springs using tool fabricated from a 12 inch piece of heavy wire with a ¼ inch hook made on one end. Remove the four cylinder retaining nuts, then pull cylinder off squarely and in line with piston. Use caution so rod does not bend. Install seal protector tool (670206) at magneto end of crankshaft and seal protector tool (670263) at pto end of crankshaft. Remove crankcase cover screws, then carefully separate crankcase cover from crankcase. Rotate crankshaft to top dead center and withdraw crankshaft through crankcase cover opening while sliding connecting rod off crankpin and over crankshaft. Refer to Fig. TP3-4. Use care not to lose any of the 23 crankpin needle bearings which will be loose. Flanged side of connecting rod (Fig. TP3-5) must be toward pto side of engine after installation. Handle connecting rod carefully to avoid bending.

Standard crankpin journal diameter is 0.5985-0.5990 inch (15.202-15.215 mm). Standard crankshaft pto side main bearing journal diameter is 0.6248-0.6253 inch (15.870-15.880 mm). Standard crankshaft magneto side main bearing journal diameter is 0.4998-0.5003 inch (12.69-12.71 mm). Crankshaft end play should be 0.004-0.012 inch (0.10-0.30 mm).

To install crankshaft, clean mating surfaces of crankcase, cylinder and

crankcase cover. Avoid scarring or burring mating surfaces.

Crankshaft main bearing in crankcase of early model engines did not have a retaining ring as shown in Fig. TP3-6. Retaining ring was installed as a running change in late model engines. To install new caged bearing in crankcase, place bearing on installation tool (670302) with the numbered side of bearing away from tool. Press bearing into crankcase until tool is flush with crankcase housing. Install retaining ring (as equipped). Place seal for magneto side onto seal installation tool (670301) so metal case of seal enters tool first. Press seal in until tool is flush with crankcase. Use the same procedure to install bearing and seal in crankcase cover using bearing installation tool (670304) and seal installation tool (670303).

New crankpin needle bearings are on bearing strips. Heavy grease may be used to retain old bearings on crankpin journal as required. During reassembly, connecting rod must not be forced onto crankpin journal as rod failure or bending will result. Apply Loctite 515 to mating surfaces of crankcase during reassembly and use seal protectors when installing lip seals over ends of crankshaft. When installing cylinder over piston, install a wooden block with a slot cut out for connecting rod under piston to provide support and prevent connecting rod damage. Exhaust ports in cylinder are on the same side of engine as muffler resting boss. Make certain cylinder is correctly positioned, stagger ring end gaps and compress rings using a suitable ring compressor which can be removed after cylinder is installed over piston. Install cylinder and push cylinder onto crankcase studs to expose 1-2 threads of studs. Install the four nuts onto exposed threads of studs, then push cylinder further down to capture nuts on studs. Tighten nuts in a crisscross pattern to specified torque.

Install muffler using fabricated tool to install springs. Install blower housing

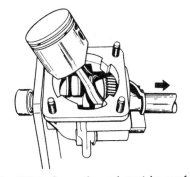

Fig. TP3-4—Connecting rod must be carefully worked over crankpin during crankshaft removal. Do not lose the 23 loose crankpin needle bearings.

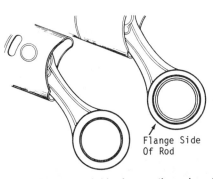

Fig. TP3-5—Flanged side of connecting rod must face pto side of engine after installation.

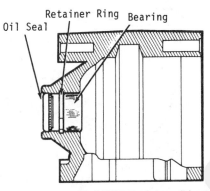

Fig. TP3-6—Early Model TC200 engines did not have retaining ring shown. Retaining ring was installed as a running change in late model engines.

base and tighten the three screws to specified torque.

Refer to Fig. TP3-7 to install governor air vane assembly. Speed adjustment lever is held in place by inserting screw into the blower housing base. Long end of governor spring hooks into the notch on neck of air vane. Short end hooks into the hole in speed adjustment lever. To decrease governed speed of engine, bend speed adjusting lever towards spark plug end of engine. To increase governed speed of engine, bend lever in the opposite direction. Throttle link is inserted into hole in the neck of the air vane and the hole closest to the throttle shaft in throttle plate.

Install carburetor, spacer, gaskets, screen and air cleaner body on engine. Tighten screws to specified torque. Install and adjust ignition module. Install blower housing/rewind starter assembly and tighten screws to specified torque. Install fuel tank.

PISTON, RINGS AND CONNECTING ROD. Standard piston diameter is 1.4327-1.4340 inch (36.39-36.42 mm). Standard width of both ring grooves is 0.050-0.051 inch (1.27-1.29 mm). Standard piston ring width is 0.46-0.47 inch (11.7-11.9 mm). Standard ring end gap is 0.004-0.014 inch (0.10-0.36 mm).

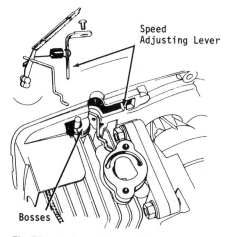

Fig. TP3-7—View of air vane governor assembly used on Model TC200 engines. Refer to text.

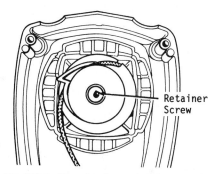

Fig. TP3-8—View showing rewind starter retaining screw.

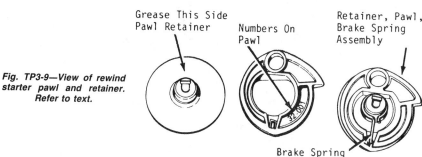

Fig. TP3-9—View of rewind starter pawl and retainer. Refer to text.

CYLINDER. Cylinder must be smooth and free of scratches or flaking. Clean carbon carefully as necessary. Standard bore size is 1.4375 inches (36.513 mm).

TECUMSEH SPECIAL TOOLS. Tecumseh special tools are available to aid in engine disassembly and reassembly are listed by use and tool part number.

FLYWHEEL PULLER 670299
AIR GAP GAGE 670297
ENGINE HOLDER 670300
SEAL PROTECTOR
    (MAG. END) 670206
SEAL PROTECTOR
    (PTO END) 670263
SEAL INSTALLER
    (MAG END) 670301
SEAL INSTALLER
    (PTO END) 670303
BEARING INSTALLER
    (MAG END) 670302
BEARING INSTALLER
    (PTO END) 670304

REWIND STARTER. The rewind starter assembly is incorporated into blower housing. Blower housing design varies according to engine model and specification number. To release rewind spring tension, remove staple in starter handle and slowly let spring tension release by winding rope onto rope sheave. Remove the 5/16 inch retainer screw (Fig. TP3-8). Remove pawl retainer and pawl (Fig. TP3-9) and extract starter pulley. Use caution not to pull rewind spring out of housing at this time. Uncoiling spring can be very dangerous. If rewind spring is damaged or weak, use caution when removing spring from housing.

To reassemble, grease center post of housing and portion of housing where rewind spring will rest. Grip rewind spring firmly with needlenose pliers ahead of spring tail. Insert spring and hook tail into housing as shown in Fig. TP3-10. Make certain spring is seated in housing before removing needlenose pliers from spring. Grease top of spring. Insert starter rope into starter pulley and tie a left handed knot in end of rope. With neck of starter pulley up, wind starter rope in a counterclockwise rotation. Place end of rope in notch of pulley and

place pulley in housing. Press down on pulley and rotate until pulley attaches to rewind spring. Refer to Fig. TP3-11. Lubricate pawl retainer with grease and place the pawl, numbers up, onto retainer. Place brake spring on center of retainer with tab locating into pawl Fig. TP3-9). Tab on pawl retainer must align with notch in center post of housing and locating hole in pawl must mesh with boss on starter pulley (Fig. TP3-12). Install retainer screw (Fig. TP3-8) and tighten to specified torque. Use starter rope to wind spring a minimum of 2 turns counterclockwise and a maximum of 3 turns. Feed starter rope through starter grommet and secure starter handle using a left-hand knot.

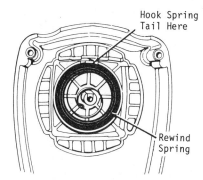

Fig. TP3-10—View of rewind spring and housing.

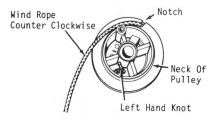

Fig. TP3-11—View showing rewind starter rope as shown and as outlined in text.

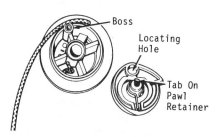

Fig. TP3-12—Boss must engage locating hole on pawl retainer. Refer to text.

TECUMSEH

4-STROKE

LIGHT FRAME MODELS

HP	Crankshaft	Bore	Stroke	Displacement
3	Horizontal	2.3 in.	1.81 in.	7.61 cu. in.
(2.24 kW)		(58.7 mm)	(46.04 mm)	(124.71 cc)
3	Horizontal	2.3 in.	1.84 in.	7.75 cu. in.
(2.24 kW)		(58.7 mm)	(46.74 mm)	(126.00 cc)
3.5	Horizontal	2.5 in.	1.81 in.	8.90 cu. in.
(2.61 kW)		(63.5 mm)	(46.04 mm)	(145.84 cc)
3.5	Horizontal	2.5 in.	1.84 in.	9.06 cu. in.
(2.61 kW)		(63.5 mm)	(46.74 mm)	(148.47 cc)
4	Horizontal	2.6 in.	1.94 in.	10.50 cu. in.
(2.98 kW)		(66.7 mm)	(49.21 mm)	172.06 cc)
5	Horizontal	2.8 in.	1.94 in.	12.00 cu. in.
(3.73 kW)		(71.4 mm)	(49.21 mm)	(196.64 cc)

MEDIUM FRAME MODELS

HP	Crankshaft	Bore	Stroke	Displacement
4	Horizontal	2.5 in.	2.25 in.	11.04 cu. in.
(2.98 kW)		(63.5 mm)	(57.15 mm)	(180.91 cc)
5	Horizontal	2.4 in.	2.25 in.	12.18 cu. in.
(3.73 kW)		(66.7 mm)	(57.15 mm)	(199.53 cc)
6	Horizontal	2.4 in.	2.50 in.	13.53 cu. in.
(4.47 kW)		(66.7 mm)	(63.50 mm)	(221.72 cc)
7	Horizontal	2.9 in.	2.53 in.	17.16 cu. in.
(5.22 kW)		(74.6 mm)	(64.29 mm)	(281.20 cc)
8	Horizontal	3.1 in.	2.53 in.	19.41 cu. in.
(5.97 kW)		(79.38 mm)	(64.29 mm)	(318.07 cc)

Engines must be identified by the complete model number, including the specification number in order to obtain correct repair parts. These numbers are located on the name plate and/or tags that are positioned as shown in Fig. T1. It is important to transfer identification tags from the original engine to replacement short block assemblies so that unit can be identified when servicing later.

MAINTENANCE

SPARK PLUG. Recommended spark plug is Champion J-8 or equivalent. Set electrode gap to 0.030 inch (0.762 mm). Spark plug should be removed, cleaned and adjusted periodically. Renew plug if electrodes are burned and pitted or if porcelain is cracked. If frequent plug fouling is experienced, check for following conditions:

a. Carburetor setting too rich
b. Partially closed choke
c. Clogged air filter
d. Incorrect spark plug
e. Poor grade of gasoline
f. Too much oil or crankcase breather clogged

CARBURETOR. Several different carburetors are used on these engines. Refer to the appropriate following paragraph for service and adjustment.

TECUMSEH DIAPHRAGM CARBURETOR. Idle mixture is adjusted at needle (10–Fig. T2). High speed mixture is adjusted at main fuel needle (14). Initial setting is 1 turn open for both needles and clockwise rotation will lean the mixture. Make final mixture adjustment with engine warm and operating with the normal amount of load. Adjust the main fuel needle (14) for smoothest operation at governed speed, then adjust idle needle (10) for smoothest operation at idle (slow) speed. Idle speed is adjusted at stop screw (9) and should be approximately 1800 rpm.

Observe the following when overhauling Tecumseh diaphragm carburetors: The carburetor model number i stamped on the mounting flange. Th fuel strainer in the fuel inlet fitting can be cleaned by reverse flushing with compressed air after the inlet needle and

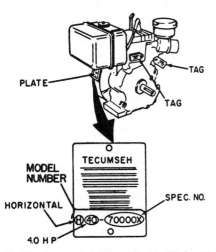

Fig. T1—Tags and plates used to identify model will most often be located in a position shown.

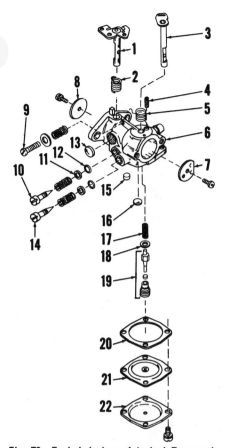

Fig. T2—Exploded view of typical Tecumseh diaphragm carburetor.

1. Throttle shaft
2. Return spring
3. Choke shaft
4. Choke stop spring.
5. Return spring
6. Carburetor body
7. Choke plate
8. Throttle plate
9. Idle speed screw
10. Idle mixture needle
11. Washers
12. "O" rings
13. Welch plug
14. Main fuel needle
15. Cup plug
16. Welch plug
17. Inlet needle spring
18. Gasket
19. Inlet needle & seat assy.
20. Gasket
21. Diaphragm
22. Cover

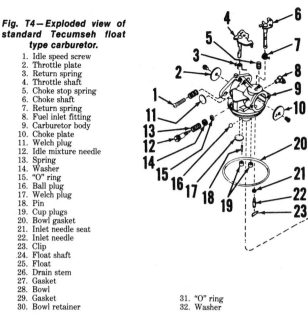

Fig. T4—Exploded view of standard Tecumseh float type carburetor.

1. Idle speed screw
2. Throttle plate
3. Return spring
4. Throttle shaft
5. Choke stop spring
6. Choke shaft
7. Return spring
8. Fuel inlet fitting
9. Carburetor body
10. Choke plate
11. Welch plug
12. Idle mixture needle
13. Spring
14. Washer
15. "O" ring
16. Ball plug
17. Welch plug
18. Pin
19. Cup plugs
20. Bowl gasket
21. Inlet needle seat
22. Inlet needle
23. Clip
24. Float shaft
25. Float
26. Drain stem
27. Gasket
28. Bowl
29. Gasket
30. Bowl retainer
31. "O" ring
32. Washer
33. Spring
34. Main fuel needle

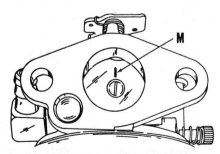

Fig. T3—The mark (M) on throttle plate should be parallel to the throttle shaft and outward as shown. Some models may also have mark at 3 o'clock position.

seat (19—Fig. T2) are removed. The inlet needle seat fitting is metal with a neoprene seat, so the fitting (and enclosed seat) should be removed before carburetor is cleaned with a commercial solvent. The stamped line on carburetor throttle plate should be toward top of carburetor, parallel with throttle shaft and facing OUTWARD as shown in Fig. T3. Flat side of choke plate should be

toward the fuel inlet fitting side of carburetor. Mark on choke plate should be parallel to shaft and should face INWARD when choke is closed. Diaphragm (21—Fig. T2) should be installed with rounded head of center rivet up toward the inlet needle (19), regardless of size or placement of washers around the rivet. On carburetor Models 0234-252, 265, 266, 269, 270, 271, 282, 293, 303, 322, 327, 333, 334, 344, 345, 348, 349, 350, 351, 352, 356, 368, 371, 374, 378, 379, 380, 404 and 405, gasket (20) must be installed between diaphragm (21) and cover (22). All other models are assembled as shown, with gasket between diaphragm and carburetor body.

TECUMSEH STANDARD FLOAT CARBURETOR. Idle mixture is adjusted at needle (12—Fig. T4) and high speed mixture at main fuel needle (34). Initial setting is 1 turn open for both needles and clockwise rotation will lean the mixture. Make final mixture adjustment with engine warm and operating with the normal amount of load. Adjust the main fuel needle (34) for smoothest operation at governed speed, then adjust idle needle (12) for smoothest operation at idle (slow) speed. Idle speed is adjusted at stop screw (1) and should be approximately 1800 rpm.

Observe the following when overhauling: Disassemble the carburetor before attempting to clean. Most commercial cleaners will damage neoprene and Viton rubber parts. Do not attempt to reuse any expansion plugs. Install new plugs if any are removed for cleaning. The fuel inlet needle valve closes against a neoprene or Viton seat which must be removed before cleaning in most commercial solvents.

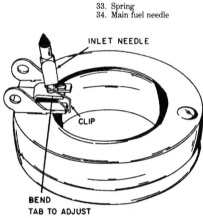

Fig. T5—View of float and fuel inlet valve needle. The valve needle shown is equipped with resilient tip and a clip. Bend tab shown to adjust float height.

Three types of fuel inlet valves are used. Some carburetors are equipped with a resilient tip on the fuel inlet needle (Fig. T5). The soft tip contacts the seating surface machined into the carburetor body to shut off the fuel. Do not attempt to remove the inlet valve seat. Some carburetors are equipped with a Viton seat (21—Fig. T4) that is located in bore of carburetor body. The rubber seat can be removed by blowing compressed air in from the fuel inlet fitting

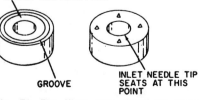

Fig. T6—The Viton seat used on some Tecumseh carburetors must be installed correctly to operate properly. All metal needle is used with seat shown.

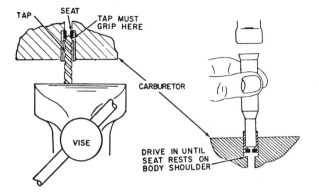

Fig. T7 — A 10-24 or 10-32 tap is used to pull the brass seat fitting and fuel inlet valve seat from some carburetors. Use a close fitting flat punch to install new seat and fitting.

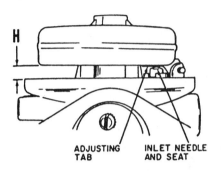

Fig. T8—Distance (H) between carburetor body and float with body inverted should be 0.200-0.220 inch (5.1-5.6 mm).

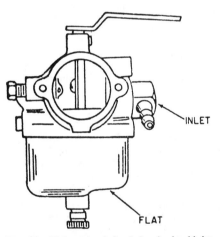

Fig. T9—Flat part of float bowl should be located under the fuel inlet fitting.

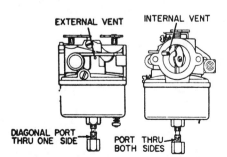

Fig. T10—The bowl retainer contains a drilled fuel passage which is different for carburetors with external and internal fuel bowl vent.

or by using a hooked wire. The grooved face of valve seat should be IN toward bottom of bore and the valve needle should seat on smooth side of the Viton seat. Refer to Fig. T6. On some carburetors, the Viton seat is contained in a brass seat fitting. Use a 10-24 or 10-32 tap to pull the seat and fitting from carburetor bore as shown in Fig. T7. Use a flat, close fitting punch to install new seat and fitting.

Install the throttle plate (2—Fig. T4) with the two stamped marks out and at 12 and 3 o'clock positions. The 12 o'clock line should be parallel with the throttle shaft and toward top of carburetor. Install choke plate (10) with flat side down toward bottom of carburetor. Float setting should be 0.200-0.220 inch (5.08-5.59 mm) and can be measured as shown in Fig. T8. Remove float and bend tab at float hinge to change float setting. The fuel inlet fitting (8—Fig. T4) is pressed into body on some models. Start fitting, then apply a light coat of "Loctite" (grade A) to shank and press fitting into position. The flat on fuel bowl should be under the fuel inlet fitting. Refer to Fig. T9.

Be sure to use correct parts when servicing the carburetor. Some gaskets used as (20 – Fig. T4) are square section, while others are round. The bowl retainer (39) contains a drilled passage for fuel to the high speed metering needle (34). A diagonal port through one side the bowl retainer is used on carburetors with external vent. The port is through both sides on models with internal vent. Refer to Fig. T10.

WALBRO. On Walbro carburetors, clockwise rotation of both the low idle mixture needle (9 – Fig. T18) and the main fuel adjusting needle (33) leans the mixture. Initial setting for both needles is 1 turn open. Make final adjustment with engine warm and running. Adjust main fuel needle until engine runs smoothly at normal operating speed. Back out idle speed screw (7), hold throttle to slowest engine speed possible without stalling and adjust idle mixture needle for smoothest operation. Read-

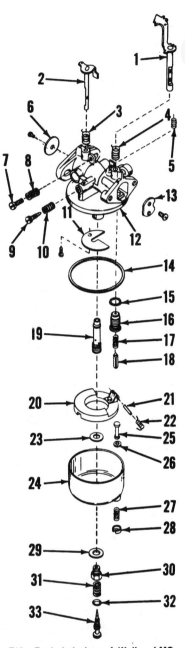

Fig. T18—Exploded view of Walbro LMG carburetor.

1. Choke shaft
2. Throttle shaft
3. Throttle return spring
4. Choke return spring
5. Choke stop spring
6. Throttle plate
7. Idle speed stop screw
8. Spring
9. Idle mixture needle
10. Spring
11. Baffle
12. Carburetor body
13. Choke plate
14. Bowl gasket
15. Gasket
16. Inlet valve seat
17. Spring
18. Inlet valve
19. Main nozzle
20. Float
21. Float shaft
22. Spring
23. Gasket
24. Bowl
25. Drain stem
26. Gasket
27. Spring
28. Retainer
29. Gasket
30. Bowl retainer
31. Spring
32. "O" ring
33. Main fuel adjusting needle

just idle speed screw so engine idles at 1800 rpm.

To check float setting, hold carburetor body and float assembly in inverted position. A clearance of 1/8-inch (3.2 mm) should exist between free end of float and machined surface of carburetor body. Refer to Fig. T19. Bend tab on float as necessary to provide correct measurement.

NOTE: If carburetor has been disassembled and main nozzle (19–Fig. T18) removed, do not reinstall the original equipment nozzle; obtain and install a new service nozzle. Refer to Fig. T20 for differences between original and service nozzles.

MECHANICAL GOVERNOR. Most engines are equipped with a mechanical (flyweight) type governor. To adjust the governor linkage, refer to Fig. T28 and loosen governor lever screw. Twist protruding end of governor shaft clockwise as far as possible on horizontal crankshaft engines. On all models, move the governor lever until carburetor throttle shaft is in wide open position, then tighten governor lever clamp screw.

Binding or worn governor linkage will result in hunting or unsteady engine operation. An improperly adjusted carburetor will also cause a surging or hunting condition.

Refer to Figs. T29, T30, T31, T32, T35, T36, T37, T39 and T40 for views of typical mechanical governor speed con-

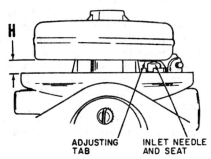

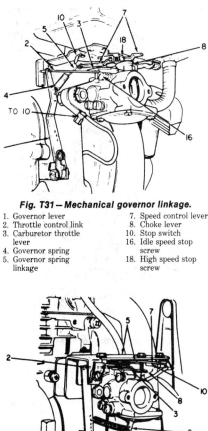

Fig. T31 — Mechanical governor linkage.

1. Governor lever	7. Speed control lever
2. Throttle control link	8. Choke lever
3. Carburetor throttle lever	10. Stop switch
4. Governor spring	16. Idle speed stop screw
5. Governor spring linkage	18. High speed stop screw

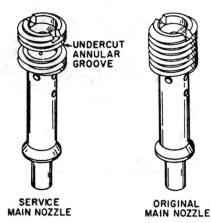

Fig. T19 — Float height (H) should be measured as shown on Walbro float carburetors. Bend the adjusting tab to adjust height.

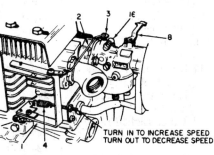

Fig. T29 — View of mechanical governor with one type of constant speed control. Refer also to Fig. T30 through T43 for other mechanical governor installations.

1. Governor lever	
2. Throttle control	4. Governor spring
3. Carburetor throttle lever	8. Choke lever
	16. Idle speed stop screw

Fig. T32 — Mechanical governor linkage. Refer to Fig. T31 for legend. Bellcrank is shown at (6).

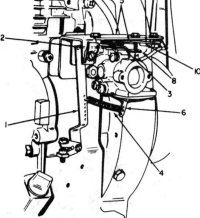

Fig. T30 — Mechanical governor linkage. Refer to Fig. T29 for legend except the following.

6. Bellcrank
7. Speed control lever   18. High speed stop screw

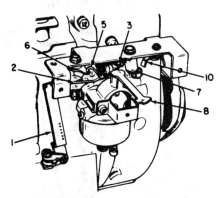

Fig. T35 — Mechanical governor linkage. Governed speed of engine is increased by closing loop in linkage (5); decrease speed by spreading loop.

1. Governor lever	
2. Throttle control link	6. Bellcrank
3. Throttle lever	7. Speed control lever
5. Governor spring linkage	8. Choke lever
	10. Stop switch

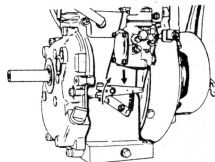

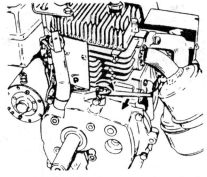

Fig. T28 — Views showing location of mechanical governor lever and direction to turn when adjusting position on governor shaft.

trol linkage installations. The governor gear shaft must be pressed into bore in cover until the correct amount of the shaft protrudes (A – Fig. T44). The correct distance (B) is 1-5/16 inches (33.3 mm) for all light frame engines. Governor shaft protrusion (D) for 4, 5 and 6 hp engines should be 1-17/64 inches (32.1 mm). Governor shaft protrusion (D) for 7 and 8 hp engines should be 1-15/64 inches (31.4 mm).

MAGNETO AND TIMING. Breaker point gap at maximum opening should be 0.020 inch (0.5 mm) for all models. Marks are usually located on stator and mounting post to facilitate timing. Ignition timing can be checked and adjusted to occur when piston is at specific location (BTDC) if marks are missing. Refer to the following specifications for recommended timing.

Models (Displacement)	Piston Position Inch (mm) BTDC
7.75 Cu. In.	0.060-0.070
(126.00 cc)	(1.524-1.778)
8.90 Cu. In.	0.050-0.060
(145.84 cc)	(1.270-1.524)
9.06 Cu. In.	0.035
(148.47 cc)	(0.889)
10.50 Cu. In.	0.035
(172.06 cc)	(0.889)
17.16 Cu. In.	0.085-0.095
(281.20 cc)	(2.159-2.413)
19.41 Cu. In.	0.085-0.095
(318.07)	(2.159-2.413)
All Other Light Frame Models	0.060-0.070
	(1.524-1.778)
All Other Medium Frame Models	0.050
	(1.270)

SOLID-STATE IGNITION. The Tecumseh solid-state ignition system does not use ignition breaker points. The only moving part of the system is the rotating flywheel with the charging magnets. As the flywheel magnet passes position (1A – Fig. T46), a low voltage AC current is induced into input coil (2). Current passes through rectifier (3) converting this current to DC. It then travels to capacitor (4) where it is stored. The flywheel rotates approximately 180 degrees to position (1B). As it passes trigger coil (5), it induces a very small electric charge into the coil. This charge passes through resistor (6) and turns on the SCR (silicon controlled rectifier) switch (7). With the SCR switch closed, low voltage current stored in capacitor (4) travels to pulse transformer (8). Voltage is stepped up instantaneously and current is discharged across the electrodes of spark plug (9), producing a spark before top dead center.

Some units are equipped with a second trigger coil and resistor set to turn the

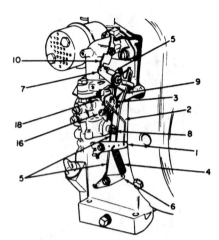

Fig. T36 – Mechanical governor linkage.

1. Governor lever
2. Throttle control link
3. Throttle lever
4. Governor spring
5. Governor spring linkage
6. Bellcrank
7. Speed control lever
8. Choke lever
9. Choke control link
10. Stop switch
16. Idle speed stop screw
18. High speed stop screw

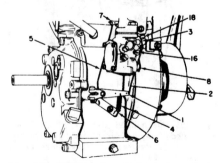

Fig. T37 – View of control linkage used on some engines. To increase governed engine speed, close loop (5); to decrease speed, spread loop (5). Refer to Fig. T36 for legend.

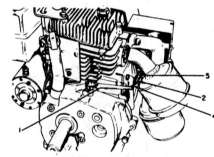

Fig. T40 – Mechanical governor linkage.

1. Governor lever
2. Throttle control link
4. Governor spring
5. Governor spring linkage

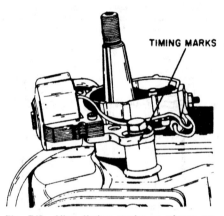

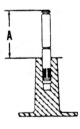

Fig. T45 – Align timing marks as shown on magneto ignition engines.

Fig. T44 – The governor gear shaft must be pressed into bore until the correct amount of shaft protrudes (A). Refer also to illustrations for correct assembly of governor gear and associated parts. See text for protrusion dimension (B or D).

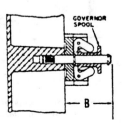

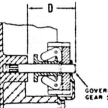

LIGHT FRAME   MEDIUM FRAME

Fig. T39 – Linkage for mechanical governor. Refer to Fig. T36 for legend. Bellcrank is shown at (6).

SCR switch on at a lower rpm. This second trigger pin is closer to the flywheel and produces a spark at TDC for easier starting. As engine rpm increases, the first (shorter) trigger pin picks up the small electric charge and turns the SCR switch on, firing the spark plug BTDC.

If system fails to produce a spark to the spark plug, first check high tension lead (Fig. T47). If condition of high tension lead is questionable, renew pulse transformer and high tension lead assembly. Check low tension lead and renew if insulation is faulty. The magneto charging coil, electronic triggering system and mounting plate are available only as an assembly. If necessary to renew this assembly, place unit in position on engine. Start retaining screws, turn mounting, plate

counterclockwise as far as possible, then tighten retaining screws to a torque of 5-7 ft.-lbs. (6.775-9.485 N·m).

LUBRICATION. Engines may be equipped with a gear driven rotor type pump or a dipper type oil slinger attached to the connecting rod.

On engines equipped with gear driven rotor oil pump, check drive gear and rotor for excessive wear or other damage. End clearance of rotor in pump body should be within limits of 0.006-0.007 inch (0.152-0.178 mm) and is controlled by cover gasket. Gaskets are available in thicknesses of 0.005 inch (0.127 mm) and 0.010 inch (0.254 mm).

On all models with oil pump, be sure to prime during assembly to assure immediate lubrication of engine. On all

models, use SAE 30 or SAE 10W-30 oil when operating in temperatures above 30°F and SAE 5W-30 or SAE 10W oil in temperatures 32°F and below.

REPAIRS

TIGHTENING TORQUES. Recommended tightening torques are as follows:

Cylinder Head
  7 HP & 8 HP models . . . . . . 170 in.-lbs.
                            (19.20 N·m)
  All other models . . . . . 160-200 in.-lbs.
                  (18.07-22.58 N·m)
Connecting Rod Nuts
(Except Durlok Type)
  3 HP & 3.5 HP . . . . 65-75 in.-lbs.
                (7.34-8.47 N·m)
  4 HP & 5 HP Light
    frame models . . . . 80-95 in.-lbs.
             (9.03-10.73 N·m)
  5 HP Medium frame . . . 86-110 in.-lbs.
             (9.71-12.42 N·m)
Connecting Rod Bolts
(Durlock Type)
  5 HP Light
    frame model . . . . 110-130 in.-lbs.
            (12.42-14.68 N·m)
  5 HP Medium frame
    & 6 HP model . . . . 130-150 in.-lbs.
            (14.68-16.94 N·m)
  7 HP & 8 HP models . . . . . . 120 in.-lbs.
             (13.55 N·m)
Crankcase Cover
  All models . . . . 65-110 in.-lbs.
            (7.34-12.42 N·m)
Ball Bearing Retaining Nut
  7 HP & 8 HP models . . . . 15-22 in.-lbs.
            (1.69-2.48 N·m)
Flywheel
  Light frame models . . . 360-400 in.-lbs.
            (40.65-45.17 N·m)
  Medium frame models . 430-480 in.-lbs.
            (48.55-54.20 N·m)
Spark Plug . . . . 250-300 in.-lbs.
            (28.23-33.88 N·m)
Magneto Stator . . . . 40-90 in.-lbs.
            (4.52-10.16 N·m)

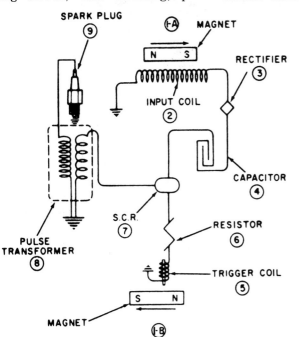

Fig. T46 — Diagram of solid state ignition system used on some engines.

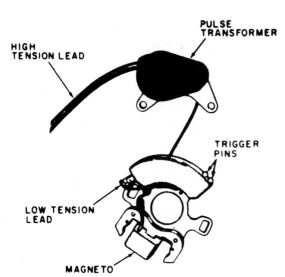

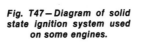

Fig. T47 — Diagram of solid state ignition system used on some engines.

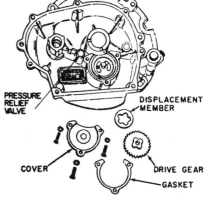

Fig. T49 — Disassembled view of typical gear driven rotor type oil pump.

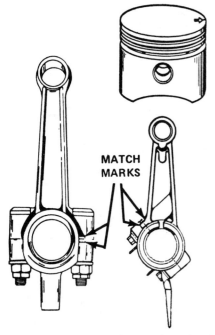

Fig. T50—Match marks on connecting rod and cap should be aligned and should be toward pto end of crankshaft.

Frame engines: 0.8610-0.8615 inch (21.869-21.882 mm) for other Light frame engines; 1.0615-1.0620 inch (26.962-26.975 mm) for Medium Frame engines. Specified inside diameter of connecting rod crankpin bearing is 1.0005-1.0010 inches (25.413-25.425 mm) for 10.5 cu. in. (172.06 cc) and 12.0 cu. in. (196.64 cc) displacement Light Frame engines; 0.8620-0.8625 inch (21.895-21.9075 mm) for other Light Frame engines; 1.0630-1.0635 inches (27.000-27.013 mm) for Medium Frame engines. Crankpin journal diameter is 1.1865-1.1870 inches (30.137-30.150 mm) for 17.16 cu. in. (281.20 cc) and 19.41 cu. in. (318.07 cc) displacement engines. Align match marks on connecting rod and cap as shown in Fig. T50. On some models, piston pin hole is offset in piston and arrow on top of piston should point toward valves. On all engines, match marks on rod and cap must be installed toward power take off (pto) end of crankshaft. Renew lock plates, if so equipped, for connecting rod cap retaining screws each time cap is removed.

PISTON, PIN, RINGS AND CYLINDER. Aluminum alloy pistons are equipped with two compression rings and one oil control ring. Specified ring end gap for all models is 0.007-0.020 inch (0.18-0.51 mm). Specified piston skirt clearance in cylinder (measured at thrust side of piston just below oil ring) is as follows:

7.61 cu. in.
(124.71 cc) . . . . 0.005-0.0065 in.
(0.127-0.165 mm)
7.75 cu. in.
(126.0 cc) . . . . 0.0025-0.0040 in.
(0.064-0.102 mm)
11.04 cu. in.
(180.91 cc) . . . . 0.0055-0.0070 in.
(0.14-0.178 mm)

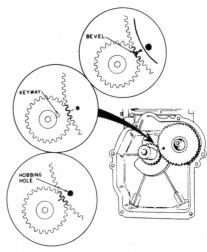

Fig. T52—The camshaft and crankshaft must be correctly timed to assure that valves open at correct time. Different types of marks have been used, but marks should be aligned when assembling.

8.90 cu. in.
(145.84 cc)
9.06 cu. in.
(148.47 cc)
10.50 cu. in.
(172.06 cc)
12.00 cu. in.
(196.64 cc) . . . . 0.0045-0.0060 in.
(0.114-0.152 mm)
12.18 cu. in.
(199.53 cc)
13.53 cu. in.
(221.72 cc) . . . . 0.0035-0.0050 in.
(0.089-0.127 mm)
17.16 cu. in.
(281.20 cc)
19.41 cu. in.
(318.07 cc) . . . . 0.004-0.006 in.
(0.10-0.15 mm)

Mounting Flange . . . . 75-110 in.-lbs.
(8.47-12.42 N·m)
Carburetor to
Intake Pipe . . . . 48-72 in.-lbs.
(5.42-8.13 N·m)
Intake Pipe to Cylinder . . . 72-96 in.-lbs.
(8.13-10.84 N·m)
Breather Screws . . . . 20-26 in.-lbs.
(2.26-2.94 N·m)

CONNECTING ROD. Piston and rod assembly is removed from cylinder head end of engine. The aluminum alloy connecting rod rides directly on crankshaft. Crankpin journal diameter is 0.9995-1.000 inch (25.387-25.400 mm) for 10.5 cu. in. (172.06 cc) and 12.0 cu. in. (196.64 cc) displacement Light

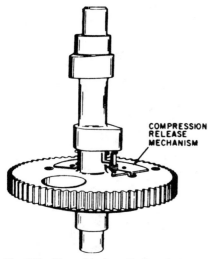

Fig. T51—View of insta-matic Ezee-Start compression release camshaft.

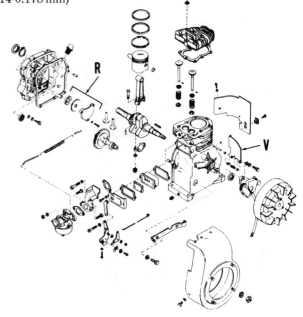

Fig. T53—View of light frame engine with horizontal crankshaft. Air vane (V) type governor and rotor type oil pump (R) are used on model shown.

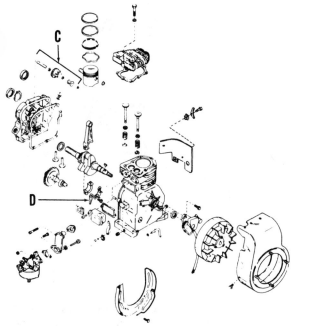

Pistons and rings are available in standard, 0.010-inch (0.25 mm) and 0.020-inch (0.51 mm) oversizes. On light frame 12.0 cu. in. (196.64 cc) displacement models, arrow on top of piston should point towards valves and match marks on connecting rod and cap should point toward pto end of crankshaft (Fig. T50).

Bore and hone cylinder and fit with next suitable oversize piston and rings if cylinder is scored, tapered or out-of-round more than 0.005-inch (0.13 mm). Standard cylinder bore is as follows:

7.61 cu. in.
(124.71 cc)
7.75 cu. in.
(126.0 cc) . . . . 2.3125-2.3135 in.
(58.738-58.763 mm)
8.90 cu. in.
(145.84 cc)
9.06 cu. in.
(148.47 cc) ·
11.04 cu. in.
(180.91 cc) . . . . 2.500-2.501 in.
(63.50-63.53 mm)
10.50 cu. in.
(172.06 cc)
12.18 cu. in.
(199.53 cc)
13.53 cu. in.
(221.72 cc) . . . . 2.625-2.626 in.
(66.68-66.70 mm)
17.16 cu. in.
(281.20 cc) . . . . 2.9375-2.9385 in.
(74.613-74.638 mm)
19.41 cu. in.
(318.07 cc) . . . . 3.125-3.126 in.
(79.38-79.40 mm)

CRANKSHAFT AND MAIN BEARINGS. Crankshaft main bearing journals are 0.8735-0.8740 inch (22.187-22.200 mm), 0.9985-0.9990 inch

(25.362-25.375 mm), 1.124-1.125 inch (28.55-28.58 mm) or 1.1870-1.1875 inch (30.150-30.163 mm) in diameter when new. On some engines, main bearing journals ride directly in the aluminum alloy bores in cylinder block and crankcase cover (mounting flange). A special tool kit is available from Tecumseh to ream cylinder block and cover so renewable main bearing bushings may be installed. Other engines are originally equipped with renewable steel backed bronze bushings and some are originally equipped with a ball type main bearing at pto end of crankshaft.

All bushing type main bearings for 0.8735-0.8740 inch (22.187-22.200 mm) diameter journals have a specified clearance of 0.0010-0.0025 inch

Fig. T54 — View of light frame horizontal crankshaft engine with mechanical governor and splash lubrication. Governor centrifugal weights are shown at (C) and lubrication dipper at (D).

(0.025-0.064 mm). Specified clearance between bushing bore and all larger diameter journals is 0.0015-0.0025 inch (0.038-0.064 mm). Specified crankshaft end play is 0.005-0.027 inch (0.13-0.69 mm) for all models.

Connecting rod crankpin diameter is 0.9995-1.000 inch (25.387-25.400 mm) for 10.50 cu.in. (172.06 cc), 11.04 cu.in. (180.91 cc) and 12.00 cu. in. (196.64 cc) displacement light frame engines. Crankpin diameter is 0.8610-0.8615 inch (21.869-21.882 mm) for all smaller displacement Light Frame engines. Crankpin diameter is 1.0615-1.0620 inches (26.962-26.975 mm) for four, five and six horsepower Medium Frame engines. Crankpin diameter is 1.1865-1.1870 inches (30.137-30.150 mm) for seven and eight horsepower Medium Frame engines. Specified connecting rod-to-crankpin bearing clearance is 0.0005-0.0015 inch (0.013-0.038 mm) for all Light Frame engines and 0.0010-0.0020 inch (0.025-0.051 mm) for all Medium Frame engines.

CAMSHAFT. The camshaft and camshaft gear are an integral part which rides on journals at each end of camshaft. Renew camshaft if gear teeth are worn or if bearing surfaces or cam lobes are worn or scored.

Specified cam lobe diameter is as follows:

10.50 cu. in.
(172.06 cc)
12.00 cu. in.
(196.64 cc) . . . Intake – 1.2939-1.2959 in.
(32.865-32.916 mm)
Exhaust – 0.9775-0.9795 in.
(24.829-24.879 mm)

Fig. T55 — View of medium frame horizontal crankshaft engine with mechanical governor (C). An oil dipper for splash lubrication may be cast onto the connecting rod cap instead of using the rotor type oil pump (R).

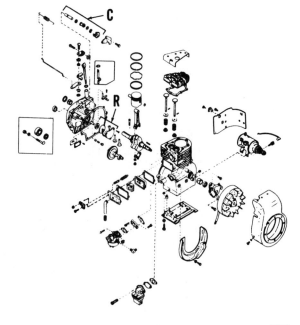

Other light frame
engines . . . . . Intake – 0.9775-0.9795 in.
(24.829-24.879 mm)
Exhaust – 0.9775-0.9795 in.
(24.829-24.879 mm)
Other medium frame
engines . . . . Intake – 1.258-1.262 in.
(31.95-32.06 mm)
Exhaust – 1.258-1.262 in.
(31.95-32.06 mm)
17.16 cu. in.
(281.20 cc) . . . . . Intake – 1.263-1.267 in.
(32.08-32.18 mm)
Exhaust – 1.263-1.267 in.
(32.08-32.18 mm)
19.41 cu. in.
(318.07 cc) . . . Intake – 1.3045-1.3085 in.
(33.134-33.236 mm)
Exhaust – 1.3045-1.3085 in.
(33.134-33.236 mm)

Cam followers (lifters) are identical for most engines; however, parts should not be interchanged once they have been used. Exhaust valve cam follower is longer than intake valve follower on some 10.50 cu. in. (172.06 cc) displacement and larger light frame engines.

On engines equipped with Instamatic Ezee-Start compression release type camshaft (Fig. T51), check compression release parts for binding, excessive wear or other damage. If any parts are damaged or excessively worn, renew complete camshaft assembly. Compo-

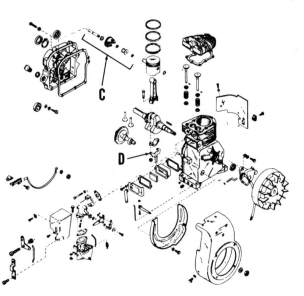

Fig. T56 – View of light frame horizontal crankshaft engine with mechanical governor and splash lubrication.

nent parts are not serviced separately for the compression release.

When installing the camshaft, align timing marks on camshaft gear and crankshaft gear (Fig. T52) on all models.

VALVE SYSTEM. Intake and exhaust valve tappet gap should be 0.010 inch (0.25 mm) (cold). Correct tappet gap is obtained by grinding end of stems squarely. Intake and exhaust valve seats are nonrenewable. Valve seat angle is 46 degrees. Valve seat width should be 3/64-inch (1.2 mm).

Valve stem guides are cast into cylinder block and are nonrenewable. If excessive clearance exists between valve stem and valve guide, ream guide and install a new valve with oversize stem.

Valve timing is correct when timing mark on camshaft gear is aligned with timing mark on crankshaft gear.

SERVICING TECUMSEH ACCESSORIES

REWIND STARTERS

FRICTION SHOE TYPE. To disassemble the starter, refer to Fig. TE17 and proceed as follows: Hold starter rotor (12) securely with thumb and remove the four screws securing flanges (1 and 2) to cover (15). Remove flanges and release thumb pressure enough to allow spring to rotate pulley until spring (13) is unwound. Remove retaining ring (3), washer (4), spring (5), slotted washer (6) and fiber washer (7). Lift out friction shoe assembly (8,9,10 and 11), then remove second fiber washer and slotted washer. Withdraw rotor (12) with rope from cover and spring. Remove rewind spring from cover and unwind rope from rotor.

When reassembling, lubricate rewind spring, cover shaft and center bore in rotor with a light coat of "Lubriplate" or

Fig. TE17 – Exploded view of typical friction shoe rewind starter.

1. Mounting flange
2. Flange
3. Retaining ring
4. Washer
5. Spring
6. Slotted washer
7. Fiber washer
8. Spring retainer
9. Spring
10. Friction shoe
11. Actuating lever
12. Rotor
13. Rewind spring
14. Centering pin
15. Cover
16. Rope
17. Roller

equivalent. Install rewind spring so that windings are in same direction as removed spring. Install rope on rotor, then place rotor on cover shaft. Make certain that inner and outer ends of spring are correctly hooked on cover and rotor. Preload the rewind spring by rotating the rotor two full turns. Hold rotor in preload position and install flanges (1 and 2). Check sharp end of friction shoes (10) and sharpen or renew

as necessary. Install washers (6 and 7), friction shoe assembly, spring (5), washer (4) and retaining spring (3). Make certain that friction shoe assembly is installed properly for correct starter rotation. If properly installed, sharp ends of friction shoes will extend when rope is pulled.

Remove brass centering pin (14) from cover shaft, straighten pin if necessary, then reinsert pin 1/3 of its length into cover shaft. When installing starter on engine, centering pin will align starter with center hole in end of crankshaft.

DOG TYPE. To disassemble the dog type starter, refer to Fig. TE18 and release preload tension of rewind spring as follows: Pull starter rope until notch in pulley half (5) is aligned with rope hole in cover (1). Use thumb pressure to prevent pulley from rotating. Engage rope in notch of pulley and slowly release thumb pressure to allow spring to unwind. Remove retainer screw (11), retainer (10) and spring (6). Remove brake screw (9), brake (8) and starter dog (7). Carefully remove pulley assembly with rope from spring and cover. Note direction of spring winding and carefully remove spring from cover. Unbolt and separate pulley halves (4 and 5) and remove rope.

To reassemble, reverse the disassembly procedure. Then, preload rewind spring as follows: Align notch in

Fig. TE18 — Exploded view of typical dog type rewind starter assembly. Some units of similar construction use three starter dogs (7).

1. Cover
2. Rope
3. Rewind spring
4. Pulley half
5. Pulley half & hub
6. Retainer spring
7. Starter dog
8. Brake
9. Brake screw
10. Retainer
11. Retainer screw
12. Hub & screen assy.

pulley with rope hole in cover. Engage rope in notch and rotate pulley two full turns to properly preload the spring.

Pull rope to full extended position. Release handle and if spring is properly preloaded, the rope will fully rewind.

WISCONSIN ROBIN

TELEDYNE WISCONSIN MOTOR
Milwaukee, Wisconsin 53246

HP	Crankshaft	Model	Bore	Stroke	Displacement
4.6	Horizontal	EY18W	2 9/16 in.	2 5/32 in.	11.14 cu. in.
(3.43 kW)			65.1 mm	54.8 mm	182.55 cc

MAINTENANCE

SPARK PLUG. Recommended spark plug is Champion L86, AC 44F, NGK B6HS or equivalent. Electrode gap is 0.020-0.025 inch (0.51-0.635 mm). Tighten spark plug to a torque of 24-27 ft.-lbs. (32.5-36.6 N.m).

CARBURETOR. Mikuni Model BV18H carburetor is used on Model EY18W engine. Refer to Fig. WR1 for exploded view. To adjust idle fuel mixture, gently seat the idle mixture needle (1), then back needle out (counterclockwise) 1½ turns. Main fuel is metered through main jet (19) and is nonadjustable. With engine operating, adjust idle speed stop screw (3) to obtain an idle speed of 1250 rpm. Make final adjustments on idle mixture needle and idle speed stop screw with engine running at normal operating temperature.

To check and adjust float setting, remove jet holder (20) and fuel bowl (17). Place carburetor body on end (on manifold flange) so that float pin is in vertical position. Move float to close inlet needle valve.

NOTE: Needle valve is spring loaded.

Float tab should just contact needle valve pin but should not compress the spring. Using a depth gage, measure distance between body flange and free end of float as shown in Fig. WR2. Distance should be 0.710-0.790 inch (18.03-20.07 mm). If not, bend tab on float lever to obtain correct setting.

GOVERNOR. The mechanical flyweight governor is mounted to and operated by the camshaft gear. See Fig.

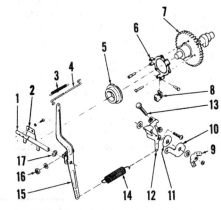

Fig. WR3 — *Exploded view of mechanical governor and linkage.*

1. Governor lever shaft
2. Yoke
3. Link spring
4. Carburetor link
5. Thrust sleeve
6. Governor plate
7. Camshaft assy.
8. Flyweights (3 used)
9. Wing nut
10. Stop plate
11. Wave washer
12. Control lever
13. Speed stop screw
14. Governor spring
15. Governor lever
16. Clamp nut
17. Retaining ring

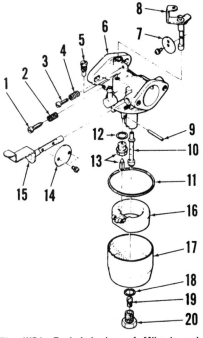

Fig. WR1 — *Exploded view of Mikuni model BV18H carburetor used on Model EY18W engine.*

1. Idle mixture needle
2. Spring
3. Idle speed stop screw
4. Spring
5. Idle jet
6. Carburetor body
7. Throttle plate
8. Throttle shaft
9. Float pin
10. Nozzle
11. Bowl gasket
12. Gasket
13. Inlet needle & seat
14. Choke plate
15. Choke shaft
16. Float
17. Bowl
18. Washer
19. Main jet
20. Jet holder

Fig. WR2 — *With fuel bowl removed, stand carburetor on manifold flange and measure float setting as shown.*

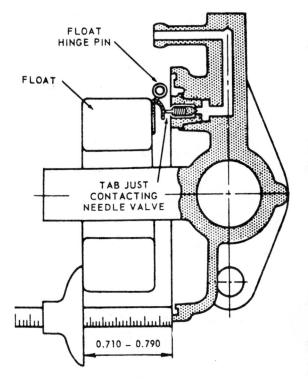

FLOAT HINGE PIN

FLOAT

TAB JUST CONTACTING NEEDLE VALVE

0.710 – 0.790

WR3. Engine speed is controlled by the tension on governor spring (14).

Before attempting to adjust governed speed, synchronize governor linkage as follows: Loosen clamp nut (16) and turn governor lever (15) counterclockwise until carburetor throttle plate is in wide open position. Then, insert screwdriver in slot in end of governor lever shaft (1) and rotate shaft counterclockwise as far as possible. Tighten governor clamp nut.

To adjust for a particular loaded rpm, hook governor spring (14) to control lever (12) and governor lever (15). Start engine, loosen wing nut (9), move control lever (12) counterclockwise and adjust stop screw (13) until the required no-load speed is obtained. If engine is to operate at a fixed speed, tighten wing nut (9). For variable speed operation, do not tighten wing nut.

For the following loaded engine speeds, adjust governor to the following no-load speeds:

Loaded RPM	No Load RPM
1800	2370
2000	2515
2200	2665
2400	2815
2600	2975
2800	3140
3000	3310
3200	3485
3400	3670
3600	3855

MAGNETO AND TIMING. Flywheel type magneto is used and breaker points and condenser are located under flywheel. Initial point gap is 0.014 inch (0.36 mm) See Fig. WR4. To check and adjust engine timing, disconnect lead wire from shut-off switch. Connect a continuity light lead to lead wire and ground other lead to engine. Slowly rotate flywheel in normal direction until light goes out. Immediately stop turning flywheel and check location of timing marks. Timing marks should be aligned as shown in Fig. WR5. If timing mark (M) on flywheel is below timing mark (D), breaker point gap is too large. If mark (M) is above mark (D), breaker point gap is too small. Carefully measure the distance necessary to align the two marks, then remove flywheel and breaker point cover. Changing point gap 0.001 (0.03 mm) will change timing mark (M) position ⅛-inch (3.2 mm). Reassemble and tighten flywheel retaining nut to a torque of 47 ft.-lbs. (63.685 N·m).

LUBRICATION. Crankcase capacity is 1¼ pints. Use SAE 30 oil when operating in temperatures above 40° F, SAE 20 oil in temperatures between 15° F and 40° F and SAE 10W-30 in temperatures below 15° F. Recom-

mended motor oil is API classification SE or SF. An oil dipper attached to the connecting rod cap provides for splash type lubrication.

CRANKCASE BREATHER. A floating poppet type breaker valve is located in the breather plate behind the valve cover plate. A breather tube connects breather into air cleaner. Restricted or faulty breather is indicated when oil seeps from gasket surfaces and oil seals.

REPAIRS

TIGHTENING TORQUES. Recommended tightening torques are as follows:

Spark plug . . . . 27 ft.-lbs. (36.58 N·m)
Connecting rod cap screws . . . 14 ft.-lbs. (18.97 N·m)
Cylinder head nuts . . . . 22 ft.-lbs. (29.81 N·m)
Flywheel nut . . . . 47 ft.lbs. (63.69 N·m)
Gear cover cap screws . . . . . . 13 ft.lbs. (17.62 N·m)

CYLINDER HEAD. Always use a new head gasket when installing cylinder head. Tighten cylinder head nuts evenly in three stages; first to 12

ft.-lbs. (16.26 N·m), then 18 ft.-lbs. (24.39 N·m) and finally 22 ft.-lbs. (29.81 N·m).

CONNECTING ROD. Connecting rod and piston assembly is removed from above after cylinder head and gear cover are removed. Specified connecting rod to crankpin clearance is 0.0021-0.0031 inch (0.053-0.079 mm) with a maximum clearance of 0.005-inch (0.13 mm). Specified rod side clearance is 0.008-0.0235 inch (0.20-0.597 mm) with maximum clearance of 0.039-inch (0.99 mm). Specified connecting rod-to-piston pin clearance is 0.0004-0.0012 inch (0.010-0.030 mm) with a maximum clearance of 0.0032-inch (0.081 mm).

When installing connecting rod and piston assembly, make certain match marks (cast ribs) on connecting rod and cap are together as shown in Fig. WR6. Install oil dipper with offset toward gear cover end of engine if engine is to be operated on a tilt toward take-off end. Mount dipper with offset toward flywheel end if operated on a tilt in that direction or with no tilt operation. Use a new lock plate and tighten connecting rod cap screws to a torque of 14 ft.lbs. (18.97 N·m).

PISTON, PIN AND RINGS. Piston is equipped with one compression ring, one scraper ring and one oil control ring. Install rings as shown in Fig. WR7.

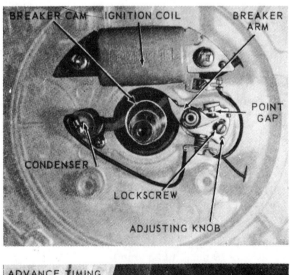

Fig. WR4 — View showing flywheel magneto. Flywheel and breaker cover are removed.

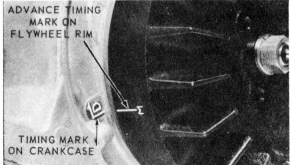

Fig. WR5 — 23 degrees BTDC timing mark (M) on flywheel aligned with timing mark (D) on crankcase.

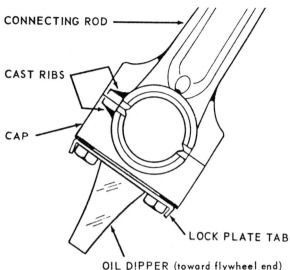

CONNECTING ROD

CAST RIBS

CAP

LOCK PLATE TAB

OIL DIPPER (toward flywheel end)
Mount toward gear cover if operating
tilt is toward take-off end.

Fig. WR6—Connecting rod and cap must be installed with cast ribs together.

shaft into position. Make certain that the marked tooth on crankshaft gear is between the two marked teeth on camshaft gear.

CRANKSHAFT. Crankshaft is supported in two ball bearings. Renew bearings if any indication of roughness, noise or excessive wear is found. Crankshaft end play of 0.001-0.009 inch (0.03-0.23 mm) is controlled by the adjusting collar located between crankshaft gear and gear cover main bearing. See Fig. WR8. Three different lengths of adjusting collars are available: 0.701-0.709 inch (17.81-18.01 mm), 0.709-0.717 inch (17.81-18.21 mm) and 0.717-0.725 inch (17.81-18.42 mm). To determine correct length of adjusting collar with gear cover removed, proceed as follows: Measure distance (A–Fig. WR8) between machined surface of crankcase face and end of crankshaft gear. Measure distance (B) between machined surface of gear cover and end of main bearing. Compressed thickness of gear cover gasket (C) is 0.007-inch (0.18 mm). Select adjusting collar that is 0.001-0.009 inch (0.03-0.23 mm) less in length than the total of A, B and C.

Specified ring end gap is 0.002-0.010 inch (0.05-0.25 mm). Specified piston ring side clearance in piston grooves is 0.0004-0.003 inch (0.010-0.08 mm). Stagger ring end gaps 90 degrees apart around piston.

Recommended piston-to-cylinder bore clearance (measured at thrust face of piston) is 0.0016-0.0032 inch (0.041-0.081 mm). Standard piston diameter at skirt thrust face is 2.5567-2.5575 inch (64.940-64.961 mm).

Pistons and piston rings are available in standard size as well as oversizes of 0.010 inch (0.25 mm) and 0.020 inch (0.51 mm).

Standard piston pin diameter is 0.5509-0.5512 inch (13.993-14.000 mm). Piston pin-to-piston fit is 0.00035-inch (0.0090 mm) tight to 0.00039-inch (0.0100mm) loose with a maximum clearance of 0.0023-inch (0.058 mm) loose. Specified piston pin-to-connecting rod clearance is 0.0004-0.0012 inch (0.010-0.030 mm) with a maximum clearance of 0.0032 inch (0.081 mm).

CYLINDER BLOCK. If cylinder wall is scored, out-of-round more than 0.003-inch (0.08 mm) or tapered more than 0.006-inch (0.15 mm), bore and/or hone cylinder to nearest suitable oversize of 0.010-inch (0.25 mm) or 0.020-inch (0.51 mm). Standard cylinder bore is 2.5519-2.5599 inch (64.818-65.021 mm).

CAMSHAFT. Camshaft rides in bores in crankcase and gear cover. When removing camshaft assembly, lay engine on side to prevent tappets from falling out. If valve tappets are removed, identify them so they can be reinstalled in their original position. Valve tappets have an operating clearance in crankcase bores of

0.001-0.0024 inch (0.03-0.061 mm) with a maximum clearance of 0.004-inch (0.10 mm). Camshaft journal diameter is 0.5889-0.5893 inch (14.958-14.968 mm).

When reinstalling camshaft, install governor thrust sleeve (5–Fig. WR3) on governor flyweights, then slide cam-

Fig. WR7—Install piston rings as shown.

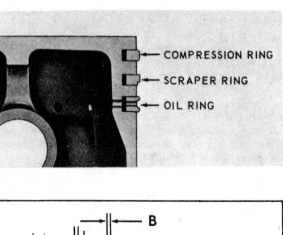

COMPRESSION RING

SCRAPER RING

OIL RING

Fig. WR8—Crankshaft end play is controlled by adjusting collar. Refer to text for procedure to determine the length of collar.

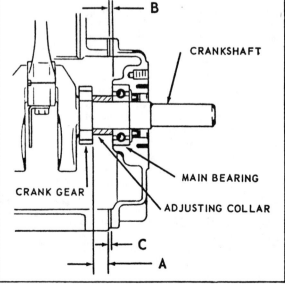

B

CRANKSHAFT

MAIN BEARING

ADJUSTING COLLAR

CRANK GEAR

C

A

After reassembly, check crankshaft end play with a dial indicator.

Standard crankpin diameter is 1.0210-1.0215 inch (25.933-25.946 mm). Specified connecting rod to crankpin clearance is 0.0021-0.0031 inch (0.053-0.079 mm) with a maximum clearance of 0.005-inch (0.13 mm). Replace crankshaft if rod clearance is excessive or if crankpin is out-of-round or tapered more than 0.0002-inch (0.005 mm).

When reassembling engine, make certain that marked tooth on crankshaft gear is between the two marked teeth on camshaft gear. When renewing crankshaft oil seals, install seals with lips toward ball bearings.

VALVE SYSTEM. Valve tappet gap (cold) is 0.006-0.008 inch (0.15-0.20 mm). Valve face and seat angle is 45 degrees. Desired seat width is 0.047-0.059 inch (1.19-1.50 mm). Specified valve spring free length is 1.4173-inch (35.999 mm) with a minimum length of 1.3582-inch (34.498 mm). Stem diameter of intake and exhaust valves is 0.273-0.274 inch (6.93-6.96 mm). Specified valve stem-to-guide clearance is 0.0016-0.0039 inch (0.041-0.099 mm) with a maximum clearance of 0.006-inch (0.15 mm). Inside diameter of new guides is 0.2756-0.2769 inch (7.000-7.033 mm). If stem-to-guide clearance is excessive, renew guides and/or valves.

WISCONSIN ROBIN

4-STROKE

Model	No. Cyls.	Bore	Stroke	Displacement
W1-145V	1	2.48 in.	1.81 in.	8.73 cu. in.
		(63 mm)	(46 mm)	(143 cc)
W1-185V	1	2.64 in.	2.05 in.	11.2 cu. in.
		(67 mm)	(52 mm)	(183 cc)

ENGINE IDENTIFICATION

All models are four-stroke, air-cooled, single-cylinder, gasoline engines with a vertical crankshaft. On all models, the engine model and specification numbers are located on the name plate on flywheel shroud. The serial number is stamped on the crankcase base. Always furnish engine model, specification and serial numbers when ordering parts.

MAINTENANCE

SPARK PLUG. Recommended spark plug for all models is a Champion CJ14 or equivalent. Specified spark plug electrode gap for all models is 0.025 inch (0.6 mm).

CARBURETOR. All models are equipped with a Mikuni float type carburetor. All models are equipped with carburetor shown in Fig. WR25. Carburetor has fixed low speed and high speed jets. Main fuel mixture is metered through main jet (15) and is nonadjustable. Adjust idle stop screw (12) to obtain an idle speed of 1250 rpm at normal operating temperature.

To check or adjust float level, remove bowl plug (22) and fuel bowl (20). Place carburetor body on end (on manifold flange) so float pin is in vertical position. Move float to close inlet needle valve.

NOTE: Needle valve is spring loaded. Float tab should just contact needle valve pin but should not compress spring.

Measure float setting as shown in Fig. WR28. Dimension "A" should be 0.492-0.571 inch (12.5-14.5 mm). Carefully bend tab on float lever to obtain correct setting.

GOVERNOR. Engines are equipped with a centrifugal flyweight type governor. Governor assembly is located in the oil pan and is driven by the camshaft gear (Fig. WR30).

To adjust external governor linkage, loosen clamp screw on governor lever (Fig. WR31). Turn speed control lever clockwise (toward high speed position) until throttle valve in carburetor is opened fully. Hold lever in this position. Insert screwdriver in slot at end of governor shaft. Turn clockwise as far as shaft can be turned. Tighten governor

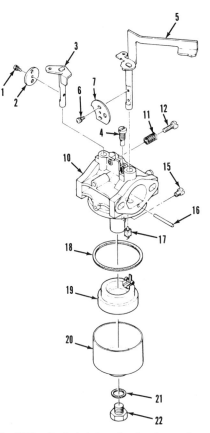

Fig. WR25—Exploded view of carburetor used on all models.

1. Screw	12. Throttle stop screw
2. Throttle plate	15. Main jet
3. Throttle shaft	16. Pin
4. Pilot jet	17. Fuel inlet valve
5. Choke shaft	18. Gasket
6. Screw	19. Float
7. Choke plate	20. Float bowl
10. Carburetor body	21. Gasket
11. Spring	22. Plug

lever clamp screw. Two different governor springs are available to obtain a variety of engine speeds. Changing governor spring location in holes will also vary engine speed.

IGNITION SYSTEM. Early models are equipped with a breaker point type ignition system. Late models are equipped with a solid-state ignition system. Refer to the appropriate paragraphs for ignition type being serviced.

Breaker-Point Ignition System. Breaker points and condenser are located behind flywheel and the ignition coil is located outside flywheel. Initial breaker-point gap for all models is 0.014 inch (0.36 mm). Specified air gap between ignition coil and flywheel is 0.020 inch (0.5 mm).

To check and adjust engine timing, disconnect lead wire from shut-off switch. Connect test lead from a continuity light to lead wire and ground remaining test lead to engine. Slowly rotate flywheel in normal operating direction until light goes out. Immediately stop turning flywheel and check location of timing marks. Timing marks should align. If timing mark on flywheel is below timing mark on crankcase, breaker-point gap is too small. Carefully measure the distance necessary to align the two timing marks, then remove flywheel and breaker-point cover. Changing point gap 0.001 inch (0.03 mm) will change timing mark on flywheel approximately 1/8 inch (3.18 mm). Reassemble and tighten flywheel retaining nut to torque specified under TIGHTENING TORQUES in REPAIRS section.

Solid-State Ignition System. Transistor type solid-state ignition system does not have breaker points. There is no scheduled maintenance. Specified air gap between ignition coil and flywheel is 0.020 inch (0.5 mm).

To test for spark, remove spark plug

lead from spark plug. Insert metal conductor into cable end, then use a suitable insulated tool and hold conductor 1/8 inch (3 mm) from cylinder shroud. Turn engine over and observe spark. A weak spark or no spark indicates a defective ignition coil. Also check for broken, loose or shorted wiring or a faulty spark plug.

LUBRICATION. Check engine oil level daily and maintain oil level at full mark on dipstick or at lower edge of filler plug.

Manufacturer recommends oil with an API service classification of SE or SF. Use SAE 30 oil when temperature is above 40° F (4° C), SAE 20 oil when temperature is between 15° F (-9° C) and 40° F (4° C) and SAE 10W-30 oil when temperature is below 15° F (-9° C).

Oil should be changed after every 50 hours of operation. Crankcase capacity is 1.3 pints (615 cc) for Model W1-185V and 1.2 pints (568 cc) for Model W1-145V.

GENERAL MAINTENANCE. Check and tighten all bolts, nuts or clamps prior or to each day of operation. Check for fuel or oil leakage and repair if necessary.

Clean dust, dirt, grease or any foreign material from cylinder head and cylinder block cooling fins after every 50 hours of normal operation. Inspect fins for damage and repair as necessary.

Cylinder head should be removed and carbon and other combustion deposits cleaned after every 500 hours of normal operation.

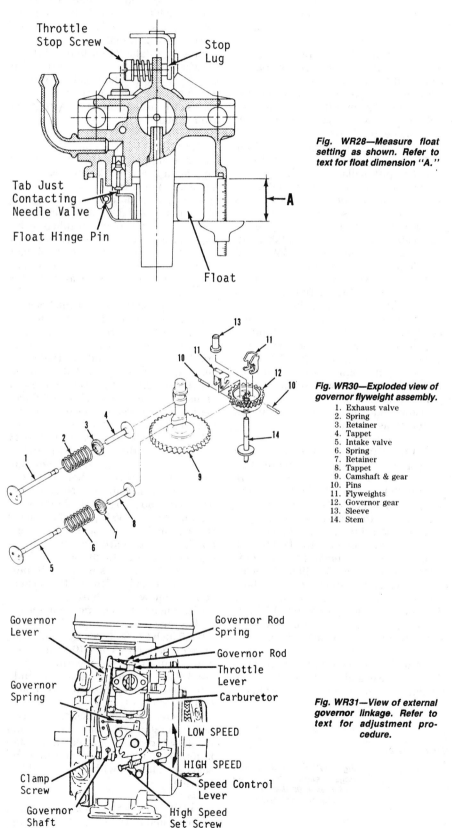

Fig. WR28—Measure float setting as shown. Refer to text for float dimension "A."

Fig. WR30—Exploded view of governor flyweight assembly.

1. Exhaust valve
2. Spring
3. Retainer
4. Tappet
5. Intake valve
6. Spring
7. Retainer
8. Tappet
9. Camshaft & gear
10. Pins
11. Flyweights
12. Governor gear
13. Sleeve
14. Stem

Fig. WR31—View of external governor linkage. Refer to text for adjustment procedure.

REPAIRS

TIGHTENING TORQUES. Recommended tightening torque specifications are as follows:

Spark plug	9-11 ft.-lbs. (12-14 N·m)
Cylinder head bolts/nuts	14-17 ft.-lbs. (19-23 N·m)
Connecting rod cap screws:	
W1-145V	8 ft.-lbs. (10.5 N·m)
W1-185V	12-14 ft.-lbs. (16-19 N·m)
Crankcase cover/oil pan	7 ft.-lbs. (9 N·m)
Flywheel nut	44-47 ft.-lbs. (60-64 N·m)

CYLINDER HEAD. Renew cylinder head if warpage exceeds 0.006 inch (0.15 mm). Always use a new head gasket when installing cylinder head. Tighten cylinder head bolts or nuts evenly and in stages until torque specified in TIGHTENING TORQUES is obtained.

CONNECTING ROD. To remove piston and connecting rod assembly, remove all cooling shrouds. Remove cylinder head and crankcase cover or oil pan.

Remove connecting rod retaining bolts and remove connecting rod and piston assembly from cylinder bore.

Connecting rod side clearance should be 0.0039-0.0118 inch (0.099-0.300 mm). If side clearance exceeds 0.039 inch (0.99 mm), renew connecting rod and/or crankshaft.

Connecting rod-to-piston pin clearance should be 0.0004-0.0012 inch (0.010-0.030 mm). If clearance exceeds 0.005 inch (0.13 mm), renew piston pin and/or connecting rod.

When installing connecting rod and piston assembly, make certain match marks (cast ribs) on connecting rod and cap are adjacent to each other as shown in Fig. WR33. Tighten connecting rod cap screws to torque specified in TIGHTENING TORQUES.

PISTON, PIN AND RINGS. All models are equipped with one compression ring, one scraper ring and one oil control ring. Install rings as shown in Fig. WR34. Stagger ring end gaps at 90 degree intervals around piston.

Piston ring end gap should be 0.0080-0.0160 inch (0.203-0.407 mm). If ring end gap exceeds 0.059 inch (1.5 mm), renew rings and/or recondition cylinder bore.

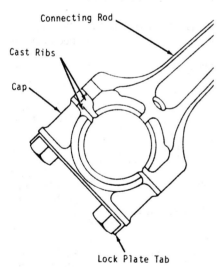

Connecting Rod

Cast Ribs

Cap

Lock Plate Tab

Fig. WR33—Cast ribs must be adjacent to each other for correct assembly.

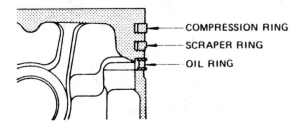

COMPRESSION RING

SCRAPER RING

OIL RING

Fig. WR34—Install piston rings as shown. Stagger ring end gaps at 90 degree intervals around piston.

Piston ring side clearance in piston ring groove should be as follows:
Top ring .... 0.0035-0.0053 in.
(0.089-0.135 mm)
Second ring ...... 0.0023-0.0041 in.
(0.058-0.104 mm)
Oil ring .... 0.0004-0.0025 in.
(0.010-0.064 mm)

If piston ring side clearance exceeds 0.006 inch (0.152 mm), renew piston rings and/or piston.

Standard piston-to-cylinder clearance is 0.0008-0.0023 inch (0.020-0.058 mm).

Standard piston diameter is 2.469-2.470 inches (62.71-62.74 mm) for Model W1-145V. If piston diameter is 2.4661 inches (62.64 mm) or less, renew piston. Standard piston diameter is 2.629-2.630 inches (66.78-66.80 mm) for Model W1-185V. If piston diameter is 2.6261 inches (66.70 mm) or less, renew piston.

Standard piston pin diameter is 0.5509-0.5512 inch (13.993-14.000 mm). If piston pin diameter is 0.5496 inch (13.96 mm) or less, renew piston pin.

Piston pin should be 0.00035 inch (0.009 mm) interference fit to a 0.00039 inch (0.010 mm) loose fit in piston pin bore. Piston pin looseness must not exceed 0.0023 inch (0.06 mm). Standard piston pin clearance in connecting rod is 0.0004-0.0012 inch (0.010-0.029 mm). If piston pin clearance exceeds 0.0047 inch (0.12 mm), renew piston pin and/or connecting rod.

Piston and ring sets are available in oversizes as well as standard.

CYLINDER BLOCK. If cylinder wall is scored, or out-of-round more than 0.0004 inch (0.01 mm), or tapered more than 0.0006 inch (0.015 mm), the cylinder should be bored to nearest oversize for which piston and rings are available.

Standard cylinder bore diameter is 2.4803-2.4811 inches (63.000-63.020 mm) for Model W1-145V. If diameter exceeds 2.4862 inches (63.149 mm), recondition cylinder. Standard cylinder bore diameter is 2.6378-2.6385 inches (67.000-67.018 mm) for Model W1-185V. If diameter exceeds 2.6437 inches (67.15 mm), recondition cylinder bore.

CAMSHAFT. Camshaft rides in bores in crankcase and gear cover/oil pan. When removing camshaft, position en-

gine to prevent tappets from falling free. If valve tappets are removed, identify them so they can be reinstalled in their original positions.

Standard camshaft journal diameter for flywheel and pto side is 0.5895-0.5899 inch (14.973-14.983 mm). If diameter is less than 0.5890 inch (14.961 mm), renew camshaft.

When reinstalling camshaft, lubricate camshaft bearing surfaces, lift valve tappets upward, then slide camshaft into position, making certain timing marks on camshaft and crankshaft gears are aligned.

CRANKSHAFT. The crankshaft on all models is supported in two ball bearing type main bearings. Renew bearings if any indication of roughness, noise or excessive wear is noted. Crankshaft end play should be 0.000-0.008 inch (0.00-0.20 mm). End play is controlled by an adjusting collar or shim located between crankshaft gear and gear cover/oil pan main bearing. Three thicknesses of adjusting collars or shims are available for each model.

To determine the correct thickness of adjusting collar or shim with gear cover removed, measure distance (A—Fig. WR36) between machined surface of crankcase face and end of crankshaft gear. Measure distance (B) between machined surface of gear cover and end of main bearing. The compressed thickness of gear cover gasket (C) is 0.009 inch (0.23 mm). Select adjusting shim or collar that is 0.001-0.009 inch (0.03-0.23 mm) less than the total of A, B and C. After reassembly, crankshaft end play can be checked with a dial indicator.

Standard crankpin journal diameter is 0.9436-0.9450 inch (23.967-24.000 mm) for Model W1-145V. If journal diameter is 0.9391 inch (23.85 mm) or less, renew crankshaft. Standard crankpin journal diameter is 1.021-1.023 inches (25.93-26.00 mm) for Models W1-185V. If journal diameter is 1.017 inches (25.83 mm) or less, renew crankshaft.

Clearance between crankpin journal and connecting rod should be 0.0015-0.0025 inch (0.038-0.064 mm). If clearance exceeds 0.008 inch (0.20 mm), renew connecting rod bearing and/or crankshaft. Maximum allowable crankpin taper and out-of-round is 0.0002 inch (0.005 mm).

When reassembling engine, make certain timing marks on camshaft and crankshaft gears are aligned after installation. When renewing crankshaft oil seals, install seals with lips toward ball bearings.

VALVE SYSTEM. Valve tappet gap (cold) should be 0.003-0.005 inch (0.08-0.13 mm).

To increase clearance, grind off end of valve stem. To reduce clearance, grind valve seat deeper or renew valve and/or valve tappet.

Valve face and seat angles should be 45 degrees. Standard seat width is 0.047-0.059 inch (1.2-1.5 mm). Maximum allowable seat width is 0.098 inch (2.5 mm).

Standard valve stem diameter is 0.256 inch (6.5 mm). If diameter is 0.2501 inch (6.35 mm) or less, renew valve.

Standard valve stem-to-guide clearance is 0.0010-0.0024 inch (0.025-0.061 mm) for intake valve stem and 0.0022-0.0039 inch (0.056-0.099 mm) for exhaust valve. Maximum allowable valve stem-to-guide clearance is 0.0118 inch (0.30 mm) for intake and exhaust valve stems.

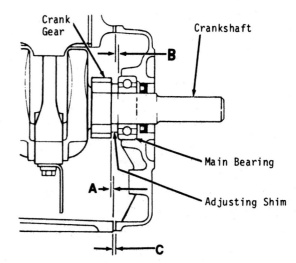

Fig. WR36—View showing location of measuring points to determine correct shim thickness for obtaining correct crankshaft end play. Refer to text.

SERVICING WISCONSIN ROBIN ACCESSORIES

REWIND STARTER

Early Style

OVERHAUL. To disassemble the rewind starter, refer to Fig. WR60 and release spring tension by pulling rope handle until about 18 inches (457 mm) of rope extends from unit. Use thumb pressure against ratchet retainer to prevent reel from rewinding and place rope in notch in outer rim of reel. Release thumb pressure slightly and allow spring mechanism to slowly unwind. Twist loop of return spring and slip loop through slot in ratchet retainer. Refer to Fig. WR61 and remove nut, lockwasher, plain washer and ratchet retainer. Reel will completely unwind as these parts are removed. Remove compression spring, three ratchets and spring retainer washer. Slip fingers into two of the cavity openings in reel hub (Fig. WR62) and carefully lift reel from support shaft in housing.

CAUTION: Take extreme care that power spring remains in recess of housing. Do not remove spring unless new spring is to be installed.

If power spring escapes from housing form a 4½ inch (114 mm) wire ring and twist ends together securely. Starting with the outside loop, wind spring inside the ring in a counterclockwise direction.

NOTE: New power springs are secured in a similar wire ring for ease in assembly.

Place spring assembly over recess in housing so hook in outer loop of spring is over the tension tab in housing. Carefully press spring from wire ring and into recess of housing.

Using a new rope of same length and diameter as original, place rope in handle and tie a figure eight knot about 1½ inches (38 mm) from end. Pull knot into top of handle. Install other end of rope through guide bushing of housing and through hole in reel groove. Pull rope out through cavity opening and tie a slip knot about 2½ inches (64 mm) from end. Place slip knot around center bushing as shown in Fig. WR63 and pull knot tight. Stuff end of rope into reel cavity. Spread a film of light grease on power spring and support shaft. Wind rope ¼ turn clockwise in reel and place rope in notch on reel. Install reel on support shaft and rotate reel counterclockwise until tang on reel engages hook on inner loop of power spring. Place outer flange of housing in a vise and use finger pressure to keep reel in housing. Hook a loop of rope in the reel notch and preload power spring by turning reel 7 full turns counterclockwise. Remove rope from notch and allow reel to slowly turn clockwise as rope winds on pulley and handle returns to guide bushing on housing.

Install spring retainer washer (Fig. WR61), cup side up, and place compression spring into cupped washer. Install return spring with bent end hooked into hole of reel hub. Place the three ratchets in position so they fit the contour of the recesses. Mount ratchet retainer so loop end of return spring extends through slot. Rotate retainer slightly clockwise until ends of slots just begin to engage the three ratchets. Press down on retainer, install flat washer, lockwasher and nut, then tighten nut securely.

New Style

OVERHAUL. To disassemble the rewind starter, refer to Fig. WR64 and release spring tension by pulling rope handle until about 14 inches (356 mm) of rope extends from unit. Use thumb pressure against ratchet retainer to prevent reel from rewinding and place rope in notch in outer rim of reel. Release thumb pressure slightly and allow spring mechanism to slowly unwind. Twist loop of return spring and slip loop through slot in ratchet retainer. Refer to Fig. WR65 and remove clip, thrust washer and ratchet retainer. Reel will completely unwind as these parts are removed. Remove compression spring

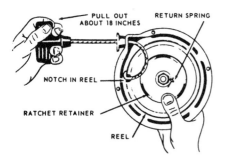

Fig. WR60—View showing method of releasing spring tension on rewind starter assembly.

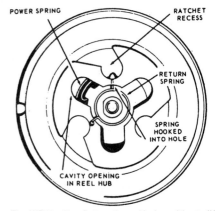

Fig. WR62—Use fingers in reel hub cavities to lift reel from support shaft.

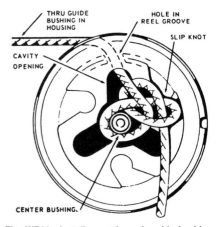

Fig. WR63—Install rope through guide bushing end hole in reel groove, then tie slip knot around center bushing.

Fig. WR61—Exploded view of rewind starter assembly used on Models EY18W and EY18-3W engines.

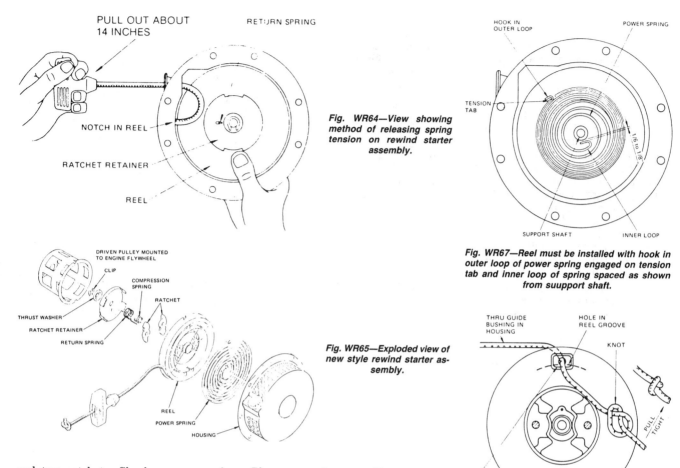

PULL OUT ABOUT 14 INCHES

RETURN SPRING

NOTCH IN REEL

RATCHET RETAINER

REEL

Fig. WR64—View showing method of releasing spring tension on rewind starter assembly.

HOOK IN OUTER LOOP

POWER SPRING

TENSION TAB

1/16 to 1/8

SUPPORT SHAFT

INNER LOOP

Fig. WR67—Reel must be installed with hook in outer loop of power spring engaged on tension tab and inner loop of spring spaced as shown from suupport shaft.

DRIVEN PULLEY MOUNTED TO ENGINE FLYWHEEL

CLIP

COMPRESSION SPRING

RATCHET

THRUST WASHER

RATCHET RETAINER

RETURN SPRING

REEL

POWER SPRING

HOUSING

Fig. WR65—Exploded view of new style rewind starter assembly.

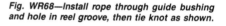

THRU GUIDE BUSHING IN HOUSING

HOLE IN REEL GROOVE

KNOT

PULL TIGHT

CAVITY OPENING

Fig. WR68—Install rope through guide bushing and hole in reel groove, then tie knot as shown.

and two ratchets. Slowly remove reel from support shaft in housing.

CAUTION: Take extreme care that power spring remains in recess of housing. Do not remove spring unless new spring is to be installed.

If power spring escapes from housing, form a 3 inch (76 mm) wire ring and twist ends together securely. Starting with outside loop, wind spring inside the ring in counterclockwise direction as shown in Fig. WR66.

NOTE: New power springs are secured in a similar wire ring for ease in assembly.

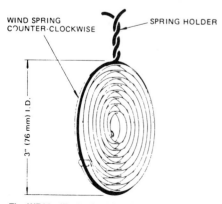

WIND SPRING COUNTER-CLOCKWISE

SPRING HOLDER

3" (76 mm) I.D.

Fig. WR66—Illustration showing fabricated spring holder used to rewind power spring.

Place new spring assembly over recess in housing so hook in outer loop of spring is over the tension tab in the housing. Carefully press spring from wire ring and into recess of housing. See Fig. WR67.

Using a new rope of same length and diameter as original, place rope in handle and tie a figure eight knot about 1 inch (25 mm) from end. Pull knot into top of handle. Install other end of rope through guide bushing of housing and through hole in reel groove. Pull rope out through cavity opening and tie a knot about 1 inch (25 mm) from end. Tie knot as illustrated in Fig. WR68 and stuff knot into cavity opening. Wind rope 2½ turns clockwise on reel, then lock rope in notch of reel pulley. Install reel on support shaft and rotate reel counterclockwise until tang on reel engages hook on inner loop of power spring. Place outer flange of housing in a vise and use finger pressure to keep reel in housing. Hook a loop of rope into reel notch and preload power spring by turning reel four full turns counterclockwise. Remove rope from notch and allow reel to slowly turn clockwise as rope winds on pulley and handle returns to guide bushing on housing. Refer to Fig. WR65 and install compression spring. Install return spring with bent end hooked into hole of reel hub and looped end toward outside. Install the

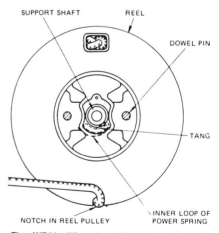

SUPPORT SHAFT

REEL

DOWEL PIN

TANG

NOTCH IN REEL PULLEY

INNER LOOP OF POWER SPRING

Fig. WR69—When installing reel in housing, engage inner loop of power spring on tang of reel. Refer to text.

two ratchets, with tips pointed in a counterclockwise direction, into the contours of the hub recesses. Mount ratchet retainer so loop end of return spring extends through slot. Rotate retainer slightly clockwise until ends of slots just begin to engage the ratchets. Press down on retainer, install washer and clip.

GEAR REDUCTION UNIT

Gear-driven speed reduction units are available on Model EY18-3W engines. See Fig. WR70 for exploded view of reduction unit. Reduction ratio is 6:1 Special crankshafts are required on reduction models. Takeoff end of crankshaft is machined to serve as the drive gear. Reduction unit is mounted directly to engine gear cover. Reduction unit may be mounted on engine in any of four positions, depending on requirements. Note that cover (9) will require shifting to maintain position of level plug (1) and fill plug (2) when unit is mounted in positions other than shown in Fig. WR70. Reduction gears are lubricated by same type of oil used in engine crankcase. Gearcase capacity

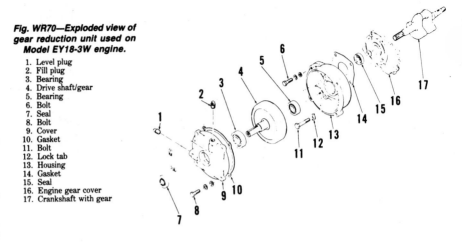

Fig. WR70—Exploded view of gear reduction unit used on Model EY18-3W engine.

1. Level plug
2. Fill plug
3. Bearing
4. Drive shaft/gear
5. Bearing
6. Bolt
7. Seal
8. Bolt
9. Cover
10. Gasket
11. Bolt
12. Lock tab
13. Housing
14. Gasket
15. Seal
16. Engine gear cover
17. Crankshaft with gear

is approximately 3/8 pint (0.18 L), filled to level plug opening. Oil change interval should not exceed 500 hours of operating time and more frequently in heavy continuous duty. Maintain level by regular periodic checks.

METRIC

CONVERSION

Cubic meters	= .02832	x Cubic Feet
Cubic meters	x 1.308	= Cubic Yards
Cubic meters	= .765	x Cubic Yards
Liters	x 61.023	= Cubic Inches
Liters	= .01639	x Cubic Inches
Liters	x .26418	= U.S. Gallons
Liters	= 3.7854	x U.S. Gallons
Grams	x 15.4324	= Grains
Grams	= .0648	x Grains
Grams	x .03527	= Ounces, avoirdupois
Grams	= 28.3495	x Ounces, avoirdupois
Kilograms	x 2.2046	= Pounds
Kilograms	= .4536	x Pounds
Kilograms per square centimeter	x 14.2231	= Pounds per square Inch
Kilograms per square centimeter	= .0703	x Pounds per square Inch
Kilograms per cubic meter	x .06243	= Pounds per cubic Foot
Kilograms per cubic meter	= 16.01890	x Pounds per cubic Foot

Metric tons (1,000 kilograms)	x 1.1023	= Tons (2,000 Pounds)
Metric tons (1,000 kilograms)	= .9072	x Tons (2,000 Pounds)
Kilowatts	= 1.3405	x Horsepower
Kilowatts	x .746	= Horsepower
Millimeters	x .03937	= Inches
Millimeters	= 25.400	x Inches
Meters	x 3.2809	= Feet
Meters	= .3048	x Feet
Kilometers	x .621377	= Miles
Kilometers	= 1.6093	x Miles
Square centimeters	x .15500	= Square Inches
Square centimeters	= 6.4515	x Square Inches
Square meters	x 10.76410	= Square Feet
Square meters	= .09290	x Square Feet
Cubic centimeters	x .061025	= Cubic Inches
Cubic centimeters	= 16.3866	x Cubic Inches
Cubic meters	x 35.3156	= Cubic Feet

MAINTENANCE LOG

MAINTENANCE LOG
